W9-AUF-220

# Critical Thinking
# in Clinical Practice

# Critical Thinking in Clinical Practice

## Improving the Quality of Judgments and Decisions

*Second Edition*

Eileen Gambrill

WILEY

John Wiley & Sons, Inc.

This book is printed on acid-free paper. ⊗

Copyright © 2005 by John Wiley & Sons. All rights reserved.

Published by John Wiley & Sons, Inc., Hoboken, New Jersey.
Published simultaneously in Canada.

No part of this publication may be reproduced, stored in a retrieval system, or transmitted in any form or by any means, electronic, mechanical, photocopying, recording, scanning, or otherwise, except as permitted under Section 107 or 108 of the 1976 United States Copyright Act, without either the prior written permission of the Publisher, or authorization through payment of the appropriate per-copy fee to the Copyright Clearance Center, Inc., 222 Rosewood Drive, Danvers, MA 01923, (978) 750-8400, fax (978) 646-8600, or on the web at www.copyright.com. Requests to the Publisher for permission should be addressed to the Permissions Department, John Wiley & Sons, Inc., 111 River Street, Hoboken, NJ 07030, (201) 748-6011, fax (201) 748-6008. e-mail: permcoordinator@wiley.com.

Limit of Liability/Disclaimer of Warranty: While the publisher and author have used their best efforts in preparing this book, they make no representations or warranties with respect to the accuracy or completeness of the contents of this book and specifically disclaim any implied warranties of merchantability or fitness for a particular purpose. No warranty may be created or extended by sales representatives or written sales materials. The advice and strategies contained herein may not be suitable for your situation. You should consult with a professional where appropriate. Neither the publisher nor author shall be liable for any loss of profit or any other commercial damages, including but not limited to special, incidental, consequential, or other damages.

This publication is designed to provide accurate and authoritative information in regard to the subject matter covered. It is sold with the understanding that the publisher is not engaged in rendering professional services. If legal, accounting, medical, psychological or any other expert assistance is required, the services of a competent professional person should be sought.

Designations used by companies to distinguish their products are often claimed as trademarks. In all instances where John Wiley & Sons, Inc. is aware of a claim, the product names appear in initial capital or all capital letters. Readers, however, should contact the appropriate companies for more complete information regarding trademarks and registration.

For general information on our other products and services please contact our Customer Care Department within the United States at (800) 762-2974, outside the United States at (317) 572-3993 or fax (317) 572-4002.

Wiley also publishes its books in a variety of electronic formats. Some content that appears in print may not be available in electronic books. For more information about Wiley products, visit our web site at www.wiley.com

ISBN-13: 978-0-471-471189
ISBN-10: 0-471-471186

Printed in the United States of America.

10  9  8  7  6  5  4  3  2  1

In memory of all the
Daisy Andersons

# Contents

# Preface

CRITICAL THINKING IN CLINICAL PRACTICE is for clinicians who want to think more clearly about the decisions they make and the context in which they make them. This second edition describes the exciting related developments in evidence-based practice (EBP) and policy and updates content as needed throughout. This book will be of value to all professionals who offer services to clients, including psychologists, psychiatrists, social workers, and counselors. Clinical practice is an uncertain enterprise. Much remains unknown about what works best with which client toward what aim, and wide variations exist in how clinicians carry out their practice. Indeed, the very criteria that should be used to evaluate outcomes are in dispute. Mistakes are inevitable, even in the best of circumstances. However, even in uncertain areas such as clinical practice, some decisions are better than others. The percentage of those that are better can be increased by avoiding common sources of error.

The spirit in which this book is written is illustrated by the author of *Straight and Crooked Thinking: Thirty-Eight Dishonest Tricks of Debate* (Thouless, 1974). The purpose of learning about sources of error is to enhance critical thinking skills, to learn to recognize errors and acquire strategies for minimizing avoidable mistakes. The emphasis here is on offering readers decision-making tools (some have been referred to as "mind tools"; Gigerenzer, 2002a) that can improve the accuracy of clinical judgments and related decisions. Surprisingly little attention is devoted in professional training programs to many sources of error that can lead clinicians astray. For example, little attention is given to informal fallacies that may result in questionable decisions, such as relying on tradition or what is popular to select practices and policies. Clinical decision making is approached as a challenging process that can be improved by acquiring skills integral to evidence-based practice, such as posing well-formed questions that guide an efficient, effective search for practice- and policy-related research. Beliefs, attitudes, and interpersonal skills that influence the effectiveness with which content and procedural knowledge are used are reviewed. Some clinicians view clinical practice as an art, rejecting as irrelevant related research. However, research findings are available in many areas that can be put to good use, both at the individual level of practice and when making policy decisions. Critical thinking and evidence-based practice are closely related; both reject authority as a guide (such as someone's status), both emphasize the importance of honoring ethical obligations, and both involve a spirit of inquiry.

## DEVELOPMENT OF THIS BOOK

A number of influences led to the writing of the first edition of this book. One was the prevalence of common errors in thinking among clinicians. Examples include making decisions based on small biased samples, not recognizing pseudoexplanations, and having a false sense of accuracy in predicting future events. Another was puzzlement about the success of colleagues who use weak rather than strong strategies when trying to influence others: Examples include using straw person arguments, misrepresenting positions, and begging the question. A third was the discovery of books such as *Straight and Crooked Thinking* (Thouless, 1974)—a well-written book describing a range of common errors as well as remedies. A fourth influence was research concerning human judgment and decision making that has been pulled together in sources such as *Human Inference* (Nisbett & Ross, 1980) and *Judgment and Choice* (Hogarth, 1980, 1987). Books such as *The Protection of Children* by Dingwall and his colleagues (Dingwall, Eekelaar, & Murray, 1983) that describe decision-making processes in case conferences provided a supplement to studies of clinical decision making by individuals. Research and theory in the area of teaching people how to think more critically were also of value.

### What's New and What's Not Over the Past 15 Years

The past years since the publication of the first edition are a fascinating mix of progress and challenges. These are described in this book. Progress and increases in critical thinking in clinical practice include the invention of the systematic review and the process and philosophy of evidence-based practice and policy in medicine and health care and its spread to other professions (Gambrill, 2006; Gibbs, 2003; Gray, 2001a; Sackett, Straus, Richardson, Rosenberg, & Haynes, 2000). There has been greater attention to pseudoscience and fads in the helping professions (Jacobson, Foxx, & Mulick, 2005; Lilienfeld, Lynn, & Lohr, 2003), to human service propaganda (Gibbs & Gambrill, 1999), to harming in the name of helping (McCord, 2003; Sharpe & Faden, 1998), to flaws in research related to clinical practice (Altman, 2002; Gray, 1997, 2001b), to fraud in related industries such as "Big Pharma" (Angell, 2004; Kassirer, 2005) and to ethical obligations of professionals, for example, to involve clients as informed participants (Edwards & Elwyn, 2001). All of these developments promise to enhance the quality of services provided to clients.

On the other hand, propaganda in the human service professions grows by leaps and bounds, including its distribution via advertisements on our television screens (e.g., Moynihan, Heath, Henry, & Gøtzsche, 2002). The Internet is both a source of accurate information and bogus claims and quackery. It is perhaps this very growth and the absurdity of some of the claims and the revelations of fraud and the play of special interests that do not match those of clients (e.g., harming in the name of helping) that has resulted in the greater attention to propaganda, harm, and fraud in the helping professions—including the creation of ways to decrease them. When parents start to be threatened with being reported to child protection services because they refuse to place their child on Ritalin, some counter-pressure is bound to happen. And when anything that sounds good comes along such as evidence-based practice, there will be those who simply apply the new label to old practices that share none of the characteristics of evidence-based practice (Gambrill, 2003a). Who will know? Who will look? Who will care?

## OVERVIEW OF THE CHAPTERS

Chapter 1 describes the vital role of decision making in clinical practice, kinds of errors that may occur and their sources, as well as the importance of thinking critically about decisions. Hallmarks of critical thinking are reviewed, including related values, attitudes, and styles, and its integral association with evidence-based practice is emphasized. Barriers to making sound decisions are discussed, including social, economic, and political influences on the helping professions. The role of emotions, goals, and information-processing strategies in making decisions is highlighted, and ways in which these may lead to errors noted; for example, discounting conflicting information in exploring the accuracy of assumptions. Clinical reasoning as a skill is discussed. Finally, the costs and benefits of critical thinking are reviewed.

Chapter 2 describes sources of influence on clinical decisions. Readers are encouraged to take a broad view of such influences—to consider the influence of political, social, and economic factors on what is defined as a personal or social problem, and what are considered suitable intervention options in relation to different kinds of problems. The influence of agency variables is also discussed; many clinicians either work in an agency or have contacts with agencies—perhaps through services that are contracted out. In addition, the helper-client relationship is discussed as this may influence decisions, as well as psychological factors such as confirmation biases that may result in misleading clients because of premature acceptance of faulty assumptions.

Reasoning is at the heart of clinical decision making—forming hypotheses about presenting concerns, gathering data to evaluate the accuracy of different views, offering arguments for assumptions, and evaluating the quality of these arguments. Chapter 3 provides an overview of different kinds of reasons (for example, hot and cold), suggests helpful distinctions (for example, between facts and beliefs), and describes different kinds of arguments and explanations.

Different views of knowledge and how to get it are discussed in Chapter 4. Questionable criteria on which to base decisions, such as testimonials and popularity, are reviewed and contrasted with scientific criteria. Readers are encouraged to review their personal epistemology. If we rely on questionable criteria to accept knowledge claims, clients may be harmed rather than helped. Thus, it is vital to review personal beliefs about knowledge and how to get it.

The influence of language and social-psychological persuasion strategies are discussed in Chapter 5. The interview is the context in which most helping efforts are carried out, and language plays a crucial part in what transpires there. Sources of error related to language are described in this chapter, including "bafflegarb," use of emotional words, and conviction through repetition.

Rarely are clinicians trained in the various kinds of formal and informal fallacies that may occur in clinical practice and compromise the quality of decisions. Informal and formal fallacies may involve overlooking, evading, or distorting facts. Although most clinicians may be familiar with some fallacies described in Chapter 6, they may not be familiar with others that may result in avoidable errors, such as inappropriate use of analogies and circular reasoning. Chapter 6 suggests how learning to identify and remedy fallacies can improve the quality of decisions.

The topics of classification, pseudoauthority, and pathological set are discussed in Chapter 7. Classification is inevitable in clinical practice. This chapter describes sources of error that may result from it, such as an incorrect classification of clients and treatment methods. Pseudoauthority is singled out for special focus because it represents a key source of potential error in clinical practice. For example, clinicians may accept knowledge based on appeals to consensus or tradition. A pathological set also is singled out for attention, because of tendencies to focus on pathology and to ignore positive attributes of clients.

Domain-specific knowledge as well as procedural knowledge is often required in making accurate clinical decisions. The importance of content and procedural knowledge (data that decrease uncertainty) is discussed in Chapter 8. This chapter emphasizes the key role of clinical education programs and the value of acquiring skills for lifelong learning. Differences between experts and novices are reviewed.

Chapter 9 provides an overview of research in the areas of judgment, problem solving, and decision making of value to clinicians, including developments in naturalistic decision making. Structuring problems is a critical phase. Research highlights the importance of situation awareness and development of expertise based on corrective feedback. The uncertainty of problem solving is emphasized and tools of value are described for decreasing common biases based on research on judgment and decision making.

Chapter 10 describes the origins, process, and philosophy of evidence-based practice. Evidence-based practice and policy are designed to facilitate well-informed, ethical decisions. They suggest a way to handle the uncertainty in making decisions in an informed, ethical manner. Considerable attention is devoted to developing tools required to do so, such as access to high-quality reviews of practice-related research. Objections to EBP are reviewed, as well as counterarguments. Controversies concerning "what is evidence" are given special attention.

Chapter 11, "Posing Questions and Searching for Answers," offers detailed guidelines for preparing well-structured questions that guide an effective, efficient search for practice- and policy-related research findings. Questions that often arise, such as "What if the experts disagree?" and "Do research findings apply to my client?" are discussed, and common errors in each phase of EBP are noted.

Guidelines for critically appraising different kinds of research, including qualitative reports, are offered in Chapter 12. Common myths that hinder critical appraisal are discussed, such as "It is too difficult for me to learn" and "All research is equally sound." Different sources of bias are reviewed and questions to raise about all research suggested. In addition, guidelines are offered for critically appraising research related to particular kinds of questions, including effectiveness questions as well as those related to description and identification of causes. Readers are referred to additional sources for further reading.

Chapter 13 describes options for collecting data. Sources of assessment data are described, as well as their advantages and disadvantages. Kinds of reliability and validity of concern in evaluating assessment measures are reviewed. Decisions in this stage influence those in later phases of working with clients. This chapter also discusses factors that influence what clinicians see and report, such as vividness, motivation, and insensitivity to sample size.

Clinicians make decisions about causal factors related to clients' concerns and desired outcomes. Factors that influence selection of causes (such as similarity between effects and presumed causes and the availability of preferred practice theories) are reviewed in Chapter 14, and guidelines are offered to enhance the accuracy of causal assumptions. These include helpful rules of thumb, such as paying attention to sources of uncertainty and examining all four cells of a contingency table.

Making choices and predictions is a routine part of clinical practice. Predictions are made about how clients will behave in the future and about the effectiveness of intervention methods. Sources of error that may decrease the accuracy of predictions are described in Chapter 15 and steps are suggested to increase accuracy, such as taking advantage of statistical tools and decreasing reliance on memory.

Clinical decisions are often made in case conferences, particularly difficult ones that involve high costs if errors are made. Tendencies in such contexts that may decrease the quality of decisions (such as the belief that all contributions are equally good, and confusion between the consistency and differential weight of signs) are discussed in Chapter 16, and guidelines are provided for enhancing the quality of discussions.

Personal obstacles that may get in the way of developing and using critical thinking skills are discussed in Chapter 17. Examples include a disinterest in critical thinking, a preference for mystery over mastery, unrealistic expectations of success, failure to reflect on excuses used for lack of quality services, and a fear of discovering errors. Social anxiety may decrease willingness to express opinions that differ from those of others. Moving beyond weak arguments requires accurate identification of errors and knowledge of remedies, as well as effective interpersonal skills for diplomatically neutralizing weak influence attempts and highlighting important issues.

Guidelines for maintaining critical thinking skills and becoming a lifelong learner are described in Chapter 18. As in other areas, having a skill does not mean that it will be used; many influences may erode critical thinking skills.

## PURPOSE OF THE BOOK

This book is not meant to be read at one sitting but is designed to be sampled over many readings. This will provide the reader with leisurely opportunities to catch errors that I no doubt have made in my thinking. Writing a book about critical thinking is a daunting prospect, given the inevitability of revealing crooked thinking. However, this book is written in the spirit that we all make errors and that the task is to learn to recognize and correct them.

It is important to note what this book attempts to do as well as what it does not do. This book does attempt to draw on a range of areas that are pertinent to critical thinking and evidence-based practice in clinical practice and to draw these together in a format that makes sense to clinicians and that can be used to enhance the quality of practice. It does *not* attempt to offer incisive reviews of the many fields that are touched on here as they relate to clinical decision making. The teaching of thinking is as old as philosophy itself, and entire domains of inquiry have been concerned with this subject. Material related to the area of clinical decision making lies in sociology, anthropology, psychology, medicine, rhetoric, philosophy, education, and popularized presentations of formal and informal fallacies, such as *Straight and Crooked Thinking* (Thouless, 1974). The potential arena of relevant sources has been a challenge of manageability. This book is not for those who are looking for a state-of-the-art presentation on artificial intelligence or who seek in-depth discussions of one of the many topics mentioned in this book. Entire books could be (and have been) written on many, if not most, of the topics discussed in this book. References are provided throughout the book to sources that offer more detail.

Strong differences of opinion exist about many of the topics discussed in this book, such as statistical versus clinical prediction and the most useful way to pursue knowledge, or whether it can be gained. The sources of error described here, especially those resulting in confirmation of favored views, will encourage biased misreadings of some of the content. There has been a historical reluctance to make clinical assumptions explicit so that their accuracy can be carefully examined. Efforts in this direction, even though described with the utmost tentativeness, often have been greeted with vigorous negative reactions that are based on misreadings of what has been presented. Consider, for example, the ongoing discussion concerning the use of actuarial methods for making clinical decisions. Even though the advantages of such methods may be described in measured terms, positions may be distorted.

## ACKNOWLEDGMENTS

I am indebted to the many authors of the excellent material from which I have drawn liberally. I thank Oxford University Press for their generosity in allowing me to reproduce material from *Social Work Practice: A Critical Thinker's Guide* (2006) that appears in Chapters 4, 10, 11, and 12. I wish to thank the participants of my workshops on making clinical decisions in both the United States and Britain, who greeted this material with such enthusiasm and inspired me to continue working in this area. These workshops supported my impression over the years that most clinicians are open to examining their reasoning processes in an atmosphere of constructive inquiry. I also want to extend my thanks to reviewers of drafts of the first edition of this book, including William E. Henry and Gracia A. Alkema of Jossey-Bass, who were consistently supportive yet critical in nudging the manuscript toward clarity and in considering the topic important. Warm thanks also to Tracey Belmont and Isabel Pratt for their enthusiastic support and encouragement regarding this second edition and to Linda Witzling and Susan Dodson for attention to production.

I thank the University of California at Berkeley for past research grants that facilitated preparation of this book as well as the funders of the Hutto Patterson Chair in Child and Family Studies. I extend a special note of appreciation to Sharon Ikami for her word-processing support and consistent warmth and good will. And, warm thanks to Gail Bigelow for her support and encouragement.

# PART I

## LAY OF THE LAND

# CHAPTER 1

# The Need for Critical Thinking in Clinical Practice

D ECISION MAKING IS AT the heart of clinical practice. You may have to decide how to assess a client's depression. What sources of information will you draw on and what criteria will you use to evaluate their accuracy? Will you rely on your intuition? Will you ask your client to complete the Beck Depression Inventory? Will you talk to family members and take a careful history? Will it help you to understand your client's depression if you give her a psychiatric diagnosis? Or, you may have to decide how to help parents increase positive behaviors of their four-year-old boy. What sources of information will you use? How can you locate valuable guidelines regarding the most effective methods? What criteria will you use to review the evidentiary status of a claim such as: "Attention-Deficit/Hyperactivity Disorder is due to a biochemical disorder?" Think back to a client with whom you have worked. Which of the following criteria did you use to make decisions (Gibbs & Gambrill, 1999):

   ____ 1. Your intuition (gut feeling) about what will be effective.
   ____ 2. What you have heard from other professionals in informal exchanges.
   ____ 3. Your experience with a few cases.
   ____ 4. Your demonstrated track record of success based on data you have gathered systematically and regularly.
   ____ 5. What fits your personal style.
   ____ 6. What is usually offered at your agency.
   ____ 7. Self-reports of other clients about what is helpful.
   ____ 8. Results of controlled experimental studies (data that show that a method is helpful).
   ____ 9. What you are most familiar with.
  ____ 10. What you know by critically reading professional literature.

In addition to complex decisions that involve collecting, processing, and organizing diverse sources of data, scores of smaller decisions are made in the course of each interview. For example, moment-to-moment decisions are made during an interview about how to respond. Options include questions, advice, reflections, interpretations, self-disclosures, and silence. Decisions are made about what concerns to focus on, what information to gather, what intervention methods to use, and how to evaluate progress. The usefulness of different outcomes must be weighed, the risks of different options must be evaluated, and probabilities must be estimated. Judgmental tasks include describing clients and situations, deciding on causes, and making predictions about outcomes. For example, a clinician may have to describe a child's injuries and decide whether these were a result of parental abuse or were caused by a fall (as reported by the mother). She will have to decide what criteria to use to make this decision, what type of data to gather, and when she has enough material at hand. If a decision is made that the injuries were caused by the parent, a prediction must be made as to whether the parent is likely to abuse the child again. Clinical errors that may occur include

- Errors in description. (Example: Mrs. V. was abused as a child [when she was not].)
- Errors in detecting the extent of covariation. (Example: All people who are abused as children abuse their own children. )
- Errors in assuming causal relationships. (Example: Being abused as a child [always] leads to abuse of one's own children.)
- Errors in prediction. (Example: Insight therapy will prevent this woman from abusing her child again [given that this is not true ].)

## THE IMPORTANCE OF THINKING CRITICALLY ABOUT DECISIONS

Clinical practice allows a wide range of individual discretion: how to structure problems, what outcomes to pursue, when to stop collecting information, what risks to take, what criteria to use to select practice methods, and how to evaluate progress. Shortcuts may be taken that may not enhance accuracy. The privacy of clinical practice (rarely is it observed by other clinicians), allows unique styles, which may or may not enhance the accuracy of decisions, depending in part on the nature of corrective feedback. Use of vague evaluation procedures may maintain styles that are not optimal. Clients may be harmed rather than helped if we do not think critically about the decisions we make. Are they well-reasoned? Are they informed by related research? Have we accepted bogus claims about the effectiveness of a practice method? As Karl Popper (1994) points out, "There are always many different opinions and conventions concerning any one problem or subject-matter. . . . This shows that they are not all true. For if they conflict, then at best only one of them can be true" (p. 39). The following findings suggest that clinical decisions can be improved:

1. There are wide variations in practices including racial disparities (e.g., Kuno & Rothbard, 2002; Smedley, Stith, & Nelson, 2003).
2. Most services provided are of unknown effectiveness. There has been little rigorous critical appraisal of most variations in practices and policies in relation to their outcomes (e.g., do they do more good than harm?).
3. Clients are harmed as well as helped. Consider for example the death of a child in "rebirthing therapy" (Janofsky, 2001; see also Diaz & deLeon, 2002; Goulding, 2004; Ofshe & Watters, 1994; Sharpe & Faden, 1998; Silverman, 1980).
4. Methods found to be harmful continue to be used (e.g., Petrosino, Turpin-Petrosino, & Buehler, 2003).
5. Methods shown to be invalid continue to be used (e.g., see Hunsley, Lee, & Wood, 2003).
6. Methods that have been found to be effective are often not offered to clients (e.g., see Olds, et al., 1998).
7. There are large gaps between claims of effectiveness and evidence for such claims. In fact, often there is counterevidence, as illustrated by mandated receivership of child welfare services in many U.S. states (contrary to claims that such services are effective).
8. Good intentions are relied on as indicators of good outcomes.
9. Research suggests that nonprofessionals are as effective as professionals in helping clients attain many outcomes (e.g., see Christensen & Jacobson, 1994; Dawes, 1994a).
10. Exposes of professional practice and policy by journalists are common.
11. Avoidable errors are common (e.g., DePanfilis, 2003; Reason, 2001).
12. Licensing and accreditation bodies such as the National Association of Social Workers (NASW) and the Council on Social Work Education rely on surrogates of competence and quality of professional education, such as the diversity of faculty and size of faculty, their degrees, and experience (Gambrill, 2002).
13. Clients are typically not informed regarding the evidentiary status of recommended services (e.g., that there is no evidence that these are effective or do more good than harm; Braddock, Edwards, Hasenberg, Laidley, & Levinson, 1999; Cohen & Jacobs, 1998; Gottlieb, 2003). And clients are not involved in designing, conducting, and interpreting critical tests of the effectiveness of services (for exceptions see Hanley, Truesdale, King, Elbourne, & Chalmers, 2001).
14. There seems to be an inverse correlation between growth of the helping professions and problems solved (see Gambrill, 2001).

The history of the helping professions shows that decisions made may do more harm than good. Consider the blinding of 10,000 babies by the standard practice of giving them oxygen at birth (Silverman, 1980). Scared Straight programs designed to decrease delinquency have been found to increase it (Petrosino, Turpin-Petrosino, & Buehler, 2003). Many clinicians carry out their practice with little or no effort to take advantage of practice-related research describing the evidentiary status of different interventions in relation to different kinds of clients. Gaps between knowledge available and what was used was a key reason for the development of evidence-based practice and care as described in Chapter 10. The histories of the mental health industry, psychiatry, psychology, and social work are replete with the identification of false causes for personal troubles and social problems. Complex classification systems with no empirical status such as those based on physiognomy (facial type) and phrenology (skull formation) were popular, including the creation of metal phrenological hats to aid in diagnosis (Gamwell & Tomes, 1995). (See Exhibit 1.1.) Reviews of the history of psychiatry reveal a long list of intrusive interventions that can best be described as torture (e.g., see Scull, 2005; Valenstein, 1988). Consider Darwin's chair, in which a patient was spun until bleeding from his or her nose.

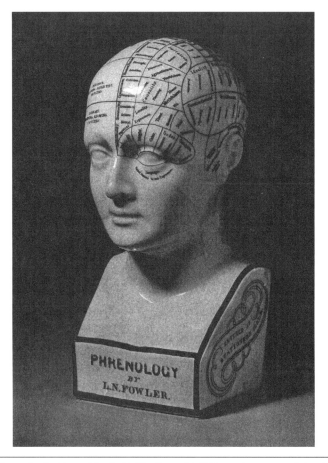

**Exhibit 1.1**   Phrenological head, by L. N. Fowler, mid-19th century, porcelain, 11 in. high. Courtesy Mrs. Erick T. Carlson. Reprinted from *Madness in America* (p. 86), by L. Gamwell and N. Tomes, 1995, Ithaca, NY: Cornell University Press.

TREATMENT OF HYSTERIA

**Exhibit 1.2** "Treatment of Hysteria," in Russell T. Trall, *Hydropathic Encyclopedia* (New York, 1868). The New York Academy of Medicine Library. Reprinted from *Madness in America* (p. 157), by L. Gamwell and N. Tomes, 1995, Ithaca, NY: Cornell University Press.

Water-based "cures" were a popular strategy (see Exhibit 1.2). A former patient, Ebenezer Haskell, said he witnessed the spread-eagle cure while in Pennsylvania Hospital for the Insane. "A disorderly patient is stripped naked and thrown on his back, four men take hold of the limbs and stretch them out at right angles, then the doctor or some one of the attendants stands up on a chair or table and pours a number of buckets full of cold water on his face until life is nearly extinct, then the patient is removed to his dungeon cured of all diseases" (cited in Gamwell & Tomes, 1995 p. 63). The remedy of the tranquilizing chair is shown in Exhibit 1.3. Epidemiologists bring to our attention different rates of use of certain kinds of interventions, such as the higher number of hysterectomies in the United States as compared with Britain. Such differences may reflect actual need, or they may result from influences that conflict with client interests (such as an overabundance of surgeons or a tendency to think for clients rather than inform them fully and let them make their own decisions). Variations in services provided for the same concern was one of the key reasons for the development of evidence-based medicine and health care (Gray, 2001b; Wennberg, 2002). The question naturally arises: "Do they all do more good than harm?"

The exposure of clinical errors and harming in the name of helping is a topic of concern to journalists as well as investigators in a variety of fields, as illustrated by reports of children maltreated by their foster parents (e.g., DePanfilis, 2003; Pear, 2004) and abuse of patients in facilities that purport to help them such as group homes for the "mentally ill" (e.g., see Levy, 2002). Thousands of patients suffer the consequences of avoidable errors in hospitals each year (e.g., see Naylor, 2002). Exhibit 1.4 illustrates types of errors. What would be considered an error today might have been considered common (and good practice) years ago. For example, many people who entered a mental hospital

**Exhibit 1.3**   "The Tranquilizing Chair," in Benjamin Rush, "Observations on the Tranquilizer," The Philadelphia Medical Museum (1811). Archives of Pennsylvania Hospital, Philadelphia. Reprinted from *Madness in America* (p. 33), by L. Gamwell and N. Tomes, 1995, Ithaca, NY: Cornell University Press.

in the fifties and spent the rest of their lives there should not have been hospitalized in the first place. Many errors reflect a confirmatory bias (seeking only data that support favored views; Nickerson, 1998). Imagine that you are a community organizer in a low-income neighborhood and believe that new immigrants moving into the neighborhood are the least likely to become active in community advocacy efforts. Because of this belief you may concentrate your attention on long-term residents. As a result, new resident immigrants are ignored, with the consequence that they are unlikely to become involved. This will strengthen your original belief.

The very nature of clinical practice leaves room for many sources of error. Decisions must be made in a context of uncertainty; the criteria on which decisions should be made are in dispute and empirical data about the effectiveness of different intervention options are often lacking. Some errors result from a lack of information about how to help clients. Empirical knowledge related to clinical practice is fragmentary, and theory must be used to fill in the gaps. Other errors result from ignorance on the part of individual clinicians—

**Exhibit 1.4**
Examples of Types of Errors in Medicine

---

**Diagnostic**

Error or delay in diagnosis

Failure to employ indicated tests

Use of outmoded tests of therapy

Failure to act on results of monitoring or testing

**Treatment**

Error in the performance of an operation, procedure, or test

Error in administering the treatment

Error in the dose or method of using a drug

Avoidable delay in treatment or in responding to an abnormal test

Inappropriate (not indicated) care

**Preventive**

Failure to provide prophylactic treatment

Inadequate monitoring or follow-up of treatment

**Other**

Failure of communication

Equipment failure

Other system failure

---

*Source:* From "Preventing Medical Injury," by L. Leape, A. G. Lawthers, T. A. Brennan, et al., 1993, *Qualitative Review Bulletin, 19*(5), pp. 144–149. Reprinted with permission.

that is, knowledge (defined here as information and procedural know-how that reduces or reveals uncertainty) is available but is not used. This lack of knowledge and skill may be due to inexperience or inadequate training. Errors also result from lack of familiarity with political, economic, and social influences on professions such as psychiatry, psychology, and social work, and with the influence of social-psychological variables in the therapeutic context. The interpersonal context within which counseling occurs offers many potential opportunities for mutual influence that may have beneficial or dysfunctional effects (see Chapter 2). Errors may occur because of personal characteristics of the clinicians, such as excessive need for approval (see Chapter 17).

Avoidable errors may result in (1) failing to offer help that could be provided and is desired by clients, (2) forcing clients to accept "help" they do not want, (3) offering help that is not needed, or (4) using procedures that aggravate rather than alleviate client concerns (that is, procedures that result in iatrogenic effects [e.g., Sharpe & Faden, 1998]). Such errors may occur in all three phases of clinical practice: assessment, intervention, and evaluation. Errors may occur during assessment by overlooking important data, using invalid assessment measures, or attending to irrelevant data; during intervention by using ineffective methods; and during evaluation by using inaccurate measures of progress. If irrelevant or inaccurate sources of data are relied on during assessment, the result may be incorrect and irrelevant accounts of client concerns and consequent recommendation of ineffective or harmful intervention methods. Important factors may not be noticed. For example, a clinician may overlook the role of physiological factors in depression. Depression is a common side effect of birth control pills and is also related to hormonal changes among middle-aged women. Failure to consider physical causes may result in inappropriate treatment decisions. Failure to seek information about the evidentiary status of different methods may result in use of an ineffective method rather than one that would help clients attain valued outcomes. We may fail to recognize important cues or our attention may drift. We may forget important intentions or attend to irrelevant content/events. Errors may result from reliance on questionable criteria such as anecdotal experience to evaluate the accuracy of claims, as discussed in Chapter 4.

Given the role of decision making in clinical practice and the variety of factors that influence the quality of decisions, it is surprising that more attention is not devoted to this content in professional training. Meehl's book *Clinical Versus Statistical Prediction* appeared in 1954. The classic "Why I Do Not Attend Case Conferences" (Meehl, 1973) identifies errors and tendencies in groups that dilute the quality of decisions. The influence of illusory correlations on clinical observation was explored in the late sixties (see, for example, L. J. Chapman, 1967; L. J. Chapman & J. P. Chapman, 1967, 1969). The tendency of clinicians to attribute problems to the person and overlook the role of environmental factors has been a topic of interest for some time (see, for example, Rosenhan, 1973). Although students in professional education programs learn to attend to some sources of error (such as factors that influence reliability and validity) and are cautioned to avoid mistaking correlation for causation, they are not exposed to the range of formal and informal fallacies described in this book. Nor are they given information about the conditions that encourage these fallacies and that increase the likelihood that their influence on decisions will slip by unnoticed. Students may not be exposed to sociological views of psychological and psychiatric concepts (e.g., Busfield, 2001; Conrad & Schneider, 1992; Goffman, 1961; Scheff, 1984a, 1984b): that the labeling of attributes or actions as symptoms of psychopathology is intimately associated with political and economic concerns and social conventions; that therapists function as "moral managers" (Sedgwick, 1982, pp. 141, 147; see Chapter 2 of this book).

Although the strategies we use to make decisions may often result in sound judgments, the task here is to identify ways in which they are not correctly used, so that errors can be avoided. Judgmental strategies are not necessarily used consciously, which is another reason it is helpful to be familiar with them. Indeed, two of the three routes to information lie outside of our awareness: perception and automatic associations. However, familiarity with sources of error is not enough. If this were true, certain kinds of errors would not recur in clinical practice. For example, many writers, both past and present, have argued that mental health professionals are too focused on pathology, that stereotypes interfere with making balanced decisions that reflect what a client can do as well as what he cannot do (see, for example, Hobbs, 1975). However, some clinicians continue to focus on individual pathology, neglect client assets, and overlook environmental causes of personal troubles. Decreasing such errors requires a systemic approach including attention to agency culture and climate as discussed in Chapter 9.

## HALLMARKS OF CRITICAL THINKING

The term *reflection* is popular. But as Steven Brookfield notes, "Reflection is not by definition critical" (1995, p. 8). Critical thinking is a unique kind of purposeful thinking in which we use standards such as clarity and fairness. It involves the careful examination and evaluation of beliefs and actions in order to arrive at well-reasoned decisions. It is

- Clear versus unclear
- Precise versus imprecise
- Specific versus vague
- Accurate versus inaccurate
- Relevant versus irrelevant
- Consistent versus inconsistent
- Logical versus illogical
- Deep versus shallow
- Complete versus incomplete
- Significant versus trivial
- Adequate (for purpose) versus inadequate
- Fair versus biased or one-sided (Paul, 1993, p. 63)

Both critical thinking and evidence-based practice encourage asking questions designed to make the invisible visible. Problems may remain unsolved because we rely on questionable criteria to evaluate claims about what is accurate, such as tradition, popularity, or authority. This was a key reason for the development of evidence-based practice (see Chapter 10). Consider a claim that recovered memory therapy works. Usually, the questions we should ask to reveal the evidentiary status of a claim are not visible, such as "What is the source?" "Works for what?" "What kind of research was conducted to test this claim?" "Could such research rigorously test the claim?" "Has anyone been harmed by this method?" (See, for example, Ofshe & Watters, 1994.) This illustrates the difference between propaganda and critical thinking. In the former, strategies such as censoring (not mentioning) alternative well-argued views and contradictory evidence are used.

Critical thinking involves clearly describing and carefully evaluating our claims and arguments, no matter how cherished, and considering alternative views when needed to arrive at decisions that do more good than harm. "One cannot tell truth from falsity, one cannot tell an adequate answer to a problem from an irrelevant one, one cannot tell good ideas from trite ones—unless they are presented with sufficient clarity" (Popper, 1994, p. 71). This means paying attention to the process of reasoning (how we think), not just the product. Critical thinking encourages us to examine the context in which problems occur (to connect private troubles with public issues; Mills, 1959), to view questions from different points of view, to identify and question our assumptions, and to consider the possible consequences of different beliefs or actions.

### CRITICAL THINKING IS INTEGRAL TO EVIDENCE-BASED PRACTICE

Critical thinking knowledge, skills, and values are integral to evidence-based practice (EBP). Critical thinking, evidence-based practice, and scientific reasoning are closely related. All use reasoning for a purpose (i.e., to solve a problem), relying on standards such as clarity, relevance, and accuracy. All regard criticism (self-correction) as essential to forward understanding; all encourage us to challenge our assumptions, consider well-argued opposing views, and check our reasoning for errors. All are antiauthoritarian. Critical appraisal skills are needed to accurately describe the extent to which a given research method can rigorously test a given practice or policy question, and many tools have been developed to facilitate this task, as described in Chapter 12. Critical thinking can protect us from being bamboozled and misled by descriptions of research and advertisements, for example for drugs. Consider the examples below. Each makes a claim concerning the effectiveness of a practice method. Are they true? What questions would you ask to evaluate the accuracy of these claims? How would you search for related research findings? Is there a high-quality review of research related to each claim?

- Eye movement desensitization therapy is effective in decreasing anxiety. (Is it?)
- "Four hours a month can keep a kid off drugs forever. Be a mentor" (*New York Times*, 12/31/02, p. A15. The Partnership for a Drug-Free America; www.drugfreedomamerica.org). (Can it?)
- Anatomically detailed dolls can be used to accurately identify children who have been sexually abused. (Can they?)
- THREE MINUTE THERAPY: Change your thinking, change your life (Edelstein, flyer distributed). (Does it work?)

Both critical thinking and EBP value clarity over obscurity, accuracy over inaccuracy, deep versus superficial analysis, and fairminded versus deceptive practices. Both value transparency (honesty) concerning what is done to what effect, including candid description of lack of knowledge (uncertainty and ignorance). Consider the statement by the editor of the *British Medical Journal:*

"The history of medicine is mostly a history of ineffective and often dangerous treatments. . . . Unfortunately there is still no evidence to support most diagnostic methods and treatments. Either the research hasn't been done or it is of too poor a quality to be useful" (Smith, 2003, p. 1307).

(For a more optimistic view see J. A. M. Gray, 2001a.) Material referred to as "evidence-based" reflects critical thinking values, knowledge, and skills to different degrees, ranging from a close relationship to little overlap, as illustrated by use of the term "evidence-based" without the substance (e.g., misrepresenting the philosophy and evolving technology of EBP, inflated claims of effectiveness, and not involving clients as informed participants; Gambrill, 2003a).

## RELATED VALUES, ATTITUDES, AND STYLES

Critical thinking is independent thinking—thinking for yourself. Critical thinkers question what others view as self-evident. They ask:

- Is this claim accurate? Have critical tests been performed? If so, were they relatively free of bias? Have the results been replicated? How representative were the samples used?
- Who presented it as true? How reliable are these sources?
- Are vested interests involved?
- Are the facts presented correct?
- Have any facts been omitted?
- Are there alternative well-argued points of view?

Critical thinkers are skeptics rather than believers. That is, they are neither gullible (believing anything people say, especially if it agrees with their own views) or cynical (believing nothing and having a negative outlook on life). This was illustrated by Susan Blackmore in a keynote address at the 1991 annual meeting of the Committee for the Scientific Investigation of Claims of the Paranormal (CSICOP) when she presented what she described as her favorite slide (a question mark) between slides of a sheep (illustrating gullibility) and a goat (illustrating cynicism). Cynics look only for faults. They have a contemptuous distrust of all knowledge. Skeptics (critical thinkers) value truth and seek approximations to it through critical discussion and the testing of theories. Criticism is viewed as essential to forward understanding.

Intellectual traits integral to critical thinking, suggested by Richard Paul, are shown in Exhibit 1.5. Critical thinking involves using related knowledge and skills in everyday life and acting on the results (Paul, 1993). It requires flexibility and a keen interest in discovering mistakes in our thinking. Truth (accuracy) is valued over "winning" or social approval. Values and attitudes related to critical thinking include openmindedness, an interest in and respect

**Exhibit 1.5**
Examples of Valuable Intellectual Traits

---

**Intellectual autonomy:** Analyzing and evaluating beliefs on the basis of reason and evidence.

**Intellectual civility:** Taking others seriously as thinkers, treating them as intellectual equals, attending to their views.

**Intellectual confidence in reason:** Confidence that in the long run our own higher interests and those of humankind will best be served by giving the freest play to reason—by encouraging people to come to their conclusions through a process of developing their own reasoning skills; form rational viewpoints, draw reasonable conclusions, persuade each other by reason, and become reasonable people despite the many obstacles to doing so. Confidence in reason is developed through solving problems though reason, using reason to persuade, and being persuaded by reason. It is undermined when we are expected to perform tasks without understanding why, or to accept beliefs on the sole basis of authority or social pressure.

**Intellectual courage:** Critically assessing viewpoints regardless of negative reactions. It takes courage to tolerate ambiguity and to face ignorance and prejudice in our own thinking. The penalties for nonconformity are often severe.

**Intellectual curiosity:** An interest in deeply understanding, figuring things out, and in learning.

**Intellectual discipline:** Thinking guided by intellectual standards (e.g., clarity and relevance). Undisciplined thinkers neither know or care when they come to unwarranted conclusions, confuse distinct ideas, or ignore pertinent evidence. It takes discipline to keep focused on the intellectual task at hand, to locate and carefully assess evidence, to systematically analyze and address questions and problems, and to honor standards of clarity, precision, completeness, and consistency.

**Intellectual empathy:** Putting ourselves in the place of others to genuinely understand them and recognize our egocentric tendency to identify truth with our views. Indicators include accurately presenting the viewpoints and reasoning from assumptions other than our own.

**Intellectual humility:** Awareness of the limits of our knowledge, sensitivity to bias, prejudice, and limitations of one's viewpoint. No one should claim more than he or she actually knows. Lack of pretentiousness and conceit, combined with insight into the strengths and weaknesses of the logical foundations of one's views.

**Intellectual integrity:** Honoring the same standards of evidence to which we hold others, practicing what we advocate, and admitting discrepancies and inconsistencies in our own thought and action.

**Intellectual perseverance:** The pursuit of accuracy despite difficulties, obstacles, and frustration; adherence to rational principles despite irrational opposition of others: recognizing the need to struggle with confusion and unsettled questions to pursue understanding. This trait is undermined when others provide the answers or do our thinking for us.

---

*Source:* Adapted from *Critical Thinking: What Every Person Needs to Survive in a Rapidly Changing World* (Rev. 3rd ed., pp. 470–472), by R. Paul, 1993, Foundation for Critical Thinking. www.criticalthinking.org. Reprinted with permission.

for the opinion of others, a desire to be well informed, a tendency to think before acting, and curiosity. It means being fair-minded, that is, accurately describing opposing views and critiquing both preferred and less preferred views using the same rigorous standards. Critical thinking discourages arrogance, the assumption that we know better than others or that our beliefs should not be subject to critical evaluation. As Popper emphasized, ". . . in our infinite ignorance we are all equal" (Popper, 1992, p. 50). These attitudes reflect a belief in and respect for the intrinsic worth of all human beings, for valuing learning and truth without self-interest, and a respect for opinions that differ from one's own (Nickerson, 1988–1989, p. 507). They also highlight the role of affective components, such as empathy for others and a tolerance for ambiguity and differences of opinion. Critical reflection stresses the value of self-criticism. It prompts questions such as Could I be wrong? Have I considered alternative views? Do I have sound reasons to believe that this plan will help this client?

## RELATED SKILLS AND KNOWLEDGE

Similar kinds of knowledge and skills are of value in problem solving and decision making, including accurately weighing the quality of evidence and arguments, identifying assumptions, and recognizing contradictions. Examples of critical thinking skills (e.g., see Ennis, 1987; Paul, 1993) are:

- Clarify problems.
- Identify significant similarities and differences.
- Recognize contradictions and inconsistencies.
- Refine generalizations and avoid oversimplifications.
- Clarify issues, conclusions, or beliefs.
- Analyze or evaluate arguments, interpretations, beliefs, or theories.
- Identify unstated assumptions.
- Clarify and analyze the meaning of words or phrases.
- Use sound criteria for evaluation.
- Clarify values and standards.
- Detect bias.
- Distinguish relevant from irrelevant questions, data, claims, or reasons.
- Evaluate the accuracy of different sources of information.
- Compare analogous situations; transfer insights to new contexts.
- Make well-reasoned inferences and predictions.
- Compare and contrast ideals with actual practice.
- Discover and accurately evaluate the implications and consequences of a proposed action.
- Evaluate one's own reasoning process.
- Raise and pursue significant questions.
- Make interdisciplinary connections.
- Analyze and evaluate actions or policies.
- Evaluate perspectives, interpretations, or theories.

We often fail to solve problems not because we are not intelligent but because we fall into intelligence traps such as jumping to conclusions. This highlights the value of acquiring strategies that avoid these "defaults" in thinking.

In addition to content knowledge, we need performance skills. For example, being aware of pitfalls in observing interaction between clients and significant others (e.g., students and teachers) will not be useful without the skills to avoid them (see Chapter 13). Critical thinking skills are not a substitute for problem-related knowledge. For example, you may need specialized knowledge to evaluate the plausibility of premises related to an argument. Consider the following example:

- Depression always has a psychological cause.
- Mr. Draper is depressed.
- Therefore the cause of Mr. Draper's depression is psychological in origin.

Even though the logic of this argument is sound, the conclusion may be false; the cause of Mr. Draper's depression could be physiological. The more information that is available about a subject that can decrease or reveal uncertainty about what decision is best, the more important it is to be familiar with this knowledge. Taking advantage of practice-related research findings is a hallmark of evidence-based practice.

Nickerson (1986a) suggests that *self-knowledge* is one of the three forms of knowledge central to critical thinking, in addition to knowledge of content related to a topic and critical thinking skills. Self-knowledge includes awareness of our style of thinking (e.g., the strategies we use), and its flaws such as, stereotypes that bias what we see and inaccurate (inflated) assessment of our competencies (Dunning, Heath, & Suls, 2005). Without self-knowledge, content and performance knowledge may remain unused. Three of the nine basic building blocks of reasoning suggested by Paul (1993) (ideas and concepts drawn on, whatever is taken for granted, and the point of view in which one's thinking is embedded), concern background beliefs that influence how we approach problems.

## BARRIERS TO MAKING SOUND JUDGMENTS

Judgments and decisions must be made in the face of uncertainty; even if all could be known, typically not enough time would be available to know all, nor may "knowing all" be needed to solve problems. The judgments that must be made are difficult ones, requiring distinctions between causes and secondary effects, problems and the results of attempted solutions, personal and environmental contributions to presenting complaints, and findings and evidence (links between clinical assumptions and findings). Physicians usually work in a state of uncertainty about the true state of the patient. They can only estimate the probability that a client has a certain illness. Uncertainty may concern: (1) the nature of the problem; (2) the outcomes desired; (3) what is needed to attain valued outcomes; (4) likelihood of attaining outcomes; and (5) measures that will best reflect degree of success. Information about options may be missing or unreliable, and accurate estimates of the probability that different alternatives will result in desired outcomes may be unknown. It may be assumed that because there is uncertainty, there is no difference between the different degrees to which a claim has been critically appraised. There are many pressures on clinicians to act more certain than they are, including the rhetoric of professional organizations that oversells the feats of clinicians, clients who seek more certainty than is possible, colleagues who make exaggerated claims of certainty, and journal articles that misrepresent findings (Doust & Delhar, 2004). Such pressures encourage our tendency to be overconfident in the accuracy of our views (Baron, 2000). A reluctance to consider errors as inevitable may result in overlooking uncertainty. We work under environmental constraints such as time pressures. Preferences may change in the very process of being asked about them. Problems that confront clients (e.g., lack of housing or day care) are often difficult ones that challenge the most skilled of helpers. Rarely is all relevant information available, and it is difficult to integrate different kinds of data. Knowledge may be available but not used.

Even when empirical information is available, this knowledge is usually in the form of general principles that do not allow specific predictions about individuals (Dawes, 1994a). For example, many convicted rapists rape again when released from prison; however, this does not allow you to accurately predict whether a particular person will rape again if released. You can only appeal to the general information (see discussion of expert testimony in Chapter 13). Problems may have a variety of causes and potential solutions. We must often settle for less than the best. The criteria on which decisions should be based are in dispute, and empirical data about the effectiveness of different options are often lacking. A desire to avoid uncertainty is a source of error.

Yet another barrier is the effort required to make sound judgments. Some barriers, such as selective perception, are common to all judgmental tasks. Others, such as the lack of agreed-on criteria for determining the accuracy of decisions, are more problematic in clinical contexts than they are in the hard sciences or in activities such as car repair. Our perception is selective; we do not necessarily see what is there to be seen (see Chapter 9). Errors may occur during perception and when thinking about what we see. The former may be more difficult to alter because of their automatic nature. We may process data in a sequential manner, although a network or web approach to the associations between variables may result in more accurate judgments. Although strategies used to simplify judgmental tasks and decrease effort may usually work well in making accurate judgments, at other times they may result in errors. Our memories may not be accurate. Data that decrease uncertainty may not be available. It is often difficult to discover whether our beliefs are compatible with one another, since they may be implicit rather than explicit. Preferences for certain views or theories may result in propaganistic attacks rather than reasoned discussion (e.g., see Gresham & MacMillan, 1997). We may give exaggerated importance to some findings to justify retention of a favored hypothesis—the ubiquitous confirmation bias, in which we seek data that support our views and ignore data that do not (Nickerson, 1998). Lack of knowledge and interfering attitudes such as fear of failure and inflated self-assessments (for example, an unjustified belief in one's background knowledge) are other limiting factors (see Chapter 17). We are often "unskilled and unaware of it" (Dunning, Heath, & Suls, 2005; Kruger & Dunning, 1999).

There are often no agreed-on criteria against which to check the accuracy of decisions in clinical practice in psychology, social work, and psychiatry—unlike in medical practice in which there are signs (e.g, temperature reading) as well as symptoms (feeling hot). The reports of a pathologist may verify clinical assumptions, although here, too, there may be more disagreement than we recognize. Clients may not and probably do not know when an avoidable error occurs, since they usually are not informed about the potential risks and benefits of different assessment, intervention, and evaluation options (Braddock et al., 1999). Clients may not be aware that methods suggested are not those that have been found to be most effective and offer little potential for attaining outcomes they value. As noted earlier, this reflects a key reason for the development of evidence-based practice—gaps between available practice-related knowledge and what practitioners draw on (Sackett, Richardson, Rosenberg, & Haynes, 1997). Nor may clients realize that a clinician's selection of outcomes to focus on may involve an error in that the choice may not address the clients' real interests—although it may serve other ends (see Chapter 2).

Economic and political interests influence decisions in interpersonal helping, as they do in fields such as medicine (see Chapter 2). Clinicians may not be aware of how these larger influences such as the pharmaceutical industry affect the very definitions of problems and recommended practice methods. Decisions are made in a particular context that influences their nature (see Chapter 2). These situations differ in how conducive they are to learning and critical thinking. Hogarth (2001) uses the term "wicked" to refer to environments that impede learning from experience. Because many clinical tasks involve the same kinds of judgments made in everyday life, replacement of research-informed views by unsupported hunches is especially easy. For most clinicians, "practice theory" is probably a mix of common knowledge, hunches, and scientific knowledge (Bromley, 1986, p. 219). There are many application challenges, such as gaining timely access to research findings related to important practice questions. Indeed, a key aim of evidence-based practice is addressing these application challenges (see Chapter 10).

Lack of understanding of and misrepresentation of science may result in rejection of this approach to critical appraisal of claims of knowledge. Some confuse this with scientism, "the belief that science knows or will soon know all the answers, and it has the corrupting smugness of any system of opinions which contains its own antidote to disbelief" (Medawar, 1984, p. 60). Hallmarks of a scientific approach toward clinical practice include looking for disconfirming evidence for favored views and considering the evidentiary status of practices and policies. It is assumed that nothing is ever proven, but that rather some claims have passed critical tests of their accuracy. Thus, a scientific approach is quite the opposite of the characteristics often attributed to it, such as "rigid," "dogmatic," "closed," or "trivial" (see Chapter 4). Within a scientific approach, it would be just as ill advised to claim that some people are psychic as it would be to claim that there is no such thing as "psychic abilities" without results from critical tests. An understanding of the scientific method is usually not available to the public. "It itself is esoteric knowledge" (Stevens, 1988, p. 382). "There is a grave crisis in science education. The basic principles of the scientific method are not being taught in a manner that enables otherwise well-educated people to apply them to problems in their daily experiences" (p. 385) (See also National Science Foundation reports, 2002). Clinicians are not immune from this educational deficit, which is so common in our culture and which accounts in large part for the ready acceptance of proposed causal factors without any evidence that they are relevant. Consider, for example, the uncritical acceptance of phenomena such as past lives, spirit guides, auras, and the occult (Shermer, 1997). Even quite elementary knowledge of scientific ways of weighing the value of evidence would call such claims into question. Clinicians may become disenchanted with science as a problem-solving method (for example, to discover what helps clients) because of being confronted repeatedly with trivializing or bogus examples of its use in professional newsletters and professional journals. Because of this, they may discard a method that is vital in finding out how to help clients and avoid harm. The tendency to ignore practice-related research may result from ineffective search skills or disappointment that more knowledge is not available.

We have a tendency to believe in initial judgments, even when we are informed that the knowledge on which we based our judgments was arbitrarily selected, for example, by the spin of a roulette wheel (Tversky & Kahneman, 1974). Clinicians tend to form impressions of clients quickly; these first impressions influence their expectations about outcomes, which in turn may affect how they respond to clients and so confirm their original impressions. As Snyder and Thomsen (1988) note, the view that these initial judgments are accurate is questionable, since different therapists may form quite different impressions of the same client (Houts & Galante, 1985; Strupp, 1958). Not only are initial beliefs resistant to new evidence, but they also are remarkably resistant to challenges of the evidence that led to those beliefs. Primacy or anchoring effects (influence by what we see or first consider) may be a result of our tendency to generate theories that bias our interpretation of additional material. Premature commitment to a position and insufficient revision of beliefs as well as a tendency to believe (often falsely) in the consistency of behavior contribute to the primacy effect.

Evidence in support of preferred theories tends to be accepted, and evidence contrary to such views tends to be discounted; different standards are used to criticize opposing evidence than to evaluate supporting evidence. Moreover, data that provide some support for and some against preferred views increase the confidence of holders of both views. For example, both students who were in favor of capital punishment and those who were not, read studies supporting and critical of their views about capital punishment and were more confident of their initial position than they were before they had read any evidence (Lord, Ross, & Lepper, 1979). The generation of data, as well as the retrieval of material, are influenced by causal assumptions. Clinicians have a tendency not to search for evidence against their views; this tendency may result in errors. The more clinicians are biased in favor of an argument and the more unaware they are of these biases, the less likely they will be to weigh (or even identify) points against an argument as carefully as they do points in favor of it. Expectations tend to be self-fulfilling: assumptions about how clients will respond encourage reactions compatible with these beliefs. Snyder and Thomsen (1988) describe the many opportunities for confirmation bias in therapeutic exchanges. They, as well as others (Pyszczynski & Greenberg, 1987), note the many stages at which confirmation biases may occur; assumptions in earlier phases influence actions in later phases. For example, a clinician may have read a report describing a client as schizophrenic. This may result in a selective search for evidence in support of this assumption and a selective ignoring of counter-evidence. The behavior of clients, their histories, and relevant current situations may be scanned selectively for data that support initial assumptions. This justification focus (searching for data that confirm initial views rather than seeking to disconfirm preferred views) is at the heart of many sources of error.

Errors may occur because certain logical-statistical principles are ignored, such as the size and representativeness of samples, the importance of base-rate data, and the importance of considering relative frequencies in assessing co-variations (see Chapter 15). Checklists are available to help us pay attention to important characteristics when critically appraising practice-related research (e.g, see Gibbs, 2003; Greenhalgh, 2001). The tendency to attribute problems to dispositional (personal) characteristics of clients and to ignore environmental factors is common in clinical practice. This is known as the *fundamental attribution error* (see Chapter 14).

The tendencies described may influence decision making in all phases of helping (for example, describing clients and their concerns, making inferences about causal factors, and making predictions about the effectiveness of different kinds of services). Specific examples of their influence and guidelines designed to avoid them are given in later chapters. Being forewarned is being prepared—the more familiar we are with sources of error that compromise the quality of decisions, the more likely we may be to avoid them. Many of these biases result in too little, in contrast to too much thinking—a "premature cessation of search" (Baron, 1985a, p. 208). The process of evidence-based practice and related tools such as systematic reviews are designed to facilitate critical appraisals of practice-related beliefs.

## CLINICAL REASONING AS A TEACHABLE SKILL

The good news is that we can learn to make better decisions, for example by learning through our mistakes. Research in a variety of areas including decision making, judgment, problem solving, creativity, and teaching of reading, writing, and reasoning relates to this topic. A rich literature is available describing efforts to enhance problem solving and decision making, including the tools and process of evidence-based practice designed to decrease gaps between a clinician's current knowledge about how to attain outcomes desired by clients and possibilities for resolution (see Chapters 10 and 11). Debiasing strategies can be acquired, as described in later chapters. We can learn how to allocate scarce resources, such as time, wisely. We can become familiar with barriers to problem solving including inaccurate self-assesments and develop skills for avoiding them. We can acquire critical thinking values, knowledge, and skills that contribute to problem solving and decision making that are described throughout this book. We can become more aware of our reasoning process, as described in Chapter 3. The term *metacognitive* refers to awareness of and influence on our reasoning processes (e.g., monitoring our thinking by asking questions such as "How am I doing?" "Is this correct?" "How do I know this is true?" "What are my biases?" "Is there another way to approach this problem?" "Do I understand this point?"). These questions highlight the importance of *self-correction* in problem solving. Related behaviors can be thought of as self-governing processes (strategies we use to guide our thinking). They can help us to use effective approaches to problem solving and to avoid common intelligence traps. Increasingly metacognitive levels of thought include: (1) *Tacit:* Thinking without thinking about it; (2) *Aware:* Thinking and being aware that you are thinking; (3) *Strategic:* Organizing our thinking by using strategies that enhance its efficacy; and (4) *Reflective:* Reflecting on our thinking (pondering how to proceed and how to improve; Swartz & Perkins, 1990, p. 52).

In a skill-based metaphor for reasoning, it is assumed that critical thinking requires a repertoire of strategies, such as anticipating questions and focusing on key information. Successful managers, for example, seek concrete information when faced with ambiguity, obtain information from a range of sources, and identify useful analogies to explain a situation (Klemp & McClelland, 1986). Mathematical problem solving, reading, and invention can be improved by teaching (Schoenfeld, 1982). Accurate estimates of risk can be made by thinking in terms of frequencies rather than probabilities (see Chapter 15). As skill is acquired in an area, knowledge tends to be stored in larger chunks, and these chunks are run off in a more automatic fashion. Consider the difference between skilled and unskilled drivers. The ability of chess masters to quickly identify effective moves depends on pattern recognition. (See discussion of primed decision making in Chapter 9.) Components of practical intelligence tend to be learned on the job. The goal of practical intelligence is to accomplish tasks in real-life settings. Different kinds of practical intelligence include managing emotions, developing and using interpersonal skills, responding to setbacks and failures, and dealing with procrastination.

## THE COSTS AND BENEFITS OF CRITICAL THINKING

Like anything else, critical thinking has advantages and disadvantages; there may be long-term benefits for short-term investments. A tendency to overemphasize immediate costs in relation to future gains may be an obstacle to critical thinking. The benefits depend on our goals and values. An interest in enhancing clinical competence, curiosity, and a desire to make ethical decisions encourage critical thinking (for example, searching for and critically appraising practice-related research).

*The Benefits of Critical Thinking*　There are many benefits of thinking critically about clinical decisions, all of which contribute to helping clients and avoiding harming them:

- Discover problem-related resources and constraints.
- See the connection between private troubles and public issues; think contextually.
- Avoid cognitive biases.
- Avoid influence by bogus claims/human service propaganda.
- Recognize errors and mistakes as learning opportunities.
- Recognize pseudoscience, quackery, and fraud.
- Focus on outcomes related to clients' complaints.
- Accurately assess the likelihood of attaining hoped-for outcomes.
- Make valuable contributions at case conferences (e.g., identify flawed arguments, suggest well-argued alternative views).
- Select programs and policies that achieve hoped-for outcomes with a minimum of harmful side effects.
- Make accurate predictions.
- Select effective plans.
- Accurately assess the effects of policies, programs, and plans.
- Make timely changes in plans, programs, and policies that have unintended negative effects.
- Use resources (e.g., time) wisely and justly.
- Respect and have empathy for others.
- Continue to learn and to enhance your skills.
- Increase your self-awareness; for example, contradictions between what you say ("I care about clients") and what you do (not keep up-to-date with research findings about clients' concerns).

Thinking critically about practice beliefs and judgments should increase the accuracy of decisions. Informal fallacies and weak rhetorical appeals used in human service propaganda will be less likely to be influential, and clinicians may be more aware of cognitive biases that influence their judgments. Enhancing the quality of reasoning should provide useful problem-solving skills, such as deciding what questions to ask, what data to gather, and what factors to relate to problems. Selection of weak or ineffective practice methods may be avoided by a search for alternative views of problems and by consulting high-quality research reviews related to specific practice methods, such as those in the Cochrane and Campbell databases. Critical thinking skills and practice in their use can be used to avoid errors, such as the *fundamental attri-*

*bution error,* in which environmental influences are overlooked, such the role of significant others (those who interact with clients and influence their behavior). Clarifying vague terms such as *addiction, abuse, dementia,* and *self-determination* may prevent misunderstandings between clinicians and their clients, as well as among clinicians, and help to avoid the "patient uniformity myth," in which clients and their problems are incorrectly assumed to be identical (Kiesler, 1966). Only when desired outcomes are clearly described may it be obvious that, given available resources, some are unattainable or conflict with other valued outcomes. Clarifying values and preferences is another benefit of critical thinking. Only when more thought is devoted to exploring preferences, for example regarding different outcomes, may these be discovered.

Thinking carefully about a decision will minimize regret. If the advantages and disadvantages of alternative courses of action are identified at an early point, they are not as likely to be a surprise after an option has been selected and acted on (Janis & Mann, 1977). Enhancing decision-making skills may help us to recapture a sense of discovery and curiosity in confronting the challenges of clinical work and in encouraging an attitude of "constructive discontent" (Koberg & Bagnall, 1976). Some clinicians may lose the sense of positive challenge over their careers as they labor in environments in which there is a poor match between resources available and tasks required. A sense of curiosity and discovery may be replaced by a mindless approach to work that is dull and dulling (Maslach, Schaufeli, & Leiter, 2001).

Familiarity with persuasion strategies and informal fallacies should upgrade the quality of decisions in all contexts: interviews with clients, case conferences, and discussions with colleagues. I was quite mystified when low-level appeals such as strawman arguments were often successful in swaying colleagues. After becoming familiar with persuasive tactics and the variety of fallacies that may occur, as well as reasons for their effectiveness, I understood their popularity and was also better prepared to handle them. Argument-analysis skills are valuable in focusing on key assumptions and identifying problems with a position (see Chapter 3). An emphasis on helping clients and avoiding harming them should encourage a collaborative, critical approach to decision making and decrease the frequency of weak appeals and adversarial tactics.

Increasing your knowledge related to decisions including skills involved in evidence-based practice, as well as critical thinking skills, should increase your effectiveness in helping clients and avoiding harm. You and your clients will be in a better position to assess whether an outcome can be pursued successfully. Some clinicians may believe that, because of the gap between resources needed to help clients and those available, their hands are tied. In some instances, this may be true; at other times, there may be options for change. It is disturbing to hear clinicians say "nothing can be done" when, in fact, if they were familiar with available knowledge, they *could* do something. It is also distressing to see clinicians using methods that do not help clients because other methods are needed (and available) to do so. Saying "nothing can be done" when this is not true leaves you helpless, and leaves clients without the benefit of the best chance of obtaining hoped-for outcomes.

Some clinicians view helping people as an art rather than a science—that there is little if any empirical knowledge of value in increasing the accuracy of decisions and that, therefore, taking the time to become familiar with and to draw on this is not only a waste of time, it will diminish the quality of service, because it interferes with the creative, spontaneous flow that is the heart of effective helping. This is not an either-or question. Both art and science are involved. For example, there is evidence in many areas that certain decisions are better than others in maximizing the likelihood of helping clients achieve outcomes they value and minimizing use of harmful methods (see, for example, Cochrane & Campbell Reviews). Perhaps you should ask yourself, "In what area would I want my dentist or doctor to be spontaneous?", to base their recommendations on what "feels best," without finding out whether what "feels best" is compatible with related research findings. Do you base decisions you make about your clients on the same criteria you would like your doctor to use when making recommendations about a serious health problem of your own? (See the list given earlier in this chapter.) If not, why so? Comparison of criteria used when making decisions that affect one's own health with those relied on with clients show that what's good for the goose (ourselves) may not be good for the gander (our clients). For example, 92 percent of respondents wanted physicians to base recommendations about treatment of a health problem on results of randomized controlled trials, but relied on criteria such as intuition with their clients. Exhibit 1.6 shows results from 86 Master's degree students in social work (Gambrill & Gibbs, 2002). Personal preferences do have a role in selecting a method from among several different ones when all methods may be equally effective—especially if the client makes the choice. And such preferences may be acted on if many methods are all equally effective or all are of unknown effectiveness.

Considerable time may be spent thinking about problems that are unsolvable (that is, there is little or nothing that can be done that would make the slightest difference). Conversely, too little thinking time may be devoted to problems that are solvable. Increasing critical thinking skills should result in a wiser allocation of thinking time. Knowledge about different kinds of decision-making strategies and the situations in which they can be used to good effect may contribute to timely, well-reasoned decisions. It is often not necessary to "optimize" (choose the best of all possible alternatives) to achieve desired outcomes. Rather, we "satisfice" (seek a satisfactory option). Simon (1983) refers to this approach as "bounded rationality" (see discussion of primed decision making in Chapter 9). In many situations, it may not be cost-effective to spend time trying to identify the optimal alternative, since there may be a range of indifference within which any one of a number of options would be satisfactory. For example, if any one of several methods can be used with equal effectiveness to enhance client participation, trying to select the

**Exhibit 1.6**
Percentage Endorsement of Criteria over Three Situations (n = 86)

| | Client (%) | Physician (%) | Ideally with Client (%) |
|---|---|---|---|
| 1. Your intuition (gut feeling) about what will be effective. | 77 (66) | 22 (19) | 38 (33) |
| 2. What you have heard from other professionals in informal exchanges. | 64 (55) | 20 (17) | 27 (23) |
| 3. Your experience with a few cases. | 73 (67) | 26 (22) | 26 (22) |
| 4. Your demonstrated track record of success based on data you have gathered systematically and regularly. | 39 (34) | 92 (79) | 91 (78) |
| 5. What fits your personal style. | 62 (53) | 3.6 (3) | 27 (22) |
| 6. What was usually offered at your agency. | 59 (51) | 3.6 (3) | 8 (7) |
| 7. Self-reports of other clients about what was helpful. | 65 (56) | 52 (45) | 64 (55) |
| 8. Results of controlled experimental studies. | 37 (32) | 92 (79) | 86 (74) |
| 9. What you are most familiar with. | 53 (45) | 19 (16) | 14 (12) |
| 10. What you know by critically reading professional literature. | 67 (58) | 88 (76) | 86 (74) |

*Source:* From "Making Practice Decisions: Is What's Good for the Goose Good for the Gander," by E. Gambrill and L. Gibbs, 2002, *Ethical Human Sciences and Services, 4*(1), p. 39. Reprinted with permission.

optimal one is a waste of time. A more systematic approach to problem solving will be required at other times.

*The Costs of Thinking Critically about Decisions*   A review of the costs of thinking suggests why so many people do not think carefully about their beliefs and the tasks they confront. There are social, psychological, and practical costs. People (including clinicians) may falsely believe that only experts can understand what is going on in a field, and that it will take too much to understand views related to decisions they must make. The media often perpetuate this belief, and scientists do too little to make their efforts accessible to those outside their field. In fact, many of the basic principles vital to examining the evidentiary status of a claim or theory are quite straightforward and easy to understand, even though these are not generally taught (see later chapters).

Consider our tendency to search our memories for one or two supporting examples when asked about the accuracy of an assumption, and to believe that these examples provide satisfactory evidence for our beliefs. It takes little training to realize that the case is far from settled. An overestimate of the costs of thinking may be combined with an underestimate of the value of further thinking and an overconfidence in the thinking already done. These tendencies result in impulsive decision making (Baron, 1985a). Reliance on a "makes-sense epistemology" (Perkins, Allen, & Hafner, 1983) encourages impulsive decisions (see discussion of empathic explanations in Chapter 3).

Making well-reasoned decisions may require additional time and effort in questioning initial hypotheses, consulting practice-related research, gathering data in real-life contexts to explore assumptions (for example, concerning the quality of parent-child exchanges), and encouraging colleagues to consider alternatives in case conferences. Addressing application problems in drawing on practice-related research is of high priority in evidence-based practice. It often takes longer to refute an argument than it does to state a position. The benefits of thinking may be in the future, whereas the costs in time, effort, and lost opportunities may be immediate (Baron, 1985a). Learning to question inferences requires the cultivation of compatible values and goals–a commitment to helping clients and avoiding harming them; for example, not using ineffective or harmful practices or policies. Effort will be required to learn how to critically appraise different kinds of research relevant to different kinds of decisions including both quantitative and qualitative research. The time and effort involved in increasing critical thinking skills can be reduced by using effective learning skills and helpful tools, as well as by encouraging compatible beliefs about knowledge, thinking, and learning that will make the process efficient and enjoyable. Once statistical tools are mastered, using them to increase the likelihood of accurate decisions will take less time than will the usual, intuitive means of making decisions (Nisbett, Krantz, Jepson, & Kunda, 1983). Time and effort devoted to critical thinking should be saved many times over in increased accuracy of decisions. Errors in assessment or intervention may be avoided.

An interest in protecting self-worth is a key factor in avoiding information that is not self-serving. Questioning our views requires recognizing the uncertainty inherent in helping clients. It requires us to abandon attitudes of smug paternalism and related justifications used to impose services on clients. It requires a tolerance of ambiguity and doubt. If self-efficacy is low, this tolerance probably has a narrow edge, resulting in neglect of sources of bias and disconfirming data. The belief that our current preferences and judgments are fine "as is" is helpful in maintaining self-esteem and value in the eyes of others. Our biases and prejudices and patterns of thinking have served us well—at least so we think. Thinking about problems and issues entails the possibility of discovering that "we were wrong"—of having to admit error. Suggesting positions and questioning the views of others carries the risk of negative reactions from colleagues. Critical thinkers may be viewed as acting "unsociably," by questioning assumptions others take for granted. If self-efficacy is low and the desire for social approval is greater than the interest in helping clients by discovering accurate answers, divergent perspectives may not be shared. Even though critical thinking skills are used with consummate diplomacy, negative reactions may result. Complementing these skills with effective interpersonal skills and creating an environment that encourages critical thinking will decrease the probability of negative reactions. Cultural differences should also be considered regarding when and how questions are raised (see Tweed & Lehman, 2002).

Careful consideration of options and assumptions may reveal ignorance and uncertainty. The complexity of some tasks clinicians confront may challenge the clearest thinker. Dilemmas include (1) the tension between the need to act despite uncertainty, and the desire for certainty and (2) the attempt to not impose personal biases while increasing client options (Lenrow, 1978). Estimating the probability that a practice method will be effective may reveal that it is relatively low. For example, in child protection agencies, social workers have to tackle problems even though they realistically estimate the chances of success to be low. The likelihood that a parent may curtail the use of cocaine that interferes with adequate parenting of her child may be 10 percent, given available resources. Still, the effort may have to be made in a context of permanency planning, in which other goals such as termination of parental rights can be pursued only after services have been provided to a parent and these have failed to alter problems. Being aware of the slim probability of effectiveness in this larger context should be helpful in highlighting the necessity of this step as well as in preventing clinicians from blaming themselves for lack of success, given that they have offered the best services possible. Not recognizing situations in which chances of success are slim may contribute to burnout.

Most decisions involve costs as well as benefits. Thinking about a decision may reveal tradeoffs that have been ignored. People, clinicians included, are engaged in two tasks: (1) they seek to know more about the world and (2) at the same time, they wish to protect themselves from the world, especially from information that might prove upsetting. As the need for defense against disturbing information gets stronger, curiosity gets weaker. Yet another cost is the time needed to critically review practice claims. Many clinicians accept practice beliefs without asking questions such as "Is it true?" "Is there any evidence that this claim is correct?" "Would another explanation offer greater leverage in helping this client?" Not asking questions saves time and effort. Also, if we do not have goals, tools, and beliefs that encourage such questions (e.g., to help clients, access to relevant databases describing practice-related research findings, and a belief that seeking this information is important), we are less likely to raise questions and seek answers. Use of critical thinking skills will increase responsibility for providing the help that can be offered to clients and decrease tendencies to blame clients for resistance. Increased responsibility in the absence of skills to act effectively is unpleasant. No wonder so many people opt for answers based on unfounded authority (see Chapter 7)—they do not realize that doing so limits their freedom (Fromm, 1963). The flip side of responsibility is freedom; giving up responsibility entails giving up freedom. Thinking critically increases freedom from the unwanted influence of other people, including researchers who misrepresent the evidentiary status of practices and policies. You will move beyond acceptance of arguments simply because they "make sense," realizing that what makes sense is not necessarily true; uncritical acceptance of practice-related claims leaves you at the mercy of what others think as well as of flaws in self-assessment of your own competence. One of the basic choices in life is whether to look or not look. Critical thinking values and skills increase your willingness to risk looking.

## HOW SKEPTICAL SHOULD CLINICIANS BE?

A thoughtful approach to decision making requires a skeptical attitude. How skeptical should clinicians be? They should be as skeptical as they have to be to maximize opportunities to help clients and avoid harm. Decisions must be made in spite of uncertainties. "Practitioners are asked to solve problems every day that philosophers have argued about for the last two thousand years and will probably debate for the next two thousand. Inevitably, arbitrary lines have to be drawn and hard cases decided" (Dingwall, Eekelaar, & Murray, 1983, p. 244). As Thouless (1974, p. 166) points out, "What we do is more important than what we think . . . So important is action that we can reasonably condemn as crooked thinking any device in thought which has as its purpose the evasion of useful or necessary action" (p. 166). We could not get through a day if we questioned every judgment. We cannot offer evidence for every belief we hold. We must trust the "experts" for many beliefs—that is, we cannot offer sound evidence for many of the everyday decisions we make. The case is different for clinicians in relation to their work: They should be able to offer cogent reasons for decisions they make regarding choice of assessment, intervention, and evaluation methods.

## SUMMARY

Decision making is at the heart of clinical practice. Decisions include classifying clients into categories, making causal assumptions, and making predictions about the effectiveness of different kinds of interventions and future behavior of clients. Unless we critically reflect on our decisions, clients may be harmed rather than helped. We may uncritically accept bogus claims in professional publications. Research suggests that some errors occur because of misuse of generally effective information-processing strategies. Tendencies that decrease accuracy include discounting conflicting evidence, failing to search for disconfirming evidence, and a bias for dispositional explanations. Clinicians who are psychoanalytically oriented tend to search for and attend to different factors than those who are behaviorally oriented; these selective searches influence decisions. Clinical practice requires the integration of information from diverse sources, which places a strain on memory and on capacities to combine different kinds of data. Unique barriers to making sound decisions arise in clinical practice because of disagreements about criteria to be used to assess the accuracy of decisions, the cultural relativity of definitions of personal troubles and social problems, and the gaps in knowledge about how to achieve given outcomes. Critical thinking skills can be enhanced and helpful strategies for improving accuracy can be acquired. Evidence-based practice offers an evolving process for integrating evidentiary, ethical, and application issues, as discussed in Chapter 10.

Critical thinking should yield long-term benefits for short-term investments. The benefits of enhancing related knowledge, values, and skills far outweigh the costs, both for you and your clients. Benefits include doing more good than harm, recapturing a sense of discovery, and learning from mistakes how to enhance success in the future. Costs include the discovery of faulty beliefs, ignorance, and uncertainty. Using critical thinking skills may result in negative reactions from colleagues and may increase personal responsibility because more accurate distinctions are possible between artificial and real constraints on helping clients. Critically evaluating the accuracy of practice- and policy-related claims requires time, effort, and skill. The process of evidence-based practice is designed to facilitate the integration of practice- and policy-related research in a user-friendly manner attentive to daily time pressures of clinicians and managers. On the other hand, the costs of forgoing critical thinking in clinical practice are substantial. "In exchange for the time saved, clinicians must preserve and encourage unwarranted complacency, unverified dogma, and self-perpetuating error" (Feinstein, 1967, p. 310). Increasing critical thinking knowledge, values, and skills may result in a change of preferred practice theory. Most importantly, it should enhance the quality of services offered to clients.

# CHAPTER 2

# Sources of Influence on Decisions
# That Clinicians Make

EITHER A BROAD or narrow view can be taken concerning factors that influence clinical decision making. The narrowest view focuses only on the interaction between clients and clinicians—how they influence each other within the clinical interview. An understanding of the variables that affect clinical decisions requires a much broader exploration of environments—past, present, and future; it is not enough to confine attention to the clinical interview. Decisions made in clinical interviews are influenced by past environments (such as professional education programs and the historical conditions within which practice theories and service-delivery systems emerge), current environments (such as the organizations in which many clinicians work and the current political, economic, and social circumstances in which personal and social problems are defined and service systems provided), and future environments (hoped-for outcomes). Practice is carried out in the context of policies and legislation that given patterns of behavior are problems, and certain remedies are appropriate.

Current policies reflect different approaches to troubled and troubling behaviors, including paternalistic reactions in which it is assumed that we have an obligation to prevent other people from harming others or themselves. That is, we may feel free or obligated to force unwanted help on others for "their own good." The particular settings in which clinicians work influence the kinds of clients and problems encountered. Only by understanding how these environments influence clinical practice can the nature of clinical decisions be understood (e.g., see Burnham, 1988). Consider the examples given in the beginning of Chapter 1. How could these happen? Why do harmful methods continue to be used? Why are methods we know to be effective not used? What external influences contributed to the death of a child from "re-birthing" therapy? Clarifying and critically examining basic assumptions is a key component of critical thinking. Recognizing underlying goals and points of view is not easy; they are often implicit rather than explicit. They may be part of the basic social fabric and related belief systems in which we live, perhaps unquestioned or even unrecognized. They may be deliberately suppressed. Related facts and figures may be hidden or distorted (Phillips & Project Censored, 2005). Many scholars argue that professionals are involved not so much in problem-solving as problem-setting (e.g., Schon, 1990). Gusfield (2003) suggests that "The development of professions dedicated to benevolence, the so-called 'helping professions,' depend upon and accentuate the definition of problem populations as 'sick,' as objects of medical and quasi-medical attention" (p. 9).

As we become immersed in the everyday world of practice, it is easy to forget about the economic, political, and social context in which personal and social problems are defined and reacted to. We may forget that problems are defined in accord with popular ideas of the times; we may forget to ask: "Who benefits and who loses from a particular view?" People have different opinions about what a problem is, who and what is responsible for it, and how it can be resolved. Consider dysfunctional gambling. Is it a learned behavior maintained by a complex reinforcement schedule? Is it a "moral failing"? The American Psychiatric Association (2000) views this as a mental disorder. Is this a disease? Is there a known etiology, a worsening without treatment, and a predictable course? Is social anxiety a "mental illness"? (for critiques, see Cottle, 1998; McDaniel, 2003). Throughout history, poverty has been variously viewed as a crime, a personal limitation, or a reflection of discrimination and oppression (social injustice). Who should receive welfare, how much, when, and for how long are vigorously debated. Are parents who mistreat their children bad people who should be imprisoned or overburdened people who should be helped? Are they themselves victims of the inequitable distribution of employment, housing, and education opportunities? Who is hurt by current definitions? Who gains? What are the costs and benefits to different involved parties of certain definitions and proposed remedies? The assumptions underlying different views of problems are based on different beliefs about human nature—why people do what they do, how they change, if they can change. For example, social reform efforts emphasize the influence of political, economic, and social conditions, such as the quality of educational opportunities. Recognizing the links between definitions of problems reflected in current policies and practices will help you identify options for and constraints on helping clients.

It is not surprising that clinicians may believe that what they do when with clients and how clients think, act, and feel during exchanges is influenced solely by the nature of the transactions during clinical interviews. Professional education programs may not provide students with an understanding of historical and structural factors that influence the development of practice (Abbott, 1988; Friedson, 1994; Larson, 1977). The attention of clinicians on a day-to-day basis is on individual clients and families; it is easy to forget to step back to view the larger picture within which clinical practice takes place. It takes an effort to step outside our usual way of viewing things and consider different perspectives. New perspectives often diverge considerably from current views, making it a challenge to accurately understand other views so that we are in an informed position to decide whether to accept or reject them. Consider the different views of and reactions to evidence-based practice (e.g., Gambrill, 2003a). Many authors define this as using effective interventions, a much different view than the philosophy and process of evidence-based practice described in original sources (see Chapter 10). The day-to-day concerns of practice may lull even informed clinicians into complacent acceptance of societal definitions of personal troubles, social problems, and proposed solutions, forgetting the relativity of these definitions and preferred approaches to resolving problems. Should the focus of drug programs be on users rather than on environmental conditions that encourage substance abuse? Isn't this like waiting until people are exposed to asbestos poisoning and then treating them (Sedgwick, 1982)? Who would lose and who would benefit from decriminalizing the use of controlled substances (MacCoun & Reuter, 2001)? Lack of attention to the larger picture encourages blaming personal problems on individuals and deflects attention from related political, economic, and social factors.

One of the purposes of this book is to encourage you to consider the social, economic, and political functions of psychiatric and psychological perspectives—to move beyond preferred practice theories to ask: Where do these theories come from? What particular views of reality do they promote? Which views do they obscure or actively suppress? Who benefits from a given view of pathology and health? Which ones (if any) have been critically tested, and to what effect? What consequences will occur if a given view is accepted or rejected? Does the pharmaceutical industry influence views of problems such as social anxiety and depression? Asking such questions will help to guard the values of freedom and reasoned consideration of key issues (Mills, 1959). It is the question that is not asked that poses the greatest danger to freedom. As Mills (1959) suggests, freedom is not just choosing among the alternatives; it is having a say about what alternatives are considered. Not considering the larger picture leaves clinicians open to influence by concepts and perspectives that they might reject if they considered the social and political repercussions of such concepts.

## CHANGING VIEWS OF PROBLEMS AND THEIR PREVALENCE

Many behaviors once condemned as sinful were later considered crimes and are now defined as medical or psychological problems. The view of "heretical actions" as sinful is still alive, as illustrated by Bishop Michael J. Sheridan of Colorado Springs, "who said in a pastoral letter that Catholics who vote for candidates who support gay marriage, euthanasia or abortion rights must confess their sin before receiving communion" (Woodward, 2004, p. A23). The changing ways in which certain behaviors have been viewed supports a contextual view of deviance. For instance, only when women gained more political and economic independence was greater attention given to battered women. Advances in knowledge often force changes in how people view a problem. It had been assumed that tuberculosis was inherited because people who lived together tended to "get it." When the bacillus responsible for tuberculosis was isolated, people were no longer blamed for developing it. Changing ideas about what is and what is not mental illness illustrate the consensual nature of psychiatric diagnoses. Homosexuality was defined as a mental illness until 1973, when the American Psychiatric Association, under pressure from gay and lesbian advocacy groups and bitter infighting, decided that it was not. Carol Tavris, as well as many other scholars, describe the changing views of women's alleged mental illnesses. In the *Mismeasure of Women* (1992), she suggests that labels such as *dependent personality disorder,* which are most often given to women, punish women for fulfilling expected roles. She contends that we should examine the conditions in society that result in so many women showing these characteristics, and alter them. Natural biological changes such as menopause are viewed as needing the help of experts to negotiate. In the past, housewives who wanted to work were often regarded as pathological (Oakley, 1976). Spirited controversies continue about the prevalence of stranger abduction of children and sexual assault against women.

Problems have careers. You could take any pattern of behavior (e.g., drug use, delinquency) and explore the different ways it has been viewed. Consider masturbation. At one time it was thought to be responsible for an enormous range of problems, including mental retardation (see Szasz, 1970). Now it is considered healthy. Cultural values, common metaphors, as well as political and economic pressures influence the decisions we make about problems. The metaphors used to describe problems influence how we view them and what solutions we propose. Consider the "war on drugs." This metaphor may encourage use of force against those who sell and use drugs, as well as feelings of "us against them." (For critiques of drug policies, see for example Szasz, 2001; Walker, 1994.)

## BAD PEOPLE OR BAD ENVIRONMENTS?

A historical understanding of the different ways in which deviance has been defined reveals the value-laden basis of definitions of individual troubles and social problems. Consider the movement from calling certain variations in behavior sinful, then criminal, then indications of mental illness (Scheff, 1984a, 1984b; Szasz, 1970). A moralistic definition of problems encourages the belief that people with these problems are bad people who deserve whatever ill fate awaits them, including "justified" punishment or enforced "treatment." Paternalistic views encourage beliefs that we are free to suggest (and even enforce) services on others for "their own good." Decisions may be based on beliefs about the moral character of clients rather than on objective accounts guided by empirically grounded theories of behavior. There is a close rela-tionship between explanation and evaluation (see discussion of empathic ex-planations in Chapter 3). One of the ongoing debates concerns the extent to which people are responsible for their problems: whether to locate the source of problems in the people who have them and to focus on changing individu-als and families, and/or to examine related environmental causes and pursue environmental reform. If someone drinks too much, is homeless, is unem-ployed, is this "her fault"? Do environmental conditions such as high unem-ployment, poor-quality education, and lack of low-cost housing contribute to these problems? Moral definitions of problems emphasize individual respon-sibility. We make decisions concerning the intentionality of an act. The ques-tion of intention highlights the moral aspect of decisions—that is, the client "knowingly" selected one way to act from a variety of options. We assume that the choice made characterizes the kind of person the client is; that is, it is a re-flection of moral character. The relation between judgments of moral char-acter and ascriptions of deviance is emphasized by sociologists and often neglected by clinicians. A concern about whether applicants for services are worthy of receiving aid has a long history in the helping professions (Leiby, 1978). Moral principles may be based on (1) common sense (what appears to be self-evident), (2) revelation (communication of values by a transcendent power), (3) socialization (learning society's values), or (4) moral reasoning (reasoning out what is right and wrong). They may emphasize (1) utility (greatest good for the greatest number); (2) beneficence, love, charity; (3) jus-tice (fair play—all rules apply equally; just desserts—a belief that there should be some equivalence between behavior and rewards or punishment); or (4) equality (equal obligations and rights). The freedom to choose is a foundation requirement of moral behavior.

## PROBLEMS AS SOCIALLY CONSTRUCTED

Some scholars argue that some state of affairs becomes a social problem when an objective "condition" exists. Others believe that social problems are socially constructed. They argue that although certain needs of the sick, poor, elderly, and very young have been recognized throughout the centuries, they have been defined differently at different times and receive more or less atten-tion at different times. Gusfield (2003) suggests that the very notion of a social problem is unique to certain times.

> The idea of "social problems" is unique to modern societies . . . modern soci-eties, including the United States, display a culture of public problems. It is a part of how we think and how we interpret the world about us, that we perceive many conditions as not only deplorable but as capable of being relieved by and as re-quiring public action, most often by the state. The concept of "social problems" is a category of thought, a way of seeing certain conditions as providing a claim to change through public actions. (Gusfield, 2003, p. 7)

Gusfield (2003) points out that there are many human problems that are not considered to be public problems, such as disappointed friendships and unrequited love.

> Again and again sociologists have pointed out how the conditions said to define the social problem are socially constructed, are only one of several possible "realities." The attempt to pose as the arbiters of standards is less and less taken for granted and more and more seen as an accompaniment to social control, to the quest for hegemony. (Gusfield, 2003, p. 15)

"Problem crusaders" (people with a particular interest in a particular view of a problem) forward particular definitions and may exaggerate potential risks and prevalence (e.g., see MacCoun & Reuter, 2001). Feminist scholars and advocates have been in the vanguard in emphasizing the relationship between personal problems and social issues ("the personal is political"). The ascribed nature of deviance is shown by changing definitions of deviance and different perspectives concerning society's responsibility in relation to groups such as the homeless, the poor, the sick, the abused, and the neglected. If deviance is an ascribed rather than inherent status, then there is room to build a case for or against ascriptions. The manner in which a case can be built is illustrated in the example given in Chapter 16. The allegation of a certain kind of character may rest on a retrospective analysis of past behavior and predictions of future behavior as well as descriptions of current behavior.

## POLITICAL, ECONOMIC, AND SOCIAL INFLUENCES ON PROBLEM DEFINITIONS AND PROPOSED REMEDIES

There are great stakes in how problems are framed, and people with vested interests devote considerable time, money, and effort to influence what others believe (e.g., see Szasz, 2001). Costs to society and involved individuals may not be apparent until later developmental stages, as illustrated in follow-up studies of antisocial children (e.g., Scott, Knapp, Henderson, & Maughan, 2001). "Problem crusaders" (people with a particular interest in a particular view of a problem) forward particular definitions and may exaggerate potential risks and prevalence. Psychotherapy is a highly political enterprise. Given the relativity of the definition of personal and social problems and differences of opinion about what kinds of help should be offered, it could not help but be so. Clinicians as well as clients are influenced by the historical period in which they live and work; for example, by current definitions of personal troubles and social problems and proposed solutions. Consider the embrace of pharmaceutical remedies for a myriad of problems in everyday life. We can better understand why certain decisions are made and more accurately assess barriers and potential for change if we understand the social, economic, and political circumstances within which the current mental health system developed and is maintained. Consider individuals who are encouraged to seek treatment for their "alcoholism." Environmental factors that contribute to drinking (such as poverty, unemployment, and the multimillion-dollar advertising of alcoholic beverages) are ignored in biomedical views of alcohol abuse. Such a view is actively promoted by research funding agencies such as the National Institute on Alcohol Abuse and Alcoholism (NIAAA) (Midanik, 2006). Who benefits and who loses from acceptance of a biomedical model of alcoholism, in which attention is focused on the individual? What is the impact of such a view on the way resources are distributed, including research funding? Lack of understanding of the larger context may contribute to questionable decisions. For example, decisions to intervene may be made when there is no justifiable reason to do so. A decision may be made not to intervene when intervention would help clients to enhance the quality of their lives, or ineffective practices or policies may be chosen. Without a contextual understanding, you may miss the relationship between the personal and the political (Mills, 1959). You may accept views that limit opportunities to help clients. Without this, it is easy to fall into "blaming clients" and focusing on "changing them" or giving them a rationale for their plights rather than altering the environmental conditions related to their problems. Thinking critically about what is defined as a problem and proposed remedies commits you to the effort and courage required to question popular assumptions and examine underlying points of view.

Economic interests influence problem definition. For example, definitions of social anxiety and depression as "brain diseases" requiring medication benefit the pharmaceutical industry (which has more lobbyists in Washington than all senators and representatives combined—as of 2002, 675). These lobbyists actively promote biomedical views of problems-in-living. Problem definition is influenced by professionals' interest in maintaining and gaining power, status, and economic resources as, well as by differences of opinion about what makes one explanation better than another. As the number of clinicians has expanded, so, too, has the number of "conditions" that need treatment. Entries in the *Diagnostic and Statistical Manual of Mental Disorders* (*DSM;* American Psychiatric Association, 2000) have expanded from 80 in 1980 to over 400 in 2000. Concerns about funding and the need to respond to and consider reactions of outside pressure groups influence agency practice. Profit making is the key aim of for-profit, and many (supposedly) nonprofit organizations. Residential psychiatric facilities for youth and nursing homes are multimillion-dollar businesses. The concern for profit rather than service is reflected in the mistreatment (e.g., unneeded hospitalization) of clients in order to make money. Morawski (1987) suggests that "The drives for cooperation, organized research, integration, and unified science undoubtedly served economic ends" (p. 168). Badinter (1980) proposes that the notion of "mother love" arose only recently, when it became necessary to convince mothers that care of their children was critical in order to provide needed human resources to maintain the state, and that the modern-day concept of mother love stemmed from idealization sponsored by the state. This view is quite different from psychological discussions of mother love. Singh (2002, 2004) argues that the medicalization of deviant child behavior as a brain disease (ADHD) allows mothers to transfer blame from themselves to their child's brain. He suggests that mothers accept such a view as a relief from the burden on them to produce ideal, high-achieving children.

The development of a discipline or profession occurs in a context of competition among professions (Abbott, 1988). Social work has long been concerned with its second-class image in relation to psychiatry and has been influenced by this concern, for example, by buying into the psychiatric view of human behavior (for example, diagnostic criteria in the *DSM;* American Psychiatric Association, 2002). Psychology has been occupied with establishing and defending its scientific credibility and gaining access to rights, such as prescription privileges, once confined to psychiatrists. They have acquired such privileges in two states (New Mexico and Louisiana). Some have argued that the prime function of mental health professionals is to encourage values compatible with a capitalistic culture (Ehrenreich & Ehrenreich, 1977). Critics of the mental health services, such as Basaglia (in Scheper-Hughes & Lovell, 1987), believe that many people (including clinicians) do not understand the economic requirements of capitalistic societies such as the United States, and the effects of these requirements (such as invalidating and controlling individuals who do not contribute to productivity: the unemployed, the disabled, and the elderly, to name but a few). Clinicians are viewed as conscious or unconscious functionaries involved in imposing an ideology of health care and treatment on clients; social scientists are viewed as offering legitimation and justification for such practices that, although they seem to be universal for all citizens, meet the needs of the dominant group and control or restrain the needs of the dominated groups (Scheper-Hughes & Lovell, 1987, p. 155); "collective social problems are redefined as smaller, localized community problems, giving people a false perspective about where the problems originate and how they might be resolved. When superficial changes are made on the community level, the larger social and political issues that are at the root of the oppression and the deviance of marginal groups are depoliticized and atomized" to protect the interests of dominant vested interests (p. 99; Berger & Luckman, 1966; see also Illich et al., 1978; Manning, 1985). Webster (1997) suggests that our focus on racial and ethnic differences obscures our shared humanness and problems common across groups, such as poverty and lack of access to health services.

Political concerns such as equality of rights or freedom from unwanted control are reframed into personal ones over which the state has power. What is a political issue is transformed into a social problem (see Mills' [1959] discussion of the relationship between the personal and political, as well as related writings by Foucault [1981], Illich [1976], Illich et al. [1978], and Szasz [2003]). "If, however, the difficulties are understood to be those of moral diversity, of contested meanings, then the problem is a political issue, and no system of training can provide help" (Gusfield, 2003). Consider again views of homosexuals. "If the condition is perceived as that of individual illness or deficiency, then there can be a social technology, a form of knowledge and skill that can be effectively learned. That knowledge is the mandate for professions licensed to 'own' their social problems" (p. 9). Some groups successfully resist an unwanted view.

> The gay rights movement is perhaps the most salient example of how the ability to mobilize has enabled a subject group to transform its status. During this century, homosexuals have been thought of as sinful and as sick, objects of condemnation or of medical benevolence. What the gay rights movement did was to resist the public designation of deviance, of abnormality, by attacking the presumed norms and denying that homosexuality constituted a social problem. In the process the phenomena of homosexuality lost its status as a 'social problem' and became a matter of political and cultural conflict over the recognition of alternative sexual styles. What had been an uncontested meaning has been transformed into a political contest. (p. 15)

It has been argued that the modern concept of the self is relatively recent in origin, being dependent on reliance on the clock (Verhave & Van Hoorn, 1984). Thus, industrialization needs of the state and technology may encourage certain views about people. Clients who have trouble getting to work on time or arriving at clinical interviews on time may have views of time different from employers or counselors. An interest in psychological factors is more prominent in rights-based cultures, such as the United States, than in duty-based cultures, such as Hindu groups in India (Shweder & Miller, 1985). In rights-based cultures, emphasis is placed on personal decision making; in duty-based cultures, moral actions are defined as those that are compatible with the natural order. We live in an era in which alternative therapies have expanded enormously, in which therapy as entertainment or as spectacle is common. Hundreds may attend a lecture by a famous clinician. Hundreds of thousands of psychological self-help books are sold every year. Some may do more harm than good, as illustrated by the many deaths that resulted from Benjamin Spock's advice to place babies on their stomachs. A focus on the individual is a hallmark of what Beit-Hallahmi (1987) calls the "non-symptomatic psychotherapy subculture," which consists of those who seek counseling not to alleviate symptoms but to facilitate self-understanding and self-improvement (p. 481). Over the past decade a "biomedical grand narrative" has come to prevail in which problems are assumed to be biochemical in origin and medication is presumed to be the answer (Clarke, Shim, Mamo, Fosket, & Fishman, 2003; Moynihan, Heath, Henry, & Gøtzsche, 2002). Ascriptions of mental illness may excuse people from being responsible for their actions, including those which harm others. The advantages of the "sick role" has long been noted. Consider acceptance of the "Twinkie" excuse—the man who killed mayor Moscone of San Francisco and supervisor Harvey Milk was considered not responsible for his actions because he had consumed many Twinkies. A number of writers argue that we live in a therapeutic culture in which we escape responsibility for the results of our actions (e.g., Farudi, 2003).

An important byproduct of critical school analysis has been greater sensitivity to the value implications of psychological theory (Gergen, 1987; Scheper-Hughes & Lovell, 1987). Take, for example, Sampson's argument (1977) that psychological theory supports individualism and discourages recognition of our interdependency. Being informed about the intellectual history of different views increases awareness of biases in a given one. Knowledge about the intellectual history of a discipline or practice perspective will increase appreciation on the part of scientifically oriented clinicians that complete objectivity is impossible, and, on the other hand, this knowledge will correct misunderstandings among intuitive clinicians about potential contributions of scientific inquiry to practice (see Chapter 4). Lack of familiarity with the history of a field leaves us prey to repeating rather than building on past debates. For example, some writers contend that current discussions of the role of thoughts are largely repetitions of earlier ones. Those who recommend the expansion of private prisons often do not mention that there were many private prisons in the early part of this century, but they were closed and care of prisoners was returned to the state because of poor and brutal treatment of prisoners (D'Iulio, 1988).

Mental health services expanded during the community mental health movement, and the number of mental health professionals increased greatly. Critics argue that this expansion was not in the interests of the clients served but, on the contrary, was in the interests of expanding boundaries of attempted imposition of normative values and containment of unproductive deviance. Basaglia wrote, "Otherwise, there is no explanation for the overemphasis on health services rather than on the quality of the treatment provided" (Scheper-Hughes & Lovell, 1987, p. 155). "If the rehabilitation goals of both institutions [prisons and asylums] were genuine, one would find rehabilitated patients and prisoners reintegrated into society" (pp. 207–208). Ivan Illich (1976) argues that hospitals and drugs harm more people than they cure. Sources of human misery that are related to environmental factors and that create deviant behavior are falsely attributed to individual characteristics ("mental illness") and thus encapsulated. Special service-delivery systems can then be created for these individuals, and these systems become a source of jobs for professionals.

Those favoring biomedical views of problems have been very successful, as illustrated by the ever-lengthening list of behaviors viewed as signs of mental illness requiring the help of experts (Clarke, Shim, Mamo, Fosket, & Fishman, 2003; Conrad & Schneider, 1992). Ivan Illich (1976) emphasized the medicalization of problems in his famous book *Medical Nemesis*. Indeed, he used the term "the medicalization of life." The pharmaceutical industry promotes concerns such as the view of depression and social anxiety as biochemical illnesses requiring medication (e.g., Moynihan, 2003; Moynihan, Heath, Henry, & Gøtzsche, 2002; Starcevic, 2002). Professional experts set the rules for what is and what is not "normal." Describing slight variations in weight as a disease increases sales of certain foods and medication (see discussion of "nondisease" in Skrabanek & McCormick, 1998). In his article "The invention of post-traumatic stress disorder and the social usefulness of a psychiatric category," Summerfield (2001) suggests that "a psychiatric diagnosis is not necessarily a disease, distress or suffering is not psychopathology, post-traumatic stress disorder is an entity constructed as much from sociopolitical ideas as from psychiatric ones and that the increase in [this] diagnosis . . . is linked to changes in the relation between individual "personhood and modern life" (p. 95). Thomas Szasz has been emphasizing such points for decades (e.g., 1961, 1987, 1994). Increased attention has been given to the concerning influence of the pharmaceutical industry forwarding biased research, including the censorship of negative results (e.g., see Angell, 2004; Beckelman, Li, & Gross, 2003).

Assumptions made by Western clinicians may be inappropriate when applied to non-Western clients (e.g., see Weisz, Sunwanlert, Chaiyasit, & Walter, 1987; Ying, 2002). Differences include the greater role of physical complaints among Asian clients, differences in how children are raised (making children sleep alone is seen as a punishment in India or Japan), and differences in the relative importance of the individual and the group (Bond, 1986; Lock, 1982; Sue & Sue, 2002). The influence of culture is often overlooked. For example, during menopause, Japanese women are apt to complain of stiff shoulders, whereas Western women complain of hot flashes (Lock, 1993). Japanese women attribute little importance to the end of menstruation, seeing it as a normal part of aging. Seeking help from a mental health center is more likely to be viewed as a stigma in Asian cultures, whereas experience in therapy is the norm in some Western communities. Problems such as agoraphobia are rarely seen in non-Western countries, and problems such as "koro" (panic reactions due to fear that one's penis or nipples will retract into the body and cause death) that occur among the Chinese are unknown in the West. Overlooking such differences may result in inappropriate decisions concerning non-Western clients.

Professional organizations influence clinical decisions in a variety of ways, both in terms of what they do and what they do not do (for example, they do not usually blow the whistle on pseudoscience—bogus claims of effectiveness in approved continuing education courses; see also Lilienfeld, 2002). They influence both private and agency-based practices by setting standards for licensing—influencing who is allowed to practice. They also influence practice by engaging in political activities to protect and expand their turf. Consider the intense struggles between psychologists and psychiatrists about who should have control over diagnosis and treatment of clients, including medication privileges (see, for example, Buie, 1987, 1989). Professional associations devote resources to legal defenses of their interests. (See also discussion of Newsspeak in Chapter 5.)

## DIFFERENT PROBLEM DEFINITIONS HAVE DIFFERENT CONSEQUENCES

Different ways of defining problems have different consequences. Thomas Szasz (1987, 1994) argues that many people who injure others and are labeled mentally ill have committed criminal offenses and should be treated accordingly. Others believe that many criminals are mentally ill and should receive psychiatric care. Views about problems and their causes affect who receives aid and who does not, as well as what is offered and the spirit in which it is offered. Defining behaviors as indicators of mental illness results in quite different consequences than does defining them as criminal. Understanding the context in which problems occur provides opportunities to destigmatize clients. Tavris (1992, 2003) argues that there has been a turning away from the environmental context of personal problems in the current focus on individual characteristics (e.g., past history of abuse, low self-esteem). This is not to say that individual past histories are not important. It is to say that contextual factors such as gender role expectations comprise a part of individual histories (see also, McGrath, Keita, Strickland, & Russo, 1990). Service models that focus on altering the behavior of battered women so that their partners will stop abusing them encourage the view that women can control the behavior of their abusive partners if they change their own behavior. Does this mean that these women are responsible for the behavior of those who batter them? Focusing on the victim discounts the social roots of domestic violence (e.g., norms that support male dominance over women; see Gilbert, 1994). A study of 6,000 sheltered women revealed that access to resources permitting independent living (e.g., transportation, child care, and a source of income after leaving the shelter) was the best predictor of whether a woman would remain away from her abusive partner (Gondolf & Fisher, 1988).

Confining attention to the clinical interview when attempting to understand sources of influence on clinical decisions is like trying to understand the circulatory system from the perspective of a single red blood cell. If clinicians are informed about the economic, social, and political factors that influence practice, they are less likely to ignore environmental factors related to personal troubles and social problems.

## THE LANGUAGE OF PROBLEM DEFINITION

The words we use influence how we think about problems and behaviors. Certain views are forwarded by "claims makers" who try to influence others to accept their perspective. More and more everyday human problems are viewed as health problems remediable by experts. "To give a name to a problem is to recognize or suggest a structure developed to deal with it. Child abuse, juvenile delinquency, mental illness, alcoholism all have developed occupations and facilities that specialize in treatment, prevention, and reform" (Gusfield, 2003, p. 8). The role of language (rhetoric) in claims making has been noted by many scholars (e.g., Szasz, 1987). Indeed, Thomas Szasz views the very notion of "mental illness" as a rhetorical device that obscures the real differences between physical illness and problems in living, such as social anxiety and depression. Consider also the role of language in the so-called "drug wars." The metaphor of war, as in the "war against drugs" makes it easier to use violent means against "them" (e.g., seizing property; see Mac-Coun & Reuter, 2001). Here, too, societal factors related to use of drugs are obscured. Labels and classifications (e.g., black, white, race, ethnicity) have policy implications and thus warrant critical review. Consider also the widespread use of medical language: healthy/unhealthy, wellness/sickness, health/disease. The word "health" has been applied to an ever-widening range of behaviors, feelings, and thoughts. Language and the ideology it reflects play a key role in obscuring economic differences. For instance, both working-class and middle-middle-class people may be labeled as middle class, creating the illusion that most people belong to the middle class. Many problems created in part by inequities in housing, job opportunities, education, health care, and the court system are treated as separate from one another, which makes it difficult to detect shared causes. DeMott (1990) suggests that differences in economic circumstances are daily translated into other terms, including moral differences. Many authors have noted the increased use of the languages of managerial approaches, consumerism, and risk management in the helping professions.

## THE INFLUENCE OF AGENCY VARIABLES

The nature of the practice setting, private or agency-based, influences options for increasing the quality of decisions. Problems and approaches to them are institutionalized in organizational structures and related mission statements. Practice is carried out in the context of currently accepted social and public policies and legislation that given patterns of behavior are problems and certain remedies are appropriate. Many practitioners work in some kind of organization, such as a community mental health center or hospital. Whether critical thinking skills are used depends on the organizational culture. Raising questions about accepted views of a profession, organization, supervisor, professor, or agency may be met with attempts to evade questions or discredit (or cajole) the questioner. Reason (1997) refers to organizational cultures in which "we don't want to know," whistle-blowers are punished, responsibility is skirted and failure is hidden, as pathological cultures. We are less likely to learn how to make better decisions in such cultures. Developing facilitating administrative and management arrangements is vital to encouraging evidence-informed practice and policy (Gray, 2001a). This includes a culture of thoughtfulness in which asking questions about practices and policies and their effects is encouraged, and clinicians have access to the tools they need to make informed decisions and to involve clients as informed participants, such as computers with access to relevant databases. Public agencies contract out services to nonprofit organizations. An understanding on the part of private practitioners about factors that influence agency-based practice will be helpful in identifying constraints on decisions.

Although there is an overlap in the factors that influence decisions in private and agency-based practice, there are differences as well. Professionals in private practice can filter out clients they do not want to work with. In a dialogue among social workers in private and agency-based practices, one private practitioner said that she refused to see anyone who had a cocaine or alcohol problem, telling them to "get rid of their habit" and then she would see them. The situation is different in agency-based practice, in which clinicians have much less control over whom they see and what they offer under managed care. Considerations regarding coercion arise in contexts in which involuntary intrusion into individual or family life occurs, such as in child protection services, enforced hospitalization of mentally ill patients, and outpatient commitment (Morrisey & Monahan, 1999). Decisions are influenced by the constraints and options created by compromises made by politicians and legislators and by those who carry out the supposed intent of policies. Sources of influence on decisions made in agencies include the following:

- Nonvoluntary aspects of the context (for example, criminal justice and child welfare settings)
- Different kinds of professionals involved
- Clients who use the agency
- Clarity of agency policy
- Criteria preferred to select service methods (e.g., scientific, popularity)
- Views about error (recognized as learning opportunities or encouraged to hide)
- Quality of learning possible (e.g., corrective feedback regarding decisions made)
- Preferred-practice theories
- Funding sources
- Procedures related to accountability
- Vulnerability to scandal (newspaper stories)
- Training of staff
- Power differentials among professionals

Biasing factors that influence decisions such as premature closure on a belief have been found in the criminal justice system (for example, Emerson, 1969), commitment hearings (Decker, 1987; Pfohl, 1978), and child protection services (for example, Dingwall et al., 1983). Agency characteristics that influence decisions include preferred views of clients, technology used, status and power differences, time pressures, and beliefs about the importance of different kinds of tasks.

*Status and Power Differences*   Power differences between agency staff and clients favor staff, especially in nonvoluntary settings. This difference allows staff and their representatives (such as attorneys) to have an influential role in the negotiation of decisions, such as whether to return a child to a parent's care. Jacobs (1985), for example, presents a case in which parental and agency reports of what would be in "the best interests of the child" differed greatly. The court had to decide who had the authoritative version. The mother wanted her daughter returned to her care. Jacobs argues that the agency's power and status were used to create a credibility for its version that was greater than the credibility of the mother's version, and that this was accomplished through "strategic written maneuvers in constructing the official court report," so that the mother's version of the best interests was discredited and the agency's version was viewed as the correct account. Identical factual evidence was given quite different interpretations consistent with the goal of the person presenting the view.

Those with power in an agency are often interested in retaining it and may view attempts to share power as threatening. This is a key obstacle in moving to evidence-based practice and social care—a reluctance, for example, to honestly share ignorance and uncertainty about the effectiveness of practice methods. An objection to a more systematic method for clinical decision making may in reality reflect a concern with keeping privileged positions. The history of psychiatric care is replete with examples of unwarranted hospitalizations (e.g., of women who wished to pursue a career) and of the invasive exercise of power by staff over hospitalized patients (e.g., Valenstein, 1986). Removing coercion and punitive environments for clients under the control of psychiatric staff has been the major aim of institutional antipsychiatric politics (Sedgwick, 1982).

*Available Resources*   Decisions about who should receive services and what services should be provided are influenced by both actual and perceived resources which, in turn, are influenced by decisions at higher levels. These include access to technological innovations that facilitate evidence-based decisions, such as the Cochrane and Campbell databases. Resources available are related to political, economic, and ideological influences. For example, some people believe that few resources were initially provided to prevent and find a cure for acquired immunodeficiency syndrome (AIDS) because this problem primarily affected minority populations. Three options are possible when resources are scarce. One is to widen the definition of a resource. For example, a clinician in private practice may decide that since no relapse-prevention program is available in his geographical area that research shows is most effective for a client with a substance-abuse problem, he will offer another kind of intervention. Widening the definition of resources may work for or against clients; it works against them if the new resources selected are not effective. The second option is to increase the threshold for deciding that treatment is required. One of the major conclusions made by Dingwall and his colleagues

(1983) following their observation of work in British child protection agencies was the reluctance of staff to identify child maltreatment. That is, professionals tailored their decisions to the resources available. These authors highlighted the relativistic nature of clinical decisions, noting that social workers are continually admonished to consider the individual needs and norms of different groups: that what may constitute child abuse in one group may not in another, and that this relativistic view prevents the system from being overwhelmed by new cases. Often, neglectful circumstances were excused even when clients did have some control over them. Swings in policy may be made because of a high-profile death of a child in care—that is, too many children may be taken into care following a death as a result of great media attention.

A third option when resources are scarce is to focus on problems for which resources are plentiful. Clinicians do not have the resources to alleviate severe material deprivation and so often focus instead on problems that they can resolve, such as interpersonal concerns. A large gap between what can be done and what is needed (whether due to lack of skills on the part of clinicians or lack of other resources) may encourage negative reactions toward clients (if their presence is a reminder of a limited ability to be of help), or problems of secondary interest to clients may be focused on. Sedgwick (1982) suggests that too often a request for greater resources "amounts to a request for some form of tardy and individualized intervention in a problem that should be met in preventative terms implicating the wider social and political system" (p. 195).

*Limited Access to Information*    Access to some environments is at the discretion of those who inhabit them, as in the case of those who can only enter clients' homes with the permission of residents. Clumsy efforts to do so may result in lack of access to the premises. Based on a review of case records, Margolin (1997) argues that the major achievement of social workers was gaining access to the privacy of clients' homes. Although some factors that limit access to information are insurmountable, others are discretionary or self-imposed. For example, a clinician may decide not to collect observational data in real-life settings regarding parent-child exchanges, even though clients agree there is time to do so and such data would be helpful in understanding interaction patterns and in identifying specific changes needed to help clients. Different kinds of professionals have access to different kinds of information. A physician in an emergency room, especially one who is not familiar with the local community in which a client resides, may ignore or not have information about a family's social situation that may be helpful in identifying the cause of a child's injuries (Dingwall et al., 1983). The physician may have access to medical evidence of child abuse but no data about social evidence or moral evidence (e. g., data about the moral character of clients). Agency policy concerning record keeping and evaluation influences the quality of information available. Vagueness rather than clarity may be preferred. Clinicians may find it difficult to continue careful evaluation in a climate that favors sloppy evaluation. Clients may not have access to their records and so are unable to correct content they believe to be inaccurate (Margolin, 1997). Staff may not have access to information needed to make informed decisions, such as high-speed computers with relevant databases.

*Preferred Views of Clients*   Settings differ in the views of clients that are encouraged. Imputations of moral character (as distinguished from objective descriptions) may be conveyed in the way clients and their actions are described as well as in treatment methods selected. Strong (1979) studied decisions made in pediatric outpatient clinics and found that parents were assumed to be honest, competent, and caring, and that the disorders of their children were assumed to be natural events. If the physicians discovered evidence that contradicted this view, they engaged in exchanges designed to reconceptualize the parent's character. The opposite tendency may now be present, in which parents are under excessive suspicion concerning a child's injuries or failure to thrive. Whether this suspicion is acted on may be tempered by the "rule of optimism" (see Chapter 7). Past studies of workers in welfare offices found that clients were often viewed as liars and manipulators (Blau, 1960). Wills (1978) suggests that this may occur because workers make dispositional attributions about the cause of client behaviors; they overlook the influence of the situation. For example, applicants are dependent on the decisions of the social worker. Clinicians prefer clients who are manageable and treatable (see later section). Their views of clients are also related to the match between staff, clients, and preferred-practice theories. The philosophy of evidence-based practice emphasizes the importance of involving clients as informed participants in decisions and considering their values and preferences. This differs from authoritarian approaches in which paternalism reigns (we know what is best for you).

*Agency Culture and Climate*   Clinical settings differ in terms of what behaviors are reinforced, ignored, or punished—in the contingencies in effect. Little positive feedback may be offered for competencies that enhance the quality of decisions. Helpful behaviors may be punished, as when clinicians are criticized for evaluating their work by collecting self-monitored or observational data or are considered obsessive because of an interest in setting clear objectives. Administrators and supervisors may attend to behaviors they do not like, neglecting behaviors they want to see more often; they focus on catching staff doing something wrong rather than catching staff performing competently. Supervisors may ignore approximations to desired outcomes, such as asking particular questions, doing a task correctly even though it is late, or completing part of a task correctly. Power relations in an agency may be concealed or denied. This is one way in which a given ideology is maintained (Thompson, 1987). For example there may be an "old boys group" or "old girls group" that makes all the important decisions. However, this may be denied by members of this group. One of the oldest ways to dilute competitive power is to divide and conquer—to create divisiveness among groups. As long as they are busy arguing with each other, they will not pose a threat.

Settings differ in pressure to conform to the majority view. For example, there may be only one psychoanalytically oriented clinician in an agency in which most staff members prefer a behavioral approach. Alternative views concerning presenting problems may be dismissed rather than explored by weighing the evidence for different views. Negative labels may be applied to people who raise questions. Rather than thank a colleague who questions a diagnosis, labels such as "uninformed" or "naive" may be applied to the "questioner" to discourage unwanted influences. Consider, for example, how whistle-blowers are often treated (Glazer & Glazer, 1991). If negative labels and innuendos stick, staff may avoid the troublemaker, not wanting to be guilty by association. Attempts to present divergent accounts may gradually wane. Decisions are often made in a brief time—even in situations in which they have weighty consequences. Studies of psychiatric commitment hearings show that only a few minutes are devoted to each decision (Decker, 1987; Scheff, 1984b). It is no wonder that decisions are not optimal in noisy offices with ringing phones and constant interruptions—the environment in which many practitioners carry out their daily work. These distractions interfere with concentration. Although some clinicians may flourish under such conditions, others are adversely affected. Whether performance is compromised depends on the skills and resources required to carry out a task. "Kant did some of his best thinking in bed with blankets wrapped around him in a special way; Dr. Johnson needed a purring cat, orange peel, and tea; and Schiller filled his desk with rotten apples" (Yinger, 1980, p. 27).

Administrators differ in the kinds of appeals and political maneuvers they favor or tolerate. Such preferences influence the quality of decisions. Just as there are a variety of methods that can be used to encourage change, there are many that can be used to decrease the likelihood of change. The term *stratagem* refers to cunning methods of achieving or maintaining an end (that is, trickery) such as manipulation of information. Only some alternatives may be presented. Data can be presented in a way that obscures rather than clarifies what is actually happening (see, for example, *How to Lie with Statistics,* Huff, 1954; Tufte, 1990). Doubts about a disliked position can be created by spreading rumors. "Once suspicions, apprehensions, or misgivings are created, people will be misled by the old adage 'where there is smoke there is fire.' However, both the smoke and the fire may be illusory" (Michalos, 1971, pp. 100–101). Stonewalling can be used to block change; verbal statements in favor of a decision may be made without doing anything to implement it. Administrators may reaffirm their agreement with an idea by setting a specific date to accomplish a certain task but take no steps to put it into effect. The maneuver of stonewalling occurs anytime someone grants a request but fails to deliver.

Staff reorganization is another stratagem. This deflects attention from other matters and may juggle responsibilities so that people with opposing views are in less advantageous positions. There are many other stratagems. An administrator may request a study to gain more data relevant to a decision which precludes action for weeks or months. In an appeal to no precedent it is assumed that if something has not been done by now, there is no good reason it should be done; the idea is that we (or you) would have discovered and corrected it by now if the disputed practice is a poor one. No evidence for or against the wisdom of the proposed change is offered. Tokenism refers to making minimal, unsatisfactory efforts and acting as if they are adequate. Impossible deadlines may be insisted on, restricting time for careful consideration of alternatives. Agreement on a small decision may be sought that can then be appealed to make subsequent larger decisions. It is often argued that the end justifies the means, that even though there are disadvantages to the route suggested, it provides a way to achieve valued outcomes and is therefore justified. It may be argued that, even though the use of aversive methods are objectionable, these are used to achieve the valued end of decreasing assaultive behavior when positive methods have been tried and have failed to achieve this goal. It may be argued that because an idea is new, it is ipso facto good. This stratagem is the converse of the no-precedent fallacy. People who use this tactic may attempt to portray an advocate of other positions, especially those that have been or are being used, as a stick-in-the-mud who is not au courant.

*Other Factors*   Personal beliefs, as well as generally accepted views in an organization or profession, influence the perceived importance of different tasks. Pressures to act quickly may result in an underestimation of the importance of careful assessment. Staff turnover may also compromise the quality of decisions. In agency-based practice, a family may have many different workers during one year. Rather than building on what has gone before, new staff members may approach a case as a tabula rasa, with little regard for prior data collected or recommendations made. Dingwall and his coauthors (1983) suggest, based on their research, that the initial tendency is to think the best about a family and then to become disillusioned over time as efforts fail.

Ignorance is not bliss in relation to understanding how our environments influence our feelings, thoughts, and behaviors. It may result in misattributions for lack of success, which may be an obstacle to improving decisions. Clinicians may blame themselves for consequences that have little or nothing to do with the quality of their clinical skills but everything to do with the agency in which they practice and the agency's environment; clients may be blamed, or blame may be mistakenly placed on environmental limitations, and options for altering these constraints may be overlooked. Not identifying the true obstacles, the clinician is unlikely to take effective action. Rather, a bad situation may be accepted prematurely. Procedures, policies, and habits that interfere with effective decision making may be accepted as a fait accompli when, in fact, change is possible.

## TECHNOLOGY DEVELOPMENT

Decisions are also influenced by available technology. Gray (2001b) suggests that the origins of evidence-based practice and policy include the Internet revolution and the invention of the systematic review. Now clinicians, administrators, and policy makers can gain quick access to high-quality reviews of research related to many questions, for example from the Cochrane and Campbell Collaboration Databases (see also Chapter 11). Examples of some Cochrane reviews are:

- Pekkala, E., & Merinder, L. (2004). Psychoeducation for schizophrenia (Cochrane Review). In *The Cochrane Library,* Issue 4. Chichester, UK: Wiley.
- Rose, S., Bisson, J., & Wessely, S. (2004). Psychological debriefing for preventing Posttraumatic Stress Disorder (PTSD) (Cochrane Review). In *The Cochrane Library,* Issue 3. Chichester, UK: Wiley.
- Spector, A., Orrell, M., Davies, S., & Woods, B. (2004). Reality orientation for dementia (Cochrane Review). In *The Cochrane Library,* Issue 3. Chichester, UK: Wiley.

Access to efficient, effective information storage and retrieval systems allows you to find information quickly on an as-needed basis (for example, a user-friendly reference management system). The influence of technology is illustrated in the following example. A young man got frostbite of his big toe while hiking in the Andes. The local surgeon advised amputation. The young man had a digital camera and took pictures of this big toe (it looked quite bad) and sent these images via the Internet to the British Mountaineering Council, which forwarded them to a vascular surgeon who examined them and advised him not to have his toe amputated but to immediately return to the United Kingdom. Here, a vascular surgeon operated—the toe was saved, and three months later the young man ran the London Marathon in just over 4 hours, dressed as a fairy (Hillebrandt & Imray, 2004). The example of our mountain climber illustrates one of the most robust findings in the literature on decision making—the role of specialized knowledge. It also illustrates the role of technology and access to it (such as the Internet). It illustrates the interplay between content and performance knowledge, goals, and technology. Without the digital camera and a computer with Internet access and without knowledge on the part of the climber about the British Mountaineering Council, the young man would have lost his big toe. Without access to a vascular surgeon with special knowledge and perhaps special equipment, his toe might have been lost.

## THE INTERACTION BETWEEN CLIENTS AND CLINICIANS

Helping clients involves an interaction between clients and therapists; it involves a social influence process in which the reactions of one party influence the reactions of the other. If we want to understand the helping process, we must explore the transaction (i.e., the interactions) between helpers and clients and the context in which it occurs. Studies of helping highlight the social influence process that takes place, even in "nondirective" approaches (Truax, 1966). Statements that match the therapist's views are reinforced; this may increase the congruence between therapist and client views (Snyder & Thomsen, 1988).

Helpers reinforce some behaviors, ignore others, and punish still others. In turn, clients influence the helpers' behavior. Clients may even report content from their dreams that is consistent with the counselor's conceptualizations (Whitman, Kramer, & Baldridge, 1963). The subtlety of these social influence processes (they may not be obvious) does not remove the fact that they occur. Margolin (1997) argues that this subtlety allows helpers to misuse their power to the detriment of their clients.

Cultural differences between clients and helpers may increase the likelihood of miscommunication. Both clients and therapists arrive at the first interview with preconceptions concerning what is a problem, what it is related to, and how it may be resolved. Some clients may screen their presentation of problems and related causes in accord with the particular orientation of an agency. As soon as the exchange begins, a trajectory may be initiated on the basis of pre-conceptions that support and stabilize initial views. Therapists' views of clients are formed relatively swiftly and may remain stable over a long period. How cli-nicians structure problems affects what they inquire about, which in turn af-fects what clients report. The type of information focused on differs among therapists of differing theoretical preferences (eclectic, cognitive-behavioral, psychodynamic, or family systems; Kopta, Newman, McGovern, & Sandrock, 1986). Given the tendency to search for evidence that confirms initial precon-ceptions, the clinician is less likely to note data that suggest competing views of problems. That is, once we arrive at a point of view of what the problem is and what factors are related to it, we may search selectively for additional informa-tion to confirm our view in the client's history, current situation, and behavior.

Counselors typically sample only a small portion of a client's repertoires (be-havior in the interview). This decreases the likelihood of discovering behavior that is not consistent with prior expectations. A psychiatrist may believe that working-class clients are not as likely to respond well to insight-oriented ap-proaches as more educated, middle-class clients, and so may recommend dif-ferent treatment approaches for working-class clients. These initial beliefs influence the nature of feedback sought and this may, in turn, alter the task en-vironment. If clinicians believe that poor, relatively nonverbal clients are not good candidates for counseling, they may not try as hard to engage such cli-ents, and, as a consequence, clients may drop out (prematurely terminate treat-ment). This may confirm original beliefs. The social nature of therapy renders this enterprise subject to a variety of influences. Past as well as current research describes a variety of negative effects that are associated with how clinicians re-late to their clients (Herron & Rouslin, 1984; Strupp & Hadley, 1985). Personal barriers to communication include a lack of respect for others and a lack of relationship skills and knowledge of when to use them. (See also Chapter 17.) Countertransference effects may result in being underprotective of clients or assuming too much responsibility for their lives. Environmental barriers include being overworked, high noise levels, and frequent interruptions. Sources of bias and error are especially likely to occur in this context because of the unequal status of the participants. Jerome Frank notes that research has not altered his earlier view of helping as an interpersonal process in which the helper's beliefs, values, and optimism overcome the client's demoralization and offer hope (Frank & Frank, 1991).

A great deal of research has been devoted to exploring the influence of the therapeutic relationship, in relation to outcome. The extensive literature on psychotherapy process and outcome continues to be characterized by controversy regarding presumed contributors to outcome. In their research summary of the therapeutic relationship and psychotherapy outcome, Lambert and Barley (2002) describe the percent of improvement as a function of different therapeutic factors: expectancy, 15 percent; common factors, 30 percent; techniques, 15 percent, and extratherapeutic change, 40 percent. Techniques refers to the specific methods used. Common factors refer to "variables found in most therapies regardless of the therapist's theoretical orientation such as empathy, warmth, acceptance, encouragement of risk taking, client and therapist characteristics, confidentiality of the client-therapist relationship, the therapeutic alliance or process factors" (Lambert & Barley, 2002, pp. 17–18). Those who described the percentage contribution of different factors to outcome are criticized on the grounds that this requires a linear view, which is not true. Lambert and Barley (2002) conclude that "Measures of therapeutic relationship variables consistently correlate more highly with client outcome than specialized therapy techniques. Associations between the therapeutic relationship and client outcome are strongest when measured by client ratings of both constructs." It is estimated that two-thirds of the observed small differences between psychotherapies in relation to outcome can be attributed to investigator allegiance (preferences of helpers for a particular method; Lambert & Barley, 2002, p. 20; Luborsky et al., 1999). Wampold (2005) sums up his views of related literature as follows: ". . . in clinical trials, the variability of outcomes due to therapists (8%–9%) is larger than the variability among treatments (0%–1%), the alliance (5%), and the superiority of an EST [empirically established treatment] to a placebo treatment (0%–4%), making it the most robust predictor of outcomes of any factor studied, with the exception of the initial level of severity" (p. 204).

The match between helpers and clients influences outcomes. Houts (1984) found that "psychodynamic clinicians" were less pessimistic in their prognosis about a client when the client's view of their problem was consistent with a psychodynamic orientation. Clients "who approach treatment passively appear to fare better with a dominant-controlling therapist than with a more passive following therapist" (Abramowitz, Berger, & Weary, 1982, p. 371). Clinicians differ in their beliefs about degree of personal responsibility for problems and solutions (McGovern, Newman, & Kopta, 1986). Negative events are more likely to be attributed to environmental factors when clients and clinicians are similar than they are when they are different (Jordan, Harvey, & Weary, 1988). The possibility of mismatches between helpers and clients has led some investigators to describe helper-client interactions as *problematic social situations* (Stone, 1979, p. 46). Waitzkin describes exchanges between physicians and patients as "micropolitical situations" in which the control of information reinforces the power relations that parallel those in the broader society, especially those concerning social class, gender, race, and age (1991, p. 54). These power imbalances highlight the importance of ethical components of evidence-based practice, such as transparency regarding what is done with what results and involving clients as active, informed participants in decisions.

Effective relationship skills increase the likelihood of establishing rapport with clients, gaining their participation, and avoiding dropout (e.g., see Patterson & Forgatch, 1985). Goldstein (1980) suggested that relationship enhancers such as empathy, warmth, and credibility increase liking, respect, and trust, which in turn increase openness and communication and strengthen the helping alliance. Strupp suggests that all forms of helping involve a relationship "characterized by respect, interest, understanding, tact, maturity, . . . a firm belief in [one's] ability to help," influence through suggestions, encouragement of open communication, self-scrutiny, honesty, interpretations of material that people are not aware of (such as self-defeating strategies in interpersonal relations), offering examples of "maturity," and "capacity and willingness to profit from the experience" (1976, p. 97). Lambert and Barley (2002) suggest that "in addition to providing the facilitative conditions in a positive alliance, therapists must avoid the negative communication patterns that detract from outcome, especially in treating more difficult clients. These styles would include comments or behaviors that are critical, attacking, rejecting, blaming, or neglectful" (Najavits & Strupp, 1994, p. 27). Therapist variables shown to be consistently related to a positive impact on treatment outcome in a review of 2000 process-outcome studies since 1950 include therapist credibility, empathic understanding, affirmation of the client, skill in engaging clients, a focus on the client's problems, and skill in directing the client's attention to the client's affect or experience (Orlinsky, Grave, & Parks, 1994). "Some therapists are better than others at contributing to positive client outcome. Clients characterize such therapists as more understanding and accepting, empathic, warm, and supportive. They engage in fewer negative behaviors such as blaming, ignoring, or rejecting" (Lambert & Barley, 2002, p. 26). Wampold (2005) concludes that "The relatively large proportion of variability in outcomes due to therapists infers that some psychotherapists consistently produce better outcomes than others; consequently, psychotherapists are a worthy locus of validation" (p. 205). The quality of the relationship is related to sharing information needed to arrive at well-reasoned decisions and encouraging clients to participate in other ways. In this sense, relationship skills are a critical ingredient of evidence-based practice. Helpers who are cold, closed down, or judgmental are not as likely to involve clients as collaborators as are those who are warm, supportive, and empathic.

Clinicians like clients who are treatable and manageable, clients who participate in the helping process, and who offer counselors success: clients who get better (Wills, 1978). "Implicit treatability criterion" include evaluations of clients' likeability and manageability (Fehrenbach & O'Leary, 1982). In a past survey of 421 psychiatrists, psychologists, and social workers, Goldman and Mendelsohn (1969) found that helpers preferred YAVIS clients: young, attractive, verbal, intelligent, and socially adept. These clinicians reported that they worked best with clients with little pathology. Such clients are more likely to be manageable and treatable than clients at the opposite pole; they are more likely to behave in ways that are consistent with someone who needs help and with "the clinician's role as a helper (though compliance with treatment expectations and behavior change) [which] are likely to result in increased perceptions of interpersonal attractiveness" (Fehrenbach & O'Leary, 1982, p. 32). Wills (1978) found that the focus on negative qualities increases with increasing experience. "Experience produces an increased emphasis on negative characterological aspects, particularly increased perception of maladjustment, and a less generous view of clients' motivation for change" (p. 981; see discussion of focusing on pathology in Chapter 7). Are professionals more accurate than others? Wills (1978) suggests they are not; "in general, there is no difference in judgmental accuracy between professionals and lay persons" (p. 981). More recent research suggests that professionals are more accurate than are lay people in identifying pathology. But, is what is identified really pathological? (See earlier discussion of the social construction of problems.) Professionals may selectively scan for negative information, whereas lay people do not have this negative focus. Views based on a negatively biased sample will obviously not be as favorable as those based on a balanced consideration of both assets and deficits; negative views result in more pessimistic predictions concerning outcomes.

Client characteristics such as severity of concerns and motivation influence outcome (Clarkin & Levy, 2004). Class, race, and ethnicity have been found to influence diagnosis and services offered. Poor people and people of color receive more severe diagnoses and are more likely to be placed on medication (e.g., see Segal, Bola, & Watson, 1996). Some writers argue that this is because clinicians reflect the values of the dominant middle class, but their clients are often working class (Scheper-Hughes & Lovell, 1987). Past research found that clients of lower socioeconomic status were less likely to be accepted in treatment, less likely to receive intensive psychotherapy, and more likely to end therapy prematurely (e.g., Hollingshed & Redlich, 1958; Parloff, Waskow, & Wolf, 1978). Socioeconomic status is related to dropout (Lambert, 2004). African American clients are less likely to be referred for individual psychotherapy and are more likely to drop out of treatment than white people (Abramovitz & Murray, 1983). (For a recent discussion of race, gender, and class as they influence practice, see Gray-Little & Kaplan, 2000.)

## PSYCHOLOGICAL FACTORS THAT INFLUENCE CLINICAL JUDGMENTS

We are influenced by our emotional reactions as well as the goals we value and the information-processing strategies we use (see Chapter 9).

*Our Emotions*   We are influenced by our emotional reactions in our day-to-day work with clients. Emotional reactions affect what we notice, what we recall, how we organize it, and what predictions we make. Even small changes in mood and arousal level may influence our judgments (e.g., see Slovic, Finucane, Peters, & MacGregor, 2002) For example, male subjects rated nudes as more attractive after a vigorous workout on an exercycle than they did before the workout (Cantor, Zillmann, & Bryant, 1975). Subjects who received a small gift rated TVs and cars more positively than those who received no gift (Isen, Shalker, Clark, & Karp, 1978). Descriptions of familiar people given while subjects were happy were charitable, loving, and generous, compared with the fault-finding descriptions given when subjects were angry (Bower & Cohen, 1982). Affect also influences memory; events are recalled that match current mood (Teasdale & Fogarty, 1979). We tend to think positive thoughts when we are in a good mood and negative experiences when we are depressed (Isen et al., 1978). Depressed people have a greater tendency to focus on themselves, to make internal attributions for negative events, and to give up after failure (Pyszczynski & Greenberg, 1985). These influences affect our judgments. For example, we remember better those events that match our current mood and ask more questions about such events. If clinicians are sad, they may attend more to risks and negative events than if they are happy, in which case they may underemphasize risks and obstacles. The clinician's mood is influenced by the client as well as by external factors, such as an argument with a significant other or an arduous commute in heavy traffic. (For a review of the effects of mood on memory and decisions, see Salovey & Turk, 1988; Schwartz, 2002.) Negative affect related to fear of failure or a seemingly insoluble problem may disrupt performance. Positive affect facilitates learning and problem solving; it seems to promote flexibility, which is an important aspect of creative thinking (Isen, 1987). Being aware of such influences may increase the likelihood that their effects on decisions will be identified.

*Our Goals*   Our decisions are influenced by our goals. We may or may not be aware of our goals. That is, certain goals may be automatically triggered in situations in which they are often pursued. And goals, reflected in intentions, may "become invulnerable to adverse situational influences" (Gollweitzer, Bayer, & McCulloch, 2005, p. 505). That is, we may pursue these even if we lose valuable opportunities in doing so. These authors refer to such goals as *automotives* "that are triggered outside of awareness by a respective situational context" (p. 504). For example, work-related goals may intrude in social situations or social goals may adversely affect work performance. We overestimate the likelihood of preferred outcomes. Janis and Mann (1977) describe many disastrous results of the influence of motivational variables on decisions, such as the 1941 failure to take preventative action despite the concrete evidence that Pearl Harbor would be attacked. Tuchman (1984) discusses other historical examples such as the decision by the Trojans not to examine the wooden horse before allowing it into their city. There are often many competing goals in a clinical context, such as saving time and effort, helping clients, performing well, and avoiding errors. (See also Chapter 9.)

*Our Information-Processing Strategies*   The information-processing strategies we use influence our decisions, and many writers emphasize these as a key source of judgmental errors. We differ in our style of approaching problems and in the way we handle uncertainty and risk. Evidence-informed practice emphasizes the importance of seeking information about the degree of uncertainty related to a decision and sharing what is found with clients (see Chapter 10). We must go beyond the information at hand in making decisions because rarely (if ever) do we have all relevant data. Simplifying strategies are used to manage data. Two tools used for this are knowledge structures (theories and preconceptions) and judgmental strategies (heuristics) such as *availability* (the accessibility of events and concepts in our perceptions, memory, or imagination) and *representativeness* (the extent to which events appear to resemble each other; see Chapter 9). An example of the influence of resemblance criteria is the tendency to predict the likelihood of given outcomes on the basis of the similarity of a predictor to an outcome. For example, if a psychologist finds that a client has a high D (depression) scale on the Minnesota Multiphasic Personality Inventory (MMPI), he or she may make a diagnosis based on this indicator, since the predictor seems representative of (similar to) the criterion. However, elevated D scores have little predictive validity when used alone. An example of the influence of availability on judgment of causal relationships (Kahneman & Tversky, 1973) is the tendency of observers to attribute behavior to characteristics of the person rather than to situational factors (the fundamental attribution error); the actor's behavior is more noticeable compared to more static situational events.

We are influenced by the relative ease of recalling behaviors or events when we try to estimate frequency. Recently, there has been a rebalancing of the value of such heuristics—that they often work well and save time and effort. Their use has been referred to as the "fast and frugal" approach to decision making (e.g., see Gigerenzer & Goldstein, 1999) and research within this perspective shows that such strategies often (but not always) suffice and even surpass more deliberative approaches. Advocates of the "fast and frugal" approach argue that rather than our limited information-processing capabilities being a handicap, they are an advantage, because they facilitate rapid decision making when confronted with the need to act based on recognition of relevant patterns. They encourage attention to cues that are most relevant in a situation (situation awareness), so avoiding errors introduced by too much information, including misleading and irrelevant data (see Chapter 9).

A number of authors describe what they term our "innumeracy," referring to our difficulties in reasoning correctly about uncertainty (Paulos, 1988). Gigerenzer (2002a) highlights four sources of uncertainty: (1) the illusion of certainty, (2) ignorance of risk, (3) miscommunication of risk, and (4) clouded thinking. The first point is addressed in Chapter 4—that is, a justification approach to knowledge in which it is assumed that we can arrive at certain truth, for example, by piling up examples. Ignorance of risk refers to being uninformed about the risks associated with different decisions, such as having a mammogram or attending an anxiety screening day. The third point, miscommunication of risk, refers to not knowing how to communicate risk in an understandable way. For example, a physician may know the risks associated with a certain test but not be able to clearly communicate his knowledge to a patient so that the patients can make an informed decision. The fourth kind of innumeracy, clouded thinking, refers to knowing the risks but not knowing how to draw correct inferences from them. "For instance, physicians often know the error rates of a clinical test and the base rate of a disease, but not know how to infer from this information the chances that a patient with a positive test actually has the disease" (Gigerenzer, 2002a, p. 25). This is a very potent foursome in that it illustrates the symbiotic relationship between professionals' and clients' innumeracy and the many opportunities for interested parties to mislead us (intentionally or not) in order to encourage us to make use of certain interventions. The foursome illustrates that professionals may be as ignorant of risks and how to calculate, communicate, and draw inferences from them, as may clients. He as well as others illustrate the negative consequences that may occur from these sources of innumeracy, such as being misinformed about the diagnostic accuracy of a test (such as a mammogram) and as a result having invasive, unnecessary interventions, such as biopsies or prophalactic mastectomies. Thus, as Gigerenzer suggests, the motto that applies is "dare to know."

*Flawed Self-Assessment*   Research in a number of areas suggests the flawed nature of our self-assessment. Such incorrect beliefs may interfere significantly with sound decisions. In a review of related literature Dunning, Heath, and Suls (2004) state: "Thus, whether people decide well in life depends, at least in part, on whether their self-assessments are accurate, that is, on how successfully they follow the classical admonition from the Delphic oracles to 'know thyself'" (p. 70). Based on their review of the literature they conclude that ". . . people's capacity to evaluate themselves and predict their behavior is usually quite modest and often much more meager than common intuition would lead us to believe" (p. 70).

## SUMMARY

Many environments affect the quality of clinical decisions in both private and agency-based practice, including past (for example, political, economic, and social influences on the development of the mental health industry), present (such as the clinical interview and current service-delivery systems), and future (anticipated changes in service delivery). What is viewed as a problem differs at different times and in different ethnic and cultural groups. Not considering the larger picture leaves decisions open to influences that you may reject if you considered their social and political repercussions. Understanding how these many environments influence clinical practice should increase understanding of the nature of clinical decisions and help us to discover options for improvement. Practice theories and professions develop in a particular historical context. The resources provided to address personal and social problems are related to these larger structural variables. The setting in which decisions are made influences decisions. In agency-based practice, the quality of decisions may be compromised by large caseloads, lack of clear agency policy concerning priorities, and contradictory demands from diverse sources. In both private and agency-based practice, preferred views of clients, available resources, and social and time pressures affect decisions. Other influences include the perceived importance of clinical tasks, goals pursued, access to different kinds of information including databases describing practice- and policy-related research, and agency cultures. Competencies that enhance the quality of decisions, such as keeping track of progress, may be ignored. Reactions that compromise their quality, such as complaining without assuming any responsibility for seeking desired changes, may be reinforced.

Certain kinds of errors occur due to misuse of generally effective information-processing strategies. We are prone to various kinds of innumeracy when reasoning about uncertainty. We are influenced by the availability of information and theories. A psychoanalytically oriented clinician may attend to different factors than one who is behaviorally oriented. These selective tendencies influence decisions. Clinical practice requires the integration of information from diverse sources, often a challenging task. Motivational and emotional reactions may also bias judgments. Data that are vivid are especially likely to be misleading. Attention may be focused on bizarre symptoms, and data that are less vivid but nevertheless important may be ignored. Tendencies that decrease accuracy include discounting conflicting evidence, failing to search for disconfirming evidence, and a bias toward dispositional explanations. The particular match between a client and a clinician and the quality of the helping relationship also affect decisions. Familiarity with sources of influence on decisions increases the likelihood that we can avoid those that compromise the quality of services clients receive.

# CHAPTER 3

# Reasons and Reasoning: The Heart of Making Decisions

C LINICAL REASONING involves making and evaluating arguments, making judgments and drawing conclusions, and forming and testing hypotheses. Considerable attention has been devoted to the description of reasoning fallacies on the part of clients, and this is a major emphasis in cognitive behavioral and rational-emotive therapy (Beck, 1976; Dobson, Backs-Dermott, & Dozois, 2000; Ellis & Dryden, 1996). Attention has also been devoted to describing fallacies that occur in clinical reasoning. See, for example, *Follies and Fallacies in Medicine* (Skrabanek & McCormick, 1998) and *Biomedical Bestiary* (Michael, Boyce, & Wilcox, 1984). These colorful titles reflect a concerning variety of fallacies that may affect the well-being of clients. Consider the following from *Biomedical Bestiary:*

| | |
|---|---|
| Nerd of Nonsignificance | Assumes there is no real relationship between two or more variables because none was found in a study. |
| Diagnostic Zealot | Overzealous peddler of the latest diagnostic test. He has fooled himself (and may fool you, too) into untested belief in the benefits of a diagnostic test. |

Examples from *Follies and Fallacies in Medicine:*

- *The ecological fallacy:* Assuming that relationships in populations occur in an individual.
- *The fallacy of obfuscation:* Use of language to mystify rather than clarify.
- *The "hush hush" fallacy:* Ignoring the fact that mistakes are inevitable.
- *The fallacy of the golden mean:* Assuming that the consensus of a group indicates the truth.

Reasoning is "largely the conversion of unconscious judgments, feelings and knowledge into something more explicit" (Scriven, 1976, p. 180). It is concerned with exploring assumptions related to premises; that is, a tentative conclusion is drawn and then assumptions related to the conclusion are reviewed to determine whether the conclusion is warranted. In evidence-based practice a key part of this review involves considering research related to information needs. Clinical reasoning involves debating with ourselves and checking our assumptions—posing well-formed questions related to important decisions, searching efficiently and effectively for related research findings, critically appraising what is found, drawing on clinical expertise to integrate information from different sources (including the client's preferences), and deciding, together with the client, what to do. The terms reasoning, problem-solving, decision making, and thinking are closely related, and the tasks they involve overlap. We must make decisions to address problems. Reasoning is an active process involving an interaction between ourselves and the situations we encounter. (See also discussion of the importance of the tasks we confront in Chapter 9.) Far from being a dull, uncreative activity, arriving at well-reasoned inferences requires skill, flexibility, and sensitivity to the different kinds of evidence relevant to different kinds of questions, for example about the effectiveness of an intervention such as cognitive-behavioral therapy for depression, or the accuracy of an assessment measure such as the Beck Depression Inventory (see Chapter 12). This does not mean that we go through Dewey's (1933) steps: (1) clarifying the problem, (2) identifying alternatives, (3) reviewing the advantages and disadvantages of each, and (4) selecting the best option and trying it out. Indeed, as we develop expertise in an area, we rapidly size up a situation based on past experiences that provided corrective feedback: that is, we move on to pattern recognition; "take the best and leave the rest," "fast and frugal heuristics" (see, for example Gigerenzer, 2005; Klein, 1998). And we use a more deliberative problem-solving style when the "take the best and leave the rest" approach does not result in a solution. For example, experts pay attention to "anomalies" that may reflect that something is amiss. (See discussion of differences between experts and novices in Chapter 8 as well as Chapter 9.) Being reasonable "takes courage, because it seldom corresponds to being popular" (Scriven, 1976, p. 5). Our emotions influence our reasoning in a variety of ways, as described in Chapter 9.

## VIEWS OF INTELLECTUAL COMPETENCE

Discussions about what makes a "good thinker" are as old as philosophy itself. Let's take a look at what one author views as knowledge, abilities, attitudes, and ways of behaving that are characteristic of a "good thinker" (Nickerson, 1987, pp. 29–30). These characteristics are integral to evidence-based practice and illustrate the close relationship between critical thinking and EBP.

- Uses evidence skillfully and impartially
- Organizes thoughts and articulates them concisely and coherently
- Distinguishes between logically valid and invalid inferences
- Suspends judgment in the absence of sufficient evidence to support a decision
- Understands the difference between reasoning and rationalizing
- Attempts to anticipate the probable consequences of alternative actions before choosing among them
- Understands the idea of degrees of belief
- Has a sense of the value and cost of information, knows how to seek information, and does so when it makes sense
- Sees similarities and analogies that are not superficially apparent
- Can learn independently and . . . has an interest in doing so
- Applies problem-solving techniques appropriately in domains other than those in which they were learned
- Can structure informally represented problems in such a way that formal techniques (for example, mathematics) can be used to solve them
- Listens carefully to other people's ideas
- Understands the difference between winning an argument and being right
- Recognizes that most real-world problems have more than one possible solution and that those solutions may differ in numerous respects and may be difficult to compare in terms of a single criterion of merit
- Looks for unusual approaches to complex problems
- Can represent differing viewpoints without distortion, exaggeration, or caricaturization
- Is aware of the fact that one's understanding is always limited
- Recognizes the fallibility of one's own opinions, the probability of bias in those opinions, and the danger of differentially weighing evidence according to personal preferences
- Can strip a verbal argument of irrelevancies and phrase it in terms of its essentials
- Understands the differences among conclusions, assumptions, and hypotheses
- Habitually questions one's own views and attempts to understand both the assumptions that are critical to those views and the implications of the views
- Is sensitive to the difference between the validity of a belief and the intensity with which it is held

There is a lively literature regarding the distinction between unskilled and skilled thinkers. "While some may see inept thinkers as limited by their repertoire of operations, others may find their encoding impoverished, while still others locate the difficulty in inadequate goals, or inadequate monitoring of them" (Nickerson, Perkins, & Smith, 1985, p. 651). A skill analogy suggests certain distinctions and concepts, such as the difference between general and specific skills. Whether there are general skills is a topic of controversy. Many investigators (e.g., Baron, 1981, 2000; Sternberg & Wagner, 1986) argue that intelligence is best approached by understanding of general coping processes rather than by the investigation of correlations among test scores. IQ tests concentrate on academic skills and have limited predictive value in relation to everyday performance (Sternberg & Wagner, 1986), as well as limited prescriptive value in terms of offering guidelines to enhance performance (Campione, 1989). There is an interest in "metacognitive" skills, which involve managing cognitive resources and monitoring cognitive performance (Nickerson, 1985, p. 142). Examples of such skills include planning and strategizing, monitoring and evaluating knowledge and performance, and recognizing the utility of a skill. These metacognitive skills involve reasoning about reasoning. Research showing that the value of strategies is typically context bound (related to a particular kind of problem) is a strike against the "economy hypotheses," in which it is proposed that great benefit can be derived from learning a few general strategies (see other sources for discussion of transfer; Halpern, 2003; Haskell, 2001). The importance of domain-specific knowledge, including both content knowledge (knowing what) as well as procedural knowledge (knowing how to carry out certain procedures), is supported by research that shows that physicians who made accurate clinical decisions in their area of expertise were not as likely to do so when they were considering problems in another specialty (Elstein et al., 1978; see Chapter 8).

A skill approach to critical thinking suggests use of rules and strategies. We can use rules or cues as a guide as to when a given skill will be of value. For example, physicians who make accurate medical assessments pay attention to information that contradicts a diagnosis (Elstein et al., 1978). They question initial assumptions when confronted with anomalies. Some writers disagree with a focus on the importance of rules; they argue that just because a person has certain rules of inference does not mean that they will be used, and that their effectiveness will depend on the model (mental simulation) drawn on (see, for example, Johnson-Laird, 1983). Research concerning naturalistic decision making supports this view (see Chapter 9). Analyses of lapses in reasoning in arguments given by three hundred subjects about social issues showed that the most common ones involved failures to evaluate or elaborate the model offered—for example, counterexamples were overlooked (Perkins, Allen, & Hafner, 1983)—an illustration of the negative consequences of a justification approach to knowledge (searching only for data that support preferred views). So, both rules and pattern recognition may be important—serving as useful for different kinds of problems. A clinician may have a certain model in mind when offering an argument but fail to use (or not have available) rules to evaluate its accuracy. Decision aids such as palm pilots and algorithms may be used as reminders (e.g., Larrick, 2005).

Thinking ability and intelligence are only partially related; either can be modified independently of the other—that is, how people use their intelligence can be altered. For example, high intelligence is no guarantee of creativity (Weisberg, 1986); even though people may be very intelligent, they may not have learned good thinking strategies. Simply knowing about a strategy is not enough. Other requirements include knowing (1) how to apply it (necessary background knowledge and specific means of putting the strategy to work are needed), (2) when to apply it, and (3) fluidity of use (strategies become automatic; Perkins, 1985, p. 352). In addition, our values must encourage its use. The way in which we view strategies (for example, their plausibility), as well as other factors, such as forgetting, influence their use.

## REASONS

Many kinds of reasons are used in clinical decision making, and different practice theories emphasize different ones. These differences affect how problems are framed and what information is gathered. (Examples of fallacies related to different kinds of reasons are offered in other chapters.) Consider the following:

1.  Bill drinks because he is an alcoholic; he has a disease.
2.  Mary's hallucinations are caused by a mental disorder—schizophrenia.
3.  Joe's antisocial behavior at school is related to the teacher's ineffective curriculum planning and classroom management skills and few recreational activities.
4.  HIV risk behaviors are due to a variety of causes, all of which contribute to their frequency and all of which must be addressed.

In examples one and two we see appeals to underlying mental disorder, to biomedical causes. In three, a social learning view is emphasized and in four, a multi-attribute view.

Different people appeal to different sources of evidence as reasons for using a practice method or policy (see discussion of controversies regarding knowledge and how to get it in Chapter 4). Clinicians often reason from analogy; that is, they look to what has happened before to discover what to do in novel situations; they seek and draw conclusions from a comparison of experiences. The analogy of psychological problems to "illness" is perhaps the best known analogy in clinical practice and one that is widely accepted, as can be seen by the popularity of viewing alcohol abuse as a disease and the popularity of psychiatric diagnoses implying a "mental disorder." Spirited, well-argued critiques of this analogy, often presented as a fact, are available to those who wish to critically appraise it (e.g., Boyle, 2002; Midanik, 2006; Szasz, 1994). Troubling behaviors, feelings, and thoughts are often attributed to many different causes. Consider number four in the preceding list. This is an example of a multicausal view. Tesh (1988) argues that such a view allows planners to focus on only one, ignoring the rest, misleading the public that a problem has been addressed.

Arguments based on analogy depend on the similarity of the cases compared. Questions of concern (Terry, 1973, p. 99) include: How many respects are similar? How many respects are dissimilar? Are the bases of comparison relevant to the issue? Is there agreement on the major points? For example, those who do not accept the disease view of alcoholism argue that problematic drinking does not have the characteristic of a disease; for example, drinking does not necessarily become worse without treatment and, for some, one drink does not lead to many (e.g., Fingarette, 1988). Analogies may be literal or figurative. Literal analogies involve comparison between classes, cases, or objects of the same kind. Figurative analogies involve comparison between unlike categories.

Clinicians generalize from samples to populations. A psychiatrist may interview three Vietnamese families and make assumptions about all Vietnamese families. The accuracy of a generalization depends on the size and representativeness of the sample and the degree of variability in a population. If there is no variability, a sample of one is sufficient. Questions of concern include: Do the examples accurately reflect characteristics of the population? What variations occur? (See also discussion of samples in Chapter 12.)

Making clinical decisions requires reasoning from signs and symptoms. Observed signs (such as slumped shoulders, downcast eyes, and tears) may be used to infer emotional states such as depression. That is, the signs are used as "signifiers" of a state. Signs may be used as indicative of a certain history. An example is the use of the "reflex dilation test" to evaluate whether children had been abused sexually by their parents (Hobbs & Wynne, 1989). A key question here concerns validity—are the signs really indicators of the state assumed. In medicine, unlike interpersonal helping, there are signs as well as symptoms. For example, if you feel hot (a symptom) your physician can take your temperature (a sign). Do we have signs in other helping professions? Some argue, for example, that magnetic resonance imaging (MRI) has revealed brain differences between those viewed as having a mental disorder and those not so labeled. Others argue that such research is deeply flawed (see, for example, "Broken brains or flawed studies?" by Leo & Cohen, 2003).

Clinicians also reason by cause—that is, they have assumptions about the causes of particular concerns such as homelessness, poverty, anxiety, substance abuse, obsessions, or marital disharmony. The study of attributions and factors that influence them is an active area of research (e.g., see Darley & Cooper, 1998). Publications such as *Skeptic* and the *Skeptical Inquirer* explore the evidentiary status of proposed causes of behavior, such as spirits from past lives. However, lack of evidence for a claim does not mean that it is incorrect. Nor does lack of evidence discourage people from believing a claim. Indeed, some clinicians believe in practice theories that have no supporting evidence. Beutler (2000a) concludes that most of the theories and approaches that are used within the community of practitioners are unsupported by empirical evidence of effects. Is the picture more positive in medicine? It depends on whom you ask. Some, such as Richard Smith (2003), past editor of the *British Medical Journal*, do not think so.

Another form of reasoning is by exclusion. Alternative accounts for a given event or behavior are identified, and the adequacy of each is examined. This involves a search for rival explanations. For example, if a client is referred to a community mental health agency because of intractable depression, one hypothesis may be that this is an unsolvable problem, given modern-day knowledge. A rival hypothesis may be that this client did not receive state-of-the-art intervention and that improvement would follow such intervention. The book *Rival Hypotheses* (Huck & Sandler, 1979) presents 100 different claims and invites readers to evaluate these in order to sharpen their skills in identifying alternative hypotheses. A search for alternative explanations is a key strategy we can use to avoid premature acceptance of a claim or explanation that may be inaccurate (see Chapter 4).

Hot and cold reasons correspond to two major routes to persuasion—by affective association (hot) or by reasoned argument (cold; e.g., see MacCoun, 1998). Many people try to persuade others by offering reasons that play on our emotions and appeal to accepted beliefs and values. Simon (1983) uses the example of Hitler's *Mein Kampf:* "Hitler was an effective rhetorician for Germans precisely because his passion and incentives resonated with beliefs and values already present in many German hearts. The heat of his rhetoric rendered his readers incapable of applying the rules of reason and evidence to his arguments. Nor was it only Germans who resonated to the facts and values he proclaimed. The latent anti-Semitism and overt anti-Communism of many Western statesmen made a number of his arguments plausible to them" (pp. 98–99). Appeals to our emotions is a key strategy used in human service advertisements. Propaganda takes advantage of emotional reasoning, as discussed in Chapter 4.

## SOME HELPFUL DISTINCTIONS

Some people confuse the use of logical principles and reasoning. Logic is concerned with the form or validity of deductive arguments. "It provides methods and rules for restating information so as to make what is implicit explicit. It has little to do with the determination of truth or falsity" (Nickerson, 1986a, p. 7). Effective clinical reasoning requires much more than logic; it requires skill in developing arguments and hypotheses, establishing the relevance of information to an argument, and evaluating the plausibility of assertions. It requires inventiveness and a willingness to change beliefs on the basis of evidence gathered. Johnson-Laird (1985) offered this example concerning who committed a murder. The victim was stabbed to death in a movie theater. The suspect was traveling on a train to London when the murder took place. Logically it seems that this suspect must be innocent: One person cannot be in two places at once. However, the only way to guarantee the truth of a conclusion is to eliminate all possible counterexamples. "Logic cannot ensure that one has considered all the different ways in which the murder might have been accomplished. Like most everyday problems that call for reasoning, the explicit premises leave most of the relevant information unstated. Indeed, the real business of reasoning in these cases is to determine the relevant factors and possibilities, and it therefore depends on a knowledge of the specific domain. Hence, the construction of putative counter examples calls for an active exercise of memory and imagination rather than a formal derivation of one expression from others" (p. 45). Similarly, logic will not be of value in deciding that a client who complains of fatigue and headaches should be screened by a neurologist to determine if there is a physical cause of these complaints; knowledge as well as logic is required (see discussion of fallacies later in this chapter).

It is sometimes assumed that reasoning and creativity have little to do with each other. Some people believe that engineers are not creative people, that they deal with well-defined relationships that simply require a great deal of tedious study and memorization to master. On the contrary, creativity and reasoning go hand-in-hand, especially in areas such as clinical decision making, which involves unstructured situations in which needed information is often hard to get or missing, and in which there may be no one best solution. Halpern (2003) suggests use of the following skills to encourage creativity:

- Define a problem in different ways
- Brainstorm to increase the number of ideas
- Maximize intrinsic motivation
- Work with people from different backgrounds
- Encourage risk taking
- Combine attributes in different ways (p. 426)

Knowledge is required to evaluate the plausibility of premises related to an argument. Take the following example: (1) Depression always has a psychological cause; (2) Mr. Draper is depressed; (3) therefore, Mr. Draper's depression is psychological in origin. The logic of this argument is sound, but the conclusion may be false because the first premise is false. The cause of Mr. Draper's depression could be physiological. Thus, knowledge is critical in offering cogent arguments. Reasoning involves the review of evidence against as well as evidence in favor of a position. Rationalizing entails a selective search for evidence in support of a belief or action that may or may not be deliberate. "[It is] easy after having made some choice that is significant in our lives to fall into the trap of convincing ourselves of the reasonableness of that choice. It is also easy to forget, with the passage of time, what the real determinants of the choice were and to substitute for them 'reasons' that make the choice seem like a good one, and perhaps a better one than it actually was" (Nickerson, 1986a, p. 14). The research of Elizabeth Loftus and others shows that memory is a reconstructive process. False memories can be implanted (Loftus, 2004). Our views of an event, such as the reasons for a divorce, may change over time (see discussion of self-report in Chapter 13). When clinicians rationalize arguments, they are interested in building a case rather than weighing evidence for and against an argument. (See discussion of hindsight bias in Chapter 15 and excuses in Chapter 17.) This is not to say that there is no interest in persuading when arguments are presented; the difference lies in a balanced consideration of multiple perspectives in viewing possible reasons and an openness to changing our mind when a better argument is offered.

It is helpful to distinguish between propaganda, bias, and points of view (MacLean, 1981). *Bias* refers to an emotional leaning to one side (see also Chapter 12). Biased people try to persuade others but may not be aware that they are doing so. They may use propaganda tactics and faulty reasoning and offer statements in a manner designed to gain uncritical or emotional acceptance of a biased position. Personal biases may make if difficult to identify biases in a statement "*Propagandists* are aware of their interests and usually intentionally disguise these." Here too, messages are couched in a way to encourage uncritical acceptance (see Chapter 4). Those with a *point of view* are also aware of their interests, but sources are described and propaganda devices and faulty reasoning are avoided; statements are made in a manner that invites critical review. Views can be examined because they are clearly stated. People with a point of view are open to clarifying their statements when asked. (See Ellul, 1965, for a fascinating discussion of propaganda.)

Reasoning does not necessarily yield the truth. "People who are considered by many of their peers to be reasonable people often do take, and are able to defend quite convincingly, diametrically opposing positions on controversial matters" (Nickerson, 1986a, p. 12). However, effective reasoners are more likely to generate assertions that are closer to the truth than ineffective reasoners. Some assumptions are more accurate than are others. The accuracy of a conclusion does not necessarily indicate that the reasoning used to reach it was sound; errors in the opposite direction may have cancelled each other out.

A number of terms reflect the difference between rigorous logical reasoning and exploratory thinking, between the generation of hypothesis and the testing of hypotheses. Examples include divergent versus convergent thinking, and problem finding versus problem solving. However, a sharp distinction between the two kinds of thinking does not hold. Assigning appropriate weight to evidence for or against a claim is a key part of what it means to be reasonable. The term evidence-based practice draws attention to the kinds of evidence (reasons) relied on to make practice and policy decisions. Distinguishing between *consistency, corroboration*, and *proof* is important in assigning proper weight. We often use "consistency" in support of an assumption; for example, we search for consistent evidence when exploring a depressed client's history of depression. An assertion should be consistent with other beliefs that are held; that is, self-contradictory views should not knowingly be entertained. Of the three criteria (proof, falsifiability, and consistency) consistency is the weakest for offering evidence. Two or more assertions may be consistent with each other but yield little or no insight into the soundness of an argument. Saying that A (a history of "mental illness") is consistent with B (alleged current "mental illness") is to say only that it is possible to believe B given A. (See discussion of use of the word *proof* in Chapter 4.)

The accuracy of assumptions may be assessed using quite different criteria, including authority (e.g., status, credentials) and mysticism (see Chapter 4). Some assertions are not falsifiable; there is no way to determine if they are false. Psychoanalytic theory is often criticized on the grounds that it is not falsifiable—that contradictory hypotheses can be drawn from the theory (Popper, 1963). However, a theory can be shown to be false given that it is falsifiable. Falsifiability is a vital characteristic of assertions.

1. It is easy to obtain confirmations, or verifications, for nearly every theory—if we look for confirmations.
2. Confirmations should count only if they are the result of *risky predictions;* that is to say, if, unenlightened by the theory in question, we should have expected an event which was incompatible with the theory—an event which would have refuted the theory.
3. Every "good" scientific theory is a prohibition; it forbids certain things to happen. The more a theory forbids, the better it is.
4. A theory which is not refutable by any conceivable event is nonscientific. Irrefutability is not a virtue of a theory (as people often think) but a vice.
5. Every genuine test of a theory is an attempt to falsify it or to refute it. Testability is falsifiability; but there are degrees of testability; some theories are more testable, more exposed to refutation, than others; they take, as it were, greater risks.
6. Confirming evidence should not count except when it is the result of a *genuine test of the theory;* and this means that it can be presented as a serious but unsuccessful attempt to falsify the theory (Popper, 1959, p. 36).

If nothing can ever be proven, as Popper argues, the least we can do is construct falsifiable theories: theories that generate specific hypotheses that can be tested. (See Chapter 4 for further discussion.) In an evidence-based approach to practice, it is assumed that the evidentiary status of a claim is related to the rigor with which it has been critically tested—for example, does a risk-assessment measure accurately predict future behavior?

It is helpful to distinguish between facts and beliefs. A belief can be defined as "confidence that a particular thing is true, as evidenced by a willingness to act as though it were" (Nickerson, 1986a, p. 2). Beliefs vary widely in their evidentiary status. Most clinicians would believe the statement "childhood experiences influence adult development." There would be less agreement on the accuracy of the assertion that "childhood experiences determine adult development." Facts are capable of being critically appraised; beliefs may not be. Sound reasons consist of those for which sound arguments can be offered. Some beliefs are matters of definition (for example, 3 + 3 = 6). Another helpful distinction is between beliefs and opinions. Beliefs are statements that, in principle, can be shown to be true or false, whereas with an opinion, it does not make sense to consider it as true or false because people differ in their preferences and opinions. An example of an opinion statement is "I prefer insight-oriented treatment." This statement appeals to preferences. An example of a belief is "Play therapy can help children to overcome anxiety." Here, evidence can be gathered to determine if this is indeed the case. Additional examples of opinions and beliefs are shown below. The first one is an opinion and the last two are beliefs.

- I like to collect payment for each session at the end of the session.
- Insight therapy is more effective than cognitive behavioral treatment of depression.
- My pet Rottweiler helps people with their problems (quote from psychologist on morning talk show, 4/6/88).

The woman who offered the last statement also described the value of her pet Rottweiler in offering support to her clients during interviews: The pet would sit by the wife when she spoke and move over to the husband and offer support to him when he spoke. We often allow our preferences to influence our beliefs, even though preferences and beliefs should be independent. Another common distinction is that between mindful action, in which an active effort is made to understand something, and automatic functioning, in which tasks are carried out fairly automatically. The effectiveness of different styles depends on whether "automatic processing" matches what is needed to solve problems; for example, does it reflect rapid pattern recognition, based on extensive experience offering corrective feedback? (See Chapter 9.)

## ARGUMENTS

There are many products of reasoning: Arguments are one. The term *argumentation* refers to the process of making claims, challenging them, backing them with reasons, criticizing these reasons and responding to the criticism offered (Toulmin, Rieke, & Janik, 1979, p. 13; see also Hansen & Pinto, 1995). In clinical practice, this process is often implicit, as different possible causes of client concerns are considered. An argument in this sense refers to the claims and reasons offered for these—that is, "a set of assertions that is used to support a belief" (Nickerson, 1986a, p. 2). This term has a different meaning in everyday use, in which it refers to disagreements between two or more people (for example, "They had an argument about who would go to the store"). Arguments involve a set of assertions, one of which is a conclusion, and the rest of which are intended to support that conclusion. For example, a clinician may argue that because a client has a history of being hospitalized for anxiety and compulsive hand-washing, current complaints about anxiety and obsessive thoughts indicate that another severe episode of compulsive hand-washing is imminent. This conclusion is based on the premise that there is a history of hospitalization for what seem to be similar problems. The purpose of arguments is often to convince someone (or oneself) that something is true, or to convince someone to act in a certain way. Another purpose is to explore the accuracy of an assumption, for example about the effectiveness of a practice method.

Arguments consist of parts; they can be taken apart as well as put together. They may be strong (convincing) or weak (unconvincing), simple or complex. A complex argument usually involves several assertions in support of one or more conclusions. Assertions may involve statements of fact ("a belief for which there is enough evidence to justify a high degree of confidence"; Nickerson, 1986a, p. 36), assumptions, or hypotheses. For example, there may be no doubt that a client was hospitalized. The term *assumption* refers to "an assertion that we either believe to be true in spite of being unable to produce compelling evidence of its truth, or are willing to accept as true for purposes of debate or discussion." A *hypothesis* is an assertion that we do not know to be true but that we believe to be testable (Nickerson, 1986a, pp. 36–37). Assumptions, hypotheses, or statements of fact may be used as premises in an argument—or, they may serve as conclusions; that is, an assertion may be a conclusion that is drawn from what precedes it and can also be a premise with respect to what follows it. "The credibility of a conclusion can be no greater than the least credible of the premises from which it is drawn, so a conclusion cannot be considered a statement of fact unless all of the premises are statements of fact. . . . If the conclusion follows from two premises one of which is considered to be a fact and the other an assumption, the conclusion should not be considered a statement of fact" (Nickerson, 1986a, p. 37). Universal assertions that contain words such as *all* or *none* are much more difficult to defend than are particular assertions that contain qualifiers such as *some*. The statement that all children of alcoholic parents have problems as adults would be more difficult to support than the more modest claim that some children of alcoholic parents have problems later.

A key part of an argument is the claim, conclusion, or position that is put forward (see Exhibit 3.1). In the statement "Mary Walsh is the person who is responsible for the abuse of this child; she had the greatest opportunity," the claim or conclusion is clear. Often, excessive wordiness makes the premises and/or conclusion difficult to identify; that is, "an eloquent speaker or writer can dress up his arguments in all kinds of ways so as to conceal their deficits and make them attractive to his audience" (Toulmin et al., 1979, p. 106). The claim here is that Mary Walsh is guilty of the abuse of the child. Claims or conclusions are often qualified—that is, some probability is expressed (for example, "I think there is a 90 percent probability that Mary Walsh abused this child"). Conclusions can be further qualified by describing the conditions under which they do, or do not, hold. A clinician may believe that she would only abuse the child "if she were under extreme stress."

A second critical feature of an argument consists of the reasons or premises offered to support the claim made. Premises can be divided into two parts—

**Exhibit 3.1**

Toulmin's Six Types of Statements in a Rational Argument

| Label | Name | Logical Function |
|---|---|---|
| C | Claim or conclusion | States a claim or a conclusion. |
| D | Data, evidence, or foundation | Offers data or foundations, i.e., relevant evidence, for the claim. |
| W | Inference warrant | Warrants or justifies the connection between data (D) and claim (C) by appealing to a rule of inference, such as an operational definition, a practical standard, or an analogy. |
| Q | Modal qualifier | Qualifies a claim or conclusion (C) by expressing degrees of confidence and likelihood. |
| R | Rebuttal or reservation | Rebuts a claim or conclusion (C) by stating the conditions under which it does not hold; or introduces reservations showing the limits within which the claim (C) is made. |
| B | Backing | Backs up, justifies, or otherwise supports an inferences warrant (W) by appealing to further evidence (empirical data, common knowledge, professional practice, scientific theory, and so on). |

Colloquially speaking:

| | |
|---|---|
| C | Answers the questions "What are you saying?" "What is it you are claiming?" "What is your conclusion?" |
| D | Answers the questions "What have you to go on?" "Where is your evidence?" "What data do you have?" |
| W | Answers the questions "How do you make that out?" "What is the connection?" "Why are you entitled to draw that conclusion?" |
| Q | Answers the questions "How sure are you?" "What confidence do you have in your claim?" "How likely is it that what you say is correct?" |
| R | Answers the questions "What are you assuming?" "Under what conditions would your argument break down?" "What reservations would you make?" |
| B | Answers the questions "What proof have you?" "What is the justification for your line of reasoning?" "Is there any support for the connection you are making?" |

*Source:* From *The Case-Study Method in Psychology and Related Disciplines* (p. 195), by D. B. Bromley, 1986, New York: Wiley. Copyright 1986 by John Wiley & Sons. Reprinted by permission.

grounds and warrants. The grounds (data or evidence) must be relevant to the claim as well as sufficient to support the claim; that is where warrants come in. Warrants concern the justification for making the connection between the grounds and the claim. The question is: Do the grounds provide support for the claim made? Warrants may involve appeals to common knowledge, empirical evidence, practice theory, and so on. Let's return to the claim that Mary Walsh is responsible for the abuse of a child. The ground is that she had the opportunity to abuse the child. The warrant is probably something of the nature that op-

**Exhibit 3.2**

The Four Combinations of True or False Premises and Conclusions in a
Valid Logical Argument

**Conclusion**

| | | True | False |
|---|---|---|---|
| | | True | False |
| **Premises** | True | Necessary<br><br>(Conclusion must be true if premises are true) | Impossible<br><br>(Conclusion cannot be false if premises are true) |
| | False | Possible<br><br>(Conclusion *may* be true even if premises are false) | Possible<br><br>(Conclusion *may* be false if premises are false) |

*Note:* Entries in the table indicate how the truth or falsity of the conclusion depends on the truth or falsity of the premises.
*Source:* From *Reflections on Reasoning* (p. 90), by R. S. Nickerson, 1986, Hillsdale, NJ: Erlbaum. Copyright 1986 by Lawrence Erlbaum Associates. Reprinted by permission

portunity is sufficient to yield abuse, clearly an inaccurate assumption. There is no firm backing for the warrant; opportunity does not an abuser make. So warrants purport to offer evidence for making the step from the grounds to the claim and the strength of the support offered should be evaluated. How reliably does the warrant offer such evidence? Are the grounds necessary or sufficient? For example, opportunity is necessary but not sufficient. (See also the discussion of clues to causality in Chapter 14.) The possible combinations of false or true premises and conclusions are shown in Exhibit 3.2.

An argument may be unsound for one of three reasons. There may be something wrong with its logical structure: (1) all mental patients are people; (2) John is a person; (3) therefore, John is a mental patient. It may contain false premises: (1) all battering men were abused as children; (2) Mr. Smith batters his wife; (3) therefore, Mr. Smith was abused as a child. It may be irrelevant or circular: (1) kicking other children is a sign of aggression; (2) Johnny kicks other children; (3) therefore, Johnny is aggressive. The last two arguments contain informal fallacies; they have a correct logical form but are still incorrect. Informal fallacies are related to the content of arguments rather than to their form. There are many varieties of informal fallacies (see Chapters 5 and 6). Arguments often contain unfounded premises. They may give the impression that they are valid arguments, but because relevant facts have not been presented correctly (they may have been left out, evaded, or distorted), they are not valid. An example of the logical error of affirming the consequence is: (1) if he has measles, he should have red spots; (2) he has spots; (3) therefore, he has measles. Denying the antecedent also involves a logical error: (1) if we don't conserve clinical resources, the supply will run out; (2) we will not waste clinical resources; (3) therefore, our supply should not run out. In none of the preceding cases does the conclusion follow from the premises. These errors involve a confusion between one-way and bidirectional implication (Nickerson, 1986a, p. 82). Contradictions are a type of implication. For example, to say that X contradicts Z is to say that if X is true, Z must be false. A premise implies another premise when the second premise must be true if the first is true. Contradictions involve a bidirectional relationship: if X contradicts Y, then Y contradicts X. However, this is not necessarily the case with implication; although X may imply Y, Y may not imply X. The *premise conversion error* occurs when the assertion "all X are Y" (all clinicians are human) is assumed to be the same as "all Y are X" (all humans are clinicians). Examples of clinical errors that result from this fallacy are illustrated in Chapter 14. (See other sources for a description of logical fallacies.)

Both deductive and inductive reasoning play a critical role in clinical decision making. Deductive arguments involve a sequence of premises and a conclusion; if the reasoning is logically valid, the conclusion necessarily follows (although it may not be true, because one or more of the premises may be false;

**Exhibit 3.3**
Distinguishing Deductive from Inductive Arguments

| *Deductive Example* | *Inductive Example* |
|---|---|
| • No animals are persons<br>• Only persons have rights<br>• Therefore, no animals have rights. | • Both psychiatrists and psychologists have professional training<br>• Psychiatrists have hospital privileges.<br>• Therefore, psychologists should also have hospital privileges. |
| • If you see one client, you've seen them all.<br>• I have seen one client.<br>• Therefore, I have seen them all. | • All clients I have seen have been demoralized.<br>• Therefore, all clients are demoralized when they first seek help. |
| Although the premises may or may not be true, if they are true, the conclusion is true as well, because, in a deductive argument, the information in the conclusion is implicitly present in the premises. Thus, adding information does not change the probability that the conclusion is true. | Although the premises provide evidence for the conclusion, it is possible that the conclusion is false even when the premises are true, because in an inductive argument the conclusion contains information not present in the premises. |
| A good deductive argument is called valid. | In an inductive argument, the probability of the conclusion may change with the addition of further information.<br><br>A good inductive argument is called strong (or plausible). |

*Source:* Adapted from *Inductive Arguments: A Field Guide* (p. 4), by K. D. Moore, 1986, Dubuque, IA: Kendall/Hunt. Reprinted with permission.

see Exhibit 3.3). Deductive arguments can produce false conclusions, either when one of the premises is false or when one of the rules of deductive inference is violated, as in the preceding example, illustrating the logical fallacy of affirming the consequent. The conclusion may be true but it is invalid, because it is arrived at by an illogical inference. Seldom are the major premises as well as the conclusion clearly stated in deductive arguments; more typically, at least one premise is missing.

Logical (deductive) arguments use deductive inferences; there are objective criteria that can be used to evaluate such arguments. With plausible (inductive) arguments, there are no objective criteria; what is convincing may differ from person to person. Key assertions can be identified in plausible arguments, as well as other assertions that are assumed to support the main one. Inductive reasoning involves generalizing from the particular to the general. It is assumed that what is true of the sample is true of all possible cases. For example, if a psychologist sees three young, successful professional men who use cocaine and who complain of stress in their work life, he or she may conclude that all young professional men who use cocaine experience stress. Thus, in inductive reasoning, we go beyond the data at hand in drawing a conclusion that we cannot affirm with certainty (see Popper's [1972] critique of induction).

## ANALYZING ARGUMENTS

Your skill in analyzing arguments will increase the quality of clinical decisions, whether considering those presented by others or your own—the latter is more challenging: "Playing prosecutor, judge, and jury when one is oneself the defendant requires an unusual degree of objectivity and commitment to the truth" (Nickerson, 1986a, p. 88). There are many excellent descriptions of how to analyze arguments (e.g., see Nickerson, 1986a; Scriven, 1976; Toulmin et al., 1979). Arguments are often incomplete. Key premises or conclusions may be missing, and a critical part of examining an argument is filling in these parts. For example, consider the following statements. What are key premises? "Sexualization for purposes of stimulation of a dead self is frequent and addictive. In general, so-called masochistic behaviors of all types are probably more often the result of the desire and need to stimulate, even through pain, affects which will counter deadness and nothingness. They can be seen as the outgrowth of a motivation to be alive (self-cohesion enhancing) rather than a desire to be dead (self-destructive). Behaviors such as promiscuity, exhibitionism, or voyeurism, seem to be sexualized attempts to fulfill nonsexual stimulating and calming self-needs, that is, mirroring, twinship, and idealization, which are necessary to help maintain a cohesive sense of self" (Chelton & Bonney, 1987, p. 41).

The following steps can be used to analyze incomplete logical arguments.

- Identify the conclusion or key assertion.
- List all the other explicit assertions that make up the argument as given.

- Add any unstated assertions that are necessary to make the argument complete. (Put them in parentheses to distinguish them from assertions that are explicit in the argument as given.)
- Order the premises (or supporting assertions) and conclusion (or key assertion) so as to show the structure of the argument. (Nickerson, 1986a, p. 87)

Since induction is based on facts, "all the principles and lines of arguments on facts apply to induction. Whenever we talk in terms of percentages, ratios, indices, the majority of cases, and the minority, we are referring to terms statistical in nature" (Huber, 1963, p. 123). These statistics are usually gathered by sampling (an inductive process). Statistics may be misleading in a number of ways that relate to the size and representativeness of the samples on which they are based. There are many different meanings of the term *representative sample* (Kruskal & Mosteller, 1981). The most common one refers to an absence of selective factors, which would render the sample unrepresentative of the population from which it is drawn (see also Chapter 12). The importance of asking for precise figures is illustrated by the varied meanings given to words referring to frequency expressions, such as *sometimes*, *often*, or *rarely*. For example, the meaning of the term *sometimes* has been found to range from 20% to 46% (Pepper, 1981). Figures may be used to mislead rather than inform. Only relative risk may be given, rather than both relative and absolute risk (see Chapter 15). Proponents of a new suicide prevention center may say that there has been a 200% increase in the number of suicides over the past year. The total increase may be two additional cases. Thus, misleading percentages may be offered. The total number of occurrences of a given event may be cited when a percentage would be more informative. A drug company may claim that more people have improved using drug X than any other drug. However, the best drug on the market may only be effective 5% of the time. Drug X may be effective 6% of the time—usually not much to write home about. Groups with a special interest in a problem may deliberately inflate the number of people affected by a problem. Questions raised when evaluating inductive arguments include the following (Huber, 1963, p. 140):

- Are the facts accurate?
- Do the examples consist of isolated or universal instances?
- Do the examples used cover a significant time period?
- Are the examples given typical or atypical?
- Is the conclusion correctly stated?
- Is the argument really of concern—the "so what" and "what harm" questions?

Consider, for example, Joel Best's (2004) critiques of the prevalence of stranger abduction. He argues that it is greatly exaggerated. Rather than reporting accurate data, those who advocate for greater attention to a problem and more

Percentage of Doctors Devoted Solely to Family Practice

| 1964 | 1975 | 1990 |
|------|------|------|
| 27% | 16.0% | 12.0% |

1: 4,232
6,212

1: 3,167
6,694

1: 2,247 RATIO TO POPULATION
8,023 Doctors

**Exhibit 3.4** The Shrinking Family Doctor in California
*Source: Los Angeles Times*, August 5, 1979, p. 3. Reprinted by permission.

funding for related services may distort the scope of the problem. They engage in "advocacy scholarship" (see also MacCoun & Reuter, 2001).

Our tendency to be influenced by vivid material makes us vulnerable to distortions created by visual material such as photographs, charts, and graphs (Huff, 1954; Tufte, 1983). Consider Exhibit 3.4, The Shrinking Family Doctor in California. Graphic displays often lie by omission—by what is left out—leaving unanswered the question "compared with what?" Only a portion of a graph may be shown, resulting in a distorted version of data. Visual representation should be consistent with numerical representation. Often it is not, as shown in Exhibit 3.4. Principles of graphical excellence suggested by Tufte (1983) include the following: (1) complex ideas are communicated with clarity, precision, and efficiency; (2) the viewer receives the greatest number of ideas in the shortest time with the least ink in the smallest space; and (3) the truth about the data is depicted (p. 51).

We should consider the context when attempting to understand the intended meaning of a claim; however, we should interpret words as they generally would be defined. And, as Scriven (1976) points out, arguments should not be dismissed simply because they are presented emotionally or because a conclusion is disliked; the emotion with which a position is presented is not

**Exhibit 3.5**

A Taxonomy of Socratic Questions

---

## Questions of Clarification

- What do you mean by _____?
- What is your main point?
- How does _____ relate to _____?
- Could you put that another way?
- Let me see if I understand you; do you mean _____ or _____?

- Could you give me an example?
- Would this be an example: _____?
- Could you explain that further?

## Questions That Probe Assumptions

- What are you assuming?
- What could we assume instead?
- You seem to be assuming _____. Do I understand you correctly?

## Questions That Probe Reasons and Evidence

- What would be an example?
- Why do you think that is true?
- Do you have evidence for that?
- What other information do we need?
- Is there reason to doubt that evidence?
- Who is in a position to know if that is so?
- How could we find out whether that is true?

- Are these reasons adequate?
- How does that apply to this case?
- What difference does that make?
- What would change your mind?

## Questions about Viewpoints or Perspectives

- What might someone who believed _____ think?
- Can/did anyone see this another way?
- What would someone who disagrees say?
- What is an alternative?

## Questions That Probe Implications and Consequences

- What are you implying by that?
- What effect would that have?
- What is an alternative?

## Questions about the Question

- How can we find out?
- What does this question assume?
- How could someone settle this question?
- Can we break this question down at all?
- Do we all agree that this is the question?
- To answer this question, what questions would we have to answer first?

- Is this the same issue as _____?
- Why is this question important?

---

*Source:* Adapted from *Critical Thinking: What Every Person Needs to Survive in a Rapidly Changing World* (Rev. 2nd ed., pp. 367–368), by R. Paul, 1992, Foundation for Critical Thinking. www.criticalthinking.org

necessarily related to the soundness of an argument. Since plausible (inductive) arguments do not have to fit any particular form, objective evaluation is more difficult than it is with deductive arguments. As with logical arguments, the truth of the premises is important to assess. (See list of Socratic Questions in Exhibit 3.5.) However, even if these are assumed to be true, clinicians may disagree as to whether they provide evidence for a conclusion. (See discussion of controversies regarding the evidentiary status of claims in Chapter 10.) Questions of concern in evaluating a logical argument include: Is it complete? Is its meaning clear? Is it valid (does the conclusion follow from the premises)? Do I believe the premises? (Nickerson, 1986a, p. 88). An argument may be worthy of consideration even though it has some defects.

Counterarguments should be considered. Are there arguments on the same issue that point to the opposite conclusion or to a somewhat different conclusion? For example, an analogy may be used to support the opposite conclusion. Are there other arguments that support the same conclusion? Consider the following claims made by astrologers to support their belief in astrology (Kelly et al., 1989). What are possible counterarguments? (1) Astrology has great antiquity and durability. (2) Astrology is found in many cultures. (3) Many great scholars have believed in it. (4) Astrology is based on observation. (5) Extraterrestrial influences exist. (6) Astrology has been proved by research. (7) Nonastrologers are not qualified to judge. (8) Astrology works.

Many statements, written or spoken, are opinions or points of view; "they frequently don't pass the test of providing reasons for a conclusion, reasons that can be separated from a conclusion" (Scriven, 1976, p. 67). The question is, Can the premises be established independently of the conclusion? Is the argument convincing?

## KINDS OF ARGUMENTS

Arguments occur in different contexts, including courts of law, case conferences, Joe's Bar, and the American Psychiatric Association's annual convention. These different contexts influence the manner in which a topic is discussed in terms of different norms, values, procedures, and requirements for and types of evidence that are acceptable or unacceptable (Bromley, 1986, p. 223). The focus in this book is on reasoning processes that influence clinical decisions, including those found in the professional literature, meetings, and case conferences. The most elaborate and detailed set of rules related to the presentation and rebuttal of arguments can be found in the field of law. For example, specific grounds are described for objecting to the introduction of certain kinds of questions. Courts of law favor an adversarial (competitive) format in which each party tries to settle a dispute in its favor. In clinical settings, a concern such as child abuse must be considered from many different perspectives (for example, medical, legal, psychological, and educational), each of which has a unique framework for viewing problems and resolutions. Aristotle distinguished three kinds of arguments: didactic, dialectical, and contentious. The hallmark of dialectical arguments is a spirit of inquiry. The aim of people involved in teaching and learning was considered to differ from the aim of those involved in competition. "... for a learner should always state what he thinks; for no one is even trying to teach him what is false; whereas in a competition the business of a questioner is to appear by all means to produce an effect upon the other, while that of the answerer is to appear unaffected by him" (Topics, 159a 25). Aims of the questioner in contentious arguments include (1) to refute the opponent—that is, to prove the point contradictory to his or her thesis; (2) to show that the opponent has committed a fallacy; (3) to lead the opponent into paradox; (4) to make the opponent use an ungrammatical expression; and (5) to reduce the opponent to babbling (Aristotle cited in Hamblin, 1970, p. 63).

Adversarial arguments are competitive in nature; that is, each party concentrates on defending one line of reasoning and attacking other lines presented. In arbitrational arguments, the focus is on arriving at a compromise resolution that is satisfactory to both parties. Neither party may be fully satisfied by the conclusion reached, but agree to abide by it. The kinds of arguments that typically occur in clinical contexts can be contrasted to arguments in scientific contexts by the time frame involved; that is, judgments in clinical contexts must be made under time pressures and without all needed information. In both professional and scientific contexts, value is (or should be) placed on a "willingness and ability to be self-critical, to deal sensibly with justifiable objections and queries from others" (Bromley, 1986, p. 233); that is, there should be dialectical arguments displaying a spirit of inquiry. This critical approach is a hallmark of evidence-based decision making (see Chapter 10; that such appraisal is not the norm can be seen in the case example in Chapter 16). Consideration of clashing viewpoints regarding an issue or question is vital to exploring the cogency of different assumptions. Popper (1994) attributes the invention of criticism to Xenophenes, who traveled outside of Greece and discovered that not everyone accepted the Gods revered in his country. Grappling with different perspectives, for example, between our current beliefs and new ideas, is vital to learning—to expanding our knowledge.

Misunderstandings and bad feelings may result when participants in a discussion do not recognize that different kinds of arguments are being used. Lawyers and social workers often have negative views of each other because of their different frameworks for argument analysis. Lawyers may view clinicians as fuzzy thinkers, and clinicians may view lawyers as inhumane and legalistic in their questioning of the accuracy of "alleged" evidence. Required characteristics Damer (1995) describes for effective rational discussion include the following:

*The Fallibility Principle:* a willingness to admit you could be wrong

*The Truth-Seeking Principle:* a commitment to search for the truth or the most defensible position on the issue. Examination of alternative positions and a welcoming of raising objections to your view.

*The Burden of Proof Principle:* This rests on the person who presents it.

*The Principle of Charity:* Arguments are presented in their strongest version.

*The Clarity Principle:* Positions, defenses, and challenges are clear.

*The Relevance Principle:* Only reasons or questions that are directly related to the merit of the position at issue.

*The Acceptability Principle:* Premises or reasons relied on meet standard criteria of acceptability.

*The Sufficient Grounds Principle:* Those who present an argument for or challenge a position should attempt to provide reasons sufficient in number, kind, and weight to support the conclusion.

*The Rebuttal Principle:* The person who presents an argument for or challenges a position should attempt to provide effective responses to all serious challenges or rebuttals.

*The Resolution Principle:* An issue should be considered resolved if the proponent for a position presents an argument that uses relevant and acceptable premises that are sufficient in number, kind, and weight to support the premises and the conclusion and provides an effective rebuttal to all serious challenges.

*The Suspension of Judgment Principle:* If no position can be successfully defended, or if two or more positions can be defended with equal strength, you should suspend judgment, or if practical considerations require a decision, proceed based on preferences.

*The Reconsideration Principle:* Participants are obligated to reconsider the issue if subsequent flaws are found in an argument. (pp. 173–186)

## EXPLANATIONS

Many different kinds of explanations are used in clinical practice, including biological, genetic, psychological, and sociological. Explaining is closely connected with judging whether something is good or bad. Different explanations suggest different reasons that may be offered for beliefs:

- Preferred kind of explanation → reasons → evidence sought/appealed to
- Example: biomedical → brain differences → different levels of dopamine in those diagnosed with a mental illness and those not so labeled

William James (1975) suggested that temperamental differences (tender versus tough-minded) account for preference for different kinds of explanations (p. 13). Optimists are more likely to prefer explanations that allow appreciable room for change, whereas pessimists are more likely to be drawn to explanations that allow little room for change. People differ in the kinds of explanations that satisfy their curiosity. Explanations are often given by defining a word in terms of other words (for example, synonyms) as in dictionary definitions. Other kinds of explanations by definition include classifying (for example, social work is a profession), offering examples, or describing operations.

Some clinicians prefer empathic explanations. (These may or may not assume a causal connection.) Techniques of empathy building include telling a story; describing circumstances; labeling character; presuming drives, instincts, and needs; and describing intentions and feelings (motives; see Exhibit 3.6). "The heart of empathy is imagined possibility" (Nettler, 1970, p. 34). The empathizer thinks, "Under these circumstances I, too, might have behaved similarly." An example of an empathic explanation is: "The reason he did it is because he hated her." Empathic explanations often involve concepts that are only variant definitions of the behavior to be explained, as shown in the following examples (Nettler, 1970, p. 71).

> Case One
> *Probation:* Why, doctor, does our client continue to steal?
> *Psychiatry:* He is suffering from antisocial reaction.
> *Probation:* What are the marks of "antisocial reaction"?
> *Psychiatry:* Persistent thievery is one symptom.

> Case Two
> *Defense:* Whether one calls him insane or psychotic, he's a sick man. That's obvious.
> *Psychiatry:* I should think that's largely a matter of terminology.
> *Defense:* Do you mean to suggest that a man could do what that boy has done and not be sick?

A preference for empathic explanations reflects a search for explanations in terms of underlying essences—essential properties. Explanations that offer less are considered useless. Popper (1983a) refers to this position as *essentialism*. Essentialists seek empathic explanations and argue about the meaning of words rather than exploring meaning through empirical inquiry.

In scientific explanations, critical appraisal of claims is emphasized, there is an active effort to seek out errors in assumptions through this appraisal (see Chapter 4). Scientific explanations are not essentialist accounts—quite the opposite. The scientific process is designed to eliminate errors, not to claim final accounts. As many writers have pointed out, ultimate claims stifle inquiry; they may function as prisons that limit our vision (Popper, 1994). Nor do scientific explanations assume that objective accounts can be offered—accounts that are not influenced by diverse meanings associated with how events are interpreted. To the contrary, in no approach is objectivity so suspect as illustrated by the variety of methods devised to attempt to avoid biases (see discussion of falsifiability in Chapter 4).

Ideological explanations are distinguished from scientific ones by their rejection of objectivity, their ready acceptance of sound and unsound premises,

**Exhibit 3.6**

Hallmarks of Different Kinds of Explanations

A. *Ideological Explanations*

1. Provide few answers for many questions (a few principles cover a wide territory).
2. Seek to clarify true meaning of "scriptures."
3. Contain a high proportion of nonfactual sentences included as declarations ("nonfactual" means ambiguous and improvable or without empirical warrant," p. 186). Values disguised as facts.
4. Contain "A high ratio of hortatory-presumptive to declarative" sentences.
5. Contain many failures of logic.
6. Deny the possibility of objectivity; (critical appraisal of claims) "all explanations of social behavior are considered to be distorted (cues include 'stating one's own motives . . . locating the 'social position' from which the competing thesis allegedly originates," p. 186).
7. Favor ad hominem arguments, which are viewed as tools, not as errors; identification of "who said it" as an important test of a statement's validity.
8. Resort to reliance on authority.
9. Seek converts; respond to criticism with emotional defenses; attack critic's motives and develop "cults" (practices that a believing group develops as its distinctive mode of "meeting the world," p. 186); may seek to force theories on others.
10. Prescribe action; have an interest in persuading rather than explaining.
11. Are action oriented.

B. *Scientific Explanations*

1. Reject ad hominem arguments as persuasive.
2. Encourage dispute of key ideas.
3. Do not encourage unexamined commitment to one side.
4. Value critical appraisal and observation.
5. Question everything.
6. Seek to reduce influence of moral judgments on observation and inference.
7. Reflect an interest in improving accuracy of judgments.

C. *Empathic Explanations*

1. Do not require proof; consider the test of empathy to be empathy (p. 49); common sense is sufficient.
2. Use vague indicators; hard "to know when one has understanding"; do not use independent tests of interpretations.
3. Accept ad hominem arguments.
4. Entangle moral judgments with understanding.
5. Have a cognitive bias; an attempt to explain behavior "as if it arose from thought alone" (p. 56); an equation of awareness with verbal reports; knowledge of others limited by excessive attention to what they say.
6. Are vulnerable to tautology; infer inner states from behaviors, and explain behaviors by reference to inner states; prove motives from acts.
7. Confuse understanding and predictive capability; consider propositions to be non-predictive.
8. Assume that understanding of individuals can offer knowledge of groups.

*Source:* Adapted from *Explanations* (pp. 49, 56, 186), by G. Nettler, 1970, New York: McGraw-Hill.

and their reliance on ethical judgments. "Ideological explanations, then, became operative as they are believed, rather than as they are verified" (Nettler, 1970, p. 179). They are *theory* driven and discount empirical findings (e.g., see Gorman, 1998). It is difficult to find a term that has a more speckled history than does *ideology*. Depending on who is talking and what they are talking about, ideology is a virtue or a sin. Criticisms of "let's drop the ideology" are used often in attempts to quiet critics. "The term 'ideology' is someone else's thought, seldom our own" (McLellan, 1986, p. 1). On the other hand, "ideology tells the point of it all. Life is no longer absurd. It describes the forces of light and darkness and names the innocent to be saved" (Nettler, 1970, p. 179).

Thompson (1987) distinguishes between two uses of the term *ideology*. One is as a purely descriptive term. For example, the beliefs of a particular clinical approach, such as psychoanalysis, can be described. In the second use, the term is "linked to the process of sustaining asymmetrical relations of power—that is, to maintaining domination" (p. 518). It is this use of ideology that has negative connotations, and it is in this sense that language is used as a medium of influence. "The difference between the scientific orientation and the empathetic and ideological outlooks, however, lies in the criteria of conceptual utility. In the latter explain ways, terms are maintained as they serve the explicators' purposes of building empathy or justifying ethical-political causes. In the scientific schema, any concept or construct is, in principle, dispensable regardless of these empathetic or ideological effects" (Nettler, 1970). Ideological explanations are used to account for "collective" behavior as empathetic ones do in the clarification of individual actions—they fill the needs of "curiosity left by the gaps in knowledge" (Nettler, 1970, p. 187). In professional contexts, scientific explanations may be preferred over ideological ones—but not always, as the most casual perusal of professional writing demonstrates.

Explanations do not necessarily involve arguments. For example, empathic and ideological explanations may not involve arguments. A client may say "I hit her because I was annoyed," or a person with a drinking problem may say, "I saw the bar and couldn't stop myself from going in and having a drink." Offering an explanation for taking some action (indicating a cause) does not necessarily offer a justification (reason) for the action taken. If, for example, a clinician claims that he or she did not obtain assessment data that is generally considered desirable to gather, and, as a result, selected an ineffective intervention method, the excuse that he or she did not have time does not provide a moral justification for inaction. The latter refers to offering reasons that "are morally adequate to support a certain conclusion or action" (Scriven, 1976, p. 219). People tend to feel that they should be able to justify (have sound reasons for) their beliefs. An inability to explain why a certain view is held may create feelings of anger or embarrassment. It's not odd that cogent reasons for a belief may not be at hand, since many of our beliefs result from automatic processes that lie outside of our awareness (see Chapter 9). Most beliefs are not examined in terms of providing explanations or justifications for them.

Prediction refers to forecasting what will happen in the future. An example is "attending Alcoholics Anonymous will help this client to remain abstinent." Explanations involve offering alleged reasons for certain behaviors or events. Thus, the explanation here may be that if this client attains peer support, she or he will be able to use self-management skills to avoid alcoholic beverages. Practice theories suggest possible explanations and predictions. The question is "How much *real* understanding, as opposed to *feeling* of understanding, do these approaches provide? How much better are the predictions that they yield than those of an intelligent observer not using these theories but using all the other background knowledge that we have about psychological or socioeconomic events?" (Scriven, 1976, p. 219). Explanations may be psychologically compelling but be quite weak from an evidentiary standpoint. For example, astrological explanations may give many people the feeling of understanding; this does not mean that these explanations are accurate.

## INDIVIDUAL AND CULTURAL DIFFERENCES

Thinking styles and skills are related to educational and socialization experiences. Stanovitch and West (2002) have studied individual differences in reasoning. Thinking and the development of thinking styles occur in a particular context, involving an interaction between an individual and a particular physical and social situation (Greeno, 1989). The results of differences in educational and socialization opportunities may be attributed inaccurately to an inherent style difference; for example, that women are naturally more subjective and intuitive in their approach to problems in contrast to men, who are more objective. Barnett and Rivers (2004) argue that similarities between men and women have been downplayed and differences exaggerated, with negative effects on both men and women. (For counterarguments, see Rhoads, 2004.) Poor people, compared to economically privileged individuals, often receive less training in the skills of rationality and objectivity and less cultivation of related beliefs, such as the belief that "knowledge is a product of individual and social intellectual construction" (Greeno, 1989, p. 139). The superordinate position of class to gender is often overlooked; that is, what is attributed to gender differences may be a matter of class differences in access to educational opportunities that nourish effective problem-solving skills. Thus, a preference for subjectivity that is attributed to personal choice may be the result of socialization experiences that "discourage critical thinking and reflective thought." The question is, what is gained and lost by such a preference? Encouraging intuitivism, depriving people of critical thinking skills, helps to maintain current power imbalances. It is to the advantage of those with economic resources to encourage individuals in less-advantaged positions to embrace an intuitive approach to the exclusion of a rational approach. (See discussion of propaganda in Chapter 4.) As some have argued, isn't it the economically privileged who benefit most from the anti-intellectual bias in the general population, in terms of protection of their privilege? Extreme subjectivism as a reaction against disliked "male styles of thinking" forgoes the option of reaping the benefits of critical appraisal. We can be critical thinkers as well as caring professionals. Effective decision making requires both creativity and critically reflective skills.

Cultural differences include norms regarding questioning authority figures (Tweed & Lehman, 2002). If this is not permitted, or frowned on, how can a staff member raise questions about agency policies that affect clients' well-being? If important questions are not raised, how can "group think" be avoided in which there is premature closure on an option (see Chapter 16). What are the options here? A shared focus on helping clients (rather than protecting the esteem of authority figures) should contribute to a culture in which asking questions is valued. Still, this may be an uphill battle, in contexts in which authority-based decision making is preferred.

## SUMMARY

Clinical decision making involves reasoning-forming hypotheses about clients' concerns, offering arguments for case formulations, and evaluating these assumptions. Reasons may be hot or cold—that is, developed by emotive associations or by reasoned argument. Reasoning does not necessarily yield the truth, nor does the accuracy of a conclusion necessarily indicate that the reasoning used to reach it was sound. Plausible reasons are more likely to be offered if distinctions are made among assumptions that have been critically tested, beliefs based only on confidence that they are true, and preferences that cannot be shown to be true or false. Effective reasoning requires much more than logic in developing and evaluating arguments to arrive at those that are well-reasoned. Domain-specific knowledge is also needed. Being familiar with the steps in argument analysis is useful in examining the quality of arguments. Different criteria are used to assess the quality of arguments in different settings. Effective reasoning requires a certain kind of attitude toward the truth—a questioning attitude and an openness to altering beliefs in light of evidence offered—a willingness to say "I don't know." Clinicians differ in the kinds of explanations they prefer, which influences the plausibility of arguments offered. Some clinicians prefer empathic and ideological explanations rather than scientific ones. The kinds of explanations that we find satisfying depends in part on the subject or question at hand. Creativity, including flexibility, and reasoning, are closely related, especially in areas such as clinical decision making, in which helpful information is often missing.

# CHAPTER 4

# Different Views of Knowledge and How to Get It: Exploring Your Personal Epistemology

Professionals are assumed to have unique knowledge as a result of special education, experience, and training. This implies that there is some knowledge to master, that some decisions are better reasoned than others. Claimed special knowledge supposedly makes those with certain degrees, training, and/or experience more effective in achieving certain outcomes than those without such "credentials." That is, the former are supposed to be "experts" in solving certain kinds of problems. Larson (1977) suggests that

> The main instrument of professional advancement, more than the profession of altruism, is the capacity to claim esoteric and identifiable skills—that is, to create and control a cognitive and technical basis. The claim of expertise aims at gaining social recognition and collective prestige which, in turn, are implicitly used by the individual to assert his authority and demand respect in the context of everyday transactions within specific role-sets. (p. 180)

Studies in medicine show that specialized content knowledge is vital to making sound decisions in many instances (see Chapter 3). Professional codes of ethics call on practitioners to draw on practice-related research. This obligates professionals to be informed about knowledge, ignorance, and uncertainty associated with decisions they make that affect clients' well-being. Our concern for helping and not harming clients obliges us to critically examine the criteria we use to evaluate knowledge claims. Evidence-based practitioners consider research findings related to decisions that affect clients' lives. But what is evidence? What is knowledge and what are underlying assumptions in different views of how to get it? How much evidence is needed to say that a treatment is "appropriate," that it should be used, and how it should be paid for?

(Eddy, 1993). What criteria should we use to decide whether a service method is ineffective? Different criteria for evaluating knowledge claims are described in this chapter, and you are invited to explore your views on this important topic—to explore your personal epistemology. The connection between evidentiary and ethical issues is highlighted, including the importance of recognizing uncertainty and fallibility in making decisions.

Evidence-based practice arose in part because of flaws in published reports of research findings, including peer reviewed journals—for example, inflated claims of effectiveness (see Chapter 10). But what is a flaw? When is it so significant that we should dismiss a claim? Traditional and current criteria include what is "standard or accepted" or what a helper believes to be in a client's "best interests." However, as Eddy notes, "the credibility of clinical judgement, whether examined individually or collectively, has been severely challenged by observations of wide variations in practices, inappropriate care, and practitioner uncertainty" (Eddy, 1993, p. 521; see also discussion of clinical and actuarial judgment in Chapter 15). The smaller the gap between the knowledge you have and the knowledge available to help clients, or to correctly determine that you cannot, the more likely you are to honor ethical obligations to help clients and avoid harm and to involve clients as informed participants in decisions made. Evidence-based practice is a process designed to reveal or decrease these gaps, as described in Chapter 10.

## DIFFERENT VIEWS OF KNOWLEDGE AND HOW (OR IF) IT CAN BE GAINED

The question, what is knowledge? has been of concern to philosophers throughout the ages. People differ in their beliefs about knowledge and how it can be gained (e.g., see Hofer & Pintrich, 2002). Many criteria are relied on in making claims of knowledge, including folklore, practice wisdom, common sense, superstition, pseudoscience, and the results of well-designed research studies. Cultural differences influence these beliefs (Nisbett, 2003). Given that we are all philosophers in making scores of decisions each day about how to act and how to solve problems, we, too should consider this question. Different ways of knowing differ in the extent to which they recognize uncertainty and are designed to weed out biases and distortions that may influence assumptions. Knowledge serves different functions, only one of which is to encourage the growth of knowledge. For example, Munz (1985) suggests that the function of *false knowledge* (beliefs that are not true and that are not questioned) is to maintain social bonds among people by protecting shared beliefs from criticism (the growth of knowledge). This may be necessary to encourage cooperation in a group. Cultures often thrive because of false knowledge. Such cultures "are doubly effective in promoting social behavior because, not being exposed to rational criticism, they enshrine emotionally comforting and solidarity-producing attitudes" (pp. 283–284). This view suggests that the growth of knowledge can only take place in certain circumstances (i.e., cultures)—those in which alternative views are entertained and all views are subject to criticism, that is, in an environment in which rationality is valued and practiced (see Glossary at end of chapter). Only in this way do beliefs confront the environment.

Certain "ways of knowing," compared to others, are designed to rigorously test guesses (e.g., about effectiveness). Frazer (1925) suggested that there is a closer connection between magic and science than between science and religion. Both magic and science attempt to predict certain events by taking certain actions, such as conducting a rain dance, hoping to make it rain. The very purpose of experimental studies and some experimental single-case designs is to avoid unwarranted assumptions about effects. (Whether they offer information about the role of methods used in the reported effects depends on the particular design used.) Karl Popper suggests that we do not know more today than we did thousands of years ago, because solving some problems only creates new ones. For example, medical advances have created new problems, such as overpopulation. Some people believe that nothing can be known "for sure." This is assumed in science. But does that mean we don't know anything? Others argue that because we know nothing for sure, we really know nothing. We should follow out the logic of each position. If we know nothing, then what is the rationale for professional education? The success of scientific methods in distinguishing between correct and incorrect assumptions in hundreds of areas shows that all methods are not equally effective in testing knowledge claims.

Raymond Nickerson (1986) defines knowledge as information that decreases uncertainty about how to achieve a certain outcome. (I would add—or reveals uncertainty.) We can ask: "What knowledge will help us to solve problems clients confront (e.g., elder abuse, a need for reliable respite care)?" Studies of the development of assumptions about knowledge (e.g., what can be known and what cannot, how we can know, and how certain we can be in knowing), suggest a scale ranging from the belief that we can know reality with certainty by direct observation, to the view that there is never certainty and that we must critically appraise and synthesize information from multiple sources (King & Kitchener, 2002; Kitchener, 1986). Karl Popper (1992) defines knowledge as problematic and tentative guesses about what may be true. It results from selective pressures from the real world, in which our guesses come into contact with the environment through a process of trial and error (Munz, 1985).

## EVALUATING KNOWLEDGE CLAIMS

The most important decisions clinicians make concern the criteria used to select and evaluate the accuracy of practice theories and claims of effectiveness. You will encounter many different theories and claims. How will you choose among them? How will you select those most likely to be of value in helping clients? Because practice-related beliefs influence our decisions, they are important to examine. The criteria you rely on influence your selection of assessment, intervention, and evaluation methods. Consider the following statements:

- Mentoring programs for youth are effective. (Are they?)
- National depression screening days do more good than harm. (Do they?)
- If you have to urinate eight or more times a day you have a condition called "irritable bladder" and should ask your doctor for medication. (Should you?)

Your beliefs about these claims will influence decisions you make.

## AVOIDING HARMING IN THE NAME OF HELPING

Relying on false claims or theories may result in harming rather than helping clients; false hope may be created and opportunities to use effective methods missed. Consider Emma Eckstein, one of Sigmund Freud's patients (Masson, 1984). He attributed her complaints of stomach ailments and menstrual problems to masturbation. Freud's colleague Fleiss recommended a nose operation, based on his belief that the sexual organs and the nose were connected. Eckstein's subsequent pain and suffering then were attributed to her psychological deficiencies. The real cause was a large wad of dressing left in her nose by mistake. Consider the many claims of effectiveness regarding intervention based on anecdotal case reports that were later shown to be false in controlled research. For example, the findings of controlled—in contrast to uncontrolled—studies of the effects of facilitated communication (FC; a method alleged to help nonverbal people talk) "have been consistently negative indicating that FC is neither reliably replicable nor valid when produced" (Jacobson, Mulick, & Schwartz, 1995, p. 754). These controlled studies showed that the communication alleged to be from previously nonverbal people was actually determined by the facilitators.

## QUESTIONABLE CRITERIA

Decisions that get in the way of helping clients may be made because of lack of knowledge about the limitations of commonly accepted criteria for evaluating the accuracy of claims. Criteria such as popularity, testimonials, newness, or tradition do not provide sound grounds on which to accept claims, often because they consider only part of the picture (e.g., only examples that support a belief). The Post-Hoc Ergo Propter Hoc fallacy is common; the false belief that if an event (dream therapy) proceeds an event (an increase in well-being), that the preceding event caused the second one. Other examples include influence based on manner of presentation and reliance on anecdotal experience.

### AUTHORITY

The source of the fallacy of authority is the mistaken assumption that status is correlated with accuracy. Appeals based on authority can be recognized by the assertion of a claim (e.g., play therapy is the best method to use with act-ing-out children) based solely on someone's status or position, with no refer-ence to empirical studies that provide evidence (Gibbs, 1991). Let us say that Ms. Sommers, a case manager for the elderly, tells her supervisor that she re-ferred Mr. Rivers to the Montview Nursing Home because Dr. Lancaster told her that this home provides excellent services—even though Dr. Lancaster of-fered no evidence that it does. Appeals to authority are a common social per-suasion strategy. Cereal companies often use famous baseball players to tout the many benefits of their cereals. Appeals to unfounded authority are com-mon in the professional literature, such as citing a famous person to support a claim when in fact he or she has not conducted any critical tests of the claim. Evidence-based practice arose as an alternative to authority-based practice (Gambrill, 1999; Sackett, Richardson, Rosenberg, & Haynes, 1997). Appeals to popularity and tradition, described next, are forms of appeals to authority. (See Chapter 7.) (For critiques of authority as a fallacy see Hansen & Pinto, 1995.)

## POPULARITY AND NUMBERS

Popularity and numbers refer to the acceptance of claims simply because many people accept them. For instance, an agency may decide to adopt psy-choanalytic methods because many other agencies use these methods. Here, too, the question is whether there is any evidence that popular methods are effective:

> How much is spent in the USA every year on magnetic devices to treat pain? $500 million, with a total worldwide market to date above $4 billion. To put that into some sort of perspective, that $500 million is just half the annual sales that the pharmaceutical industry defines as a "blockbuster." And what do you think is the evidence for magnets affecting pain? You guessed it. None. There is a trial in a Cochrane review of interventions for plantar heel pain, and that was nega-tive, and poor. A new, well-conducted, randomised trial provides a powerful negative, and a great example of trial design. (Magnetic insoles for foot pain. http://www.jr2.ox.ac.uk/bandolier, *Bandolier,* Jan. 2003)

Consider use of residential care for adolescents alleged to have substance abuse and psychiatric problems. Schwartz (1989) argues that there is no evi-dence that such programs are effective, even though huge sums of money are spent on them. A reliance on popularity is similar to a reliance on consensus (what most people think). But what most people think may not be correct.

## TRADITION

Tradition (what has been done in the past) may be appealed to support claims. For example, when asked why she was using genograms, a social worker may answer, "That's what our agency has used for the past five years."

Advertisers often note how long their product has been sold, suggesting that this establishes its effectiveness. Because a method has been used for many years does not mean it is effective. In fact, it may be harmful. Consider Scared Straight programs, designed to decrease delinquency. These have been found to increase delinquency (Petrosino, Turpin-Petrosino, & Beuhler, 2003). Practice may be based on what helpers believe is important. Testing as well as guessing is needed (systematic exploration) to determine the accuracy of these beliefs.

## NEWNESS

Newness (the latest method) is often appealed to, as in "We are using the new coaddiction model with all our clients." Simply because something is new or innovative does not mean it is effective. After all, everything was new at some time.

## MANNER OF PRESENTATION

We are often persuaded that a claim is correct by the confident manner in which it is presented. This fallacy occurs when (1) a speaker or writer claims that something is true of people or that a method is effective; (2) persuasive interpersonal skills are used (e.g., building the self-esteem of audience members, joking); and (3) data describing the effectiveness of the method is not reviewed (Gibbs, 1991). Being swayed by the style of presentation underlies persuasion by the material's entertainment value. How interesting is a practice view? Does it sound profound? Does it claim to empower clients? Here, too, the question is whether there is any evidence for the claims made.

## GOOD INTENTIONS

We may accept claims of effectiveness because we believe that those who make them have good intentions, that they want to help clients. But, as the history of the "helping professions" shows, good intentions and services that help clients and avoid harm do not necessarily go together (e.g., see Sharpe & Faden, 1998; Valenstein, 1986). Consider the following:

- People have died as a result of a "rebirthing."
- Scared Straight programs for delinquents increase future delinquency.
- Babies were blinded as a result of being given oxygen at birth.
- Creating false memories resulted in innocent people being accused of sexual abuse.

Clients have been killed as a result of using methods assumed to be helpful. Programs that have been critically tested and found to be ineffective or harmful continue to be used (e.g. Petrosino, Turpin-Petrosino, & Beuhler, 2002).

> Of all tyrannnies a tyranny sincerely exercised for the good
> of its victims may be the most oppressive.
>
> It may be better to live under robber barons
> than under the omnipotent moral busybodies.
>
> The robber baron's cruelty may sometimes sleep,
> his cupidity may at some point be satiated;
>
> but those who torment us for our own good
> will torment us without end, for they do so
> with the approval of their own conscience.
>                           —C. S. Lewis, "The Humanitarian Theory of Punishment"

## WHAT MAKES SENSE

You may have read that expressing anger in frustrating situations is helpful in getting rid of your anger. This may make sense to you. But is it true? In fact, research on anger suggests that it does not have this happy effect (see Averill, 1982; Tavris, 1989). Explanations always "make sense" to the person who accepts them. People's thinking is logical if seen on its own premises (Renstrom, Andersson, & Marton, 1990, p. 556). Whether these premises are accurate is another question. What about common sense? This may refer to cultural maxims and shared beliefs or shared fundamental assumptions about the social and physical world (Furnham, 1988). One problem here is that different maxims often give contradictory advice.

## ENTERTAINMENT VALUE

Some claims are accepted simply because they sound interesting, even though interest value does not indicate accuracy.

## EMOTIONAL INFLUENCES

When evaluating claims, we are easily swayed by our emotions, and politicians and advertisers take advantage of this. They may appeal to our self-pity, self-esteem, fears, and self-interest (e.g., Slovic, Finucane, Peters, & MacGregor, 2002). Vivid testimonials and case examples play on our emotions. For example, a TV commercial for an alcohol treatment center may show an unkempt, depressed man with a drinking problem, and describe the downward spiral allegedly caused by drinking, including the loss of job and family. We may then see him in the Detox Treatment Center, which is clean and whose staff seem caring and concerned. Next we see our client shaved, well dressed, employed, and looking happy and healthy. Words, music, and pictures may contribute to the emotive effect. Because of the commercial's emotional appeal, we may overlook the absence of evidence for the effectiveness of the Detox Treatment Center.

## CASE EXAMPLES

In the case example fallacy, conclusions about many clients are made based on a few unrepresentative examples (e.g., see Loftus & Guyer, 2002). The case example fallacy involves faulty generalization. What may be true in a few cases may not be at all true of many other cases. Gibbs (1991) suggests three reasons why case examples so readily snare the unwary: (1) the detailed description of case examples has considerable emotional appeal, especially in comparison to the dull data from large representative samples that may be reported in the literature; (2) we become immersed in the details of a particular case and forget that what may be true of this case may be untrue of others; and (3) cases that "prove the point" can always be found. Case examples are easy to remember because they have a story-like quality. Often, extreme examples are selected, making them easy to remember, even though they are unrepresentative of other cases. We tend to overestimate the probability of detailed examples. This is one example of the misunderstanding of probability that can lead us astray. Aronson (2003) notes that anecdotal case reports may be a valuable source of promising hypotheses, for example, regarding adverse events and possible causes, and may provide telling counterexamples that disprove an hypothesis. He also suggests that anecdotes may be used to demonstrate diagnostic methods, how to handle challenging clinical situations, or to remind or educate us about important clinical possibilities.

## TESTIMONIALS

Testimonials are reports by people who have used a product or service that that product or service is effective. For example, someone who has attended Alcoholics Anonymous may say, "I tried it and it works." The testimonial is a variant of the case example fallacy and is subject to the limitations of case examples in offering evidence for a claim; neither case examples or testimonials provide comparative information needed to evaluate whether an assumption is true or false. Testimonials may include detailed, vivid descriptions of the method used, the distressing state of affairs prior to its use, and the positive results. Testimonials are widely used in advertising. The problem with testimonials is not that the report about an individual's personal experience with a given method is not accurate, but the further step of making a claim that this experience means that the method works.

## EXPERIENCE

Professionals often appeal to their anecdotal experience to support claims of effectiveness. (Relying on a carefully documented track record of success is quite different, as this offers a systematic record.) A counselor may state, "I know cognitive behavioral methods are most effective with depressed clients because they are effective with my clients." Experience in everyday practice and beliefs based on this are the key source of what is known as *practice wisdom.* Although anecdotal experience (practice wisdom) does provide an important source of "guesses" about what is effective, it is not a sound basis for evaluating claims of effectiveness; it cannot critically test the accuracy of a claim.

*Problems with Learning from Experience*    Experience does not necessarily result in improved performance. In fact, it may have the opposite effect (see also Chapter 9). Experience does not offer systematic data about what works with what clients with what problems. It may decrease rather than enhance the identification of creative options, as shown in a study by Johnson (1972) in which people who did not work in a spark-plug factory identified more alternative uses for spark plugs than personnel who worked in the factory. Thus, learning may become "context bound." Expertise is not necessarily a monotonic function of experience. For example, third- and fourth-year residents did not perform as well as either first- or second-year students or experts in interpreting some X-rays (see Lesgold et al., 1988). Possible reasons for such findings include vacillation between old (but inaccurate) representations of problems and new (perhaps "untrusted") views about what is accurate. Experience alone may not offer the tactical guidance and necessary representation of problems that is required for practice to be beneficial (Dawes, 1994a; Perkins, 1987). Practice may occur in what Hogarth (2001) refers to as a "wicked" environment that does not offer corrective feedback. Even if some improvement does occur without tactical coaching, it may not match the potential gains of what would be possible with guidance.

The key problem with relying on experience as a guide to the evidentiary status of a claim (e.g., is it true?) is the lack of comparison (Dawes, 1988). An interest in comparison is a hallmark of scientific thinking. Our experience is not a sound guide because it is often restricted and biased. For example, a child welfare worker may assume that few child abusers stop abusing their children because she sees those who do not stop abusing their children more than those who do stop. Her experience with this biased sample results in incorrect inferences about the recurrence of child abuse (i.e., an overestimate). When relying on experience we may not recognize that conditions have changed; that what worked in the past may no longer work in the present. For example, Western-style mental health services may not be appropriate for many clients. In addition, we tend to recall our successes and forget our failures. That is, we tend to selectively focus on our "hits." Unless we have kept track of both our hits and our misses we may arrive at incorrect conclusions. We tend to be overconfident in the accuracy of our beliefs, perhaps because of our interest in predicting what happens in our world (Baron, 2000). This interest can encourage an illusion of control in which we overestimate how much control we really have. Also, as Dawes (1988) points out, we tend to create our own experience. If we are friendly, others are likely to be friendly in return. If we are hostile, others are likely to be hostile. Dawes refers to this as "self-imposed bias in our own experience" (p. 106).

Another problem with relying on experience to test the accuracy of claims concerns the biased nature of our memory of what happened. We tend to remember what is vivid, which often results in biased samples. We alter views about the past to conform to current moods or views. We don't know what might have happened if another sequence of events had occurred. Overlooking this, we may unfairly praise or blame ourselves (or someone else). A psychologist might say, "If only I had focused more on the teenager, Mario and his mother would have returned for a second interview." But maybe if he had concentrated more on the teenager, Mario would have walked out in the first interview. Where is the comparison? Relying on experience opens us to accepting irrelevant causes. We may assume that mental illness results in homelessness because many homeless people are mentally ill. But does it? So experience, while honing skills in many ways, especially in environments in which we gain corrective feedback (see Chapter 9), may have negative effects, such as a reluctance to consider new ideas and an unwarranted overconfidence in the extent to which we can help clients. Indeed, one advantage of being a novice may be a greater willingness to question beliefs. King (1981) suggests that "severely critically handling of experience was an important part of scientific method, applicable to clinical practice as well as to research investigation" (pp. 303–304). These concerns call for caution about generalizing from the past and present to the future.

## INTUITION

Intuition is another criterion used to evaluate the accuracy of claims. *Webster's New Collegiate Dictionary* (1988) defines intuition as "the direct knowing or learning of something without the conscious use of reasoning." Intuitions (inferences) may refer to looking back in time (interpreting experience) or forward in time (predictions). For example, we may make a "diagnosis" of a client or we may predict that she will act in a certain manner in the future. Jonathan Baron defines intuition as "an unanalyzed and unjustified belief" (1994, p. 26) and notes that beliefs based on intuition may be either sound or unsound. (See also Baron, 1998.) They may reflect experience providing corrective feedback (informed intuition). Or they may be based on experience that does not provide such feedback, or pure speculation (uninformed intuition). Basing beliefs on uninformed intuition may result in harm that could have been prevented. Intuition, in contrast to analytical thinking, cannot be defined by a description of steps used in the process (Hammond, 1996, p. 60). This does not mean that intuition is wrong. As Hogarth (2001) suggests, it means "that nonintuitive processes are *deliberative* and can be *specified* after [or before] the fact. Logic and analysis can be made transparent. Intuition cannot without effort." (See discussion of cognitive task analyses of expert decision makers in Chapter 9.) Someone may ask, "How did you know that this method would be effective?" The answer may be: "My intuition." The view that intuition involves a responsiveness to information that, although not consciously represented, yields productive insights, is compatible with the differences found between experts and novices. Experts rely on pattern recognition that they no longer may be able to describe. No longer remembering where we learned something encourages attributing solutions to "intuition." When asked what made you think that "*Y*" service would be effective, your answer may be, "Intuition." When asked to elaborate, you may offer sound reasons reflecting knowledge of related research and appropriate inference rules. That is, you used far more than uninformed hunches.

Intuition cannot show which method is most effective in helping clients; a different kind of evidence is required for this. It, too, like anecdotal experience, lacks a comparison. Relying on intuition or what "feels right" is ethically questionable when other grounds, including a critical examination of intuitive beliefs, will result in better-informed decisions. Decisions based on intuition may be inconsistent; this inconsistency may not be evident because no one keeps track of the decisions made, the grounds for making them, and their outcomes. The greater the number of factors that must be considered in arriving at a well-reasoned decision and the more that is known about the relevance of considering them, the less likely is intuition to offer the best guide for decisions. (See discussion of actuarial compared to consensus-based methods in Chapter 15.) Attributing judgments to "intuition" decreases the opportunities to teach practice skills; one has "it" but doesn't know how or why "it" works. If you ask your supervisor, "How did you know to do that at that time," and she says, "My intuition," this will not help you learn what to do.

Hogarth (2001) suggests that we can develop our intuition most effectively by using a scientific approach in which we make maximal use of feedback. Science offers a particular way of learning about our world, a particular way of trying to solve problems (Popper, 1972). It is a method in which we learn from our errors, that is, corrective feedback. A key step is becoming aware of the limitations of experiential (intuitive) learning: "1) people discover for themselves that it is to their benefit to 'take greater control of their processes,' and, 2) they must understand at an intellectual level why learning from experience has limitations" (Hogarth, 2001, p. 224). In making the scientific method intuitive, he suggests that we seek feedback, explore connections, and accept conflict when making choices. Thus, ". . . even though intuitive learning takes place largely tacitly, only by being aware of the process can we manage it (by being aware, e.g., of whether an environment is 'kind'—provides valuable feedback or 'wicked'—provides misleading or no feedback). Otherwise, we leave what we learn to chance" (p. 215). The terms *kind* or *wicked* refer to different kinds of feedback environments, a kind one being one which provides helpful feedback, and a wicked one which does not. In the latter, we can be misled if we rely on intuition. "Wicked" learning structures are those that do not contribute to learning. Thus, the accuracy of intuition is related to the kind of feedback we get from our environments. Hogarth urges us to learn to observe better, to speculate more intelligently about what we see, to think carefully about how we can generalize from experience, and to always be willing to test our ideas. He suggests that "each of these requires different skills to counteract and compete with our normal, tacit, automatic way of learning." Important questions that need to be asked about the connections observed include: "Are these significant or due to chance? What do they mean relative to what we already know?" (p. 227). Ideally, as Hogarth (2001) notes, these habits of learning would become second nature; they would occur without effort. They themselves would become tacit. Examples include strategies discussed in later chapters, such as asking "Could I be wrong?" "Is there another way to look at this?" "Have I left anything out?" Different questions may be of value in different stages of problem solving to avoid common errors.

Thus, the environments in which we grow up and spend our time influence how we reason. If we change our environments we can change how we think. A key question is: How can I make the kind of feedback I acquire in my everyday work more helpful in educating my intuition? One of the obstacles to use of evidence-based practices and policies is the quality of feedback we get about our decisions. Often, the kind of feedback provided is exactly opposite of what is needed to "educate our intuition." For example, those who work in intake units in child welfare agencies typically do not find out what happens to their cases; they get no feedback regarding the accuracy of their decisions, for example, to remove a child from their home or not. Hogarth (2001) notes that rarely do emergency room personnel see the outcomes of their decisions. He calls this a classic case of the wicked learning environment. It is also true of interviewing job candidates. We typically do not know what would have happened if we had hired those whom we rejected. The value of learning from feedback emphasizes the importance of avoiding confirmation biases that do not allow us to test whether our intuition is correct. In contrast, in a falsification approach to learning, we question ourselves; we ask "Could I be wrong?" (See later discussion.)

## UNCRITICAL DOCUMENTATION

Simply because something appears in print does not mean that it is true. Similarly, just because a claim is accompanied by a reference is not a good reason for assuming that it is accurate. Unless the report describes the evidence for this statement, it is uncritical documentation. For all we know, this statement could be someone's uninformed opinion.

## SCIENCE AND SCIENTIFIC CRITERIA

Our concern for helping and not harming clients obliges us to critically evaluate claims about what is true. Some of the results of not doing so are described in our daily newspapers. Consider the withdrawal of the arthritis drug Vioxx because of side effects such as strokes.

## MISUNDERSTANDINGS AND MISREPRESENTATIONS

We are confronted with many varied images of science—what it is, how it is done, what its consequences are. There is an extensive literature describing beliefs about science and how they are developed and how they change (Bell & Linn, 2002). Surveys show that most people do not understand the basic characteristics of science (Miller, 1987; National Science Foundation, 2002). Science educators may emphasize deterministic models rather than the uncertainty involved in understanding the relationship between variables. This discourages a useful view of uncertainty (as indicating limits of understanding) and encourages a common distortion of "science" as deterministic in a dogmatic sense. Misconceptions include the following:

- There is a search for final answers.
- Intuitive thinking has no role.
- It is assumed that science knows, or will soon know, all the answers.
- Objectivity is assumed.
- Chance occurrences are not considered.
- Scientific knowledge is equivalent to scientific thinking.
- The accumulation of facts is the primary goal.
- Linear thinking is required.
- Passion and caring have no role.
- There is one kind of scientific method.
- Unobservable events are not considered.

Bell and Linn (2002) note that "When textbooks attempt to synthesize historical accounts of discovery, they often omit controversy and personality" (p. 324). These accounts may overemphasize and give an incorrect illusion of a logical progression of uncomplex discovery when indeed the history is quite different: "serendipitous, personality-filled, conjectural, and controversial" (p. 324). "Scientific journal articles often erase controversy from the record, leaving the disputes and discussions behind the closed doors of the scientific laboratory" (p. 324). Lack of understanding of science is responsible for the "sterile study fallacy" in which a study is disregarded because it focuses on a narrow aspect of some subject. This criticism reflects a lack of appreciation for the developmental nature of knowledge; one study represents but one step among many that will be required to understand a problem, such as substance abuse. Removing a study from its programmatic context may misrepresent its role in the overall picture. (Critics can, of course, selectively pick out studies that do not contribute much, if anything, to knowledge development, and ignore those that do.)

Misunderstandings about science may result in ignoring this problem-solving method and the knowledge it has generated to help clients enhance the quality of their lives. Misunderstandings and misrepresentations of science are so common that D. C. Phillips, a philosopher of science, entitled one of his books *The Social Scientist's Bestiary: A Guide to Fabled Threats to and Defenses of Naturalistic Social Science* (1992). (See also Phillips, 1990.) Even academics confuse logical positivism (discarded by scientists long ago) and science as we know it today. Logical positivism emphasizes direct observation by the senses. It is assumed that observation can be theory free. It is justification focused, assuming that greater verification yields closer approximations to the truth. This approach to knowledge was discarded decades ago because of the induction problem (see later discussion of justification/falsification), the theory-laden nature of observation, and the utility of unobservable constructs. Theories are conjectures about what may be true. We always have theories. "There is no pure, disinterested, theory-free observation" (Popper, 1994, p. 8). Science is often misrepresented as a collection of facts or as referring only to controlled experimental studies. Many people confuse science with pseudoscience, bogus science, and scientism (see the glossary at the end of this chapter). Some people protest that science is misused. Saying that a method is bad because it has been or may be misused is not a cogent argument. Anything can be misused. Some people believe that critical reflection is incompatible with passionate caring. Reading the writings of any number of scientists, including Loren Eiseley, Carl Sagan, Karl Popper, and Albert Einstein, would quickly put this false belief to rest. Consider a quote from Karl Popper: "I assert that the scientific way of life involves a burning interest in objective scientific theories—in the theories in themselves, and in the problem of their truth, or their nearness to truth. And this interest is a *critical* interest, an *argumentative* interest" (1994, p. 56).

A scientific approach may be criticized on the grounds that it cannot capture the full meaning of psychological experiences—that scientific accounts are trivial, unrepresentative accounts. A trivial account, by definition, cannot account for events of interest. A scientific approach to practice requires use of a broad range of methods that faithfully represent significant aspects of the phenomena under investigation. There is no doubt that social science and professional journals are replete with research reports that are irrelevant or distort the events under investigation (e.g., see Armstrong, 1980; Lipton & Hershaft, 1985). This does not mean that such an approach is not useful. Indeed, history shows that critical tests of common practices have prevented further harms for clients (e.g., the blinding of babies; Silverman, 1980). It does indicate that, like anything else, it can be appropriately or inappropriately applied. For example, clients may be randomly assigned to different groups, overlooking critical individual differences that call for selective matching of clients to particular services. The bogus presentation of research findings was a key reason for the development of evidence-based practice as described in Chapter 10. Statistics are often used inappropriately (Best, 2004; Huff, 1954). Far from reinforcing myths about reality, as some claim (e.g., Karger, 1983, p. 204), science is likely to question them. All sorts of questions that people may not want raised may be raised, such as: "Does this residential center really help residents? Would another method be more effective? Does what I'm doing really help clients?

How accurate is my belief about _____?" Many scientific discoveries, such as Charles Darwin's theory of evolution, clashed with (and still does) some religious views of the world. Consider the church's reactions to the discovery that the earth was not the center of the universe. Only after 350 years did the Catholic church agree that Galileo was correct in stating that the earth revolves around the sun. Objections to teaching evolutionary theory remain common (see *Reports* published by the National Center for Science Education). An accurate understanding of science will help you distinguish among helpful, trivializing, and bogus uses. Bogus uses may create and maintain views of problems and proposed solutions that leave unchanged or decrease the quality of life for clients (Scheper-Hughes & Lovell, 1987).

## WHAT IS SCIENCE?

Science is a way of thinking about and investigating the accuracy of assumptions about the world. It is a process for solving problems in which we learn from our mistakes. Science rejects a reliance on authority (e.g., pronouncements by highly placed officials or professors) as a route to knowledge. Authority and science are clashing views of how knowledge can be gained. The history of science and medicine shows that the results of experimental research involving systematic investigation often frees us from false beliefs that harm rather than help and decrease our susceptibility to fraudulent claims. There are many ways to do science and many philosophies of science. The terms *science* and *scientific* are sometimes used to refer to any systematic effort—including case studies, correlational studies, and naturalistic studies—to acquire information about a subject. All methods are vulnerable to error, which must be considered when evaluating the data they generate. Nonexperimental approaches to understanding include natural observation, as in ethology (the study of animal behavior in real-life settings), and correlational methods that use statistical analysis to investigate the degree to which events are associated. These methods are of value in suggesting promising experiments as well as when events of interest cannot be experimentally altered, or if doing so would destroy what is under investigation. Where does magic fit in? Magic has been defined by anthropologists "as an intervention designed to reduce anxiety at times of uncertainty" (Frazer, 1925, p. 364); for example, doing a rain dance. Frazer (1925) suggested that there is a much closer relationship between magic and science than between science and religion. In both magic and science there is an interest in predicting the environment, for example.

The view of science presented here, critical rationalism, is one in which the theory-laden nature of observation is assumed (i.e., our assumptions influence what we observe) and rational criticism is viewed as the essence of science (Miller, 1994; Phillips, 1987, 1992; Popper, 1972). (See Exhibit 4.1.) Concepts are assumed to have meaning and value even though they are unobservable. Popper's view of science can be summed up in four steps: (1) we

**Exhibit 4.1**

Contrasts between Two Philosophies of Science—The Verificationist Philosophy and the Refutationist Approach Propounded by Popper

| Verificationist | Refutationist |
|---|---|
| Certainty is possible. | Certainty is impossible. |
| Science is based on proof. | Science is based on disproof. |
| Observation reveals truth. | Observation involves interpretation. |
| Recognition of facts precedes formulation of theories. | Formulation of theories precedes recognition of facts. |
| A good theory predicts many things. | A good theory forbids many things. |
| A good theory is probable: it has been repeatedly confirmed. | A good theory is improbable yet it has repeatedly failed to be refuted. |
| A prediction is more informative the more it conforms to experience. | A prediction is more informative the more it is risky or deviant from expectations. |
| Induction is the logical foundation of science. | Deduction is the logical foundation of science. |
| Inductive inference is logical. | Induction is illogical. |
| A theory can be validated independently, and absolutely. | A theory can be corroborated only relative to other theories. |
| Among competing theories, the preferable is the one which has been more often verified. | Among competing theories of equal refutability, the preferable is the one which has withstood more diverse tests. |
| Theories become more scientific the more they have been proven true by objective observations. | Theories become more scientific as they are made more refutable both through reformulations and technological advances in methods. |

*Source:* From "Popperian Refutation in Epidemiology," by M. Maclure, 1985, *American Journal of Epidemiology, 121*(3), pp. 343–350. Reprinted with permission.

select a problem; (2) we try to solve it by proposing a theory as a guess about what may be true; (3) we critically discuss and test our theory, and (4) which always reveals new problems. ($P_1 \rightarrow$ Th $\rightarrow$ test $\rightarrow$ Error—$P_2$). Creative, bold guesses about what may be true are essential to the development of knowledge, especially guesses that can be refuted; that is, you can find out whether they are false. This view of science emphasizes the elimination of errors by means of criticism: "Knowledge grows by the elimination of some of our errors, and in this way we learn to understand our problems, and our theories, and the need for new solutions" (Popper, 1994, p. 159). The growth of knowledge is not in accuracy of depiction or certainty but in an increase in universality and abstraction (Munz, 1985). That is, a better theory can account for a wider range of events. By testing our guesses, we eliminate false theories and learn a bit more about our problems. Corrective feedback from the physical world allows us to test our guesses about what is true or false. We learn which of our guesses are false. Evolutionary epistemologists highlight the two different histories of science: the creation of theories (e.g., through random variation) and their selection (by testing; Munz, 1985).

*Scientific Statements Are Refutable/Testable*   The scientific tradition is the tradition of criticism (Popper, 1994, p. 42). Karl Popper considers the critical method to be one of the great Greek inventions. Scientific statements are those that can be tested (they can be refuted). Consider the question, How many teeth are in a horse's mouth? You could speculate about this, or you could open a horse's mouth and look inside. If an agency for the homeless claims that it succeeds in finding homes for applicants within 10 days, you could accept this claim at face value or systematically gather data to see whether this claim is true. Bunge (2003) suggests the following possibilities:

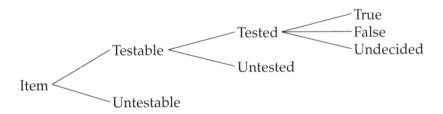

The essence of science is creative, bold guessing and rigorous testing in a way that offers accurate information about whether a guess (conjecture or theory) is accurate (Asimov, 1989). Popper argues that "The growth of knowledge, and especially of scientific knowledge, consists of learning from our mistakes" (1994, p. 93). It is assumed that we can discover approximations to the truth by means of rational argument and critical testing of theories and that the soundness of an assertion is related to the uniqueness and rigor of the relevant critical tests. Some tests are more rigorous than others (they control for more biases) and so offer more information about what may be true or false. Theories differ in the extent to which they have been tested and in the rigor of the tests used. The question raised will suggest the research method required to explore it (see Chapter 12). Every research method is limited in the kinds of questions it can address successfully. Purpose will suggest the kinds of evidence needed to test different kinds of claims. Thus, if our purpose is to communicate the emotional complexity of a certain kind of experience (e.g., the death of an infant), then qualitative methods are needed (e.g., detailed case examples, thematic analyses of journal entries, open-ended interviews at different times).

A theory should describe what cannot occur as well as what can occur. If you can make contradictory predictions based on a theory, it cannot be tested. If you cannot discover a way to test a theory, it is not falsifiable. Testing may involve examining the past, as in Darwin's theory of evolution. Some theories are not testable (falsifiable). There is no way to test them to find out if they are correct. Psychoanalytic theory is often criticized on the grounds that it cannot be falsified, that contradictory hypotheses can be drawn from the theory. As Karl Popper points out, irrefutability is not a virtue of a theory, but a vice. Theories can be falsified only if specific predictions are made about what can happen and also about what cannot happen.

Many people accept a justificationist approach to knowledge development, focusing on gathering support for (justifying, confirming) claims and theories (see Exhibit 4.1). Let's say that you see 3,000 swans, all of which are white. Does this mean that all swans are white? Can we generalize from the particular (seeing 3,000 swans, all of which are white) to the general, that all swans are white? Karl Popper (and others) contend that we cannot discover what is true by means of induction (making generalizations based on particular instances) because we may later discover exceptions (swans that are not white). (In fact, black swans are found in New Zealand.) Popper maintains that falsification (attempts to falsify, to discover the errors in our beliefs) by means of critical discussion and testing is the only sound way to develop knowledge (Popper, 1992, 1994). (For critiques of Popper's view of knowledge, see for example Kuhn, 1996.) Confirmations of a theory can readily be found if one looks for them. Popper uses the criterion of falsifiability to demark what is or could be scientific knowledge from what is not or could not be. For example, there is no way to refute the claim that "there is a God," but there is a way to refute the claim that "assertive community outreach services for the severely mentally ill reduces substance abuse." We could, for example, randomly distribute clients to a group providing such services and compare outcomes with those of clients receiving no services or other services. Although we can justify the selection of a theory by its having survived more risky tests concerning a wider variety of hypotheses (it has not been falsified), compared with other theories that have not been tested or that have been falsified, we can never accurately claim that this theory is "the truth." We can only eliminate false beliefs.

*The Search for Patterns and Regularities*   It is assumed that the universe has some degree of order and consistency. This does not mean that unexplained phenomena or chance variations do not occur or are not considered. For example, chance variations contribute to evolutionary changes (e.g., see Lewontin, 1995; Strohman, 2003). And uncertainty is assumed. Since a future test may show an assumption to be incorrect, even one that is strongly corroborated (has survived many critical tests), no assertion can ever be proved. This does not mean that all beliefs are equally sound; some have survived more rigorous tests than have others.

*Parsimony*   An explanation is parsimonious if all or most of its components are necessary to explain most of its related phenomena. Unnecessarily complex explanations may get in the way of detecting relationships between behaviors and related events. Consider the following two accounts:

1. Mrs. Lancer punishes her child because of her own unresolved superego issues related to early childhood trauma. This creates a negative disposition to dislike her oldest child.

2. Mrs. Lancer hits her child because this temporarily removes his annoying behaviors (he stops yelling) and because she does not have positive
   parenting skills (e.g., she does not know how to identify and reinforce acceptable behaviors).

The second account suggests specific behaviors that could be altered. Unless
clarified, concepts such as "unresolved superego issues" and "negative disposition" may not yield guidelines for discovering the potential to help clients.

*Scientists Strive for Objectivity*    Basic to objectivity is the critical discussion and
testing of theories (eliminating errors through criticism). "What we call scientific objectivity is nothing else than the fact that no scientific theory is accepted
as dogma, and that all theories are tentative and are open all the time to severe
criticism—to a rational, critical discussion aiming at the elimination of errors"
(Popper, 1994, p. 160). The theory-laden nature of observation is assumed; observation is always selective (influenced by our theories and related concepts).
We are influenced by our evolutionary history in how we see and react to the
world as well as by the culture in which we have grown up. We see what we expect to see. Scientists are often wrong and find out that they are wrong by testing their predictions. In this way, better theories (those that can account for more
findings) replace earlier ones. Science is conservative in insisting that a new
theory account for previous findings. Science is revolutionary in its calling for
the overthrow of previous theories shown to be false, but this does not mean that
the new theory has been established as true. (For critiques of the view that ad-
vancing knowledge means abandoning prior knowledge, see Phillips, 1987.)

Although the purpose of science is to seek true answers to problems (statements that correspond to facts), this does not mean that we can have certain
knowledge. Rather, we may say that certain beliefs (theories) have (so far) survived critical tests or have not yet been exposed to them. And, some theories
have been found to be false. An error "consists essentially of our regarding as
true a theory that is not true" (Popper, 1992, p. 4). We can avoid error or discover it by doing all that we can to discover and eliminate falsehoods (p. 4).
The study of errors when making decisions has received much greater attention in the past years (See Chapter 9).

*A Skeptical Attitude*    Scientists are skeptics. They question what others view
as fact or "common sense." They ask for arguments and evidence. They do not
have sacred cows.

> Science . . . is a way of thinking. . . . [It] invites us to let the facts in, even when
> they don't conform to our preconceptions. It counsels us to consider hypotheses
> in our heads and see which ones best match the facts. It urges on us a fine bal-
> ance between no-holds-barred openness to new ideas, however heretical, and
> the most rigorous skeptical scrutiny of everything—new ideas and established
> wisdom. (Sagan, 1990, p. 265)

Scientists and skeptics seek criticism of their views and change their beliefs when they have good reason to do so. Skeptics are more interested in arriving at accurate answers than in not ruffling the feathers of supervisors or administrators.

*Other Characteristics*    Science deals with specific problems that may be solvable (that can be answered with the available methods of empirical inquiry). For example, is intensive in-home care for parents of abused children more effective than the usual agency services? Is the use of medication to decrease depression in elderly people more (or less) effective than cognitive-behavioral methods? Examples of unsolvable questions are, "Should punishment ever be used in raising children?" "Are people inherently good or evil?" Saying that science deals with problems that can be solved does not mean, however, that other kinds of questions are unimportant or that a problem will remain unsolvable. New methods may be developed that yield answers to questions previously unapproachable in a systematic way. Science is collective. Scientific knowledge is publicly reviewed by a community. Scientists communicate with one another, and the results of one study inform the efforts of other scientists.

## THE DIFFERENCE BETWEEN SCIENCE AND PSEUDOSCIENCE

The term *pseudoscience* refers to material that makes science-like claims but provides no evidence for them (see Exhibit 4.2; e.g., see Lilienfeld, Lynn, & Lohr, 2003; Pope, 1998; Sarnoff, 2001). Surveys of college students reveal a variety of pseudoscientific beliefs (e.g., see Wilson, 2001). (See also Gallup Organization, 2001; Shermer, 1997.) Pseudoscience is characterized by a casual approach to evidence (weak evidence is accepted as readily as strong evidence). Hallmarks include the following:

- Discourages critical examination of claims/arguments.
- The trappings of science are used without the substance.
- Relies on anecdotal evidence.
- Is not self-correcting.
- Is not skeptical.
- Equates an open mind with an uncritical one.
- Falsifying data are ignored or explained away.
- Relies on vague language.
- Is not empirical.
- Produces beliefs and faith but not knowledge.
- Is often not testable.
- Does not require repeatability (e.g., see Bunge, 1984; Gray, 1991; Jarvis, 1990).

**Exhibit 4.2**
Comparison of Attitudes and Activities of Scientists and Pseudoscientists

| Typical Attitudes and Activities | Scientist | | | Pseudoscientist | | |
|---|---|---|---|---|---|---|
| | Yes | No | Optional | Yes | No | Optional |
| Admits own ignorance, hence need for more research | X | | | | X | |
| Finds own field difficult and full of holes | X | | | | X | |
| Advances by posing and solving new problems | X | | | | X | |
| Welcomes new hypotheses and methods | X | | | | X | |
| Proposes and tries out new hypotheses | X | | | | | X |
| Attempts to find or apply laws | X | | | | X | |
| Cherishes the unity of science | X | | | | X | |
| Relies on logic | X | | | | | X |
| Uses mathematics | X | | | | | X |
| Gathers or uses data, particularly quantitative data | X | | | | | X |
| Looks for counterexamples | X | | | | X | |
| Invents or applies objective checking procedures | X | | | | X | |
| Settles disputes by experiment or computation | X | | | | X | |
| Falls back consistently on authority | | X | | X | | |
| Suppresses or distorts unfavorable data | | X | | X | | |
| Updates own information | X | | | | X | |
| Seeks critical comments from others | X | | | | X | |
| Writes papers that can be understood by anyone | | X | | X | | |
| Is likely to achieve instant celebrity | | X | | X | | |

*Source:* From "What Is Pseudoscience?" by M. Bunge, 1984, *The Skeptical Inquirer, 9*, p. 41. Copyright 1984 by Committee for the Scientific Investigation of Claims of the Paranormal. Reprinted with permission.

A critical attitude, which Karl Popper (1972) defines as a willingness and commitment to open up favored views to severe scrutiny—is basic to science, distinguishing it from pseudoscience. Indicators of pseudoscience include irrefutable hypotheses and a reluctance to revise beliefs even when confronted with relevant criticism. It makes excessive (untested) claims of contributions to knowledge. Results of a study may be referred to in many different sources until they achieve the status of a law without any additional data being gathered. Richard Gelles calls this the "Woozle Effect" (1982, p. 13). Pseudoscience is a billion-dollar industry (Dawes, 2001). Products include self-help books, "subliminal" tapes, and call-in advice from "authentic psychics" who have no evidence that they accomplish what they promise (Beyerstein, 1990; Druckman & Bjork, 1991). Pseudoscience can be found in all fields, including multiculturalism (e.g., Ortiz De Montellano, 1992) and clinical psychology (Lilienfield et al., 2003; see also later discussion of propaganda).

A good part of the prestige of the helping professions rests on their alleged scientific base. This does not represent the practice of many clinicians and researchers who, knowingly or not, embrace a pseudoscientific perspective. They use the trappings of science without the substance (Bunge, 1984). Examples include use of invalid assessment measures and ineffective or harmful services (e.g., see Jacobson, Foxx, & Mulick, 2005; Lilienfeld et al., 2003). The picture presented both to professionals and to the public in terms of "what is known" often far exceeds reality. Inflated claims about what is "known" abound throughout the history of the helping professions (e.g., Colman, 1987; Gardner, 1957; Kohn, 1988; Leo & Cohen, 2003; Medawar, 1979). Gaps between what was claimed as true and the rigor of related research was a key contributor to the development of evidence-based practice. Such misrepresentations are not benign. They result in intrusive, unnecessary services and encourage paternalistic coercion in the name of helping. Basaglia suggests that the ideology and "trappings" of science are used to pull the wool over people's eyes in suggesting a credibility of claims that does not exist (Scheper-Hughes & Lovell, 1987).

Clinicians, in their role as part or the "public," are not immune from the influence of bogus claims in the media as well as in professional sources such as newsletters, books, the Internet, and journals. The battle for acceptance of critical appraisal of claims as of value in assessing their accuracy that has been won in the physical sciences and in many areas of medicine has not yet been won in the interpersonal helping professions. Medawar (1984, p. 58) argues that quasi-scientific psychologies "are getting away with a concept of truthfulness which belongs essentially to imaginative literature" and that this represents "a style of thought that will impede the growth of our understanding of mental illness." He describes this approach as "poetism," which "stands for the belief that imaginative insight and a mysteriously privileged sensibility can tell us all the answers that are truly worthy of being sought or being known" (p. 60). A sound grounding in the differences between science and pseudoscience is vital to avoid influence by bogus claims. The terms *science* and *scientific* are often used to increase the credibility of a view or approach, even though no evidence is provided to support it. The term *science* has been applied to many activities that in reality have nothing to do with science. Examples are "scientific charity" and "scientific philanthropy." The term "evidence-based" is often applied to material that shares none of the characteristics of the philosophy and process of EBP as described in Chapter 10. Proseletizers of many sorts cast their advice as based on science. They use the ideology and "trappings" of science to pull the wool over our eyes in suggesting critical tests of claims that do not exist. Classification of clients into psychiatric categories lends an aura of scientific credibility to this practice, whether there is any evidence that it is warranted or that it is helpful to clients (e.g., see Houts, 2002; Kirk & Kutchins, 1992a; Kutchins & Kirk, 1997). For example, is it really true that half of Americans develop a mental disorder sometime during their lives (see *The National Psychologist*, July/August, 2005, p. 23). The misuse of appeals to science to sell products or encourage certain beliefs is a form of propaganda.

## ANTISCIENCE

Antiscience refers to rejection of scientific methods as valid. For example, some people believe that there is no such thing as privileged knowledge; that is, that some is more sound than others. Typically, such views are not related to real-life problems and to a candid appraisal of the results of different ways of solving a problem. That is, they are not problem-focused, allowing a critical appraisal of competing views. Antiscience is common in academic settings (Gross & Levitt, 1994; Patai & Koertege, 2003) as well as in popular culture (e.g., John Burnham, *How Superstition Won and Science Lost*, 1987). Many people confuse science, scienticism, and pseudoscience, resulting in an antiscience stance (see Glossary at the end of this chapter). Popper (1994) argues that we must value truth, the search for truth, the approximation to truth through the critical elimination of error, and clarity in order to overcome the influence of other values (e.g., trying to appear profound by using obscure words or jargon; p. 70).

### Relativism

Relativists argue that all methods are equally valid in testing claims (e.g., anecdotal reports and experimental studies). It is assumed that knowledge and morality are inherently bounded by or rooted in culture (Gellner, 1992, p. 68). "Knowledge or morality outside culture is, it claims, a chimera. . . . Meanings are incommensurate, meanings are culturally constructed, and so all cultures are equal" (p. 73). Postmodernism is a current form of relativism. Gellner argues that in the void created, some voices predominate, throwing us back on authority, not a criterion that will protect clients' rights and allow clinicians to be faithful to their code of ethics. If there is no means by which to tell what is accurate and what is not, if all methods are equally effective, the vacuum is filled by an "elite" who are powerful enough to say what is and what is not (Gellner, 1992). Gellner argues that the sole focus on cognitive meaning in postmodernism ignores political and economic influences. He argues that postmodernism "denies or obscures tremendous differences in cognition and technical power" (pp. 71–72). He points out that there are real constraints in society that are obscured within this recent form of relativism (postmodernism) and suggests that such cognitive nihilism constitutes a "travesty of the real role of serious knowledge in our lives" (p. 95). Gellner argues that this view undervalues coercive and economic constraints in society and overvalues conceptual ones. "If we live in a world of meanings, and meanings exhaust the world, where is there any room for coercion through the whip, gun, or hunger?" (p. 63).

Gellner (1992) argues that postmodernism is an affectation: "Those who propound it or defend it against its critics, continue, whenever facing any serious issue in which their real interests are engaged, to act on the non-relativistic assumption that one particular vision is cognitively much more effective than others" (p. 70). Consider, for example, the different criteria social workers want their physicians to rely on when confronted with a serious medical problem compared to criteria they say they rely on to select service methods offered to clients. They rely on criteria such as intuition and experience with a few cases when making decisions about their clients, but want their physicians to rely on the results of controlled experimental studies and demonstrated track record of success based on data collected systematically and regularly when making decisions about a serous medical problem of their own (Gambrill & Gibbs, 2002).

## QUACKERY

Quackery refers to the promotion and marketing, for a profit, of untested, often worthless, and sometimes dangerous health products and procedures, by either professionals or others (Jarvis, 1990; Young, 1992).

> People generally like to feel that they are in control of their life. Quacks take advantage of this fact by giving their clients things to do—such as taking vitamin pills, preparing special foods, meditating, and the like. The activity may provide a temporary psychological lift, but believing in false things can have serious consequences. The loss may be financial, psychological (when disillusionment sets in), physical (when the method is harmful or the person abandons effective care), or social (diversion from more constructive activities). (Barrett, Jarvis, Kroger, & London, 2002, p. 7)

Barrett and his colleagues (2002) suggest that victims of quackery usually have one or more of the following vulnerabilities: (1) lack of suspicion; (2) desperation; (3) alienation (e.g., from the medical profession); (4) belief in magic; or (5) overconfidence in discerning whether a method works. Advertisers, both past and present, use the trappings of science (without the substance) to encourage consumers to buy products (Pepper, 1984). Indicators of quackery include the promise of quick cures, the use of anecdotes and testimonials to support claims, privileged power (only the great Dr. _____ knows how to _____), and secrecy (claims are not open to objective scrutiny). Natale (1988) estimated that in 1987 Americans spent $50 million on subliminal tapes, even though there is no evidence that they offer what they promise (Druckman & Bjork, 1991). For every claim supported by sound evidence, there are scores of bogus claims in advertisements, newscasts, films, TV, newspapers, and professional sources, making it a considerable challenge to resist their lures. McCoy (2000) describes a cornucopia of questionable medical devices. Reasons suggested by William Jarvis (1990) for why some professionals become quacks include the profit motive (making money) and the prophet motive (enjoying adulation and discipleship resulting from a pretense of superiority). The history of quackery is quite fascinating (Porter, 2002). There is a museum of medical quackery in Minneapolis, Minnesota. Quacks probably have existed as long as people have. They may award themselves degrees or obtain degrees from bogus institutions. They use a variety of strategies to woo people. Quackery takes advantage of a variety of propaganda methods designed to encourage beliefs and actions with the least thought possible.

## PROPAGANDA

Quackery and pseudoscience make use of propaganda strategies (see Exhibit 4.3). Jacques Ellul (1965) views propaganda as "principally interested in shaping action and behavior with little thought" (p. 278). A major function of propaganda is to squelch and censor dissenting points of view (e.g., see Rank, 1984). Its purpose is not to inform but to persuade. Interrelated kinds of propaganda in the helping professions include deep propaganda that obscures political, economic, and social contingencies that influence problem-related behaviors claimed by a profession (e.g., alcohol use, depression) and the questionable accuracy of basic assumptions, for example relabeling problems in

**Exhibit 4.3**
Mental Illness Model and Rank's (1984) Fourfold Classification of Propaganda

---

**Overemphasize the positive aspects of preferred model**

Inflated claims of success in removing complaints (puffery)

Inflated claims of success in preventing problems (puffery)

**Hide and minimize negative aspects of preferred model**

Harmful effects of neuroleptic drugs

Questionable reliability and validity of psychiatric classification systems

**Overemphasize negative aspects of opposing views**

Associate alternative approaches with negative terms (mechanistic, dehumanizing)

Allege that positive effects of alternative approaches are only temporary

**Hide and minimize positive aspects of opposing views**

Ignore research showing that nonprofessionals are as effective as professionals with many problems (e.g., see Dawes, 1994).

Ignore positive results achieved by alternative approaches

living as mental disorders that require the help of experts. It also includes inflated claims of effectiveness regarding assessment, intervention, and evaluation methods that woo clients to professionals and professionals to professions, perhaps because of profit and/or prophet motives (Jarvis, 1990). There are troubling gaps between the obligations of researchers to report limitations of research, prepare systematic reviews, and accurately describe well-argued alternative views, and what we find in published literature. Common propaganda methods include inaccurate generalizations, emotional reasoning, creation of fear, appeals to self interest, and censorship of alternative views and contradictory evidence (see prior discussion of questionable criteria).

Censoring of competing views and counter-evidence is common in certain areas such as AIDS and drug research (e.g., see Angell, 2004; Brewer et al., 2003; Kondro & Sibbald, 2004; Moran, 1998). Internet sources, including those of government agencies such as the National Institute of Health, may censor well-argued competing views; they claim that social anxiety and ADHD are "brain diseases," not mentioning alternative well-argued views (e.g., Web-MDHealth). Consider, for example, the propagandistic nature of The International Consensus Statement on ADHD (Barkley et al., 2000). Rather than addressing cogent criticisms of the diagnosis of ADHD (attention-deficit/hyperactivity disorder) and related recommended interventions, Barkley, Cook, and Diamond et al. (2002) dismiss criticisms as dangerous myths. Indeed, this brief statement (most pages contain a series of signers and references) is replete with propaganda strategies such as begging the question and hiding problems in views presented. Others view the labeling of thousands of little boys (mostly) as having ADHD as a cultural phenomenon, not a biomedical one (e.g., see Timimi, 2002; Timimi & Taylor, 2004; Singh, 2002). Censorship thrives at all levels of education (e.g., see Ravitch, 2003). Ad hominem arguments are directed toward the opponents of the preferred biomedical view promoted, rather than ad rem arguments. Here too, as with fraud, websites and organizations have been developed to counter material viewed as propaganda (e.g., National Coalition Against Censorship). The inflation of knowledge claims (puffery) is a key propaganda strategy (Rank, 1984). The resultant harms of professional propaganda are varied and may ripple out to others for decades.

Those who market ideas attempt to forward a view, not through a balanced and accurate presentation of related evidence and alternative views, but through reliance on strategies such as vague, emotional, distorted presentations of disliked positions, presentation only of data that support a favored position, and question begging. Skrabanek and McCormick (1998) illustrate the many false promises made in the name of prevention: that is, if we avoid certain risky behaviors, we will live longer, have a higher quality of life, and so on. They view the hyper-inflated claims and promises in the prevention area as a crusade; they remind us of the ideological simplicity of the quasi-religious crusades against the old enemies of sex, drugs, gluttony, and sloth. They suggest that the self-righteous intolerance of some wellness zealots borders on health fascism. Historically, humans have been at greatest risk while being improved in the best image of their possibilities as seen by somebody else" (p. 113). Although many public health experts would have us believe that taking certain steps to improve our health will prolong or enhance the quality of our life, typically, this is far from known; it is far from certain (see also Nettleton & Bunton, 1995).

Treatment programs may misrepresent the nature of their services and their outcomes (e.g., O'Hagan, 2003). The interpersonal helping industry is a huge one, consuming billions of dollars a year in direct and third-party payments. Those who have products to sell, including residential centers, pharmaceutical companies, and professional organizations promoting their training programs, take advantage of sophisticated marketing strategies to encourage purchase of their products. Strategies range from the obvious, such as advertisements in professional journals, to the subtle, such as offering workshops or conferences without identifying the funding source of these conferences. It is estimated that pharmaceutical companies spend between $8,000 and $11,000 per medical student per year to market their products to these individuals. A review of advertising on marketing brochures distributed by drug companies to physicians in Germany revealed that 94% of the content in these had no basis in scientific evidence (reported in Tuffs, 2004). Drug companies promote the creation of new "diseases" such as social anxiety and Premenstrual Dysphoric Disorder to increase markets for their medications (Parry, 2003). Economic interests of pharmaceutical companies in advocating a biomedical view of problems, such as social anxiety as "mental illnesses," encourage use of propaganda methods such as simply asserting that social anxiety is a "mental illness" requiring medication (Antonuccio, Burns, & Danton, 2002; Bekelman, Li, & Gross, 2003; Moncrieff, 2003; Starcevic, 2002). Websites sponsored by this industry contain material such as the following:

> If you think you are suffering from depression, panic disorder, obsessive compulsive disorder (OCD), posttraumatic stress disorder (PTSD), or Premenstrual Dysphoric Disorder (PMDD) know that you're not alone. In the United States, millions of people have these disorders. It is important to know these medical conditions are treatable. Read some of the articles and brochures below to learn about options for improving your mental health. (12/8/03, www.pfizerforwomen .com)

Psychological and biomedical views ignore contextual factors. This may be the most insidious effect of promoting pharmaceuticals directly to consumers. The message is that problems such as social anxiety and depression are brain diseases that are biomedical in origin and that can be treated with medication. This ignores and hides contributors such as lack of employment, high-cost housing, and poor schools. It ignores the social context of human experience and the unique causes of and ways distress is experienced and the resulting differences in how it should be approached. Presenting pitches for a product in an article form (advertorials) may lull readers into uncritical acceptance of promotional material (Prounis, 2004). Recently, more attention is being given in professional education programs to helping students understand marketing strategies used and how to avoid unwanted influences (Wilkes & Hoffman, 2001). Related courses encourage clinicians to critically appraise claims, including those in human service advertisements in journals (see also Gibbs & Gambrill, 1999). Much of continuing education in psychiatry is funded by the pharmaceutical industry (Angell, 2004). Screening days for anxiety and depression are often funded by this industry. Organizations such as National Alliance for the Mentally Ill (NAMI) and Children and Adults with Attention-Deficit/Hyperactivity (CHADD) obtain funding from this industry.

## FRAUD

Fraud is the intentional misrepresentation of the effect of certain actions, such as taking a prescribed drug to decrease depression, or to persuade people to part with something of value (e.g., money). It does this by means of deception and misrepresentation, drawing on a variety of propaganda ploys such as the omission of relevant information such as harmful side effects (e.g., see Miller & Hersen, 1992; Sackett & Oxman, 2003; Smith, 2005; Sparrow, 2000). Fraudulent claims (often appealing to the trappings of science) may result in overlooking effective methods or being harmed by remedies that are supposed to help (e.g., Jacobson, Foxx, & Mulick, 2005). Gould (cited in Jensen, 1989) included fraud (manufacture of evidence, presenting fiction as fact) as one of four pathologies of science. The three others were propaganda (selective presentations of evidence), prejudice, and finagle. The latter refers to minor hoaxes and intentional errors in data description or recording that result in a misrepresentation of findings. Scientific prejudice involves use of different standards of evidence for preferred and disliked views. That is, less rigorous standards are used for preferred views. Fraud is so extensive in some areas that special organizations have been formed, newsletters written, and Internet sites created to help consumers evaluate claims (e.g., *Health Letter* published by the Public Citizens Research Group; see also junkscience.com, Federal Trade Commission, National Council Against Health Fraud, Center for Media Education [CME]).

The Attorney General of the State of New York, Eliot Spitzer, filed a civil suit accusing the drug giant GlaxoSmithKline of committing fraud by concealing negative information about Paxil, a drug used to treat depression.

The suit says that the company conducted five clinical trials of Paxil in adolescents and children, yet published only one study whose mixed results it deemed positive. The company sat on two major studies for up to four years, although the results of one were divulged by a whistle-blower at a medical conference in 1999 and all of the studies were submitted to the Food and Drug Administration in

2002 when the company sought approval for new uses of Paxil. At that time it became apparent that Paxil was no more effective than a placebo in treating adolescent depression and might even provoke suicidal thoughts. (When drug companies hold data; *New York Times*, June 6, 2004)

In another report it was noted that Pfizer Inc. "agreed to pay $430 million in fines and plead guilty to charges that a company it acquired four years ago promoted a drug for non-approved uses, in part by plying doctors with favors to get them to talk up the medication" (Harris, 2004). Pennsylvania's attorney general sued 13 pharmaceutical companies for alleged deceptive pricing and sales practices (4/11/04). In June of 2004 the editors of leading medical journals and the American Medical Association called on drug companies to register all their clinical trials on a website.

## KNOWLEDGE VALUED IN EVIDENCE-BASED PRACTICE

The phrase *evidence-based practice* (EPB) draws attention to the kind of evidence needed to rigorously test different kinds of practice-related claims (see Chapter 10). What is needed depends on what kind of question it is; for example, does it concern the effectiveness of a treatment method or predictive accuracy of a risk assessment measure? (see Chapter 12). Knowledge valued in evidence-based practice includes how to critically test claims related to important practice and policy questions, such as "Is this assessment measure valid?"; "Does this parent training program help clients to enhance positive parenting skills?" Such knowledge can help us to avoid biases that may provide misleading conclusions. It can help us to avoid fooling ourselves that we have knowledge when we do not. Have claims been critically examined in relation to their consequences for clients? Mistakes (what kind occur, when they occur, what contributes to them, and how we can minimize them) are viewed as a vital kind of knowledge, as is knowledge about application obstacles and how we can overcome them, such as creating technological innovations, enhancing communication skills, and increasing self-knowledge that forwards integration of practice and research.

Clinicians work under uncertainty. Yet they must act. Awareness of the degree of uncertainty associated with a decision is one kind of knowledge. Knowledge that decreases or reveals the degree of uncertainty about how to attain outcomes that clients value is emphasized in evidence-based practice: guesses (theories) that have survived critical tests of their efficacy in resolving problems. Thinking carefully about practice-related claims will keep the inevitable uncertainty involved in working with clients in view. We are less likely to promote bogus claims that may harm clients if acted on. The importance of specialized content knowledge and skills is one of the major findings from research in problem solving and decision making, including professional decision making (see Chapter 8). Both content and performance knowledge are important. Other kinds of knowledge valued in EBP include clinical expertise to identify and integrate information about the unique circumstances and characteristics of a client, including his or her preferences, values, and expectations, and local circumstances in making decisions. Knowledge of common biases that may lead us astray is another kind of valued knowledge, as is knowledge about tools, such as decision aids that help us to make sound decisions (see Chapter 9), and knowledge of clients' characteristics, circumstances, and values. Knowledge concerning ethical obligations is another kind of knowledge valued in EBP.

## KNOWLEDGE VALUED IN AUTHORITY-BASED PRACTICE

Criteria used to select knowledge in authority-based practice are quite different: popularity, tradition, status, degrees or credentials. Peter Munz (1985) defines *false knowledge* as beliefs that are not true and that are not questioned. This refers to "pieces of knowledge held consciously which have little direct bearing on physical survival" (p. 74). Such beliefs "can be held or discarded regardless of the environment in which people who hold them are living. Nevertheless, they are frequently used for a useful function: ". . . as a social bond so that societies can be formed with defined members, and these societies can survive because the defined membership makes cooperation and division of labor possible" (p. 74). In this kind of society, membership "depends on being able to give the correct answers to a catechism," beliefs "are not available for criticism and therefore cannot be examined. They are held dogmatically" (p. 74).

## CRITICAL APPRAISAL OF PRACTICES AND POLICIES AS AN ETHICAL OBLIGATION

Karl Popper (1994) argues that relying on unexamined claims about what is true reflects an arrogance that is at odds with a compassion for others. Valuing "truth, the search for truth, the approximation to truth through the critical elimination of error, and clarity" (p. 70) is needed to overcome the influence of other values (e.g., trying to appear profound by using obscure words or jargon; see also the discussion of obstacles to critical thinking in Chapter 1). If criticism is the route to knowledge, we must value truth over certainty, ignorance, and prejudice, and clarity over obscurity; we must value getting closer to the truth more than winning arguments and maintaining status. The philosophy of evidence-based practice emphasizes the close relationship between evidentiary and ethical obligations. It is a way to handle uncertainty constructively for the client's benefit—to deal "with inadequate information in ways that can help to identify really important uncertainties, uncertainties that are often reflected in dramatic variations in clinical practices and which cry out for coordinated efforts to improve knowledge" (Chalmers, 2004). Ethical obligations require clinicians to draw on practice-related research, to be competent, and to accurately inform clients about the risks and benefits of recommended services and alternatives. The intellectual attitudes of empathy, courage, curiosity, open-mindedness, and reliance on standards such as clarity (Paul, 1993) contribute to making ethical decisions. Popper (1992) suggests that we are all equal in our vast ignorance. "It is important never to forget our ignorance. We should therefore never pretend to know anything, and we should never use big words. What I call the cardinal sin . . . is simply talking hot air, professing a wisdom we do not possess" (p. 86). We have "the obligation never to pose as a prophet" (p. 206). Valuing truth over prejudice and ignorance requires critical testing of claims and conclusions. Only through criticism can we discover our errors and perhaps learn how to do better in the future. A candid recognition of and active search for mistakes keeps the inevitable uncertainty involved in trying to help clients clearly in view, and encourages us to keep track of our mistakes as a way to improve services (McIntyre & Popper, 1983).

Valuing truth calls for making well-reasoned decisions—you can make a sound argument for them. For example, claims have survived risky predictions and are compatible with and informed by research findings. Critical discussion with oneself as well as with others is necessary for making well-informed decisions. Principles that Karl Popper highlights as the basis of every rational discussion are:

1. The principle of fallibility: perhaps I am wrong and perhaps you are right. But we could easily both be wrong.
2. The principle of rational discussion: we want to try, as impersonally as possible, to weigh up our reasons for and against a theory: a theory that is definite and criticizable.
3. The principle of approximation to the truth: we can nearly always come closer to the truth in a discussion which avoids personal attacks. It can help us to achieve a better understanding; even in those cases where we do not reach an agreement. (Popper, 1992, p. 199)

Valuing truth requires basing decisions on data as well as theory when necessary to solve problems. Guesses about the causes of problems should be checked against data gathered in real life. Only by collecting observational data in problem-related circumstances, such as the classroom or residential setting, may informed guesses be made about the causes of complaints and related circumstances. Collecting systematic data concerning outcomes provides a guide for decisions and allows us to discover whether we are helping, harming, or having no effect. It allows clients to find out whether the quality of their lives has improved, remained the same, or diminished. Anthony Flew (1985) contends that the sincerity of our interest in helping clients is reflected in the efforts we make to find out whether we do help them.

## THE BURDEN OF KNOWLEDGE

One topic that seems to have been slighted in the literature on the integration of practice and research concerns the burden of knowledge; for example, the negative consequences of information that all is not as it should be regarding the quality of services provided to clients (e.g., see Sagan, 1987). We are exposed to reports showing harming in the name of helping, for example adverse events that a professional knew about but did not say or do anything about. My students routinely report concerning lapses in agency practices—often ongoing events in their agency—about which nothing is being done and which are not being discussed. Examples include the following:

- A medical social worker who knows that a client who is dying is not receiving proper pain medication and the medical director will not alter the pain medication schedule.
- A social worker who works in a legal advocates office who knows that a client has been required to attend a drug treatment program, even though it is known that the client has no drug problem—a mistake was made by the person who prepared the report for the court. This parent will not regain custody of her children until she attends this drug treatment program for her alleged drug use.

Even among beginning master's students there is a surprising acceptance of troubling practices and policies based on the assumption that nothing can be done. Such descriptions would often be accompanied by embarrassed laughter and a shrugging off of the possibility that anything could be done. Rarely was the description of the practice, policy, or mistake accompanied by statements such as the following:

- I am going to do something about this.
- We must do something about this.
- I am going to bring this up to my agency team.
- We must work together to change this.

If recognizing unnecessary burdens and harms to clients creates negative feelings (stress, anxiety, sadness for the plights of others, perhaps shame that nothing is being done), then forgetting provides relief. When we cannot act in the face of avoidable suffering, is not forgetting an adaptive reaction?

## SUMMARY

Professionals are assumed to have special knowledge that helps them to effectively address certain kinds of problems. There are many views of knowledge, what it is, and how to get it. Some, compared to others, are more likely to result in sound decisions. Thus, thinking about knowledge and how to get it, reviewing your personal epistemology, is vital to being a professional. If we rely on questionable criteria for evaluating practice- and policy-related claims, clients may be harmed rather than helped, false hope may be created, harmful effects experienced, and effective methods forgone. Some clinicians rely on authority as a guide; for example, what high-status people say, what is popular (how many people use a method) or tradition (what's usually done). These criteria do not provide sound guides. Avoiding confirmation biases (searching only for data that confirm our views and ignoring data that do not) requires seeking evidence against favored views and considering well-argued alternative perspectives. Critical appraisal will help you to identify flaws in your thinking, such as referring a client to agencies that use ineffective practices and programs. You are more likely to acquire knowledge and skills that help you to help your clients if you take an active role in critically appraising what you read, hear, and believe. Sound criteria for making practice decisions include well-reasoned arguments and critical tests that suggest that one option is more likely than another to result in outcomes clients value.

## GLOSSARY

**antiscience**   Rejection of scientific methods as valid.

**critical discussion**   "Essentially a comparison of the merits and demerits of two or more theories (usually more than two). The merits discussed are mainly the *explanatory power* of the theories . . . the way in which they are able to solve our problems of explaining things, the way in which the theories cohere with certain other heavily valued theories, their power to shed new light on old problems and to suggest new problems. The chief demerit is inconsistency, including inconsistency with the results of experiments that a competing theory can explain" (Popper, 1994, pp. 160–161).

**cynicism**   A negative view of the world and what can be learned about it.

**eclecticism**   The view that we should adopt whatever theories or methodologies that are useful in inquiry, no matter what their source and without undue worry about their consistency.

**empiricism**   The position that all knowledge (usually excluding that which is logical or mathematical) is in some way "based on" experience. Adherents of empiricism differ markedly over what the "based on" amounts to— "starts from" and "warranted in terms of" are, roughly, at the two ends of the spectrum of opinion (Phillips, 1987, p. 203).

**evidence**   "Ground for belief, testimony or facts tending to prove or disprove any conclusions" (Oxford English Dictionary, 1994).

**false knowledge**   Beliefs that are not true and that are not questioned (Munz, 1985).

**falsification approach to knowledge**   The view that we can discover only what is false, not what is true.

**hermeneutics**   'The discipline of interpretation of textual or literary material, or of meaningful human actions" (Phillips, 1987, p. 203).

**justification approach to knowledge**   The view that we can discover the truth by seeking support for our theories.

**knowledge**   Problematic and tentative guesses about what may be true (Popper, 1992, 1994); "guess work disciplined by rational criticism" (1992, p. 40). Criticism is "the crucial quality of knowledge" (Munz, 1985, p. 49).

**logical positivism**   The main tenet of logical positivism is the verifiability principle of meaning: "Something is meaningful only if it is verifiable empirically (i.e., directly, or indirectly, via sense experiences) or if it is a truth of logic or mathematics" (Phillips, 1987, p. 204). The reality of theoretical entities is denied.

**nonjustificationist epistemology**   The view that knowledge is not certain. It is assumed that although some claims of knowledge may be warranted, no warrant is so firm that it is not open to question (see Karl Popper's writings).

**paradigm**   "A theoretical framework that influences the problems that are regarded as crucial, the ways these problems are conceptualized, the appropriate methods of inquiry, the relevant standards of judgment, etc." (Phillips, 1987, p. 205).

**phenomenology**   "The study of, in depth, of how things appear in human experience" (Phillips, 1987, p. 205).

**postmodernism**   Disputes assumptions of science and its products. All grounds for knowledge claims are considered equally questionable (see, for example, Rosenau, 1992; Munz, 1992).

**postpositivism**   The approach to science that replaced logical positivism decades ago (see, for example, Phillips, 1987, 1992).

**pseudoscience**   Material that makes science-like claims but provides no evidence for them.

**quackery**   The promotion of products and procedures known to be false or which are untested, for a profit (Pepper, 1984).

**rationality**   An openness to criticism. "A limitless invitation to criticism is the essence of rationality" (Munz, 1985, p. 50). Rationality consists of making mistakes and eliminating error by natural selection (p. 16).

**relativism**   Relativists "insist that judgments of truth are always relative to a particular framework or point of view" (Phillips, 1987, p. 206). This point of view prevents criticism from outside a closed circle of believers.

**science**   A process designed to develop knowledge by critically discussing and testing theories.

**scientific objectivity**   Scientific objectivity is solely the critical approach (Popper, 1994, p. 93). It is based on mutual rational criticism in which high standards of clarity and rational criticism are valued (Popper, 1994, p. 70). See also **Critical discussion.**

**scientism**   A term used "to indicate slavish adherence to the methods of science even in a context where they are inappropriate" and "to indicate a false or mistaken claim to be scientific" (Phillips, 1987, p. 206). Scientism refers to the view that "authority should be conferred upon knowledge and the knower, upon science and the scientists, upon wisdom and the wise man, and upon learning and the learned" (Popper, 1992, p. 33).

**skepticism**   A provisional approach to claims; the careful examination of all claims.

**theory**   Myths, expectations, guesses, and conjectures about what may be true. A theory always remains hypothetical or conjectural. "It always remains guesswork. And there is no theory that is not beset with problems" (Popper, 1994, p. 157).

**theory ladenness (of perception)**   "The thesis that the process of perception is theory-laden in that the observer's background knowledge (including theories, factual information, hypotheses, and so forth) acts as a 'lens' helping to 'shape' the nature of what is observed" (Phillips, 1987, p. 206).

**truth**   "An assertion is true if it corresponds to, or agrees with, the facts" (Popper, 1994, p. 174). We can never be sure that our guesses are true. "Though we can never justify the claim to have reached truth, we can often give some very good reasons, or justification, why one theory should be judged as nearer to it than another" (Popper, 1994, p. 161).

# PART II

# COMMON SOURCES
# OF ERROR

# CHAPTER 5

# The Influence of Language and Persuasion Strategies

T WO COMMON SOURCES of error involve use of language and the influence of social-psychological persuasion strategies. Clinicians use words to describe people and events, to describe relationships between behavior and events, and to express evaluations. Language is used in posing and "thinking" about clinical questions and in processing material read in professional books and articles. Although considerable attention has been devoted to problematic use of language on the part of clients, less attention has been devoted to exploration of how common sources of error influence clinicians in their daily practice. The words clinicians use not only shape their own experiences and actions but those of their clients as well. The tendency of clinicians to say "Yes, I know this" without becoming knowledgeable about the specific ways language and persuasion strategies influence clinical decisions is an obstacle to avoiding these sources of error. Here, too, as with other sources of error described in this book, having a name for a fallacy highlights its uniqueness, and may help us to recognize and plan how to avoid it.

## THE INFLUENCE OF LANGUAGE

Many critical thinking skills involve recognition of the ways in which language may affect decisions (Halpern, 2003; Johnson, 1946). Language plays an important role in clinical practice. Discussions between clients and practitioners and the nonverbal reactions that accompany these are a key component in most practice frameworks. Use of language is also integral to decisions made during case conferences and in court presentations, as well as in interpretations of clinical records. All writing in the professions and the social sciences can be viewed as rhetorical in that a position is advanced and a point of view is presented that is then reviewed for its soundness (Edmondson, 1984). The term *rhetoric* has varied definitions: (1) "the art of using words effectively in speaking or writing; now, the art of prose composition (2) artificial eloquence; language that is showy and elaborate but largely empty of clear ideas or sincere emotion" (*Webster's New World Dictionary,* 1988). It is in the latter sense that the term is in ill-repute. It is not unusual, for example, to hear someone say "we need less rhetoric and more straight facts." When rhetoric is defined in its broader sense, as in the first definition above, it is an important area of study and skill, especially in helping professions that rely heavily on the spoken and written word.

Three basic reasons that language may compromise the quality of decisions include carelessness, lack of skill in writing and thinking, and deliberate intent on the part of a speaker or writer. The many functions that language serves complicate understanding of spoken or written statements. One function is description. Description of clients, procedures used, and progress achieved is an integral part of clinical records. The aim of descriptive statements is to inform (for example, "Mr. Larkin has been hospitalized three times."). We can find out whether they are true or false. Another function is to persuade others to believe or act differently. Clinicians attempt to persuade clients to act, think, or feel differently in problem-related situations by talking to them. Use of language is a critical influence when considering the evidentiary status of different assessment or intervention strategies, whether talking to oneself or to colleagues. A third function of language is purely expressive—to express some emotion or feeling or to create such a feeling without trying to influence future behavior. Other statements direct or guide us, as in "Call the parental stress hotline." A given statement may serve several functions; not only may a speaker or writer have more than one purpose in mind when making a statement, but the listener or reader also may have more than one in mind, which may or may not match those of the speaker. The context is used to interpret the speaker's or writer's purpose. Language also has presymbolic functions, such as affirming social cohesion (as in "Isn't it a nice day?"). Lack of understanding of this function may result in naive assumptions about the triviality of conversation, as Hayakawa (1978) notes in his "Advice to the Literal-Minded" (p. 85). Only if we correctly understand the motive behind a sentence may we translate it correctly.

Words differ in their level of abstraction. At the lowest level are definitions in extensional terms. The extensional meaning of a word refers to what it points to in the physical world; it is what the word stands for. A psychiatrist could point to the disheveled clothes of a person admitted to an emergency psychiatry unit, or to the behavior of pushing a nurse. Many words have no extensional meaning—that is, there is nothing we can point to. In operational definitions, a rigorous attempt is made to exclude nonextensional meaning, as in the definition of length in terms of the operations by which it is measured. The intentional meaning of a word refers to what is connoted or suggested. Clinicians may act toward people, objects, or events in accord with the intentional (affective) connotations associated with a name. For example, reactions to terms such as "sociopath" or "welfare recipient" may go far beyond the extensional meaning of these terms without recognizing that this is happening. Definitions describe our linguistic habits; they are statements about how language is used. The higher the level of abstraction, the less the utility of referring to a dictionary definition to capture meaning, especially intentional meaning.

## FALLACIES RELATED TO LANGUAGE

Problems related to use of language that influence the quality of clinical decisions are described in the following, together with suggested remedies. This list is by no means exhaustive, and readers are referred to other sources for greater detail (e.g., Halpern, 2003; Hayakawa, 1978; Thouless, 1974). Carelessness is often responsible for foggy writing and speaking—not taking the time and thought to clearly state inferences and reasons for them.

*Predigested Thinking*    This term refers to the tendency to oversimplify complex topics, issues, or perspectives into simple formulas that distort content, such as describing Freudian theory as reducing everything to sex or describing behavioral theory as favoring mechanistic stimulus-response connections. Stereotyping is a form of predigested (oversimplified) thinking. Perhaps one of the most striking examples of oversimplification is the assertion that a wide variety of problems are caused by "chemical imbalances in the brain." The brain is very complex. Compared with what there is "to know"; we know little about it, contrary to claims such as: "We have found . . ." "This shows that . . ." "We now know . . ." What is a "chemical imbalance"? How does this relate to electricity in the brain? How do different chemicals interact? Oversimplifications of complex views and topics may lead to errors and get in the way of further research. Varieties of oversimplifications of complex concepts include use of words that obscures the differences between different entities, words that suggest that some phenomenon is unchanging when it does change, and words that suggest differences that do not exist.

Analogues used to simplify material may result in a disregard for the real complexity of concerns; for example, development of hallucinations or a severe phobia. Consider a diagnosis of social anxiety based on reports of a client—that she is fearful in social situations and avoids them. Describing this as a "mental disorder" (assuming that such concerns are caused by brain diseases) and prescribing medication, ignores the environmental context in which such reactions develop and are maintained that, if changed, may decrease related distressing reactions. It may misrepresent or ignore interaction among variables, and as Woods and Cook (1999) note, create "a false sense of understanding and inhibit pursuit of deeper understanding" (p. 152). Simplifying strategies do not always help us to solve problems, although overall, they may do so as discussed in Chapter 9.

Referring to hundreds of different behaviors, feelings, and thoughts as "mental disorders" (diseases) is an oversimplification; for example, it ignores the continuous nature of the vast majority of related behaviors, such as drinking alcohol or anxiety. Consider shyness. Eighty percent of people are shy in some situations. Are certain forms of "social anxiety" a "mental disorder"? (see *DSM IV-TR*, 2000). Another example of a common oversimplification is reflected in the following answer of a doctoral student during a discussion of twin studies: "We know the environment was the same because the twins were raised in the same home." Is it the same home for each of these individuals? Research suggests that it is not, that even twins have different environments. As Lewontin (1991, 1995) suggests, we each construct (not adapt to) our environments. Clinicians are sometimes guilty of reducing an answer to a simple formula, such as "rapists will rape again." A practitioner who does not believe that evaluation of client progress can be done in a way that is meaningful may say, "evaluation is mechanistic," or "it trivializes concerns," or "it does not represent the true complexity of human problems." Such views overlook the fact that evaluation can be carried out in an irrelevant or relevant manner. The latter requires skill in working together with clients to select important, feasible, and sensitive progress indicators. Such views also overlook resources for dealing with the complexity of evaluating client progress in terms of identifying measures that accurately reflect progress (or its lack). (See for example descriptions of assessing quality of life.)

Another example is the statement that "a scientific approach to clinical questions offers trivial answers." What is the meaning of "a scientific approach" here? What is a "trivial answer"? Predigested thinking in the form of slogans may be used to encourage actions, such as "support community care." The history of the community mental health movement reveals that such slogans were used often, despite the minimal available community care for patients (Sedgwick, 1982). Slogans are easy to remember and so are readily available to influence us at an emotional level. The use of predigested thinking obscures complexities and so may encourage inaccurate inferences. This kind of thinking is common because of indifference, lack of information, and idleness, and the fact that it often offers a practical guide for life. The tendency to simplify complex matters may help to account for ignoring the undistributed middle (substituting *all* for *some*) and the readiness to accept an extension of a position.

We can guard against predigested thinking by avoiding mental idleness, which encourages us "to accept mental food well below the limits of our digestion" (Thouless, 1974, p. 164). The remedy is to consider the actual complexity of the issue at hand as needed to arrive at accurate accounts. Recognizing the complexities related to a question may increase tolerance for other positions. The emotional appeal of predigested thinking and the fact that it often provides a practical guide for daily life make it difficult to challenge. For example, a clinician may object to the oversimplistic presentation of Freudian theory that "everything is related to sex." The other person may protest that the objections raised are too "learned," that "nothing will convince him that art, romantic love, and religion are just sex, which is generally agreed by everybody to be the teaching of Freud" (Thouless, 1974, p. 161). Note the reaffirmation of the original position (begging the question) and the appeal to consensus. As Thouless notes, if this is a discussion with other people, the user of predigested thinking can usually rely on "having their sympathy, for his opponent will seem to be a person trying to make himself out to be too clever and who makes serious argument impossible by throwing doubt on what everyone knows to be true" (pp. 161–162). The only recourse here may be to state an argument so clearly that the inadequacies of a position are quite obvious. So, challengers of predigested thinking who wish to take a more careful look at a point under discussion should be prepared that some people may not like this; negative reactions can be avoided by posing inquiries in a tactful manner and by emphasizing common interests, such as helping clients achieve outcomes they value.

*Pseudotechnical Jargon/Bafflegarb*   Jargon can be useful in communicating in an efficient manner if listeners (or readers) share the same meaning of technical terms. However, jargon may be used to conceal ignorance and "impress the innocent" (Rycroft, 1973, p. xi; see also Tavris, 2001). Consider the earlier discussion of misleading oversimplifications, such as claims that problems are due to "chemical imbalances in the brain." An economic incentive may perpetuate obscure writing; for example, highly specialized jargon in the legal profession increases the need to hire lawyers who can understand it. We tend to be impressed with things we cannot understand. Professors tend to rate journals that are hard to read as more prestigious than journals that are easier to read (Armstrong, 1980). Of course, it is possible that the more prestigious journals discuss more complex subjects that require more difficult language. This possibility was tested by Armstrong. Portions of management journals were rewritten to increase readability without changing the content; unnecessary words were eliminated, easy words were substituted for difficult ones, and sentences were broken into shorter ones. A sample of 32 management professors were asked to rate as easy or difficult versions of four such passages and also rate them on a scale of "competence" ranging from 1 to 7. They knew neither the name of the journal nor the name of the author. Versions that were easier to read were considered to reflect less competent research than were the more difficult passages.

Obscurity may be desirable in some circumstances, such as when exploring new possibilities. However, in most situations that arise in clinical practice, obscurity is not an advantage; it is often a cloak for vagueness. Examples of pseudotechnical jargon include *psychic deficiencies, structural frame of reference,* and *generational dysfunctions.* The proliferation of terms adds to pseudojargon in psychotherapy. Consider, for example, terms that Firestone and Seiden (1987) present as similar to "microsuicide."

- indirect suicide
- masked suicide
- partial suicide
- hidden suicide
- installment plan suicide

- parasuicide
- slow suicide
- chronic suicide
- embryonic suicide

Who has not suffered from "bureaucratese"—turgid, unnecessarily complex descriptions that yield only to the most persistent of readers (or listeners)? Examples include "mumblistic" (planned mumbling) and "profundicating" (translating simple concepts into obscure jargon; Boren, 1972). The remedy is to simplify and clarify. Examples of rules suggested by Orwell (1958) include the following:

1. Never use a metaphor, simile, or other figure of speech which you are used to seeing in print.
2. Never use a long word when a short one will do.
3. If it is possible to cut a word out, always cut it out.
4. Never use the passive when you can use the active.
5. Never use a foreign phrase, a scientific word, or a jargon word if you can think of an everyday English equivalent.
6. Break any of these rules sooner than say anything outright barbarous. (p. 143)

The potential for obscure terms to become clear can be explored by asking questions such as "What do you mean by that?" "Can you give me an example?" Asking such questions when reading case records and practice-related literature is a valuable rule of thumb (see list of Socratic questions in Exhibit 3.5).

Obscure language often remains unquestioned because of worries that the questioner will look ignorant or stupid. The risks of lack of clarification should be considered, as well as the risks of revealing a lack of knowledge. Writers and speakers should clarify their terms, bearing in mind appropriate levels of abstraction. If they don't, it may be because they cannot. They should be thankful that someone cares enough to want to understand their position and that lack of clarity is discovered. Not all people will be open to questions, especially those who use vague language to hide aims or lack of knowledge they would rather not reveal. "The great enemy of clear language is insincerity. When there is a gap between one's real and one's declared aims, one turns as it were instinctively to long words and exhausted idioms like a cuttlefish squirting out ink" (Orwell, 1958, p. 142). Some people will become defensive and try to put others down for asking simpleminded questions, perhaps using their prestige to do so. They may share Humpty Dumpty's attitude: "When I use a word" Humpty Dumpty said, in a rather scornful tone, "it means just what I choose it to mean neither more nor less." "The question is," said Alice, "whether you *can* make words mean so many different things." "The question is," said Humpty Dumpty, "who is to be master, that's all." (Lewis Carroll, 1946, *Through the Looking Glass,* p. 229). A question could be asked in such a straight-forward manner that if the person still cannot understand it, his own lack of astuteness is revealed (Thouless, 1974).

*Use of Emotional or Buzzwords or Images*   Professionals, as well as advertisers and politicians, make use of emotional words and images, as illustrated in the letter to the editor, National Association of Social Workers (NASW) *News:*

| *Example* | *Comments* |
|---|---|
| The conspiracy of silence continues to state implicitly that social workers, because of their training and clinical expertise, cannot possibly be impaired by alcohol and drug abuse. As long as this conspiracy exists, impaired social workers will be afraid to seek help and to come out into the open about their addiction, just as I am ("Letter to the Editor," 1986, p. 15). | The term "conspiracy" is highly pejo-rative, as is "impaired." No evidence is offered that there is a "conspiracy of silence," or for the assumption that the "conspiracy" stops social work-ers from disclosing their "addiction." No evidence is offered for the assump-tion that people assume that social workers "cannot have a substance abuse problem because of their train-ing and expertise." It is assumed that substance abuse is "an addiction." |

Emotional terms are rife in the turf battles between psychologists and psychi-atrists: Consider the opening sentence in an article in the *Psychiatric Times:* "Clinical psychology is in a war for survival against American psychiatry" (Buie, 1987, p. 25). Research regarding the role of emotions on our behavior lies in many fields, including social psychology, learning, and clinical psy-chology. Our emotions offer rapid, often automatic information linked to fight-or-flight reactions. Our emotional reactions influence our decisions and how we respond to new material, or if we seek out certain material (Slovic, Fin-ucane, Peters, & MacGregor, 2002). Emotions and perceptions may precede thoughts; associated cues, which are automatic in nature (they occur without our awareness) influence behavior (Gilovich & Griffin, 2002). Indeed, auto-matic perceptions and associative responses comprise two of the three pro-cesses for making judgments (see Chapter 9).

Proverbs, similes, or metaphors that have emotional effects may be used to describe or support a position. They may be of great value in developing new ideas about how to solve problems. On the other hand, they may obscure rather than clarify a problem or issue; they may create a feeling of under-standing without an accompanying increase in real understanding. Points against a disliked (and perhaps misunderstood) position may be referred to as ammunition, and points in favor of a preferred position referred to as rea-soned and humanistic considerations. Clinicians who do not believe that clini-cal practice can be evaluated may refer to such efforts as mechanical, and may appeal to an inappropriate analogy geared to demonstrate just how inappropriate it is to evaluate practice, such as saying that evaluation of practice entails treating people like cars—mechanistically, simplistically. (For further discussion of the influence of metaphors see Lakoff & Dean, 2004; Sontag, 1991.) Examples of the use of emotionally toned words can be seen in the excerpts from a case conference in Chapter 16.

The use of emotionally toned words is not always dysfunctional; however, in the context of trying to make correct inferences, such words may interfere with clear thinking (for example, they may interfere with identifying useful options). A vigilance about possible effects of emotional words should encourage use of terms that are more neutral, less value laden. Biases that may influence clinical decisions can be coaxed out by exploring reactions to terms such as *nursing home resident* and *developmentally disabled youth*. Noting the possible biasing effects of emotional terms and using more neutral ones may increase the quality of clinical decisions in all venues, including case conferences and discussions with oneself.

*Labeling*   Labels often are applied incorrectly. The term "evidence-based practice" is often used to describe practices which do not reflect the philosophy of evidence-based decision making as described in original sources (see Chapter 10, as well as a list of distortions of "evidence-based practice" in Exhibit 6.1, Chapter 6). A label such as *behavior modification* may be used inaccurately to describe a program that is just the opposite of what a behavioral program would be like (see discussion of faulty classification in Chapter 7). Pseudo-explanations are one result of unexamined use of labels. Stigmatizing labels often are applied to clients that have few, if any, implications for selection of effective treatment methods (see discussion of labeling in Chapter 7).

*The Assumption of One Word, One Meaning*   Words have different meanings in different contexts. As Hayakawa (1978) has bluntly put it, "Ignoring of contexts in any act of interpretation is at best a stupid practice. At its worst, it can be a vicious practice" (p. 56), as when, for example, a sentence is taken out of context. Differences that exist in the world may not be reflected in different use of words, or differences in language may not correspond to variations in the world. Misunderstandings arise when different uses of a word are mistaken for different opinions about a topic of discussion. "Unless people mean the same thing when they talk to each other, accurate communication is impossible" (Feinstein, 1967, p. 313). Two people discussing "addiction" may not have the same definition of this term, and a muddled discussion may result. One way to avoid this is to define key terms. The following dialogue illustrates how the same word may have different meanings.

> *Counselor:* I think you have an addiction to alcohol.
> *Client:* I don't think so.
> *Counselor:* You drink every day.

*Client:* But it doesn't interfere with my life. I'm happily married and like my job. Just because I drink every day doesn't mean I'm addicted.

*Counselor:* I think it does.

Results of assessment are often presented in vague terms, such as *probable*, or *cannot be excluded*, which have a wide range of meaning to different clinicians (Bryant & Norman, 1980). Definition of terms such as *panic reaction* or *dementia* may be shared initially but diverge as discussion proceeds. Clinicians may differ in how they define certain intervention methods. Confusion can be avoided by checking definitions of key concepts.

*Use of Vague Terms*  Vague terms are common in clinical contexts: *uncommunicative, aggressive, immature, drug dependency, dependent patient, dysfunction, family therapy, social work intervention, family oriented modality, psychic deficiencies, dysfunctional alignments,* and *proper boundary lines*. If terms are not clarified, different meanings may be used, none of which may reflect the real world. Fashionable phrases or terms often become vague phrases in time. Examples include supportive therapy and case management. Two individuals with different meanings of the term "evidence-based practice" may make little progress in discussing related advantages and disadvantages because of different views of this term. Clichés and "unoriginal remarks do have their uses in terms of highlighting similarity between people; that those present are on the 'right-side' so to speak" (Hayakawa, 1978). It is when hackneyed phrases and clichés are used carelessly to communicate new ideas and perspectives that they become problematic. (For a general discussion of vagueness see Keefe, 2000.)

*Reification, Word Magic*  Here it is mistakenly assumed that a word corresponds to something real; in fact, "the existence of a word does not guarantee the existence of any corresponding entity" (Fearnside & Holther, 1959, p. 68). The term *aggressive,* used as a summary term for specific actions, may also be used to refer to an aggressive disposition, which is believed to be responsible for these actions. This disposition then comes to be thought of as an attribute of the person (Bromley, 1977). Staats and Staats (1963) refer to this as the use of pseudoexplanations. Noting the circularity of such terms reveals that no new information is offered and that no evidence other than the behavioral referents described support the influence of this higher-order concept. Perhaps the most common example of word magic in clinical psychology, psychiatry, and social work, is the term "mental illness." Because we use the word, we assume the associated entity exists when it may not. I do not mean to say that troubling behaviors, thoughts, or feelings are not real. They are. But the alleged "mental illness" may not be. (See also Didi-huberman, 1982.)

In *Schizophrenia: A Scientific Delusion?* Mary Boyle (2002) describes how language used (such as repeated use of the word "clinical"), kinds of arguments presented, and benefits, both touted and actual, intersect to maintain an illusion that a coherent entity called *schizophrenia* exists, and that the methods used to identify it are unproblematic. As Boyle (2002) notes, it is easy to believe that what is referred to by a word actually exists—particularly if authority figures such as psychiatrists use the term and act as if it is unproblematic. She illustrates the problematic nature of terms such as "mental illness" and "mental disorder" on both methodological and conceptual grounds. She gives many examples of how the discourse of science is used to create a false impression of objectivity and rigor, for example by using specialized terminology that is often unfamiliar to lay readers as well as to many in the mental health profession. She notes that terms are often misused (e.g., "base rate") in a manner that favors the assumption that schizophrenia exists as a unique entity, that it is a "mental disorder," and that it is biochemical in origin. Appeals to the language of neuroscience are rife.

Boyle (2002) suggests that narratives of scientific progress are used to imply that advances are being made when they are not (see also Houts, 2002). For example, even though biochemical correlates have not yet been discovered, claims are made that they soon will be. She points out that the language of medicine is also appealed to, and that this combines with the language of science in a potent rhetorical mix to give illusions of objectivity, knowledge, and progress. Scores of books contain the word "schizophrenia" in the title. Thousands of articles contain this word, and we see it daily in the press. Our tendency to rely on "experts," and to believe that if there is a word, it refers to something in the real world (reification), combines with other factors, such as lack of time or interest in digging deeper, a desire to understand our environments with little effort (e.g., the causes of troubled or troubling behavior), and an interest in escaping from responsibility for our behavior or troubles by attributing them to a mental disorder. This is a powerful mix. (See also critiques of ADHD, such as Singh, 2002; Timimi & Taylor, 2004.)

*Influence of Semantic Linkages and Cuing Effects*   This ranges from the subtle to the obvious. A familiar example is the tendency to think in terms of opposites, such as *good/bad* or *addicted/nonaddicted*. Such thinking obscures the situational variability of behavior as well as the individual differences in behavior, feelings, or thoughts that may occur in a given context. For example, consider the term *addiction*. Patterns of substance use and abuse vary widely; the description of a client as addicted is not very informative. This does not indicate what substances are used, with what frequency, in what situations, nor offer any information about the functions served by ingestion of such substances (although within some practice perspectives all clients who are "addicted" are assumed to have similar personality dynamics, which purport to account for the addiction, and a description of the exact nature of the addiction may not be considered important). Decisions concerning degree of responsibility for an action differ depending on whether a person is the subject of the sentence, as in: "Ellen's car hit the fireplug," compared to "The fireplug was hit by Ellen's car" (Loftus, 1979, 1980). (See also Loftus, 1997, 2004.) Familiarity with the influence of semantic linkages and cuing effects may help us to avoid related errors. Statements can be rearranged to see if this yields different causal assumptions.

*Confusing Verbal and Factual Propositions*   Questions (such as "What is a borderline personality?") often involve disputes about use of words, as if they were questions of facts. Discussions of the meaning of mental illness are often conducted as if there were an independent, objective reality to be discovered, rather than with the realization that what will be accepted as referents for this term is at issue—a constructed reality, not a discovered reality. What must be established by critical inquiry is presuming as fact, as in the fallacy of begging the question (see Chapter 6). Questions of fact cannot be settled by arguments over the use of words. The problem of how to use a word is different from the problem of what is a fact. Pointing out the lack of objective criteria is helpful when there is a confusion between verbal and factual propositions.

*Misuse of Verbal Speculation*   This refers to the use of "speculative thinking to solve problems which can only be solved by the observation and interpretation of facts" (Thouless, 1974, p. 78). Speculation is valuable in discovering new possibilities, but it does not offer information about whether these insights are correct; that is, what is cannot be deduced from what ought to be, nor can vague terms referring to client behavior or situational contexts of interest be clarified simply by thinking about them. For example, if a client is described as a drug abuser and no information is provided about what this means, speculation will not be helpful. Facts gathered from some reliable and valid source are needed (see Chapter 13). Misuse of speculation occurs often in clinical practice and is not without its effects, since assumptions influence what we attend to. Thus, a little unchecked speculation can be a dangerous thing. The process of evidence-based practice encourages critical appraisal of speculation that may influence the quality of clients' lives.

*Conviction through Repetition*   Simply hearing, seeing, or thinking about a statement many times may increase belief in the statement. As Thouless (1974) notes, we tend to think that what goes through our mind must be important. A willingness to challenge even cherished beliefs helps to combat this source of error. Popper (1992) suggests that "We are all equal in our vast ignorance." Recognizing this may help us to question our beliefs. Valid inferences cannot be made on the basis of repeated affirmation, conviction, or the manner in which something is said. "If our examination of the facts leads to a conclusion which we find to be inconceivable, this need not be regarded as telling us anything about the facts, but only about the limits of our powers of conceiving" (Thouless, 1974, p. 80). Conviction through repetition may be attempted in case conferences to influence group members. For example, a client may be continually referred to as mentally incompetent, when in fact no evidence has been offered. Pointing out the danger of repeating unsupported assertions may be helpful in discouraging such descriptions.

Simply repeating a position increases the likelihood of its acceptance, especially if the statement is offered in a confident manner by a person of prestige and has a slogan quality that plays on our emotions. Repetitions of a statement are more effective if they are varied; we are less likely to discover that no reasons are provided as to why we should believe or act in a certain manner (Thouless, 1974). Consider the constant repetition in the media, professional journals, books, conferences, human service advertisements, and websites of the term "mental illness" and biomedical accounts of related behaviors (e.g., Clarke, Shim, Mamo, Fosket, & Fishman, 2003). This biomedical view of problems dominates these many venues. Only the motivated, the skeptical, the critical thinker will raise questions and seek out well-argued alternative views (e.g., see Leo & Cohen, 2003). The economic support of the American Psychiatric Association, and billions spent on promotion of biomedical accounts of client concerns by "Big Pharma," daily expose the public to the medical view of human behavior, including the funding of research (Angell, 2004; Kassirer, 2005). I do not mean to say that biomedical causes are not implicated in some behaviors, thoughts, or feelings. No doubt they are. But as Szasz (1994) suggests, if that is discovered, would not related disorders pass over into the field of neurology (as in certain kinds of dementia)?

*Bold Assertions*   People often act as if they have a conclusive argument when they do not. They may simply assert a position with no attempt to provide any evidence for it. A clinician may protest, "Mr. Greenwood is obviously a psychopath who is untreatable." A confident manner and bold assertions often accomplish what should be achieved only by offering sound reasons for a position. Words that are cues for this tactic include: *unquestionable, indisputably, the fact is, the truth is.* Bold assertions are a form of *begging the question;* the truth or falsity of the point is assumed (see Chapter 6). This informal fallacy, like many others, takes advantage of our tendency to be lulled into accepting a position because of the confidence with which it is described. Evidence should be requested for the position asserted. An example of a bold assertion is "We know that social work is effective. More than any other single profession, we see the youth in the settings where we work. We know what is needed and what works" ("From the President," [National Association of Social Workers], 1986, p. 2). In fact, there is considerable debate about this, and some research suggests the opposite (harming in the name of helping, e.g., McCord, 2003). Indeed, concerns about the gap between practice- and policy-related research and what practitioners draw on was a key reason for the development of evidence-based practice and health care.

*Primacy Effects*   We are influenced by what we see or hear first. This is referred to as the *primacy* or *anchoring* effect (Nisbett & Ross, 1980). What we hear or see first influences what we attend to, and thus influences our causal attributions. It narrows the range of data that is attended to. The influence of initial suggestions is shown by an experiment in which four groups of clinicians diagnosed a client under different conditions (Temerlin, 1968). One group was informed that the person was sane, one group was told that they were selecting scientists to work in research, one group (the control group) received no suggestions, and one group (the experimental group) was informed that the interviewee was mentally ill. Diagnoses were made by psychiatrists and clinical psychologists, who listened to a tape-recorded interview. The diagnoses differed greatly. All 25 psychiatrists and most of the clinical psychologists (22 of 25) in the experimental group made a diagnosis of mental illness. The majority of clinicians in the control group stated that the interviewee was mentally healthy. These results illustrate not only the influence of primacy effects on presumptions of illness but also concerns regarding psychiatric diagnoses. (See discussion of labels in Chapter 7.)

*Newsspeak*   *Newsspeak* refers to "language that distorts, confuses, or hides reality" (MacLean, 1981, p. 43). Examples from the media include *neutralized* (meaning, killed), *misspoke* (meaning, lied), and *air support* (meaning, bombing and strafing). *Newsspeak* refers to the intentional abuse of language to obscure the truth. Orwell (1958) wrote, "In our time, political speech and writing are largely in defense of the indefensible . . . political language has to consist of euphemisms, question begging, and sheer cloudy vagueness" (p. 136). Newsspeak occurs in the mental health industry as well, as illustrated in the following examples:

| *Statement or Term* | *Translation* |
| --- | --- |
| Fiscal constraints call for retrenchment. | Some people are going to be fired; clinics will be closed. |
| New policies have been put in place to ensure better services for clients. | All services will be provided by psychiatrists. |
| Improve your practice tenfold. | Attend Dr. X's workshop. |
| Pregnancy crisis center. | Prolife centers, which are anti-abortion. |
| Community care in place of warehousing. | Patients will be discharged from mental hospitals even though no adequate community care is available. |

The goal of protecting professional interests requires presenting one's own profession in a uniquely favorable light in comparison with other professions (Friedson, 1973). Political and economic aims increase the likelihood that stratagems will be used that distort material presented. Misleading or unfair headlines may be used; editors and publishers are aware that many more people read the headlines than read the material under the headlines. Thus, even if the small print presents an accurate view, the headlines may be misleading. Readers rarely are aware of what is not discussed in professional newsletters (see discussion of suppressed evidence in Chapter 4). Too seldom are the pros and cons concerning an issue presented, even though readers would benefit from this. Other sources of hidden bias include bias in the source of material, through selection or omission of material, in placement, in words, in selection of photographs, and hidden editorials (content presented as disinterested descriptions that actually give a biased account, advocating one particular position) (Cirino, 1971). Use of these devices may or may not be deliberate. Whether deliberate or accidental, they may have biasing effects. Familiarity with commonly used strategies and ways to avoid or counter these should be helpful in avoiding distorting influences (see also Chapter 6).

*Other Sources of Fallacy Related to Language*   Insisting on a specific definition of a term is inappropriate if this obscures the complexity of a situation. Vagueness of terms may be an advantage in the early stages of thinking about a topic, to discover approaches that otherwise may not be considered. Not recognizing that words differ in level of abstraction may create confusion and needless arguments. Both the one word-one meaning fallacy and the assumption that definitions are things reflect a confusion among (or ignorance of) different levels of abstraction. Metaphors may lead to faulty attributions and thus contribute to incorrect selection of intervention programs.

In the *fallacy of composition*, it is assumed that what is true of a part is also true of the whole. An example is the assumption that because each staff member in a psychiatric hospital is skilled, the hospital as a whole is an effective treatment center. A clinician may assume that because a young man has been caught stealing money at home he also engages in other criminal activities. The more vivid the particular behavior or person singled out for attention (that is, the more vivid the part), the more likely it is that generalizations will be made from the part to the entire person. In the *fallacy of division*, it is assumed that what is true of the whole is true of all the parts. A client may assume that because a clinic has a good reputation, every counselor on the staff is competent, but this is not necessarily true.

Ferreting out the nature of an argument is often difficult because of *excessive wordiness*. (Consider the example given in Chapter 3 under the section on analyzing arguments.) *Confusing factual and emotional uses of words* can result in errors. Offering descriptions is but one of the many functions of language. Persuading people to act is a common aim in many kinds of discourse, including professional contexts, and this is often accomplished through emotive use of language. Distinguishing between the emotive and informative uses of language should be helpful in avoiding influence by emotional terms.

The *eloquence* with which an argument is presented, whether in writing or in speech, is not necessarily related to its cogency; words that move and charm may not inform. To the contrary, eloquence may lull our critical powers into abeyance. Consider the Dr. Fox lecture. An actor who could convincingly present a "professional" manner was hired to give a lecture to psychiatrists, psychologists, social worker educators, psychiatric social workers, and other educators and administrators on the application of mathematics to human behavior (Naftulin, Ware, & Donnelly, 1973). Dr. Fox was introduced with an impressive list of qualifications and gave an eloquent lecture. Indeed, he knew nothing about the subject, but no one detected the ruse. Thus, a confident manner may accompany nonsense. Some clinicians are excellent orators and engaging writers. However, efforts to use methods they describe may prove frustrating because of a lack of clarity. A focus on the eloquence of a presentation may decrease motivation to examine arguments because one tends to focus on the words alone. Given the scarcity of eloquence, it is hard to resist a desire for more. Best of all is the combination of eloquence and clarity. A summary of ways in which language may influence inferences is offered in Exhibit 5.1. Examples of skills suggested by Diane Halpern (2003) for making effective use of language include the following:

- Recognize and avoid inappropriate use of emotional language, labeling, name calling, ambiguity, and vagueness.
- Detect misuse of definitions, reification, euphemism, and bureaucratese.
- Consider the goals of a communication, the background knowledge of the listener, and the context, when deciding what and how to communicate.
- Pay attention to framing effects (see Chapter 15).
- Use analogies appropriately (examine similarity and its relationship to a conclusion).
- Give a variety of examples when thinking about members of a category, so that you do not think about people in a category in terms of a prototype.
- Recognize when an anchor may bias your judgments about a quantity or cost, and consider alternative anchors.
- Use active questioning and explaining as a skill for comprehension.
- Practice retrieving information to increase the accuracy and fluidity of retrieval.
- Use graphic organizers (linear arrays, hierarchies, networks, matrices, flowcharts; Halpern, 2003, p. 133).

## THE INFLUENCE OF SOCIAL PSYCHOLOGICAL PERSUASION STRATEGIES

Persuasive attempts are common in clinical contexts. Clinicians try to persuade clients to carry out agreed-on tasks and try to convince other profes-

**Exhibit 5.1**
Sources of Errors Related to Use of Language

1. Assumption of one word, one meaning.
2. The fallacy of composition.
3. The fallacy of division.
4. Use of vague terms.
5. Shifting definitions of terms.
6. Reification (acting as if an abstract concept actually exists).
7. Influence by semantic linkages and cuing effects.
8. Predigested thinking.
9. Confusing verbal and factual propositions.
10. Use of pseudotechnical jargon.
11. Misuse of speculation (assuming that what is can be discovered by merely thinking about a topic).
12. Conviction through repetition.
13. Insistence on a specific definition that oversimplifies a situation.
14. Influence through emotional words.
15. Use of a confident manner and bold assertions.
16. Judgments based on primacy effects.
17. Newsspeak.
18. Excessive verbiage.
19. Misuse of labels.
20. Confusion of different levels of abstraction.
21. Confusion between descriptive and emotive uses of words.
22. Careless use of language.
23. Eloquence without clarity.

sionals to offer needed resources. Conversely, clinicians are the target of persuasive attempts by clients, colleagues, friends, family members, as well as by professional organizations, the pharmaceutical industry, and the mass media (e.g., see Angell, 2004; Burnham, 1987). The essence of persuasion is influencing someone to think or act in a certain manner. There is an extensive literature on persuasion (e.g., see Brock & Green, 2005; Dillard & Pfau, 2002; Wosinka, Cialdini, & Barrett, 2001). Persuasion may occur intentionally or unconsciously, as a part of the interpersonal context in which exchanges take place. Both beliefs and actions are influenced by persuasion efforts, which may be masked in terms of their intent to influence. Knowledge about social-psychological persuasion strategies is important for clinicians, both in resisting unwanted effects that dilute the quality of decisions and in effectively using persuasive appeals toward clinically desired ends. Competence in the use of influence is a key component of "practical intelligence." One route to persuasion is based on thoughtful consideration of arguments related to a topic. This review could, of course, be biased, because of one or more of the information-processing errors described in other chapters. The other major route is through emotional associations or inferences based on peripheral cues in the persuasion context, such as our mood or the status of the person offering a "pitch" (Petty & Cacioppo, 1986, p. 191). In the first route, there is an elaboration process; we are motivated to think about arguments for and against a position.

Persuasion by affect (the "affect heuristic") comes into play when we do not engage in elaboration and are influenced not so much by what people say but by extraneous variables, such as how attractive they are or how confidently they present their views (e.g., see Slovic, Finucane, Peters, & MacGregor, 2002). Persuasion strategies based on liking and authority attain their impact largely because of affective associations. The elaboration likelihood model suggests that we must be both motivated and able to engage in the cognitive effort to critique information regarding a topic, person, or idea (see Petty, Cacioppo, Strathman, & Priester, 2005). Within this model it is suggested that a given variable may serve as a cue as to what to believe by influencing the amount of elaboration we engage in, or it may bias the direction of elaboration (Fabrigar, Smith, & Brannon, 1999). Here we have yet another example of different ways to reach a decision—quickly based on emotions or in a more deliberative, thoughtful manner. What we use is the subject of considerable research and is of great interest to advertisers of products.

Becoming familiar with persuasion strategies and decreasing automatic influence by these tactics should upgrade the quality of your clinical decisions. Compliance-induction strategies will be more readily identified, and thus you will be in a better position to decide if going along with the strategies will diminish or enhance the quality of decisions. (See Cialdini, 2001, for an entertaining, well-written, and empirically based description of such strategies.) In everyday life, the principles on which these strategies are based provide convenient shortcuts that often work for us. We don't have time to fully consider the merits of each action we take or "pitch" we hear—we take shortcuts that often work for us (see Chapter 9). These compliance-induction strategies thus take advantage of our natural human tendencies. However, people can exploit them for their own purposes; our automatic reactions work in their favor. "All the exploiters need do is to trigger the great stores of influence that exist in a situation and direct them toward the intended target. . . . Even the victims themselves tend to see their compliance as due to the actions of natural forces rather than to the designs of the person who profits from that compliance" (Cialdini, 1984, p. 24). Thus, these strategies offer others the ability to manipulate without the appearance of manipulation. (See also Cialdini & Sagarin, 2005.)

The principle of liking is one of the most frequently used persuasive strategies. We like to please people we know and like; we like to comply with their requests. Clinicians prefer clients who are likeable (see Chapter 2). The liking rule is often used by people we do not know, to gain our compliance. Factors that encourage liking include physical attractiveness, similarity, compliments, familiarity, and cooperation (see discussion of the influence of client characteristics in Chapter 2). "Compliance professionals are forever attempting to establish that we and they are working for the same goals, that we must 'pull together' for mutual benefit, that they are, in essence, teammates" (p. 182). The "good guy/bad guy" routine takes advantage of the liking rule—we like the good guy (in contrast to the bad guy), so we comply with what he wants. The rule of liking also works through conditioning and association. Workshops that advertisers wish clinicians to attend are associated with positive qualities such as "big names" (for example, Albert Ellis). Clinicians will be more receptive to new material if they like the person presenting it. Associating "pitches" with food, as in the "luncheon technique," is a well-known strategy (Razran, described in Cialdini, 2001, p. 167). Concerns about disapproval are often responsible for a reluctance to offer counterarguments to popular views in case conferences.

Another persuasion strategy is based on a desire to be (and appear) consistent with what we have already done. (This is *not* a trait of creative people.) A colleague may argue that because insight therapy was used to help a client with her depression, it should also be used to help her with her substance-abuse problem. A clinician may be reluctant to alter a service plan, even though such a change will help to achieve client-desired outcomes because of a fear of appearing inconsistent to a client. Being consistent usually works for us. "But because it is so typically in our best interests to be consistent, we easily fall into the habit of being automatically so, even in situations where it is not the sensible way to be" (Cialdini, 1984, pp. 68–69). Consistency can protect us from troubling realizations we would rather not think about. Since automatic consistency "functions as a shield against thought" (p. 72), it can be exploited by people who want us to comply with their requests. Gaining commitment sets the consistency rule into effect. "Commitment strategies are . . . intended to get us to take some action or make some statement that will trap us into later compliance through consistency pressures" (p. 75). An advertisement for a clinical workshop on a new intervention method may urge readers to reserve a space now—to ensure a place (scarcity principle)—and send a refundable deposit of $10.00 (commitment). A clinician may encourage a reluctant spouse to come in for "just one interview," hoping to persuade him to enter a course of relationship counseling.

Obtaining an initial concession or offering a favor may be used to gain compliance through the influence of the reciprocity rule; we feel obliged to return favors. A colleague who is eager to receive referrals may refer some clients to other clinicians. Offering concrete help at an early point may be used to encourage clients to participate in a counseling program. It may be difficult to counter or neutralize the influence of reciprocation, since we often do not know whether an offer is an honest one or the first step in an exploitation attempt. The rule of reciprocity "entitles a person who has acted in a certain way to a dose of the same thing" (Cialdini, 1984, p. 65). Thus, if an action is viewed as a compliance device instead of a favor, this rule will not work as an ally. The reciprocity rule lies behind the success of the "rejection-then-retreat technique," in which a small request follows a large request—the small request is viewed as a "concession," and is likely to be reciprocated by a concession from the other person. For example, when college students were asked to serve as chaperones for a group of juvenile delinquents on a day trip to the zoo, 83 percent of those requested refused. However, when this was first preceded by a larger request—which they refused (to spend 2 hours a week for 2 years as a counselor to the delinquent), three times as many students agreed to the smaller request (Cialdini, 1984, pp. 50–51). The contrast effect is also at work here (see later discussion).

Informal fallacies appealing to pseudoauthority take advantage of our tendency to go along with authorities (see examples in Chapter 6). Many appeals to authority are symbolic, such as certain kinds of titles; they connote rather than offer any content supporting the credibility of the authority. Some appeals to authority attempt to influence through fear, as in the advertisement for professional liability insurance in Exhibit 5.2. The test format is designed to convey a sense of "authority." Notice that no facts and figures are presented in relation to what percent of social workers are sued for what reasons. Types of strategies used are noted on the table. Understanding the basis for the effectiveness of informal fallacies that appeal to pseudoauthority should be helpful in resisting appeals that compromise the quality of decisions.

**Exhibit 5.2**
Self-Test Advertisement for Professional Liability Insurance.

*Test Yourself*

Answer the following questions to find out whether you need malpractice coverage.

| Yes  No | | Type of Strategy |
|---|---|---|
| 1. __ __ | I am a practicing social worker. | (setting the stage) |
| 2. __ __ | I don't have my own coverage if I'm sued for malpractice. | (fear induction) |
| 3. __ __ | I let my malpractice coverage drop. | (fear induction) |
| 4. __ __ | I've heard about other social workers being sued. | (fear induction) |
| 5. __ __ | I know I need my own liability insurance, even though my employer provides it. | (neutralization of counterarguments) |
| 6. __ __ | I'm aware that malpractice suits against social workers have considerably increased over the past few years. | (fear induction) |
| 7. __ __ | I don't want to worry about being sued. | (fear induction) |

*Source:* From 1987, *NASW News, 32*(4), p. 17. Copyright 1987 by National Association of Social Workers. Reprinted with permission.

The scarcity principle rests on the fact that opportunities seem more valuable when their availability is limited (Cialdini, 1984, p. 230). A prospective client who is informed that a clinician has no time to take on any new clients for 2 months may value the chance to work with this clinician even more. A nursing home intake worker may say, "If you don't decide now, space may not be available" (which may not be true). Here too, as with the impulse to use other shortcuts, it is accurate in its basic thrust; things that are scarce are usually more valuable; also, freedom is lost as opportunities become less available. Cialdini (1984) provides a good example of the influence of the scarcity principle:

> One set of customers heard a standard sales presentation before being asked for their orders. Another set of customers heard the standard sales presentation plus information that the supply of imported beef was likely to be scarce in the upcoming months. A third group received the standard sales presentation and the information about a scarce supply of beef, too; however, they also learned that the scarce supply news was not generally available information. It had come, they were told, from certain exclusive contacts that the company had. Thus the customers who received this last sales presentation learned that not only was the availability of the product limited, so also was the news concerning it—the scarcity double whammy. . . . Compared to customers who got only the standard sales appeal, those who were told about the future scarcity of beef bought more than twice as much. But the real boost in sales occurred among the customers who heard of the impending scarcity via "exclusive" information. They purchased six times the amount that the customers who received only the standard sales pitch did. (Cialdini, 1984, p. 239; based on Knishinsky, 1982)

Actions are often guided by the principle of social proof—that is, finding out what other people think is correct. (Creative people are not as likely to follow this principle.) This principle also provides a convenient shortcut that often works well; however, if it is accepted automatically, it can result in errors. A clinician may decide that since most clinicians refer clients to Alcoholics Anonymous, he or she will do so as well. The danger in appealing to the principle of social proof is the "pluralistic ignorance phenomenon" (Cialdini, 1984, p. 129): The majority view may be (and often is) incorrect. As with other social-psychological sources of influence, this one is more effective under some conditions than under others. Uncertainty increases the effects of this principle; we are more likely to go along with what other people do in ambiguous situations. Similarity also influences the impact of social proof; this principle operates most powerfully when we observe the behavior of people who are similar to ourselves. Observation of the behavior of people who are similar offers "the greatest insight into what constitutes correct behavior for ourselves" (Cialdini, 1984, p. 140). False evidence may be provided to influence people through the principle of social proof, such as claiming (without evidence) that hundreds have benefited from use of a new therapy.

We are also influenced by the contrast effect. A client who is fairly cooperative may be viewed as extremely cooperative following an interview with a
very resistant person. Men assign more negative ratings of pictures of potential blind dates when they are watching *Charlie's Angels* on TV than when they
are watching some other program (Kenrick & Gutierres, 1980).

## SUMMARY

Misuse of language contributes to inaccurate clinical decisions. Careless
use of language is perhaps the greatest source of error. Confusion about the
different functions of language may result in muddled discussions, as may
confusion among different levels of abstraction. If terms are not clarified, confused discussions (or thinking) may result, due to the assumption of one word,
one meaning. Reification of terms (using a descriptive term as an explanatory
term) offers an illusion of understanding without providing any real understanding. Technical terms may be carelessly used, resulting in "bafflegarb" or
"psychobabble"—words that sound informative but are empty and not helpful for making sound decisions. We are often unaware of the influence of emotional terms. Labels, for example, have emotional connotations that influence
us in ways that do not necessarily enhance the accuracy of decisions. We are
influenced by primacy effects (by what we hear first) and are often guilty of
the misuse of verbal speculation (assuming that what is can be discovered by
merely thinking about it). Knowledge of fallacies related to use of language
and care in using language while thinking, listening, writing, or reading
should improve the quality of decisions.

Clinicians both use and are influenced by social-psychological persuasion
appeals in their everyday practice. A thorough knowledge of these strategies
can be of value in avoiding sources of influence that decrease the accuracy
of decisions. Learning how to recognize and counter persuasion strategies
(such as attempted influence based on liking and appeals to consistency,
authority, or scarcity) should increase well-reasoned decisions.

# CHAPTER 6

# Formal and Informal Fallacies: Mistakes in Thinking and How to Avoid Them

FALLACIES THAT FREQUENTLY OCCUR in clinical (as well as other) contexts are described in this chapter as well as in Chapter 5. Informal fallacies may be used to avoid critical appraisal of claims. The term *fallacy* refers to an error or mistake in thinking. Becoming familiar with fallacies and acquiring effective ways to avoid them should enhance the quality of clinical decisions. Familiarity with the names of fallacies can be helpful in identifying them and in pointing them out to others. The focus of attention concerning fallacies typically has been on clients: assessment of their thinking patterns and the identification of how distortions in their thinking are related to personal problems they experience (see, for example, Beck, 1976; Burns, 1999; Ellis & Grieger, 1977). The focus here is on clinicians, educators, researchers, and peer reviewers—on how formal and informal fallacies may compromise the quality of decisions they make, for example whether to and how to describe well-argued alternative views of controversies that affect clients. Errors that may result include assuming that pathology exists when it does not, missing pathology that is present, and selection of ineffective practice methods. Practice- and policy-related research findings may be ignored because they are associated with a disliked practice perspective, resulting in harming in the name of helping.

There have been many attempts to classify the different kinds of fallacies and a variety of systems have been suggested (Hamblin, 1970). "Not the least of the merits of a really good classification of fallacies would be that it could be used in the formulation of appropriate points of order. . . . It should be made possible in principle, as Bentham wished, that the perpetrator of fallacy be greeted with voices in scores crying aloud 'Stale! Stale! Fallacy of Authority! Fallacy of Distrust!' and so on" (p. 284; for descriptions of fallacies, see for example, Damer, 1995; Engel, 1994; Kahane & Cavender, 1998; Thouless, 1974). The term *trick* or *stratagem* refers to informal fallacies that are often used deliberately as persuasion strategies, although they also may occur because of sloppy thinking or lack of critical thinking skills. Fallacies may be intentional or unintentional. Intentional fallacies could be called deceptions. Does it make a difference? It may in terms of what must be done to avoid their influence. Gibbs and Gambrill (1999) include three reasoning-in-practice games designed to increase awareness of fallacies in reasoning when making clinical decisions. Gibbs (2003) includes interactive videos that offer practice in spotting such fallacies. The list at the end of this chapter includes a catalogue of flaws in thinking discussed here and in other chapters that may interfere with making sound decisions.

## FALSE EVEN THOUGH VALID

Some arguments are false even though they are valid. A valid argument is one whose premises, if true, offers good or sufficient grounds for accepting a conclusion.

*Doubtful Evidence*   One kind of "false even though valid" argument is that in which conclusions are accepted even though the premises are questionable. For example, it may be assumed that problems have a biochemical cause based on findings described in flawed studies of neuroimaging (Leo & Cohen, 2003). That is, someone may insist that the form of an argument is valid while ignoring the possible (or probable) inaccuracy of the premises. Clinicians often refer clients to other practitioners; they make decisions about the competence of colleagues. It may be assumed that "All psychologists are competent. Max is a psychologist. Therefore, Max is competent." If the premises are true, the conclusion is true. However, the truth of the first premise is debatable, and because one of the premises is doubtful, the argument is unsound, and a client may be referred to a clinician who is not competent to offer needed services. (An argument must be both valid and have accurate premises for it to be sound.) Because the argument stands or falls on whether a false premise is accepted, those who use doubtful evidence often try to distract readers or listeners from examining the premises; they may even try to use a "below the belt" technique such as ridicule.

Many facts are unknowable by anyone (for example, the exact number of gay/lesbian people who live in the United States). Some facts are potentially knowable or are known by someone, but are not known by the person who is using doubtful evidence. Doubtful evaluation refers to the insertion of an "unsupported controversial value judgment into an argument as a premise" (Kahane, 1971, p. 9). This may be confused with simple opinion statements, which are not really arguments (see Chapter 3). Examples of such statements are, "behavioral methods are superficial" and "psychoanalytic methods are overly complex in their view of causative factors." Some arguments contain premises that are contradictory, so even if the form of the argument is accurate, the conclusions cannot be true. The contradictory nature of the premises may not be obvious because of vagueness.

*Suppressed Evidence*    The suppression of evidence is one of the most widely and successfully used strategies. (See also discussion of propaganda in Chapter 4.) These "errors of omission" allow people to create false impressions and mislead others without actually lying. For example, in a recent newspaper article a pharmaceutical representative claimed that their drug was responsible for decreasing surgery for stomach ulcers. No mention was made that the decreased need for surgery was mainly due to the discovery that ulcers were caused by a bacterium. A drug company may run 10 trials to examine the effectiveness of a drug, only 2 of which are positive, and send only these to the FDA for approval. It may test many people on a placebo and drop all placebo reactors before randomly distributing remaining subjects to a placebo and drug condition (Antonnucio, Burns, & Danton, 2002). It may not share information that use of an antidepressant results in a significant risk of suicide (Healy, 2003). One kind of evidence that is often not shared with clients is information about the evidentiary status of recommended intervention methods in relation to other options (Braddock et al., 1999). That is, a clinician may suggest to the client that "x" intervention is best without informing the client that other options are available that may have greater empirical support concerning their effectiveness. This may influence decisions of clients to go along with the method proposed. In such situations, clients are involved as uninformed participants, in violation of professional codes of ethics that call for informed consent.

A drug company may not inform people that use of a drug results only in a two point drop in the Hamilton Depression Scale and that the other eight point drop is matched by a placebo group—and that people are still depressed. Clients are often unaware of what is not offered to them and so are in a disadvantaged position to request alternative methods. One remedy here is for the client to ask the practitioner whether there are alternative methods and, if the answer is yes, to seek information about their evidentiary status. Information concerning the false-positive and false-negative rates regarding a diagnostic measure may not be reported in an article describing this measure. Without these data, clinicians may make incorrect decisions because of overestimating the accuracy of a measure. Reviews of web sites regarding screening for breast cancer found that the negative effects of overdiagnosis and overtreatment are often not mentioned (Jørgensen & Gøtzsche, 2004; Thornton, Edwards, & Baum, 2003). Only relative rates may be given, omitting information about absolute rates (see Chapter 15).

Presenting only facts that serve one's own purpose while ignoring other relevant data is especially insidious, because readers or listeners are often unaware of information left out (MacLean, 1981, p. 37). It is a form of propaganda (see Chapter 4). There may be a conscious effort to suppress evidence. For example, someone may not just have a point of view that he is open to examining, but be interested in persuading us of the truth of a conclusion by appealing to our emotions. However, not considering important evidence related to a claim may be unintentional; it may occur because of unrecognized biases and preconceptions (see discussion of partiality in use of evidence in Chapter 14). The more educated the readers or listeners are, the more likely it may be that a tactic such as suppressed evidence is used rather than an obvious ploy, such as use of emotional language.

Published sources contribute to influence by suppressed evidence, by failing to discuss well-argued alternative views of issues and by not including corrections of inaccurate reports. Boyle (2002), for example, identifies many examples of suppression of contradictory data in her book *Schizophrenia: A Scientific Delusion*? Many books, articles and media reports attest to censorship of negative results regarding the effects of certain drugs on the part of pharmaceutical companies (e.g., see Angell, 2004). A sophisticated campaign may be mounted to suppress data contradictory to a preferred position, as illustrated in the following excerpts from an article describing court proceedings concerning the death of a smoker (Janson, 1988, p. A13):

> "Evidence presented by the plaintiff," Judge Sarokin said, "particularly that contained in documents of the defendants themselves, indicates the development of a public relations strategy aimed at combating the mounting adverse scientific reports regarding the dangers of smoking."
>
> "The evidence indicates further that the industry of which these defendants were and are a part entered into a sophisticated conspiracy. The conspiracy was organized to refute, undermine and neutralize information coming from the scientific and medical community and, at the same time, to confuse and mislead the consuming public in an effort to encourage existing smokers to continue and new persons to commence smoking."
>
> Judge Sarokin noted that evidence had been introduced showing that results of industry-sponsored research adverse to the industry's goals had been "suppressed and concealed."
>
> "At least one scientist testified as to threats made to him if he published his findings, and there was other evidence of attempts to suppress or coerce others," he said.

The remedy to the use of suppressed evidence depends partly on whether the suppression is intentional or unintentional. The goal is to identify unmentioned information that bears on the accuracy of a claim. Possible options include (1) seeking information from alternative sources, such as talking to people holding other views or reviewing information on various web sites, especially those with a reputation for rigorous appraisal, such as the Cochrane and Campbell databases; (2) exploring negative as well as positive effects of a decision; and (3) asking speakers if there is anything else we should know before making a decision, such as important consequences of a proposed view that have not been mentioned, or alternative options; speakers may not be willing to lie and so share suppressed views and relevant evidence, or they may be unwilling to appear uninformed at a later date by having failed to do so under direct questioning.

## IRRELEVANT APPEALS

Some common irrelevant appeals are described in the sections that follow. Irrelevant appeals include fallacies in which the wrong point is supported or when a conclusion established by premises is not relevant to the issues being discussed. These are informal fallacies, that is, none involve a formal mistake. Many such fallacies achieve their effect by taking advantage of one or more of our natural tendencies, such as wanting to please others or going along with what others think (the principle of social proof).

*Ad Hominem Arguments*   Here, the background, habits, associates, or personality of an individual are attacked or appealed to, rather than his or her argument. Rather than arguing *ad rem* (to the argument), someone argues *"ad hominem,"* to the person proposing it. The appeal or attack may be subtle or obvious. You may suggest that an advocacy group should be made up of community residents because they have had experience with advocacy and are eager to work together. Another staff member may respond "But how can you say this? You haven't completed your clinical training program yet." Rather than addressing your argument, he is commenting on your education. This example illustrates that ad hominem appeals may function as diversions—an attempt to sidetrack people. Consider the ad hominem attacks directed toward Jeffrey Masson (1988), author of the controversial book *Against Therapy;* rather than addressing the arguments made in the book, some writers chose to make negative statements about the author. The theories of Jung may be rejected because of his alleged racism and anti-Semitism; this rejection is made on an ad hominem basis: these alleged characteristics do not necessarily bear on the cogency of his theory. Improper appeals to authority to support a position are a kind of ad hominem argument. The effectiveness of ad hominem arguments depend partially on the principle of liking (disliking), as well as the principle of authority (see Chapter 5).

Is an ad hominem attack or appeal ever relevant? (For a detailed discussion see relevant readings in Hansen & Pinto, 1995.) If an attack on the presenter of the argument is related to the issue at hand, then in some cases it may be relevant. For example, someone could be shown to offer unreliable accounts on most occasions. However, this person may be offering a correct account this time. Thus, the credibility of the person presenting an argument is important to consider. Ad hominem arguments are surprisingly effective for a variety of reasons, only one of which is failure to identify the fallacious nature of the argument. Others include the following:

- Implicit agreement with the implications about the individual
- Agreement with the conclusion of the argument with little concern for its correctness
- Unwillingness to raise questions, cause a fuss, or challenge authorities who may counterattack
- Social pressures in group settings—not wanting to embarrass others

The remedy in relation to ad hominem arguments is to point out that the appeal made provides no evidence for or against a claim.

Guilt (or credit) by association is a variation of an ad hominem argument—judging people by the company they keep. A youth accused of theft may associate with a gang known to engage in a variety of criminal activities. Such association offers indirect, circumstantial evidence—it does not offer direct support for the argument that he is guilty. The best use of circumstantial or indirect evidence is as a cue for further exploration. There may be a grain of truth in assessing an argument by considering the associates of the person proposing it. However, not all of an individual's friends may be disreputable or uninformed (or reputable or informed, in the case of assumptions of credit). And, even if they all are (either one or the other), the individual may still speak the truth. An attempt to discredit a position may be made by associating it with a disliked institution, value, or philosophy, as in the statement that behavioral methods are antihumanistic or psychoanalytic methods are antifeminist. "Imposter terms" or "euphemisms" may be used to make an unpopular view or method acceptable. For example, use of long-term lockups in a prison may be referred to as behavior modification. Dumping patients into the community from mental hospitals may be called "community care." As Nickerson (1986a) points out, we are more likely to agree with institutions and philosophies we favor—however, it is unlikely that we will agree with every facet, and similarly, it is unlikely that we would disagree with every aspect of a disliked view. So, "Credit or discredit by association becomes a fallacy when it is applied in a blind and uncritical way. Whether or not a particular view is one that is held by a specific individual, institution, or philosophy that we generally support (or oppose) is very meager evidence as to the tenability of that view" (Nickerson, 1986a, p. 116).

In the bad seed fallacy, it is assumed that a person's character or habits are passed on to his descendants (Michalos, 1971, p. 54); that because a client's parents acted in a certain way, that is why the client acts in this manner. The bad seed fallacy is quite common in clinical contexts. A striking example of guilt by association is shown in the excerpts from a case conference given in Chapter 16. Genetic factors do play a role in influencing behavior; however, the correlations presented are typically far from perfect and, in any case, may not support a causal connection (Strohman, 2003).

An argument may be made that a position is not acceptable because the person's motives for supporting the issue are questionable. For example, a proposal that a new suicide prevention center be created may be denied on the grounds that those who propose this are "interested parties"—that they will profit from such a center by gaining needed jobs. In fact, the accuracy or inaccuracy of the view proposed cannot be determined from an examination of the motives of those who proposed it, but only from an examination of the evidence presented in its favor. It may be argued that because our intentions or motives are good, a claim is true. A psychologist may wish to place a child on Ritalin even though there is little evidence that this is indicated. He may protest that his intent is to help this child. Appeals to good intentions are the opposite of the assumption of suspect motives. In both cases, evidence is needed that the claim is correct; motives, whether altruistic or otherwise, are not evidence.

The fallacy of special pleading involves favoring our own interests by using different standards for different people, as in "I am firm, thou art obstinate, he is pigheaded" (Thouless, 1974, p. 11). A clinician may claim that she does not have to evaluate her work as carefully as other clinicians because of her lengthy experience.

A discrepancy between a person's behavior and his principles may be invalidly used against him. For example, an argument may be dismissed on the grounds that the person's behavior is not consistent with his argument. A clinician who is not sympathetic to behavioral methods may say to his behavioral friend, "If behaviorists know so much about how to change behavior, why are you still smoking when you want to stop?"

Another kind of false claim of inconsistency is when a charge is made that a person's behavior is not consistent with his principles when his principles have changed. It may be argued that because a clinician held a certain view many years ago, he holds the same view today. Altering a position does not necessarily entail inconsistency. It depends on whether a person states that his position has changed and explains the reasons for these changes. Not recognizing that people often have rational grounds for changing their opinions results in a false charge of inconsistency. This fallacy takes advantage of our desire to be consistent and to expect others to be consistent as well. (See discussion of persuasion in Chapter 5.)

Objections to a position or action may be countered with "You'd do it, too, if you had an opportunity," as in "You would refer difficult clients to someone else if you could." This argument does not provide evidence for (or against) a position.

*Vacuous Guarantees*   A warrant may be offered for a claim that is without substance. Self-help books have long been criticized for offering unsupported, vacuous guarantees of effectiveness (Rosen, 1982). For example, an advertisement in a professional journal directed to mental health facilities and substance abuse centers assures potential customers interested in consultation, training, and supervision that "it works," that they "custom-design safe programs," that "I can, you can, together we can." No criteria are described as to what is meant by "it works" or what a "safe program" consists of. No evidence is offered in support of claims made. The costs in time and money of holding people responsible for vacuous claims may outweigh any benefits.

The fallacy of ignorance involves the assumption "that the absence of evidence for (against) a claim must be counted as evidence for (against) it" (Michalos, 1971, p. 52). A clinician may argue that because there is no evidence showing that "directed aggression" (hitting objects such as pillows) does not work, it should be used. The fact that no one can think of a course of action that is better than one proposed may be used as an argument that the proposed course is a good one. In fact, they could all be bad. It is hard to believe that this fallacy would ever work (that is, influence people), but it does, as do some other weak appeals—such as simply asserting that a position is true.

An example of the fallacy of appeals to will is to say that "if he really wanted to . . . he would." It would be hoped that clinicians, with their more sophisticated conceptualizations of motivation (compared with laymen), would not use appeals to will. However, I have heard clinicians say, "If she was interested in getting better, she'd come in for counseling." Appeals to "will power" offer no information about how to create desired changes. Wishful thinking involves the assumption that because some condition ought to be, it is the case—without providing any support for the position. This fallacy could also be included under the category of begging the question. Statements made about declassification (hiring staff without advanced clinical degrees) are often of this variety. That is, it is assumed that declassification is bad; no evidence is presented to support the position by showing, for example, that hiring staff without graduate degrees results in lower quality services for clients. "We continue to hear about professional caregivers coming into conflict with case managers who lack the requisite training to perform the complicated tasks involved in assessment and evaluation" ("From the President," 1987, p. 2). No evidence is provided that case managers without professional training lack the requisite skills to perform the tasks described and the conflict alluded to is assumed to reflect negatively on the case managers rather than on "professional caregivers."

Attacking the example is a relatively transparent strategy—the example given of a position is attacked rather than the position itself. The example offered might not be an apt one. A remedy here is to point out that a successful attack on the example does not take away from the possible soundness of a position, and to offer a better example. This fallacy is the opposite of the use of a suspect particular case as proof for a generalization (see later discussion). It may be argued that two wrongs make a right—that because other people do something, it is all right to do the same. Common practice is a variety of this fallacy. It may be argued that it is all right not to keep up with practice-related empirical literature because other clinicians do not do so.

## EVADING THE FACTS

Fallacies that evade the facts, such as begging the question, appear to address the facts but do not: "Such arguments deceive by inviting us to presume that the facts are as they have been stated in the argument, when the facts are quite otherwise" (Engel, 1982, p. 114).

*Begging the Question*   This refers to assuming the truth or falsity of what is at issue; that is, trying to settle a question by simply reasserting a position. This tactic is surprisingly effective often because it is accompanied by appeals to authority. Such appeals take advantage of persuasive bases, such as liking (we are less likely to question poor arguments of people we like), authority (we accept what experts say), and social proof (we are influenced by what other people do). Consider the statement, "The inappropriate releasing of mentally ill patients must be ended." The speaker assumes that releasing mentally ill patients is inappropriate, instead of offering evidence to show that it is. Presenting opinions as facts is a common variant of this fallacy. Michalos (1971) has identified seven ways to beg the question, some of which overlap with improper appeals to authority (see Chapter 7). Question-begging descriptions can be used as a clue that relevant facts are being evaded.

Alleged certainty may be used to encourage readers or listeners to accept a claim without any evidence that the claim is accurate. The claim is presented as if it were obvious, in the hope that our critical senses will be neutralized. Examples are (1) "No one doubts the number of alcoholics in the United States today." (2) "It is well accepted that therapy works."

Appeals to consensus may be made with no evidence provided that there is a consensus concerning a position. This appeal, as well as the appeal of alleged certainty, takes advantage of the principle of social proof (our tendency to believe that what most other people think or do is correct). A clinician may say that "use of play therapy with autistic children is the accepted method of choice." Even if evidence for a consensus is offered, that does not mean that the position is correct. Consensus is a notoriously unreliable ground on which to believe a claim.

Speakers or writers are guilty of using question-begging epithets when they add evaluative terms to neutral descriptive terms—the aim is to influence through emotional reactions. For example, "Fairview Hospital opened today" is a simple declarative statement. "The long-needed Fairview Hospital opened its doors today" includes evaluative epithets. Examples of question-begging can be seen in the descriptions of Mary Walsh in Chapter 16. Variations of this fallacy include the use of emotive language (see Chapter 5), loaded words, and verbal suggestion. Emotional terms may be used to attempt to prejudice the facts by using evaluative language that supports what we want to demonstrate but have not shown. "By overstatement, ridicule, flattery, abuse and the like, they seek to evade the facts" (Engel, 1982, p. 120).

Circular arguments are a form of question-begging, as in the following example (Engel, 1982, p. 142).

> People can't help what they do.
> Why not?
> Because they always follow the strongest motive.
> But what is the strongest motive?
> It is, of course, the one that people follow.

This argument is circular in saying that A is so because of B and B is true because of A. The conclusion that a speaker or writer is trying to establish is used as a premise or presupposed as a premise. Such circular arguments may seem so transparent that they would never be a problem in clinical practice. However, they occur in clinical practice. Consider the following dialogue.

> Mr. Levine can't control his outbursts.
> Why is that?
> Because he is developmentally disabled.
> Why do you say that he is developmentally disabled?
> Well, because he has outbursts when he is frustrated.

Attributing the cause of outbursts to the developmental disability offers no information about how to alter the frequency of the outbursts.

A clinician may alter a definition or question a diagnosis rather than admit that a counterexample to a position has been identified. Believers in the disease view of alcoholism contend that drinkers who can return to limited nonproblem drinking were never "true alcoholics." "In its extreme, this argument maintains that even individuals who have suffered distinct alcohol withdrawal symptoms must have been misclassified as alcoholics" (Sobell & Sobell, 1982, p. 156). As Michalos (1971) points out, "facts cannot shake the generalization because the truth is guaranteed by definitions."

Apriorism is a form of question-begging in which a position is claimed as true (prior to any investigation) because it is necessary according to a particular view of the world (or of clinical practice). Consider the assertion of psychiatrists that they should supervise treatment of patients (implying that psychologists and other kinds of mental health professionals, such as social workers, would work under their supervision) and that to arrange services otherwise (to allow other kinds of professionals to work autonomously) would lower the quality of service offered to clients. The view of practice that is assumed is that training as a psychiatrist is superior to other kinds of professional training. This is not necessarily true. What is needed is a description of evidence for and against the position advanced.

Unfounded generalizations may be used to support a conclusion. For example, someone may say, "Offering positive incentives for desired behaviors is dehumanizing because it is behavioral." The assumptions are that behavioral methods are dehumanizing and that offering positive incentives for desired behaviors is behavioral. Since the truth of the wider generalizations is questionable, the particular example is questionable. A supervisor could beg the question of whether practice should be evaluated on the grounds that this violates client confidentiality. When a more general claim is assumed, the accuracy of this claim should be examined.

Complex, leading, or trick questions with indirect assumptions may be used. A question may be asked in such a way that any answer will incriminate the speaker (for example, "Do you still beat your wife?" or "Where do you keep your cocaine?"). This is the interrogative form of the fallacy of begging the question; the conclusion at issue is assumed rather than supported. "Complex questions accomplish this by leading one to believe that a particular answer to a prior question has been answered in a certain way when this may not be the case" (Engel, 1982, p. 122). These questions bring with them assumptions that influence how they will be answered. The remedy is to question the question. Because of their leading nature, some questions would be ruled out in a court of law, given that lawyers were on their toes. Such questions are also fallacious "because they assume that one and the same answer must apply to both the unasked and the asked question as in the example of 'Isn't Dr. Green an unthinking feminist?'" (p. 124). If the question is divided into its parts, different answers may apply: Is Dr. Green a feminist? Is she unthinking? Thus, the remedy is to divide the original question into its implied components and answer each one at a time.

Complex questions are often used to encourage clients to comply with a request, as in the example of a staff member who is having trouble getting a patient to take a bath. Rather than asking him if he wants to take a bath tonight, she might say, "Do you want to take a bath now or at seven?" Another variation of complex questions is requesting explanations for supposed facts that have not been supported, as in "How do you account for extrasensory perception (ESP)"? Since there is controversy about whether ESP exists, and many people believe that research exploring such phenomena has yielded negative results (see, for example, Blackmore, 1987), there may be no extraordinary effects to explain, perhaps just fallacies or questionable experimental designs to be uncovered.

One way to respond to a criticism is to ignore it—that is, to simply proceed as if the statements had never been made. This tactic can be successful if no one is present who will object, perhaps because everyone agrees with the original position. One form of ignoring the issue is to claim there is no issue. The question may be swept aside as irrelevant, trivial, or offensive.

## OVERLOOKING THE FACTS

Relevant facts are often neglected, as in the fallacy of the sweeping generalization, in which a rule or assumption that is valid in general is applied to a specific example to which it is not valid (Engel, 1982, 1994). It might be argued that since expressing feelings is healthy, Susan should do it more, because it will increase her self-esteem and make her happier. However, if expressing feelings will result in negative consequences from significant others (such as work supervisors and her husband), the general rule may not apply here. This kind of fallacy can be exposed by identifying the rule involved and showing that it cannot be applied accurately to the case at hand. (Another name for this fallacy is the fallacy of accident; Toulmin et al., 1979, p. 161.) The fallacy of hasty generalization is the opposite of the one above; here, an example is used as the basis for a general conclusion that is not warranted. For example, if a psychologist has an unpleasant conversation with a social worker and says "Social workers are difficult to work with," the generalization to all social workers might be inaccurate. This fallacy is also known as the fallacy of hasty conclusion (Kahane, 1971), and it has many variants. All have in common making unwarranted generalizations from small or biased samples. This fallacy entails a disregard for the law of large numbers. (See Chapter 13 and prior discussion of suppressed evidence and of either/or thinking.)

## DISTORTING FACTS/POSITIONS

A number of informal fallacies distort positions. Famous people may be misquoted or views misrepresented (see discussion of incorrect classification of procedures in Chapter 7). In straw man arguments, a position similar to but different from the one presented is attacked; an argument is distorted and the distorted version is then attacked. Such arguments are often seen in the discussion of disliked practice theories. Examples of distortions of the philosophy of evidence-based decision making, as described in original sources, can be seen in Exhibit 6.1. Distorted presentations of Skinner's views are common, such as the incorrect view that he believes in stimulus-response Watsonian behaviorism (e.g., see Todd & Morris, 1983). Incorrect assertions may then be criticized. Inaccurate descriptions may be used to give a misleading view of what indeed occurred, as in the statement that "there is an epidemic of drug use" when in fact there has been a modest increase or no increase at all (MacCoun, 2001; see also Best, 2004). Clinicians may believe extreme (but inaccurate) statements that support their biases. Advocacy in place of accurate presentation of data is common (Best, 2004). Consider also misleading descriptions of evidence-based practice (Gibbs & Gambrill, 2002).

Forcing an extension may be intentionally used by someone aware of the fact that it is usually impossible to defend extreme positions; that is, most positions have some degree of uncertainty attached to them, like the statement that insight therapy is useful with many (not all) clients. The original position may be misstated in an extreme version (insight therapy is effective with all clients) and this extreme version then criticized. The original, less extreme position should be reaffirmed.

The *fallacy of false cause* involves arguments that suggest that two events are causally related when no such connection has been demonstrated. It may be argued that because one event followed another, the latter caused the former. A client may state that because she had a bad dream the night before, she made a bad mistake the next day (see Chapter 14).

An argument may be made for a conclusion that is not the one under discussion. While seeming to counter an argument, irrelevant statements advance a conclusion that is different from the one at issue. Other names for this fallacy include *red herring, irrelevant conclusion, ignoring the issue,* and *diversion.* This fallacy can be quite deceptive because the irrelevant argument advanced often does support a conclusion and so gives an impression of credibility to

**Exhibit 6.1**
Fallacies in Misrepresentations of Evidence-Based Practice (EBP)

| Distortion | Reply |
|---|---|
| 1. EBP stems from behaviorism and positivism. | 1. It does not stem from either. |
| 2. EBP ignores client values. | 2. Attending to client values and preferences is a hallmark of EBP. |
| 3. EBP ignores clinical expertise. | 3. Clinical expertise is used to integrate information from diverse sources. |
| 4. EBP simply substitutes another form of authority. | 4. This indeed could happen by distorting EBP and is illustrated by uses of the term "evidence-based" without the substance; EBP is an alternative to authority-based practices and policies. |
| 5. EBP is a cookbook approach. | 5. EBP involves the use of clinical expertise to consider unique client characteristics and circumstances and available resources. |
| 6. EBP is simply a cost-cutting tool. | 6. A review of the evidence related to a concern may result in more money being spent. |
| 7. EBP is limited to clinical research. | 7. A variety of research is drawn on, depending on the question raised, including qualitative research. |
| 8. Research shows it cannot be done. | 8. Research suggests that it can be done (e.g., see Chapter 10). |
| 9. EBP results in therapeutic nihilism. | 9. If no evidence is found, this is shared with clients and practice theory is drawn on to guide decisions. |
| 10. There is nothing new about EBP. | 10. Not true—see Chapter 10. |
| 11. We are already doing it. | 11. Not true—see Chapter 10. |
| 12. No evidence is available that can guide practice. | 12. Many questions have been critically examined. See, for example, Cochrane and Campbell databases. |
| 13. EBP assumes that professionals are rational agents. | 13. One of the very reasons EBP originated was because clinicians often do not draw on practice-related research. |
| 14. Only randomized controlled trials are drawn on. | 14. A wide variety of research is drawn on to match the question raised. |
| 15. It only applies if evidence is found. | 15. See no. 9 above. |
| 16. Effectiveness is a matter of personal opinion. | 16. See Chapter 12. |
| 17. You can always find evidence for a point of view. | 17. See Chapter 12. |
| 18. All methods are of equal value in arriving at the truth. | 18. See Chapter 12. |

*Note:* Based on Gibbs and Gambrill (2002); Straus and McAlister (2000). See Chapter 10 for a description of evidence-based practice and care as described in original sources.

the person offering it, and the illusion of a lack of cogency for the original argument, but the argument does not address the conclusion at issue (Engel, 1994). An example is, "the advocates of reality therapy contend that if we adopt their practice methods, clients will be better off. They are mistaken, for it is easy to show that reality therapy will not cure the ills of the world." There are two different points here: (1) whether reality therapy is effective and (2) whether it will "cure the ills of the world." Showing that the latter is not true may persuade people that the first point has also been shown to be untrue. The fallacy of irrelevant thesis is a version of forcing an extension. Notice that distortion of a position can make it look ridiculous and so easily overthrown. If the presenter of the original, more modest view is duped into defending an extreme version, he or she will likely fail.

*Inappropriate Use of Analogies*    Analogies can be helpful in understanding clinical problems and in selecting treatment methods. Analogies often are used in daily life to decide what to do in novel situations; that is, we try to identify a familiar experience and use it to make decisions in new contexts. Analogies often are used to clarify meanings. For example, the Freudian theory of motivation is sometimes likened to a hydraulic system, in which repressed forces are kept in check by defenses, and if these are removed, repressed content will emerge. Analogies can be helpful if they compare two phenomena that are indeed similar in significant ways; the more familiar event can be helpful in highlighting aspects of the less familiar event that should be considered. However, if the two events differ in important ways, then the analogy can interfere with understanding. Two things may bear a superficial resemblance to each other but be quite unlike in important ways. Consider the question "Should couples have sex before marriage?" A response might be "You wouldn't buy a car without taking it out for a test drive, would you?" (Bransford & Stein, 1984, p. 88). Some people who hear this argument simply say, "Oh, yes, you have a point there." Others will see that the analogy is inappropriate; marriage is significantly different from buying a car. The soundness of the analogy must always be explored. It is only a guide; it becomes dangerous "when the conclusions to which it points are regarded as certain" (Thouless, 1974, p. 171). Does "mental illness" (disease/disorder) match the characteristics of a disease? Does it have (1) a known etiology, (2) a predictable course, and (3) get worse without treatment? Peele (1999) and Fingarette (1988) argue that alcohol abuse is not a disease; that is, it does not have these characteristics. Consider also schizophrenia. Its etiology is unknown (contrary to bold assertions by some to the contrary, and candidly acknowledged by others, including the Surgeon General of the United States in 1999). It does not have a predictable course, and it does not necessarily get worse without treatment (indeed, about one third of people labeled as schizophrenic get better over time).

Argument by mere analogy refers to the use of an analogy "to create conviction of the truth of whatever it illustrates, or when it implies that truth in order to deduce some new conclusion" (Thouless, 1974, p. 169). When an argument from analogy is reduced to its bare outline, it "has the form that because some thing or event N has the properties a and b which belong to M, it must have the property c which also belongs to M" (p. 171). Arguments from analogy may sometimes be difficult to recognize; that is, the analogy may be implied rather than clearly stated. The mind of a child may be likened to a container that must be filled with information. This analogy carries implications that may be untrue, such as that we have sharply limited capacities. So "the use of analogy becomes crooked argumentation when an analogy is used not as a guide to expectations, but as proof of a conclusion" (Thouless, 1974, p. 176). Analogies create vivid images that are then readily available. They may oversimplify concerns in a misleading manner. Their vividness may crowd out less vivid but more accurate analogies and discourage a review of possible limitations of the analogy. There is thus an emotional impact; analogies play upon our emotions. We forget that, although they may be a useful guide to what to look for, "They are never final evidence as to what the facts are" (Thouless, 1974, p. 175). They are one of many devices for creating conviction, even though there are no rational grounds for the conviction. Arguments from mere analogy can be dealt with by noting at what point the analogy breaks down.

In argument from forced analogy, an analogy is used to advance an argument when there is so little resemblance between the things compared to ever expect that they would resemble each other in relation to the main point under discussion. One example is "delusional processes are like a machine run amok." Those who use such analogies are often aware of their influence in creating beliefs, despite the absence of rational grounds for such beliefs. Forced analogies are often used in public speeches where their deficiencies cannot be readily pointed out. The remedy consists of examining just how closely the analogy really fits the matter at hand. Thouless (1974) recommends trying out other analogies and noting that these carry as much force as the original one.

## DIVERSIONS

Many informal fallacies succeed by diverting attention away from the main points of an argument. Some of the informal fallacies already discussed could be so classified, such as red herring and ad hominem arguments, in which attention is focused on the person making the argument rather than the argument itself. Trivial points or irrelevant objections may be focused on. "If you find that you are being worsted, you can make a diversion—that is, you can suddenly begin to talk of something else, as though it had a bearing on the matter in dispute" (Schopenhauer, n.d., p. 29). Here the diversion is not to a new question (as in the fallacy of irrelevant thesis), but to a question related to the prime question under consideration. In any discussion, a number of points may be raised, one or more of which may not be true. In this fallacy, some trivial point is addressed and shown to be incorrect and it is assumed that the main question has been disposed of. Showing the inaccuracy of a fact that is actually not relevant to a position can create the impression that the entire argument is incorrect. Certainly all points related to an argument should be examined; however, this is just the beginning of an evaluation of a position. Witty comments and jokes can be used to divert attention from the main point of an argument or from the fact that little evidence is provided for a position. A joke can be made that makes a valid position appear ridiculous or poorly conceived. Attempts to defend a position in the face of such a response may seem pedantic. The remedy is to point out that, although what has been said may be true (or humorous), it is irrelevant.

In an appeal to ignorance, a "why?" is met with a "why not?" (Michalos, 1971, p. 81). In the fallacy of answering questions with questions, hypothetical questions are introduced that provide a distraction from important points. Questions cannot be true or false, so continued questioning is not informative. Certainly, some questions are vital to evaluation of arguments. However, in arguments they are never an end in themselves. In other contexts, such as an exchange between Buddhist monks, another end may be sought (see Engel, 1982, p. 82).

Creating anger is another way to distract people. Emotional language can be used to create anger, anxiety, or blind adherence to a position, and to distract us from noticing flaws in an argument. Anger may be created by inflammatory statements about a position or by ad hominem attacks. The focus may shift to insults rather than the issues under discussion. Anger may be distracting also if others become angry.

Appeals to anxiety and fear are widely used to distract listeners and readers from the main issues. In an article entitled "Marketing: A Lifeline For Private Practice," readers are told that "as more social workers go into private practice, and as competition between them and other mental health professionals heats up, marketing becomes a necessary survival tool" (*NASW News*, Oct. 1987, p. 5). Notice the term *survival*, appealing to the scarcity principle (see Chapter 5). The principle of social proof is one of the bases of appeals to anxiety—"You will be out of step with 'everyone else' if you don't agree with an accepted position." Thus, appeals to anxiety and fear may draw on any one of the sources of persuasion, as illustrated in Exhibit 6.2 (see also Chapter 5).

**Exhibit 6.2**
Use of Persuasion Tactics to Create Fear and Anxiety

| Social-psychological principle | Anxiety-arousing appeal |
|---|---|
| Liking | You don't like me if you don't go along with my position (and therefore I won't like you as much). |
| Consistency | You're inconsistent with your beliefs if you don't agree with me. |
| Reciprocity | I helped you out in the past, now you're not fulfilling your obligation to return the favor if you don't support my position. |
| Authority | Other people (namely me) know what is best. |
| Scarcity | We won't have this opportunity for long; it's now or never. |
| Social proof | Everyone (but you) accepts this position; what's the matter with you? |

Appeals to fear are used by psychiatrists in their battle against psychologists to retain and expand their turf. For example, they may predict that the quality of services will decrease if psychologists receive hospital admission privileges (Buie, 1989). Appeals to pity or friendship may also direct attention away from careful examination of evidence for a claim (see Chapter 5).

## THE USE OF CONFUSION

Some fallacies work by confusion: "If you can't convince them (or if you don't know what you're talking about), confuse them." People may attempt to create confusion by citing a counterexample to a position, saying that "the exception proves the rule." It does no such thing. Finding an example that does not fit a rule may be informative about the boundaries within which a rule is applicable, but may say nothing about the truth or falsity of the rule in question. (See discussion of the fallacy of the sweeping generalization earlier in this chapter.) Excessive verbiage is a common means of creating confusion—talking about many different things and then stating a conclusion that supposedly stems from all of them. Excessive words used in the presentation of arguments, whether written or spoken, make the task of argument analysis difficult. Irrelevancies, unstated premises, and implicit assumptions must be culled out in order to reveal the actual premises and conclusions.

Use of pseudoarguments takes advantage of our tendency to assume that if someone is talking (or writing), he or she must be making sense. That is, we tend to think that we have missed the point and that we are limited in our lack of understanding; we "tend to put the burden of comprehension on ourselves" (Michalos, 1971, p. 79). If excessive verbiage is complemented by prestige, the use of pseudoarguments is even more likely to confuse and mislead. We are misled by our tendency to go along with what authorities say. Another persuasive influence at work here may include liking—if we like someone, we are more prone to agree with what they say and to think they are saying something of value.

Equivocation involves playing on the double meaning of a word in a misleading or inaccurate manner (see Hamblin, 1970). "If someone informs you that Simon Butcher is independent, exactly what has he told you? Is he politically, religiously, economically, or socially independent? Is he a free thinker or a free lover? Is he a lover of free thinking or does he just think about loving freely? The fallacy of *equivocation* would be committed if someone began with a premise attributing independence in one sense to Butcher and concluded from that that Butcher possessed independence in an entirely different sense" (Michalos, 1971, p. 71).

People may claim a lack of understanding to avoid coming to grips with an issue, or try to confuse issues by repeatedly asking for alternative statements of a position (Michalos, 1971, p. 75). This tactic, like some others, such as arousing anger, may be used to gain time to consider a position better in terms of what to do next in order to prevail. Feigned lack of understanding is often combined with use of power, as when an instructor tells a student that he does not understand the point being made. Often there is an implication that the other person's point of view is irrelevant or silly anyway. A possible remedy here may be to ask the person exactly what aspect of the argument is confusing.

## SUMMARY

Both formal and informal fallacies may dilute the quality of clinical decisions. Some arguments are false even though they are valid. A valid argument is one whose premises, if true, offer good or sufficient grounds for accepting a conclusion. The incorrectness of premises may be overlooked, resulting in poor decisions. Most fallacies are informal ones; that is, they do not involve a formal mistake. There are many different kinds of informal fallacies. Ad hominem arguments may be used, in which the background, habits, associates, or personality of the person (rather than the arguments) are criticized or appealed to. Variants of ad hominem arguments include guilt (or credit) by association, the bad seed fallacy, appeals to faulty motives or good intentions, special pleading, and false claims of inconsistency. Vacuous guarantees may be offered, as when someone assumes that because a condition ought to be, it *is* the case, without providing support for the position.

Fallacies that evade the facts (such as begging the question) appear to address the facts, but do not. Variants of question begging include use of alleged certainty, circular reasoning, use of unfounded generalizations to support a conclusion, complex, trick, or leading questions, and ignoring the issue. Some informal fallacies overlook the facts, as in the fallacy of the sweeping generalization, in which a rule or assumption that is valid in general is applied to a specific example for which it is not valid. Other informal fallacies distort facts or positions; in straw person arguments, a position similar to (but significantly different from) the one presented is described and attacked. The informal fallacies of false cause, forcing an extension, and the inappropriate use of analogies also involve the distortion of facts or positions. Diversions may be used to direct attention away from a main point of an argument. Trivial points, irrelevant objections, or emotional appeals may be made. Some fallacies work by creating confusion, such as feigned lack of understanding and excessive talk that obscures arguments. Knowledge of formal and informal fallacies decreases the likelihood that clinical decisions will be influenced by these sources of error.

## A CATALOG OF FAULTY INFERENCES

1. *Fallacy of representativeness.* Assuming that two or more things or events are related simply because they resemble each other.

    Foxes have remarkable lungs. Therefore the lungs of a fox will remedy asthma.

2. *Irrelevant conclusion.* A conclusion is irrelevant to the reasoning that led to it.

> I don't think Mr. Jones abused his child. He acts like a normal father; he even spends time on the weekend repairing his car.

3. *Fallacy of division.* Assuming that what is true of the whole is necessarily true of each individual part of the whole.

> Staff at the Mixer Community Mental Health Center are psychoanalytically oriented. Mary M., who works there, is psychoanalytically oriented.

4. *Fallacy of labeling.* Labeling yourself or others when the label is unjustified by the circumstances, or when the label is inappropriately used as a reason for behavior or lack of behavior (Sternberg, 1986, p. 96).

> You have worked hard to help a client, to little avail. You say to yourself "I'm a failure."

5. *Hasty generalization.* Considering only exceptional cases and generalizing from those cases to a rule that fits only those exceptions.

> Bill and a friend were discussing the director of their agency. Bill said, "He is a total failure because he has not increased funding for our agency."

6. *Overlooking the role of chance.* Assuming that an outcome due to chance is related to past occurrences.

> My next baby must be a boy. We've had five girls.

7. *Personalization.* Assuming you are the cause of some event for which you were not primarily responsible, or taking personally a statement that is not directed toward you.

> A client failed to keep an agreement that you believe he could have kept. You say to yourself, "It's my fault."

8. *Magnification/minimization.* Magnifying our negative characteristics or mistakes or minimizing positive characteristics or accomplishments.

> Mrs. Silvers (a supervisor) congratulated Max on his success with his client. He said "Oh, it's really not a big thing."

9. *Fallacy of composition.* Assuming that what is true of parts of a whole is true of the whole.

> Jane is behaviorally oriented. Therefore, staff at her agency are behaviorally oriented.

10. *"Should" statements* (*e.g., "I must do this," "I should feel that," "They should do this"*) are fallacies when they are used as the sole reason for behavior.

> A supervisor tells her staff: "You should evaluate your practice."

11. *False cause.* Relying on the mere fact of coincidence of temporal succession to identify a cause.

    John worked in a large office. He applied for a promotion, but a woman received it, He said to himself, "It's clear that the woman was promoted and not me because she is a woman."

12. *Invalid disjunction* (either/or-ing). Considering only two options when more than two should be considered.

    We must either hospitalize him or leave him to wander the streets.

13. *Fallacies based on availability.* Accepting the first explanations for an event that occurs to you without considering other, less obvious, or readily available explanations.

    I can see he is an angry man by how he acts in the office. I think he is guilty of abusing his wife.

14. *Argument from ignorance.* Assuming that something is true simply because it has not been shown to be false, or that it is false simply because it has not been shown to be true.

    You don't have any proof that your method works. Therefore, I don't think it does.

15. *Mental filter.* Picking out some small aspect of a situation (often a negative one) and focusing on this so that the "bigger picture" is ignored. All events are viewed through the filter of one aspect of the situation.

    I just don't like the way my director dresses.

16. *Emotional reasoning.* Using our emotions or feelings as evidence of a truth.

    This is true because I feel it is true.

17. *Appeal to authority.* Arguing that a claim is true based purely on an authority's status with no reference to evidence.

    "Dr. Monston said . . ."

18. *Argumentation ad populum.* Assuming that "if everyone else thinks this way, it must be right." Appeal to popularity.

    Everyone is using this new method. I think we should use it, too.

19. *Argumentum ad hominem.* Attacking or praising some aspects of a person's character, lifestyle, race, religion, sex, and so on, as evidence for (or against) a conclusion, even when these circumstances are irrelevant to the situation being examined.

    He has a point. But look at how he is dressed.

20. *Inference by manner of presentation* (how believable is this person?).

    She gave a convincing talk. I'm going to use her methods.

21. *Appeal to experience.*

    I've seen thirty clients and used x successfully with all of them. It works!

22. *Appeal to tradition.*

    That's the way we have always done it. We should continue to use these methods.

23. *Influence by testimonials.*

    I believe it works because Mrs. Rivera said she tried it and it helped.

24. *Appeal to newness.*

    It's the latest thing. We should try it, too.

25. *Assume hard-headed—therefore, hard-hearted.*

    She can't really care about her clients if she spends that much time questioning our agency's methods.

26. *Assume that good intentions result in good services* (e.g., protect clients from harm).

    In response to a question from a client about an agency's effectiveness, you say: "We really care about our clients."

27. *Weak documentation.*

    Accepting a claim based on vague, undocumented evidence.

———————

Source: See, for example, Robert J. Sternberg (1986). *Intelligence applied: Understanding and increasing your intellectual skills,* San Diego, CA: Harcourt Brace Jovanovich; Thouless (1974). *Straight and crooked thinking. Thirty-eight dishonest tricks of debate.* London: Pan Books.

# CHAPTER 7

# Classification, Pseudoauthority, and Focusing on Pathology

A DDITIONAL SOURCES OF FALLACY that have special relevance to clinical decision making are discussed in this chapter. These include fallacies related to classification; appeals to pseudoauthority; a pathological set; and the rule of optimism.

## FALLACIES RELATED TO CLASSIFICATION

Classification (sorting objects, events, or people into different categories and giving different names to these categories) is necessary in everyday life as well as in clinical practice (e.g., see Taylor & Rutter, 2002). Among the potential benefits of classification are selection of effective treatment methods and standard usage of terms. Predictions or new discoveries may result from classification. For example, Mendeleef's classification of the elements according to their atomic weights and chemical properties enabled the prediction of the discovery of unknown elements. Causal relationships may not necessarily be implied by classification. Indeed, the introduction to the *Diagnostic and Statistical Manual of Mental Disorders* (*DSM*; American Psychiatric Association, 2000) states that the psychiatric labels described neither suggest etiology or service guidelines. A belief that classification systems accurately reflect the world can lead clinicians astray. "Science and common sense inquiry alike do not discover the ways in which events are grouped in the world; they invent ways of grouping" (Abercrombie, 1960, p. 113). Faulty classification may occur when the classification is not exhaustive or exclusive, is not adequate to the purpose for which it was created, or does not permit precise divisions, resulting in serious marginal cases (e.g., see Shorter & Tyrer, 2003). Labels that point to effective interventions are helpful. Meehl (1973) suggests that not applying the correct label may prevent clients from receiving appropriate intervention. Labels can normalize client concerns (Grunebaum & Chasin, 1978). For example, parents who have been struggling to understand why their child is developmentally slow may view themselves as failures. Recognition that this "slowness" is a result of a specific kind of disability can be a great relief. Too often, however, labels, although they may sound sophisticated, offer little or no information about what to do to help a client. In addition, labels often have iatrogenic effects; they medicalize, stigmatize, and pathologize clients (Morgan, 1983).

Classification requires overlooking differences among people, events, or objects and focusing on similarities. At lower levels of abstraction, difficulties may not be great in making correct classifications. It is at the higher levels of abstraction that problems often occur, and cause errors such as inappropriate stereotyping. Even at lower levels, sloppy thinking may lead to inaccurate generalizations, such as "a rose is a rose"; in the context of a competition among rose growers for the most beautiful rose of the year, a rose is certainly not a rose. Even the same rose may differ from day to day. The context influences the features attended to in categorizing an event, object, or behavior; these may differ from person to person and time to time. For example, Rosenhan's (1973) research suggests that once a "normal" person enters a psychiatric hospital he or she will continue to be viewed as mentally ill. Overlooking cultural differences may result in misdiagnosis, neglect of problems, or overestimation or underestimation of pathology (Sue & Sue, 2002; Westermeyer, 1987).

Classification is of great interest in psychology and related fields. An enormous literature is devoted to the development of measures that will permit the reliable and valid classification of clients into different categories. For example, hundreds of reports have appeared on the Minnesota Multiphasic Personality Inventory (MMPI). Hundreds of alleged disorders are described in the *Diagnostic and Statistical Manual of Mental Disorders* and spirited discussions take place about adding or removing entries. Items listed in the *DSM* have grown by leaps and bounds. Houts (2002) notes that there has been a 300 percent increase over 4 decades in the number of "mental disorders" included in the *DSM*. Diagnostic labels must be applied to clients as a requirement for third-party payments. Clinical labels are used as shorthand terms to refer to specific behaviors. A teacher may use the term Attention-Deficit/Hyperactivity Disorder (ADHD) to refer to the fact that a student often gets out of his seat at school and talks out of turn in class. She may use this label as a summary term to refer to these behaviors. Even though psychiatric labels are said *not* to carry treatment implications in everyday practice, they often *do* have this use. That is, a label is used as a diagnostic category that carries implications for resolving a client's problems. Where a label connotes more than a cluster of behaviors, it involves additional assumptions about the person labeled, which supposedly will be of value in altering the situation. For example, a counselor, after verifying that a student does engage in these behaviors, may agree that he "has ADHD," meaning that he has a "mental disorder," and therefore should be placed on medication. That is, inferences are based on observed behavior that a condition of ADHD exists, and intervention recommendations stem from these inferences. In fact, the label is based simply on the observed behaviors. This is an example of the use of a descriptive term as a pseudoexplanatory term (see also Chapter 13). Even if criteria described in the *DSM* are accurately used ("Six or more . . . symptoms of inattention," as well as "Six [or more] symptoms of hyperactivity-impulsivity have persisted for at least six months to a degree that is maladaptive and inconsistent with developmental level"; p. 92), and "some impairment from the symptoms is present in two or more settings," inferences about causation based on these occurrences may be inaccurate. For example, rather than being caused by a "brain disorder," related behaviors may be a result of environmental contingencies (e.g., see Baldwin, 1999; Timimi, 2002).

The consensus base on which diagnoses are identified is often downplayed or obscured by the scientific narrative within which diagnoses are framed. For example, Houts (2002) suggests that "the field of modern psychopathology has garnered authority and legitimacy, both professional and civic, by casting its knowledge claims within a master narrative of scientific discovery and progress" (p. 23). Critiques of the brain disease view of troubled, troubling, and dependent behaviors note that basic assumptions are often ignored, such as "What is a disease?" "Are troubling behaviors 'diseases'?" (e.g., Szasz, 1994). The consensual nature of diagnostic categories is reflected in controversies about adding the terms *self-defeating personality disorder, sadistic personality disorder,* and *premenstrual syndrome* (later changed to late luteal phase dysphoric disorder). Opponents argued that a diagnosis of sadistic personality disorder would offer a legal defense to child abusers and wife beaters and that women would be stigmatized by the addition of late luteal phase dysphoric disorder. Debates concerning other labels illustrate the consensual nature of diagnosis. For example, the term *learning disability* included different referents at different times on the list of skills a learning-disabled person may have difficulty acquiring. Former definitions included listening, speaking, reading, writing, reasoning, and mathematics, and more recently, social skills. The U.S. Education Department, concerned with the increase in the number of students identified as learning disabled, warned that inclusion of social skills deficiencies would increase the number of children classified as learning disabled and eligible for special education services (Landers, 1987, p. 350). (See also Merrell & Walker, 2004.) This category has been further expanded over the past years. Cantor (1982) suggests that psychiatric diagnostic knowledge conforms better to a fuzzy prototype description, in which categories are described by a set of correlated features, than it does to a small set of necessary and sufficient defining features, as in the normative descriptions in the *DSM*. According to the classical model, categorization is simply a matter of presence or absence of all of the defining features of a category. By contrast, the prototype model views categorization as a probabilistic process of assessing degree of similarity of a particular target to each of the prototypes for a set of relevant categories—categorization is a matter of degree (Cantor, 1982, p. 33).

Labeling theorists stress the relativity with which labels are used in accord with changing societal views about what is proper and improper behavior (Lemert, 1951; Scheff, 1984a, 1984b). It is argued that labels reflect moral judgments based on societal definitions of what is normal and abnormal. The relation between judgments of moral character and ascriptions of deviance is emphasized by sociologists as well as by those who have been critical of accepted psychiatric practices (see Chapter 2). In the labeling theory of mental illness, "symptoms of mental illness" are conceptualized as a kind of "nonconformity: the violation of residual rules" (Scheff, 1984b, p. 188). The term *residual rules* refers to all of those situations in which a conventional label of deviance, such as drunkenness, cannot readily be found. Scheff (1984b) suggests that it is here, in this residual category, that the label "mental illness" is applied. Rule breaking may occur for a variety of different reasons, only some of which (a small percentage according to labeling theorists) are a true result of "disease."

A question of concern to labeling theorists is "from whatever cause, why are some [symptoms] short-lived or self-limited and others stable?" (Scheff, 1984b, p. 189). They suggest that societal reactions to residual rule breaking stabilize the symptoms and result in a career of deviance. Thus, within labeling theory, the label itself is considered to be partially responsible for the continuation of and increase in deviant acts. Labeling is viewed as a behavior that varies from culture to culture, from person to person, and from time to time, and which has social functions in relation to regulating the boundaries between accepted and unaccepted behavior. This stance is very different from a psychiatric one, in which there is a search for an objective diagnostic label for a client that justifies certain consequent actions, such as reimbursement for services (see *DSM-IV-R*, 2000). In the former instance there is a concern that labeling stigmatizes clients and encourages deviant behavior, and diverts attention from client strengths and related environmental factors; also, that it results in "blaming the victim" and deflects attention away from social, economic, and political conditions that encourage deviant behavior. In the psychiatric enterprise, services offered may not benefit clients, but, to the contrary, may result in loss of freedom and independence (Scheper-Hughes & Lovell, 1987; Szasz, 2003). Critics of the mental health industry argue that, rather than fulfilling promises of alleviating human suffering, professions such as psychiatry, psychology, and social work have helped to create institutions and practices that classify, define, and control behavior (including coercive efforts) and fulfill the interest of dominant groups (Basaglia in Scheper-Hughes & Lovell, 1987, p. 151). There is, however, a symbiotic relationship between those applying labels and those who are labeled, for example, the latter escape responsibility for their behavior and the former have a reason for lack of success (e.g., making a diagnosis of "borderline personality").

*Incorrect Classification of People*   Incorrect classification of people may result in inappropriate selection of intervention methods. Classification may result in false-positives or false-negatives. The consequences of a false-positive (for example, saying someone is a danger to society when he or she is not) or a false-negative (that is, deciding someone is not a danger to others when he or she is) depend on the situation. Physicians are trained to be conservative in their judgments of pathology—that is, when in doubt, to err in the direction of a false-positive judgment. They are trained to accept the norm that judging a sick person to be well is worse than judging a well person to be sick (Scheff, 1963; see later discussion of fallacies related to a pathological set). The accuracy of classification is related to the reliability and validity of measures used to make them. Concerns about the reliability and validity of *DSM* categories have been described by many critics (see, for example, Houts, 2002; Kirk & Kutchins, 1992a; Kutchins & Kirk, 1997). The less reliable and valid a measure, the greater the likelihood of incorrect classification. Overestimating the accuracy of measures and ignoring base rate data (the frequency with which a sign or symptom occurs in a population) increase the likelihood of inaccurate classification (see Chapter 15). Hundreds of behaviors are now labeled as mental disorders. There is a "creep" to their use. For example, the label "Posttraumatic Stress Disorder," originally developed to refer to shell-shocked Vietnam War veterans, is now applied also to relatively minor stresses (Summerfield, 2001). Donovan (2004) refers to this as "the erasure of degrees of suffering and fear" (p. 153).

Diagnostic labels are typically imprecise. They say too little about positive attributes, potential for change, and change that does occur, and they say too much about presumed negative characteristics and limits to change. Someone who carries a negative label such as *schizophrenic* often is regarded as if he possesses only the characteristics of this category (Rosenhan, 1973). Negative labels may result in the neglect of environmental conditions that need attention, and do not reflect rapid changes that often take place; that is, even though changes occur, the same label (such as *retarded*) may be retained. Acceptance of a label may prematurely close off consideration of options. The tendency to use a binary classification system, in which people are labeled as either having or not having something (for example, as being an alcoholic or not), obscures the many patterns to which vague terms may refer and isolates those labeled from normal people. A continuous distribution is transformed into a binary one. Labels that limit exploration do not have to be fancy ones like *hyperactive* or *paranoid;* they can be everyday terms like *old lady.* Lack of agreement among professionals in their use of labels has already been noted.

Psychiatric classification systems have been criticized for blaming the victim for his plight rather than examining the social, economic, and political circumstances related to concerns (Ryan, 1976). Past and current critiques of the *DSM* raise concerns about the extent to which this system of classification assumes that mental disorder is an inner condition of the individual and ignores environmental causes of personal problems (e.g., McReynolds, 1989; Tavris, 1992). Although Axis IV (psychosocial and environmental problems) is included in the *DSM,* in everyday practice little attention may be given to this. The notion of psychiatric classification implies the existence of objective criteria. The history of psychiatry shows that objectivity is difficult. Even when empirical data are available, such information may be ignored in the definition of diagnostic categories, and criteria used are often judgmental (Houts, 2002; McReynolds, 1989). Many writers, both past and present, have argued that psychiatric classification serves the interests of the ruling majority (Sedgwick, 1982; Szasz, 1994). "Categories and labels are powerful instruments for social regulation and control, and they are often employed for obscure, covert, or hurtful purposes: to degrade people, to deny them access to opportunity, to exclude 'undesirables' whose presence in some way offends, disturbs familiar custom, or demands extraordinary effort" (Hobbs, 1975, p. 11 ). The fact that assignment of a deviant status and subsequent actions partially depend on social class supports the social control function of labels. Reiman (2004) argues that the wealthy are protected by their wealth from having their crimes recognized, and if recognized, prosecuted with the same vigor with which poor people are prosecuted. The wealthy have powerful options to protect themselves from being labeled as a "criminal" and prosecuted as criminals, for example, access to high-quality lawyers. So too does such protection accrue to the rich, compared to the poor, in avoiding psychiatric labels. Those who receive psychiatric or criminal labels are those who are observed in deviant acts, sometimes because they are poor and so have little access to privacy.

Basaglia (in Scheper-Hughes & Lovell, 1987, p. 105) suggests that those labeled "are forced as deviants into an ideological category that defines them, continues to create them, and controls them." New labels are created to stigmatize behavior that deviates from the norm. "Whoever is exuberant is labeled overly emotional. . . . Whoever stands up for himself suffers from a combativeness that could turn into protest and contentiousness" (p. 112). "Confronted with new forms of deviance and abusive behavior, which might be symptoms of an unbearable, abnormal life, lists and technical terms are found to categorize them. This may be brought up to date with a vague reference to a hypothetical 'social' factor, which supposedly guarantees that the problem will be confronted in contemporary modern terms. In the meantime, prisons and asylums continue to preserve their marginal, class character" (p. 218). Szasz (2003) suggests that those who try to resist involuntary commitment as mental patients are then labeled "paranoid." Classification magnifies and strengthens differences between people, perpetuating the isolation of deviants from others. Critics of the *DSM* raise concerns about the growing number of behaviors classified as mental disorders. For example, McReynolds (1989) suggests that it seems inappropriate to view children's problems in reading, spelling, and arithmetic as psychiatric disorders. Is enuresis really a mental disorder? It is included in the *DSM*.

*Use of Vague Terms*   Refutation of a claim may be impossible because the claim is vague. A distinction can be made between vague and ambiguous terms, in that ambiguous terms can be clarified by describing the context in which the term is used. Vague terms remain imprecise even when the context is clear (Michalos, 1971, p. 89). Examples of vague clinical terms include *supportive therapy, family systems theory, resistance,* and *sociopath.* Although some terms may have more precise meanings, this does not mean they are used precisely; that is, they may mean different things to different people, resulting in different classifications and decisions (see discussion of the one word, one meaning fallacy in Chapter 5).

*False Dilemma*    It may be proposed that there are just two possibilities in relation to a question when, in fact, there are many. A clinician may argue that either a client is mentally disturbed or he is not. Such accounts get in the way of discovering individual variations. This fallacy often occurs in conjunction with other fallacies, such as the straw person argument, which offers a distorted view of a position (Kahane, 1995). A continuum may be involved rather than a polar representation, as in family versus individual therapy, drug dependent versus drug independent, dysfunctional versus functional, and sick versus well. Contrary statements may be presented as if they were contradictory statements (Engel, 1982). Contrary statements are two statements that cannot both be true but may both be false. Contradictory statements are those that cannot both be true nor can they both be false (for example, "either today is New Year's Day or it is not"). The fallacy of the false dilemma presents two contraries as two contradictory statements. Engel (1982) classified this under fallacies of presumption, since facts are overlooked—namely, the fact that choices are not limited to only two alternatives. This fallacy is known also as the either/or fallacy and black-and-white fallacy. A remedy is to point out other possibilities that have been ignored.

*Incorrect or Misleading Classification of Procedures*    Errors in classification may be due to incorrect use of terms. Consider the following statements that appeared under the title "Human Subjects at Risk of Torture, U.S. Style," in the *California NASW News* (Montenegro, 1988, p. 5), which is distributed to social workers in California: "Information provided by the Prisoners Rights Union reveals that the Bureau of Prisons has built a high security unit (HSU) for women in Lexington, Kentucky, based on guidelines provided by experts in brainwashing and behavior modification techniques. HSU is designed to isolate inmates from the outside world. No personal clothing is allowed. Nothing can be placed on the walls. One hour per day is allowed in an opaque fenced yard with no view of the outside world. . . . A recent sleep deprivation experiment involved waking the women every half hour throughout the night. Rules are changed arbitrarily at random time intervals. This tactic was used by Hitler's SS" (Montenegro, 1988, p. 5). The conditions described are quite the opposite of characteristics of a behavioral approach. Hallmarks of the latter include an emphasis on the use of positive reinforcement, arranging environments that are as similar as possible to real-life settings, and offering multiple opportunities for positive reinforcement of desired behaviors. Thus, prolonged isolation would not be a part of a behavioral program; sleep deprivation would not be used. I wrote to the editor requesting further information and received a brochure titled "Buried Alive in the Lexington Women's Control Unit" (n.d.) published by the National Campaign to Abolish the Lexington Women's Control Unit (294 Atlantic Ave., Brooklyn, NY 11201). This source described the Lexington Unit as "a behavior modification unit characterized by systematic use of sensory deprivation, extreme isolation and degradation." According to the brochure, the Bureau of Prisons learned about "new techniques of behavior modification . . . in part, from Professor Edgar Schein of MIT, who spent five years doing research for the CIA on the brain washing techniques used by North Korea and China against American POWs in the Korean war" (Dillinger, 1988, p. 18). However the procedures described are the opposite of a behavioral approach, which involves a constructional approach to change (e.g., see Alberto & Troutman, 2002; Crone & Horner, 2003; Goldiamond, 1984; McGimsey, Greene, & Lutzker, 1995; Pryor, 1984).

If incorrect classification of procedures results in clients being deprived of helpful methods, those effects are worrisome. Korzybski (1980) was so concerned with the effects of spreading false information that he recommended licensing of public workers and speakers. "Even at present no professor, teacher, lawyer, physician or chemist, is allowed to operate publicly without passing an examination to show that he knows his subject. . . . At present public writers or speakers can hide behind ignorance. . . . They may 'mean well'; yet, by playing upon the pathological reactions of their own and those of the mob, they may 'put over' some very vicious propaganda and bring about very serious suffering to all concerned. But once they would have to pass an examination to get their license as public speakers or writers, they could not hide any longer behind ignorance. If found to have misused the linguistic mechanism, such an abuse on their part would be clearly a willful act, and 'well meaning' would cease to be an alibi" (Korzybski 1980, p. 486). The history of psychiatry is replete with euphemisms for cruel and unusual punishment of psychiatric patients (Valenstein, 1986). The pleasant-sounding term *community care* often means that the patient is released from an institution to fend for himself. Sources of social control are often called revolutionary new views or innovative methods. New but distrusted methods may receive the "kiss of death" by being inordinately praised as marvelous when the intention is to "cool them out." A hallmark of evidence-based practice is being accurate and honest about the degree of knowledge, ignorance, and uncertainty associated with practice methods and policies used (see Chapter 10).

*Fallacy of Stereotyping*    Clinicians often represent people as examples of categories and, on the basis of this classification, entertain certain feelings toward and expectations about them that influence how they respond to these individuals. The past and present clinical literature offers a rich source of stereotypes, such as the *schizophrenagenic mother* (now dismissed by most clinicians), *codependent partner, sociopath,* and *personality disorder.* The fallacy of stereotyping refers to treating a description as if it represents all the individuals in a group of which it may (or may not) be a fairly typical example (Scriven, 1976,

**Exhibit 7.1**
Venn Diagrams Illustrating Relationships between *A*s and *B*s for Different Premises

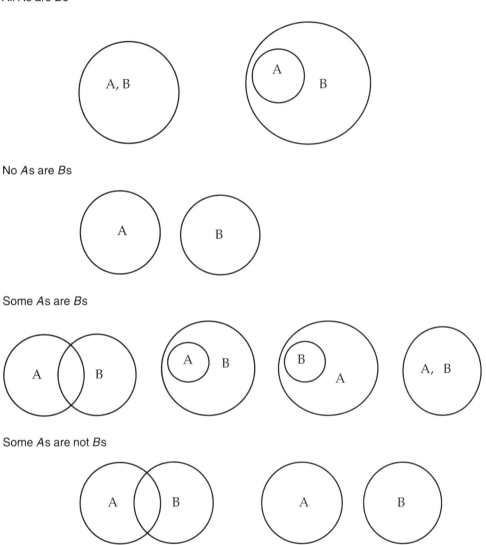

All *A*s are *B*s

No *A*s are *B*s

Some *A*s are *B*s

Some *A*s are not *B*s

*Source:* From *Cognition and Cognitive Psychology* (p. 360), by A. J. Sanford, 1985, Hove, East Sussex, England: Erlbaum. Copyright 1985 by Lawrence Erlbaum. Reprinted with permission.

p. 209). Consider the "homeless." There are many different kinds of homeless people who may benefit from different kinds of services. Similarly, there are many different patterns of substance abuse, ranging from once-a-week cocaine use by a middle-class white-collar worker to daily use by a teenager. Possible classifications can be illustrated by diagrams (see Exhibit 7.1). Stereotypes may be cultural—that is, shared by many people in a society.

Other stereotypes are unique to certain individuals, based on their past experiences. Stereotypes are often inaccurate in that they reflect only one of many aspects of an individual. They influence what we see, since we tend to seek information that supports them. The influence of stereotypes can be seen in a study by Duncan (1976). Subjects watched a videotape of a discussion between two men during which one of the men shoved the other. The race of the actors was varied in different versions. Subjects were asked to classify a behavior whenever they received a signal from the experimenter. More subjects classified the Black protagonist's behavior as violent than so classified the White protagonist's behavior, especially if the person shoved was white. Brian Nosek and his colleagues (Nosek, Banaji, & Greenwald, 2002) developed The Implicit Association Test (a computer-based test of implicit attitudes). Data collected on 600,000 test takers indicated that both White and Black participants had an implicit preference for white faces and names. Preferences shown on the test were greater than those indicated, revealing implicit biases to test takers, which is a key purpose of the test—to reveal that we have thoughts, feelings and behaviors that are not compatible with what we think, we feel, and do.

The influence of labels on stereotyping is also illustrated by a study in which information about socioeconomic background was varied. One group of subjects was informed that a child was from a high socioeconomic background, and another group of subjects was informed that the child was from a low socioeconomic background (Darley & Gross, 1983). Both groups watched a videotaped performance of the child taking an academic test. Subjects who had received information that the child was from a high socioeconomic background rated her capabilities well above grade level; subjects in the other group rated the child's abilities as below grade level. In both groups, subjects indicated that the ability test was used as evidence to support their ratings. This study offers another example of the influence of stereotypes on judgments; hypotheses are tested in a biased manner. Much greater attention is given to class-based stereotypes in the United Kingdom compared to the United States. This study, as well as other research, shows the unequal treatment of the poor compared to the wealthy. The extent to which class-based stereotypes are ignored in the United States can be seen in the 704-page book *The Psychology of Stereotyping* (Schneider, 2004), where we do not find class mentioned in the index, although we do find some attention to socioeconomic status in the book (e.g., p. 525). We find gender, race, and ethnicity in the index, but no listing for class.

There is an extensive literature exploring the influence of stereotypes in clinical practice (for example, regarding race, ethnicity, gender, and class; e.g., see Snowden, 2003; Tavris, 1992). The danger of stereotyping is that ways in which individual clients do not fit a stereotype may be overlooked and incorrect clinical decisions may be made as a result, such as selecting an ineffective intervention or deciding to intervene when there is no good reason to do so. For example, a behavior, thought, or feeling may be normative. This is not to say that intervention is not called for if a behavior pattern is normative. Clearly this is not true. Consider, for example, the low level of positive feedback and the high level of negative feedback that many secondary school teachers offer their students. This pattern may be normative but is certainly not desirable, and a school psychologist may strive to reverse it.

*Other Sources of Fallacy*   Classification often offers an illusion of objectivity. For example, consider use of the term *normal*. The view of normal as the condition of the average man or woman acquires the meaning of the healthy condition. If the statistically normal condition is accepted as equivalent to the psychologically healthy condition (Trotter, 1916), the result may be inappropriate recommendations for clinical intervention (for people who vary from the statistical norm). The vagueness of the word *normal* and the tendency of professionals to link the term with healthy are discussed by Abercrombie (1960) in her work with medical students. (See also the section on reification in Chapter 5.)

In the fallacy of the continuum, it is argued that because there is a continuous distribution of gradations between two extremes, there is no real difference. Staff members in a residential treatment center for adolescents may argue that hitting residents is really no different from yelling at them. A common argument attempting to justify the use of torture makes use of this fallacy; saying that all governments take steps to protect the integrity of their countries and sometimes encroach on the rights of its citizens. There is a refusal to recognize a shift from a quantitative to a qualitative difference. In the slippery-slope fallacy, a position is opposed on the grounds that, if it is acted on, it will result in a series of inevitable negative consequences which indeed are not inevitable. A clinician may argue (incorrectly) that if a client's overidentification with her father is focused on, a series of negative effects will follow, such as increased anxiety and depression. A decision may be made not to offer services to one needy group of clients on the basis that this would require provision of services to all other needy groups. A familiar example is the domino theory: If Vietnam falls, all of Southeast Asia will fall into Communist hands.

## APPEALS TO PSEUDOAUTHORITY

Many weak appeals work by taking advantage of common human tendencies (Cialdini, 2001). One example is the use of pseudoauthority. We grow up learning to respect authority, and those who use appeals to illegitimate authority take advantage of this tendency. Appeals to pseudoauthority also take advantage of the principle of social proof. Decisions are based on what other people think is correct (as in appeals to traditional wisdom and to consensus). Evidence-based practice is an alternative to authority-based practice, as described in Chapter 10. Proper appeals to authority should be distinguished from improper ones. The following rules of thumb can be used to distinguish proper from improper appeals.

- Remember that an authority in one area is not necessarily an authority in other areas.
- Do not accept the opinions of authorities when experts disagree or there is little known in a field. For example, experts often disagree about the sanity of a defendant; therefore, it would be unwise to accept the opinion offered by any one person.
- Examine the evidence, reasons, and arguments when experts disagree. If psychiatrists claim that a client is psychotic, find out why they believe this and evaluate the reasons given.
- Review the track record of the expert (Kahane, 1995).

Inappropriate appeals to authority can take quite subtle forms in the area of clinical decision making, and occur during clinical interviews as well as in case conferences, in discussions among colleagues, and during moments of self-reflection. Data supporting a position may be described in detail, whereas data counter to it may be mentioned only in passing or not at all (see discussion of suppressed evidence in Chapter 4). The remedy to appeals to pseudoauthority is to point out that no evidence is offered in support of the appeal, or to request or seek such evidence.

Appeals to pseudoauthority are another kind of informal fallacy—that is, they may occur without any formal error. Michalos (1971) identifies 16 varieties of pseudoauthority. A number that occur in clinical situations are reviewed in the sections that follow. Some of the informal fallacies discussed under the influence of language in Chapter 5 could be included here as well, such as the use of pseudotechnical jargon. Appeals to authority are often used to present preferred positions with a false aura of credibility.

*Popular Sentiments*   The feelings and attitudes of a group may be appealed to in order to gain acceptance for a position. In the statement "As members of the American Psychological Association, we know that," the appeal is to a respected professional group. Stereotyped descriptions of an out-group (as in the statement "Sophisticated diagnostics are eschewed in narrow behavioristic approaches") appeal to the sentiments of an in-group. Although appeals to popular sentiment may make people feel better, superior, or complacent, they do little to advance the quality of arguments. Such appeals are particularly insidious in a clinical setting, where they may bolster personal beliefs about what is normal and what is deviant without the clinician recognizing this connection (see later section on fallacies related to a pathological set). The remedy for appeals to popular sentiments is to point out that no evidence is offered for the position stated.

*Misleading Aura of Authority*   Most of the material printed in the media consists of secondary information: "Most news is given to reporters, not discovered by them" (Kahane, 1971, p. 153). However, the material is often presented in a way that makes it seem as if it were based on firsthand experiences. Opinions may be presented as facts, as in the statements "reality therapy works" or "codependents need help." Here one should ask questions like "What evidence is provided for the statement?" The kind of evidence that is relevant depends on the kind of claim made (see Chapter 12). References cited in support of a comment in an article may in fact provide none. For example, a claim may be made that a certain kind of counseling has been shown to be effective, followed by a series of references which, in fact, contain no data supporting the claim. Gibbs and Gambrill (1999) refer to this as "uncritical documentation." Reliance on secondary sources amplifies such errors. Other ways in which a misleading aura of authority may be given is by use of impressive-sounding but vague terms and by obtuse descriptions of data analysis methods or clinical procedures in place of straightforward clear accounts (which may reveal a lack of evidence for claims made). The call for transparency in evidence-based practice, including clear descriptions of limitations of research studies, should discourage hiding of research flaws that may result in inaccurate conclusions that, in turn, result in poor clinical decisions, such as use of ineffective or harmful interventions.

*Popular People and Irrelevant Authority*    The authority of popular people may be appealed to in order to support a claim. A writer may cite Freud far more often than is necessary in a manuscript submitted to a psychoanalytic journal, hoping that such name-dropping will lend an aura of credibility to the work. This tactic is often used in advertising. For example, a famous baseball player may be shown talking about the positive attributes of a cereal. Gullible viewers may not realize that an outstanding baseball player is not necessarily an expert in evaluating cereal. This appeal (as well as the next one) is a type of ad hominem argument (see Chapter 6).

*Titles and Supposed Experts*    In some variants of this use of pseudoauthority ("Doctors report that," "Studies show that"), we may not even be informed which particular person is responsible for the statement (Michalos, 1971). The studies cited were supposedly conducted by scrupulous, well-trained researchers. The possession of a credential or degree in an area may indicate some level of knowledge in a subject. The question is, does this background by itself substantiate the claim made by the bearer of these credentials? Appeals to authority can be buttressed by use of pseudotechnical jargon geared to impress listeners with the speaker's erudition. (See discussion of pseudoscience in Chapter 4.) The remedy is to ask the person to explain points more simply.

*Traditional Wisdom*    It is often assumed that what is old is best, with no evidence offered in support of the view other than people used that method in the past. An example is "That's the way I've always done it." Reluctance to question such appeals in case conferences may be related to not wishing to accept an unpopular view, or to appear contrary or difficult. Appeal to traditional wisdom may be combined with other kinds of appeals to authority, as in the statement "Historians have found that this has been the custom for many centuries" (reference to supposed experts). Or, it may be combined with question-begging definitions. A clinician may say, "The traditional role of women is the proper role because it is the traditional role" (Michalos, 1971, p. 40). One antidote to persuasion by appeals to traditional wisdom is being informed about the history of science or medicine, which offers countless examples of times when the majority view or traditional wisdom was incorrect, often, resulting in harm to people (see, for example, Broad & Wade, 1982; Gardner, 1957).

*Appeals to Consensus and the Authority of the Many*   This variant is also referred to as the appeal to large numbers (Michalos, 1971) and the fallacy of popularity (MacLean, 1981). It refers to attempted support of a claim by saying that many people agree with a position (see discussion of social proof in Chapter 5). "We view a behavior as more correct to the degree that we see others performing it" (Cialdini, 1984, p. 117). Alcoholics Anonymous may claim that its success is demonstrated by the thousands of people who have taken part in their program. But what percentage of those who participate in such programs stop drinking, and for how long? Appeals to consensus and traditional wisdom may block the acceptance of new methods for years or decades. Consider, for example, the neglect of Semmelweiss' discovery that puerperal fever could be eliminated "by having doctors wash their hands in a chlorine solution before examining the mother" (Broad & Wade, 1982, p. 137). His work was ignored for years, resulting in thousands of unnecessary deaths. The authority of the psychiatric profession is often appealed to to bolster claims, as in "Most psychiatrists believe that psychotropic medication is of benefit for clients."

*Provincialism*   Provincialism is a variety of the use of traditional wisdom and popular sentiment. It appeals to the tendency to identify with an in-group and to assume that the familiar is better or more important, when it may not be. Valuable ideas and the values that they reflect are ignored. A feminist counselor may assume that all women clients want to be liberated and fail to consider the preference of some clients who want to maintain a traditional female role. Imposition of Western views of psychological problems and proposed remedies on non-Western clients is a form of provincialism in clinical practice. Provincialism is carried to an extreme in cases in which beliefs are based on loyalty to a position rather than on evidence. Or, a counselor may withhold offering skills to a client that are usually not learned in a culture, such as certain kinds of assertive behaviors—even though the client could benefit from them and it could be done in a culture-sensitive manner. This appeal, as well as plain folks and bandwagon appeals that are variants on it (see the following), exerts influence through the principle of social proof (see Chapter 5). The plain folks appeal is at the opposite end of the spectrum from snob appeal and the appeal of pseudo-jargon (MacLean, 1981, p. 39). This tactic works (if it works) by associating the appearance of simplicity and straightforwardness with a particular view of reality. In fact, there may be little relation between reality and this appearance.

*Bandwagon Appeal*   In the *bandwagon appeal*, it is assumed that everybody is behind something: What is implied is that everybody who "knows what's best" supports a position. An article about a topic that is controversial may start with "We all know that." This tactic takes advantage of our tendency to be influenced by what other people do: If other people do it it must be good or right (the principle of social proof). This kind of pitch partly accounts for the fads and fashions in psychotherapy. There are a number of questions that should be raised, such as "Is everybody doing it?" Probably not. Even if many people do act in a certain way or accept a certain belief, that does not mean they are correct. History is replete with infamous examples of the acceptance by many of incorrect ideas. Take, for example, the hundreds of papers by scientists and doctors in the early twentieth century concerning "N-rays"—these were "discovered" in many places, including the human brain (Nye, 1980). Popular clinical approaches are not necessarily those that really help clients achieve valued outcomes (e.g., see Jacobson, Foxx, & Mulick, 2005).

*Imaginary Authority*   Reference may be made to imaginary evidence; that is, a speaker or writer may refer to evidence that does not exist. A psychologist may report that he has seen many clients with anorexia and so he can speak with authority about this disorder, when in fact he has seen one such client. An infamous example of the use of imaginary authority is the extraordinary case of Sir Cyril Burt. This is perhaps the most well-known and flagrant example of "the failure of psychologists to spot dogma masquerading as objective truth" (Broad & Wade, 1982, p. 203). Burt invented data to support his views. "He used his mastery of statistics and gift of lucid exposition to bamboozle alike his bitterest detractors and those who claimed his greatness as a psychologist" (p. 204). He submitted articles in favor of his views under an assumed name and published them in the *British Journal of Statistical Psychology,* of which he was editor for sixteen years. He not only made up data, he invented coauthors "from the vasty deep of his tormented imagination and clothed them so well in the semblance of scientific argument that the illusion fooled all his fellow scientists for as much as thirty years" (p. 204). Some argue that the fabrication of data is becoming more common, as pressures mount to publish and competition for funding becomes keener. For a spirited (and concerning) discussion see, for example, Sackett and Oxman (2003; for discussions of fraud and error in science see Miller & Hersen, 1992; Judson, 2004). The claims of an authority may be changed or completely misrepresented; a sentence may be taken out of context or minor parts of a sentence may be presented as major parts. Consider, for example, the misrepresentations of Skinner's views (e.g., Todd & Morris, 1983). This illustrates that claims may be attributed to a famous person who never said or wrote such a thing, even by well-known scholars. How many people have read all of a person's writings to check such claims? How many readers check sources cited in support of statements made in the professional journals and books? Research findings are often misrepresented (e.g., see Altman, 2002; Lipton & Hershaft, 1985). Indeed, this was one of the key reasons for the development of evidence-based practice.

*Other Kinds of Appeals to Pseudoauthority*   Some writers and speakers refer to the authority of a proverb, maxim, cliche, or aphorism (a concise statement of a principle, truth, or sentiment), instead of offering evidence related to their position. These sayings have a ring of truth that encourages their acceptance (see discussion of empathic explanations in Chapter 3). They can usually be interpreted in a variety of ways and thus may seem "psychologically compelling." When asked why he does not carefully evaluate his work with clients, a clinician may say that "capturing human experience is like trying to describe a beautiful smell; it is not possible." Metaphors and similes may be helpful in suggesting solutions to clinical problems, as well as in offering clients a view of concerns that encourages maintenance of gains—as in the metaphor of a journey used by Marlatt and Gordon (1985) in their relapse prevention program (see also Lakoff & Dean, 2004; Lakoff & Johnson, 1980).

Views may be presented as those of a vague or mysterious and generally respected group or ideal (Michalos, 1971). A clinical supervisor may argue that to challenge her views is to challenge the very authority required to maintain high-quality training programs—that is, to challenge idols. A clinician may support his use of an unfocused approach to therapy by saying that this reflects a humanistic approach to counseling, in which client values are respected and nourished. Snob appeal (authority of a select few) takes advantage of our feeling that we are special—one of a select few. In the past, psychologists were not permitted entry into psychoanalytic training programs: Acceptance required a medical degree, a restriction that ensured privileged entry to psychiatrists. Historians of social work have noted the tendency of social workers to identify with psychiatrists in order to bolster their image. People can sometimes be seduced into going along with a position in an uncritical way (without examining the soundness of the position) by the allure of association with an elite group. Persuasive strategies based on elitism may be combined with strategies based on the principle of liking—for example, friendly overtures may be made toward typically ignored or disliked colleagues to win their support.

In an appeal to faith, we are asked to accept a position based on faith alone—when evidence for or against the claim should be produced. A counselor may tell a client who questions her selection of intervention, "Trust me, I have your interests at heart." This may be combined with an appeal to expertise or longevity: "I've been a psychiatrist for twenty years."

## FALLACIES RELATED TO A PATHOLOGICAL SET

Clinicians tend to emphasize client pathology (e.g., see Ganzach, 2000). Although there is a great deal of talk and writing about empowerment of clients and focusing on client strengths, when you examine what is done in everyday practice, what is done may not reflect this focus. The psychiatric classification system (*DSM*) describes hundreds of mental disorders. It focuses on behaviors viewed as pathological based on a consensus about the classification and diagnosis of mental disorders. Third-party payment requires use of this system.

Such a focus on pathology encourages undue attention to what is wrong with people. Lack of cooperation on the part of clients may be attributed to their deficiencies. This search for personal causes of resistance discourages recognition of environmental obstacles, including lack of transportation or day care for children, and reflects a lack of appreciation for the difficulty of achieving change. Resistance is a natural part of any effort to change. Many writers, both past and present, have noted the recycling of sickness ideology under new euphemisms (such as *clinical population,* which is considered to be qualitatively different from nonclinical populations; Bandura, 1978). Such terms continue to select out as unique those people with a given behavioral pattern who seek or are sent for help from the much larger group of people with the same pattern (such as excessive use of alcohol) who do *not* seek help. More and more behaviors and related risk factors are referred to as "sicknesses" requiring the help of experts (e.g., see Moynihan, Heath, Henry, & Gøtzsche, 2002). Meehl (1973) referred to the tendency to focus on pathology as the "sick-sick" fallacy. Professional training increases this tendency (Wills, 1978). A review of 71 courses on psychopathology from 58 different schools of social work showed that such courses typically present a biomedical view of behavior, ignoring well-argued alternative viewpoints (Lacasse & Gomory, 2003). Should not graduate education expose students to different viewpoints and critique preferred views?

It is important to accurately identify pathology, especially if treatment implications follow. However, this should be balanced by a search for client assets and potential for change. Undue attention to pathology results in a neglect of client assets, creates undue pessimism about the possibility of positive outcomes, and may stigmatize clients if negative views are conveyed to clients, significant others, and authorities (see Mirowsky & Ross, 1989). For example, a negative label may make it more likely that a client will be involuntarily hospitalized (or imprisoned) and less likely that helpful services are offered. Negative impressions may be difficult to alter; research in a number of areas, including social interaction, reveals that negative events carry more weight than do positive events (e.g., Rook, 1984; Wills, Weiss, & Patterson, 1974).

*Factors That Encourage an Overemphasis on Pathology*  Factors that encourage an overemphasis on pathology include the practice theories emphasized during graduate education, an interest in protecting oneself from failure, (you can blame lack of success on the client's disorder), reliance on metaphors such as adjustment and mental health, lack of awareness of political, social, and economic influences on what is defined as a problem, lack of (or ignoring) empirical information about base rates and individual differences, and an interest in appearing erudite. Professional training may bias students toward pathology, not only by what it includes but also by what it excludes (for example, political functions of varying definitions of deviance, a working knowledge of basic behavioral principles describing relationships between our behavior and the environment [e.g., see Reid, Patterson, & Snyder, 2002], and information re-

**Exhibit 7.2**
Negative Labels and Positive Counterparts

| Negative Label | Positive Counterparts |
|---|---|
| Paranoia | Perspicacity (sensitive to the motives and feelings of others); perceptive identification and neutralization of hostile intentions |
| Depression | Elan vital |
| Substance abuse | Creative substance use |
| Obsessive-Compulsive Disorder | Effective attention to detail; good attention span |
| Exhibitionism | Freedom from undue modesty |
| Multiple personality | A creative mixture of personas |

garding base rates and individual differences). Practice theories may focus on discovering pathology in both the client's history and current functioning. Students are introduced to the *DSM*, which describes hundreds of different ways in which behaviors, thoughts, and feelings may be pathological. They may not be informed regarding criticism of the *DSM*, lending an indoctrination quality to this introduction rather than an educational quality (LaCasse & Gomory, 2003). Labels for describing behavior at the opposite pole are usually tepid (such as *well adjusted, normal*). Some more lively labels are suggested in Exhibit 7.2.

An emphasis on dispositional attributions for problems and a tendency to ignore environmental causes (the fundamental attribution error) encourages a pathological view of clients; people rather than their environments are blamed for problems of living (see discussion of dispositional bias in Chapter 14). The common occurrences of negative experiences in the history of both individuals who do not seek counseling and those who do make it quite easy to discover pathogenic experiences that are assumed to be responsible for clients' complaints and render the causative character of these symptoms questionable. Renaud and Estess (1961) interviewed 100 men who were selected because there was no indication that they had any problems. They had no history of either mental or psychological conflict and did not complain of any problems. The men were functioning as normal or superior on all objective indices. They were in good health, had attained superior educational and occupational status, and had positive relationships with others, both in their personal and work lives. The interviews held with these 100 men were similar to clinical intake interviews. These interviews revealed all kinds of traumatic events and experiences that could well be considered pathogenic and were at least as serious as experiences in the histories of psychiatric patients.

Clinicians are influenced by the values of the society in which they live. Some clinicians have not been exposed to a political and social perspective on deviance—to the fact that what is considered to be a social or personal problem is consensual and relative (that is, ascribed), rather than inherent (fixed). What is considered *pathological* changes with the times and differs in different cultures. Only in 1975 did the American Psychiatric Association decide that homosexuality was not a sickness. The fact that a professional organization decides what is and what is not a mental illness illustrates the consensual basis of psychiatric labels. Without exposure to material describing the social, economic, and political functions of deviance, including crimes and psychiatric disorders (e.g., Reiman, 2004; Scheff, 1984; Sedgwick, 1982; Szasz, 1994) as well as class, ethnic, and racial differences in the expression of related behaviors, their detection, and subsequent responses of involved officials and helpers, clinicians are likely to be overly acceptant of current popular conceptions of pathology and health (see Chapter 2). Without effective skills for handling the inevitable uncertainty and lack of success involved in clinical practice. it is easy to fall into acceptance of a pathological focus as a protection against failure (Houts, 2002). Negative pronouncements offer a reason for lack of success in remedying or preventing problems.

The terms "healthy" and "unhealthy" have been extended to an ever-wider range of behaviors, thoughts, and feelings (McCormick, 1996). Personal beliefs about what is normal may encourage a focus on pathology. For example, some psychiatrists continue to believe that homosexuality is an illness despite the decision of the American Psychiatric Association that it is not. How many practitioners carefully review their personal biases in relation to given behaviors? How many accept a view of deviance as ascribed rather than inherent? Many biases are implicit, and it is thus easy for clinicians to unknowingly impose their beliefs about what is normal, what is "healthy," and what is good on clients. Since their beliefs usually mirror commonly accepted norms of proper and improper behavior, little in the way of contradiction may challenge personal beliefs. For example, a heterosexual counselor may be consulted by a lesbian couple who want to have a child by artificial insemination. A counselor with a traditional view of family life may respond differently to this request than may a counselor with a broader view of healthy family life. Meehl (1973) suggests that "Many family psychiatrists have a stereotype of what the healthy family ought to be; and if anybody's family life does not meet this criteria, this is taken as a sign of pathology" (p. 237). This tendency is increased by the fact that practitioners tend to be from the middle class and many of their clients are poor or "working class." Meehl notes that clinicians will say, "Yes, we know about that." Knowing about something is not enough—both related skills and values and contingencies that encourage their use are also needed.

Inferences of pathology may occur because of lack of familiarity with normative data concerning behaviors, thoughts, or feelings—that is, from a lack of knowledge regarding base rates and the range of individual variability of a behavior. Imposition of a clinical label on clients further removes them from individuals considered normal. Clinical case studies reported in the professional literature often focus on pathology and neglect positive attributes of individuals and families and their environments (see, for example, Kazak & Marvin, 1984). Information about people who do well despite challenges, such as caring for a developmentally disabled child, is often absent (see also Anthony & Cohler, 1987). Lack of knowledge about historical differences in how a certain pattern of behavior is viewed may encourage pathologizing clients.

Consider "social anxiety disorders." In her interesting book *Shrinking Violets and Casper Milquetoasts*, McDaniel (2003) describes the changing views of reticent, shy behavior (see also Cottle, 1998). A clinician may be familiar with normative data but ignore this in making decisions. Ignoring information about base rates and individual difference in environmental challenges increases the likelihood of pathologizing clients and making inaccurate clinical judgments. For example, most people are shy in some social situations. Thus, this reaction is normative. Normative data may be ignored because of one or more of the other reasons discussed in this section. In our increasingly diverse society, ethnic and cultural differences may result in the imposition of biased views of health on clients. To the extent to which clinicians are unaware of such differences or ignore them, clients may suffer from arbitrarily imposed views of health. Another reason clinicians may overemphasize pathology is the biased sample of people they encounter; for example, those with rare patterns of behavior, such as severe depression, are overrepresented in the clinical population.

Vague metaphorical descriptions of exotic pathology may appear profound; clear descriptions of complaints and related factors may appear simpleminded. Describing vague, exotic inferences about the presumed causes of a problem may offer an illusion of astuteness and gain the attention of listeners. Whether they are accurate and helpful in minimizing problems is another question.

## THE RULE OF OPTIMISM

In some contexts, such as criminal justice settings and child welfare agencies, overattention to pathology may be replaced by the "well-well fallacy," to protect the service system from being overwhelmed. The constraints imposed by managed care may encourage lack of attention to dysfunctional behaviors that should be addressed, as may the rule of optimism. This is the opposite of the "sick-sick fallacy" and might be called the "well-well fallacy." It refers to the tendency not to see pathology or behavior that harms others when it is actually there. Dingwall et al. (1983) argue that this rule is used in child protection agencies because the resources of the system would be depleted if all families that needed state intervention were taken into the system. This rule states that the least discrediting interpretations of observed conduct will be used (p. 218). These authors identify cultural relativism as one vehicle through which the rule of optimism is carried out—the view that "any style of child rearing may be justified as a valid cultural statement which should not be illiberally suppressed" (p. 218). The following dialogue illustrates cultural relativism (Dingwall et al., 1983, p. 84).

*Social Worker:* Her father was very annoyed and beat her with a strap.

*Senior SW:* With a strap?

*Social Worker:* Oh, this sort of thing happens in this community.

*Senior SW:* This violence is very difficult to prove and we have to accept that it is just part of the West Indian culture.

Dingwall and his colleagues found that the more familiar a professional was with a particular area in which a family lived, the more likely such reactions were. Appeals may be made to natural love; the parent/child relationship is viewed as a natural rather than as a social phenomenon, with the implication that a charge of mistreatment is equivalent to an allegation that the parents involved do not share in our common humanity. As with cultural relativism, behaviors are recognized as deviant but there is no allegation of moral liability. These two views "combine to produce an attitude of acceptance towards parental accounts and a sense that an accusation of parental failure is a matter of almost inconceivable gravity" (1983, p. 218). They combine to eliminate the majority of potential cases by "allowing front-line workers to prefer an optimistic reading of client behavior" (p. 82). They also save the taxpayer a great deal of money by not addressing the social conditions related to questionable parenting practices). These authors offer an example in which a child was clearly made a scapegoat. Because her parents demonstrated a capacity for loving relationships with their other children, the agency did not intervene (p. 87). The following excerpt describes a health visitor overlooking a quite prominent black eye on a baby. The researcher who accompanied the health visitor to the home wrote this:

> This baby has a fairly large and extremely obvious black eye. From what I could gather the health visitor made no comment to the mother about it nor did the nursing auxiliary (who was helping with a routine domiciliary hearing test) . . . HV went off to speak to another mother (in the same house). . . . While HV was doing this, the nursing auxiliary was talking to the other mum and saying things like, "Amy's at a very difficult age." The mother said to her, "I nearly strangled her last night." I pricked up my ears rather and then the mother said to the nursing auxiliary, "I expect you are wondering how she got her black eye." The nursing auxiliary didn't really take much notice and the mother says, "It was my fault." The nursing auxiliary continued to sort of coo and chuckle at the baby. . . . The mother went on to talk about something else. Once we were in the car I asked HV if she had said anything about the black eye to the mother. She said not. She thought some explanation would be given and she didn't think that this was a bashed baby. The nursing auxiliary made no reference to the fact that the mother had tried to speak to her about it and we let the subject drop. HV, however, referred to this later and again the next day. (next day) HV once again brought up the child with the black eye. It seems to be preying on her mind that she didn't ask this mother about it and she tried to explain to me again why she didn't think that this mother would batter her child. (Dingwall et al., 1983, p. 100)

Just as clinicians may misinterpret the significance of signs that are there, they may misinterpret the importance of signs that are absent (see discussion of nonoccurrences in Chapter 14).

Dingwall and his colleagues highlight the elasticity of the rules of cultural relativism and natural love. "What may seem like eccentricities or perversions are elevated into valid cultural statements" (1983, p. 88). Reliance on these rules encourages acceptance of clients' accounts or conclusions "that the fault lies within them, for failing to sufficiently empathize with the alleged deviant." These authors point out that use of these principles helps to solve the problems faced by helpers. That is, cultural relativism and natural love can be invoked to bridge the gap between ideals and the realities of practice. At a higher level, they serve to maintain current imbalances in resources between those who are poor and those who are not. The rule of optimism may be used to rationalize insufficient services to clients insured by managed care systems. This rule should be balanced against concern to protect clients from serious harm, such as restoring a child who has been abused to parents who again abuse him or her.

The fallacy of prevention is another form of the rule of optimism. That is, potential benefits of behaviors alleged to decrease risk of certain diseases are greatly inflated, obscuring the uncertainty of achieving such outcomes (Skrabanek & McCormick, 1998).

## SUMMARY

Clinicians classifiy clients. Factors that may compromise the accuracy of classification are often forgotten in the pressures of everyday practice, resulting in errors such as inappropriate stereotyping and false dilemmas. Pathological labels may be accepted as describing reality with little understanding of the ascribed nature of these labels and the political, economic, and social functions they serve—for example, to control and regulate undesired behaviors. Clinicians base their selection of practice knowledge on various kinds of authority, some of which are sound (sound evidence is offered for the claim) and many of which appeal to pseudoauthority (such as popular sentiment, traditional wisdom, and consensus). Clinicians often have a pathological set; they search for deficiencies and neglect client assets. This creates undue pessimism about the possibility of change and may stigmatize clients. Factors that contribute to this tendency include practice theories that emphasize pathology and ignore the role of environmental contingencies, lack of familiarity with the political, social, and economic functions of psychiatric labels, ignorance of norms and the range of individual differences, and protection against failure. An opposite rule, the rule of optimism, may come into play when resources would be overwhelmed by recognizing all the problems and needs that are present. This also serves a function in saving funds that would be required to address the social and economic conditions related to many social and personal problems, such as child maltreatment, depression, and substance abuse.

# PART III

# DECISION AIDS

---

CHAPTER 8

# Content and Procedural Knowledge

C RITICAL THINKING SKILLS are not enough to make well-reasoned clinical decisions—specialized knowledge may also be needed. This may concern the following:

- Developmental norms related to given age groups
- Normal and deviant interaction patterns in relation to given concerns, such as parent-child interactions
- Indicators of psychopathology
- Evidentiary status of assessment measures and protocols related to given concerns
- Strategies for enhancing client participation
- Evidentiary status of given intervention methods and protocols
- Risk indicators for suicide attempts
- Accuracy of different measures of progress
- Procedures for encouraging generalization and maintenance

Fox and Swazey (1974) suggest that there are three major causes of failure: (1) lack of available information about the problem; (2) failure to get it; (3) failure to recognize one's own ignorance. Gaps between practice-related knowledge and what is used by clinicians was a key reason for the development of evidence-based practice, as described in Chapter 10. "Reasoning does not occur in a vacuum. Although logic has to do with the forms of argument as distinct from their content, the arguments we encounter in real life have content as well as form, and being able to judge the truth or falsity of that content, clearly a knowledge-based ability, is essential to effective reasoning in any but the most abstract sense" (Nickerson, 1985, p. 359; see also discussion of naturalistic decision making in Chapter 9). The term *knowledge* refers to information that decreases or reveals uncertainty about how to attain a certain outcome (Nickerson, 1986a). The importance of knowledge of content was one of the major findings of the study of diagnostic decision making among physicians (Elstein et al., 1978). As Nickerson (1988) points out, "To think effectively in any domain one must know something about the domain and, in general, the more one knows the better" (p. 13). Specialists who make accurate decisions in their area of expertise may not display expertise when making decisions outside of their field. There are different kinds of problems, and different aspects of decision making differ in their importance in relation to the kind of problem. For example, in some medical problems, if you diagnose the problem, all else falls in place. In other cases, diagnosis offers little guidance. Empirical literature related to clinical decisions has increased, as have tools to get access to useful information, such as the process of evidence-based practice (see Chapter 10). Practice guidelines, including assessment protocols and treatment manuals, have been developed in many areas. A key application challenge, taken on directly in evidence-based practice, concerns helping practitioners to gain timely access to research findings related to decisions that must be made; time pressures emphasize the value of efficient methods. Material is of little value if it cannot be located when needed. An information management system (storage and retrieval) is vital (Gray, 2001a).

Knowledge that is helpful in making accurate inferences includes content or topical knowledge (facts related to a domain and concepts that contribute to understanding problems), procedural knowledge ("how-to"), and self-knowledge (such as awareness of personal assets and limitations in processing information). For example, being informed regarding dysfunctional and constructive communication patterns in families offers a conceptual framework for translating concerns such as "poor communication" into a picture that may clarify client concerns. Practice-related claims and beliefs differ along many dimensions, including their evidentiary status and the intensity with which they are believed. They differ in how easy it is to critically appraise their accuracy. There may be uncertainty about something that can be determined, such as the existence of Freud, or personal uncertainty about the exact indeterminacy of an event that is determinate, such as the probability of a coin that is unbiased coming up heads. It may be impossible to decide an issue because it lies outside the rules of the system—for example, what kind of chairs chess players should sit on. Clinicians as well as clients may be bamboozled into accepting bogus claims about practice methods by the emotive persuasiveness of human service advertisements and rhetorical presentations in the media, as well as in professional contexts, such as conferences (see Chapters 4 and 5). Claims may be draped in the trappings of science to increase credibility. Consider appeals to the scientific status of psychiatric classification systems and interventions that do not match empirical findings (e.g., see Houts, 2002; Kutchins & Kirk, 1997; Petrosino et al., 2003). Critical thinking skills can be used to increase the percentage of accurate data acquired relative to unsupported or incorrect data.

## IS KNOWLEDGE IMPORTANT IN THE INTERPERSONAL HELPING PROFESSIONS?

As suggested earlier, research exploring decision making in medicine highlights the importance of specialized knowledge (e.g., Elstein et al., 1978). The process of evidence-based practice is designed to help you to discover information that may help clients attain outcomes they value. The development of treatment manuals and practice guidelines assumes that specialized knowledge contributes to successful outcomes. (See related discussion in Norcross, Beutler, & Levant, 2006.) Studies comparing the relative effectiveness of "lay helpers" (people with no specialized training in interpersonal helping) with trained practitioners show that nonprofessionals are as effective as professionals in attaining a variety of outcomes valued by clients (Christensen & Jacobson, 1994; Dawes, 1994a). Strupp and Hadley (1979) found that a college professor of English who was friendly and supportive but with no specialized training in working with clients was more effective than trained professionals in helping clients. Garb (1998) concludes that "overall results on presumed expertise, experience, training, and validity are disappointing" (p. 17). Lack of differences between professionals and untrained individuals in many situations may be related to common "nonspecific factors" shared by many helping efforts, such as warmth and empathy (Lambert & Barley, 2002; Wampold, 2001). Both trained clinicians and naive subjects display biases, such as incorrect assumptions regarding associations between certain signs and symptoms. For example, reports of undergraduate students about covariations of symptoms with signs in "clinical data" that contained no systematic relationship duplicated those of experienced clinicians (Chapman & Chapman, 1969). Both naive subjects and clinicians reported that patients who were suspicious of others tended to distort drawings of the eyes; that dependent clients tended to make feminine or childlike drawings; and that impotent clients drew figures with broad shoulders. Gigerenzer (2002a) describes various sources of "innumeracy," such as the illusion of certainty and ignorance and miscommunication of risk.

If little is known in an area, there might not be much difference in effectiveness between trained and untrained helpers; so-called "common factors" and characteristics of particular practitioners may assume preeminence and eliminate differences in effectiveness between professionals and nonprofessionals. Nonprofessionals may be even more empathic and warm. If graduate education encourages excessive focus on pathology, untrained helpers may have an edge. Training in the *DSM* increases use of such diagnostic categories (Pottick, Wakefield, Kirk, & Tian, 2003). On the other hand, when specialized knowledge is available, its use, combined with nonspecific helping skills, should give the edge to professionals who are familiar with this knowledge and who also possess high levels of relationship skills. The more empirically based domain-specific knowledge is available, the more important it is to consider this in making decisions. For example, knowledge about the degree of effectiveness of different kinds of services in relation to achieving a given outcome will decrease the likelihood that potential success will be underestimated or overestimated. And, no matter what the current state of knowledge, ignorance, and uncertainty regarding a decision, shouldn't professionals share this with clients to fulfill informed consent requirements?

## DIFFERENCES BETWEEN NOVICES AND EXPERTS

Research in the areas of problem solving in physics and mathematics indicates that experts differ from novices both in quality of outcomes achieved (experts are superior) and in processes used. Experts pay more attention to problem definition and structure problems at a deeper (more abstract) level compared to novices, who tend to accept problems as given (Voss, 1989). For example, experts in physics tend to sort problems in relation to abstract laws and principles, whereas novices sort problems in relation to surface structure (i.e., concepts directly stated in the problem); experts categorize problems by using essential information required to discover a solution, whereas novices attend to the superficial aspects of problems (Chi, Feltovich, & Glaser, 1980). Experts learn about possible causes associated with a given behavior, sign, or syndrome; this has been referred to as the "logical competitor set" (Feltovich, Johnson, Moller, & Swanson, 1984). For example, someone well trained in contingency analysis (detecting relationships between behaviors and environmental circumstances) can recognize patterns of interaction when observing parents and children or residents and staff (Dishion & Granic, 2004). Experts develop skill at *meta-reasoning*. This may include planning a problem-solving approach, considering competing hypotheses, asking questions that prime the use of helpful data, and reviewing assumptions in terms of their consistency with the evidence at hand. Expert problem solving takes advantage of new possibilities as they arise; it is opportunistic (Lesgold et al., 1988). Being aware of what we know and what we do not know is an ingredient of expertise. Experts compared to novices possess domain-specific knowledge in an area and can more rapidly identify what information is needed to solve a problem. Indeed, they seem to use a different reasoning process compared to novices, based on many experiences providing corrective feedback. Differences between experts and novices described by Salas and Klein (2001) include:

- They know more (for example, more strategies).
- They demonstrate superior performance, mainly in their own areas of expertise.
- They know better how to use what they know; they are faster than novices at solving problems.
- What they know is better organized, enabling speedy recognition of patterns.
- They represent problems at a deeper level compared to novices.

- What they know is more accessible; they have superior short-term and long-term memories.
- They have better learning skills.
- They are more likely to carry out an "executive review" of their reasoning process—to assume simultaneously the roles of doer and observer—if there is time to do so.

Skills and knowledge, suggested in Phillips, Klein, and Sieck (2005), include the following:

- Perception skills (making fine discriminations).
- Mental models: representations of the world that reflect broader and deeper knowledge compared to novices—"they know how tasks and subtasks are supposed to perform, how equipment is supposed to function, and how teams are supposed to coordinate" (p. 300).
- Sense of typicality and association: Experts have a "repertoire of patterns" (p. 30); they can quickly recognize and accurately interpret information. "The repertoire of patterns that allow experts to recognize situations as typical, also enables them to spot information that is expected but missing from the picture, and to detect anomalies that are present but not expected" (p. 301).
- Routines.
- Declarative knowledge.
- Running mental simulations: imagining different patterns of events "by combining what they know to be true with what might be based on what they see in the new situation" (p. 301).
- Spotting anomalies and detecting problems: Experts spend more time analyzing situations.
- Finding leverage points.
- Managing uncertainty.
- Taking one's own strengths and limitations into account.

Experts do not necessarily perform better than novices in unstructured problem areas such as psychology and psychiatry (Johnson, 1988). For example, Goldberg (1959) compared the ability of psychiatrists with that of their secretaries in diagnosing brain damage by using the Bender-Gestalt test. There was no difference between these two groups. And no relationship was found between individual diagnostic accuracy and degree of confidence. (See also Hinds, 1999.) People, whether familiar with a domain or not, have difficulty integrating diverse sources of information, as is required in clinical decisions, and tend to make certain kinds of errors (such as being inconsistent in how data are combined), which may decrease the accuracy of judgments. Clinicians as well as lay people often have incorrect views about probability and change. Experts as well as novices are prey to a variety of illusions, such as the illusion that one can have control over an outcome when this is not possible, and make a variety of errors even in their own area of expertise (see Hammond, 1996).

Information derived from interviewing experts has been used to develop computerized expert systems; judgments given are codified into rules, which are referred to as the knowledge base. A program is then developed that will simulate and (it is hoped) improve on human reasoning (e.g., see Groen & Patel, 1988). Such systems have been used to diagnose disease, to select antibiotics, and to play chess. Gains suggested from the development and evaluation of artificial intelligence systems include encouraging clear description of the processes involved, understanding the complexity of judgmental tasks, the importance of knowledge of the task environment, and the importance of controlling relevance (Medin, 1989). Dreyfus and Dreyfus (1986) argue that artificial intelligence systems have not lived up to their promise because experts do not use rules to arrive at their decisions; therefore, it will do little good to interview the experts because they cannot describe how they arrive at their decisions. (See also critique in Hammond, 1996.) The experts themselves do not know what they know and therefore cannot tell it to investigators eager to identify the rules used to construct expert systems. Instead of using rules, Dreyfus and Dreyfus believe that the expert recognizes "thousands of special cases" (p. 108). They suggest that when experts are asked how they arrive at their decisions, they are forced to abandon the thinking system they use and revert to the level of novices, describing rules they no longer use. They suggest that experts no longer have access to these rules. Keep in mind that Dreyfus and Dreyfus are focusing on unstructured problems—those in which the goal, the relevancy of information, and the effects of decisions are unclear (p. 36); these are the kinds of problems clinicians deal with.

Skill in solving unstructured problems seems to require a great deal of experience with the domain. Experience permits the building of an extensive library of distinguishable situations. Chase and Simon (1973) estimate that a chess master can recognize 50,000 types of positions. Not only may these positions have no names, but they do not seem capable of being described verbally. Thus, Dreyfus and Dreyfus (1986) argue that expert behavior is not governed by rules and is not abstract. Many other investigators share this view; they argue that the basis of diagnostic expertise is the possession of a large memory store of symptom patterns, each of which is associated with a diagnosis and a course of action (see, for example, Feltovich et al., 1984). Research concerning naturalistic decision making also suggests this view (Klein, 1998; Zsambok & Klein, 1997). Based on extensive interviews with highly experienced firefighters, nurses, and paramedics, Klein (1998) argues that expert decision-makers do not rely on formal rules or a careful comparison of different options or formal decision models, but instead quickly size up a situation based on informed intuition, to identify important cues relying on the similarity of the new situation to others previously experienced. Klein calls this "primed decision making"; it is one model of decision making in naturalistic situations (for other models, see Zsambok and Klein, 1997).

Interviews with experts show that it is difficult for them to identify the cues they use. For example, an experienced pediatric nurse looked at a baby and said "This baby is in trouble" (which was true). When asked why, she may say "I just knew it." It took a while for her to identify specific characteristics of the baby's features she used as cues. Such research highlights the importance of *situation awareness*, that is, having an accurate understanding of what is occurring in a situation from moment to moment as circumstances change (see also Durso & Gronlund, 1999). Thus, expertise is closely related to "pattern recognition," based on extensive experience offering corrective feedback concerning what is the best course of action. This experience allows experts, compared to novices, to see different things, such as opportunities for problem solution (leverage points). Ineffective reasoners may fail to note relevant features, such as unexpected anomalies, or attend to irrelevant ones. Useful strategies may include dividing a problem into subproblems and recognizing that a problem is similar to certain kinds of past problems—there is a similar story. Thus, research shows that experienced decision makers do not follow a "rational model" of decision making, in which one defines the problem, identifies options, evaluates them, and then makes a decision. Rather, they seem to quickly size up a situation and decide on an option. Klein (1998), as well as others, emphasizes the importance of experience that provides corrective feedback as a "source of power"—a background we can take advantage of in future situations to make sound decisions. In this view we will not acquire expertise by reading books. We must practice in real-life situations and receive corrective feedback regarding the consequences of our decisions. This description of expertise highlights the critical role of procedural in addition to content knowledge.

Klein (1998) notes that experts see the world differently. They see things the rest of us cannot. Often experts do not realize that the rest of us are unable to detect what seems obvious to them (p. 147). What is visible to experts that is not visible to others includes:

- Patterns that novices do not notice
- Anomalies—events that did not happen and other violations of expectancies
- The big picture (situational awareness)
- The way things work
- Opportunities and improvisations
- Events that either already happened (the past) or are going to happen (the future)
- Differences that are too small for novices to detect
- Their own limitations (Klein, 1998, pp. 148–149)

He argues that these characteristics are related to pattern matching and mental simulation. "Pattern matching" (intuition) refers to the ability of the expert to detect typicality and to notice events that did not happen and other anomalies that violate the pattern. Mental simulation refers to quickly running things through one's mind as to what could happen in real time, in real-life situations. By recognizing "typicality" (a certain kind of pattern), experts identify when this pattern is violated—that is, when there is an anomaly that should be attended to. Indeed, failure to recognize anomalies is related to escalation toward a major mistake. Based on his study of decision makers in real-life situations, he argues that:

- Experience counts.
- Expertise depends on perceptual skills: . . . "Learning takes many cases to develop."
- The computer metaphor of thinking is incomplete.
- Skilled problem solvers and decision makers are themselves scientists and experimenters. They are actively searching for and using stories and analogues . . . to learn about important causal factors. . . .
- Skilled problem solvers and decision makers are chameleons. They can simulate all types of events and processes in their heads.
- Sources of power [such as situation awareness and pattern-recognition] operate in ways that are not analytical. They are generative, channeling decision making from opportunity to opportunity rather than exhaustively filtering through all the permutations. They enable the decision maker to redefine goals and also to search for ways to achieve existing goals. They trade accuracy for speed, and therefore allow errors. (p. 287)

"Sources of power" emphasized include the following:

1. Intuition (pattern recognition, having the big picture, achieving situation awareness).
2. Mental simulation (seeing the past and the future).
3. Using leverage points to solve ill-defined problems.
4. Seeing the invisible (perceptual discriminations and expectancies).
5. Storytelling.
6. Analogical and metaphorical reasoning.
7. Reading people's minds (communicating intent).
8. Rational analysis.
9. Team learning (drawing on the experience base of a team). (p. 288)

Other kinds of judgments and abilities he identifies include the following:

1. Judging the typicality of the situation.
2. Judging typical goals.
3. Recognizing typical courses of action.
4. Judging the solvability of a problem.
5. Detecting anomalies.
6. Judging the urgency of a problem.

7. Detecting opportunities.
8. Making fine discriminations.
9. Detecting gaps in a plan of action.
10. Detecting barriers that are responsible for gaps in a plan of action. (p. 288)

Experts draw on both the past and the future in making decisions in the present. "The ability to see the past and the future rests on an understanding of the primary causes of the domain and the ability to apply these causes to run mental simulations. This is one way to distinguish true experts from people who pretend to be experts. The pretenders have mastered many procedures and tricks of the trade; their actions are smooth. . . . However, if they are pushed outside of the standard pattern, they cannot improvise. They lack a sense of the dynamics of the situation. They have trouble explaining how the current state of affairs came about and how it will play out" (p. 156). Different decision tasks require different "time horizons" (how long we should look into the future to make a decision). Experts prepare themselves for changing situations. Klein offers the example of the term "flying behind the plane" in aviation that is used to describe people who are so wrapped up in what they are doing that they are insensitive to what lies ahead (p. 155). "It describes people who are either so novice or so overworked or have such poor situation awareness that they are not generating expectancies; they are not preparing themselves properly" (p. 155). Klein also suggests that experts are better at seeing both outside and inside. The role of self-knowledge and self-reflection has been emphasized by scholars in the area of critical thinking and decision making (e.g., Nickerson, 1986; Paul, 1993). Certainly Socrates was the preiminent advocate of self-knowledge—particularly in relation to one's own vast ignorance. Experts are better at critiquing themselves when things are slipping away. Because their content knowledge is better organized, they have more free time compared to a novice who is still struggling to integrate different bits of knowledge, and who therefore lacks time to look ahead and backward in ways that facilitate decision making in the present.

Research regarding naturalistic decision making has implications for learning how to make better decisions—for becoming an expert. It suggests that the best way to become an expert is to have repeated practice opportunities with corrective feedback. This focus is reflected in problem-based learning, in which students are repeatedly confronted with how to solve problems of real-life concern to clients in real time. (See later discussion.) Thus, as Klein (1998) suggests, we can "learn like experts, rather than trying to teach [people] to think like experts" (p. 169). This view of expertise highlights the close connection between methods used by scientists and methods used in developing expertise such as it trying out things, seeing if it works, and carefully examining what happens. This view of decision making and problem solving is compatible with what has been found about the causes of error (see Chapter 9).

Challenges in developing expertise include the following: (1) situations are dynamic (changing), (2) we have to predict human behavior (it is often unpredictable), (3) often we lack opportunities for corrective feedback, (4) the task does not have enough repetition to build a sense of typicality (e.g., see Shantau, 1992, p. 282). Doesn't this characterize most encounters with clients?

## WHAT COMPETENCIES CONTRIBUTE TO SUCCESS?

We must identify competencies before we decide how to assess them. For example, what cues does an experienced nurse use to recognize that an infant is "in trouble"? Methods used range from those that appeal to authority, such as simple pronouncements and consensus on the part of unrepresentative samples of individuals, to systematic research exploring links between certain content knowledge, performance skills and values, and hoped-for outcomes. Concerns that arise in both stages include reliability (e.g., agreement among different raters of the performance of the same person) and validity (are competencies related to client outcomes)? Clarity of description of criterion levels related to outcomes, and generalization: Do competencies developed in class and/or one practice setting generalize to others?

Barrows (1994) suggests that if we concentrate on producing students who provide effective, efficient, ethical services to clients, all else would follow. This is an outcome-focused approach to identification of competencies. Agreement based on consensus is often used to identify competencies. Lists of competencies based on consensus give an illusion of knowledge. Indeed, they get in the way of identifying what knowledge, skills, and values are critical in offering high-quality services and attaining hoped-for outcomes via systematic investigation. Many competencies start with the word "knows," "understands," or "is able to." But what does this mean? What would someone who "knows different family system theories" or "understands different family system theories," do, compared to someone who did not know or understand? What criteria would we use to tell the difference? What would someone who "knows" accomplish compared to someone who did not know? I may know how to define "positive reinforcement" but be unable to help a parent to increase the frequency with which she reinforces her child, even a fully cooperative client. That is, I may have *inert knowledge*—content knowledge unaccompanied by performance knowledge. Identifying competencies required to achieve a valued outcome (involving clients as active participants) may require a task analysis, in which those who are successful are observed and specific patterns of behavior are identified, including their sequence and contexts. It may require talking to "experts" to find out what they are thinking when making certain decisions—a cognitive task analysis, as described earlier in this chapter. Here, goal attainment in real-life situations is the criterion of competent performance. Base rates of success by "experts" is important to consider, because some outcomes are difficult to attain, even by highly competent individuals.

# HOW SHOULD WE ASSESS PROFESSIONAL COMPETENCE?

Clinicians differ in the criteria they use to assess the accuracy and completeness of their knowledge. Possibilities include what feels okay; what seems to work; how knowledge compares with that of colleagues; and what makes sense and what's possible to know, given constraints of time, energy, and competing priorities. Some clinicians prefer an approach in which content is valued if it seems intuitively relevant (that is, without critical tests of its accuracy) and if it is compatible with preferred practice theories or if it "feels" right. Others believe that critical appraisal of claims is vital to discover what is effective and what is not. Selecting material based on what "feels right" or what matches a preferred theory may be misleading. The criterion of standard of practice is used to determine whether a certain method is appropriate in lawsuits. Does appeal to this criterion protect clients from harm? If little is known about a topic, there's not much to learn. However, the opposite may be true. Considerable information may be available related to an important decision you and your clients must make, for example concerning parent training, depression, or anxiety. Cochrane and Campbell systematic reviews are available related to many questions.

Methods for assessing competencies differ in how specific and detailed they are, ranging from global assessments to lists of specific clusters of competencies in a variety of areas (e.g., see Erault, 1994). The former have been found by some investigators to be more valid (Regehr, Freeman, Robb, Missiha, & Heisey, 1999). The repeated finding that self-report does not correlate highly with actual performance should encourage us to move beyond surrogate measures such as self-report, reported self-efficacy, views of supervisors, and grades (Ward, Gruppen, & Regehr, 2002). Facilitators tend to overestimate the skills of their students (Whitfield & Xie, 2002). Medicine has taken the lead in using standardized patients. These are individuals who are trained to display certain behaviors, such as presenting certain symptoms to a physician and responding in certain ways depending upon the physician's questions and actions. Standardized clients can be trained to a very high level of reliability; that is, to perform in the same way over different practitioners. Such clients offer advantages of assessing quality of services while controlling for variation and case mix (Luck & Peabody, 2002). Use of standardized clients offers the possibility of discovering different ways to achieve the same outcome—that is, to discover the varied ways in which a given outcome can be attained, allowing for individual styles. You could review your content and procedural knowledge in an area to discover gaps. Can you "fluidly" carry out valuable assessment or intervention methods? Is your understanding of a practice theory accurate? Comprehension is a matter of degree. You may have complete understanding of some concepts, a moderate degree of comprehension of others, and no understanding or inaccurate views of others. You may be familiar with only a small percentage of knowledge available concerning a topic, not because of any inherent limitations on your part, but because of the kinds of learning environments you have encountered, including graduate education. Each offered only some percentage of knowledge that would be helpful in clinical practice and, in the bargain, probably also offered misinformation.

## TO KEEP UP-TO-DATE OR NOT

Gaps between available knowledge and what professionals draw on was a key reason for the development of evidence-based practice (see Chapter 10). Sheldon and Chilvers (2000) found that only 18 percent of social services staff had consulted practice-related literature in the past 6 months. This neglect has also been found among other professionals, including psychologists (e.g., Cohen, Sargent, & Sechrest, 1986). Plausible but surmountable excuses for neglecting valuable sources include: It takes too much time, I cannot find good articles or books, I do not remember what I read, and I do not know how to acquire procedural knowledge to complement knowledge of content. Evidence-based practice suggests methods to decrease the costs of searching and increase the payoffs, for example, by posing well-structured questions that facilitate an effective, efficient search for related research findings, taking advantage of the work of others (e.g., Cochrane and Campbell reviews) and learning how to critically appraise different kinds of practice- and policy-related research. Poor excuses may be based on overgeneralizations, such as: all research is fatally flawed (some is and some is not), the writing is bad (often, but not always, true), nonclinical samples are used (findings are often relevant for clinical samples as well), they do not know what they are talking about (they often do), and some research is fabricated (most is not): see also discussion of objections to EBP in Chapter 10 and discussion of excuses in Chapter 17.) Is reading (or listening or thinking) always a good idea? On the basis of decision-making research, one might conclude that sometimes not reading is better, since we tend to select material that supports our biases, are influenced by irrelevant material, and may alter our memories based on inaccurate information we hear about later (see Chapter 9). So reading is not necessarily a help. It depends on what we read and how.

## DECIDING WHAT INFORMATION TO SEEK AND WHERE TO SEEK IT

We make decisions about what to read, see, and hear, and where to seek it. We make decisions about web sites to consult, what journals (if any) to read, how to read, what to discuss with colleagues, what workshops to take, and what lectures to attend. You could review your knowledge related to important practice questions by talking to people who are knowledgeable in an area or by seeking out related research. Our decisions influence what we offer to clients. Thus, what we read or the workshops we attend is more than a personal matter; these decisions influence the quality of services we provide to clients. The quality of our search skills influence what we discover (see Chapter 11). The Internet and resources such as the Cochrane and Campbell Collaboration databases of systematic reviews facilitate discovery of research findings. We approach reading, listening, or watching with different goals. These may include discovering how to encourage client participation, helpful assessment measures, effective intervention methods for attaining certain outcomes, or how to prevent relapse. Confirmation biases and an interest in saving time and effort encourage us to search for and read material with which we already agree—unless we have and use debiasing strategies to avoid such one-sided approaches. We select material that reflects our preferred practice framework. Behaviorists tend to read articles written by behaviorists. Psychoanalysts read articles in psychoanalytical journals, attend psychoanalytical conventions, and speak to other psychoanalysts. These preferences, if acted on, protect us from contact with well-argued alternative views—not always a happy outcome for clients. In evidence-based practice, helpers search for information related to specific decisions they and their clients must make. A variety of criteria influence our decisions about what to seek and what to ignore.

*Credibility as a Guide*   Selection of what to read will be influenced by judgments of credibility. Credibility refers to degree of belief. As Phillips (1992) suggests, anything can be credible, possible to believe. People differ in the criteria they use to assess credibility (the accuracy of claims). Degree of conviction is not necessarily correlated with the accuracy of a statement. Criteria that may be used include the following:

- *Authority:* believed because of who said it (for example, Freud, Skinner, your supervisor)
- *Liking:* believed because your friends believe it
- *Consensus:* believed because it is the dominant view in a field
- *Fear:* believed because of fear of being different or left out
- *Empathy:* believed because it feels right. (See discussion of empathic explanations in Chapter 3 and intuition in Chapter 4)
- *Scientific:* accepted tentatively (until disconfirmed) because an assumption or claim has survived critical tests (see Chapter 4)

*Mysticism*   Claims may be accepted on the basis of criteria such as divine revelation, altered states of consciousness, or inspiration (see discussion of empathic explanations in Chapter 3). Some subsample of such beliefs may reflect an inability to identify associative cues that we detect but cannot verbally describe. Beliefs based on mysticism lack "a high degree of intra- and inter-judge reliability" (Thorngate & Plouffe, 1987, p. 67). However, there may be consensus within a group (not between groups) because of conformity and habit rather than common mystical experience. Reliance on variations of mysticism by people in all walks of life is striking, as illustrated in publications such as the *Skeptical Inquirer* and *The Skeptic.* "Consider the number of scientists who pray for inspiration and insight rather than perspiration or foresight to guide them" (p. 75; see also www.junkscience.com).

*Critical Rationalism*   Rationalism comprises a part of scientific reasoning (see Chapter 4). Premises are assessed by scientists through critical testing and observation. Premises may neither be intuitively obvious (solid objects are comprised of atoms) nor testable by observation and/or measurement (such as, "Freud would have changed some of his major conceptions if he had access to research over the past twenty years").

*Anecdotal Empiricism (Experience)*   Some clinicians favor anecdotal empiricism: "a claim to knowledge is assessed as credible if it is similar to, or congruent with, recalled anecdotes from personal experience; otherwise it is deemed incredible" (Thorngate & Plouffe, 1987, p. 69). Anecdotal empiricism requires little effort or time. One reason that reliance on this form of empiricism results in errors is that the vividness of our experiences may have little or no correlation with the true frequency or importance of an event (see discussion of experience in Chapter 4).

*Analogy*   Accuracy may be assessed in terms of how well the structure or form of the claim, rather than its content, agrees or is compatible with views judged to be accurate. We tend to anthropomorphize what we see. Different kinds of analogies include metaphors, similes, and models. Advantages of analogies include their value in understanding new events, thoughts, or ideas. Disadvantages include being led astray by superficial similarities.

*Authority*   Most knowledge is not firsthand—it is secondhand, and thus the source should be considered in estimating accuracy. We may evaluate the credibility of an authority by use of one or more of the other criteria discussed in this section. Authority may be ascribed on the basis of irrelevant variables, such as gender and number of academic degrees (see Chapter 7). Whether the claim of an authority should be accepted depends on how important a topic is to us. Gullibility serves important functions, such as preserving a sense of optimism about people, preserving social bonds with other believers, accepting beliefs as entertainment, and avoiding time spent on checking claims that are not important. The nature of the claim must be considered. Metaphor and mysticism will not be of value in checking the claim that a client has been hospitalized for schizophrenia on two occasions. Scientific methods will not be of use in assessing the credibility of the claim that "life is like a tree" or "a bird in the hand is better than two in the bush." Convenience is also a criterion. More than one criterion is often used, as when the accuracy of a claim based on authority is assessed by appealing to another criterion, such as critical appraisal. Conflicts may occur between the head and the heart (mysticism and critical rationalism), and between what we see and whether it makes sense. Choice is complicated by conflicts within epistemologies; for example, conflicting data often are generated within an empirical framework.

*Clarity*   The importance of clarity depends on our goals and what is needed to attain them. Some people value what they cannot understand, perhaps assuming that because of the imminence of the author, it has a profundity we cannot grasp. Sokol (1998) took advantage of this in his bogus manuscript, which was published. That is, we may believe that if we cannot understand something, it is profound—that what is clear is simple-minded. (See also discussion of the Dr. Fox effect in Chapter 5.) Perhaps one reason is that we can use obscure knowledge to impress our colleagues. Appearing knowledgeable about topics others know little about may have indirect benefits, such as speaking invitations (Thorngate & Plouffe, 1987). We may not realize how little we understand about material, accepting empathic explanations (see Chapter 3) and not testing their utility by applying this knowledge to real-life problems and seeking corrective feedback. Both the media and professional sources contain descriptions that appear informative but are not. Social problems may be attributed to obscure social conditions with no description of these conditions or the factors responsible for maintaining them. (See also later discussion of active versus passive reading.) Tesh (1988) suggests that complex multivariate models of causality allow any given advocacy or research group to focus on only one, ignoring the rest. Burnham (1987) argues that the popularization of science by journalists in fragmented bits and pieces is one of the major reasons for the widespread acceptance of superstitious beliefs.

*Is It Important? Will It Help Us to Help Clients?*   If material is not considered useful, it probably is not sought. Psychological importance must be considered also. "Knowledge can also be important because it promotes understanding, provides a sense of order, continuity, elation or peace, establishes a locus for the expression of emotion, inflates or guards the ego, develops or maintains a favored (usually positive) self-image" (Thorngate & Plouffe, 1987, p. 79).

*Interest-Knowledge as Entertainment*   We are more likely to read material if we find it interesting. Motivation is a key variable in learning; for example, interesting presentation of content encourages us to read or listen. Thorngate and Plouffe (1987) suggest that valuable knowledge should be digestible (comprehensible), edible (credible), and nutritious (important; p. 85). Content in professional sources, such as journals, may not reflect these characteristics. Rather it "is by tradition, if not by necessity, stripped of its wonder, ground to an emotional pulp, and distributed in plain brown envelopes. It is food for the cortex not the soul. It is meant to bypass the senses and the passions. It has the subtlety and all the excitement of weak tea" (Thorngate & Plouffe, 1987, p. 88). Here, too, this does not have to be. Scientific reports can and should be written in an engaging yet informative manner.

## ACTIVE VERSUS PASSIVE LEARNING

We differ in our preferred learning styles, in the quality of our learning skills, and in our beliefs about how (or if) knowledge can be gained. Jarvis (1990) argues that a key hallmark of objectivity is being willing to say "I don't know." A willingness to examine practice beliefs, to say "I don't know," encourages an openness to new knowledge. Biases such as the tendency to interpret what is read (or heard) in accord with preferred views emphasizes the value of active versus passive reading, in which we question our assumptions. Clinicians are no less immune to the influence of confirmation biases (Nickerson, 1998) than any other group. The suppression of information, whether intentional or not, is a source of error because we do not know what is omitted. It is not only others who withhold information. We ourselves are in part responsible for the quality of our knowledge and skill. We ourselves are a source of suppressed information via our decisions about what to read and whom to listen to. We ourselves arrange a large part of our knowledge and gaps in it. Our learning style affects the ease of acquiring knowledge. Personal, social, and cultural views of knowledge, thinking, and learning influence what knowledge we acquire (Greeno, 1989; Tweed & Lehman, 2002). We each have a "personal epistemology" (beliefs about what knowledge is and how or if it can be gained) that influences whether we seek information, what we seek, and how we evaluate it (e.g., Hofer & Pintrich, 2002; see also Chapter 4).

The introduction of new material may be followed by the statement "It doesn't feel right." Feelings about what is true are not necessarily good guides to what is true. Some clinicians believe that they learn best through experience; just getting in and working with clients. Often this style is not complemented by conditions needed for experience to be helpful, such as corrective feedback. (See discussion of the limits of experience in Chapter 4 and learning from intuition in Chapter 9.) Faulty beliefs about how we learn will get in the way of keeping up with new information and putting this to use. Clinicians may not be well educated in the use of effective learning strategies. This is unfortunate, since clinical practice often involves helping clients to learn new skills, as does continued upgrading of clinical skills.

Reading or listening can be active or passive. We learn and remember more if we use an active process in which relationships between our previous views (our background knowledge) and new information are explored (Weinstein & Rogers, 1985). Conditions of learning include the following:

- Clear identification of objectives (what is to be learned)
- Clear description of content and procedural knowledge already available
- Sequential steps that match available skill levels
- Clear, relevant means of monitoring progress
- Model presentation accompanied by instruction concerning skills to be learned, the reasons for using these, and the conditions under which they are useful
- Multiple practice opportunities with corrective feedback (e.g., Bransford, Brown, & Cooking, 1999; Hogarth, 2001)

The prevalence of confirmation biases (the tendency to accept beliefs that match preferred views) highlights the value of active learning (a deep approach to learning) versus passive learning (a surface approach). Differences between these approaches are shown below (Entwistle, 1987, p. 16).

The deep approach involves:

- Intention to understand
- Vigorous interaction with content
- Relation of concepts to everyday experience
- Relation of new ideas to previous knowledge
- Relation of evidence to conclusion
- Examination of the logic of the argument

The surface approach involves:

- Intention to complete task assignments
- Memorization of information
- Failure to distinguish principles from examples
- Treatment of the task as an external imposition
- Focus on discrete elements without integration
- Nonreflectiveness about purpose or situation

Surface approaches encourage assimilation of new material; new concepts are integrated into existing frameworks, with relatively small changes in overall views. Deep approaches are needed to create large changes in conceptual views (Prosser, 1987). Conflicts between current background and new knowledge are more likely to occur in deep approaches; they are important in the development of new ideas (Dewey, 1933; Sigel, 1979).

Passive learning often results in "inert knowledge" (Whitehead, 1929). There are two kinds of inert knowledge. One kind is conceptual knowledge unaccompanied by procedural knowledge. This has been referred to as the *"parroting problem"* (Bereiter & Scardamalia, 1985, p. 65); a principle may be recited but not applied correctly. For example, the correct definition of insight may be given, but examination of clinical work may reveal a lack of understanding of this concept. Only when we are asked to apply knowledge can our "procedural understanding" be assessed. The second kind of inert knowledge is information that is available but not used. Knowing when to apply relevant knowledge is one of the characteristics that distinguishes experts from novices. Experts can retrieve useful knowledge from their memories; they have more effective "metamemory" search skills. The two kinds of inert knowledge represent the difference between a behavior deficit (lack of a competency) and a prompting or motivational deficit (a skill is available but not used). The problem of inert knowledge highlights the importance of seeking learning opportunities that enhance procedural as well as content knowledge. Confusion between the entertainment value of information and its value in helping clients and avoiding harm (how useful is it in clinical contexts) encourages the development of inert knowledge. Active reading differs from passive reading in a number of ways. In the former we are active in posing and answering questions about what we read:

- What is the evidence for this claim?
- Is this true for all people, including my clients?; Is it important?
- Can I use this information to help clients?
- Is there anything missing in this argument?
- What is the main point of this section?
- How does this relate to other well-argued views and related evidence about this topic?
- How can I remember this information or store it so I can find it when I need it?

Examples of helpful learning strategies are described in the following. Using these should enhance learning as well as enjoyment of the process. (See also later discussion of problem-based learning.)

*Comprehension Monitoring*   Comprehension monitoring includes asking questions about content, paraphrasing, noting progress, identifying trouble-some content, summarizing information, and reviewing the adequacy of explanations offered. Self-talk, including questions, is used to guide comprehension (e.g., Meichenbaum & Asarnow, 1979). Is an explanation accompanied by a well-argued, evidence-informed account, or does it simply paraphrase a problem to be explained or offer a vague account? Comprehension monitoring is especially important in self-learning, since no one else is available to review knowledge acquired (unless an interactive computer program is used). In programs using a comprehension monitoring approach, students learn basic strategies of "playing teacher." Involvement increases the likelihood that effective responses will be made to obstacles, such as not understanding a word or sentence. For example, one common error is to react to difficulties in learning as an occasion to skip material rather than try to understand it. Lack of comprehension may occur because of a poor match between the background knowledge of readers and content in the text. Compared with novices, experts approach material with different background knowledge. "Experts are probably better able to monitor their comprehension within their areas of specialization than are novices because: (a) systematization of knowledge produces chunks which unite facts into higher order structures; (b) more detailed and organized structures create expectations on the part of the learner; and (c) experts have more explicit knowledge about the organizational principles (structures) involved in a body of knowledge" (Weinstein & Rogers, 1985, p. 621).

Memorization without understanding is not enough to make use of knowledge. Effective learners "identify and define problems with their ability to understand the significance of new information . . . they actively apply particular strategies and *look* at the effects" (Bransford & Stein, 1984, p. 68). Questions of value when reviewing practice-related research include the following (see also Chapter 12):

- Are concepts clearly defined?
- Are measures valid and reliable and is related data clearly described?
- Is it clear how concepts are derived from a theory?
- Is the derivation appropriate?
- Are data collection methods clearly described?
- Is the study design clearly described?
- Are sampling procedures clearly described? Are they adequate?
- Is the study design appropriate to the question pursued?
- Are appropriate control or comparison groups included?
- Are data-collection methods free of bias?
- Are the data-analysis methods appropriate?
- Are follow-up data available? If so, for how long?
- Were changes clinically impressive?
- Are conclusions warranted?
- Are well-argued alternative explanations for results likely?
- Can findings be generalized to other situations?

Checklists are available for reviewing the quality of different kinds of research pertinent to a clinical question (e.g., Geyman, Deyo, & Ramsey, 2000; Gibbs, 2003; Greenhalgh, 2001; Guyatt & Rennie, 2002).

*Elaboration Strategies*  Elaboration strategies include "adding mental imagery, reading to answer questions, noticing categories, attending to hierarchical structure, and finding examples to illustrate principles" (Nickerson et al., 1985, p. 304). Klein (1998) emphasizes the value of stories and metaphors that capture effective decisions in the past. You may draw a concept map or prepare a flow chart. There is an active search for relations, and new content is related to old information. Current views (background knowledge) may be discarded as no longer accurate. Reading a systematic review showing that a method is ineffective (if not harmful) should result in no longer using it. "Effective learners attend to factual content, but they also try to understand the significance or relevance of facts" (Bransford & Stein, 1984, p. 56). Counterexamples are sought. Such strategies increase interconnections among material and so increase options for recall. We introduce our background knowledge through implicit assumptions we make about material in terms of its compatibility, evidentiary status, and usefulness for helping clients. The more clear we are about what these assumptions are, the more clearly we can compare different views. Hagert and Waern (1986) suggest that readers approach a text with different rules of inference and knowledge; because they have different strategies, they process inferential tasks in different ways. Thus, "the reader or reasoner constructs his or her own interpretation of the text, which thereby [may] assume quite a different meaning from that intended by the author" (p. 112).

*Avoiding Confirmation Biases*   Be sure to search for research findings that may disconfirm your assumptions; this will help you to avoid confirmation biases (searching only for data that supports your view) and related negative conse- quences, such as offering clients ineffective or harmful services. Data that do not support preferred beliefs and practice theories are likely to be overlooked and may even be misinterpreted as data that support preferred views. Too much credit is given to data that support preferred views. Consider the study by Lord et al. (1979), in which two studies concerning the deterrent effects of capital punishment (one offering supportive evidence and the other offering negative evidence) were read by Stanford University students who had previ- ously indicated whether they believed in capital punishment as a deterrent to potential murderers. The studies involved two different designs. Regardless of the design used, students found the study supporting their own position to be more convincing and better conducted than the study opposing their position. (Conditions were counterbalanced across direction and belief.) Furthermore, after reading both studies, students were more certain of the accuracy of their original position than they were before they read either of the studies. Read- ing only material that matches our assumptions is unlikely to counter our expectations, which is one of the triggers for learning (Hayes-Roth, Klahr, & Mostow, 1981).

*Other Helpful Habits*   Identifying goals when reading or listening encourages a focus on material of interest and is helpful in avoiding the distractions of ir- relevant details. The process of evidence-based practice, in which we pose well-structured answerable questions related to information needs that con- cern important decisions, (such as discovering what intervention will be most effective to decrease social anxiety), provides a guide (see Chapter 10). Effec- tive readers attend to hierarchical relations—how content can be organized in terms of multiple linkages. These organizational strategies often involve "deep processing" (in contrast to superficial descriptions), in which key prin- ciples are used to structure problems. Tree diagrams may be useful to illustrate the relationship among hierarchically ordered events (see Chapter 15).

One way to understand new material is to try to communicate understand- ing in writing. "The experienced writer sees writing as a technique for learn- ing and discovery, whereas the novice tends to view it as a chore analogous to 'tidying up' [fixing sentence structure and words]" (Bransford & Stein, 1984, p. 104). Writing can be divided into two major kinds, both of which are used in clinical practice. One involves description of events. For example, a record may contain a description of exchanges between family members. Common deficiencies in this kind of writing include confusion between description and inference and a lack of descriptive detail, such as clear examples (see Chapter 13). The second kind of writing involves presenting positions and making and supporting inferences. Striking deficiencies in this kind of writing have been found. Studies in the United States indicate that only about 20 percent of students are able to write an acceptable, persuasive essay (National Assessment of Educational Programs, 1981). Problems included failure to offer support for positions, making unwarranted generalizations, and lack of illustrative examples. (See also Paul, Elder, & Bartell, 1997.) The environment in which reading (and listening) takes place influences how much is learned. Concentration (and thus comprehension) may be compromised by interruptions, noise, and fatigue.

*Be Charitable*   "The principle of charity requires that we look for the best, rather than the worst, possible interpretation of material" (Scriven, 1976, p. 71). This approach increases the likelihood that useful applications of material are identified and decreases the likelihood that valuable content is prematurely discarded. People often respond to differences in a defensive or rejecting way rather than by viewing differences as opportunities to explore new ideas and discover new options. Material may be rejected because of the label attached to it. A clinician who is behaviorally oriented might pass by an article with the term *psychoanalytic* in its title; those who are psychoanalytically oriented may feel a cold chill when seeing the word *behavioral*. It is important to look beyond labels to the quality of information that is offered. Labels tell us too little about too much and imply too much about too little (Hobbs, 1975). The advantages of looking for applications rather than limitations are illustrated by a study in which two groups of engineers were given different instructions in viewing new material. Engineers who were asked to focus on how content could be used came up with more creative ideas than did those who were asked to identify its limitations (Hyman, 1961). A charitable approach is especially important when reading material regarding disliked (but potentially valuable) practice theories.

## REMEMBERING WHAT WE READ

Active reading using elaboration and comprehensive monitoring strategies increases the likelihood that we will remember material. Rehearsal of information and use of different modes of representation during rehearsal increase recall. Learning can be planned or unplanned (as in incidental learning). Problems attributed to memory difficulties may be due to lapses of attention as well as decisions about how to distribute attention. Items that appear first and last in a list tend to be recalled. These effects are known as the *primacy* and *recency* effects, respectively. Items in the middle of a list tend to be forgotten. The manner in which information is arranged in our memory also influences recall; the more associations we have with certain content, the easier it is to remember.

Some strategies for enhancing memory, such as rehearsal and elaboration, can be used when information is first encountered. Others are helpful when trying to recall material. Very negative and stressful emotions hinder accurate perception and memory. The nature of a task influences the effects of stress; if a habit is well learned, it is less susceptible to disruption by stress or fatigue. Deliberately attending to certain features enhances memory for those features. Important information can be entered into a user-friendly referencing or notation system to be referred to later. (See other sources for more detail, e.g., Baddeley, Conway, & Aggleton, 2002; Cowan, 2005; Halpern, 2003.)

## PROBLEM-BASED LEARNING

The importance of developing professionals who are lifelong learners is highlighted by research that shows that the typical professional program produces graduates who do not keep up with the literature; this results in knowledge becoming rapidly out of date, with all the implications of this for clients. Content knowledge is emphasized in many clinical courses: learning *what* rather than *how*. Traditional approaches to professional education reflect a certain theory of education and the assessment of its quality and success. It reflects a certain view of knowledge and how it can be gained and how it can be put to good use in the real world. It reflects a theory in which we assume that we can pour knowledge into students—the bucket theory of education. In the traditional format of education, students are given the *products* of the process of investigation rather than being involved in the process of creating the products themselves, so that they can not only understand this process, but experience the excitement and the challenges of wrestling with problems that make a difference in the lives of their clients. Many have criticized this theory, including Dewey (1933), Lipman (2003), Perkins (1992), and Perkinson (1993). Such criticisms are compatible with research findings in related areas such as professional education, human judgment, and decision making (see Chapter 9).

A key problem with the bucket theory is that what is poured in may not be poured out when needed in the form necessary to solve problems. Perkinson (1993) argues that knowledge does not come to us from without: "We are not buckets into which knowledge can be dumped." He suggests that such attempts result in "Knowledge becoming true beliefs—knowledge that the student will retain tenaciously, knowledge that will not grow." Content knowledge is of limited value if it is not complemented by procedural knowledge—how and when to use it in practice and how to automatize procedures so they can be used efficiently. Research suggests that traditional continuing education programs are *not* effective (e.g., Thomson O'Brien et al., 2003). Learning-how-to-learn skills are critical for clinicians but are often not taught in clinical training programs. There is a remarkable concordance in the areas of problem-solving, professional decision making, critical thinking, and education on the value of active learning, in which students focus on problem solving. King and Kitchener (2002) emphasize the value of offering opportunities to discuss and analyze ill-structured problems, teaching students how to gather and evaluate data, encouraging students to discuss controversial issues, and helping them to explore their assumptions about knowledge and how it is gained.

**Exhibit 8.1**
Paradigms in Learning

| Old | New |
|---|---|
| Knowledge-based | Problem-based |
| Knowing what one should know | Knowing what one does not know |
| Intuition very powerful | Ability to generate and define a question and to search for, appraise, and act on the evidence to solve it |
| Learning for received wisdom | Ability to question received wisdom |
| Learning almost complete at end of formal training—only a finite amount of knowledge to be absorbed | Life-long learning—there is always new knowledge to be absorbed |
| Learning dominated by knowledge from experience | Learning involves complementing experience with knowledge from research |

*Source:* J. A. M. Gray (2001a). *Evidence-based healthcare: How to make health policy and management decisions* (2nd ed., p. 328). New York: Churchill Livingstone. Reprinted with permission.

Problem-based learning (PBL) was initiated at the McMaster University Faculty of Health Sciences in Canada. Students are placed in small groups of five or seven, together with a tutor who is trained in group process as well as in skills involved in evidence-based practice, such as posing well-structured questions and searching effectively and efficiently for related literature (see Exhibit 8.1). Barrows (1994) identifies six characteristics of problem-based learning.

1. Learning is student-centered.
2. Client concerns are the focus and stimulus for learning.
3. Learning takes place in groups of about five to eight students.
4. Teachers are facilitators or guides.
5. Problems are a vehicle for the development of problem-solving skills.
6. New information is acquired through self-directed learning.

This kind of problem-based learning in medicine has spread throughout the world. Those who initiated the program were concerned that medical students were inundated by vast amounts of information and that traditional modes of professional education eroded rather than facilitated clinical reasoning ability (Barrows, 1994).

Problem-based learning emphasizes the *process* of problem-solving and decision making, the need to help practitioners to integrate practice and external research findings (if any) with the unique circumstances and characteristics of clients, including their values and preferences, and to develop the tools to help them to do so. This focus suggests different professional competencies and different professional practice and educational formats—evidence-based practice and problem-based learning, as described by Sackett and his colleagues

(Sackett, Strauss, Richardson, Rosenberg, & Haynes, 2000). They were influenced by the fact that traditional education methods such as workshops, texts, and peer review journals were not effective (e.g., Davis et al., 1999; Thomson O'Brien et al., 2003: see discussion of the origins of evidence-based practice in Chapter 10). This process reflects an educational theory in which it is assumed that we learn by actively engaging with problems we confront—by offering repeated opportunities to integrate knowledge from diverse areas that bear on a hoped-for-outcome and in which we continually confront our information needs (our ignorance) and learn how to address them. This model focuses on making decisions about real clients, in real time, in real circumstances. The focus is on the *process* of decision making. One advantage of this view is identification of resources needed to make informed decisions. For example, how can we get rapid access to high-quality reviews of research that may help us to make informed decisions? Let's say that a clinician works with adolescents at risk for delinquency. Her supervisor suggests that she place a youth in a cognitive behavioral prevention program. She has read in a professional newsletter that this program is very effective. How can this clinician find out if this is true? With access to needed databases and effective information-retrieval skills and the support of her agency to take the time needed to consult related research findings (or access to a knowledge resource agency staff person), she should locate the article by Poulin, Dishion, and Burraston (2001). This is a 3-year follow-up study of programs aggregating high risk adolescents in cognitive behavioral programs. The authors report harmful (iatrogenic) effects. That is, youth placed in such programs experienced negative outcomes. The information she found suggests that she should search for another kind of program.

A problem focus grounds content squarely on practice concerns, highlights key decisions and related questions and options, and links curriculum areas such as research and practice, policy and practice, and knowledge about human behavior and the environment in a manner that reflects the needs of everyday practice decisions. It highlights common errors in different decision phases as well as biases common to all phases, such as confirmation biases, as well as resources needed. It emphasizes the unstructured and uncertain nature of problem solving. Repeated practice opportunities are provided to learn how to handle uncertainty in a constructive and ethical manner. Focusing on problems of concern to clients and/or significant others in no way implies that client strengths are overlooked. It would be a poor problem solver indeed who did not take advantage of both personal and environmental resources. Enhancing self-directed learning skills is a key goal of problem-based learning. For reviews of the effectiveness of PBL see Colliver, 2000; Smits, Verbeek, & de Buisonjé (2002), and Campbell Collaboration Review (www.campbellcollaboration.org). Wood (2003) suggests that problem-based learning provides a more stimulating and challenging educational environment. Only if we confront real-life problems can we see if our approach is effective or not. Focusing on problems of concern to clients in educational activities is compatible with an approach to learning in which it is assumed that we learn through our mistakes. In *Teachers Without Goals, Students without Purposes,* Perkinson (1993) suggests that learning or growth is up to the student: "it is the student who must modify, or refine, his or her existing knowledge when he or she recognizes its inadequacies" (p. 16). In problem-based learning these inadequacies are repeatedly confronted. Teachers and tutors serve as facilitators in this process.

## BECOMING A LIFELONG LEARNER

Professional development requires life-long learning. Perkinson (1993) notes that many teachers including Socrates emphasized that "all education is self-education; the student educates himself or herself. The teacher's task is simply to facilitate this self-education" (p. 20) by providing an educational environment that is *free, critical*, and *supportive*. "Students must become critical of their own performances and their own understandings—while remaining confident in their ability to do better—if they are to continue growing" (pp. 40–41). The need for such an approach is emphasized by research showing how flawed our self-assessments often are (Dunning, Heath, & Suls, 2004). This philosophy of education is reflected in problem-based learning and its goal: to develop lifelong learners. Knowledge and skills in critically appraising the evidentiary status of practice and policy-related literature is vital. As described in Chapter 10, flaws in the published literature was one reason for the development of evidence-based practice. In place of accurate descriptions of research limitations and findings, we often find opinions masquerading as facts, straw man arguments, question begging, suppression of evidence against favored views, and methodological flaws.

Many obstacles to critical thinking (such as lack of motivation, impulsive decisions, and procrastination) are related to a lack of self-management skills. (See also Chapter 17.) Students should emerge from clinical programs with expertise in self-management, including skills in self-reinforcement and planning self-change programs to enhance their competencies. Research concerning the differences between effective and ineffective problem solvers highlights the critical role of self-regulatory skills, such as monitoring performance and seeking feedback. Self-management, as well as contingency management skills, will be required to maintain and enhance critical thinking skills in work environments that do not support or are actively hostile to the use of such skills. Steps that can be taken to prevent knowledge from becoming inert include using it, training others, using prompts, arranging effective incentives for its use, and engaging in "deep processing" concerning the value of knowledge and skills in helping clients and avoiding harming them. Prompts, such as checklists, decision aids, and incentives may be needed to foster use of valuable knowledge and skills (see Chapter 11). Agency policies and practices concerning continuing education programs influence the quality of learning opportunities. Gains in knowledge and its use on-the-job are more likely if such programs include ingredients that facilitate learning, retention, and generalization of new skills on-the-job.

## The Problem of Belief Perseverance

A key challenge is replacing old beliefs with new ones when new information contradicts old beliefs. We tend to cling to old beliefs and for reasons that seem and often are good: they have worked for us, they are familiar, and they give us a sense of control over the environment. Beliefs can survive significant logical and empirical challenges. Consider the failure of debriefing. Subjects continued to believe in initial estimates that affected their judgments even after they were informed that these initial estimates were wrong (Ross, Lepper, & Hubbard, 1975). Subjects were asked to distinguish real from fictitious suicide notes and were provided with false feedback in relation to their performance. All participants were debriefed following this phase of the study; they were informed that the feedback they had received was false and that they had been assigned to one of three conditions: success, failure, or average performance. Debriefing was not successful in altering perception of performance. Subjects assigned to the success condition continued to rate their performance and abilities more favorably than did the other two groups. Subjects assigned to the failure condition continued to rate themselves as lacking in ability and as unsuccessful. The perseverance effects of initial impressions have been found with observers also.

Why are beliefs so persistent? One reason concerns information-processing factors, for example biased search, recall, and integration of evidence (Einhorn, 1980a). Although motivational and emotional factors may play a role, they do not seem to account for the research findings described previously. Confirmation biases, such as discounting contradictory information by offering alternative explanations, come into play. Offering explanations for beliefs makes these more enduring. "Thus the subject who suddenly finds herself confronted with evidence of her superior or inferior ability at discriminating suicide notes might search for some aspect of her background or personality that might account for such a talent or deficiency. The seemingly successful subject, for example, may credit her performance to her familiarity with the self-revealing poetry of an author who later committed suicide; the apparent failure may cite her own cheerful and optimistic disposition as an impediment to the empathetic set of task demands" (Einhorn, 1980a, pp. 26–27). Beliefs are more likely to be altered if concrete information based on firsthand experience is provided that is compatible with current knowledge. Here, too, we see the importance of a true clinical apprenticeship that would offer such opportunities. Popular clinical beliefs receive consistent support from material in professional sources, especially those we selectively choose from the many available. Only by a deliberate search will we discover divergent views.

## THE INFLUENCE OF PROFESSIONAL
## EDUCATION PROGRAMS

A number of changes could be made in clinical programs to upgrade the quality of decision-making as suggested earlier in the chapter in the discussion of PBL. (See also Hakel, 1997; Hoge, Tomdora, & Stuart, 2003; McFall, 1991.) Richard McFall was so concerned about the quality of clinical psychology programs that he initiated a separate qualifying procedure (see Herbert, 2002). Many sources of error that influence clinical judgments, such as confirmation biases, are universal, and we bring unique, dysfunctional habits from our personal lives into our professional lives. There is a lack of attention in professional education to decision-making competencies, including recovery from errors. Instructors may not be familiar with fallacies and biases that influence decisions, or may embrace an intuitive approach to practice and ignore analytic skills (e.g., see Medawar, 1984, pp. 58–60). Economic, structural, and political factors that influence how problems are defined and handled may be ignored, including the influence of Big Pharma. We should learn how to spot and counter human service propaganda (see Chapter 4) and dysfunctional stratagems (see Chapters 5 and 6). We should acquire political skills, such as how to form coalitions, that would help us to achieve changes that benefit clients and create learning environments. A lack of such skills is one reason for the sense of helplessness and hopelessness among many clinicians in agency-based practice. Lipman (2003) highlights the importance of a community of inquiry. An educational environment in which controversial issues are routinely discussed and in which well-argued, conflicting points of view are welcomed encourage critical thinking skills. Discussing the pros and cons of different courses of action and related alternative accounts should encourage us to welcome discussions in an atmosphere in which participants take responsibility for describing their views and related evidence.

Clinical internships may not offer sustained guided experience with high-quality corrective feedback. Clinical supervisors may rely on indirect measures of trainees' skills in the form of process notes, brief written reports, or descriptions during supervisory meetings or case conferences, forgoing opportunities to listen to tape recordings of interviews with clients or to observe staff working with clients. Too rarely do students have multiple opportunities to observe trained staff working with clients, although such observation without tactical guidance may provide little help in any case. Model presentation without explicit instructions about the principles modeled may be ineffective (Palincsar & Brown, 1984). Mentors should share information about *how* they arrived at decisions as well as what the decisions are, so that novices have access to a model of the clinical reasoning process "in action." Helpful questions should be modeled, both questions asked of clients and questions asked covertly. Research suggests the importance of active coaching, including offering guidance, requiring explanations, and evaluating progress (Campione, 1989). Clinical supervisors often reconstruct their thinking process "after the fact" during supervisory discussions; such reconstruction may not portray the reasoning process that actually occurred. Few professional education programs require students to develop expertise in contingency analysis: skill in identifying and altering the relationships between environmental events and behaviors of interest, drawing on related empirical research in both applied and laboratory settings. They are thus handicapped in understanding how the environment (including the reactions of other people) influences behavior, and tend to misattribute outcomes and behaviors that are the result of environmental consequences to personal characteristics. Lack of such knowledge and skill may contribute to the dispositional bias—focusing on characteristics of clients and ignoring environmental variables (see Chapter 14). Programs vary in how they train students to evaluate their work with clients, ranging from reliance on vague, global methods to ongoing monitoring using specific, relevant progress indicators. Ongoing evaluation of specific, relevant, progress indicators contributes to timely clinical decisions.

## SUMMARY

Domain-specific knowledge and skills may be vital in making well-reasoned decisions. Practice- and policy-related research relevant to practice has increased, which makes choices as to whether to seek and use this knowledge more significant in relation to consequences for clients. Clinicians now have more help in gaining rapid access to practice- and policy-related research findings with the invention of the systematic review and the process of evidence-based practice. The accuracy of our self-assessment of our knowledge influences the decisions we make. If relevant information is available, possible discrepancies between what we "know" and what can be known may be large. If considerable information is available but little is used, clients may be harmed rather than helped. Clinicians differ in their goals in selecting material to read and workshops to attend. Some focus on entertainment value. Others focus on acquiring knowledge that can be used to help clients. Decisions about what to read, see, or hear are influenced by comprehensibility, credibility, ease of access of material, and judged importance. They are influenced by our values and goals, such as a concern for helping clients and avoiding harm. Clinicians differ in the criteria used to assess the value of material. Some rely on scientific criteria—has a claim been critically tested, and if so, to what effect? Others rely on anecdotes, what's new, or appeals to authority (status of the purveyor of a claim). Preferences regarding criteria influence what is learned and thus what is offered to clients.

Our skill in learning how to learn, as well as our attitudes about knowledge and learning, influences the gap between our current information and what is available that could contribute to well-reasoned decisions. Active learning skills, such as comprehension monitoring and elaboration skills, enhance learning. Asking "What's missing?" and "Is there evidence that this claim is true?" decreases acceptance of bogus claims that limit the quality of services offered to clients. Use of the principle of charity when reading or listening decreases the likelihood that valuable content will be prematurely discarded. The nature of professional education programs influences the quality of clinical decisions. Inclusion of a high-quality mentoring experience, as well as material concerning sources of formal and informal fallacies, contingency analysis, and the influence of social, political, and economic influences on the mental health industry, all discussed in an atmosphere that encourages critical appraisal of different positions, should enhance the quality of decisions and contribute to development of lifelong learning skills. It should encourage asking questions about claims and a willingness to say "I don't know." Professional education programs should provide students with effective learning-how-to-learn skills, including self-management skills of value in continuing to learn and overcoming obstacles to making well-reasoned decisions, such as procrastination and lack of perseverance. Problem-based learning and evidence-based practice provide an educational format and a decision-making process designed to integrate evidentiary, ethical, and application issues in real time.

# CHAPTER 9

# Taking Advantage of Research on Judgment, Problem Solving, and Decision Making

C LINICAL DECISION MAKING requires choosing among different (often competing) goals and related courses of action. The list of options (the "menu") related to a decision differ in number, variety, and whether they include feasible options that will help clients to attain outcomes they value. Lists differ in their "noise level" (number and vividness of irrelevant and misleading options). Misleading items may be in the list (those that direct you and your clients in unhelpful directions). Invalid assessment methods that do not measure what they presume to measure may be included. (See critiques of the Myers-Briggs Type Indicator, use of anatomically detailed dolls, projective drawings, and the Rorschach Inkblot Test; Hunsley, Lee, & Woods, 2003.) Decision making has been investigated in a variety of situations, including the laboratory (in which conditions can be controlled), as well as in interviews of experts and review of archival data. Characteristics of naturalistic decision-making settings include "time pressure, high stakes, experienced decision makers, inadequate information (information that is missing, ambiguous, or erroneous), ill-defined goals, poorly defined procedures, cue learning, context (e.g., higher-level goals, stress), dynamic conditions, and team coordination" (Klein, 1998, p. 4; Orasanu & Connolly, 1993). Related research reveals two different kinds of intuition—*informed* intuition, based upon extensive experience providing corrective feedback, and *uninformed* intuition, which is not accompanied by such experience. There are different models of judgment and decision making:

> . . . normative models of thinking specify an ideal standard. The idea is to figure out what kind of thinking would bring us closest to achieving our personal goals,

or the personal goals we would have "on reflection"—that is, after thinking about them carefully and well. Descriptive models specify what people in a particular culture actually do and how they deviate from the normative models. Prescriptive models are designs or inventions, whose purpose is to bring the results of actual thinking into closer conformity to the normative model. If prescriptive recommendations derived in this way are successful, the study of thinking can help people to become better thinkers. (Baron, 2000, p. 33)

Prospect theory concerns decisions that do not follow normative ideals (see, for example, Kahneman & Tversky, 1984). Some authors emphasize the importance of both cognitive scripts as well as judgmental strategies for decision making (e.g., Elstein, 2000; Hamm, 2003). Connelly and Beach (2000) describe subject matter expertise as essentially "off-line," and distinct from decision-making expertise in Traditional Decision Theory. In image theory, "subject-matter expertise is central to the decision apparatus itself" (p. 762).

One of the purposes of decision making is to reveal possibilities (Baron, 2000). As Jonathan Baron (1994) points out, the whole point of good thinking is to increase the probability of good outcomes. A good outcome is one that decision makers value; it results in valued goals (Baron, 2000). Klein (1998) suggests that effective decision makers do the best they can with what is knowable. Clearly this is not always done. Deficiencies identified in nursing students' decision-making skills included not making effective or efficient use of available information, errors in estimating risk and uncertainty, and difficulties selecting among alternative courses of action. Shanteau and his colleagues (Shanteau, Grier, Johnson, & Berner, 1991) taught decision-making skills in a classroom to these nurses. Training occurred both in the classroom and in the hospital. Different scenarios were used to test for improvement in the three problems among 115 nurses. Responses of nurses in a control group and nurses who received the training were compared to the responses on the test scenarios of seven expert nurses. The results showed that the students receiving training compared more closely with the data on the scenarios to the expert nurses as compared with the control group subjects. However, there was no improvement in accuracy of probability assessments (see also Poses, Cebul, & Wigton, 1995). Decisions differ in terms of how quickly they must be made, how rich the store of experience is in relation to the person making the decision, the kind of feedback offered, and the time there is to consider the match between choices and outcomes (Connelly & Beach, 2000). New goals may emerge during the course of decision making (Klein, 1998). Differences in how problems are framed (for example, to avoid negative events or to achieve positive benefits), how questions are posed, and how responses are gathered (either by closed or open questions) influence judgments (Fischhoff, Slovic, & Lichtenstein, 1980). Outcome should be distinguished from the process used to achieve it; that is, a poor outcome may result from a good decision-making process. There are different kinds of problems, and different aspects of decision making differ in their importance in relation to the kind of problem. For example, in some medical problems, if you diagnose the problem, all else falls in place. In other problems, diagnosis offers little guidance.

Our knowledge and skills regarding a decision we must make may be incomplete and/or inaccurate. We may have *buggy knowledge*—an incorrect model of how something, or some situation, functions. We may rely on misleading oversimplifications and resist acquiring a model offering a deeper understanding because we view our current model as adequate, when it is not (Spiro et al., 1988). Not only is it important to have relevant information, it must also be organized so that we can take advantage of it when needed. It must allow us to adapt fluidly as needed, in real life, in real time.

There is a rich literature on judgment, problem-solving, and decision making in many different fields (e.g., see Baron, 2000; Gilovich, Griffin, & Kahneman, 2002; Koehler & Harvey, 2005; Salas & Klein, 2001). This indicates that:

- Expertise varies greatly.
- Domain-specific knowledge is important: both problem-related knowledge and self-knowledge influence success.
- Experts use different reasoning processes compared to novices (e.g., pattern recognition, mental simulations).
- Problem structuring is a critical phase: Some ways of structuring problems are better than others.
- Creative as well as critical thinking is required.
- Repeated practice providing corrective feedback is critical to developing informed intuition that allows us to respond effectively: Skill in learning from experience is important, not experience per se, including learning from errors.
- Our goals influence our actions.
- We readily fall into a number of "intelligence traps"; jumping to conclusions (deciding on one option too soon) and overlooking promising alternatives are common errors; errors of omission and commission occur.
- Experts, compared to novices, organize knowledge in a different way, and approach problems on a more abstract level and can more readily identify anomalies and additional information that would be helpful.
- Situation awareness is important (attending to important cues).
- Local rationality must be considered (the problem context).
- The strategies we use influence our success.
- We may have the skills and knowledge required to solve problems but not use them.
- Monitoring progress is important; for example, to catch false directions.
- Beliefs about what knowledge is and how to get it (our personal epistemology) influence success.
- How we decide to allocate our resources influences success (e.g., time spent in overall planning).
- We can learn to become better problem solvers.

Successful compared to unsuccessful problem solvers think more about their thinking. They critically review their assumptions and reasoning. They are their own best critics. They pay attention to data that contradict their assumptions. They ask questions about the accuracy of data, such as: What evidence supports this claim? What evidence contradicts it? Has it been critically tested? With what results? Are there well-argued alternative views? There is often a lack of match between the decisions we make and whether these are optimal in terms of rules of probability. For example, our judgments do not follow the laws of probability for maximizing expected utility. Such deviations are viewed as cognitive illusions or fallacies by some and as adaptive strategies by others (see later discussion).

## PROBLEM SOLVING IS UNCERTAIN

Defining problems and making decisions in the helping professions is an uncertain activity. Uncertainty may concern: (1) the nature of the problem; (2) the outcomes desired; (3) what is needed to attain them; (4) likelihood of attaining outcomes; and (5) measures that will best reflect degree of success. Information about options may be missing, and accurate estimates of the probability that different alternatives will result in desired outcomes may be unknown. Preferences may change in the very process of being asked about them. Problems that confront clients (e.g., lack of housing or day care) are often difficult ones, which challenge the most skilled of helpers. They are often unstructured and untidy (Adams, 1974). Rarely is all relevant information available, and it is difficult to integrate different kinds of data. Knowledge may be available but not used. The true prevalence of a behavior or its natural history may not be known. The probabilities of different outcomes given certain interventions may be unknown. Every source of information has a margin of error that may be small or large. We often do not know how great the range of error is or if it is random or biased.

Even when a great deal is known, this knowledge is usually in the form of general principles that do not allow specific predictions about individuals (Dawes, 1994a). For example, although many convicted rapists rape again when released from prison, this does not allow you to accurately predict whether a particular person will rape again if released. You can only appeal to the general information (see critique of expert testimony in Chapter 8). Physicians usually work in a state of uncertainty about the true state of the patient. They can only estimate the probability that a client has a certain illness. Problems may have a variety of causes and potential solutions. Barriers that may be present are illustrated in Exhibit 9.1. Overlooking ignorance and uncertainty encourages attitudes (e.g., overconfidence) and problem-solving styles (e.g., jumping to conclusions) that may get in the way of helping clients, or delude clients that help is at hand when it is not. This also will result in misinforming clients.

**Exhibit 9.1**
Barriers to Problem Solving

1. Limited Knowledge
- is available about the prevalence of a problem.
- is available about the causes of a problem.
- is available about what methods will be most effective in solving a problem.

2. Information Processing Barriers
- We can only consider so many different kinds of data at one time.
- Inaccurate memory
- We tend to process information sequentially rather than contextually.
- We may rely on misleading "rules."
- Reliance on questionable criteria to evaluate claims

3. Task Environment
- Lack of resources
- Value on winning rather than learning
- Overvalue of tradition (as preferable to change)
- Taboo topics (e.g., questioning claims)
- Distractions (constant interruptions)
- Time pressures
- Reluctance to examine the results of policies, programs, and practices
- Autocratic decision-making style

4. Motivational Blocks
- Value winning over discovering approximations to the truth
- Vested interest in an outcome
- Interest in predicting our environment
- Cynicism

5. Emotional Blocks
- Fatigue
- Anger
- Anxiety
- Low tolerance for ambiguity
- Inability to "incubate"
- Lack of zeal
- Appeal of vivid material

6. Perceptual Blocks
- Defining problem too narrowly
- Overlooking alternative views
- Stereotyping
- Judging rather than generating ideas
- We see what we expect to see

**Exhibit 9.1** *Continued*

7. Intellectual Blocks
- Reliance on questionable criteria to evaluate claims
- Failure to think critically about beliefs
- Inflexible use of problem-solving strategies
- Lack of accurate information
- Limited use of problem-solving languages (e.g., illustrations, models)

8. Cultural Blocks
- Disdain for intellectual rigor
- Valuing John Wayne thinking (strong pro/con positions with little reflection)
- Fear that the competition of ideas would harm the social bonding functions of false beliefs (see Chapter 4)

9. Expressive Blocks
- Inadequate skill in writing and speaking clearly
- Social anxiety

*Source:* Adapted from *Conceptual Blockbusting: A Guide to Better Ideas* (3rd ed.), by J. L. Adams, 1986, Reading, MA: Addison-Wesley.

## SITUATIONS CHANGE

Situations evolve. They are not static. They may change from minute to minute, hour to hour, day to day, or week to week. Our initial hunch and the actions we take based on it influence later decisions. A second interview with a client may reveal an additional concern, such as substance abuse. Unless we recognize new information and rethink our initial hypotheses, we may make poor decisions. "Debugging strategies" may be needed to remind ourselves to attend to important changes in a situation that may call for new approaches to overcome an initial mindset or framing of a situation. Woods and Cook (1999) suggest that situation assessment and plan formulation are interlinked; that is, as we change our views of the situation, we consider what plans we may use to deal with it. Failure to revise our views (becoming fixated on a certain hypothesis) is a key source of poor decisions. Elstein et al. (1978) found that the difference between expert diagnosticians and those who were not as accurate was that the experts held hypotheses tentatively, and were open to revising them as new information that they sought emerged.

## STRUCTURING PROBLEMS IS A CRITICAL PHASE

Problem definition (clarifying and deciding how to structure a problem) is a critical step. Experts pay more attention to problem definition and structure problems at a deeper (more abstract) level compared to novices, who tend to accept problems as given (see Chapter 8). Different theories involve different problem spaces (i.e., how a problem is represented). Consider homelessness. This could be viewed as: (1) the client's own fault (he or she is lazy); (2) a family problem (relatives are unwilling to help); (3) lack of low-cost housing; (4) a problem with service integration (services are not integrated); (5) due to a mental disorder; (6) a result of our basic economic structure (e.g., unskilled jobs have decreased); (7) discrimination based on racial prejudice; and (8) some mix of these possibilities. Only by clarifying and redefining (restructuring) a problem may it be solved, or may you discover that there is no solution. Creative (bold guesses) and contextual thinking will often be needed to describe the "problem space" in a way that yields a solution. Only in this way may you discover interrelationship among different levels of influence (e.g., individual, family, community, agency, service system).

> A problem well stated is a problem half solved. —Charles F. Kettering

## OUR GOALS AND CONFLICTS AMONG THEM INFLUENCE OUR SUCCESS

We differ in our goals when making decisions. Some clinicians focus on helping clients. Others may be distracted from such goals because of time pressures. Meta-goals suggested for decision making include "Maximizing decision accuracy, minimizing cognitive effort and negative emotions both when making a decision as well as following a decision, and maximizing how easy it is to justify a decision" (Payne & Bettman, 2005, p. 126). Goal conflict is a critical concern in many areas, including aviation, medical settings (such as anesthesiology), and child welfare practice. Competing goals in child welfare settings may include providing services to parents and respecting their wishes, guarding the well-being of children who cannot protect themselves, and protecting oneself from lawsuits. As one goal is pursued, another may be forgone. "Because local rationality revolves around how people pursue their goals, understanding performance at the sharp end depends on tracing interacting multiple goals and how they produce tradeoffs, dilemmas, and double binds" (Woods & Cook, 1999, p. 160). We know little about how tradeoffs are usually represented or resolved in given situations. Consider a staff member in an agency who was required to make daily visits to the home of a father of a child who was physically abused. He arrives at the house and is told by the father that the child is sleeping and is fine. What are the tradeoffs here? Tradeoffs include dealing with an irate father whose statements are questioned by the request to see the child, time pressures to get on to other visits, and trying to protect the well-being of the child—is this child safe?

Vested interests in certain outcomes influence our decisions. We may assign exaggerated importance to some findings to protect a favored hypothesis. We are subject to wishful thinking (i.e., our preferences for an outcome increase our belief that it will occur) and to the illusion of control (simply making a prediction may increase our certainty that it will come true). Lack of interest in having a carefully thought out position or a wish to appear decisive (i.e., a "John Wayne" style) may compromise the quality of reasoning, as may a preference for mystery over mastery. An interest in understanding and predicting our environment encourages a readiness to overlook uncertainty and offer explanations for what are in fact chance occurrences. Such explanations may influence our decisions. We may have unrealistic expectations and a desire for quick success.

## OUR AFFECTIVE REACTIONS INFLUENCE DECISIONS

Our moods and affective reactions to different people or events influence our decisions. Slovic and his colleagues (2002) refer to reliance on feelings of goodness and badness in guiding judgments as the *affect heuristic*. Such feelings may affect us outside of our awareness. (See also Raghunathan & Pham, 1999.)

## TASK DEMANDS INFLUENCE DECISIONS

The setting in which decisions are made influences our decisions. Task demands are emphasized in fast and frugal models of decision making (see later discussion). The concept of local rationality captures the idea that cognitive activity needs to be considered in view of the demands placed on practitioners by characteristics of the problems that occur. "The expression of expertise and error, then, is governed by the interplay of particular problem demands inherent in the field of activity and the resources available to bring knowledge to bear in pursuit of the critical goals" (Woods & Cook, 1999, p. 161). The marketing pressures of managed care and related ethical dilemmas have received considerable attention over many years. Knowledge that may be available and needed often remains unused. Variations of a problem may occur. Different clinicians confront different problems. Some features of situations increase problem demands, such as time pressures, sources of irritability, conflicting goals, and unanticipated variations in pacing (Woods & Cook, 1999). Understanding demands that arise "can reveal a great deal about the knowledge activation, attentional control or handling of multiple goals that is needed for successful performance" (p. 161). The notion of rationality favored by authors such as Gigerenzer, Klein, and Simon emphasizes the match between the problems we confront and the environment in which they occur. This focus is also reflected in research that shows that the causes of errors are typically *systemic* (Reason, 1997, 2001); they are usually *not* caused by one person or one environmental characteristic. Rather, they are related to a number of such characteristics (see later discussion of errors). The emphasis on the contextual nature of decision making has implications for the extent to which a given decision-making procedure is generalizable with positive outcomes over a number of different situations; it depends on the similarity and the nature of the decisions and the contexts in which they are made.

## SITUATION AWARENESS IS VITAL

Decision makers have to make decisions about where to focus their attention (Durso & Gronlund, 1999). This is an evolving process, characterized by many changes (LaBerged, 1995). Situation awareness refers to the interlinking of pattern recognition and environmental factors. (See discussion of experts and novices in Chapter 8.) The intersection of the two, points to a variety of

**Exhibit 9.2**
Types of Cognitive Underspecification

| Domain | Type of Underspecification | Consequences |
|---|---|---|
| Perception | Attenuated, ambiguous, or incomplete sensory data. | False recognition of contextually high frequency object or event. |
| Action | Absence of positive attentional involvement at branch point in an action sequence that is required to deviate from habitual practice. | Unintended action taking the form of a contextually typical high frequency routine. |
| Memory | When automatic retrieval of known item fails, a conscious search is conducted with very fragmentary retrieval cues. | Recurrent retrieval of wrong item, which shares features with target, and which is more frequent than target in the search context. |
| Category generation | Only the semantic category is specified, and subjects are required to output as many exemplars as they can in a given period. | Output order corresponds closely to frequency of item encountered. High frequency items are emitted first. |
| Semantic knowledge retrieval | Underspecification may arise from either incomplete calling conditions or incomplete domain knowledge, or both. | Elicitation of the most commonly encountered items within the semantic context of search. |
| Planning, problem solving, decision making, design | Underspecification is intrinsic in these activities. Sources: (1) uncertainty about the future; (2) inadequate knowledge of effects and side effects of planned actions; (3) resource limitations on serial processing; (4) "keyhole" view of the problem space as a whole; and (5) imperfect understanding of statistical and logical principles. | A strong tendency to "fight the last war" (i.e., to apply proven, high frequency solutions to novel problems). |

*Source:* Adapted from J. T. Reason (1992). Cognitive underspecification: Its variety and consequences. In B. J. Baars (Ed.), *Experimental slips and human error* (p. 76). New York: Plenum. Reprinted with permission.

ways in which our thinking may go astray. Relevant knowledge may only be available if accurate pattern recognition occurs. If task demands are excessive, there may not be time to search our memories for patterns that facilitate successful task accomplishment. Woods and Cook (1999) use the term *mindset* to refer to attentional control and loss of situational awareness, framing effects, the representation effect, and juggling multiple lines of thought and activity in time, including breakdowns in workload management and thematic vagabonding. The latter refers to a loss of coherence, in which multiple interacting themes are treated superficially and independently—so we jump incoherently from one theme to the next. This may be because either a mindset is too difficult to interrupt, our attention is influenced by irrelevant stimuli, or a breakdown occurs in setting priorities or making tradeoffs. For example, we may focus on irrelevant tasks; we may lose situation awareness. Irrelevant stimuli may intrude, resulting in distractions. This may occur because a preferred way of approaching a problem is incomplete; it omits vital cues. Various kinds of "cognitive underspecification" can be seen in Exhibit 9.2.

We may use standardized, routinized methods when these are not what is needed in a particular situation. We may not pay attention to the unique features of a situation, and so fail to realize that a change in approach is needed. One question here is: How much evidence should you require that a cue is wrong and should be overridden? There are many opportunities to misrepresent a situation before making a decision that may only be obvious after we make it and compare our initial perspective with what resulted. In simulated aviation scenes "less effective crews tended to simplify the situations they faced and were less sensitive to the constraints of the particular context they faced. Less effective crews were 'controlled by the task demands' and did not look ahead or prepare for what would come next. As a result, they were more likely to run out of time or encounter other cascading problems" (Woods & Cook, 1999, p. 155). Thus, how we direct our attention and what criteria we use to shift it is vital.

## CONFIRMATION BIASES ABOUND: PARTIALITY IN THE USE OF EVIDENCE

We tend to seek and overweigh evidence that supports our beliefs and ignore and underweigh contrary evidence (Nickerson, 1998). That is, we try to justify (confirm) our assumptions rather than to falsify them (seek counterexamples and test them as rigorously as possible). This is an example of partiality in the use of evidence, which can result in avoidable errors. Consider the study by Snyder and Swann (1978) in which students were asked to test the hypothesis that a person was either an extrovert or an introvert. Those who believed a person was an extrovert asked questions that prompted data in support of their view. Students who assumed that the person was an introvert selected questions that would prompt answers supporting this view. Both created a *self-fulfilling prophecy.* This study was replicated with counselors with similar results (Dallas & Baron, 1985). That is, therapists selected questions that offered confirming evidence for their assumptions. Studies of medical reasoning show that *overinterpretation* is a common error. This refers to assigning new information to a favored hypothesis rather than exploring alternative accounts that more effectively explain data, or remembering this information separately (Elstein et al., 1978). Data that provide some support for and against opposing views increase confidence for holders of both views (Lord, Ross, & Lepper, 1979). As a result of considering only one hypothesis (e.g., that a child's behavior is a result of sexual abuse) and ignoring an alternative hypothesis (e.g., that he or she has not been so abused), false allegations of sexual abuse have occurred (Ceci & Bruck, 1995; DeYoung, 2004). Clinicians assign labels to clients based on the *Diagnostic and Statistical Manual of Mental Disorders IV-TR* (American Psychiatric Association, 2000). These labels may result in a selective search for data that confirm the label; contradictory data may be ignored. We use different standards to criticize opposing evidence than to evaluate supporting evidence. Confirmation biases may influence judgments in all phases of work with clients; defining problems, deciding on causes, and selecting service plans. Such biases are not found among experts (Klein, 1999).

## WE USE SIMPLIFYING STRATEGIES (HEURISTICS)

Our information is typically incomplete. We can consider only so much information at one time. The consequences of this may include: (1) selective perception (we do not necessarily see what is there); (2) sequential (rather than contextual) processing of information; (3) reliance on heuristics (strategies) to reduce effort (e.g., frequently occurring cues, vivid case examples); and (4) faulty memory (our memory is inaccurate). In his discussion of bounded rationality over half a century ago Simon (1955) suggested that we use heuristics (simplifying strategies) to solve decision problems. Nisbett and Ross (1980) and others, such as Tversky and Kahneman (1973), also suggested that we use heuristics as shortcuts (rules of thumb) for making decisions in the everyday world. They focused on circumstances in which we violate probability rules and rational decision making, emphasizing errors that result from use of simplifying heuristics such as availability and representativeness. More recently there has been a shift to highlighting the adaptive nature of our decision making as it fits certain environments (fast and frugal heuristics; Gigerenzer, 2005; Klein, 1998). Gigerenzer (2005) argues that many events that have been viewed as cognitive illusions are reasonable judgments, given the environmental structure. A key question is "Are the decisions that result those most likely to help clients attain outcomes they value?"

## AVAILABILITY

We often rely on what is available (e.g., a preferred practice theory or a vivid example). Biases related to availability are shown in Exhibit 9.3. The accessibility of events/concepts in our perception, memory, or imagination influ-

**Exhibit 9.3**
Examples of Bias Related to Availability

*Availability.* Influence by the accessibility of data. For example, we may judge the probability of an event by how easy it is to recall or imagine it.

| Preconceptions and Preferred Practice Theories | Influence by Our Assumptions about Behavior/People |
|---|---|
| Vividness | Concrete and salient data stand out more and are given more weight than are abstract data (e.g., statistical reports) or events that do not occur. |
| Confirmation biases | We seek data that confirm our favored views and ignore contradictory data. |
| Anchoring and insufficient adjustment | Influence by initial judgments or data and underadjustment of these based on new information. |
| Recency effects | Influence by data seen, heard, or read most recently. |
| Frequency, familiarity, imaginability | Influence by how easy it is to imagine an event, by how familiar we are with it, or how often we see, hear, or think about it. |
| Fundamental attribution error | Attributing behavior to personal characteristics and overlooking environmental influences (the former are more vivid). |
| Resources available | Basing decisions on resources available rather than client need. |
| Emotional influences | Influence by our mood or feelings about a person/event. |
| Motivational influences | Influence by our preferences for certain outcomes. |
| Illusory correlation | Incorrect assumption that two or more variables covary. |

*Source:* From *Human Inference: Strategies and Shortcomings of Social Judgment,* by R. Nisbett and L. Ross, 1980, Englewood Cliffs, NJ: Prentice Hall. See also Tversky & Kahneman (1974).

ences our decisions (Tversky & Kahneman, 1973). We structure problems based on past experiences. We tend to see what we think we will see, and seek information that is consistent with our preconceived notions; we tend to disregard conflicting evidence. We focus on items that are easy to recognize and rely on readily recalled examples. Let us say that one of your clients has a substance abuse problem and that you recently went to a workshop on self-esteem. This concept (self-esteem) is readily available in your thoughts. You may associate self-esteem with your client's problems and believe that low self-esteem is mainly responsible for this person's substance abuse. Availability influences our judgments about causal relationships (Kahneman & Tversky, 1973). For example, observers tend to attribute the cause of other people's behavior to characteristics of the person rather than to situational factors (Batson, O'Quin, & Pych, 1982). The "actor's" behavior is more noticeable compared to more static situational events (see later discussion of observer-actor effects). We tend to exaggerate our own contributions to tasks; information about them is more available to us (Nisbett & Ross, 1980). The recognition heuristic emphasizes the value of frequently occurring cues in making swift decisions. Many factors that are *not* correlated with the frequency of an event influence how important it seems, such as how visible it is, how vivid it is, and how easily it can be imagined (that is, how available it is). We tend to overestimate the prevalence of illnesses that receive a great deal of media attention and underestimate the prevalence of illnesses that receive little media attention (Slovic, Fischhoff, & Lichtenstein, 1982).

## The Influence of Preconceptions and Preferred Theories

Preconceptions and theories influence how client problems and possible resolutions are viewed. Often these are helpful. At other times they involve systematic errors (those in a biased direction, in contrast to random errors that may cancel each other out) and result in incorrect inferences. "The impact of preconceptions is one of the better-demonstrated findings of twentieth-century psychology" (Nisbett & Ross, 1980, p. 67). Consider the classic study in which teachers are told that certain children in their classroom did very well on a nonverbal intelligence test that predicts intellectual blooming (Rosenthal & Jacobson, 1992). These children showed superior gains over the next 8 months. Actually, they were randomly selected. Many similar studies show that if teachers have low expectations about students the students will perform poorly, and if they have high expectations the students will perform well. Differences in expectations create different interactions. For example, teachers pay greater attention to students for whom they have high expectations (see Rosenthal 1994a). Our preconceptions and theories affect which concepts and beliefs are available; they influence what events we notice or inquire about. These theories are more available compared to others. The generation as well as the retrieval of data may be biased by preconceptions. Beliefs about the causes associated with a problem may result in selective inquiry during assessment. Practitioners who are psychoanalytically oriented search for different types of data compared to those who use a cognitive-behavioral practice model (Kopta, Newman, McGovern, & Sandrock, 1986).

Preconceptions can lead to incorrect inferences when (1) a theory is based on poor grounds (there is not adequate reason to believe that it is relevant); (2) a theory is used unconsciously; and (3) use of the theory "preempts examination of the data" (Nisbett & Ross, 1980, p. 71). All three biases are common in clinical practice. Practitioners often hold theories that have no empirical support as dearly as theories that do have support; they are often unaware of preconceptions that influence their decisions, and often do not check out their preconceptions by examining outcomes. Overconfidence in and availability of a theory increase the likelihood of biased preconceptions. The more ambiguous the data are, the more descriptions are influenced by preconceptions. We may be unaware of preconceptions that influence our decisions. We may not critically evaluate the accuracy of our beliefs. Much of our understanding of the world is theory-based rather than data-based; our interpretations are inferences based on guesses about what may be true. Unwarranted confidence in a theory increases the chance of incorrect views. We are particularly likely to be overconfident of our judgments about people. Only if we critically examine our assumptions may we identify flaws in our thinking and discover better options.

## VIVIDNESS

We are influenced by the vividness of material in collecting, organizing, and interpreting data. Vivid information is more likely to be remembered than pallid information—thus, it is more available (Nisbett & Ross, 1980). The influence of vividness is illustrated by the finding that college students who spoke to four people were more swayed by the reports of these four individuals concerning the desirability of different psychology courses than were students who read a printout describing the course evaluations of 500 students (Borgida & Nisbett, 1977). Factors that contribute to vividness include emotional interest of material; the extent to which it provokes imagery and is concrete; and its sensory, temporal, or spatial proximity. Vivid case examples and testimonials are easy to recall and crowd out data that, although less vivid, may be more informative, such as information on baseline rates of certain behaviors. Behaviors such as hitting and yelling are more vivid compared to polite requests and following instructions. The client in the interview is more vivid than his or her home and neighborhood, which you may not see; this may contribute to our tendency to make the fundamental attribution error.

Practitioners often appeal to their experience: "I have seen this in my own practice." Clinicians may continue to use certain tests despite their questionable reliability and validity. In a survey of 500 clinical psychologists, they indicated that, in decisions about using a test, personal clinical experience with a test was more important than were data on reliability and validity (Wade & Baker, 1977). These clinicians emphasized the "subjective, insightful and experiential nature of the testing process" (p. 874). They gave more weight to their personal clinical experiences than to experimental evidence. (See also Lilienfeld, Lynn, & Lohr, 2003.) If a suspected murderer is called a "vicious killer," we may more readily believe that he was responsible for alleged crimes. Rook (1984a) proposes that the heavy impact of negative exchanges in relationships that are basically positive may be due to the fact that positive exchanges become the expected background in such relationships; they are taken for granted and are less vivid. Events that do not take place are not as vivid. This type of information tends to be overlooked when it can be crucial. Sherlock Holmes solved a case based on the fact that a dog did not bark at an intruder.

> Vision is the art of seeing things invisible. —Jonathan Swift

Vivid information can be misleading, especially when duller but more informative material is not considered. Helpers often discount statistical information by citing a single case that supposedly contradicts this information. A vivid case example, unless it is known to be typical, ought to be given little weight in making decisions. "The vividness of information is correlated only modestly, at best, with its evidential value" (Nisbett & Ross, 1980, p. 60). A single example certainly should be given less weight than accurate relevant statistical information that contradicts the example. If vividness reflects valuable clues, then relying on this should facilitate speedy, accurate decisions.

## ANCHORING AND INSUFFICIENT ADJUSTMENT

We tend to believe in initial judgments, even when we are aware that the knowledge we have access to has been arbitrarily selected (e.g., by the spin of a roulette wheel). Adjustments from initial values are often inadequate. We often form impressions of clients quickly (Houts & Galante, 1985). For example, helpers make assumptions about clients' manageability and treatability that may influence questions asked and methods considered (Wills, 1978, 1982). Nisbett and Ross (1980) attribute primacy effects to our tendency to generate theories that bias the interpretation of data. These effects are encouraged by *premature commitment* to one assumption and insufficient revision of beliefs, as well as the tendency to believe (often falsely) in the consistency of behavior across different situations. One way to avoid anchoring effects is to consider an alternative estimate at another extreme.

## RECENCY EFFECTS

We are also influenced by recency—what we last see or hear. You may attend a workshop on child abuse and as a result suspect child abuse more readily in families. This, too, is a kind of influence based on availability.

# REPRESENTATIVE THINKING: MISUSE OF RESEMBLANCE CRITERIA

We often make judgments based on the degree to which a characteristic seems to be representative of (resemble or be similar to) another characteristic or schema (theory); Tversky & Kahneman, 1974). Biases related to representativeness can be seen in Exhibit 9.4. We have beliefs about what types of causes are associated with certain effects. We often assume that causes resemble their effects, when this may not be so (e.g., see Gilovitch & Savitsky, 2002). This heuristic involves the use of resemblance or "goodness of fit" criteria when making decisions, such as classifying clients into diagnostic categories, deciding on the causes of problems, and predicting what clients will do. Representative thinking is mainly an associative process in which the associations we have with a certain characteristic (such as African-American or homosexual) influence our judgments. Overestimating the relationship between abuse as a child and abuse of one's own children reflects reliance on resemblance criteria. Consider some other examples:

**Exhibit 9.4**
Biases Related to Reliance on Representativeness

| | |
|---|---|
| *Representativeness.* Misuse of resemblance criteria: influence by the similarity of events (e.g., the probability of an event is estimated by how closely it resembles a population). | |
| Ignoring sample size | We tend to overlook nonrepresentativeness of data (it may not reflect population characteristics). |
| Stereotyping | Treating a description as if it represents all the individuals in a group (when it does not). |
| Overconfidence | Excessive belief in the accuracy of our judgments. |
| Reliance on consistency | Search for consistent rather than informative data. |
| Overlooking regression effects | Forgetting that extreme scores return to mean levels. |
| Ignoring base rates | We tend to overlook the prevalence of a behavior/event in a population. |
| Ignoring predictive validity | Overlooking questionable validity of data we rely on in making judgments (e.g., predictions). |
| Misconceptions | Inaccurate belief that events are related when they are not (e.g., the belief that a series of heads in a coin toss means that the next toss will be a tail). |

*Note:* Some sources of error are discussed in later chapters.

- Foxes have remarkable lungs. Therefore, the lungs of a fox will remedy asthma.
- Turmeric (which is yellow) will cure jaundice.
- Unwillingness to discuss homosexual feelings reflects excessive interest in them. (Here and in the next two examples we see the assumption of opposites.)
- A generous action reflects underlying stinginess.
- Permissiveness when raising children leads to radicalism as adults.

The problem is, similarity is *not* influenced by a number of factors we should consider: (1) whether a person/object belongs in a certain group; (2) the probability that an outcome was a result of a particular cause; and (3) the probability that a process will result in a certain outcome. Reliance on representative thinking may yield incorrect beliefs about the degree to which: (1) outcomes reflect origins; (2) instances are representative of their categories; and (3) antecedents are representative of consequences. In representative thinking, some characteristic "triggers" an associated theory, belief, or schema. An example given by Howitt (1992) is assuming that a man abused his stepson because there is a correlation between being a stepfather and abuse of children. Consider also the example of a college admissions committee reviewing applicants given by Dawes (1988). One applicant was outstanding in all areas; however, she misspelled a word on her application. One committee member believed that this indicated that she was dyslexic, and her application was denied. Let's call misspelling a word $c$ and the associated schema (dyslexia) the symbol $S$. We can then ask about *conditional* probabilities: What is the probability of $c$ given $S$ or $S$ given $c$? The probability that members of $S$ have characteristic $c$ [$p(c \mid S)$] is likely. People with dyslexia often do misspell words. However, the probability that the characteristic $c$ implies membership in $S$ (dyslexia) is given by the conditional probability $p(S \mid c)$ (the probability that people with characteristic $c$ are members of $S$), which is the *inverse* of $p(c \mid S)$. As Dawes points out, it is true that misspelling is a characteristic of dyslexia. However, probably many more students cannot spell certain words who are *not* dyslexic than who are dyslexic. Thus, "The basic problem with making probability judgments on the basis of representative characteristics is that the schema accessed [dyslexia] may in fact be *less* probable, given the characteristic, than one not accessed when the schema not accessed has a much greater *extent* in the world than the accessed one" (Dawes, 1988, p. 70). The number of people who are *not* dyslexic is much larger than the number of people who *are* dyslexic. The problem is that when a schema (i.e., dyslexia) is accessed (considered), the actual extent of the class is usually not, resulting in faulty decisions. As Dawes points out, representative thinking does not distinguish between the probability of $c$ given $S$ and the probability of $S$ given $c$. Most associations are *not* symmetric. We can draw on rules of probability theory to avoid errors caused by representative thinking.

Associative thinking may occur unnoticed (automatically, mindlessly) unless we question our assumptions, search for alternative possibilities, and review the evidentiary status of practice-related claims. Nisbett and Ross (1980) argue that we "are far more confident than is warranted in [our] ability to judge the plausibility of specific cause-effect relationships based on superficial resemblance of features" (p. 117). Causes and effects may bear little or no resemblance to one another. Reliance on representativeness results in errors when we use clues that do not accurately predict an outcome. For example, we may incorrectly assume that because a homeless child is similar to another client we just saw, similar causes are involved. Often, as in recognition-primed decision making, our associations reflect accurate information about important frequencies that help us to make sound decisions. However, reliance on superficial resemblance may lead us astray in making inferences about causes. Other schemas (views) that may be far more likely are *not* considered.

## IGNORING SAMPLE SIZE

Clinicians deal with samples of behavior. Helpers often rely on small samples of self-report data gathered in an interview (a sample from one source). These samples may be biased and therefore misleading. Assessing the representativeness of samples to a population is a key helping skill. How likely is it that a sample (e.g., of behaviors, thoughts, feelings) accurately represents the population from which it is drawn? How likely is it that what you see during 1 hour in a residential center accurately reflects the usual pattern of interaction between staff and residents? Relying on similarity when making judgments about the extent to which a sample is representative of a population may result in incorrect estimates.

## STEREOTYPING

We have biases about certain groups, individuals, or behaviors that influence our judgments. Stereotypes are a kind of preconception. They influence what we do and what we believe (e.g., see Schneider, 2004). They save us time. We do not have to think about all the ways in which a client may not fit our conception. Stereotypes can be created remarkably quickly. For example, the fact that children were told that a visitor to their school was clumsy resulted in many of the children holding him responsible for knocking over a cake (when in fact he had not; Leichtman & Ceci, 1995). Stereotyping is an incorrect assessment of variability, "a set of people who are labeled as belonging to a given group is presumed to be more homogeneous than is in fact the case" (Holland, Holyoak, Nisbett, & Thagard, 1986, p. 245). It is a false estimate of the complexity of a group. The *fallacy of stereotyping* (Scriven, 1976, p. 208) consists of treating a description as if it represents all the individuals in a group of which it may (or may not) be a fairly typical sample. We tend to overestimate the variability of in-groups (groups of which we are a member). Thus, we might assume too much knowledge from a sample of in-group members on some dimension about which we have little information. We tend to underestimate the degree of variability in "out-groups" (groups of which we are not a member). For example, people who are not gay or lesbian may underestimate the degree of variability among people who are gay or lesbian. On the other hand, gay men and lesbians may overestimate the degree of variability of gay or lesbian people. Underestimating the variability of groups with which we are not familiar results in believing that we learn more (than we in fact do) from experience with one member of that group. If you have never before met a Native American you may be inclined to make greater generalizations about what all Native Americans are like than if you have met many. If you have met many Native Americans from only one of the hundreds of different tribes, you may underestimate the degree of variability of behavior, values, and norms in other tribes. If we underestimate the degree of variability we may lose a chance to identify clues about what a person is like or may do in certain situations. If we search only for evidence that supports a stereotype, we may miss more accurate alternative accounts. For example, Ceci and Bruck (1995) note that "Failure to test an alternative to a pet hunch can lead interviewers to ignore inconsistent evidence and to shape the contents of the interview to be consistent with their own beliefs" (p. 80).

## MEMORY AS RECONSTRUCTIVE

We rely on our memory when processing and organizing data. Research shows that memory is a reconstructive process. "With the passage of time, with proper motivation, with the introduction of special kinds of interfering facts, the memory traces may change" (Loftus, 1980, p. 37; see also Ceci &

Bruck, 1995; Loftus & Ketcham, 1994; Lynn et al., 2003). We tend to recall our successes and overlook our failures. This is one reason "intuition" may lead us astray. False memories can be created through biased interviewing methods (Ceci & Bruck, 1995; Ofshe & Watters, 1994). Simply being asked a question repeatedly can result in memories of events that did not happen (Ceci, Crotteau-Huffman, Smith, & Loftus, 1994, 1995). Our memories change in accord with our stereotypes. Consider a study in which subjects were read a description of some events in a woman's life (Gahagan, 1984, p. 93). Some subjects were told later that the woman had met a lesbian and started a homosexual relationship with her. Other subjects were told that she met a man and initiated a relationship with him. A third group received no information about sexual relationships. A week later, all participants were asked to recall details of the woman's earlier life. Subjects who were told that she had initiated a homosexual relationship showed strong distortion effects in their recall in accord with stereotypes about "typical characteristics of lesbians" (p. 93).

Memory may be imperfect because events were not accurately noted in the first place. Even if we accurately observed a sequence of events, our memory of these events may not remain accurate. Although some details may be accurately recalled, we may make up events to fill in gaps in our memory, to create what seem to be logical sequences of actions. We then imagine that we really saw these events. We thus may have false memories (e.g., see Roediger & Bergman, 1998). The illusion of having a memory of an event can be created by including inaccurate descriptive data in a question. We may forget what happened in the past because of interfering events, which decrease attention to detail so that certain characteristics may not be noticed. Drugs and alcohol also affect memory. Another possibility is motivated forgetting, in which negative events are forgotten and positive ones remembered; happy times from a vacation tend to be recalled and sad times tend to be forgotten (Loftus, 1980, p. 711). Gamblers tend to remember instances when they have won and to forget about the times when they lost. Clinicians tend to recall their successes and to forget their failures. High anxiety interferes with remembering events; high arousal decreases attention to detail so that events may not be noticed. Considerable attention has been devoted to the study of memory (e.g., see Schacter, 1999) including discovery of strategies to jog memory. Methods explored include multiple probes, use of different question forms, hypnosis, and monetary incentives (Loftus & Ketcham, 1994; see also Baddeley, 1997; Halpern, 2003).

## MANY INFLUENCES LIE OUTSIDE OUR AWARENESS

We are not necessarily aware of what influences the decisions we make, such as our goals or emotional reactions. The role of unconscious influences on our judgments, especially unrecognized environmental ones, is one of the better-supported findings within psychology. Two out of three sources of influence on our behavior (perception and associations) lie outside of our awareness. We may be unaware of contextual influences on the very goals we pursue in a situation (Gollwitzer, Bayer, & McCulloch, 2005). Gilovich and Griffin (2002) note that "cognition evolved after (and out of) perception. Organisms must proceed and act before—or more pressingly then—they need to think, and that this has implications for the quality with which these functions are carried out" (p. 10). Noticing an event does not mean that its influence is appreciated; appreciation requires awareness of a cause-effect relationship. Biasing influences may not be remembered—that is, "the influence of some event need not depend upon memory for its initial occurrence" (Bowers, 1984, p. 238). If we are not aware of our biases, we are less able to avoid them. We are typically unaware of the heuristics we use in responding rapidly to feedback in changing environments. The down side is that if our decisions are poor ones, then the automatic nature of the process makes it difficult to learn that we are wrong, and in what ways. Lack of recognition of our unawareness is responsible in part for biases such as the false consensus effect (overestimating the commonness of our own reactions; Pronin, Puccio, & Ross, 2002).

## THERE ARE DIFFERENT DECISION-MAKING STYLES

Many different decision-making styles are used, including rational styles that involve systematic thinking and careful consideration of assumptions and related evidence, intuitive styles that rely on inner experience, and some mix of the two. Hammond (2000) views these as being on a continuum. We differ in how spontaneous our styles are. Some people tend to think carefully, other are more spontaneous. Some are avoidant; that is, they try to avoid making decisions. Stanovich and West (2000) suggest that there are basically two kinds of decision-making styles: (1) an automatic style used with little effort, and (2) a more deliberate, intentional analytic style. The original emphasis by Nisbett and Ross on the functional utility of simplifying heuristics was lost over the years, until the primed decision model emphasizing "fast and frugal" heuristics received more attention by authors such as Gigerenzer (2005) and Klein (1998). Such a strategy "is fast because it can solve the problem within a few seconds, and it is frugal because it requires little information" (p. 63). Research concerning naturalistic decision making shows that steps presumed to be of value in a rational model of problem solving and decision making, in which we identify alternatives, estimate the probability that each alternative will yield hoped-for outcomes, assign values to different options, and select the alternative with the greatest value, are often impossible to satisfy and are not needed to solve problems (Salas & Klein, 2001; Zsambok & Klein, 1997). Rather a "take the best and leave the rest" approach may be enough (Gigerenzer, 2005). Experienced problem solvers quickly appraise a situation and select a plan (see also Chapter 8). Consider the recognition heuristic: "If one of two objects is recognized and the other is not, then infer that the recognized object has the higher value with respect to the criterion" (p. 68; see also Goldstein & Gigerenzer, 1999). This view is a continuation of Simon's (1982) bounded rationality—that satisficing is sufficient in many situations—that the time and effort required to identify many alternatives and evaluate their soundness is not only unnecessary in many situations to arrive at a sound decision, it may actually result in more errors, perhaps because too much information is considered; cues that are most valuable are lost in a sea of data. Rather, primed decision making based on past experiences providing corrective feedback helps us to immediately recognize important patterns (Klein, 1998).

Gigerenzer suggests that there are two kinds of search: an optimizing and a heuristic search. In the former there is a kind of sequential analysis. In the second, in which we may use social- or reason-based heuristics, we do not try to optimize. He suggests that we exploit characteristics of particular environments to make sound decisions. What is needed is to identify cues that point to a sound course of action. Too much information may decrease our effectiveness by creating distracting "noise" that results in overlooking central clues that enable speedy action (e.g., Zsambok & Klein, 1997). Gigerenzer (2005) suggests that a rule functions as a heuristic when it has three qualities: (1) It exploits our evolved capacities; that is, "a heuristic is *simple* relative to the evolved or learned capacity of an organism" (p. 63). This simplicity "allows making *fast, frugal, transparent* and *robust* judgments" (p. 64). (2) It exploits structures of environments; "evolved capacities can make a heuristic simple, while the structure of the environment can make it smart" (p. 64). "Ecological rationality implies that a heuristic is not good or bad, rational or irrational per se, only relative to an environment. It can exploit certain structures of environments, or change an environment" (p. 64). He argues that all heuristics are domain specific to some degree, designed to solve certain kinds of problems. (3) A third feature is that "heuristics are distinct from optimization models" (p. 64). Optimization refers to the idea that we try to attain the optimal solution to a problem. A "take the best" approach is a form of one-reason decision making consisting of three building blocks: (1) a search rule, (2) a stopping rule, and (3) a decision rule:

1. *Search by validity:* search through cues in order of their validity, look up the cue values of the cue with the highest validity first.
2. *One reason stopping rule:* if one object has a positive cue value 1 and the other does not or is unknown then stop search and proceed to step 3. Otherwise include this cue and return to step 1. If no more cues are found, guess.
3. *One-reason decision making:* predict that the object with the positive cue value 1 has a higher value on the criterion. (Gigerenzer & Goldstein, 1999, p. 74)

Fast and frugal heuristics can be illustrated in a flow chart or decision tree where there are a series of different decisions related to a problem; for example, is a child being abused or not? (see Chapter 15).

In their overview of research in this area, Gilovich and Griffin (2002) conclude that the "fast and frugal" writers overlook limitations of this approach in some situations. They note that shifting from probabilities to frequencies in the presentation of problems does not always result in easier, more accurate decisions (see Chapter 15). Gilovich and Griffin (2002) as well as Connelly and Beach (2002) propose a rapprochement between different views of decision making. Just as it may be misleading not to recognize differences between views, it is misleading to make the opposite kind of error. Current research suggests a dual process model. What is emerging is not an either/or view of different ways of making decisions, but an integrative view in which two different processes operate: One, which may often be effective in everyday decision making in which we rapidly arrive at decisions, and another that is more analytic and can override the former and does so as needed, particularly on the part of experts. "The two-systems view helps to clarify the differences and similarities between the 'heuristics and biases' program and the 'fast and frugal heuristics' program" (p. 16). Gilovich and Griffin (2002) suggest that "It is clear, then, that there is no deep-rooted conflict between an evolutionary perspective on human cognition and the heuristics and biases approach. . . . Both are concerned with understanding the psychological mechanisms people employ to solve a variety of important real-life problems. Both acknowledge that many cognitive problems essential to survival are typically solved with efficiency and precision. And both can accept the existence of pockets of (particularly informative) bias and error in human judgment" (p. 10).

## CREATIVITY AND INTUITION PLAY AN IMPORTANT ROLE

Successful problem solvers draw on their creative talents to discover options for solving problems. "The scientist and the artist, far from being engaged in opposed or incompatible activities, are both trying to extend our understanding of experience by the use of creative imagination subjected to critical control, and so both are using irrational as well as rational faculties. Both are exploring the unknown and trying to articulate the search and its findings. Both are seekers after truth who make indispensable use of intuition" (Magee, 1985, pp. 68-69; see also discussion of intuition in Chapter 4). Styles, attitudes, and strategies associated with creativity include:

- Readiness to explore and to change
- Attention to problem finding as well as problem solving
- Immersion in a task
- Restructuring of understanding
- A belief that knowing and understanding are products of one's intellectual efforts
- Withholding of judgment
- An emphasis on understanding
- Thinking in terms of opposites

- Valuing complexity, ambiguity, and uncertainty, combined with an interest in finding order
- Valuing feedback but not deferring to convention and social pressure
- Deferring closure in the early stages of creative tasks
- Commitment, as reflected in long hours devoted to work and total engagement
- Recognizing multiple perspectives on a topic (e.g., see Halpern, 2003; Nickerson, Perkins, & Smith, 1985; Weisberg, 1986)

## DOMAIN-SPECIFIC KNOWLEDGE AND SKILLS ARE IMPORTANT

Studies of decision making among physicians emphasize the importance of knowledge of content related to problems. The "possession of relevant bodies of information and a sufficiently broad experience with related problems to permit the determination of which information is pertinent, which clinical findings are significant, and how these findings are to be integrated into appropriate hypotheses and conclusions" were foundational components related to competence in clinical problem solving (Elstein et al., 1978, pp. x–xi). As Nickerson (1988) points out, "To think effectively in any domain one must know something about the domain and, in general, the more one knows the better" (p. 13). *Content knowledge* includes facts, concepts, principles, and strategies that contribute to problem solving. *Procedural knowledge* includes the skills required to implement content knowledge. Let's say that you have been asked to help homeless people form self-help groups. What facts may be important to know? What theories and related concepts will be helpful? What skills do you need to use this knowledge effectively? (for example, critical appraisal skills for evaluating the soundness of related research; see Chapter 12). Knowledge that could be helpful may remain unused (inert). We may not remember what we know or transfer useful strategies from one area to another. Perhaps we never understood facts, concepts, or strategies in the first place. Content knowledge without performance skills to put this into use remains unused. This is known as the *"parroting problem"*; we can describe what should be done to solve a problem but cannot put this knowledge into effect. (See also discusson of experts compared to novices in Chapter 8.) Experts, compared to novices in an area, possess domain-specific knowledge and can move rapidly to identify what information is needed to solve a problem. They have valuable "scripts" that guide decision making (Hamm, 2003). Experts seem to use a different reasoning process compared to novices, based on many experiences providing corrective feedback.

## WE TEND TO MAKE CERTAIN KINDS OF ERRORS

What is an error? Consider this example from a study of error in ophthalmology:

A young boy with an enlarging right lower eyelid mass underwent three biopsies over an 8 month interval. The biopsies each showed chronic inflammation with eosinophils and necrosis. The anatomical diagnosis was descriptive and included the comment "consistent with eosinophilic granuloma." Treatment with external beam radiation on three separate occasions and several courses of a corticosteroid was unsuccessful. Usually eosinophilic granulomas are very sensitive to radiotherapy. When the pathology slides were reviewed elsewhere, the diagnosis of fungal cellulitis was made. The boy eventually lost his right eye, eyelids, facial skin and orbit. *Areas of concern:* A boy lost nearly a third of his face because three biopsies were misinterpreted as eosinophilic granuloma and cultures of the inflamed tissues were never taken. (Margo, 2005, p. 418)

Lipshitz (1997) defines decision errors as "deviations from some standard decision process that increases the likelihood of bad outcomes" (p. 152). Woods and Cook (1999) suggest that "the label human error involves investigating how knowledge was, or could have been brought to bear in the evolving infinite" (p. 150). For example, we may use an oversimplification of value in some contexts that is not of value in others. They suggest that, by definition, experts do not make errors because they are doing the best that could be done under the circumstances. Studies of decision making in professional contexts reveal a variety of errors, such as incorrect definitions of problems (e.g., missing physical causes). There are different systems for classifying errors in diagnosis. One highlights different dimensions of professional competence, such as faulty cognition and technical or integrative skills. Another emphasizes cognitive processes such as faulty hypotheses generation and information gathering (Kassirer & Kopelman, 1989; see also Margo, 2005). Research regarding expert political judgment concerning real-world events within individuals' domains of expertise shows that they often fall prey to the following errors or biases:

1. *Overconfidence.* Large gaps between the subjective probabilities assigned to outcomes and the objective probabilities of those outcomes occurring.
2. *Cognitive conservatism.* They are too slow to update their beliefs.
3. *Certainty of hindsight.* Mistakes may be denied. "They tend to recall assigning higher subjective probabilities to those . . . outcomes that occur than they actually assigned before learning what occurred."
4. *Theory-driven standards of evidence and proof.* They "generally impose higher standards of evidence and proof on dissonant claims than they do on consonant ones." They use a double standard.
5. *Systematic evidence of incoherence in subjective probability judgments.* They "often judge the likelihood of the whole to be less, sometimes far less, than the sum of its parts." (Tetlock, 2003, pp. 233–234)

Reason (2001) distinguishes among mistakes, violations, lapses, and slips that may occur during planning, recalling intentions, carrying out a task, or monitoring (see Exhibit 9.5). A *violation* entails knowingly omitting an important step. A *lapse* involves not recalling an intention to carry out an important task at the needed time. A *slip* entails unwittingly omitting an important task in a sequence and/or not detecting it. Common errors in different problem-solving phases can be seen in Exhibit 9.6. Studies of decision making in child welfare show the effects of *ratcheting* (persisting with a point of view in spite of evidence that it is wrong) and *templating* (inappropriately applying correlational data to individual clients; Howitt, 1992). Errors may occur both in structuring problems and in drawing inferences. Medical students and even some practicing physicians hold various kinds of oversimplifications that create misconceptions (Feltovitch, Spiro, & Coulson, 1989). Examples are:

- Seeing different entities as more similar than they actually are.
- Treating dynamic phenomena as static.
- Assuming that some general principle accounts for all of the phenomena.
- Treating multidimensional phenomena as unidimensional or according to a subset of dimensions.
- Treating continuous variables as discreet.
- Treating highly interconnected concepts as separable.
- Treating the whole as merely the sum of its parts. (Feltovich, Spiro, & Coulson, 1993, cited in Woods & Cook, p. 152)

Nisbett and Ross (1980) argue that most inferential and judgmental errors are due to the overuse of generally correct intuitive strategies (such as the application of preexisting knowledge) and the underuse of certain formal, logical statistical strategies (see earlier discussion of simplifying strategies in this chapter). They suggest that "In ordinary social experience, people often look for the wrong data, often see the wrong data, often retain the wrong data and often make wrong inferences on the basis of their understanding of the data" (p. 12). Investigators differ in how prevalent they believe such tendencies to

**Exhibit 9.5**
Summary of the Possible Cognitive Processes Involved
in Omitting Necessary Steps from a Task

| Level of Failure | Nature of Failure | Failure type |
|---|---|---|
| Planning | (a) A necessary item is unwittingly overlooked. | Mistake |
| | (b) The item is deliberately left out of the action plan. | Violation |
| Intention storage | The intention to carry out the action(s) is not recalled at the appropriate time. | Lapse |
| Execution | The actions do not proceed as intended and a necessary item is unwittingly omitted from the sequence. | Slip |
| Monitoring | The actor neither detects nor corrects the prior omission. | Slip |

*Source:* J. Reason (1997). *Managing the risks of organizational accidents* (p. 96). Brookfield: Ashgate. Reprinted with permission.

**Exhibit 9.6**

Problem-Solving Phases and Common Errors

| Step | Common Errors |
|---|---|
| 1. Clarify the problem. | • Jump to conclusions (overlook alternative views)<br>• Seek to justify views rather than critically evaluate them<br>• Ignore environmental causes<br>• Gather irrelevant data<br>• Underestimate available problem-related scientific knowledge<br>• Overestimate personal problem-related knowledge<br>• Rely on invalid data (e.g., small biased samples)<br>• Disregard conflicting evidence<br>• Stereotyping |
| 2. Search for solutions. | • Overlook options<br>• Look only for data that confirm assumptions<br>• Overlook constraints<br>• Overlook resources<br>• Not revising views based on new information<br>• See other items under Step 1. |
| 3. Decide on a plan. | • Overlook promising options<br>• Overlook constraints<br>• Don't fully inform clients about options and their potential costs and benefits |
| 4. Implement plans. | • The "dilution" effect (i.e., offer ineffective version of plans)<br>• Do not arrange for corrective feedback about outcome |
| 5. Evaluate results. | • Use vague outcome measures<br>• Use inaccurate measures<br>• Do not gather both subjective and objective measures<br>• Post-hoc fallacy (assume that because there is a change; services were responsible)<br>• Overlook harmful effects<br>• Not revising plans as needed based on outcome data |
| 6. Try again? | • Give up too soon<br>• Fail to critically examine favored views |

*Source:* Adapted from *Social Work Practice: A Critical Thinker's Guide,* by E. Gambrill, 2006, New York: Oxford.

be in real-life contexts, as discussed earlier in this chapter. Motivational and informational sources of error interact in various ways. We are most likely to miss biases in situations in which we are biased for (or against) a certain point of view and the informational source contains the same bias. Bias can intrude at any point in the judgmental process and may also occur because of interactions between different stages of data processing (Hogarth, 1980). "First, the acquisition of information from both the environment and memory can be biased. The crucial issue here is how certain information does or does not become salient. How we direct our attention influences what we see (and what we miss). Second, the manner in which we process information can be biased; for example, we may attempt to simplify a situation by using a misleading strategy. Third, the manner in which we are required to respond can introduce bias. Finally, the outcomes of our judgments can create bias in both: (1) interpretation of their significance (for example, is the outcome attributable to one's actions or simply a chance fluctuation?); and (2) learning relationships for predictive validity" (p. 158). There are individual differences in susceptibility to errors and biases: "Cognitive style—the strength of respondents' preferences for explanatory closure and parsimony—moderated the magnitude of several effects. Specifically, respondents who valued closure and parsimony highly were more prone to biases that were rooted in excessive faith in the predictive and explanatory power of their preconceptions— biases such as overconfidence, cognitive conservatism, certainty of hindsight and selective standards of evidence and proof... more 'open-minded,' lower-need-for-closure respondents . . . wound up being too imaginative and assigning too much subjective probability to too many scenarios (with the result that subjective probabilities summed to well above 1.0)" (Tetlock, 2003, p. 234).

Many errors occur because of confirmation biases (searching only for data in support of a preferred view) and reliance on questionable criteria such as popularity of a view for evaluating the accuracy of claims. Research on error in a variety of contexts shows that it is typically due to systemic factors, including poor training and poor interface between technology and human factors (e.g., Bogner, 1994; Reason, 1997, 2001; see Exhibit 9.7). Often there is a cascade effect, in which one error, if not caught and countered, leads to another, in a chain that results in an unwanted consequence (Woolf, Kuzel, Dovey, & Phillips, 2004). This highlights the value of identifying the kinds of errors that occur in relation to a decision, so that early ones in a chain can be caught, so cutting off the rest of the chain from occurring. "Because there are a set of contributors, multiple opportunities arise to redirect the trajectory away from disaster . . . an important part of safety is enhancing opportunities for people to recognize that a trajectory is heading closer to a poor outcome and to recover before negative consequences occur" (Woods & Cook, 1999, p. 144). This pattern suggests that "the label 'human error' should serve as the starting point for investigating how systems fail, not as a conclusion" (p. 144). The cause of errors is usually *systemic* (see Gambrill & Shlonsky, 2001; Reason, 1997).

**Exhibit 9.7**
Errors: Examples of Possible Contributing Factors

- Unfamiliarity with a potentially important situation which is novel or occurs infrequently
- Shortage of time for error detection and correction
- High level of noise (irrelevant cues)
- Mismatch between designer's and user's model of system
- No obvious means of reversing an unintended action
- A channel capacity overload, particularly one caused by the simultaneous presence of non-redundant information
- A need to unlearn a technique and apply one that requires the application of an opposing philosophy
- The need to transfer specific knowledge from one task to another without loss
- Ambiguity in required performance standards
- A mismatch between real and perceived risk
- Poor, ambiguous, or ill-matched system feedback
- No clear, direct, and timely confirmation of an intended action from the portion of the system over which control is to be exerted
- Operator inexperience—for example, a new employee
- An impoverished quality of information conveyed by procedures and person-to-person interaction
- Little or no independent checking or testing of output
- A conflict between immediate and long-term objectives
- No diversity of information input for accuracy checks
- A mismatch between the educational level of an individual and task requirements
- An incentive to use other, more dangerous procedures
- Unreliable instrumentation that is not recognized as such
- A need for absolute judgments that are beyond the capabilities or experience of an employee
- Unclear allocation of function and responsibility
- No obvious way to keep track of progress during task
- Little or no intrinsic meaning in a task
- High-level emotional stress
- Ill-health, especially fever
- Low workforce morale
- Inconsistency of meaning of displays and procedures
- Additional team members over and above those necessary to perform tasks satisfactorily

*Source:* Adapted from *Managing the Risks of Organizational Accidents* (pp. 142–143), by J. Reason, 1997, Brookfield, VT: Ashgate. Reprinted with permission.

In errors of commission we *do* something that decreases the likelihood of discovering valuable options. We may:

- Look only for data that confirm our beliefs.
- Jump to conclusions.
- Stereotype people or theories.
- Misinterpret cues.
- Assume that correlation reflects causation.
- Prematurely discard a valuable opinion.

In errors of omission we *fail* to do something, which decreases the likelihood of discovering valuable options. We may:

- Not question initial assumptions.
- Fail to pose well-structured questions related to information needed to make decisions.
- Fail to seek out and critically appraise problem-related research findings.
- Ignore the role of environmental causes.
- Overlook cultural differences.
- Overlook client assets.

These two kinds of errors are interrelated. For example, jumping to conclusions (an error of commission) can occur only if you do not question initial assumptions (an error of omission). These errors may result in: (1) inaccurate descriptions, (2) incorrect estimates of covariations, (3) inaccurate descriptions of causal relationships, or (4) inaccurate predictions. Common defaults in thinking emphasized by David Perkins (1995) include:

- *Hasty thinking:* Impulsive and mindless; we don't reflect on what we think or do.
- *Narrow thinking:* Tendency to think in a narrow context; we overlook the "big picture" (e.g., my-side bias).
- *Fuzzy thinking:* Imprecise, unclear; we overlook key differences; we do not question vague terms (e.g., "support," "ego strength").
- *Sprawling thinking:* Wandering aimlessly in a disorganized manner without integrating data from diverse sources; we bounce from one view to another without ever deciding on an overview. (p. 153)

They occur because of a lack of attention to planning, monitoring, and critical questioning. Consider the *Barnum effect*. This refers to accepting vague personality descriptions about ourselves that could be true of just about anybody. The very nature of clinical practice leaves room for many sources of avoidable error. Some errors result from a lack of information about how to help clients. Empirical knowledge related to clinical practice is fragmentary and theory must be used to fill in the gaps. Decreasing gaps between available knowledge and its use is emphasized in evidence-based practice, including the design of innovative ways to decrease this gap (Greenhalgh et al., 2004).

## WE CAN LEARN THROUGH OUR MISTAKES

Mistakes are inevitable and provide valuable learning opportunities *if* corrective feedback is provided (see discussion of acquiring expertise in Chapter 8). Failures and mistakes (less-than-hoped-for success) offer information that may yield better guesses next time around. They help us to learn about the nature of the problem (Popper, 1994).

> Only through our efforts can we learn; and only he will learn who is ready to appreciate and even to cherish the errors of others as stepping stones towards truth, and who searches for his own errors: who tries to find them, since only when he has become aware of them can he free himself from them. (Popper, 1992, p. 149)

Popper (1998) suggests the following obligations:

1. To recognize that mistakes will be made; "it is impossible to avoid making mistakes."
2. To recognize that it is our duty to minimize avoidable mistakes.
3. To learn how to do better from recognizing our mistakes.
4. To be on the lookout for mistakes.
5. To embrace a self-critical attitude.
6. To welcome others pointing out our mistakes; we need others to discover and point out our mistakes; criticism by others is a necessity.
7. Objective criticism "would always be specific"; would give specific reasons why specific statements or specific hypotheses appear to be false or specific arguments invalid. It must be guided by the idea of getting nearer to objective truth. In this sense it must be impersonal, but also sympathetic. (pp. 64–65)

Unavoidable mistakes are those that could not have been anticipated. They occur despite taking advantage of available knowledge and critical thinking skills—in spite of making and acting on well-informed judgments. You may have worked with caregivers of an elderly relative to identify activities the relative enjoys but find that they do not function as reinforcers. Even though you and your clients do your best to identify reinforcers, you cannot know whether particular events will function as reinforcers until you try them out. Avoidable mistakes are mistakes that could have been avoided; for example, by being better informed regarding practice-related research findings and by thinking more critically about assumptions and their possible consequences, or by arranging a reminder to help you to remember an important task. They may occur because of faulty decision-making styles, such as jumping to conclusions, and/or agency policies and procedures that interfere with sound decision making, such as an autocratic administrative style. We may forget to carry out an important step in a practice guidance. We may not monitor progress so that we can detect need for change in a program. One of your greatest challenges in becoming a successful problem solver is reappraising the value of mistakes. We are often taught to hide rather than reveal them. Hiding them makes it less likely that we will avoid them in the future.

Wu and his colleagues (2003) surveyed 254 internal medical house officers regarding their most significant mistake and their response to it. Kinds of mistakes included errors in diagnosis (33%), prescribing (29%), evaluation (21%), communication (5%), and procedural complications (11%). "Patients had serious adverse outcomes in 90% of the cases, including death in 31% of cases" (p. 221). "House officers who accepted responsibility for the mistake and discussed it were more likely to report constructive changes in practice. Residents were less likely to make constructive changes if they attributed the mistake to job overload. They were more likely to report defensive changes if they felt the institution was judgmental" (p. 221). Learning what caused a mistake can be difficult. For example, Margo (2005) found high interrater reliability in classifying diagnostic errors among three ophthalmologists, but marked disagreement about the root causes of the errors.

## FAILURES ARE INEVITABLE

Calls for "ensuring" certain outcomes are often made by politicians and administrators, such as "To ensure that no child be harmed in care." This is not possible. Even in the best of circumstances, given the uncertainty surrounding problems we confront and missing options for altering circumstances, failure to protect clients will occur. Some failures are avoidable, as suggested by the research by DePanfilis (2003) based on reviews of case records of children in care. Others are not. Calling for a perfection that is not possible can be demoralizing and can impede looking closely at outcomes (since we know we are unlikely to find such perfection). And bad outcomes do not necessarily reflect poor decisions. Illusions that we can always succeed are likely to result in feelings of regret that hinder rather than facilitate better decisions in the future (e.g., see Kahneman, 1995). Reactions to commission (acting) are associated with greater regret than are reactions to omission (failing to act).

## PERSPECTIVE MAKES A DIFFERENCE: SELF VERSUS OTHERS

We have limitations in perspective taking. We differ in our perception of others and our perception of ourselves; we tend to make dispositional assumptions about others and infer environmental influences for our own behavior. This has a number of implications for empathy. Pronin and Ross (1999) explored the views of men and women after the end of a relationship. Participants perceived their own efforts in initiating a breakup as "significantly clearer, and less characterized by 'mixed signals' than the efforts of the person who initiated the breakup with them" (cited in Pronin, Puccio, & Ross, 2002, p. 646). This difference in perspective has been called "naive realism." It is an epistemological stance with the following characteristics (p. 647):

- I see stimuli, issues, and events as they are in objective reality and my social attitudes, beliefs, preferences, priorities, and the like follow from a relatively dispassionate . . . apprehension of the information or evidence at hand.
- Other rational social perceivers generally share my judgments and reactions—provided that they have had access to the same information that gave rise to my views, and provided that they too have processed that information in a reasonably thoughtful and open minded fashion.
- The failure of a given individual or group to share my judgments and reactions arises from one of three possible sources: (1) the individual or group in question may have been exposed to a different sample of information . . . (2) the individual or group in question may be lazy, irrational, or otherwise unable or unwilling to proceed in a normative fashion from objective evidence to a reasonable conclusions; and (3) the individual or group in question may be biased (either in interpreting the evidence or in proceeding from evidence to conclusions) by ideology, self interest, or some other distorting influence.

Implications of this kind of epistemology, suggested by Pronin et al. (2002) include overconfidence in our ability to persuade others and the *false polarization* effect (overestimating differences in views with adversaries; see also Ross & Ward, 1996). Consequences of insider-outsider differences and the naïve realism perspective noted by these authors include the following: (1) we perceive our own self-knowledge and insight to be more accurate and complete than that of others, (2) we perceive our knowledge of others to be more accurate and complete than other people's knowledge of ourselves, (3) we perceive the discrepancy between our self-knowledge and other people's knowledge of ourselves to be greater than the corresponding discrepancy between other people's self-knowledge and our knowledge of these other people, and (4) we perceive our group's knowledge of other groups to be more accurate and complete than other group's knowledge of our group (see also Dunning, Heath, & Suls, 2004). Human service propaganda takes advantage of this self–other distinction.

## THERE ARE CULTURAL DIFFERENCES

Some authors argue that "East Asians [Chinese, Japanese, and Koreans] have a more holistic, field-dependent attention mode and Westerners have a more focused analytic, field-independent attention mode" (Choi, Choi, &

Norenzayan, 2005, p. 511). Comparisons of Westerners and East Asians, including Chinese, Japanese, and Koreans on different kinds of cognitive tasks suggest a number of differences. Two modes of thinking were identified. In analytic thinking there is a "detachment of the object from its context, a preference to focus on attributes of the object and to assign the object to categories based on these attributes, and a tendency to use rules about the categories to predict and explain the object's behavior. Holistic thinking involves an orientation to the context as a whole, attention to relationship between the object and the context, and a preference for explaining the behavior of the object based on such relationships. Holistic thinking relies on experience rather than logic, and includes a dialectical orientation, meaning that there is an emphasis on change and a tolerance for contradiction" (p. 511). Westerners possess a greater sense of control and "tend to explain behavior in terms of internal attributes, whereas East Asians explain behavior in terms of the interaction between internal attributes and situational factors. As a consequence, East Asians are less susceptible to the fundamental attribution error" (p. 511), the tendency to attribute behavior to dispositions of a person and to overlook situational factors (see also Chapter 14). These authors argue that East Asians have a more complex idea of causality. "Westerners are likely to confront conceptual conflicts or contradictions and 'polarize' their decision, that is, make a principled choice between opposing positions. In contrast, East Asians opt to avoid conflicts or contradictions and are quick to find a compromise solution between opposing positions" (p. 512). They suggest that cultural variations in analytic compared to holistic styles predict group differences in information search, including what information is relevant, where to locate it, and how to combine it (p. 512). See also *The Geography of Thought* (2003) by Richard Nisbet.

## SELF-IMPOSED BARRIERS

Some barriers to problem solving are self-imposed, such as failures to revise our views when needed. The accuracy of our beliefs about the problems we confront affects our success in helping clients, as do our beliefs about ourselves (e.g., whether we think we can make a difference). Only if we are aware of our assumptions can we critically examine them; for example, pose related questions and seek and critically appraise relevant research. Motivational barriers include lack of interest in helping clients. You may believe that good intentions are enough to protect clients from harmful or ineffective services, although history shows they are not (see Chapter 1). Emotional barriers include fear of making mistakes and a low tolerance for uncertainty. Our moods influence how we process information (Bless, 2001; Finucane, Alhakami, Slovic, & Johnson, 2000). We may fear taking risks or feel helpless in the face of great need. Intellectual barriers include inflexible use of problem-solving strategies that results in getting caught in "loops" (see Exhibit 9.1). Focusing on justifying our beliefs rather than on critiquing them is a major obstacle. This encourages confirmation biases, in which we seek only data that support our assumptions. A preoccupation with finding *the* cause of a problem can be a barrier, rather than asking *how* behaviors or events can be altered to attain desired outcomes (Feinstein, 1967). We may have ineffective interpersonal skills. Information that can contribute to sound decisions is unlikely to be shared with unempathic, judgmental helpers. Research concerning the causes of error in aviation as well as in medicine highlights the importance of effective communication and the values that contribute to this. For example, arrogance on the part of the captain of an airplane may result in ignoring concerns raised by a copilot, which in turn results in a near-miss or a crash. (See also Chapter 17.)

## WE CAN LEARN TO BECOME BETTER DECISION MAKERS

We can draw on related research to learn how to make better and more timely decisions. Fast and frugal heuristics offer an optimistic light on decision making in situations in which speed is of the essence. It relates decision making to the characteristics of the environment in which it occurs. In addition to providing valuable guidelines for clinical practice, such research is also of value in understanding how things go wrong; for example, procrastinating in making a decision (see Chapter 17). We can learn how to allocate our resources, such as planning time wisely and becoming familiar with barriers to problem solving and developing skills for avoiding them. We can acquire critical thinking values, knowledge, and skills that contribute to problem solving and decision making that are described throughout this book, as well as skills involved in the process of evidence-based practice (e.g., see Villanueva, Burrows, Fennessy, Rajendran, & Anderson, 2001). We can acquire strategies for decreasing automatic stereotypes—for example, about the homeless (Gollwitzer, Bayer, & McCulloch, 2005), and become more aware of how we think—and make it a rule to "consider the opposite" (Larrick, 2005).

The term *metacognitive* refers to awareness of and influence on our reasoning processes (e.g., monitoring our thinking by asking questions, such as "How am I doing?" "Is this correct?" "How do I know this is true?" "What are my biases?" "Is there another way to approach this problem?" "Do I understand this point?"). These questions highlight the importance of *self-correction* in problem solving. Related behaviors can be thought of as self-governing processes (strategies we use to guide our thinking). They can help us to use effective approaches to problem solving and to avoid common intelligence traps. Increasingly metacognitive levels of thought include: (1) *Tacit:* Thinking without thinking about it; (2) *Aware:* Thinking and being aware that you are thinking; (3) *Strategic:* Organizing our thinking by using strategies that enhance its efficacy; and (4) *Reflective:* Reflecting on our thinking (pondering how to proceed and how to improve; Swartz & Perkins, 1990). Repeated practice opportunities involving real-life decisions in a context of corrective feedback contribute to developing expertise (see Chapter 8). We can, as Hogarth (2001) suggests, educate our intuition. We can take advantage of problem-based learning methods and become informed about how our work environments affect learning (e.g., see Richman-Hirsch, 2001).

## SUMMARY

Decision making is integral to helping clients. We make scores of decisions every day. Some are well reasoned. Others are not. We can take advantage of research concerning problem-solving, decision making, and judgment to make better decisions—those that are likely to help clients attain outcomes they value. We often rely on availability and representativeness as simplifying strategies. When our first judgment fails we may use a more systematic approach. No matter what our intelligence, we are likely to fall into a variety of intelligence traps unless we develop values, knowledge, and skills that help us avoid them. Personal blocks to problem solving include emotional barriers, such as fear of taking risks, and motivational barriers, such as lack of interest in helping clients. Environmental blocks include noisy offices, time pressures, and authoritarian administrative decision-making styles. Cultural blocks include a professional culture that punishes those who question bogus claims of effectiveness. We are subject to a variety of cognitive biases, such as looking only for data that support our beliefs (confirmation biases) and being influenced by misleading data. The good news is that we can become more effective problem solvers by taking advantage of de-biasing strategies, including the process of evidence-based practice. We can learn how to avoid errors that get in the way of helping clients attain outcomes they value and avoiding harm; for example, by taking advantage of practice- and policy-related research findings.

# CHAPTER 10

# Evidence-Based Practice: A Philosophy and Process for Thinking Ethically and Critically about Decisions

T HE GOAL OF CRITICAL THINKING is to arrive at well-reasoned decisions. Evidence-based practice (EBP) describes a process for facilitating this aim. It describes a philosophy and process designed to forward effective use of professional judgment in integrating information regarding each client's unique characteristics, circumstances, preferences, and actions, and external research findings. "It is a guide for thinking about how decisions should be made" (Haynes, Devereaux, & Guyatt, 2002, p. 1). Critical thinking and evidence-based practice require a willingness to say "I don't know"—to acknowledge that there may be a gap between your current knowledge and skills and what is needed to make sound decisions. It is a process for handling the uncertainty surrounding decisions that must be made in real-life, in real-time. Sources of uncertainty include limitations in current knowledge, lack of familiarity with what knowledge is available, and difficulties in distinguishing between personal ignorance and lack of competence and actual limitations of knowledge (Fox & Swazey, 1974). Uncertainties may be related to lack of information about problem-related causes, clients' ambivalence about pursuit of certain goals, and whether resources are available to help clients. A willingness to acknowledge that "I don't know," combined with taking steps to see if needed information is available, increases the likelihood that important uncertainties can be decreased or identified (Chalmers, 2004). This helps us to honor ethical obligations to involve clients as informed participants.

Although its philosophical roots are old, the blooming of EBP as a process attending to evidentiary, ethical, and application issues in all professional venues (education, practice/policy, and research) is fairly recent, facilitated by the Internet revolution. It is designed to break down the division between research, practice, and policy—highlighting the importance of attending to

253

ethical issues. Evidence-based practice and health care arose because of troubling gaps between available knowledge and what is used by professionals. Gray (2001a) suggests that "at present, the process is marked by the following characteristics":

- overenthusiastic adoption of interventions of unproven efficacy or even proven ineffectiveness;
- failure to adopt interventions that do more good than harm, at a reasonable cost;
- continuing to offer interventions demonstrated to be ineffective;
- adoptions of interventions without adequate preparation such that the benefits demonstrated in a research setting cannot be reproduced in the ordinary service setting;
- wide variation in the rates at which interventions are adopted or discarded. (p. 366)

Critical thinking is integral to this process. In both critical thinking as well as EBP, attention is given to ethical issues. If we examine the values inherent in critical thinking suggested by Paul (1993; see Chapter 1), we see that they reflect those highlighted by the orginators of EBP. Honesty and transparency (clear description of what is done to what effect) are emphasized in both. This applies to all venues of interest in the helping professions: professional education, practice and policy (what is done to what effect), and related research (its design, conduct, and reporting).

Descriptions of EBP differ in their breadth and attention to ethical issues, ranging from the broad, systemic philosophy and related evolving technology envisioned by its originators (e.g., Gray, 1997; Sackett, Richardson, Rosenberg, & Haynes, 1997) to narrow, fragmented views and total distortions (Gambrill, 2003a). For example, views of evidence-based decision making are promoted that ignore hallmarks of this process, such as involving clients as informed participants. Given these many different views, it is important to review the vision of EBP and health care as described by its creators. Otherwise, potential benefits to clients and professionals may be lost. EBP involves the "conscientious, explicit and judicious use of current best evidence in making decisions about the care of individual [clients]" (Sackett et al., 1996). It involves "the integration of best research evidence with clinical expertise and [client] values" (Sackett, Straus, Richardson, Rosenberg, & Haynes, 2000, p. 1; see Exhibit 10.1). Recently, more attention has been given to client preferences and actions because what clients do (e.g., carry out agreed-on tasks or not) often differs from their stated preferences and our estimates of preferences are often wrong (Haynes, Devereaux, & Guyatt, 2002).

EBP describes a process for and a new professional educational format (problem-based learning) designed to help practitioners to link evidentiary, ethical, and application issues. It is assumed that professionals often need information to make decisions—for example, concerning risk assessment or

**Exhibit 10.1**
An updated model for evidence-based decisions

Clinical state and circumstances

**Clinical expertise**

Patients' preferences
and actions

Research evidence

*Source:* From "Clinical Expertise in the Era of Evidence-Based Medicine and Patient Choice [Editorial]," by R. B. Haynes, P. J. Devereaux, and G. H. Guyatt, 2002, *ACP Journal Club, 136*, pp. A11–14. Reprinted with permission.

what services are most likely to help clients attain outcomes they value. Sackett et al. (1997) estimated that about two questions arise for every three patients physicians see, and that 30 percent of all questions remain unanswered (p. 8). We do not know how many questions arise in the course of work of other professionals or how many of these remain unanswered. As Gray (2001a, p. 354) suggests, when evidence is not used, important failures in decision making occur:

- ineffective interventions are used
- interventions that do more harm than good are used
- interventions that do more good than harm are not used
- interventions that are ineffective or do more harm than good are not discontinued

Clinical expertise includes use of effective relationship skills and the experience of individual helpers to rapidly identify each client's unique circumstances, characteristics, and "their individual risks and benefits of potential interventions and their personal values and expectations" (Sackett et al. 2000, p. 1). Using clinical expertise, practitioners integrate information about a client's unique characteristics and circumstances, with external research findings, client expectations and values, and their preferences and actions (Haynes, Devereaux, & Guyatt, 2002; Sackett et al., 1997). Client values refer to "the unique preferences, concerns and expectations each [client] brings to an . . . encounter and which must be integrated into . . . decisions if they are to serve the [client]" (Sackett et al., 2000, p. 1). Evidence-based health care refers to use of best current knowledge as evidence in decision-making about groups and populations (see Gray, 2001a). Professional codes of ethics call for key characteristics of EBP, such as drawing on practice/policy related research and involving clients as informed participants.

## AN ALTERNATIVE TO AUTHORITY-BASED PRACTICE

Evidence-based decision making arose as an alternative to authority-based decision making, in which consensus, anecdotal experience, or tradition are relied on to make decisions (see Exhibit 10.2). Although misleading in the incorrect assumption that evidence-based practice means only that decisions made are based on evidence of their effectiveness, use of the term does call attention to the fact that available evidence may not be used or the current state of ignorance shared with clients. It is hoped that professionals who consider related research findings regarding decisions and inform clients about them will provide more effective and ethical care than those who rely on criteria such as anecdotal experience, available resources, or popularity. The following examples illustrate reliance on authority-based criteria for selection of service methods:

> Ms. Riverton has just been to a workshop on eye movement desensitization therapy. The workshop leader told the participants that this method "works and can be used for a broad range of problems." Ms. Riverton suggests to her supervisor at the mental health clinic where she works that agency staff should use this method. When asked why, she said because the workshop leader is a respected authority in the field.

> Mr. Davis read an editorial that describes the DARE programs as very effective in decreasing drug use. No related empirical literature was referred to. He suggests to his agency that they use this method.

In the first example the authority of a workshop leader is appealed to. In the second, the authority of an author of an editorial is appealed to. Evidence-based decision making involves use of quite different criteria; a key one is information about the accuracy of practice- and policy-related claims. EBP draws on the results of systematic, rigorous, critical appraisals of research related to different kinds of questions, such as "Is eye movement desensitization effective for certain kinds of problems?" "Are DARE programs effective?" For example, review groups in the Cochrane and Campbell Collaborations prepare comprehensive, rigorous reviews of all research related to a question.

**Exhibit 10.2**

Differences between Authority-Based and Evidence-Based Practitioners

| Authority-Based Practice | Evidence-Based Decision Making |
|---|---|
| • Clients are not informed or are misinformed. | • Clients are involved as informed participants. |
| • Ignores client preferences ("We know best"). | • Seeks and considers client values and preferences. |
| • Does not pose specific questions about important decisions that must be made and does not search for and critically appraise what is found and share results with clients. | • Poses clear questions related to information needs, seeks related research findings, critically appraises them, and shares what is found with clients and others. |
| • Motivated to appear well informed, to preserve status and reputation. | • Motivated to help clients and to be an honest and competent broker of knowledge and ignorance. |
| • Ignores errors and mistakes. | • Seeks out errors and mistakes; values criticism as vital for learning. |
| • Accepts practice- and policy-related claims based on misleading criteria such as tradition, expert consensus. | • Relies on rigorous criteria to appraise practice claims and select practices and policies (e.g., those that control for biases). |
| • Relies on self-report of clients or anecdotal observations. | • Seeks out valid information concerning progress with a focus on outcomes of concern to clients. |

## THREE PHILOSOPHIES OF EVIDENCE-BASED PRACTICE

Evidence-based practice and social care involve a philosophy of ethics of professional practice and related enterprises, such as research and scholarly writing, a philosophy of science (epistemology—views about what knowledge is and how it can be gained), and a philosophy of technology. Ethics involves decisions regarding how and when to act; it involves standards of conduct. Epistemology involves views about knowledge and how to get it— or if we can. The philosophy of technology involves questions such as: Should we develop technology? What values should we draw on to decide what to develop? Should we examine the consequences of a given technology? Evidence-based practice encourages the integration of research and practice—for example, by highlighting the importance of clinicians critically appraising research reviews and developing a technology to help them to do so; "the leading figures in EBM [evidence-based medicine] . . . emphasized that clinicians had to use their scientific training and their judgment to interpret [guidelines], and individualize care accordingly"(Gray, 2001b, p. 26). EBP encourages clinicians to think for themselves—to develop critical appraisal skills. It offers practitioners and administrators a philosophy that is compatible with obligations described in professional codes of ethics, as well as an evolving technology for integrating evidentiary, ethical, and practical issues. The uncertainty associated with decisions is acknowledged, not hidden. EBP requires considering research findings related to important practice/policy decisions and sharing what is found (including nothing) with clients. Transparency and honesty regarding the evidentiary status of services is a hallmark of this philosophy. For example, on the back cover of the seventh edition of *Clinical Evidence* (2002), the continually updated book distributed to physicians, it states that "it provides a concise account of the current state of knowledge, ignorance, and uncertainty about the prevention and treatment of a wide range of clinical conditions." In what books describing practices in psychology, psychiatry, or social work do we find such a statement? To the contrary, we find books entitled *What Works in Child Welfare* (Kluger, Alexander, & Curtis, 2002) and *A Guide to Treatments That Work* (Nathan & Gorman, 2002).

## STEPS IN EVIDENCE-BASED PRACTICE

Steps in evidence-based practice include the following:

1. Convert information needs related to practice decisions into answerable questions (see Chapter 11).
2. Track down, with maximum efficiency, the best evidence with which to answer them.
3. Critically appraise that evidence for its validity, impact (size of effect), and applicability (usefulness in practice).
4. Apply the results of this appraisal to practice/policy decisions. This involves deciding whether evidence found (if any) applies to the decision at hand (e.g., is a client similar to those studied, is there access to services described) and considering client values and preferences in making decisions as well as other applicability issues.
5. Evaluate our effectiveness and efficiency in carrying out steps 1 through 4 and seeking ways to improve them in the future (Sackett et al., 2000, pp. 3–4).

Evidence-based practitioners take advantage of efficient technology for conducting electronic searches to locate the current best evidence regarding a specific question. There is an emphasis on information literacy and retrivability (Gray, 2001a).

## DIFFERENT KINDS OF QUESTIONS

Different questions require different kinds of research methods to critically appraise proposed assumptions (e.g., Greenhalgh, 2000; Guyatt & Rennie, 2002; Sackett et al., 2000). These differences are reflected in the use of different "quality filters" to search for research findings as described in Chapter 11. Kinds of questions include the following (see Chapter 11 for examples of well-structured questions):

- *Effectiveness:* Do job training programs help clients get and maintain jobs? Are there harmful effects of such programs?
- *Prevention:* Do Head Start programs prevent school dropout?
- *Screening (risk/prognosis):* Does this measure accurately predict suicide attempts?
- *Description/Assessment:* Do self-report data provide accurate descriptions of parenting practices?
- *Harm:* Does (or will) this intervention harm clients?
- *Cost:* How much does this program cost, compared to others?
- *Practice guidelines:* Are these practice guidelines valid and are they applicable to my client/agency/community?
- *Self-development:* Am I keeping up-to-date? How can I keep up-to-date?

## DIFFERENT STYLES OF EVIDENCE-BASED PRACTICE

Sackett and his colleagues (2000) distinguish between three different styles of EBP, all of which require integrating external research findings with the client's unique personal characteristics and environmental circumstances. All require Step 4 (see prior list of steps in EBP) but they vary in how other steps are carried out. They suggest that for problems encountered on an everyday basis, you should invest the time and energy necessary to carry out both searching and critical appraisal of reports found. For level 2 (problems encountered less often), they suggest that you seek out critical appraisals already prepared by others who describe and use explicit criteria for deciding what evidence they select and how they decide whether it is valid. Here, Step 3 can be omitted and Step 2 restricted to sources that have already undergone critical appraisal. A third style applies to problems encountered very infrequently, in which we "blindly seek, accept, and apply the recommendations we receive from authorities" (p. 5). As they note, the trouble with this mode is that it is "blind" to whether the advice received from the experts "is authoritative (evidence-based, resulting from their operating in the appraising mode) or merely authoritarian (opinion-based, resulting from pride and prejudice)" (p. 5). One clue they suggest to distinguish which style is being used is a reluctance to describe related documentation. Lack of time may result in using style 2 with most problems.

## EXAMPLES OF EVIDENCE-BASED DECISION MAKING

Claire provides counseling in a school in which many youth are referred for anger management problems. Her answerable question is: In youth with anger management problems, is group anger management training compared to individual counseling more effective in helping youth to control their anger? Notice that the question has the four parts typical of a well formed question: (1) a client group; (2) an intervention; (3) some comparison; and (4) the hoped-for outcome. This is an effectiveness question, so Claire was on the lookout for research studies that were most likely to control for biases that are a part of all research, but more so in some designs than in others; she was on the lookout for a high-quality review of related randomized controlled trials—a systematic review (see Chapter 12). She searched in the Cochrane and Campbell databases; psychinfo; and ERIC, and found a meta-analysis of anger management programs for youth, which suggested that group counseling was effective in helping youth to decrease angry outbursts. She decided to use this approach in her work with clients, and the youth said that they preferred a group approach.

Dr. Price works in a mental health crisis center. The administrator of this agency sent a memo to staff stating that he had heard that brief psychoanalytic debriefing was effective in decreasing Posttraumatic Stress Disorder following a crisis, and suggested that his staff use this method. Dr. Price decided to see if this was accurate. He formed the following question: In clients experiencing a potentially traumatic event, is brief, one-hour psychoanalytic debriefing compared to no service more effective in preventing Posttraumatic Stress Disorder? Here again we have an effectiveness question and here again we see a four-part answerable question. He looked in the same databases mentioned earlier and found the systematic review prepared by Rose, Bisson, and Wessely (2004). To his surprise, this review concluded that not only was this method not effective, there was some indication that it had harmful effects; one study reported that those receiving such counseling were *more* likely to experience stressful reactions a year later. Based on this review, he sent an e-mail to his colleagues questioning the use of this method for clients.

Ms. Roberts works in an agency offering services to the frail elderly. Many of her clients are diagnosed with dementia. Her question was as follows: In clients with dementia, is reality orientation more effective than individual counseling in decreasing symptoms of dementia? She made it a habit to search first in the Cochrane and Campbell databases and discovered the review by Spector, Orrell, Davies, and Woods (2004), which suggested that reality orientation is effective in achieving these outcomes. She did not find any studies comparing the two interventions. She decided to refer her clients to programs that used reality orientation.

Helen works in a family service center. A mother has consulted her about her child who is still wetting the bed at night (he has enuresis). He is five years old. Her question is: In children age five, what percentage still wet the bed at night? She looked first in the National Health Service web site and in five minutes located a description of the baserate of bedwetting on the part of young children.

Richard works in a child protection agency that requires him to use a risk assessment measure to estimate the likely recurrence of child abuse among parents alleged to have abused their children. The method used by his agency is a consensus based instrument—that is, it is based on the opinions of a group of experts on what they consider risk factors. His question is as follows: Among parents alleged to have abused their children, are actuarial compared to consensus-based measures most accurate in predicting the likelihood of future abuse? Notice again that this is a four-part question: (1) a client group, (2) a particular predictive measure, (3) another kind of risk measure, and (4) the hoped-for outcome. He looked in www.childwelfare.com and located an article by Baird and Wagner (2000) that compared the reliability and validity of these two kinds of risk measures. This article concluded that the actuarial method was the most accurate. Actuarial measures are based on empirical relationships between certain factors and the likelihood of an outcome, such as abuse (see Chapter 15 for further discussion).

These examples illustrate distinctive features of evidence-based decision making. The clinicians posed well-structured, answerable questions related to their information needs that guided an effective and efficient electronic search. Searches can be done in the office with modem-equipped computers using appropriate search methods, including Boolean logic ("or", "and"), relevant databases, and quality filters designed to locate the best evidence for a particular kind of question (see Chapter 11). Critical appraisal skills are used to review what is found. Many sources are available to guide this appraisal, which include user-friendly checklists for different kinds of questions (e.g., see Greenhalgh, 2001). A search for research findings may reveal that a practice method is harmful. You may discover that there is no research that critically appraises the effectiveness of a practice method, or that the research is too weak to draw an inference, and you and your clients must base decisions on other criteria, such as well-reasoned practice theory. All these are findings related to important decisions that you and your clients must make and should be shared with clients.

The more one reads about current-day practices in the helping professions, the clearer it is that helping efforts do not have the characteristics of evidence-based practice. Literature suggests that professionals do not draw on practice-related research findings to inform practice decisions (e.g., see Rosen, Proctor, Morrow-Howell, & Staudt, 1995). Not keeping up with new research findings related to important decisions renders knowledge increasingly out of date. As a result, decisions may be made that harm rather than help clients (e.g., see Jacobson, Foxx, & Mulick, 2005; Ofshe & Watters, 1994). Many clinicians do not honor obligations described in professional codes of ethics regarding informed consent (e.g., see Braddock, Edwards, Hasenberg, Laidley, & Levinson, 1999). Lack of transparency regarding limitations of research remains common, as does the publication of fragmented, biased reviews.

## ORIGINS OF EVIDENCE-BASED DECISION MAKING

Sackett and his colleagues (2000) suggest four realizations made possible by five recent developments for the rapid spread of evidence-based medicine. Realizations include (1) practitioner need for valid information about decisions they make, (2) the inadequacy of traditional sources for acquiring this information (e.g., because they are out-of-date, frequently wrong, overwhelming in their volume, variable in their validity), (3) the gap between assessment skills and clinical judgment "which increase with experience and our up-to-date knowledge and performance which decline" (p. 2), and (4) lack of time to locate, appraise, and integrate this evidence (p. 2). There were increasing gaps between information available on the Internet that could be of value to clients and clinicians in making informed decisions and what was drawn on. Five developments allowed improvement in this state of affairs:

1. The development of strategies for efficiently tracking down and appraising evidence (for its validity and relevance).
2. The creation of systematic reviews and concise summaries of the effects of health care (epitomized by the Cochrane Collaboration).
3. The creation of evidence-based journals of secondary publication.
4. The creation of information systems for bringing the forgoing to us in seconds.
5. The identification and application of effective strategies for life-long learning and for improving our clinical performance. (Sackett et al., 2001, p. 3)

## STUDY OF VARIATIONS IN SERVICES OFFERED

EBP and health care originated in medicine in part because of variations in services offered and their outcomes (Wennberg, 2002). Variations in services naturally raise questions such as "Are they of equal effectiveness?" "Do some harm?"

## GAPS AMONG ETHICAL, EVIDENTIARY, AND APPLICATION CONCERNS

Services found to be effective are often not used and services of little value offered. Although interlinked in professional codes of ethics and accreditation standards, ethical and evidentiary issues are often worlds apart in practice. Sheldon and Chilvers (2000) found that 18 percent of social workers surveyed ($n = 2,285$) had read nothing related to practice within the last 6 months. If professionals are not familiar with the evidentiary status of alternative practices and policies, they cannot pass this information on to their clients; they cannot honor informed consent obligations. If some alternatives are more effective than others in helping clients, and practice proceeds based on ignorance of this information, clients are deprived of opportunities to achieve hoped-for outcomes. How can clients exercise self-determination if they are uninformed or misinformed about the evidentiary status of recommended services? Currently, gaps between what research suggests is effective and what services are provided are hidden. For example, rarely do child protection staff compare services offered by agencies to which they refer clients for parent training with what research suggests is effective and then share this information with clients. Clients are typically not informed that recommended services have no evidentiary base or have been found to be ineffective or harmful.

## INCREASED ATTENTION TO HARMING IN THE NAME OF HELPING

The history of the helping professions shows that common practices thought to help people were found to harm them (e.g., see Sharpe & Faden, 1998; Valenstein, 1986). Such reports increased awareness that services designed to help clients, including assessment measures, may result in negative effects. For example, routine use of mammograms results in a high rate of false positives, with consequent unnecessary anxiety and invasive procedures such as biopsies (Gigerenzer, 2002a; Thornton, Edwards, & Baum, 2003).

## LIMITATIONS OF TRADITIONAL METHODS OF KNOWLEDGE DISSEMINATION

Gray (2001b) highlights the role of troubling gaps between obligations of researchers to report limitations of research, prepare systematic reviews, and accurately describe well-argued alternative views, and what we find in published literature. We find:

- Inflated claims: Professional propaganda.
- Biased estimates of the prevalence of a concern: Propagandistic advocacy in place of careful weighing of evidence.
- Hiding limitations of research.
- Preparing fragmented, incomplete literature reviews.
- Ignoring counterevidence to preferred views.
- Ignoring well-argued alternative perspectives and related evidence.
- Pseudoinquiry: Little match between questions addressed and methods used to address them.
- Ad hominem rather than ad rem arguments.
- Ignoring unique knowledge of clients and service providers in making decisions about the appropriateness of practice guidelines.

Examples of flaws and fallacies in the medical literature described in *Biomedical Bestiary* (Michael, Boyce, & Wilcox, 1984) include *significance turkey* (lauds significant results even if they are not clinically significant; even if a finding is statistically significant, is it large enough to make any real difference to clients?); and *test bloater* (a person who has unwavering (and unwarranted) enthusiasm for predictive utility of a new test. Poor-quality research continues to appear in professional journals (Altman, 2002). There are many reasons for this including the special interests of those who fund research, such as pharmaceutical companies, and censorship of findings (e.g., see Bodenheimer, 2000; Deyo, Simon, & Omenn, 1997).

In discussing the origins of EBP, Gray (2001b) emphasizes the increasing lack of confidence in data of potential use to clinicians: peer review, which he subtitles *feet of clay*, and flaws in books, editorials, and journal articles. Examples include submission bias, publication bias, methodological bias, abstract bias, and framing bias. In place of critical, systematic reviews of research we find incomplete, uncritical reviews (e.g., see Oxman & Guyatt, 1993). Most reviews do not tell us how they researched, where they searched, what criteria they used to review studies, and do not search for published as well as unpublished reports. Conclusions drawn based on unsystematic reviews are often quite misleading. As Rosenthal (1994) suggests in his description of hyperclaiming (telling others that proposed research is likely to achieve goals that it will not) and causism (implying a causal relationship when none has been established), "Bad science makes for bad ethics" (p. 128). Chalmers (1990) argues that failure to accurately describe research methods used is a form of scientific misconduct.

## EVOLUTION OF THE SYSTEMATIC REVIEW

Recognition of limitations in narrative reviews of research related to practice questions encouraged development of the systematic review for synthesizing research findings. Such reviews "state their objectives, ascertain as much of the available evidence as possible, use explicit quality criteria for inclusion or exclusion of studies found, use explicitly stated methods for combining data, produce reports which describe the processes of ascertainment, inclusion and exclusion, and combining data" (Gray, 2001b, p. 25). Differences between traditional and systematic review can be seen in Exhibit 10.3.

**Exhibit 10.3**

Examples of Difference between Inclusive, Rigorous (Systematic) Reviews and Authoritarian Reviews

| Authoritarian Reviews | Systematic Reviews |
|---|---|
| 1. The search process is not described. | 1. The search process is clearly described. |
| 2. The review omits many related studies. | 2. All currently available research related to a practice question, both published and unpublished in all languages, is sought. |
| 3. Criteria used to review research regarding different kinds of practice questions are not described. | 3. Criteria used to appraise research related to different kinds of practice questions are clearly described. |
| 4. Criteria used to appraise the quality of studies are not rigorous. | 4. Criteria used to appraise research are rigorous (e.g., were evaluators of outcome blind to group assignment?). |
| 5. Readers are not provided with sufficient information about each study to judge its quality for themselves. | 5. Readers are provided with enough information about each study to judge its quality for themselves. |
| 6. Inflated claims of effectiveness and validity. | 6. Claims are accompanied by descriptions of related evidence. |

## The Internet Revolution

As Gray (2001b) notes, "The Internet stimulated the development of a number of software tools which allowed international organizations such as the Cochrane Collaboration to function effectively" (p. 25). The Cochrane Collaboration was created to prepare, maintain, and disseminate high-quality research reviews related to a specific practice/policy question. The Internet provides rapid access to research related to practice guidelines, including databases that facilitate speedy searches. New search methods using Boolean terms (and/or) facilitate searches on the Internet (see Chapter 11).

## Other Factors

Gray (2001b) attributes part of the appeal of EBP to clinicians and to clients.

> It also came as a shock that even the knowledge, where it was available, was often deficient (or commonly not even utilized by doctors who had been left behind the knowledge frontier). They therefore welcomed EBM enthusiastically and it is remarkable how quickly that access to information has turned the table on professional expertise and power. It is no longer feasible to feign knowledge: patients are just as likely to have searched for the evidence before they consult a clinician. (p. 27)

Economic considerations were a factor. No matter what system of care exists, resources are limited with subsequent pressures to use them justly and wisely, including considering both individuals and populations (do all residents with a particular need have access to similar quality care?). Gray (2001b) also notes the contributions of key individuals such as David Sackett (e.g., see Sackett et al., 1997) and the role of the National Health Service Research and Development Program in encouraging an evaluative culture.

## HALLMARKS AND IMPLICATIONS OF THE PHILOSOPHY OF EVIDENCE-BASED PRACTICE AND CARE

The philosophy and related technology of EBP has implications for all individuals and institutions involved with helping clients, including educators, researchers, practitioners/policymakers, and those who provide funding (see Exhibit 10.4). Research, practice, and educational issues are closely intertwined. For example, poor-quality reviews of research related to practice and policy questions may result in bogus "practice guidelines" that result in poor-quality services for clients. Clinicians may be misinformed about the evidentiary status of practice and policy claims, and so harm rather than help clients. Hallmarks and implications are interrelated. For example, promotion of transparency contributes to both knowledge flow and honoring ethical obligations.

**Exhibit 10.4**

Interrelated Hallmarks and Contributions of Evidence-Based Decision Making

1. *Move away from authority-based practices and policies.*
   - Clearly describe gaps among evidentiary, ethical, and practical concerns.
   - Be honest brokers of knowledge and ignorance; clearly describe limitations of research; accurately describe well-argued alternative views and evidence against favored views.
   - Avoid pseudoinquiry (research that cannot critically test questions raised).
   - Avoid influence by and promotion of human service propaganda.
   - Avoid questionable criteria for making decisions, such as status, popularity, tradition, what's new.

2. *Honor ethical obligations.*
   - Focus on client concerns and hoped-for outcomes.
   - Attend to individual differences in client circumstances and characteristics, including client values and preferences.
   - Involve clients as informed participants.
   - Clearly describe limitations of practice and policy research.
   - Describe and take proactive steps to minimize errors.
   - Minimize harming in the name of helping.
   - Consider populations as well as individuals in the distribution of scarce resources.
   - Provide clear descriptions of services used and to what effect, be accountable.

3. *Promote transparency and accountability regarding what is done to what effect.*
   - Describe variations in services and their outcomes.
   - Recognize ignorance and the uncertainty associated with helping.
   - Encourage rigorous testing and appraisal of practice-related claims.
   - Avoid inflated claims.
   - Reveal gaps between research regarding the causes of problems clients confront and services provided.
   - Involve clients as informed participants.
   - Blow the whistle on pseudoscience, propaganda, quackery, and fraud.

4. *Encourage a systemic approach for integrating ethical, evidentiary, and application issues.*
   - Highlight application challenges and explore how to decrease them.
   - Involve clients as informed participants in decisions made.
   - Attend to management practices and policies that influence services (e.g., criteria used to purchase services).
   - Consider the implications of scarce resources on services purchased; consider populations as well as individuals.
   - Educate professionals who are life-long learners.
   - Educate professionals who can spot and avoid the influence of human service propaganda.

**Exhibit 10.4** *Continued*

5. *Maximize knowledge flow* (see also number 3).

- View knowledge as a resource to be shared rather than a commodity to be guarded.
- Increase use of available knowledge.
- Welcome criticism.
- Prepare, maintain and disseminate high-quality critical appraisals of practice/policy research findings related to specific questions (e.g., Cochrane and Campbell Collaborations).
- Teach helpers and clients how to rapidly locate and critically appraise practice/policy related research.
- Provide resources needed to search for practice-related research findings.
- Create professional education programs that develop lifelong learners.
- Implement accountable agency complaint systems that contribute to service improvement.
- Create effective programs for identifying errors and their causes and use this information to minimize avoidable errors that may harm clients.

*Source:* From *Social Work Practice: A Critical Thinker's Guide* (2nd ed.), by E. Gambrill, 2006, New York: Oxford. Reprinted with permission.

## Move Away from Authoritarian Practices and Policies

The key contribution of EBP is moving from authority-based professions to those in which ethical obligations to clients and students are honored and critical appraisal and honest brokering of knowledge and ignorance thrive (Gambrill, 1999). A preference for authoritarian beliefs and actions is by no means limited to clinicians. It flourishes among researchers and academics as well. Examples include misrepresenting views, hiding limitations of research studies, ignoring counterevidence to preferred views, and not involving clients and clinicians as informed participants in decisions made (e.g., about whether to use a certain practice guideline). Indicators of the authority-based nature of practice include large gaps between what is said and what is done (e.g., professional codes of ethics and current practices and policies); for example, basing decisions on criteria such as consensus and tradition, lack of informed consent, and censorship of certain kinds of knowledge, such as variations in services and their outcomes (Gambrill, 2001).

## Honor Ethical Obligations

Evidence-based practice has ethical implications for practitioners and policymakers as well as for researchers and educators (see Exhibit 10.5). Hallmarks include focusing on client concerns and hoped-for outcomes, attending to individual differences in client characteristics and circumstances, considering client values and expectations, and involving clients as informed participants

**Exhibit 10.5**
Contributions of Evidence-Based Practice to Honoring Ethical Obligations to Clients

| Ethical Obligation | Contribution |
| --- | --- |
| A. *Professional Helpers* | |
| 1. Help clients and avoid harm. | 1. Encourage and facilitate access to practice and policy related research findings to maximizes the likelihood of success and minimize the likelihood of harm. |
| 2. Maximize autonomy/self determination. | 2. Minimize coercion and involve clients as informed participants regarding risks and benefits of recommenced methods and alternatives. Accurately describe the evidentiary status of recommended methods and alternatives. |
| 3. Respect and integrity. | 3. Minimize coercion and involve clients as informed participants regarding risks and benefits of recommended methods and alternatives. Accurately describe the evidentiary status of recommended methods and alternatives. |
| 4. Competence. | 4. Have the knowledge and skills required to provide services that maximize success. Keep up-to-date with practice-related knowledge. |
| 5. Accountability. | 5. Arrange for on-going feedback about progress. |
| 6. Promote social justice. | 6. Advocate for changes in social conditions that contribute to personal problems. |
| 7. Lifelong learning. | 7. Develop tools to help practitioners become life-long learners who keep up-to-date with practice and policy related research and share this with clients. |
| B. *Researchers* | |
| 1. Accurately describe research findings in professional sources. | 1. Encourage use of educational programs that create life-long learners. |
| 2. Use research methods that can critically test questions posed. | 2. Encourage good match between research methods used and questions pursued. |
| 3. Attend to outcomes of value to clients. | 3. Involve clients in design and/or interpretation and critiques of research. |
| C. *Educators* | |
| 1. Help students to become life-long learners. | 1. Encourage use of educational programs that create lifelong learners. |

**Exhibit 10.5** *Continued*

| | |
|---|---|
| 2. Be honest up-to-date brokers of knowledge and ignorance. | 2. Accurately describe both preferred and disliked views and related research findings. |
| 3. Involve students as informed participants. | 3. Accurately describe biases, special interests and scope of knowledge. |
| 4. Treat students equitably. | 4. Do not show favoritism. |
| 5. Competence. | 5. Possess knowledge claimed. |

*Source:* From *Social Work Practice: A Critical Thinker's Guide* (2nd ed.), by E. Gambrill, 2006, New York: Oxford. Reprinted with permission.

in decision making (see prior list of steps). Ignoring practice- and policy-related research findings and forwarding bogus claims of effectiveness violates our obligation to provide informed consent, and may result in wasting money on ineffective services, harming clients in the name of helping them, and forgoing opportunities to attain hoped-for outcomes. A striking characteristic of EBP and related developments is the extent to which clients are involved in many different ways (e.g., see Entwistle, Renfrew, Yearley, Forrester, & Lamont, 1998). One is reflected in the attention given to individual differences in client characteristics, circumstances, actions, values, and preferences in making decisions (e.g., see earlier description of EBP). A second is helping clients to develop critical appraisal skills. A third is encouraging client involvement in the design and critique of practice/policy-related research (e.g., Hanley et al., 2001). A fourth is attending to outcomes clients value and a fifth is involving them as informed participants. A sixth is recognizing their unique knowledge in relation to application concerns.

The client-focused nature of evidence-based decision making requires helpers to attend to client interests; what are *their* desired outcomes; what information would *they* like; what are *their* preferences regarding practices and policies. Sharpe and Faden (1998) describe the struggle in medicine—a continuing one—to focus on client outcomes and highlight how recent this focus is and what a contentious issue it has been and continues to be. A concern for involving clients in making decisions that affect their lives emphasizes the importance of informed (in contrast to uninformed or misinformed) consent. EBP involves sharing responsibility for decision making in a context of recognized uncertainty. Although professional codes of ethics call on practitioners to inform clients regarding risks and benefits of recommended services and alternatives, this is typically not done. Decisions concerning the distribution of scarce resources is a key ethical concern in the helping professions; this requires consideration of populations as well as individuals. Decisions concerning populations may pose hardships for individual clients. EBP encourages programmatic research regarding error, both avoidable and unavoidable, its causes and consequences for clients and other involved parties, and exploration of methods designed to minimize avoidable errors, including agencywide risk management programs (e.g., see Reason, 1997, 2001). A careful review of the circumstances related to mistakes allows us to plan how to minimize avoidable ones. Such attention helps us to minimize harming in the name of helping.

## MAKING PRACTICES, POLICIES, AND THEIR OUTCOMES TRANSPARENT

Evidence-based practice encourages transparency of what is done to what effect in all venues of interest, including practice and policy, research, and professional education. EBP is a democratic endeavor, in which clients are appraised of the evidentiary status of services (e.g., the likelihood that they will do more good than harm). There is candidness and clarity in place of secrecy and obscurity. These characteristics are at odds with authority-based practice (e.g., see Chalmers, 1983; Gambrill, 2001). For example, is there evidence for the following claims:

- Scared Straight programs decrease delinquency.
- Brief psychoanalytic crisis intervention programs prevent posttraumatic stress syndrome.
- Eyewitness testimony can be trusted.
- Genograms are valuable in achieving client goals.
- Screening for depression on the part of general practitioners contributes to identification of clients in need of services.
- Anger management programs for adolescents are effective.

Involvement of clients as informed participants in decisions increases transparency. Transparency calls for blowing the whistle on pseudoscience, fraud, quackery, and professional propaganda (see Chapter 4). Increased transparency will highlight gaps between resources needed to attain hoped-for outcomes as suggested by related research and what is used, and thus may encourage advocacy on the part of clients and professionals for more effective services (e.g., see Domenighetti, Grilli, & Liberati, 1998). It will reveal services that are ineffective, allowing a more judicious distribution of scarce resources (see Eddy, 1994a, 1994b). It will reveal gaps between causes of client problems (e.g., poverty) and interventions used and promoted as of value. Identification of gaps will suggest ways to rearrange resources. For example, why pay for unneeded training or ineffective services? Transparency will reveal the extent to which different kinds of ethical obligations are met, such as involving clients as informed participants. It will reveal impossible tasks; consider the unrealistic requirement to "ensure" that children in protective care will not be harmed. This cannot be done. Transparency encourages clear language, which should discourage propagandistic ploys that hide what is done to what effect. There is no longer a need to veil the lack of evidentiary status for practices and policies, the lack of focus on client outcomes, and failure to consider client preferences.

Increased transparency also has implications for the conduct, reporting, and dissemination of research findings. It requires accurate description of well-argued alternative views and related evidence and encourages rigorous testing of claims. Biases intrude, both on the part of researchers when conducting and reporting research and when preparing research reviews (e.g., see MacCoun, 1998), as well as on the part of practitioners when making decisions. The use of rigorous criteria to evaluate research studies is encouraged by the prevalence of incomplete reviews, resulting in faulty conclusions that mislead both helpers and clients. EBP calls for candid descriptions of limitations of research studies and use of methods that critically test questions addressed; it calls for systematic reviews rather than authoritarian ones (see Cochrane and Campbell Collaborations protocols). A key contribution of EBP is discouraging inflated claims of knowledge that mislead involved parties and hinder the development of knowledge. Consider terms such as "well established," and "validated," which convey a certainty that is not possible (see Chapter 4). Bogus claims based on uncritical appraisals of related research hinder exploration and may result in harmful practices and policies.

## ENCOURAGE A SYSTEMIC APPROACH FOR INTEGRATING PRACTICAL, ETHICAL, AND EVIDENTIARY ISSUES

Evidence-based practice describes a process designed to encourage integration of ethical, evidentiary, and application concerns. It involves a *systemic* approach to improving quality of services including: (1) efforts to educate professionals who are lifelong learners, (2) involving clients as informed participants, (3) attending to management practices and policies that influence services (i.e., evidence-based purchase of services), (4) considering the implications of scarce resources, and (5) attending to application challenges, such as:

- The development of strategies for efficiently tracking down and appraising evidence (for its validity and relevance).
- The creation of systematic reviews and concise summaries of the effects of health care (illustrated by the Cochrane and Campbell Collaboration databases).
- The creation of evidence-based journals of secondary publication.
- The creation of information systems for bringing the foregoing to us in seconds.
- The identification and application of effective strategies for life-long learning and for improving our clinical performance. (Gray, 2001b)

Quality of services are unlikely to improve in a fragmented approach—that is, without attending to *all* links in the system of service provision. Gray (2001a) suggests that performance ($P$) is directly related to an individual's motivation ($M$) and competence ($C$) and inversely related to the barriers ($B$) that individual has to overcome: $P = M \times C / B$. EBP encourages the creation of tools and training programs designed to develop and encourage use of critical appraisal skills (see Chapter 12). Related literature describes a wide variety of efforts to address application concerns (e.g., see Chapter 11).

## MAXIMIZE KNOWLEDGE FLOW

EBP and social care are designed to maximize knowledge flow. Exploring ways to diffuse and disseminate knowledge encourages knowledge flow, and related literature is rich in the variety of efforts described (e.g., Greenhalgh, Robert, MacFarlane, Bate, & Kyriakidou, 2004; Sackett & Straus, 1998). In a culture in which knowledge flow is free, puffery (inflated claims of knowledge) is challenged and such challenges are welcomed. Evidence-based decision making emphasizes the importance of collaboration among interested parties, and its advocates have actively pursued the development of a technology and political base to encourage this—for example, involving clients in the design and interpretation of research projects (Hanley et al., 2001). Gray (2001a) suggests that evidence-based organizations should include systems that are capable of providing evidence and promoting the use of evidence, including both explicit (created by researchers) and tacit (created by clinicians, clients, and managers). Clinicians and clients are involved as informed participants—there is no privileged knowledge in the sense of not sharing information about the evidentiary status of recommended practices and policies. Such sharing poses a direct threat to those who forward bogus claims and carry out pseudoinquiry, perhaps to gain funding and maintain status. Benefits of a free, efficient, knowledge market include:

1. Critical appraisal of knowledge claims.
2. Honoring informed consent obligations.
3. Increased staff morale, because decisions will be more informed and staff are rewarded for sharing knowledge and are free to discuss problems and learn from colleagues and others throughout the world.
4. Increase in the ratio of informed to uninformed or misinformed decisions.
5. Recognizing uncertainty. This is often swept under the rug, resulting in blaming staff for not acting on knowledge that does not (or did not) exist.
6. Reducing bogus claims of knowledge that may result in harm to clients. We often find little match between questions addressed and use of methods that can critically test them, together with hiding limitations and inflated claims of effectiveness regarding "what has been found."
7. Lack of censorship of well-argued alternative views and counterevidence regarding popular views.

Identifying errors and mistakes and related factors and using this information to minimize avoidable mistakes contributes to knowledge flow. Thus, as

Popper (1998) suggests, we have an obligation to recognize and learn from our mistakes. We have an obligation:

- To recognize that mistakes will be made; "it is impossible to avoid making mistakes" (p. 63).
- To recognize that it is our duty to minimize avoidable mistakes.
- To learn how to do better from recognizing our mistakes.
- To "be on the lookout" for mistakes (p. 64).
- To embrace a self-critical attitude.
- To welcome others pointing out our mistakes; "we need other people to discover and correct some of our mistakes . . ." (p. 64); criticism by others is a necessity.
- "Rational (or objective criticism) must always be specific: it must give specific reasons why specific statements, specific hypotheses appear to be false, or specific arguments invalid. It must be guided by the idea of getting nearer to objective truth. In this sense it must be impersonal, but also sympathetic" (pp. 64–65).

We learn from our mistakes, and we lose valuable learning opportunities by overlooking them. Research regarding errors shows that systemic causes (e.g., quality of staff training, agency policy) contribute heavily to mistakes and errors (e.g., Reason, 1997, 2001). Accountable complaint systems are another way to maximize knowledge flow. Evidence-based agencies encourage knowledge flow by using services found to maximize the likelihood of attaining outcomes clients value and not using services of unknown effectiveness or those found to do more harm than good.

## ALTERNATIVES TO EVIDENCE-BASED PRACTICE

There are many alternatives to evidence-based decision making. We could guess, use our intuition, toss a coin, ask our colleagues, or scan journals. Alternatives are suggested in Exhibit 10.6. Given that EBP as described in this chapter is not the norm today, it is clear that alternative methods are popular and pose an obstacle to drawing on critical thinking skills to integrate evidentiary, ethical, and application concerns.

## OBJECTIONS TO EVIDENCE-BASED PRACTICE, AND COUNTERARGUMENTS

All innovations have advantages and disadvantages; evidence-based practice is no exception. Many challenges confront helpers who want to practice in an evidence-based manner, such as gaining access to research findings related to important questions and critically appraising this knowledge in a timely manner (see Chapter 11). Straus and McAlister (2000) suggest that some limitations of EBP are universal in helping efforts, such as lack of scientific evi-

**Exhibit 10.6**
Alternatives to Evidence-Based Practice

| Basis for Clinical Decisions | Marker | Measuring Device | Units of Measurement |
|---|---|---|---|
| Evidence | Randomized controlled trial | Meta-analysis | Odds ratio |
| Eminence | Radiance of white hair | Luminometer | Optic density |
| Vehemence | Level of stridency | Audiometer | Decibels |
| Eloquence (or elegance) | Smoothness of tongue or nap of suit | Teflometer | Adhesion score |
| Providence | Level of religious fervor | Sextent to measure angle of genuflection | International units of piety |
| Diffidence | Level of gloom | Nihilometer | Sighs |
| Nervousness | Litigation phobia level | Every conceivable test | Bank balance |
| Confidence | Bravado | Sweat test | No sweat |

*Source:* From "Seven Alternatives to Evidence Based Medicine," by D. Isaacs and D. Fitzgerald, 1999, *British Medical Journal, 319*, p. 1618. Reprinted with permission.

dence related to decisions and challenges in applying evidence to the care of individuals. Barriers they suggest include the need to develop new skills and limited funds and resources. Some objections result from misunderstandings of EBP. (This section is based on Gibbs & Gambrill, 2002.)

1. *It ignores or denigrates clinical expertise.* One objection to EBP is that it ignores the role of clinical expertise—for example, in forming a helping relationship and integrating information from diverse sources.

*Counterargument:* The very definition of EBP and Step 4 shows that drawing on clinical expertise is key in EBP.

> Thus, knowing the tools of evidence-based practice is necessary but not sufficient for delivering the highest quality of [client] care. In addition to clinical expertise, the clinician requires compassion, sensitive listening skills, and broad perspectives from the humanities and social sciences. These attributes allow understanding of [clients' concerns] in the context of their experience, personalities, and culture. (Guyatt & Rennie, 2002, p. 9)

Sackett and his coauthors (1997) note that evidence-based practice involves the integration of "individual clinical expertise with the best available external clinical evidence from systematic research" (p. 2).

> Good doctors use both individual clinical expertise and the best available external evidence and neither alone is enough. Without clinical expertise, practice risks becoming tyrannized by external evidence, for even excellent external evidence may be inapplicable to or inappropriate for an individual patient. Without

current best external evidence, practice risks becoming rapidly out of date, to the detriment of patients. (Sackett et al., 1997, p. 20)

An ongoing concern is how to use clinical expertise to integrate external research findings, information about client characteristics and circumstances, including client preferences and actions, in order to maximize the likelihood of attaining hoped-for outcomes (Haynes, Devereaux, & Guyatt, 2002).

2. *It ignores client values and preferences.*

*Counterargument:* Step 4 of the process of EBP highlights the attention paid to clients' values and expectations.

3. *It is a cookbook approach.*

*Counterargument:* Consideration of client values and expectations, as well as the extent to which research findings apply to a particular client, show that it is not a cookbook approach.

> By individual expertise we mean the proficiency and judgment that individual clinicians acquire through clinical experience and clinical practice. Increased expertise is reflected in many ways, but especially in more effective and efficient diagnosis and in the more thoughtful identification and compassionate use of individual patients' predicaments, rights and preferences in making clinical decisions about their care. (Sackett et al., 1997, p. 2)

Considering the extent to which research findings apply to a particular client and considering client values and preferences are hallmarks of EBP.

> External clinical evidence can inform, but can never replace, individual clinical expertise and it is this expertise that decides whether the external evidence applies to the individual [client] at all and, if so, how it should be integrated into a clinical decision. Similarly, any external guideline must be integrated with individual clinical expertise in deciding whether and how it matches the [client's] clinical state, predicament, and preferences and thus whether it should be applied. (Sackett et al., 1997, p. 4)

4. *It is only a cost-cutting tool; it saves money.* Some contend that EBP is simply a way to save money, to help the managed care industry make more money.

*Counterargument:* Straus and McAlister (2000) and Sackett et al. (1997) note that EBP may increase, not decrease cost. For example, research may show that a more expensive service is more effective than less expensive services. Hallmarks of EBP, such as considering the values and expectations of clients, involving clients as informed participants in decisions that affect their lives, and making what professionals do to what effect transparent, should help to mute influences by third-party payment systems that contribute to ignoring outcomes of interest to clients and using less costly and less effective methods.

5. *It is limited to clinical research.*

*Counterargument.* Many kinds of research are drawn on, including epidemi-ological research regarding the base-rate of certain problems or characteristics (see prior description of the different kinds of questions that arise in practice).

6. *It is an ivory tower concept—it can't be done.*

*Counterargument.* Audits and surveys of clinicians suggest that EBP can be practiced in medicine (e.g., see Ellis, Mulligan, Rowe, & Sackett, 1995), and professional codes of ethics call for many of the steps involved in EBP (e.g., re-spect, self-determination, and integrating practice-related literature). Such codes obligate professionals to address challenges to implementing EBP.

7. *It results in therapeutic nihilism.* Another objection is that professionals and clients are left helpless if a careful search for practice-related research findings reveals that no research is available suggesting what services may be of most value.

*Counterargument.* EPB calls on professionals to search for practice-related research findings and share what is found (including nothing) with clients to involve clients in decisions made as informed participants. If no research find-ings are located, clients are so informed, and helpers may proceed by drawing on practice theories and describing their hypothetical views about problem-related factors and related service implications to clients.

8. *There is nothing new about EBP.* For decades texts in the helping profes-sions have called on practitioners to apply research findings in their practice.

*Counterargument.* EBP describes a unique philosophy and related technol-ogy for integrating research and practice and honoring ethical guidelines fa-cilitated through innovations such as the Internet. Advances in electronic bibliographic databases and ways to access them make EBP possible. Consider also the development of the systematic review. Databases are now available that consist of study syntheses, such as the Cochrane and Campbell Libraries of Systematic Reviews (see Chapter 12). Such advances have been applied to practice primarily during the past decade. They are new. So, too, are checklists guiding critical appraisal of different kinds of research studies and critical ap-praisal programs designed to help both professionals and clients critically re-view research (Spittlehouse, Acton, & Enock, 2000).

9. *We are already doing it (i.e., teaching and using EBP).*

*Counterargument.* Sackett and his coauthors (1997) argue that "The argu-ment that 'everybody already is doing it' falls before evidence of striking vari-ations in both the integration of patient values into our clinical behavior and in the rates with which we provide interventions to our patients" (p. 3). Many (most?) practitioners do not search for external research findings related to important practice decisions. Many (most) do not inform clients about the criteria they use to select service methods, nor describe the risks and benefits of recommended services and alternatives (e.g., see Braddock, et al., 1998). Those who teach EBP teach students a *process* of solving problems designed to create lifelong learners. Professional education in fields such as social work, counseling, and psychology generally do not reflect characteristics of such problem-based learning. (See Chapter 8.)

10. *No evidence will be found regarding many questions helpers pose; there is conflicting evidence.*

*Counterargument.* Professional codes of ethics require professionals to search for practice-related research findings and to share what is found with clients (including nothing). It has a close connection with informed consent. Searchers may find slim pickings regarding many questions. However, careful searches will yield useful information regarding some questions, and ethical obligations require helpers to draw on practice-related research. If different reports suggest different conclusions, we should compare the rigor of these reports (see later discussion of controversies regarding evidence).

11. *Evidence-based practice assumes that professionals are rational agents.* Webb (2001) suggests that EBP assumes that professionals are rational agents. He suggests that "By underplaying the values and anticipations of social workers 'at the level of ideas' it [EBP] ignores the processes of deliberation and choice involved in their decision making" (p. 67).

*Counterargument.* Indeed, this process and related choices are highlighted (see prior description of EBP). The very reasons for the origin of EBP suggests that professionals are not rational agents; that in spite of intentions to provide competent, ethical services informed by related research findings, they do not do so. Literature describing biases, follies, and fallacies in practice described in this book suggest that we are not rational agents (e.g., see also Skrabanek & McCormick, 1998). It is true that "opinion based judgment is viewed as inferior to evidence-based decision making" (Webb, 2001, p. 62).

12. *Only randomized controlled trials are drawn on.* A common objection to EBP is that the only admissible evidence is a randomized controlled trial.

*Counterargument.* It is true that there is a preference for methodologies that critically appraise claims. Different questions require different methods to critically test them. Research drawn on depends on the question (see Chapter 12).

13. *It only applies if evidence is found.*

*Counterargument.* Research findings related to practice decisions are sought and critically appraised and what is found (including nothing) is shared with the client; clients are involved as informed participants. EBP is a decision-making approach designed to handle uncertainties in a constructive, honest manner within the context of a supportive relationship.

14. *Effectiveness is a matter of personal opinion.* Some suggest that what is viewed as effective is simply a matter of opinion.

*Counterargument.* EBP emphasizes consideration of the values and expectations of clients regarding goals, methods used, and outcomes. Efforts are made to minimize the play of opinion in the critical appraisal of practice- and policy-related research by use of rigorous criteria to evaluate such research and exhaustive search procedures, used, for example, in Cochrane and Campbell Reviews.

15. *Evidence-based practice is derived from behaviorism and positivism.* Webb (2001) suggests that EBP is derived from behaviorism and positivism.

*Counterargument.* Some writers confuse logical positivism and science as we know it today. The former approach to the development of knowledge, with its assumptions of theory-free observation, was abandoned decades ago (see Chapter 4). Evidence-based practice was initiated in medicine. Its origin has nothing to do with behaviorism.

16. *Clients don't want to be or cannot be informed.* Another objection is that clients don't want to be informed about the evidentiary status of different alternatives, don't use the information if given, or can't understand the information.

*Counterargument* Although this may apply to some people, it does not to most (see Chapter 11). Some clients are not voluntary participants. This does not remove the obligation to honor opportunities for autonomous acts in nonautonomous situations (Faden, Beauchamp, & King, 1986). And in involuntary settings such as child protection, don't clients have a responsibility to participate in an informed manner in making decisions that affect the well-being of their children? User friendly (e.g., clear, jargon-free) descriptions of practice methods and creation of decision aids facilitate client understanding (O'Connor, 2001).

17. *We don't know how to measure outcomes.*

*Counterargument.* Clients have real-life concerns allowing identification of related outcomes, both subjective and objective, and tracking of progress indicators (see Chapter 11). And how can intervention be carefully planned if outcomes are vague? The incentives maintaining selection of vague outcomes pose considerable challenges, such as obscuring ineffective or harmful actions. Clear description of service variations and their outcomes and involving all parties as informed, active participants, including selection of outcome measures, should help to ethically address conflicts about what measures to use.

18. *You can always find evidence for a favored point of view.* Some claim that if you look diligently enough, you can always find a study that will support your conclusion, and you can always find fault with a study that does not.

*Counterargument.* Ethical reviewers seek all published and unpublished research that meets standards for inclusion in a review, regardless of whether that research supports or refutes their assumptions.

19. *EBP limits professional autonomy.*

*Counterargument.* Shouldn't professionals welcome limits on their discretion if these benefit clients? Professional status is not permission to do whatever one wishes to do, as reflected in codes of ethics.

20. *EBP does not match current agency technology, policy, or practices.* Agency personnel do not have the time, resources, training, or inclination to implement EBP.

*Counterargument.* Encouraging practitioners to try to integrate evidentiary, ethical, and application issues may clash with current practices in agencies.

For example, in authority-based agencies, staff may be punished for asking questions about the effectiveness of agency services. And resources required for EBP may be lacking. However, professional codes of ethics require us to draw on practice-related research and to inform clients. Thus, we are obligated to advocate for agency practices that promote services that are faithful to these codes. Technological innovations contribute to provision of such services. Instead of resisting change, because it is inconsistent with current practices, don't we have an obligation to pursue it if it results in more effective, more ethical services?

21. *Teaching people how to think is no different than teaching them what to think.*

*Counterargument.* EBP requires skill in posing answerable questions related to important decisions that must be made and critically appraising related research findings. A question may be: Will children who may have been sexually abused, who are interviewed using an anatomically correct doll, give more accurate accounts of what happened than children interviewed by another method? Such an approach differs greatly from telling professionals which procedures to follow (e.g., you should use anatomically correct dolls when conducting child sex abuse interviews, and here is how you do it). In the former, the emphasis is on *how* to draw a conclusion. In the latter, the emphasis is on *what* to think and do.

22. *Evidence-based practice is the latest disguise for authority-based practice.*

Shahar (1997) suggests that, at worst, EBP is "a disguise for a new version of authoritarianism in medical practice" (p. 109), or the emperor's new clothes (Shahar, 1998).

*Counterargument.* Indications that EBP will be used as a new cloak for authority-based practice include material labeled as evidence-based that is not. The same product is offered in a different wrapper. For example, consider entries in the *Journal of Evidence-Based Social Work.* An article on "Treatment of anorexia nervosa and bulimia nervosa" (2004) states that its purpose is "to describe the most widely used treatment of and review the existing literature on the effectiveness of the identified treatments" (Cohen, Simpson, & Bride, 2004, p. 27). The authors do not describe where they searched, how they searched, or the criteria used to critically appraise related research, as called for in a systematic review. In addition to those who seek to forward EBP as envisioned by its originators, in an atmosphere of open, rigorous critical inquiry (transparency and accountability), there will be those who adopt the external features of EBP (e.g., its language) and forgo the substance as the latest guise for authoritarian practice (Gambrill, 2003a). But, this path is not inevitable.

23. *There is no evidence that EBP is more effective than traditional methods.*

*Counterargument.* Results of studies conducted concerning the effectiveness of evidence-based practitioners are in a positive direction. A review of the impact of postgraduate teaching of EBP suggests that clinically integrated teaching is more effective than standard teaching. The former improved knowledge, skills, attitudes, and behaviors (Coomarasamy & Khan, 2004). Shin, Haynes, and Johnston (1993) compared graduates of evidence-based training programs taught by problem-based learning (McMaster University; $n = 41$) with graduates of traditional programs (University of Toronto; $n = 41$) regarding how they would treat high blood pressure. Graduates of the traditional program were less knowledgeable and became more so with years since graduation. McMaster graduates were more up-to-date with current best practices and remained so over the years since graduation. In a controlled trial with post-test only, Bennett et al. (1987) found differences in both diagnostic accuracy and therapy decisions favoring the experimental group ($n = 45$ and 35). Studies of the effects of information provided by on-site libraries reported positive changes in care, including length of stay for patients (Klein, Ross, Adams, & Gilbert, 1994; Marshall, 1992).

24. *Recognizing the uncertainty related to decisions undermines placebo effects.*

*Counterargument.* This concern should be balanced against concerns regarding informed consent requirements, scarcity of resources such as money to provide services, and possible creation of dependence on helpers (Jarvis, 1990). The authors of a systematic review of clinical trials in which patients were randomly assigned to either placebo or no treatment concluded that there was little evidence that placebos had powerful clinical effects (Hrobjartsson & Gotzsche, 2001a, 2001b).

25. *Helping clients is an art.* Some argue that helping clients is an art that cannot be clearly described or evaluated; that one "has it" or absorbs it from a skilled mentor. They view helping clients as an art that is not amenable to objective investigation regarding procedures used (i.e., they are in some sense ineffable), the extent to which clients attain outcomes they value, and the extent to which professional education contributes to effective services.

*Counterargument.* Related research shows that helping clients is both an art and a science. Certain aspects of the "art" have been identified via research on the therapeutic "alliance"—for example, empathy and other communication skills (e.g., see Hubble, Duncan, & Miller, 1999; Norcross, 2002a). Literature exploring the behavior of experts compared to novices suggests some of the key aspects of the "art of practice." Examples include not being overly influenced by lack of perfect correlation between client characteristics and a prototype of a problem (Kassirier & Kopleman, 1991) and rapid identification of patterns based on many models (e.g., see Ericsson & Smith, 1991; Salas & Klein, 2001; see Chapter 9). Further research is likely to identify additional components of the "art" of practice. Studies showing that nonprofessionals are as effective as professionals in helping clients attain many outcomes (e.g., see Dawes, 1994a; Lambert & Ogles, 2004) suggest that if helping is an art, nonprofessionals also possess this "art." And research suggests that "It's art for them and science for us." That is, professionals rely on questionable criteria, such as intuition, when making recommendations about clients—but want professionals from whom they seek help for a serious medical problem to rely on criteria such as randomized controlled trials (see Chapter 1). Problems in integrating clinical expertise with external research findings are recognized and struggled with in EBP (see Chapter 11). If helping clients is an art, doesn't training require an apprenticeship experience in which the student works closely with an expert over a long period? Such an apprenticeship is not provided in many clinical programs.

26. *All methods are equally valuable in arriving at the truth.* Some argue that all ways of knowing are equal in revealing what services help clients, what services harm them, and what may be of no effect.

*Counterargument.* If this is so, what is the basis for claims that professionals possess special knowledge and skills of unique value to helping clients? Also, as Gellner (1992) notes, in the vacuum left by discarding evidentiary criteria, an elite will decide what is best (true) and what is not (see Chapter 4). And as described earlier, research suggests that we use different criteria in different situations in making decisions.

27. *Terms such as evidence-based are deeply misleading regarding knowledge.*

The term "evidence-based" was carefully chosen to highlight the importance of considering practice-related research findings. However, as stated, it seems to imply that decisions will be based on "evidence" rather than that there will be a search for evidence, and the results (including nothing), will be shared with clients. Misuses of the term to refer to practices which do not involve such searching and sharing reveal the reality of this concern. Shahar (1997) argues that "the noun *evidence* delivers forceful promises of truth" (p. 110) when in fact we cannot discover truth via induction (bean counting, piling up studies regarding a question) but can only falsify our theories. That is, our theories remain conjectures that may be shown to be false in the future (see discussion of different approaches to knowledge in Chapter 4). Given this, we should avoid terms such as "proved," "well-validated," "established," which imply a certainty about knowledge.

*Counterargument.* Perhaps a different term, such as *evidence-informed practice* (Chalmers, 2005) would be better—for example, more likely to avoid misuses of the term EBP. However, the literature describing the philosophy and technology of EBP and health care in original sources is readily available for anyone who cares to review it. The literature highlights the importance of critically appraising claims.

28. *Medicine differs too much from other professions, such as psychology and social work, to serve as a guide.*

*Counterargument.* Medicine, like other professions, requires complex decisions in uncertain environments. It is true that there are *signs* as well as *symptoms* in medicine, unlike the other interpersonal helping professions. That is, if we feel warm (a symptom) we can take our temperature (a sign) to check on this. However, similarities outweigh the differences, including a reluctance to face uncertainty, the play of political and economic influences, and ethical obligations. The more one reads in medicine, the more complex decisions seem to be. Medical experts argue that the typical physician works in an atmosphere of uncertainty. Physicians, too, must struggle with deciding how (or if) research findings apply to a particular client. Here, too, self-reports may be unreliable and misleading, and there may be missing information. Informed consent obligations apply to all helping professions.

## CONTROVERSIES REGARDING EVIDENCE

The degree of rigor that should be used to evaluate claims of effectiveness and the extent to which clients should be involved as informed participants are key controversies, reflected in material in which the title "evidence-based practice" appears. Both the origins of EBP and objections to it reflect different views of "evidence." There are many kinds of evidence (see Exhibit 10.7). Davies (2004) suggests that a broad view of evidence is needed to review policies, including (1) experience and expertise, (2) judgment, (3) resources, (4) values, (5) habits and traditions, (6) lobbyists and pressure groups, and (7) pragmatics and contingencies. He argues that we should consider all of these factors in making decisions about whether to implement a policy. Davies identifies six kinds of research related to evidence of policy impact: (1) implementation, (2) descriptive/analytical, (3) attitudinal, (4) statistical modeling, (5) economic/econometric, and (6) ethical. Concerns about inflated claims of effectiveness based on biased research studies was a key reason for the origin of EBP and health care. Inflated claims obscure uncertainties that, if shared, may influence client decisions. When do we have enough to recommend a practice or policy? Do criteria for "having enough" differ in relation to different kinds of decisions?

### Use of Different Criteria for Evaluating Practice and Policy Claims

Different opinions about how much we "know" reflect use of different criteria. Consider the statement of Richard Smith, past editor of the *British Medical Journal* (2003) that hardly anything is known in medicine compared to the statement by Gray (2001a) that over 60 percent of methods used in medicine and psychiatry are evidence based. Who is correct? What would we find if we examined the references to psychiatry cited by Gray? How should these differences be handled? Many reviews use the criteria developed by the American Psychological Association (APA) Division 12, Clinical Psychology Taskforce—that two well-designed RCTs showing positive outcomes represent a well-established service. Within a fallibilistic approach to knowledge (see Chapter 4) we would say that a claim has been critically tested in two well-controlled randomized controlled trials and has passed both tests. This keeps uncertainty in view. What criteria should be used to evaluate different views of evidence? Given the history of the helping professions (e.g., bogus claims of effectiveness and harming in the name of helping), isn't the most ethical road to make measured rather than inflated claims, so that professionals are not misled and in turn, mislead clients?

Do professionals use the same criteria to evaluate the evidentiary status of claims that affect their personal well-being as they do to evaluate claims that affect their clients? Research suggests that they do not, as discussed in Chapter 1. Differences of opinion regarding "what evidence is" can be seen in the

**Exhibit 10.7**
Different Kinds of "Evidence"

- Legal regulations
- Ethical guidelines
- Folklore
- Common sense
- Practice wisdom; received wisdom (experiences, beliefs, and skills of professionals)
- Cultural
- Superstition
- Medical
- Society's values
- A social care system, rules, resources, and finances
- Research findings, for example regarding prevalence and incidence of a problem
- Description of a client's circumstances or career of a problem
- Experiences of clients, practitioners, or researchers

professional literature as well as in the media. Consider the book *What Works in Child Welfare* (Kluger, Alexander, & Curtis, 2002). The editors say they originally had a question mark after the title but: "We decided to eliminate the question mark from the title because, despite its limitations, this book is a celebration of what works in child welfare" (p. xix). Leaving off the question mark is a red flag that the rigor of appraisal reflected in a book is quite different than that found in, for example, Cochrane and Campbell Collaboration reviews. The authors do not clearly describe where they searched, how they searched, or what criteria were used to critically appraise different kinds of research reports. We are given no information at many points as to the length of the follow-up. Contrast such a grandiose title with the statement on the back of the 7th edition of *Clinical Evidence* (2003) described earlier. Don't editors and authors mislead readers, clinicians, and researchers by leaving off the question mark? Do uncritical reviews of the literature contribute to helping clients and involving clients as informed participants?

*Systematic Compared to Traditional Reviews of Research*   A key way in which views of evidence-based practice differ is in the degree of rigor in evaluating knowledge claims. Such differences are illustrated by the different conclusions concerning the effectiveness of Multisystemic Family Treatment (Henggler & Lee, 2003). Multisystemic therapy is widely touted as effective (e.g., see Lehman, Goldman, Dixon, & Churchill, 2004). Thomlison (2003) states that "Of particular note is the fact that MST is at Level 1 effectiveness with eight randomized, controlled trials" (p. 547). Level 1 effectiveness refers to "Well-supported, efficacious treatment with positive evidence from more than two randomized clinical trials." Based on a critical appraisal of reviews of MST,

Littell (2005) concludes that such programs have few if any significant effects on measured outcomes compared with usual services or alternative treatment. Littell followed the guidelines developed by the Campbell and Cochrane Collaborations in preparing her review. She found that few reviews reported information on attrition in primary studies, whether outcome measures were blind, or included an intent to treat analysis. Concerns identified in the eight studies that met inclusion criteria and that were included in a subsequent analysis were inconsistent reports on the number of cases randomly assigned; unyoked designs; unstandardized observation periods within studies; unclear randomization procedures; and subjective definitions of treatment completion. Only one study met the criterion of a full intent-to-treat analysis, with a well defined follow-up. This review, as well as many others, show that unsystematic reviews come to different conclusions than do systematic reviews—typically, the former conclude that an intervention was successful when systematic reviews conclude that there is no evidence for claims of effectiveness.

Another term used is "best evidence." For example, if there are no randomized controlled trials regarding an effectiveness question, then we may consult a hierarchy of evidence in relation to the rigor of critical appraisal of a claim and move down the list (see Chapter 12). This indeed is what we must do in the everyday world, since most interventions have not been critically tested. Thus, instead of well-designed randomized controlled trials regarding an intervention, we may have to rely on findings from a pre-post test. As this example illustrates, the term "best evidence" could refer to tests that differ greatly in the extent to which they critically appraise a claim.

## SUMMARY

Current practices and policies in the helping professions reveal troubling gaps between obligations described in professional codes of ethics and what is done and between responsibilities of researchers and scholars to be honest brokers of knowledge and ignorance and what we find—inflated claims, hiding limitations of research conducted. Clients are often harmed rather than helped because of neglect of research findings, and clients are typically not involved as informed participants. There are controversies about what "evidence" is and when is there enough to make a claim of effectiveness. Evidence-based decision making suggests a problem-solving process designed to decrease these gaps, to integrate ethical, evidentiary, and application concerns. It is assumed that we and our clients often need information to make important decisions—for example, about how to decrease risk of child abuse or what method is most likely to help a client attain a job. EBP describes a philosophy and process designed to help practitioners to gain needed information and to become lifelong learners. It is a *process* in which the uncertainty in making decisions is highlighted, efforts to decrease it are made, and clients are involved as informed participants. It is as much about the ethics of and pressures on academics and researchers as it is about the ethics and pressures on practitioners and agency administrators.

Evidence-based decision making calls for honest brokering of knowledge and ignorance—for example, clear descriptions of criteria used to make decisions. It encourages us to attend to ethical obligations (draw on practice/policy related literature, involve clients as informed participants, focus on outcomes clients value), and to be systemic (for example, address application obstacles such as agency cultures). Professional codes of ethics require characteristics of EBP, such as drawing on practice/policy related research and involving clients as informed participants. The idea of integrating practice and research in professional contexts is not new, nor is attention to ethical issues as they relate to evidentiary ones. What is new about EBP and care is the description of an evolving philosophy and process designed to interlink evidentiary, ethical, and evidentiary concerns in all professional venues (practice/policy, research, and professional education).

As with all innovations, objections will and should be raised. There are many challenges and obstacles to integrating evidentiary, ethical, and application concerns. Some objections arise because of lack of knowledge about the philosophy and process of EBP. It is important to distinguish between objections based on incorrect views of EBP and those based on an accurate understanding. Otherwise, we may prematurely discard promising approaches and lose opportunities to address real challenges. Differences of opinion regarding how rigorous to be in reviewing practice- and policy-related research continue. In the everyday world of practice, "best practice" may have to be based on shaky evidentiary grounds. Evidence-based practice encourages clinicians to be honest about these grounds, so clients can be involved as informed participants in decisions made.

# CHAPTER 11

# Posing Questions and Searching for Answers

T HE STEPS IN EBP may sound as if they are easy to carry out, but that is often not the case. Special training, repeated guided practice, and related tools and resources are needed to carry out the steps of EBP in real time. Even then, as suggested in earlier chapters, many obstacles remain, such as authoritarian agency cultures. The first step in evidence-based practice is a willingness to say "I don't know"—to recognize the uncertainty in making decisions. As Chalmers (2004) suggests, evidence-based practice is a way of dealing honestly with uncertainty. Not all clinicians are willing to acknowledge the inherent uncertainty in helping clients. Not teaching physicians about clinical uncertainty has been referred to as "the greatest deficiency of medical education throughout the twentieth century" (quoted by Djulbegovic 2004; Ludmerer, 1999). A second step is to acquire expertise in carrying out the steps in EBP. Examples of related skills include the following:

1. to define and identify the sources of evidence appropriate to a particular decision that must be made;
2. to carry out a search . . . without the help of a librarian and find at least 60% of the reviews or research studies that would have been found by the librarian;
3. to construct simple search strategies using Boolean operators (*"and"* and *"or"*) . . . [and to be able to do this for a variety of interventions and service characteristics], including effectiveness, safety, acceptability, cost-effectiveness, quality, and appropriateness;
4. to download the end products of a search onto reference management software. (Gray, 2001a, p. 329)

Skills are needed in evidence management, searching, appraisal, and storage (Gray, 2001a). What skill level is best to pursue? Guyatt and Rennie (2002)

**Exhibit 11.1**
External Factors Contributing to Barriers That Impair a Professional's Performance,
and Their Solutions

| External Causes | Solutions Out of the Power of Clinicians |
| --- | --- |
| Poor quality of research producing biased evidence | Better training of research workers and stringent ethics committee |
| Studies too small to produce unequivocal results | Promotion of systematic reviews |
| Unpublished research unavailable to clinicians | Publication of all research findings by pharmaceutical companies |
| Publication biases towards positive findings | Prevention of publication bias |
| Articles that cannot be found because of inadequate indexing | Better indexing |
| Failure of research workers to present evidence in forms useful to clinicians | Tougher action by journal editors |
| Inaccessible libraries | Extension of access to the World Wide Web to all clinicians |

*Source:* From *Evidence-Based Health Care: How to Make Health Policy and Management Decisions* (2nd ed., p. 355), by J. A. M. Gray, 2001a, New York: Churchill Livingstone. Reprinted with permission.

recommend the highest possible skill levels: "Only if you develop advanced skills at interpreting the [practice- and policy-related] literature will you be able to determine the extent to which these attempts are consistent with the best evidence. Second, a high level of EBP skills will allow you to use the original literature effectively, regardless of whether pre-appraised synopses and evidence-based recommendations are available" (p. 208). (See also Guyatt, Meade, Jaeschke, Cook, Haynes, 2000.) Challenges include gaining timely access to external research findings related to important practice and policy questions and critically appraising this knowledge (see Exhibits 11.1 and 11.2). And competence does not guarantee good performance; the distinction between performance and competence is an old and continuing concern. Developing technology to address application problems has been a key contribution of evidence-based practice. This is an ongoing challenge. A review of 102 trials of interventions designed to help health professionals deliver services more effectively and efficiently shows that there are "no magic bullets" (Oxman, Thomson, Davis, & Haynes, 1995).

## POSING WELL-STRUCTURED, ANSWERABLE QUESTIONS RELATED TO PRACTICE DECISIONS

A key step in evidence-based practice is translating information needs related to practice and policy decisions into answerable questions that facilitate the search for related research in relevant databases (e.g., Sackett et al., 2000). Reasons include the following (e.g., see Gibbs, 2003):

**Exhibit 11.2**
Internal Factors Contributing to Barriers That Impair a Professional's Performance,
and Their Solutions

| Internal Causes That Even a Busy Clinician Can Modify | Solutions for the Busy Clinician |
| --- | --- |
| Out-of-date textbooks | Don't read textbooks for guidance on therapy. |
| Biased editorials and reviews | Don't read editorials and reviews for guidance on therapy, except Cochrane [and Campbell] reviews and reviews in DARE. |
| Too much primary research (the average clinician needs to read 19 articles a day to keep up) | Read good-quality reviews rather than primary research. |
| Reviews difficult to find | Improve searching skills. |
| Inability to spot flaws in research | Improve appraisal skills. |
| Difficulty in retrieving evidence identified as useful | Develop skills to use reference management software. |
| Translating data about groups of clients in research papers into information relevant to an individual client | Develop/improve understanding of baseline risk and NNT and ability to explain how research results apply to an individual client. |
| Insufficient time | Be more discerning about what to read by developing a good scanning strategy. |

*Source:* From *Evidence-Based Health Care: How to Make Health Policy and Management Decisions* (2nd ed., p. 355), by J. H. Gray, 2001, New York: Churchill Livingstone. Reprinted with permission.

- Vague questions lead to vague answers; specific questions are needed to gain specific answers to guide decisions.
- If we do not pose clear questions about decisions, we may be less likely to seek and discover helpful research findings and change what we do; we may harm clients or offer clients ineffective methods.
- It is a countermeasure to arrogance, which interferes with learning and the integration of practice and research; if we seek answers we will discover how tentative answers are and how much we do not know.
- It can save time during an electronic search. The better formed the question, the more quickly may related literature or the lack of it be revealed.
- It is necessary for self-directed, lifelong learning.

Research in medicine suggests that physicians answer only a small percentage of questions that arise by consulting relevant research sources (e.g., Ely et al., 1999; Gorman & Helfand, 1995). We have no such information in psychology, psychiatry, or social work. There is a tendency to underestimate the difficulty in carrying out this step. The better formed the question, the greater the efficiency of searching should be.

## FOUR-PART ANSWERABLE QUESTIONS

Sackett el al. (1997, 2000) suggests posing four-part answerable questions that describe the population of clients (P), the intervention you are interested in (I), and what it may be compared to (including doing nothing) (C) and hoped-for outcomes (O) (PICO questions). Gibbs (2003) refers to these as COPES questions (see Exhibit 11.3). First, they are Client Oriented. They are questions clinicians pose in their daily practice that affect clients' welfare. Second, they have *Practical* importance. They concern problems that arise frequently in everyday practice. For example, child protection service workers must assess risk. Asking the question about what types of clients present the greatest immediate risk for child abuse is a critical one. Third, COPES (PICO) questions guide an *electronic* search for related research findings. The process of forming a specific question often begins with a vague general question and then proceeds to a well-built, answerable question. Fourth, hoped-for outcomes are identified. Synonyms can be used to facilitate a search (e.g., see Gibbs, 2003; Glasziou, Del Mar, & Salisbury, 2003). For example, if abused children are of concern, other terms for this may be "maltreated children," or "mistreated children." Sackett et al. (1997) suggest that a well-formed, answerable question should meet the following criteria:

- It concerns a problem of concern to clients.
- It affects a large number of clients.
- It is probably answerable by searching for related research findings.

Posing well-formed questions is more the exception than the rule in most professional venues. Initial background reading may help you to focus your question, and you may quickly locate relevant research by using a major search engine such as Google (see later example).

## DIFFERENT KINDS OF QUESTIONS

Different kinds of questions (about effectiveness, prevention, risk, assessment, or description) require different research methods to critically test them (see Chapter 12). A variety of questions may arise with one client or family. Let's say you work in a hospice and counsel grieving parents who have lost a child. *Descriptive* questions include "What are the experiences of parents who lose a young child?" "How long do these last?" "Do they change over time, and if so, how?" Both survey data and qualitative research, such as focus groups, in-depth interviews, and participant observation can be used to explore such questions. Research may be available that describes experiences of grieving parents based on a large, randomly drawn sample of such parents. A research report may describe the experiences of clients who seek bereavement counseling using in-depth interviews. Questions concerning *risk* may arise,

**Exhibit 11.3**

Kinds of Questions and Corresponding Components of a Well-Structured Question

| Question Type | Client Type and Problem | What You Might Do | Alternate Course of Action | Hoped-for Outcome |
|---|---|---|---|---|
| | Describe a group of clients of a similar type. Be specific. | Apply a treatment to prevent a problem; measure to assess a problem; survey clients; screen clients to assess risk. | Describe the main alternative. | Outcome of intervention or prevention? Valid measure? Accurate risk estimation: Accurate estimation of need? |
| Effectiveness | Disoriented aged persons who reside in a nursing home | Reality orientation therapy | Compared to validation therapy | Which results in better orientation to time, place, and person? |
| Prevention | Sexually active high-school students at high risk for pregnancy | Exposure to baby—think-it-over | Compared to didactic material on the proper use of birth control methods | Which group has fewer pregnancies during an academic year and more knowledge of birth control methods? |
| Assessment | Elderly nursing home residents who may be depressed or have Alzheimer's disease or dementia | Complete a Depression screening test | Compared to a short mental examination test | Which measure most efficiently and reliably discriminates between depression and dementia? |
| Description | Children | Raised with depressed mothers | Compared to mothers who are not depressed | Which group will have the greatest prevalence of developmental delays? |
| Prediction/risk | Preschool children | With antisocial behavior | Compared to children who do not display such behavior | What is the risk of antisocial behavior in adolescence? |
| Harm | Adults | Participate in a Depression screening program | Compared with those who do not participate | Which results in the least harm? |
| Cost-benefit | Offering parenting classes to mothers whose children have been removed from their care | Purchase service from another agency | Compared to offering such training in-house | Which is more cost effective? |

*Source:* The Effectiveness, Prevention, and Assessment questions are from *Evidence-based Practice for the Helping Professions* (p. 50), by L. E. Gibbs, 2003, Pacific Grove, CA: Thomson/Brooks Cole. The format for all questions is based on *Evidence-based Medicine: How to Practice and Teach EBM* (p. 29), by D. L. Sackett, W. S. Richardson, W. Rosenberg, and R. B. Haynes, 1997, New York: Churchill Livingstone.

such as "In parents who have lost a young child, what is the risk of depression?" as well as questions about *effectiveness:* For parents who have lost a young child, is a support group, compared to no service, more effective in decreasing depression? *Prevention* questions may arise. For parents who have lost a young child, is brief counseling, compared to a support group, more effective in preventing depression from interfering with care of other children?

*Effectiveness Questions*   Many questions concern the effectiveness of service methods, such as given kinds of anger-management programs. Consider the 9/11 disaster at the World Trade Center. Let us say that an agency administrator wants to find out what methods (if any) may be of value in decreasing related stress reactions. The answerable question might be posed as "In people recently exposed to a catastrophic event, would brief psychological debriefing or nothing avoid or minimize the likelihood of posttraumatic stress disorder?" In this case we are dealing with an effectiveness question and ideally would discover a systematic, high-quality review or meta-analyses of randomized, controlled trials related to our question. You may discover the Number Needed to Treat (NNT)—how many clients would have to receive an intervention for one to be helped. (See Bandoher's user-friendly guide describing how to calculate NNT, see also Furukawa, 1999.) A search of the Cochrane database would reveal the Rose, Bisson, and Wessely (2004) review of brief psychological debriefing in avoiding Posttraumatic Stress Disorder. This critical appraisal of seven randomized, controlled trials showed that in six trials, there was no benefit of debriefing, and one study showed an increase of Posttraumatic Stress Disorder after a year. Thus, the administrator searching for effective methods would *not* be inclined to recommend such brief counseling, since critical tests found it to be either ineffective or harmful.

*Prevention Questions*   Prevention questions direct attention to the future. These include questions about the effectiveness of early childhood visitation programs in preventing delinquency at later developmental stages (e.g., Olds et al., 1998). Examples are: "In young children, do early home visitation programs, compared with no service, influence the frequency of delinquency as adolescents?" "For parents who have lost a young child, is bereavement counseling or a support group most valuable in decreasing prolonged dysfunctional grieving?" Here too, well-designed randomized controlled trials control for more biases than do other kinds of studies (see later discussion in Chapter 12).

*Prediction (Risk/Prognosis) Questions*   Professionals often attempt to estimate risk; for example, of future child maltreatment. A key question here is: What is the validity of the risk assessment measure? For example, what is the rate of false positives (clients incorrectly said to have some condition, such as be suicidal), and false negatives—clients inaccurately said not to have this characteristic (not be suicidal). A four-cell contingency table is of value in reviewing the accuracy of such measures (see Chapter 14). A well-built risk prognosis

question is: In abused or neglected children placed in foster care, will an actuarial risk assessment measure, compared to a consensus-based model, provide the most accurate predictions regarding reabuse when children are
returned to their biological parents? (See Baird & Wagner, 2000.)

*Assessment Questions*   Clinicians use a variety of assessment measures, such
as the Beck Depression Inventory and the Conflict Tactics Scale (e.g., see Corcoran & Fischer, 2000; Jordan & Franklin, 2003). These measures differ in their
reliability (for example, consistency of responses in absence of change) and validity (whether they measure what they purport to measure) see Chapter 13
for further discussion of reliability and validity). Inflated claims regarding the
accuracy of assessment tools are common (see Lilienfeld, Lynn, & Lohr, 2003).
The sample used to gather data and provide "norms" on a measure (scores of
a certain group of individuals) may be quite different than clients with whom
you work, and so these norms may not apply. A well-built assessment question
is: "In detecting frail elderly people who appear depressed, is the Beck Depression Inventory or the Pleasant Events Schedule most accurate?"

*Description Questions*   Professionals also seek descriptive information, such
as the experiences of caregivers of frail elderly relatives. A description question is: "In those who care for dying relatives, what challenges arise and how
are they handled?" Some description questions call for qualitative research.
For example, questions concerning in-depth experiences related to given
events, such as loss of an infant or living in a nursing home, call for research
methods that can provide such accounts, such as in-depth interviews and focus groups. In-depth surveys may yield related information. Other kinds of
description questions require survey data; descriptive data involving large
samples regarding problems and their causes is often of value to professionals. Survey data may provide information about the percentage of grieving
parents who continue to grieve in certain ways with certain consequences over
the years. It may provide information about the percentage of divorces and
other consequences and describe how parents cope with them. Here, too, we
should consider the quality of related research.

*Questions about Harm*   Decisions may have to be made about how many
people have to receive some assessment measure or service for one to be
harmed. This is known as *number needed to harm* (NNH). Related questions are:
"How many people would we have to screen to identify one person who could
benefit from help?" and "How many of these would be harmed by simply taking the test who are not at risk?" As Gray (2001a) suggests, any intervention,
including assessment methods, may harm as well as help.

*Questions about Cost-Benefit*   Limited resources highlight the importance of
cost-benefit analyses. What is the cost of offering one service compared to an-

other, and how many people benefit from each service? Criteria for reviewing cost-benefit studies can be found in many sources (e.g., Guyatt & Rennie, 2002).

*Questions about How to Encourage Lifelong Learning*   Integrating practice and research requires lifelong learning. An example of a question here is: "In newly graduated professionals, will a journal club, compared to a 'buddy system,' be most effective in maintaining evidence-based practice skills?"

## COMMON ERRORS

Errors that may occur when posing answerable questions include having more than one question in a question, trying to answer the question before stating it clearly, and posing vague questions. Gibbs (2003) notes that students often do not draw a distinction between a practice or policy question (useful to guide a search) and a research question (specific to answering a question by collecting data). Criteria suggested by Gibbs for research question answerability include the following:

1. Is a question of fact.
2. Who is selected.
3. Method is stated.
4. Study design is evident.
5. Dependent variable is identified.
6. "Where" of evaluation is cited.
7. "When" of treatment is stated.
8. "When" of outcome is specified.
9. Is single-barreled.
10. Is simple and direct.
11. Demonstrates feasibility.
12. Specifies conditions needed to answer question. (Gibbs, 1991, p. 114)

Novices may pose different questions compared to experts in an area where they are familiar with practice-related research regarding prevalence of a concern (such as depression) and the complexity of related factors, such as lack of social support, negative thoughts, recent losses, poor nutrition, and so on. A lack of assessment knowledge and skills may contribute to posing misleading questions and overlooking important individual differences in a client's circumstances or characteristics. For example, posing an effectiveness question before discovering factors that contribute to depression (such as "In adults who are depressed, is cognitive-behavioral therapy, compared to medication, most effective in decreasing depression?") may overlook the fact that, for this client, recent losses in social support are uppermost, which suggests a different question, such as "In adults who are depressed because of a recent loss in social support, is a support group or individual counseling more effective in decreasing depression?"

## OBSTACLES

Literature concerning EBP suggests that posing answerable questions can be difficult. Thus, one obstacle is thinking it is easy and giving up when difficulty occurs. Ely and his coauthors (2002) conducted a qualitative study investigating obstacles to answering physicians' questions about patient care with evidence. Participants included 9 academic/generalist doctors, 14 family doctors, and 2 medical librarians. They identified 59 obstacles. Those related to formulating questions included the following:

- Missing client data requiring an unnecessarily broad search for information. Ely and his coauthors note that questions that include demographic or clinical information and information about client preferences may help to focus the search; the kind of information that would be of value will vary depending on the question, and may not be clear until the search is underway.
- Inability to answer specific questions with general resources. A specific question was "What is this rash?" and vague cries for help, such as: "I don't know what to do with this client," cannot be answered by a general resource.
- Uncertainty about the scope of the question and unspoken ancillary questions. For example, it may not be apparent that the original question should be expanded to include many ancillary questions.
- Obstacles related to modifying the question:
  (a) uncertainty about changing specific words in the question
  (b) unhelpful modifications resulting from flawed communication between a doctor and a searcher
  (c) the need for modifications apparent only after the search has begun
  (d) difficulty modifying questions to fit a three- or four-part question format (client, intervention, comparison, and outcome)
  (e) trying to solve too many questions at once (trying to answer the question while posing it is another obstacle)

Posing clear questions may be viewed a threat. Questions are not benign, as illustrated by the fate of Socrates. Staff who pose questions in their agency may create discomfort among other staff, perhaps because they are doing something unfamiliar or perhaps because others view such staff as impertinent or disloyal to the agency or profession. Supervisors may not have experience in posing answerable questions and wonder why it is of value; learning to do so has probably not been a part of their education. Other obstacles include lack of needed tools to follow through on searches, lack of motivation to consider criteria on which decisions are made, and fears that there are more questions than answers.

## OPTIONS FOR DECREASING CHALLENGES

Options for addressing challenges include providing repeated guided experience in posing both clinical and research questions during professional education programs and providing continuing education opportunities that provide such skills. Learning by doing is emphasized in EBP. The more we use a skill, the more facility we gain with it, if we have access to corrective feedback. Unless we try to perform a certain skill we cannot determine our baseline competency level; posing answerable questions may sound easy, but can be quite difficult. Similarly, searching for related research findings may sound easy until we try to do it and run into obstacles. Answerable questions related to information needs that frequently arise could be crafted and shared with colleagues. The need for change in a question is often revealed in the next step. Gibbs (2003) and Sackett et al. (2000) provide detailed guidelines for posing different kinds of answerable questions.

## SEARCHING EFFECTIVELY AND EFFICIENTLY FOR PRACTICE- AND POLICY-RELATED RESEARCH FINDINGS

A careful search requires actively seeking information that challenges (disconfirms) our assumptions as well as for information that supports them. Sackett et al. (2000) identified different styles of evidence-based practice (see Chapter 10). In one we always look up information related to decisions and in another we depend on secondary sources. They suggest that practice-related research should always be sought and critically appraised with questions that often arise. It is perhaps at this step that the most revolutionary changes have occurred to help searchers, including development of the systematic review (see Chapter 12), creation of Internet databases such as the Cochrane and Campbell Collaboration, libraries, and descriptions of search procedures of value in locating information quickly. In addition to the development of the systematic review, the availability of the Internet has revolutionized the search for information, making it more speedy and more effective. The importance of locating information quickly is indicated by guidelines in the health area that this should be possible to do within 16 minutes. Gray (2001a) suggests that resources related to this step include the support of a librarian and access to relevant databases, the World-Wide Web, and a personal computer with reference management software so that material can be stored systematically. Sources differ in the degree of "quality-control" regarding accuracy of reporting of the evidentiary status of claims. Keep in mind that one of the reasons for the development of EBP was flaws in published research—inflated claims and incomplete searches—for example, omitting studies regarding negative or harmful effects.

A search strategy consists of identifying important search terms. Let us say you are interested in locating randomized controlled trials concerning brief psychological debriefing to prevent posttraumatic stress. Terms selected might be "stress," "psychological debriefing," and "controlled trials." Gibbs (2003) suggests using a thesaurus to identify related terms. For example, you may include child maltreatment, child abuse, and child neglect. Ease of searching depends greatly on ready access to relevant databases. Efficient, effective searching requires knowledge and experience in using Boolean search terms. Examples include "and," which retrieves only articles with *both* words (child abuse *and* single parents), and "or," which locates all articles with either word (alcohol abuse *or* cocaine abuse). Searches may be limited in a variety of ways—for example, by date. Parentheses can be used to group words (such as *frail* and *elderly*). Brackets and quote marks must be used depending on the particular database used. The term NOT excludes material containing certain words. Synonyms and key words can be combined by placing parentheses around OR statements such as (parent training OR parent education). Truncating with asterisks (*) is often used, as in (reduce*) for reduction. Other search tactics include [ti]—locate by title.

Preparing well-formed answerable questions will facilitate a search process; the better formed the question, the more likely it is that the terms entered into a search engine will be those most relevant to information needs. Gibbs (2003) suggests the following steps in the search procedure:

1. Form a well-structured answerable question (see Exhibit 11.3).
2. Clarify this question to guide an electronic search.
3. Select the appropriate quality filters related to question type.
4. Plan a search strategy.
5. Select the most appropriate bibliographic databases.
6. Conduct your search.
7. Evaluate the results and revise the strategy as needed.

Information needs identified in working with clients suggest questions and related searches of value. These can form the basis of Critically Appraised Topics (CATS) shared with others. A CAT is a brief (one page) summary of the question raised, what was found, and the implications for clinical practice. Sackett and his colleagues (2000) recommend including "the three- or four-part clinical question that started the process, and the search terms that were used to locate the paper. Next is a summary of the study methods and a table summarizing the key results. Any issues important to bear in mind when applying the CAT (such as rare adverse effects, costs, or unusual elements of the critical appraisal) are inserted beneath the results table" (Sackett et al., 2000, p. 88).

## USE OF QUALITY FILTERS

Different kinds of questions require different kinds of research to critically appraise them, and related terms are of value in preparing a search as dis-

**Exhibit 11.4**
Quality Filters for an Effective Search

| Effectiveness Questions | Prevention Questions | Risk/ Prognosis Questions | Assessment Questions | Description Question | Synthesis of Studies |
|---|---|---|---|---|---|
| random* | random* | risk | inter-rater | random* | meta-anal* |
| OR | OR | assessment | OR | select* | OR |
| controlled | controlled | OR | inter- | OR | meta-anal* |
| clinical trial* | clinical trial* | predictive | observer | survey | OR |
| OR | OR | validity | OR | OR | meta-anal* |
| control | control | OR | true positive | representative | OR |
| group* | group* | predictive | OR | sample | systematic |
| OR | OR | value | specificity | AND | review* |
| evaluation | evaluation | OR | OR | client | OR |
| stud* | stud* | receiver | false positive | satisfaction | synthesis of |
| OR | OR | operat | OR | OR | studies |
| study design | study design | OR | false | patient | OR |
| OR | OR | ROC | negative | satisfaction | study |
| statistical | statistical | OR | OR | OR | synthesis |
| significan | significan | sensitivity | sensitivity | needs | |
| OR | OR | OR | OR | assessment | |
| double-blind | double-blind | specificity | predict | to retrieve | |
| OR | OR | OR | OR | qualitative | |
| -placebo | placebo | false positive | receiver | studies: | |
| | AND | OR | operat | qualitative | |
| | prevent | false | OR | analys OR | |
| | | negative | ROC | content | |
| | | OR | AND | analys | |
| | | prognos | (assess | OR in depth | |
| | | AND | OR | Interview | |
| | | predict | diagnos*) | OR in-depth | |
| | | | | Interview | |
| | | | | OR | |
| | | | | participant | |
| | | | | observation | |
| | | | | OR | |
| | | | | focus group | |

*Source:* Based on *Evidence-based Practice for the Helping Professions* (p. 100), by L. E. Gibbs, 2003, Thomson Brooks-Cole and *PDQ Evidence-based Principles and Practice,* by A. McKibbon, A. Eady, & S. Marks, 1999, Hamilton, UK: B. C. Decker. Reprinted with permission.
*Note:* Quality filters are listed in descending order of their utility.

cussed earlier (see also Chapter 12). Such terms are referred to as *quality filters.* The use of quality filters that pertain specifically to the type of question posed will facilitate the search process. Examples are shown in Exhibit 11.4. Gibbs (2003) calls these methodology-oriented locators for an evidence search (MOLES). If a question concerns effectiveness, quality filters include terms such as random or controlled trials, meta-analysis, or systematic review. Systematic reviews and meta-analyses include a search for and critical appraisal of related studies (see later discussion in this chapter). A search strategy consists of identifying important search terms, as discussed earlier. Ease of searching depends greatly on ready access to relevant databases.

Searches can be facilitated by selecting key search terms referring to each part of an answerable question; client type, proposed course of action, alternative action, and intended result. Thus, a search includes a three- or four-part answerable question (Sackett et al., 1997) and quality filters which allow access to relevant databases. You can keep track of how many "hits" you obtain in each database by recording these in a search log (Gibbs, 2003). If your search strategy results in too many hits, you can narrow the search by using more specific terms and more quality filters. If you get too little, you can widen the search by using more general terms. Gibbs (2003) recommends taking time to prepare a search strategy. People differ in how they search. Some try a "quick and dirty" search first—for example, by entering search terms in a search engine. Sometimes this is productive. At other times, only a systematic search process may identify key studies related to a question.

## RELEVANT DATABASE

Searches will be more productive by focusing on sources that contain high-quality reviews. Different databases have different rules about exactly how search terms should be entered for maximum effect, and you should seek specific information from other sources about how to use these most effectively. Experience in using relevant bibliographic databases is an important skill. An onsite infomatist may be available to guide your search.

*The Cochrane Library*   The Cochrane Collaboration prepares, maintains, and disseminates high-quality reviews of research related to a particular practice question. It focuses on health concerns; however, many reviews are relevant to a wide variety of professionals. Examples are "Psychoeducation for schizophrenia" (Pekkala & Merinder, 2004); "Psychological debriefing for preventing Posttraumatic Stress Disorder" (Rose, Bisson, & Wessely, 2004). The Cochrane Library is an electronic publication designed to supply high-quality evidence to those providing and receiving care and those responsible for research, teaching, funding, and administration, at all levels. The Cochrane database includes thousands of systematic reviews. It is distributed on a subscription basis. Cochrane and Campbell Collaboration reviews are based on a search for all high-quality research, published and unpublished, in all languages, concerning a particular question, and critical appraisal of what is found. Journals are hand-searched. Abstracts of reviews are available without charge and can be searched. Reviews are prepared by people who are also re-

**Exhibit 11.5**

Examples of U.S. Federal Agencies and Departments

Agency for Healthcare Research and Quality (AHRQ): http://www.ahrq.gov/

Best Practices Initiative, Department of Health and Human Services: http://www.osophs.dhhs.gov/ophs/Best/Practice/default.htm

Centers for Disease Control and Prevention (CDC): http://www.cdc.gov/

Center for Information Technology : http://www.cit.nih.gov/home.asp

Centers for Medicare and Medicaid Services : http://cms.hhs.gov/default.asp

Center for Scientific Review (CSR): http:www.csr.hih.gov

Educational Research and Improvement: http://www.ed.gov/offices/OERI/index.html

Faith-Based and Community Initiatives Office: http://whitehouse.gov/government/fbci

Food and Drug Administration (FDA): http://www.fda.gov/

General Accounting Office (GAO): http://www.gao.gov/

Health Resources and Services Administration: http://www.hrsa.gov/

Justice Programs Office: http:ojp.usdoj.gov/

National AIDS Policy Office: http://www.whitehosue.gov/onap/aids.html

National Center for Complementary and Alternative Medicine (NCCAM): http://nccam.nih.gov/

National Center for Research Resources (NCRR): http://www.ncrr.nih.gov/

National Center on Minority Health and Health Disparities (NCMHD): http://ncmhd/nih.gov/

National Clearing House on Child Abuse and Neglect Information: http://nccanch.act.hhs.gov.nccanch/

National Council on Disability: http:www.ncd.gov/

National Criminal Justice Reference Service (NCJRS): http://www.ncjrs.org

National Health Information Center: http://www.health.gov/NHIC/

National Institute of Child Health and Human Development (NICHD): http://www.nichd.nih.gov/

National Institute of Mental Health (NIMH): http://www.nimh.nih.gov/

National Institute on Aging (NIA): http://www.nia.nih.gov/

National Institute on Alcohol Abuse and Alcoholism (NIAAA): http:www.niaaa.nih.gov/

National Institute on Deafness and Other Communication Disorders (NIDCD): http://www.nidcd.nih.gov/

National Institute on Drug Abuse (NIDA): http://www.nida.nih.gov/

National Institutes of Health (NIH): http://www.nih.gov/

National Library of Medicine (NLM): http://www.nlm.nih.gov/

Office of Justice Programs: http://www.ojp.usdoj.gov

Office of Scientific and Technical Information: http://www.osti.gov/ostipg.html

Office of the Surgeon General: http://www.osophs.dhhs.gov/ophs

Special Education and Rehabilitative Services: http://www.ed.gov/about/offices/list/osers/index.htm

Substance Abuse and Mental Health Services Administration: http://www.samhsa/gov/index/aspx

sponsible for identifying and incorporating new evidence as it becomes available. Entries include completed reviews, available in full-text, as well as protocols that are expressions of intent and include a brief outline of the topic and a submission deadline. Reviews are prepared and maintained based on standards in *The Reviewers' Handbook,* which describes the process of creating Cochrane systematic reviews. It is revised often to ensure that it remains up-to-date. The Cochrane Library also includes a Controlled Trials Register and The Cochrane Review Methodology Database, which is a bibliography of articles concerning research synthesis and practical aspects of preparing systematic reviews.

*The Campbell Collaboration*   The Campbell Collaboration is patterned after the Cochrane Collaboration; it prepares reviews related to education, social intervention, and criminal justice. Coordinating groups include communication and dissemination, crime and justice, education, social welfare, and a methods group. Like the Cochrane Collaboration, detailed instructions are followed for preparing high-quality reviews, and reviews are routinely updated. They, like the Cochrane Collaboration, have an annual conference, and both are attended by methodologists as well as those interested in particular problem areas (www.campbellpenn.com).

*Other Sources*   The UK National Health Service Centre for Reviews and Dissemination (CRD), located at the University of York, prepares and disseminates research on the effectiveness and cost-effectiveness of specific health-care interventions, health-care delivery, and health-care technology from high-quality health research for decision makers and health consumers (see also prior description of Database of Abstracts of Reviews of Effects (DARE) (www.york.ac.uk/inst/crd/darehp.htm). Libraries are a key resource. Librarians should be skilled at what is known as *infomatics,* searching for information related to a certain question in an efficient manner. Newspapers are another source. Governmental agencies provide free statistical information of potential value. (See examples of U.S. federal agencies and departments in Exhibit 11.5.) SIGLE (System for Information on Grey Literature in Europe) can be used to locate hard to find and nonconventional literature. Some sites are available only by subscription, but a library near you may have a subscription. Examples of databases relevant to interpersonal helping professions include: PsychInfo, Social Science Citation Index, Social Work Abstracts, Sociological Abstracts, ERIC, Evidence-based mental health, MEDLINE, EMBASE, CINAHL (nursing and allied health professionals), Health Technology Assessment Program, Bandolier, Effective Health Care Bulletin, and Clinical Evidence. Bandolier is a monthly journal that contains "bullets" of evidence-based information. Internet access is free of charge. Other databases, together with their subject coverage and focus, are listed in the following.

- *Netting the Evidence.* This web site describes where to find information on the Internet on using evidence in practice.
- *Evidence-Based Healthcare.* Its purpose is to provide managers with the best evidence available about the financing, organization, and delivery of healthcare.
- *Be Evidence-Based.com.* This is a database of research findings provided by the Center for Evidence-Based Social Services in the United Kingdom.
- World Wide Web Resources for social workers (www.nyu.edu/social workers/wwwfsw).
- *www.childwelfare.com.* This site was developed by Duncan Lindsey at UCLA and contains information related to child welfare.
- *AMED.* Alternative medicine, including complementary medicine, physiotherapy, occupational therapy, rehabilitation, podiatry, and palliative care (United Kingdom).
- *British Nursing Index.* Nursing, midwifery, and health visiting (United Kingdom).
- *CANCERLIT.* Cancer, including treatment together with information on epidemiology, pathogenesis, and immunology (United States).
- *ASSIA* (Applied Social Sciences Index and Abstracts) is an indexing and abstraction tool covering health, social services, economics, politics, race relations, and education. It currently contains 225,000 records from 650 journals in 16 different countries.

*The Internet*    Search engines such as Yahoo, Alta Vista, Ask Jeeves, and Google provide another source for locating practice-related research findings. For example, a search on Google to locate the prevalence of enuresis among young children found the answer in 5 minutes. On Google, Amanda Penick entered the search words "enuresis and prevalence," which turned up the web site for the National Institute of Health. She entered the same terms in "Medline," which identified a Cochrane Review on Alarm Interventions for nocturnal enuresis in children by Glazener, Evans, and Peto (2005). Fifteen to twenty-five percent of children five years of age wet the bed.

Sources include web sites concerned with a unique topic (Attention-Deficit/Hyperactivity Disorder [ADHD]); those concerned with fraud and quackery; those prepared by businesses (e.g., www.zoloft.com) and web sites concerned with harm (Americaniatrogenics.com). Material differs greatly in quality (accuracy of reports of research findings; e.g., Kunst, Groot, Latthe, Latthe, & Khan, 2002). Just because a source has a reputation for providing accurate appraisals does not guarantee that all material will be accurately presented. Thus, "buyer beware" applies. Criteria that can be used to appraise the likelihood that material is accurate include the source (does it have a reputation for critical appraisal and accurate presentation of well-argued alternative views), clarity of writing, completeness of description of studies (e.g., sample size, measures used), and references that provide opportunities to follow up sources.

## EXAMPLES OF CENTERS AND ORGANIZATIONS

The National Health Service (NHS) Research and Development Centre for Evidence-Based Medicine at the John Radcliffe Hospital in Oxford was the first of several similar centers around the United Kingdom. The aims are to promote an evidence-based approach and to provide support and resources to those who wish to make use of them (www.cebm.net). There are many other centers that can be located through the Internet.

## COMMON ERRORS

Errors at this stage are related to the clarity and degree of precision of questions posed; they may be too narrow or too broad, resulting in too few or too many reports. Giving up too soon is a common error; it takes persistence to reframe search strategies more effectively. Lack of information about valuable web sites may result in overlooking helpful resources.

## OBSTACLES AND EVOLVING REMEDIES

There are a number of obstacles that get in the way of discovering practice- and policy-related research. You may not be aware of important databases and may not have access to knowledgeable librarians. There may be no high-quality evidence related to a practice question. Gray refers to this as the *relevance gap* (Gray, 2001a). Another is failure to publish research results—the *publication gap*. A third is difficulty in finding published research—the *hunting gap*. Other gaps include the *quality gap* and the *good intention gap* (p. 101). Of the 59 obstacles to EBP identified by Ely and his colleagues (2002), 5 they considered most important involved search problems:

- Excessive time required to locate information
- Difficulty selecting an optimal search strategy
- Failure of a seemingly relevant resource to cover the topic
- Uncertainty about how to know when all relevant evidence has been found
- Inadequate synthesis of multiple sources of evidence into a conclusion that is clinically relevant

The resources that enable an efficient search illustrate challenges that lie in the path of the clinician or client who would like to make evidence-based decisions (see also Exhibits 11.1 and 11.2). For example, there may be no library in an agency, let alone a librarian. There may be no access to relevant databases. The importance of immediate access to needed databases is illustrated by the failure to use agency-based libraries even though they are conveniently located. There may be no access to a reference management system. Ongoing exploration of search strategies that yield the highest quality studies is a high priority. Only via providing access to a knowledge manager, as suggested by Gray (1998), may speedy access to relevant information be possible. This person's role would be to locate and critically appraise practice- and policy-related research findings in a timely manner. Searching widely is one way to protect yourself from influence by bogus presentations from a single source. For example, material on the web site of the American Psychiatric Association may be compared with material on the web site of the International Center for the Study of Psychiatry and Psychology (ICSPP). You may get ideas from browsing the Internet about how to pose a question to search for related reviews (www.icspp.com).

## CRITICALLY APPRAISING WHAT YOU FIND

Critically appraising the quality of different kinds of research is a key competency in EBP. The notion of a hierarchy of evidence is integral to evidence-based practice and policy. As emphasized earlier, the kind of research that may provide evidence differs, depending on the question. Some questions call for qualitative research methods, such as in-depth interviews. Questions pertaining to intervention, prevention, harm, or testing the accuracy of a diagnostic method, may most carefully be explored using randomized controlled trials. Often, a mix of qualitative and quantitative research may be best. Skill in critically appraising research related to different kinds of questions should be acquired during professional education programs. Resources to gain this information include books such as Gibbs (2003), Guyatt and Rennie (2002), Greenhalgh (2001), and Sackett et al. (2000; see also Chapter 12). The EBM toolkit is a Canadian-based collection of resources to support the practice of evidence-based medicine. It includes critical appraisal checklists, methodological filters, and other resources, located at http://www.med.ualberta.ca/ebm/ebm.htm.

Workshops are available at a number of different sources. The Critical Appraisal Skills Program (CASP) in Oxford has been offering training programs for many years (Institute of Health). The purpose of CASP is to help health service decision makers, and those who seek to influence decision makers, to develop evidence management skills—for example to find, critically appraise, and change practice in line with research findings. CASP has also developed an interactive CD-ROM, which can be used in conjunction with workshops, video-conferencing, as a stand-alone package, or to support learning, hopefully diffusing skills to a wider audience and providing opportunities for independent practice and learning. (See also WISDOM center.)

There is no perfect study. All research has flaws that may compromise its value in exploring a question. Biases that may limit the value of findings are always of concern. Questions to ask of all research reports include the following:

- Is there a clear research question?
- Is the study design appropriate? Does it match the question?

- What is the sample size and source?
- Are measures used valid and reliable?
- Are claims made accurate?
- Is the data analysis appropriate?
- Does the study offer information that can guide practice and policy decisions?

The research methods used may be appropriate for the question, and rigorous, but the findings may not apply to your clients or locale because of the sample or setting involved or the measures used.

## COMMON ERRORS

Common errors include: (1) not critically appraising what you find, (2) becoming disheartened when you find little available, and (3) misinterpreting a lack of evidence that a method is effective as evidence that it is not effective.

## OBSTACLES AND EVOLVING REMEDIES

You can save time by drawing on high-quality critical appraisals of evidence related to a question when these are available (for example, the Cochrane and Campbell databases). Palm Pilots are available for evaluating tests as well as for other goals (e.g., Clinical Decision-Making Calculators). Take advantage of checklists that will help you to critically appraise different kinds of research (e.g., Greenhalgh, 2001).

## USING CLINICAL EXPERTISE TO INTEGRATE EXTERNAL RESEARCH FINDINGS WITH OTHER RELEVANT INFORMATION AND APPLYING THE FINDINGS

Here you must decide whether external research located applies to your client, and consider his or her preferences and whether you have access to needed resources (e.g., see Glasziou & Irwig, 1995). Is is important? Thus, this step requires integration of a number of different kinds of information, drawing on clinical expertise. It requires integrating information concerning external research findings with characteristics of the client including their values and expectations, and his or her circumstances, and a consideration of application problems such as lack of resources, and deciding what to do together with the client. Evidence-based practice involves the "integration of best research evidence with clinical expertise and [client] values (Sackett et al., 2000, p. 1).

> Increased expertise is reflected in many ways, but especially in more effective and efficient [assessment] and in the more thoughtful identification and compassionate use of individual [clients'] predicaments, rights and preferences in making clinical decisions about their care. (Sackett et al., 1997)

Without clinical expertise, practice risks becoming tyrannized by external evidence, for even excellent external evidence may be inapplicable to or inappropriate for an individual patient. Without current best external evidence, practice risks becoming rapidly out of date, to the detriment of patients. (p. 2)

In non-compensatory views, what is considered a strength on one particular dimension cannot make up for a weakness on another. In compensatory rule-based integration, it can; that is, we can trade off between different kinds of attributes.

Many application barriers may enter at this stage. Indeed, gathering information about their frequency and exact nature will be useful in planning how to decrease obstacles. Examples reported by my students include:

- Chaotic working space—shared phone, desk, and computer, and no private space for confidential conversations.
- Disparity between practice standards taught in school and (lower) agency expectations.
- The lack of planning of interventions on the part of administrators and program coordinators. This leads to counselors and support staff mainly working in crisis to deal with issues that arise. Also, without time for planning, support staff does not research promising practices that others may be using to address issues. Additionally, they do not look for any evidence as to the effectiveness of possible interventions before implementation.
- Providers feeling overwhelmed by the problems/issues that clients bring. This may be due to a large caseload, lack of resources to refer clients to, or the multitude of issues that clients are dealing with.
- Unsupportive administration (i.e., not attentive to line workers' needs, micromanagement).
- Unclear mission/goal of organization/agency (confusion of what we are supposed to provide).
- Poor interagency communication and collaboration.

A review of research findings related to important practice questions and related information needs may reveal that little or nothing is known. This will be true for many problems, including in medicine (Greenhalgh & Young, 1998). Information may be available about certain kinds of clients but these clients may differ greatly from your client, and so findings may not apply. Resources available will limit options. Here, too, our obligations to inform clients and to consider their preferences provide a guide (e.g., helpers should clearly describe limitations in applying research findings in a particular situation). Questions include (Glasziou, Del Mar, & Salisbury, 2003): Do research findings apply to my client? That is, is a client similar to clients included in related research findings? Can I use this practice method in my setting (e.g., are needed resources available?) If not, is there some other access to programs found to be most effective in seeking hoped-for outcomes? What alternatives are available? Will the benefits of service outweigh harms of service for this client? What does my client think about this method? Is it acceptable to clients? What if I don't find anything?

## DO RESEARCH FINDINGS APPLY TO MY CLIENT?

A great deal of practice-related research consists of correlational research (e.g., describing the relationship between certain characteristics of parents and child abuse) and experimental research, describing differences among different groups (e.g., experimental and control). In neither case may the findings apply to a particular client. There is a continual strain between the scientific investigation of different events, such as child abuse, and dealing with the individual client. The focus of practice is on the individual client; science deals with generalities. Samples used in research studies may differ from a client. Norms on assessment measures may be available but not for people like your client. For example, your clients may be Latino and available norms may be for Caucasians. These norms may not represent responses of Latinos. Note, however, that norms should not necessarily be used as a guidelines for selecting outcomes for individual clients; outcomes they seek may differ from normative criteria and norms may not be optimal (e.g., low rates of positive feedback from teachers to students in classrooms). We must always consider the possible difference between those who participated in research related to a question of concern and our client. Will these differences influence the potential costs and benefits of an intervention? Certain differences may result in more harm than good if an intervention is used with a particular client.

The unique characteristics and circumstances of a client may suggest that a particular practice method should not be used because negative effects are likely or because such characteristics would render an intervention ineffective if it were applied at a certain time. For example, referring clients to parent-training programs who have a substance abuse problem may not be effective. Thus, there may be other problems (often referred to as comorbid) that influence the effectiveness of a method). The unique factors associated with a problem such as depression may influence the effectiveness of a given method (e.g., medication, increasing pleasant events, decreasing negative thoughts). Your knowledge of behavior and how it is influenced and what principles of behavior have been found to apply to many individuals may provide helpful guidelines. Decisions regarding whether practice guidelines are valid are thus separate from whether they are applicable to a particular client, agency, or community. Questions suggested by Sheldon, Guyatt, and Haines (1998) about whether an intervention applies to an individual client are as follows:

1. Is the relative risk reduction that is attributed to the intervention likely to be different in this case because of client characteristics?

2. What is the [client's] absolute risk of an adverse event without the inter-vention?
3. Is there [some other problem] or a contraindication that might reduce the benefit?
4. Are there social or cultural factors that might affect the suitability of [a practice or policy] or its acceptability?
5. What do the [client and the client's] family want?

## ARE THEY IMPORTANT? THE "SO-WHAT QUESTION"

If findings apply to your client, are they important? Would they really make a difference in the decisions you and your clients make about how to attain hoped-for outcomes?

## HOW DEFINITIVE ARE THE RESEARCH FINDINGS?

Reviews found may be high-quality systematic reviews or narrative re-views. In the former there may be strong evidence not to use a practice method (e.g., see reviews of Scared Straight Programs by Petrosino, Turpin-Petrosino, & Beuhler, 2003) or strong evidence to use one (for example, early home-visiting programs for children; Olds et al., 1998). Often there will be uncer-tainty about whether an intervention will do more good than harm.

## WILL POTENTIAL BENEFITS OUTWEIGH POTENTIAL RISKS AND COSTS?:

Every intervention, including assessment measures, has potential risks as well as potential benefits—for example, a false positive or negative result. Will the benefits of an intervention outweigh potential risks and costs? We can es-timate this in a number of ways: relative risk reduction (RRR), absolute risk re-duction (ARR), and number needed to treat (NNT). We could compute the odds ratio (see Exhibit 11.6). The percentage of clients better in the control and better with treatment can be plotted on a L'Abbè plot of data for ready visual inspection (see Bandolier worksheet for calculating NNT). How many clients have to receive a harm reduction program to help one person? Interventions differ greatly in the NNT, ranging from 2 (fear of flying—standard exposure versus waiting list control) to hundreds (aspirin versus placebo for hip surgery = 232: www.cebm.utononto.ca/glossary/nntsPrint.htm, retrieved 3/10/04). Is there any information about NNH (the number of individuals who would have to receive a service to harm one person)? A nomogram can be used to cal-culate the number needed to treat based on absolute risk in the absence of treatment (Guyatt & Rennie, 2002). "Using ARR and its reciprocal, the NNT, incorporates the influence of the changing baseline risk. If all we know is the ARR or the NNT, however, we remain ignorant of the size of the baseline risk For example, an ARR of 5% (and a corresponding NNT of 20) may represent

**Exhibit 11.6**
Estimating the Size of the Treatment Effect

*The 2 x 2 Table*

|  | Outcome + | Outcome − | Risk of Outcome: |
|---|---|---|---|
| Treated (Y) | a | b | Y = a/(a+b) |
| Control (X) | c | d | X = c/(c+d) |

*Relative risk*, or *Risk ratio* (RR), is the ratio of risk in the treatment group (Y) to the risk in the control group (X): RR = Y/X

$$\frac{a/(a + b)}{c/(c + d)}$$

*Relative risk reduction* (RRR) is the percent reduction in risk in the treated group (Y) compared to controls (X):

RRR = 1 − RR + 1 − Y/X x 100% or
RRR = [(X − Y)/X] x 100%

$$\frac{c/(c + d) - a/(a + b)}{c/(c + d)}$$

*Absolute risk reduction* (ARR) is the difference in risk between control group (X) and the treated group (Y):

AAA = X − Y

$$\frac{c}{c + d} - \frac{a}{a + b}$$

*Number needed to treat* (NNT) is the inverse of the ARR:

NNT = 1/ARR = 1(X − Y)

$$\frac{1}{ARR}$$

*Odds ratio* (OR)

$$\frac{a/b}{c/d} = \frac{ad}{cb}$$

*Source:* Adapted from G. Guyatt and D. Rennie (2002). *Users' guide to the medical literature: A manual for evidence-based clinical practice.* Chicago: American Medical Association.

reduction of the risk of death from 10% to 5% (a RRR of 50%) or from 50% to 45% (a RRR of 10%)" (Guyatt & Rennie, 2002, p. 360).

## HOW DO CLIENT PREFERENCES AND VALUES COMPARE TO THE PROPOSED SERVICES AND THEIR RESULTS?

Clients may not want to carry out a plan that seems to have the best chance of removing complaints. Thus, the acceptability of plans must be considered. This will influence adherence to important procedural components associated with success. Helping clients discover their preferences may require involving them in a decision analysis. Decisions aids are available for some decisions. The lack of correlation between what someone says he or she wants (their preferences) and what he or she does (their actions) highlights the difficulties of helping clients to discover their preferences. We often don't know what we want, and our preferences change in accord with a variety of factors, including the time at which we are asked about them in relation to a decision that has been made and the visibility of the consequences thereof. This is considered to be such a big issue, with so little related research, that the latest model of evidence-based practice carves out preferences and actions as a separate area to be considered (see Chapter 10). For example, although many people may say they wish to achieve a certain goal, when in fact given instructions about how to start to plan their life to do so, their actions often do not reflect their stated preferences. That is, they don't do anything. In view of tendencies of some clients to match the goals and values of their therapists and other sources of behavioral confirmation in the helping process, and in view of the influence of subtle influences such as question wording and order on the expression of preferences, a variety of methods of inquiry should be used, rather than relying on one method which may result in inaccurate accounts. Different surface wordings of identical problems, influence judgments. Gains or losses that are certain are weighed more heavily than those that are uncertain.

Decision aids can be used to inform clients about risks and benefits of options (see, for example, Barratt, Howard, Irwig, Salkind, & Houssami, 2005; O'Connor et al., 2002). Such aids can "personalize" information by allowing clients to ask questions important to them. In can also highlight important issues often overlooked, such as asking about absolute risk. Eddy (1990) suggests use of a cost utility matrix to help clients arrive at individual decisions. Formats include interactive videos, personal computers, audiotapes, audioguided workbooks, and pamphlets. Occasions when discovering client preferences is especially important include those in which:

- Options have major differences in outcomes or complications.
- Decisions require making trade-offs between short-term and long-term outcomes.
- One choice can result in a small chance of a grave outcome.
- There are marginal differences in outcomes between options. (Kassirer, 1994)

Clients differ in how "risk adverse" they are and in the importance given to particular outcomes. Presentation of risks and benefits may be quite misleading (e.g., see Jørgensen & Gøtzsche, 2004). How decisions are "framed" (in terms of gains or losses) influences decisions (e.g., Edwards, Elwyn, Mathews, & Pill, 2001). Benefits of decision aids noted by O'Connor (2001) include the following:

- Reducing the proportion of clients who are uncertain about what to choose.
- Increasing clients' knowledge of the problem, options, and outcomes.
- Creating realistic expectations (perceived probabilities) of outcomes.
- Improving the agreement between choices and a client's values.

**Exhibit 11.7**
Evidence-Informed Client Choice

Agency: _____

Client: _____

Date: _____

Referral agency: _____

Program within agency: _____

Staff member within agency who will offer program: _____

A. *Related External Research*

___ 1. Research shows that this program will help people like me to attain hoped-for outcomes.

___ 2. This program has never been rigorously tested in relation to hoped-for outcomes.

___ 3. Research shows that other programs that help people like me have been critically tested and found to attain hoped-for outcomes.

___ 4. Research shows that this program is likely to have harmful effects (e.g., decrease hoped-for outcomes).

B. *Agency's Background Regarding Use of this Method*

___ 1. The agency to which I have been referred has a track record of success in using this program with people like me.

___ 2. The staff member who will work with me has a track record of success in using this method with people like me.

*See for example "Evidence-informed Patient Choice," by V. A. Entwistle et al., 1998, *International Journal of Technology Assessment in Health Care, 14,* pp. 212–215.

- Reducing some elements of decisional conflict (feeling uncertain, uninformed, unclear about values, and unsupported in decision making).
- Increasing participation in decision making without adversely affecting anxiety (p. 101; see also O'Connor et al., 2002).

Client satisfaction with use of decision aids is more uncertain. Scales have been developed to measure client involvement (Elwyn, Edwards, Wensing, Hood, Atwell, & Grol, 2003). We can also involve our own clients as informed participants (see Exhibit 11.7).

## CAN THIS PRACTICE METHOD BE USED EFFECTIVELY IN MY AGENCY?

Can a plan be carried out in a way that maximizes success? Are needed resources available? Do providers have the skills required to carry out plans? Can needed resources be created? Are those responsible for offering services competent to do so? How do you know? Competence in applying a method does not necessarily reflect competence to teach others, such as parents (McGimsey, Greene, & Lutzker, 1995). Consultation skills are required to teach others successfully, such as providing a rationale for methods used, demonstrating steps while describing them, arranging role-plays for each step, and providing corrective feedback. There may be vital differences in provider adherence to practice guidelines that decrease the safety and effectiveness of an intervention. Current service patterns may limit options. Questions Sackett et al. (1997) suggest for deciding whether to implement a guideline include the following (p. 182):

1. What barriers exist to its implementation?
   • Can they be overcome?
2. Can you enlist the collaboration of key colleagues?
3. Can you meet the educational, administrative, and economic conditions that are likely to determine the success or failure of implementing the strategy?
   • Credible synthesis of the evidence by a respected body
   • Respected, influential local exemplars already implementing the strategy
   • Consistent information from all relevant sources
   • Opportunity for individual discussions about the strategy with an authority
   • User-friendly format for guidelines
   • Implementable within target group of clinicians (without the need for extensive outside collaboration)
   • Freedom from conflict with:
     • Economic incentives
     • Administrative incentives
     • Patient expectations
     • Community expectations

Problems may have to be redefined from helping clients attain needed resources to helping them to bear up under the strain of not having them, or involving clients with similar concerns in advocacy efforts to acquire better services.

### ARE ALTERNATIVE OPTIONS AVAILABLE?

Are other options available—perhaps another agency to which a client could be referred? Perhaps self-help programs are available. Here, too, familiarity with practice-related research can facilitate decisions.

### WHAT IF THE EXPERTS DISAGREE?

We rely on the assertions of experts, those with presumed special knowledge, on an everyday basis. Given this dependence, how can we make wise decisions regarding the accuracy and candidness with which an expert describes controversies and uncertainties? In some situations we could seek and review the quality of evidence for ourselves. In some cases checking the evidentiary status of claims by experts is fairly easy. Suppose a lecturer claims that psychiatric classifications are valid categories and provide intervention guidelines. You could check this by reading critiques of this classification system (e.g., Houts, 2002; Kutchins & Kirk, 1997) and by reading the introduction to the *DSM* in which its purpose is described. At other times checking the accuracy will require greater effort, such as critically reviewing the quality of a review concerning a service method. At other times it may not be possible, due to time constraints. How dependent are you on the advice of experts in your work? How can you check the expertise (knowledge) and ethics (honesty regarding controversies and uncertainties) of an expert? How do recommendations of clinical experts compare to what is suggested, based upon results of carefully controlled research? (Antman, Lau, Kuplenick, Mosteller, & Chalmers, 1992). Indicators of honesty include: (1) accurate description of controversies in an area, including methodological and conceptual problems; (2) accurate description of well-argued disliked views; (3) critical appraisal of both preferred and alternative views; (4) inclusion of references to sources cited, so readers can look these up.

## WHAT IF CLIENTS PREFER AN UNTESTED METHOD?

What if your client prefers a method that has not been tested or that has been tested and has been found to be ineffective or harmful? Most interventions used by professionals in the interpersonal helping professions have not been tested; we don't know if they are effective, not effective, or are harmful. Certainly you should not use a method shown to be harmful. What about untested methods? If there is an effective method you could describe the costs and benefits of using this compared to an ineffective method. Untested methods are routinely offered in both health and social care. Whether you should offer them depends on many factors, including acceptability to clients and scarcity of resources in your agency.

## WHAT IF I DO NOT FIND ANY RELATED RESEARCH?

What if there is no research that can guide decisions? What do you do if you have searched for information related to an important question and find nothing? Let us assume that your search has been a high-quality one and that no one else could find anything either. You should share what you find (including nothing) with your clients and draw on empirically grounded practice theory to guide your work. Providing effective, empathic responses is called for here. Evidence-based practice involves sharing ignorance and uncertainty as well as knowledge in a context of ongoing support, and drawing on practice theory to guide decisions in the context of shared uncertainties.

## WHAT IF RELATED RESEARCH IS OF POOR QUALITY?

This will be a common finding. Consider, for example, the review of research regarding family preservation programs by Lindsey, Martin, and Doh (2002). This shows that such programs, promoted as effective by "advocacy research," are not effective. Many other areas could be cited concerning lack of effectiveness of programs assumed to help clients, including intensive case management services for the elderly found to do more harm than good—mortality increased (Blenkner, Bloom, & Neilson, 1971). Other examples of harm in the name of helping include Scared Straight programs (Petrosino et al., 2003). Your search will often reveal that there is uncertainty regarding the effectiveness of a method. The term "best practice" is used to describe a hierarchy of evidence. Available resources may be low on this hierarchy in relation to critical tests of a practice method. However, this may be the best that is available. For example, if there are no randomized controlled trials regarding an effectiveness question, then we may move down the list. This is what we must do in the everyday world, since most interventions used in fields such as psychology and social work have not been critically tested. Thus, instead of well designed randomized controlled trials regarding an intervention, we may have to rely on findings from a pre-post test which is subject to many rival explanations regarding the cause of change (see Chapter 12). The term "best evidence" could refer to a variety of different kinds of tests that differ greatly in their ability to critically test claims. Some guidelines claim that if there are two well-designed randomized controlled trials that show a positive outcome, this represents a "well-established claim." Can two trials establish a claim? Isn't it less misleading to say that a claim has been critically tested in two well-controlled trials and has passed both tests? This keeps uncertainty in view. Whatever you find, you should share with your clients, and will have to draw on practice theory as needed.

## WHAT IF RESEARCH IS AVAILABLE BUT IT HAS NOT BEEN CRITICALLY APPRAISED?

One course of action is to critically appraise the literature for yourself. In the everyday world, you may not have time to do this. Perhaps you can contact someone who works in the field. If this concerns a problem that occurs often, involve interested others in critically appraising it. In the United Kingdom, physicians can contact a source that will carry out a search for research findings related to a question. Questions asked are tracked and those that are raised often can guide selection of topics for systematic reviews (Glasziou, 2005; personal communication).

## BALANCING INDIVIDUAL AND POPULATION PERSPECTIVES

One of the most challenging aspects of practice is considering both individuals and populations. Ethical issues regarding the distribution of scarce resources are often overlooked. However, there is only so much money and time. Decisions made about populations often limit options of individuals.

## COMMON ERRORS

Common errors in integrating information from diverse sources are related to common cognitive biases discussed throughout this book, such as over-confidence, influence by redundant information, and confirmation biases. Eagerness to help clients may encourage unfounded confidence in methods suggested. Lack of reliability and validity of information is often overlooked, resulting in faulty inferences. Jumping to conclusions may result in oversimplification of the causes of a client's concerns. Or, the opposite may occur, as in posing a variety of different causes, none of which provide intervention implications. Lack of evidence may be shared with the client in an unempathic manner. Many components of EBP are designed to minimize biases such as "jumping to conclusions," for example, by using "quality filters" when reviewing external research findings related to a question.

## OBSTACLES AND EVOLVING REMEDIES

Helping professionals to learn from their experience in ways that improve the accuracy of future decisions is a key priority. EBP highlights the play of bias and uncertainty involved in helping clients and attempts to give helpers and clients the knowledge and skills to handle them honestly and constructively. Consider the attention given to training both clients and helpers in critical appraisal skills and use of "quality filters" in reviewing research findings related to practice questions (see Exhibit 11.4). Biases intrude both on the part of researchers when preparing research reviews and at the practitioner level when making decisions (e.g., see Chapters 9 and 12). Consider assessment. Here clinicians have to decide what particular characteristics of clients and their contexts to attend to and how to weigh them. They have to decide what other information to gather and how they will do this (see Chapter 13). Availability (e.g., preferred practice theory) and representativeness (e.g., stereotypes) biases may interfere with integration of individual expertise, external evidence, and client values and expectations.

We can draw on research on decision-making and related theory to discover common errors in integrating different kinds of data. Hogarth (1987) proposes four sources of mistakes: (1) selective perception, (2) imperfect information processing, (3) inaccurate calculations due to cognitive limitations, and (4) incorrect reconstructions of events because of biases and faulty memory or both. The time and effort devoted to making a decision should depend on the potential consequences in relation to making a faulty or good decision and what is needed, based on our prior experience. Experts in an area can rely on primed decision making as a result of extensive experience offering corrective feedback (see Chapter 8). One problem arises when someone who does not have this expertise thinks they do and imposes, perhaps by selective attention, an inaccurate view on a situation. They may generalize a decision-making method to a situation to which it is not useful. We can draw on literature investigating expertise to identify promising directions for research and take advantage of guidelines described in the critical thinking literature to minimize biases (see Chapters 8 and 9), including "educating our intuition" (see Chapter 4). Use of hand-held computers to guide decisions may be of value in decreasing errors and common biases—for example, by providing reminders to check certain things. Computer-based decision aids can be used to prompt valuable behaviors, to critique a decision (for example, purchasing services from an agency that does not use evidence-informed practices), to make a differential diagnosis, to match a client's unique circumstances and characteristics with a certain service program, to suggest unconsidered options, and to interpret different assessment pictures (Guyatt & Rennie, 2002). And just as the narratives of clients may help us to understand how we can improve services, so the narratives of practitioners may help us to identify challenges and opportunities to providing quality services to clients (e.g., see Greenhalgh & Hurwitz, 1998). Use of clinical pathways and Palm Pilots with built-in decision aids, such as flow charts, can be helpful, and many are already in use in the health area.

## EVALUATING AND LEARNING FROM WHAT HAPPENS

Evaluating the effects of services has many advantages: (1) both you and your clients receive ongoing feedback about degree of success; (2) plans can be changed in a timely manner, depending on outcomes; (3) positive feedback increases clients' motivation; and (4) the relationship between services and outcomes can be explored (e.g., see Lambert, Whipple, Vermeersh, Smart, Hawkins, Nielsen, & Goates, 2002). Evaluation helps you and your clients to make informed decisions about the next steps you should take and to avoid faulty decisions based on incorrect estimates of progress and related factors. Timely corrective feedback is essential to catching and correcting harmful unintended effects at an early point. For example, one of my students had her field placement in a hospital. She discovered that a young girl with beta thalassemia (an inherited chronic illness) was not doing well, even though she was following her prescribed treatment regime. The student discovered this because she monitored both the girl's compliance and the results of her lab tests. The lack of expected match between compliance and the lab results led to the discovery that a treatment change recommended a year before had never been implemented, a discovery that may have saved this girl's life. Clients have a right to know whether they benefit from or are harmed by services. Involving clients as informed participants and preventing avoidable harm are ethical obligations of professionals. Fulfilling these obligations includes tracking outcomes of importance on an ongoing basis, using valid measures rather than relying on misleading surrogates, such as process measures (number of sessions attended). Reliance on surrogate end points may be misleading (Gotzsche, Liberati, Torri, & Rossetti, 1996).

Different choices have different opportunity costs, such as not discovering early on that services have harmful effects. "All genuine evaluations produce findings that are better than speculation" (Berk & Rossi, 1990, p. 34; see also Rossi, Lipsey, & Freeman, 2003). Some evaluation methods are more likely than others to avoid biases that get in the way of accurately estimating progress and what was responsible for it. (See Chapters 4 and 12.) Ways to fool yourself and your clients about degree of progress include selecting measures because they are easy to use even though they are not related to client concerns and are not sensitive to change.

Concerns about cost, acceptability to clients, and feasibility will limit options. You will often have a choice between feedback that can improve the soundness of future decisions and feedback that prevents "de-bugging" (identifying and remedying errors; Bransford & Stein, 1984). Measures used should be *relevant* (meaningful to clients and significant others), *specific* (clearly described), *sensitive* (reflect changes that occur), *feasible* (possible to obtain), *unintrusive* (not interfere with service provision), *valid* (measure what they are supposed to measure), and *reliable* (show consistency over different measurements in the absence of change).

There is a rich literature suggesting valid, feasible ways to evaluate different kinds of outcomes, including complex ones, such as quality of life. This includes different kinds of single-case designs to answer questions such as: "Is there change?; Is one intervention better than another (e.g., relaxation training compared to decreasing negative thoughts)?; Is there change within a session (for example, in anxiety)?" Such designs differ from case studies and anecdotal reports in carefully tracking clearly described outcomes of interest over time (see Bloom, Fischer, & Orme, 2003). Advantages of single-case designs include flexibility and detailed information concerning a single individual. Requirements include clear description of hoped-for outcomes and their repeated measurement in phases, such as baseline and intervention. Inclusion of a baseline allows you and your clients to compare results with pre-intervention levels of a concern. Experimental N of 1 trials are ideal in discovering what method works best for a given client when the external research is murky or does not apply well to a client. Here, you and your clients agree to test a practice method regarding its effectiveness in attaining outcomes clients value. Following a baseline, alternative services are offered, or a service and a placebo. N of 1 trials may be done in a haphazard way. If so, as Sackett and his colleagues (2000) note, conclusions about effects may be quite misleading because:

1. Many concerns are self-limited and improve on their own.
2. Extreme levels of a measure or symptom, if untreated and remeasured later, often return to or toward the normal range.
3. The placebo effect can lead to substantial relief of symptoms.

4. Our own and our client's expectations can bias our conclusions about whether a treatment worked.
5. Clients may exaggerate the benefits of treatment. (pp. 150–151)

In all of the above, any treatment applied in the interim, even if quite useless, will appear efficacious (p. 151). See other sources for further details.

Objections to obtaining corrective feedback often are related to misconceptions about careful evaluation, such as the view that this requires selection of trivial outcomes or measures—the belief that rigor requires rigor mortis. Related literature demonstrates that this is not so. Clients like the feedback they receive from careful evaluation (Campbell, 1988). In a quality assurance review program that graphed the progress toward each goal for more than 2,000 psychiatric patients, clients reported that they appreciated the careful evaluation of progress (Bullmore, Joyce, Marks, & Connolly, 1992). The alternative to careful evaluation is basing decisions on "guesstimates" (uninformed guesses) that may mislead both you and your clients.

### SOURCES OF ERROR IN ESTIMATING PROGRESS AND MAKING JUDGMENTS ABOUT RELATED CAUSES

Biases that may lead us astray in estimating progress and what was responsible for it include the following:

- Being swayed by hindsight bias (see Chapter 15)
- Being overconfident
- Engaging in wishful thinking
- Having an illusion of control
- Overlooking the role of chance (coincidences)
- Overlooking confounding causes, such as regression effects (see Chapter 15)
- Attributing success to our own efforts and failure to other factors
- Seeking only data that support preferred views (confirmation bias)
- Relying on observed rather than relative frequency (see Chapter 15)
- Overlooking the interaction between predictions and their consequences (see Chapter 15)
- Mistaking correlation for causation (see Chapter 14)
- Relying on misleading criteria such as testimonials (see Chapter 4)

What you think is a result of intervention may be the result of a confounding factor such as maturation or history (see Chapter 12). Positive outcomes may be due to the act of treatment rather than the treatment itself (i.e., a placebo effect). Negative as well as positive placebo effects may occur. The former have a negative impact on outcome and/or result in negative side effects. These may be related to subtle signs of inattention. One or more of the following reactive effects may contribute to the placebo effect:

- *Hello-goodbye effect:* Clients present themselves as worse than they really are when they seek help and as better than they really are when the service has ended. This leads to overestimating progress (Hathaway, 1948).
- *Hawthorne effect:* Improvements may result from being the focus of attention, for example, going to a well-known clinic or being seen by a famous therapist.
- *Rosenthal effect:* We tend to give observers what we think they want—to please people we like or respect.
- *Observer bias:* The observer's expectations may result in biased data.
- *Social desirability effect:* We tend to offer accounts viewed as appropriate. For example, clients may underreport drinking.

Extreme values tend to become less extreme on repeated assessment. If you do unusually well on a test, you are likely to do less well the next time around. Conversely, if you do very poorly, you are likely to do better the next time. These are called *regression effects*. There is a regression (a return) toward the mean (your average performance level). Overlooking these effects can lead to faulty judgments.

We tend to attribute success to our skills and failure to chance. Use of vague or irrelevant feedback obscures the true relationship (or lack thereof) between our judgments and outcomes. We tend to focus on our "hits" and overlook our "misses." To accurately estimate your track record (or anyone else's), you must examine both "hits" and "misses" as well as what would have happened without intervention (see Chapter 17). We tend to forget that actions taken as a result of predictions influence the outcomes.

Familiarity with common biases may help you avoid them and their negative effects, such as continuing harmful or ineffective programs. Many of these biases also influence decisions in other helping phases (e.g., assessment). Ongoing tracking of progress provides feedback that can correct inaccurate views due to one or more bias. The vaguer the outcome measures, the more likely that bias will creep in, because there is less chance for corrective feedback.

## OBSTACLES AND EVOLVING REMEDIES

Lack of time and training in selecting relevant, feasible progress indicators interferes with evaluation that can guide decision making. Fears about revealing lack of progress or harmful effects may discourage careful evaluation. Evaluation is a highly political process; it is not for the timid (Baer, 2003). Some of my masters students tell me that they are not allowed to evaluate services in their agency. As Oxman et al. (1995) suggest there are no magic bullets. Calls for accountability and the transparency of results that this requires, as well as selection of user-friendly, valid tools for assessing progress, will facilitate evaluation. Client involvement may be critical to making services and outcomes more visible to all interested parties (e.g., see Exhibit 11.8). (See Domenighetti,

Grilli, & Liberati, 1998.) The philosophy of evidence-based practice encourages the participation of clients as informed participants. Keeping track of the questions you ask, the critical appraisal of related research and client progress over time, will be of value in learning how to improve future decisions. (See discussion of CATS.)

## EVALUATING YOUR SKILLS IN EVIDENCE-BASED PRACTICE

Questions that encourage self-development of evidence-based practice knowledge and skills are illustrated in Exhibit 11.8. Gray (2001a) suggests use of the following prompts when reviewing your scanning strategy:

- How many hours each week do I want to spend scanning for new knowledge?
- What sources of knowledge do I want to scan regularly?
- What sources of information will I exclude?
- How can I ensure that I do not miss important new knowledge using this strategy?
- What checklists can I use to ensure that I stick to my scanning objectives? (A weekly checklist is useful.)
- Is there anyone else who could develop, or has developed already, a scanning strategy with whom I could share the load?
- How can I review the benefits and weaknesses of this strategy at the end of the year? (p. 111)

Try your hand by completing Exhibit 11.9. Gray (2001a) emphasizes the importance of information storage and retrieval skills; if you can't find information when you need it, it is not of value to clients. Possibilities include a user-friendly computer reference system.

## THE QUESTION OF MOTIVATION

Some helpers seem to be motivated already. But, if we are not, how do we get motivated? Does being aware of harming in the name of helping help us to get motivated? Many professionals seem to be quite aware of harm in the name of helping but do not seem to think this applies to their practices and policies. Our motivation is related to our values and our skills in "getting motivated." We must believe that it is important to prevent harming in the name of helping and to provide services most likely to benefit clients (given that they are acceptable to clients), to "be motivated," and related environmental contingencies must support this commitment. We must be willing to recognize gaps in our background knowledge and what may be available—to recognize our ignorance. We must be willing to acknowledge uncertainty—to say "I don't know." We also must have the "courage to fail" (Fox & Swazey, 1974); the

## Exhibit 11.8
### Self-Evaluation Questions

**Asking Answerable Questions**

1. Am I asking any practice questions at all?

2. Am I asking well-formed (4-part) questions?

3. Am I using a "map" to locate my knowledge gaps and articulate questions?

4. Can I get myself "unstuck" when asking questions?

5. Do I have a working method to save my questions for later answering?

6. Is my success rate of asking answerable questions rising?

7. Am I modeling the asking of answerable questions for others?

**Finding the Best External Evidence**

1. Am I searching at all?

2. Do I know the best sources of current evidence for decisions I make?

3. Do I have immediate access to searching hardware, software, and the best evidence for questions that arise?

4. Am I finding useful external evidence from a widening array of sources?

5. Am I becoming more efficient in my searching?

6. How do my searches compare with those of research librarians or colleagues who have a passion for providing best current care?

**Critically Appraising Evidence for Its Validity and Usefulness**

1. Am I critically appraising external evidence at all?

2. Are the critical appraisal guides becoming easier for me to apply?

3. Am I becoming more accurate and efficient in applying critical appraisal measures such as pretest probabilities, NNTs?

**Integrating Critical Appraisal with Clinical Expertise and Applying the Results**

1. Am I integrating my critical appraisals in my practice at all?

2. Am I becoming more accurate and efficient in adjusting some of the critical appraisal measures to fit my clients?

3. Can I explain (and resolve) disagreements about management decisions in terms of this integration?

4. Have I conducted any clinical decision analyses?

5. Have I carried out any audits of my diagnostic, therapeutic, or other EBP performance?

*Source:* From *Evidence-based Medicine: How to Practice and Teach EBM* (pp. 220–228), by D. L. Sackett, S. E. Strauss, W. S. Richardson, W. Rosenberg, and R. B. Haynes, 1997, New York: Churchill Livingstone. Reprinted with permission.

**Exhibit 11.9**
Posing Questions and Searching for Answers

*Important decision you must make:*

_____

_____

_____

*Answerable question related to this decision:*

_____

_____

_____

*Question type:* ___ Effectiveness ___Risk/Prognosis ____Description ____ Assessment

___Prevention ___ Other (please describe): _____

_____

_____

_____

*Your best answer before searching for external evidence:*

_____

_____

_____

*Resources used:*

_____

_____

_____

*Your best answer based on a review of external research:*

_____

_____

_____

_____

*Source:* From *Critical Thinking for Social Workers: Exercises for the Helping Professions* (2nd ed., p. 242), by L. Gibbs and E. Gambrill, 1999, Thousand Oaks, CA: Pine Forge Press. The format is based on a description in Sackett, Richardson, Rosenberg, and Haynes (1997). Reprinted with permission.

courage to recognize that we will make mistakes, and a commitment to learn from them.

If we work in environments in which supervisors and administrators have little interest in determining whether clients are helped or harmed (indeed, they may block such efforts), it may be difficult to maintain values and behaviors related to evidence-based practice. We may get worn down as our efforts are not reinforced, or are punished, for example, by supervisors. We may even forget valuable ways of acting, such as asking hard questions—we may come to think of such questions as irrelevant or out of place. Questions that can help us to remain faithful to our ethical principles include:

- Will it help clients if I promote assessment measures of dubious or untested validity?
- Will it help clients if I hide the evidentiary status of service programs?
- Will it help clients if I use outcome measures that are not valid?
- Will it help clients if I attribute troubled or troubling behavior to alleged pathological characteristics of clients ("mental disorders") and ignore environmental factors empirically shown to influence related behaviors?

## SUMMARY

Key steps in EBP include posing well-formed, answerable questions regarding information needed to make important decisions; seeking efficiently and effectively electronically for related research; critically appraising what is found (or drawing on high-quality critical reviews prepared by others); using practice expertise to integrate diverse sources of information, including knowledge about the clients' values, expectations, preferences, and available resources; making a decision together with clients about what to do, trying it out, evaluating what happens, and learning from this experience how to do better the next time. These steps increase the likelihood that you and your clients will be well informed about the kinds and levels of uncertainties associated with decisions. Although the steps involved in evidence-based practice may sound simple and straightforward, they are often difficult and sometimes impossible to carry out successfully in the real world. There are many challenges to evidence-based practice, including challenges in learning new skills and acquiring access to needed resources, such as high-quality training programs and needed databases, and arranging for ongoing feedback to keep skills well honed. Access to a skilled informatist and to efficient search engines is vital. The more the guided practice and provision of needed tools, the more likely the steps can be carried out in a way that honors ethical obligations to make well-reasoned decisions and to accurately inform clients regarding the evidentiary status of recommended services. Perhaps the greatest challenge is a willingness to recognize gaps in your current knowledge regarding decisions that must be made and what may be "out there"—a willingness to say "I don't know," and a commitment to your clients to see what is out there.

# CHAPTER 12

# Critical Appraisal of Practice-Related Research: The Need for Skepticism

S IMPLY BECAUSE SOMETHING appears in print does not mean that it is accurate. Indeed, flaws in published research were key to the development of evidence-based practice and policy, as described in Chapter 10. Thornley and Adams (1998) reviewed data in 2,000 trials on the Cochrane Schizophrenia Group's register and found consistently poor quality of reporting, which they suggest "is likely to have resulted in an overly optimistic estimation of the effects of treatment" (p. 1181). Less rigorous studies report more positive findings compared to research that controls for biases. Consider the history of facilitated communication. This intervention method is designed to increase verbal communication among people with disabilities. Initial anecdotal and pre-post reports suggested that this was effective. Later, more rigorous studies found no effect (Jacobson, Mulick, & Schwartz, 1995). Less rigorous studies of family preservation programs report positive results; rigorous studies found no effects (Lindsey, Martin, & Doh, 2002). And, as Rosenbaum (2002) suggests, we should also be skeptical of the skeptics. Just because someone says a study is flawed does not mean that it is. Learning to critically appraise different kinds of research studies for yourself frees you from misleading influences by others, including researchers, academics, and journalists, allowing you to accurately inform your clients about the potential of given options for attaining outcomes they value. Encouraging clinicians to do this is a key aim of evidence-based practice.

Being informed about different kinds of research and their advantages and disadvantages, including biases that result in misleading results, will help you to draw on practice- and policy-related research in an informed manner. This kind of research savvy is closely related to honoring ethical obligations to clients. Without this you may recommend ineffective or harmful methods and overlook effective programs. And you will be a pushover for those who use social psychological persuasion strategies and informal fallacies to influence

**Exhibit 12.1**
The Major Types of Studies Found in the Medical Literature

*Source:* Critical Appraisal of the Literature, W. F. Miser, *Journal of the American Board of Family Practice* 1999, 12, 315–337. Reprinted with permission.

what you do (see Chapters 5 and 6). For example, phrases such as "has not been established" may really mean that a medication has been tested with equivocal results (Meier, 2004). Drawing on rigorous appraisals of research related to practice and policy decisions and creating tools and training programs designed to facilitate this are hallmarks of EBP. Gaining access to practice-related research will help you and your clients to make more informed decisions, some of which will increase the likelihood that clients attain outcomes they value and avoid services that result in harm. Professional codes of ethics call on clinicians to draw on practice-related research and to involve clients as informed participants.

There are many kinds of research reports (see Exhibit 12.1). They differ in their purpose (the questions raised) and the likelihood that the method used

**Exhibit 12.2**
Types of Studies

The types of studies that give the best evidence are different for different types of questions. In every case, however, the best evidence comes from studies where the methods used maximize the chance of eliminating bias. The study designs that best suit different question types are as follows:

| Question | Best Study Designs | Description |
|---|---|---|
| INTERVENTION | Randomized controlled trial | Subjects are randomly allocated to treatment or control groups and outcomes assessed. |
| ETIOLOGY AND RISK FACTORS | Randomized controlled trial | As etiololgy questions are similar to intervention questions, the ideal study type is an RCT. However, it is usually not ethical or practical to conduct such a trial to assess harmful outcomes. |
| | Cohort study | Outcomes are compared for matched groups with and without exposure to risk factor (prospective study). |
| | Case-control study | Subjects with and without outcome of interest are compared for previous exposure or risk factor (retrospective study). |
| FREQUENCY AND RATE | Cohort study | As above. |
| | Cross-sectional study | Measurement of condition in a representative (preferably random) sample of people. |
| DIAGNOSIS | Cross-sectional study with random or consecutive sample | Preferably an independent, blind, comparison with "gold standard" test. |
| PROGNOSIS AND PREDICTION | Cohort/survival study | Long-term follow-up of a representative cohort. |
| PHENOMENA | Qualitative | Narrative analysis or focus group; designed to assess the range of issues (rather than their quantification). |

*Source:* From *Evidence-based Medicine Workbook* (p. 41), by P. Glasziou, C. Del Mar, and J. Salisbury, 2003, London: BMJ. Reprinted with permission.

can provide accurate information about the question (see Exhibit 12.2). Examples include:

*Analytic:* Designed to make causal inferences about relationships—for example, between certain risk factors, such as poverty, and an outcome such as child abuse. Two or more groups are compared.

*Descriptive:* Designed to provide information about the prevalence or incidence of a concern—for example, "mental disorder," or about the distribution of certain characteristics in a group.

*Prospective:* Subjects are selected and followed up.

*Retrospective:* Events of interest have already occurred (children have been abused) and data are collected from case records or recall, as in case-control studies.

*Contemporary Comparison:* Groups which experience a risk factor at the same time are compared.

Different kinds of research design control for different kinds of biases, which may result in misleading conclusions (for example, about causal relationships) to different degrees (see Exhibit 12.2). Sackett (1979) identified 35 different kinds of biases in case-control studies. Many excellent sources provide more detail, including the user-friendly book *How to Read a Paper* (Greenhalgh, 2001) and sources that provide more detail, such as Dawes et al. (1999), Dixon, Munro, and Silcocks (1998), Gibbs (2003), Geddes, Tomlin, and Price (1999), Geyman, Deyo, and Ramsey (2000), and Guyatt and Rennie (2002).

## COMMON MYTHS THAT HINDER CRITICAL APPRAISAL

A variety of myths may hinder critical appraisal of the quality of research on which practice recommendations are made.

### IT IS TOO DIFFICULT FOR ME TO LEARN

The ease of identifying some key characteristics of rigorous studies regarding certain kinds of practice questions is suggested by the fact that social workers wanted their physicians to rely on the results of randomized controlled trials when making recommendations about treatment methods (Gambrill & Gibbs, 2002). However, individuals relied on weak criteria, such as intuition, when making decisions about their clients. A variety of quality assessment checklists and scales have been developed to evaluate the rigor of different kinds of research. These range from quite detailed ones (e.g., CONSORT guidelines—see Altman et al., 2001; Geyman, Deyo, & Ramsey, 2000; Gibbs, 2003), to those that are less detailed (e.g., Crombie, 1996; Greenhalgh, 2001; web site of the Center for Review and Dissemination, University of York; evidence-based toolkit on the Internet). Failure to satisfy a critical feature (such as blind assessment of outcome) suggests that overall scores should not be used, since one critical flaw may be cancelled out by many less important characteristics.

### ALL RESEARCH IS EQUALLY SOUND

You may be a relativist—at least regarding clients. Different views of knowledge and how or if it can be gained are discussed in Chapter 4. All research is not equally informative. Research designs differ in the questions that can be carefully explored; they differ in the extent to which biases are controlled for, that may contribute to incorrect conclusions that may harm clients if acted on. A variety of errors can be and are made in designing and interpreting research. Because of this, you may conclude that a method was effective when it was not; it may even be harmful. You may conclude that a method was not effective when it is effective. A research design may be used that cannot critically test the question raised. Chalmers (2003) defines reliable studies as "those in which the effects of policies and practices are unlikely to be confused with the effects of biases or chance" (p. 28). Less rigorous studies report more positive results than do more rigorous studies (see, for example, Lindsey, Martin, & Doh, 2002; Schulz et al., 1995). Michael, Boyce, and Wilcox (1984) describe flaws and fallacies in the medical literature such as "diagnostic zealot" (someone who promotes a test in the absence of evidence that it is valid).

## I SHOULD TRUST THE EXPERTS

You will often have to depend on the experts. Depending on expertise is risky because experts may all be biased in a certain direction. That is, they may share a bias toward a commonly favored view of a certain problem and how to minimize it. In fact, experts in an area prepare more biased reviews than do individuals who are well-trained in methodological issues but who do not work in that area (Oxman & Guyatt, 1993). But you can learn about criteria of value in discovering whether a person is an honest expert. Do they, for example, use clear language that you can understand? Do they describe well-argued alternatives and describe contradictory evidence to preferred views?

## INTUITION IS A BETTER GUIDE

Myths that hinder critical appraisal include the belief that intuitive beliefs about what may help people do not result in harmful consequences. But harm occurs because of reliance on such criteria. Chalmers (2003) points out that "as Donald Campbell (1969) noted many years ago, selectively designating some interventions as 'experiments'—a term loaded with negative associations—ignores the reality that policy makers and practitioners are experimenting on other people most of the time. The problem is that their experiments are usually poorly controlled. Dr. Spock's ill-founded advice [to let babies sleep on their stomachs] would probably not be conceptualized by many people as a poorly controlled experiment, yet that is just what is was" (p. 30). As a result, many babies died. "The clinician who is convinced that a certain treatment works will almost never find an ethicist in his path, whereas his colleague who wonders and doubts and wants to learn will stumble over piles of them" (Medical Ethics, 1990, p. 846, quoted in Chalmers, 2003, p. 30; see discussion of informed and uninformed intuition in Chapter 4).

## ONLY CERTAIN KINDS OF RESEARCH MUST BE RIGOROUS

Another myth is that only certain kinds of research must be rigorous to avoid biased results. A concern to avoid biases that may result in misleading conclusions is relevant to *all* research, including qualitative research. For example, a number of authors describe errors resulting from not checking assumptions via use of various kinds of qualitative research (see later discussion of qualitative research).

## ONE OR TWO STUDIES CAN YIELD CONCLUSIVE FINDINGS

Yet another myth is that one or two well-controlled studies yield the "truth." Such an assumption reflects a justification approach to knowledge, in which we assume that certainty is possible (see Chapter 4).

## A STUDY MUST BE PERFECT TO BE USEFUL

Yet another myth is that a study must be perfect to yield valuable findings. All studies are flawed. The question is, are the flaws so great that they preclude any sound conclusions?

## QUANTITATIVE RESEARCH IS BEST/QUALITATIVE RESEARCH IS BEST

Another myth is that quantitative research is better than qualitative research, or vice versa. It depends on the question. And pursuit of many questions is informed by both kinds of research. Consider, for example, *Labeling the Mentally Retarded* (1973) by Jane Mercer, in which community surveys, official records, and unstructured interviews were all used.

## THE QUESTION OF BIAS

The notion of bias is central to critically appraising the quality of practice- and policy-related research. Bias is a systematic "leaning to one side" that distorts the accuracy of results. Bias can be of two types: (1) systematic, in which errors are made in a certain direction; or (2) random fluctuations. It has long been of interest. Consider Francis Bacon's (1685) four idols of the mind:

> The Idols of the Tribe have their foundation in human nature itself, and in the tribe or race of men. For it is a false assertion that the sense of man is the measure of things . . . and the human understanding is like a false mirror, which receiving rays irregularly, distorts and discolors the nature of things by mingling its own nature with it.
>
> The Idols of the Cave are the idols of the individual man. For everyone (besides the errors common to human nature in general) has a cave or den of his own, which refracts and discolors the light of nature; owing either to his own proper and peculiar nature; or to its education and conversation with others; or

to the reading of books, and the authority of those whom he esteems and ad-
mires; or to the differences of impressions, accordingly as they take place in a
mind preoccupied and predisposed or in a mind indifferent and settled.

There are also Idols formed by the intercourse and association of men with
each other, which I call Idols of the Market-place, on account of the commerce
and consort of men there. And therefore the ill and unfit choice of words won-
derfully obstructs the understanding. . . . But words plainly force and overrule
the understanding . . . and throw all into confusion, and lead men away into
numberless empty controversies and idle fancies.

Lastly, there are Idols, which have immigrated into men's minds from the various dogmas of philosophies and also from wrong laws of demonstration. These
I call Idols of the Theater, because in my judgment all the received systems are
but so many stage-plays, representing worlds of their own creation after an un-
real and scenic fashion.

Biases occur in the design of research, in how it is conducted and interpreted, and in how it is used (Kirsch & Sapirstein, 1999; MacCoun, 1998).
There are publication biases. For example, studies reporting negative results
are less likely to be published than studies reporting positive results: "Studies
that show a statistically significant effect of treatment are more likely to be
published, more likely to be published in English, more likely to be cited by
other authors, and more likely to produce multiple publications than other
studies" (Sterne, Egger, & Smith, 2001, p. 198). Examples of biases in published research include the following: "submission bias (research workers are
more strongly motivated to complete, and submit for publication, positive results), publication bias (editors are more likely to publish positive studies),
methodological bias (methodological errors such as flawed randomization
produce positive biases), abstracting bias (abstracts emphasize positive results), framing bias (relative risk data produce a positive bias)" (Gray, 2001b,
p. 24). The steps involved in evidence-based practice are designed to decrease
confirmation biases, such as looking only for data that support a preferred
theory.

## BIAS AND VALIDITY

Biases may influence both internal and external validity. *Internal validity*
refers to the extent to which a design allows you to critically test and come up
with an accurate answer concerning the causal relationships between some intervention and an outcome. Threats to internal validity have been masterfully
described by Campbell and Stanley (1963; see Exhibit 12.3). (See also Shadish,
Cook, & Campbell, 2002.) These threats are rival hypotheses to the assumption that a service method was effective, for example. Biases include *selection
bias* (e.g., biased allocation to experimental and control groups), *performance
bias* (unequal provision of care apart from the methods under evaluation), *detection bias* (biased assessment of outcome), and *attrition bias* (biased occurrence and handling of deviations from a protocol and loss to follow-up). Such

**Exhibit 12.3**
Possible Confounding Causes (Rival Explanations) for Change

1. *History.* Events that occur between the first and second measurement, in addition to the experimental variables, may account for changes (e.g., clients may get help elsewhere).

2. *Maturation.* Simply growing older or living longer may be responsible, especially when long periods of time are involved.

3. *Instrumentation.* The way that something is measured changes (e.g., observers may change how they record).

4. *Testing effects.* Assessment may result in change.

5. *Mortality.* There may be a differential loss of people from different groups.

6. *Regression.* Extreme scores tend to return to the mean.

7. *Self-selection bias.* Clients are often "self-selected" rather than randomly selected. They may differ in critical ways from the population they are assumed to represent and differ from clients in a comparison group.

8. *Helper selection bias.* Social workers may select certain kinds of clients to receive certain methods.

9. *Interaction effects.* Only certain clients may benefit from certain services, and others may even be harmed.

*Source:* Based on *Experimental and Quasi-experimental Designs for Research*, by D. T. Campbell and J. C. Stanley, 1963, Chicago: Rand McNally.

sources of bias are rival hypotheses to claims—for example, that a particular service method resulted in observed outcomes. *Confounders* may occur—variables that are related to a causal factor of interest and some outcome(s) which are not represented equally in two different groups. "Zero time bias" may occur, in which people in a prospective study are enrolled in a way that results in systematic differences between groups (as in prospective cohort studies). Well-designed randomized controlled trials contain more control for different kinds of biases compared to weaker studies, such as quasi-experimental studies. Unless a study is replicated we are not sure whether there were problems (flaws) that resulted in misleading findings. History illustrates that many results based on a single study could not be replicated and were found to be false. An example is cold fusion.

*External validity* refers to the extent to which you can generalize the findings in a study to other circumstances. These other circumstances may include other kinds of clients (e.g., age, risk factors, severity of problem), settings, services offered (e.g., timing, number of sessions [dosage], other concurrent services), kinds of outcomes reviewed, or length of follow-up (Jüni, Altman, & Egger, 2001, p. 42). To what extent can you generalize the causal relationship found in a study to different times, places and people, and different operational definitions of interventions and outcomes? Farrington (2003) uses the term *descriptive validity* to refer to "the adequacy of the presentation of key features of an evaluation in a research report." Unblinded rating of outcome can result in misleading conclusions of effectiveness.

The literature on experimenter and subject biases highlights the importance of research that controls for these (e.g., Rosenthal, 1994). For example, we tend to give socially desirable responses, to present ourselves in a good light. Knowing a hypothesis creates a tendency to encourage the very responses that we are investigating. Experimenter effects are not necessarily intentional; even when we do not intend to skew results in a certain way, this may occur. Experimenter biases influence results in a number of ways. If the experimenters know the group a subject is in, they may change their behavior—for example, subtly lead the person in a certain direction. This is why it is vital in randomized controlled trials for raters of outcome to be blind—unaware of the group to which a person is assigned.

## QUESTIONS TO ASK ABOUT RESEARCH

Certain questions are important to raise across all research because of the potential for flaws that may result in misleading conclusions. These include concerns about the size and source of samples used, whether there is a comparison group, the accuracy and validity of measures used, and the appropriateness of data analysis. Answers to these characteristics will shed light both on the internal and external validity of a study. Methodological quality criteria suggested by Cook and Campbell (1979) as well as Shadish, Cook, and Campbell (2002) include four criteria: statistical conclusion validity, internal validity, construct validity, and external validity. The term *validity* refers to the accuracy of assumptions in relation to causes and effects. Classic criteria for assuming a causal relationship include: (1) the cause precedes the effect, (2) the cause is related to the effect, and (3) other plausible alternatives of the effect can be excluded (John Stuart Mill, 1911). As Farrington (2003) notes, "If threats to valid causal inference cannot be ruled out in the design, they should at least be measured and their importance estimated" (pp. 51–52). Too often the limitations of studies are not mentioned, are glossed over, or are minimized. Keep in mind that flaws in traditional methods of dissemination, including peer-reviewed journals, were one of the reasons for the origins of evidence-based practice (Altman, 2002). Poor reporting of a randomized control trial does not necessarily mean that a trial was poorly constructed; it may be only poorly reported (e.g., see Soares et al., 2004).

### Is the Research Question Clear?

Do the authors clearly describe their research question, or is this vague or confusing? Examples of clear research questions are: "What factors contribute to the re-abuse of children returned to their biological parents?" or "Do substance abuse programs to which parents are referred help them to decrease alcohol consumption compared to no intervention?" Unclear questions do not allow for clear tests at the point of data analysis, set in advance, so all are clear on key concerns.

## WHAT KIND OF QUESTION IS IT?

Does the article address the effectiveness of a practice method? Is it an assessment question? Does it describe a new risk assessment measure for depression in the elderly? What kind of question does it concern? (See Exhibit 11.3 in Chapter 11.)

## IS IT RELEVANT TO MY CLIENTS? IS IT IMPORTANT?

Does the question apply to your clients? If you knew the answer, could you and your clients make more informed decisions? Does it concern outcomes of interest to your clients? Have key ones been omitted? Is the setting similar to your practice setting? Are the clients similar?

## WHO SPONSORED THE STUDY?

Sponsorship of a study may suggest possible biases (see also discussion of propaganda in Chapter 4). Sponsorship of research or a continuing training program by a company with vested interest in a product, such as a pharmaceutical company, may encourage biased material (e.g., see Bhandari et al., 2004).

## DOES THE RESEARCH METHOD USED MATCH THE QUESTION RAISED?

Can the research method used address the question? Different questions require different research methods (see Exhibit 12.2). That is why discussing whether qualitative or quantitative research is best is unproductive—it depends on the question. Oxman and Guyatt (1993) suggest a scale ranging from 1 (not at all) to 6 (ideal) in relation to the potential that a research method can critically test a question. Critically testing certain kinds of questions requires a comparison. A hallmark of randomized controlled trials is distributing clients to two or more different conditions. An intervention group (cognitive-behavioral therapy for depression) may be compared to a no-treatment group or to a comparison group (interpersonal therapy). Only if we have a comparison can we identify which might be better than the other. If all we have is a pre-post test describing how depressed people are before and after some intervention, there is no comparison with a group receiving no service or a different service. Thus, there could be a variety of other reasons for any changes seen (see Exhibit 12.3).

## IS THE STUDY DESIGN RIGOROUS?

The general research method may be appropriate but be carried out in a sloppy, unrigorous manner that allows the play of many biases (see, for example, MacLehose, Reeves, Harvey, Sheldon, Russell, & Black, 2000; Schulz, Chalmers, Hayes, & Altman, 1995; see also other questions in this section).

## What Is the Sample Size and Source?

Most research involves a sample that is assumed to be characteristic of the population from which it is drawn. Selection biases are one kind of bias related to how subjects were selected. Does the sample on which a study was based offer a sound opportunity to answer questions raised? (Some research deals with an entire population, such as all graduates of the University of California at Berkeley's social work master's degree program in the year 2004.) A key question is, "Can we accurately generalize from a sample to the population from which it is drawn, or from one population to another (other year)?" Does the sample represent the population to which generalizations will be made? Questions that arise include the following:

- Is the sample selection process clearly described?
- How was the sample selected?
- From what population was it selected?
- Is it representative of the population?
- Were subjects lost for follow-up?

The answers to these questions provide clues about biases that may limit the value of a study to answer questions. For example, small samples drawn by convenience, rather than by random selection, in which each individual has an equal chance of selection, may not provide information that reflects characteristics of the population of interest. Often researchers do not clearly describe the source of their sample. A number of "filtering" decisions may be made to obtain a final sample. Consider the complexity of the source of samples of child welfare clients in some studies. CONSORT guidelines for reporting randomized controlled trials includes a flowchart for describing samples used (Altman et al., 2001). We can see how many people were excluded at different points and for what reasons. Readers can review for themselves possible sources of bias in the final sample, on which conclusions are based.

Sample size and the critical testing of hypotheses are closely related. That is, some studies do not find effects—not because there are no effects to be found, but because the sample size does not have the power to test whether there is an association or not. As Farrington (2003) notes, "a statistically significant result could indicate a large effect in a small sample or a small effect in a large sample" (p. 52). Researchers should base selection of their sample size on the power needed to obtain a significant result. On the other hand, use of a large sample may yield many significant differences, which may not be illuminating. Clear description of the source of samples used is important in qualitative as well as quantitative research.

## Are Measures Used Reliable and Valid?

Measures of concepts, such as self-esteem and substance abuse, are used in research. Do they measure what they purport to measure? Are they relevant to your clients? The validity and accuracy of measures are key concerns in all research. Reliability refers to the consistency of ratings—for example, between different administrations of an assessment measure for an individual at different times (stability), or between two observers of an interaction at the same time (interrater reliability). Validity refers to the extent to which a measure reflects what it is designed to measure. There are many different kinds, as discussed in Chapter 13. Reliability places an upward boundary on validity. That is, a measure cannot be valid if it is not reliable (cannot be consistently assessed). And a measure may be reliable but invalid, perhaps because of shared biases among raters—including peer reviews of manuscripts. Research using one kind of data (self-report) may present an inaccurate picture. For example, observation of children's behavior on the playground to identify instances of bullying may not match a student's self report.

### Did Authors Report Attrition (Dropout Rates)?

In many studies, some subjects drop out over the course of the study. This number should be reported, and is reflected in "intention-to-treat" analysis. This is "An analysis of a study where participants are analyzed according to the group to which they were initially allocated. This is regardless of whether or not they dropped out, fully complied with the treatment, or crossed over and received the other treatment. It protects against attrition bias" (Center for Reviews and Dissemination, University of York, UK 4/4/04).

### Was There Any Follow-Up—If So, How Long?

An intervention may be effective in the short term but not in the long term. How long were subjects followed up? The effects of many programs are short term.

### Are Procedures Clearly Described?

Are practice methods used clearly described? If not, it will not be possible to replicate them. For example, in effectiveness studies, only if methods are clearly described can readers determine exactly what was done, and if methods were offered in an optimal manner.

### Are the Data Analyses Sound?

Statistics are tools used to explore whether there is a relationship between two or more variables. We ask what is the probability of finding an association by chance in samples of different sizes (e.g., see Hoyle, Harris, & Judd, 2002). We do this by estimating the probability of getting a result in a sample of a certain size (p. 461). The null hypothesis (the assumption that there is no difference between two variables that we think are associated, or two groups that we think will differ) is tested. We could make two kinds of errors here. We may assume that there is a relationship when there is not (Type I Error) or assume there is no relationship when there is (Type II Error). The term *statistical significance* refers to whether a test falls below a five percent probability. Practitioners and administrators should have some rudimentary knowledge of statistics, so that they can ask cogent questions in terms of the adequacy of statistical analyses. Researchers as well as practitioners make mistakes in how they word findings. For example, rather than stating that there was "no statistically significant difference," they may say that there was "no difference/change" (Weisburd, Lum, & Yang, 2003). Statistical testing is not without controversy (see Altman, Machin, Bryant, & Gardner, 2000; Oakes, 1986). Complex statistical methods will not correct major flaws in the design or conduct of a study. This is why care in planning studies is so important.

In addition to insufficient sample size to critically test the relationship between two or more variables, another problem is the use of inappropriate methods of statistical analysis. Incorrect statistical methods may be used, leading to bogus claims. Different statistical tests make different assumptions about variables in relation to their underlying distribution. A statistical method may be used that requires interval data (reflecting continuous data in which points are separated by equal intervals) for ordinal data, in which you can rank order differences but, in fact, don't have any idea about how much difference there is between points. It's like using a rubber ruler. Many constructs are continuous. Consider drinking—one could have no drinks, one drink, or many drinks per day. However, often this is treated as a binary variable (categorically defined); either one is or is not an alcoholic; a continuous variable is transformed into a binary one. Data is lost in changing a continuous variable to a dichotomous one—individual variations are omitted. Research texts describe a number of problems in relation to inappropriate use of statistical tests, such as mining or fishing (running many tests to see if any would be significant). For example, you may read an article that uses many different variables with a large sample and claims that it found 15 significant differences. The question is: How many correlations were run? A certain percentage would be significant by chance.

## ARE CLAIMS MADE ACCURATE?

Problems in any of the characteristics previously described, such as samples and measures used, may not allow clear conclusions. Inflated claims are common. That is why is it important to learn how to critically appraise research findings for yourself. Do claims made match the kind of design used? For example, many authors use pre-post tests. Such a design cannot tell us whether the intervention was responsible for the results because there is no comparison group. Yet the author may say, "Our results show that X was effective." This is a bogus claim.

## ARE FINDINGS CLINICALLY IMPORTANT?

Will research findings be of value in helping clients? How many clients would have to receive an intervention (be screened or receive a treatment) for one to be helped or harmed? (See discussion of Number Needed to Treat and Number Needed to Harm in Chapter 11.) People differ in their views about when there is "enough evidence" to recommend use of service or to recommend that a program not be used because it is harmful. For example, even a modest reduction in future delinquency may be important (e.g., Weisburd, Lum, & Yang, 2003). Many kinds of evidence come into play in making decisions (see Chapter 10). What may be true of a group may not be true of a given individual. Thus, aggregate studies must be interpreted with caution in relation to generalizing to an individual. Otherwise you may make the *ecological fallacy*—assume that what is true of a group is true of an individual.

## DID THE AUTHORS DESCRIBE ANY SPECIAL INTERESTS AND THEIR BIASES?

Research shows that special interests may bias results (see Chapter 4). Therefore we should be informed about any special interests of authors that may bias conclusions, including the development of practice guidelines. For example, did a drug company fund the study? Midanik (2006) describes the influence of the biomedical view of alcohol abuse on funding patterns.

## LEVELS OF EVIDENCE

The concept of levels of evidence is integral to evidence-based practice. This draws attention to the fact that different kinds of research related to a certain kind of question offer different degrees of control regarding potential biases that may limit conclusions that can be drawn. One hierarchy regarding levels of evidence for studies of effectiveness is the following:

1. Experimental studies (e.g., RCT (randomized controlled trial) with concealed allocation).
2. Quasi-experimental studies (e.g., experimental study without randomization).
3. Controlled observational studies.
   3a. Cohort studies
   3b. Case control studies
4. Observational studies without control groups.
5. Expert opinion—for example, based on consensus (Center for Research Development, University of York).

A systematic review (SR) is at the top of the list for all questions, including qualitative reviews (see for example comparison of the results of meta-analysis of randomized controlled trials and recommendations of clinical experts (Antman, Lau, Kopeklnick, Moesteller, & Chalmers, 1992). Many different hierarchies have been proposed. Such hierarchies should not be rigidly used. Glasziou, Vandenbroucke, and Chalmers (2004) note that ". . . criteria designed to guide inferences about the main effects of treatment have been uncritically applied to questions about etiology, diagnosis, prognosis, or adverse effects" (p. 39). A key point they make is that whatever the kind of report, including case studies, it is important to do a systematic review rather than using a haphazard selection of cases. They emphasize that balanced assessments should draw on a variety of types of research and that different questions require different types of evidence (see also GRADE working group, 2004; Sinclair, Cook, Guyatt, Pauker, & Cook, 2001).

## QUESTIONS ABOUT EFFECTIVENESS, HARM, AND PREVENTION

How can we discover if a practice or policy does more good than harm? We could ask our colleagues what they think. But on what do they base their views? Examples of effectiveness questions are:

- In youth with antisocial behavior, is group cognitive behavioral training or individual counseling more effective in decreasing such behaviors and increasing positive behaviors?
- In young adults diagnosed with AIDS, is education and group support, compared to individual counseling, more effective in increasing safe-sex behaviors?

A key concern with testing effectiveness questions is: Is there a comparison group that allows us to determine whether different results would be attained with different groups? For example, has a medication for depression been compared with a placebo? Just as we can ask about number needed to treat (NNT), we can ask about number needed to harm (NNH). That is, how many people would have to receive a service for one to be harmed? Many studies do not offer any information about possible harms of interventions, including assessment and diagnostic measures. Petrosino, Turpin-Petrosino, and Finckenauer (2000) conducted a meta-analysis of randomized experiments regarding recidivism data concerning Scared Straight programs. This indicated that this program was harmful; that is, the experimental group had higher recidivism rates. More recent reviews, including more studies, have arrived at the same conclusions. (For more detail regarding assessment of harm see Guyatt & Rennie, 2002, p. 84.)

### RANDOMIZED CONTROLLED TRIALS

In experimental designs such as randomized controlled clinical trials there is a comparison between different groups, which may include an experimental group that receives a special treatment (the independent variable) and a control group, in which there is no special treatment. Or a comparison group receiving a different service may be used; two different services may be compared. Factorial experimental designs explore the effects of more than one independent variable. Interaction effects are often of great interest here—for example, between personality, peer rejection of youth, and school environment. Random distribution of subjects to different groups using an effective randomization procedure is a key feature of rigorous experimental designs. Random distribution of subjects to groups is designed to minimize selection bias—differences in outcomes due to differences in subjects in different groups. (See CONSORT guidelines, www.consortstatement.com.) You should always review *how* subjects were randomly distributed to groups, because some methods of random distribution do not guard against selection biases that may skew results.

> Randomisation in clinical trials is the use of a chance procedure, such as coin tossing or computer-generated random numbers, to generate an allocation sequence. It ensures that participants have a prespecified (very often an equal) chance of being assigned to the experimental or control group. This means that the groups are likely to be balanced for known as well as unknown and unmeasured confounding variables. To protect against selection bias, concealment of the randomly-generated allocation sequence is essential. This is because foreknowledge of group assignments leaves the allocation sequence subject to possible manipulation by researchers and participants. Randomisation without allocation concealment does not guarantee protection against selection bias. (Center for Research and Dissemination, University of York, 4/4/04)

Without a comparison group (for example, a group that did not receive a service), we do not know what would have happened in the absence of a service (see Exhibit 12.4). This is a key problem in pre-post studies. Failure to question the effectiveness of an intervention has been responsible for much harm in the past, include the blinding of 10,000 babies by giving them oxygen at birth (Silverman, 1980). Joan McCord (1978) investigated the effectiveness of special services to youth designed to prevent delinquency, and found that such services resulted in more harm than good (see McCord, 1978, 2003). "Had there been no control group, evaluators might have concluded that the program was beneficial because so many of the treatment boys were better adjusted than anticipated. Or because two-thirds reported beneficial effects for themselves, evaluators might have judged that the program was effective. But these judgments would have been contrary to objective evidence that the program resulted in adverse outcomes for many of the participants" (2003, p. 22). Consider also the effects of placing a number of youth with troublesome behavior in one group; this practice has been found to have negative effects (Poulin, Dishion, & Burraston, 2001).
Blinding is another method designed to decrease bias.

> Blinding is used to keep the participants, investigators and outcome assessors ignorant about which interventions participants are receiving during a study. In

**Exhibit 12.4**
Validity Screen for an Article about Therapy

| | | |
|---|---|---|
| 1. Is the study a randomized controlled trial? | Yes (go on) | |
| How were patients selected for the trial? | | |
| Were they properly randomized into groups using concealed assignment? | | |
| 2. Are the subjects in the study similar to mine? | Yes (go on) | No (stop) |
| 3. Are the participants who entered the trial properly accounted for at its conclusion? | Yes (go on) | No (stop) |
| Was follow-up complete and were few lost to follow-up compared with the number of bad outcomes? | | |
| Were patients analyzed in the groups to which they were initially randomized (intention-to-treat analysis)? | | |
| 4. Was everyone involved in the study (subjects and investigators) "blind" to treatment? | Yes | No |
| 5. Were the intervention and control groups similar at the start of the trial? | Yes | No |
| 6. Were the groups treated equally (aside from the experimental intervention)? | Yes | No |
| 7. Are the results clinically as well as statistically significant? | Yes | No |
| Were the outcomes measured clinically important? | | |
| 8. If a negative trial, was a power analysis done? | Yes | No |
| 9. Were other factors present that might have affected the outcome? | Yes | No |
| 10. Are the treatment benefits worth the potential harms and costs? | Yes | No |

*Note:* A "stop" answer to any of the question should prompt you to seriously question whether the results of the study are valid and whether you should use this intervention.
*Source:* From "Critical Appraisal of the Literature," by W. F. Miser, 1999, *Journal of the American Board of Family Practice, 12,* pp. 315–333. Reprinted with permission.

single blind studies only the participants are blind to their group allocations, while in double-blind studies both the participants and investigators are blind. Blinding of outcome assessment can often be done even when blinding of participants and caregivers cannot. Blinding is used to protect against performance and detection bias. It may also contribute to adequate allocation concealment. However, the success of blinding procedures is infrequently checked and it may be overestimated. (Center for Reviews and Dissemination, University of York, U.K.)

Farrington (2003) suggests that the SMS developed by Sherman et al. (2002) is the most influential methodological quality scale in criminology. This scale was used to rate prevention programs using 10 criteria on a scale from 0 to 5: (1) adequacy of sampling, (2) adequacy of sample size, (3) pretreatment measures of outcome, (4) adequacy of comparison groups, (5) controls for prior group differences, (6) adequacy of measurement of variables, (7) attrition, (8) post-intervention measurement, (9) adequacy of statistical analyses, and (10) testing of alternative explanations. Brounstein and his colleagues (Brounstein, Emshoff, Hill, & Stoil, 1997) used this scale to review 440 evaluations. Only 30 percent received a score of 3 to 5, on a scale ranging from 0 (no confidence in results), to 5 (high confidence in results: Farrington, 2003, p. 57). It is difficult to carry out experiments in applied settings. However, we should not overlook the fact that many investigators *do* manage to carry out controlled studies that provide rigorous tests of claims in real-life settings. See, for example, Cochrane and Campbell databases. N of 1 randomized controlled trials involve the detailed description of an individual over a period of time and provide useful information about effectiveness (see Chapter 11). Questions Guyatt and Rennie (2002) suggest for deciding on the feasibility of such a study include: "(1) Is the client eager to collaborate? (2) Does the program have a rapid onset and offset? (3) Is an optimal duration of service feasible? (4) What important targets of service should be measured? and (5) What dictates the end?" (p. 278).

Effect size is one statistic used to describe the effects of an intervention in an experimental study. This indicates the strength of a relationship between, or among, two or more variables. Effect sizes range from 0 to 1. Larger effect sizes suggest stronger relationships. Cohen (1977) suggests that small effect sizes are about .2; medium ones about .5; and large effect sizes about .8 or greater. Effect sizes should be reported. These can be calculated in different ways, all of which are designed to describe the relationship between the effect found in the intervention group and the effect found in a comparison group. One is to divide the mean difference between the experimental and control group in a study by the standard deviation of the control or alternative treatment group. The narrower the confidence interval, the stronger the effect size (see later discussion; the odds ratio refers to the odds of an event happening in one group, expressed as a proportion of the odds of that event happening in another [e.g., control] group). An odds ratio of 1.0 indicates that there is no relationship. (See also discussion of relative and absolute risk reduction and number needed to treat in Chapter 12.)

In quasi-experimental studies allocation of participants to different groups is arranged by the researcher, but there is no genuine randomization and allocation concealment; thus, selection biases are of concern as well as a number of other biases depending on the design (see Exhibit 12.3). Pre-post studies are one variety; they do not include a comparison group, so we cannot determine causation. Time series designs are another kind of quasi-experimental study (see Campbell & Stanley, 1963).

## OBSERVATIONAL STUDIES

In observational studies, unlike RCTs, assignment of subjects to different groups is not under the control of the investigator. Different groups are self-selected or are "natural experiments." Subjects are not randomly assigned to different services or exposed to different kinds of risks. Such exposure or service occurs by choice or circumstance. Examples include exposure to lead in houses and to family violence. Those who are exposed and those who are not exposed may differ in important ways, thus introducing selection biases.

> An observational study concerns treatments, interventions, or policies and the effects they cause and in this respect it resembles an experiment. A study without a treatment is neither an experiment nor an observational study. Most public opinion polls, most forecasting efforts, most studies of fairness and discrimination, and many other important empirical studies are neither experiments nor observational studies. (Rosenbaum, 2002, pp. 1–2)

Experimental studies may be impossible to conduct because of ethical or logistic reasons. They may not be necessary. They may be inappropriate or inadequate. Important roles for observational methods suggested by Gray (2001a), based on Black (1994) include the following:

1. Some interventions have an impact so large that observational data are sufficient to show it.
2. Infrequent, adverse outcomes would be detected only by RCTs so large that they are rarely conducted. Observational methods such as postmarketing surveillance of medicines are the only alternative.
3. Observational data provide a realistic means of assessing the long-term outcome of interventions beyond the time scale of many trials. An example is long-term effects of neuroleptic medication.
4. Clinicians often will be opposed to an RCT; observational approaches can be used to show clinical uncertainty and pave the way for a trial.
5. Some important aspects of care cannot be subjected to a randomized trial for practical and ethical reasons. (Adapted from Black, 1994)

Observational studies include (1) cohort studies, (2) case control studies, (3) pre-post studies, and (4) case series. This order reflects the level of evidence provided regarding effectiveness questions, although there are exceptions (see discussion, for example, of case control studies). Observational studies may be descriptive or analytical. Analytical studies include cohort and case control studies. Observational studies differ in their *ecological validity;* that is, the extent to which the study is carried out in contexts that are similar or identical to the everyday life experiences of those involved. A variety of strategies are used to detect hidden biases in observational studies, such as inclusion of a number of control groups to try to identify hidden covariates (characteristics that influence the results other than the one focused on). And as Rosenbaum (2002) suggests "even when it is not possible to remove bias through adjustment or detect bias through careful design, it is nonetheless possible to give quantitative expression to the magnitude of uncertainties about bias, a technique called *sensitivity analysis"* (p. 11).

*Cohort Studies*   In cohort studies, a group of individuals which has experienced a certain situation (for example, witnessed domestic violence) is compared with a group which has not been so exposed. Both groups are followed up to determine the association between exposure and an outcome (such as subsequent abuse of one's own children). Cohort studies are prospective and analytical. Because of lack of random assignment they are prone to a number of biases, such as lack of control over risk assignment and uneven loss to follow-up. Cohort studies are often used to describe different kinds of risk. Questions to ask include the following (Gray, 2001a; CRD, University of York).

- Is there sufficient description of the groups (how they were recruited) and the distribution of prognostic factors?
- Are the groups assembled at a similar point in relation to (for example) their disorder progression? (Were decisions made that could have included or excluded more severe cases?)
- Is the intervention/treatment reliably ascertained?
- Were the groups comparable on all important confounding factors?
- Was there adequate adjustment for the effects of these confounding variables?
- Were measures used valid?
- Was a dose-response relationship between intervention and outcome demonstrated?
- Was outcome assessment blind to exposure status?
- Was the presence of co-occurring disorders considered?
- Was follow-up long enough for the outcomes to occur?
- What proportion of the cohort was followed up?
- Were dropout rates and reasons for dropout similar across intervention and unexposed groups?

Gray (2001a) notes that "the main abuse of a cohort study is to assess the effectiveness of a particular intervention when a more appropriate method would be an RCT" (p. 150).

*Case Control (Case-Referent) Studies*   In a retrospective case-control study we start with people who have a particular characteristic (a certain illness) and look back in time in relation to certain outcomes. Samples may be small in such studies yet suggest strong relationships. Consider the case-referent study reporting a relationship between the drug diethylstilbestrol (DES) given to pregnant women and vaginal cancer. Herbst, Ulfelder, and Poskanzer (1971) included 8 women who had vaginal cancer and 32 who did not in relation to use of DES during pregnancies. Seven had taken DES in the group with vaginal cancer and none had taken it in the referent group. This study illustrates the value of case-referent studies regarding rare conditions or for risk factors that have long development phases. Suggested criteria for reviewing case control studies are:

- Is the case definition explicit?
- Has the illness state of clients been reliably assessed and validated?
- Were the controls randomly selected from the population of the cases?
- How comparable are the cases and controls with respect to potential confounding factors?
- Were interventions and other exposures assessed in the same way for cases and controls?
- How was the response rate defined?
- Were the nonresponse rates and reasons for nonresponse the same in both groups?
- Is it possible that overmatching has occurred, in that cases and controls were matched on factors related to exposure?
- Was an appropriate statistical analysis used (matched or unmatched)?" (CRD, University of York, Phase 5, p. 11)

*Cross-Sectional Study*   In a cross-sectional study, a snapshot is taken of people at a particular time. Such studies may be used to describe the frequency or rate of a behavior or to try to identify the relationship between one or more factors and a problem, such as child abuse. Unfortunately, such research does not show which came first.

*Pre-Post Study (Before and After)*   Responses are compared before and after some intervention. Such designs do not provide information about the causal relationship between an intervention and an outcome unless, perhaps, the change is very large and is replicated.

*Case–Series*   Another kind of clinical study consists of describing characteristics of a series of case examples. Because of the lack of comparison we cannot make assumptions about causes. Questions for reviewing case-series studies include the following:

- Is the study based on a representative sample selected from a relevant population?
- Are the criteria for inclusion explicit?
- Did all individuals enter the study at a similar point in their disorder progression?
- Was follow-up long enough for important events to occur?
- Were outcomes assessed using objective criteria or was blinding used?

- If comparisons of sub-series are being made, was there sufficient description of the series and the distribution of prognostic factors? (CRD, University of York, Phase 5, p. 11)

A case report is essentially an anecdotal report—a description of a single case. Such reports differ greatly in their rigor.

## SYSTEMATIC REVIEWS AND META-ANALYSES

In systematic reviews there is a search for all evidence related to key practice questions and a critical assessment of what is found. For example, Cochrane review groups search in all languages for research reports, published and unpublished, related to a specific question. The search process is carefully described, so that readers are appraised of how this was conducted. (See also Campbell Collaboration reviews.) Authors describe how they searched, where they searched, and what criteria they used to appraise the quality of studies. Systematic reviews involve the following basic components: (1) stating the objectives of the research, (2) defining eligibility criteria for studies to be included, (3) identifying all potentially eligible studies, (4) applying eligibility criteria, (5) assembling the most complete data set feasible, (6) analyzing this data set, using statistical synthesis and sensitivity analysis, if appropriate and possible, and (7) preparing a structured report of the research (Chalmers, 2003, p. 25). Rigorous reviews "are designed to minimize the likelihood that the effects of interventions will be confused with the effects of biases and chance" (Chalmers, 2003, p. 22). Systematic reviews are of value in relation to all questions. There are vast differences between authoritative (incomplete, uncritical) and rigorous, exhaustive reviews—garbage in, garbage out. A meta-analysis is a systematic review that includes quantification of effect sizes in the summarization of results.

Differences in the rigor of research reviews are illustrated by reviews of multi-systemic therapy. Most sources, including those edited or written by well-known clinical researchers such as Kazdin and Weisz (2003), describe this as an effective treatment. Littell's (2005) review concludes that such programs are not effective (see Chapter 10). Which is correct? This illustrates the use of different criteria in arriving at conclusions about what is effective. Preparing sloppy reviews and disregarding the impossibility of discovering what is true and what is false by induction (see Chapter 4), encourages inflated claims of effectiveness that provide misleading conclusions. A key contribution of systematic reviews is encouraging an exhaustive search for research findings related to important practice and policy questions, a clear description of the search process used to locate studies, rigorous review of each study located, a clear description of the criteria used to appraise research reports and routine updating. (See Cochrane Collaboration Guidelines, Rev. Man.) Not wasting data is one aim of thorough reviews. Oxman, Cook, and Guyatt (1994) suggest the following criteria for assessing the methodological rigor of reviews:

1. Did the overview address a focused, practice-related question?
2. Were the research methods reported?
3. Was the search comprehensive?
4. Were the inclusion criteria reported?
5. Were criteria for inclusion appropriate?
6. Was selection bias avoided?
7. Were the validity criteria reported?
8. Was validity assessed appropriately?
9. Were the methods used to combine studies reported?
10. Were the findings combined appropriately?
11. Does it list, in tabular form, indices of effect size?
12. Do the conclusions match the data reported?
13. What was the overall scientific quality of the review?
14. Can the results be applied to my clients?
15. Were all important outcomes considered?
16. Are the benefits worth the harms and costs?

(See also Exhibit 12.5.) Little if any of this information is given in incomplete reviews. Without this, readers are not provided with the detail needed to make up their own minds about the evidentiary status of claims.

There is no way to get around the time it takes to carefully appraise each research report reviewed. Critical appraisal of a study takes a great deal of time. That is probably why it is often not done. The abstract and discussion sections of reports become the least important and the method and results sections become of key concern (Rosenthal, 2001). The logo of the Cochrane Collaboration illustrates a program that is effective (see Cochrane web site). This visual description allows you to quickly see how many studies fall to the left or to the right of the midline. It is called a "forest plot" (see Exhibit 12.6). The solid line running down the center indicates the point where there is no difference between treatment and control groups (an ODDS ratio of 1). The odds ratio refers to the odds of an event in an exposed group compared to the odds of the same event in a group not exposed. Odds refers to the ratio of probability of occurrence to nonoccurrence of the event (Guyat & Rennie, 2002, p. 81). Each horizontal line represents one trial, and the length of each line represents the confidence interval (CI). This shows the precision of the estimate. The shorter this is, the less the variability of results in a study. The longer it is, the greater the variability. If a confidence interval crosses the vertical line, then the range of estimated effects of the treatment include the possibility both of getting better and of getting worse. Generally, if the whole CI is on the left of the line, the treatment improves the situation. The confidence interval "quantifies the uncertainty in measurement. It is usually reported as a 95% CI, which is the range of values within which we can be 95% sure that the true value for the whole population lies" (Sackett et al., 2000, p. 245). The odds ratios and 95 percent confidence intervals for effects of home visiting on child injury (Roberts, Kramer, Suissa, 1996) are illustrated

**Exhibit 12.5**
Steps in Determining the Validity of a Meta-Analysis

| | | |
|---|---|---|
| 1. Was the literature search done well? | | |
|     a. Was it comprehensive? | Yes | No |
|     b. Were the search methods systematic and clearly described? | Yes | No |
|     c. Were the key words used in the search described? | Yes | No |
|     d. Was the issue of publication bias addressed? | Yes | No |
| 2. Was the method for selecting articles clear, systematic, and appropriate? | Yes | No |
|     a. Were there clear, pre-established inclusion and exclusion criteria for evaluation? | Yes | No |
|     b. Was selection systematic? | Yes | No |
|        i. Was the population defined? | Yes | No |
|        ii. Was the exposure/intervention clearly described? | Yes | No |
|        iii. Were all outcomes described and were they compatible? | Yes | No |
|     c. Was selection done blindly and in random order? | Yes | No |
|     d. Was the selection process reliable? | Yes | No |
|        i. Were at least two independent selectors used? | Yes | No |
|        ii. Was the extent of selection disagreement evaluated? | Yes | No |
| 3. Was the quality of primary studies evaluated? | Yes | No |
|     a. Did all studies, published or not, have the same standard applied? | Yes | No |
|     b. Were at least two independent evaluators used and was the inter-rater agreement assessed and adequate? | Yes | No |
|     c. Were the evaluators blinded to authors, institutions, and results of the primary studies? | Yes | No |
| 4. Were results from the studies combined appropriately? | | |
|     a. Were the studies similar enough to combine results? | Yes | No |
|        i. Were the study designs, populations, exposures, outcomes, and direction of effect similar in the combined studies? | Yes | No |
|     b. Was a test for heterogeneity done and was its *p* value nonsignificant? | Yes | No |
| 5. Was a statistical combination (meta-analysis) done properly? | | |
|     a. Were the methods of the studies similar? | Yes | No |
|     b. Was the possibility of chance differences statistically addressed? | Yes | No |
|        i. Was a test for homogeneity done? | Yes | No |
|     c. Were appropriate statistical analyses performed? | Yes | No |
|     d. Were sensitivity analyses used? | | |
| 6. Are the results important? | Yes | No |
|     a. Was the effect strong? | Yes | No |
|        i. Was the odds ratio large? | Yes | No |
|        ii. Were the results reported in a clinically meaningful manner, such as the absolute difference or the number needed to treat? | Yes | No |
|     b. Are the results likely to be reproducible and generalizable? | Yes | No |
|     c. Were all clinically important consequences considered? | Yes | No |
|     d. Are the benefits worth the harm and costs? | Yes | No |

*Source:* From "Applying a Meta-analysis to Daily Clinical Practice," by W. F. Miser, 2000, in *Evidence-based Clinical Practice: Concepts and Approaches* (p. 60), edited by J. P. Geyman, R. A. Deyo, and S. D. Ramsey, Boston: Butterworth Heinemann. Reprinted with permission.

**Exhibit 12.6**
Odds Ratios and 95% Confidence Intervals for Effect of Home Visiting on Child Injury

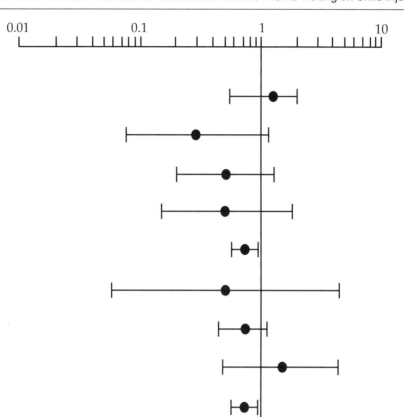

*Source:* From "Does More Visiting Prevent Child Head Injury? A Systematic Review of Randomized Controlled Trials," by I. Roberts, M. S. Kramer, and S. Suissa, 1996, *British Medical Journal, 312,* pp. 29–33. Reprinted with permission.

in Exhibit 12.6). The pooled estimate shown at the bottom is 0.74. Criticisms of meta-analysis suggested by Rosenthal (2001) include the following:

1. Retrievability bias.
2. Overemphasis on a single value rather than a description of central tendency and variability in findings.
3. Glossing over important details.
4. Overlooking heterogeneity of studies.
5. Overlooking heterogeneity of outcomes and the potential contributions of moderating variables (such as psychotherapy).
6. Inclusion of poorly designed studies that contain many sources of bias.

7. Inclusion of multiple dependent variables (outcomes) with different effect sizes, perhaps due to variables such as different laboratories. (Workshop on meta-analysis, March 2000, University of California–Berkeley; see also Lipsey, 2003)

## QUESTIONS ABOUT PREVALENCE AND INCIDENCE (FREQUENCY AND RATE)

Making informed decisions may require accurate information regarding the incidence and prevalence of a concern. *Prevalence* refers to the number of people in a population who currently have a condition or attribute. *Incidence* refers to the number of people in a population who develop an attribute within a year. Prevalence and incidence are of interest in trying to understand the frequency of a certain condition. Epidemiology is "The study of the distribution and determinants of health-related states or events in specified populations, and the application of this study to control of health problems" (Last, 1988, p. 42). Descriptive epidemiology is the study of the occurrence of illness or other health-related characteristic (e.g., person, place, or time). Analytic studies examine associations—for example, between certain risks and outcomes. Descriptive studies do not test hypotheses. Analytic studies do test hypotheses.

Let us say that a parent seeks help because she is worried about her child being abducted by a stranger. She has read a report in the newspaper saying that stranger abduction is common and parents should be careful. Because of this she rarely allows her children to go out unaccompanied. She and her husband disagree about this—he believes that his wife is over-concerned, and because of this, is depriving their child of freedom and opportunities to learn and grow. As with other decisions, we can translate information needs into well-formed, answerable questions that allow us to search electronically, efficiently, and effectively for related literature. The following questions may guide a search for related literature:

- In suburban neighborhoods, what is the incidence and prevalence of stranger abduction of young children?
- Does the media exaggerate the prevalence of stranger abduction?

Other kinds of questions that are relevant here include: "For young children, are there effective, preventative steps that can be taken to decrease stranger abduction?" "Under what circumstances does stranger abduction occur?" Quality filters for description questions can be seen in Exhibit 11.4. A search of the literature reveals that the prevalence of stranger abduction is often exaggerated by the media (Best, 1988). Ecological studies are descriptive in nature and use data collected for a variety of purposes, including administrative needs. An example is comparison of the different rates of child abuse in different communities that have different levels of social support. Both cohort studies and cross-sectional studies may be used to gather information about frequency or rate.

## QUESTIONS ABOUT CAUSES

A well-formed question might be: "In elementary school children who are a classroom management problem, what are common causes?" We could use a variety of methods to try to identify related factors. We could create a survey and ask teachers what they think. We could compare this with results of a descriptive and functional analysis of classroom contingencies (e.g., Watson & Steege, 2003). The latter form of investigation suggests that being under- or over-challenged may contribute to disruptive behavior in a classroom (problems in curriculum design) and/or classroom contingencies may maintain such behavior (being reinforced for inappropriate behavior and ignoring desired behaviors; Baldwin, 1999). Would a survey reveal the same thing? See Exhibit 12.7 for questions to raise concerning articles about causation.

### SURVEYS

Surveys are used for many purposes, including describing the prevalence of certain conditions, such as depression, to gather people's views about quality of care and services, and to try to identify causes using complex statistical tools, such as regression analysis. The purpose of correlational research is to investigate the relationship between two or more variables using statistical analysis. Pearson product-moment correlation coefficients are typically used as the statistic to represent the degree of association. This ranges from −1 to +1, both indicating a perfect correlation. For example, we may ask: "What is the

**Exhibit 12.7**
Validity Screen for an Article about Causation

| | | |
|---|---|---|
| 1. Was a clearly defined comparison group or those at risk for having the outcome of interest included? | Yes (go on) | No (Stop) |
| 2. Were the outcomes and exposures measured in the same way in the groups being compared? | Yes (go on) | No (Stop) |
| 3. Were the observers blinded to the exposure of outcome and to the outcome? | Yes (go on) | No (Stop) |
| 4. Was follow-up sufficiently long and complete? | Yes (go on) | No (Stop) |
| 5. Is the temporal relationship correct? (Does the exposure to the agent precede the outcome?) | Yes (go on) | No (Stop) |
| 6. Is there a dose-response gradient? (As the quantity or the duration of exposure to the agent increases, does the risk of outcome likewise increase?) | Yes (go on) | No (Stop) |
| 7. How strong is the association between exposure and outcome? (Is the relative risk or odds ratio large?) | Yes (go on) | No (Stop) |

*Note:* A "stop" answer to any of the questions should prompt you to seriously question whether the results of the study are valid and whether the item in question is really a causative factor.
*Source:* W. F. Miser (1999). Critical appraisal of the literature. *Journal of the American Board of Family Practice, 12,* 315–333.

relationship between college grade-point average (GPA), scores on the Graduate Record Examination (GRE), and performance in graduate school?" Do GPA and GRE scores predict performance in graduate school? Correlational designs differ in their ecological validity (the extent to which findings can be generalized to other groups). We cannot draw causal assumptions based upon correlational data; associations do not necessarily reflect causal relationships (see Chapter 14). There may be some other variable that is responsible for the association. It could even be that there is reverse association. Gray (2001a) suggests the following questions in critically appraising a survey:

- How was the population to be surveyed chosen? Was it the whole population or a sample?
- If a sample, how was the sample chosen? Was it a random sample or was it stratified, to ensure that all sectors of the population were represented?
- Was a validated questionnaire used? Did the authors of the survey mention the possibility of different results being obtained by different interviewers, if interviewers were used?
- What procedures were used to verify the data?
- Were the conclusions drawn from the survey all based on the data or did those carrying out the survey infer conclusions? *Inference is acceptable, but it must be clearly distinguished from results derived solely from the data.* (p. 153)

## QUESTIONS REGARDING EXPERIENCES

Examples of questions that arise here include:

- In social workers in child welfare agencies, what are current sources of strain and perceived causes?
- In elderly clients entering a nursing home, what are feelings and thoughts?

Qualitative research may be of many different kinds, including case studies, narrative analyses, focus groups and participant observation. There is a concern to describe people's experiences as they see them. Clinicians must understand events from a client's point of view in order to plan, together with the client, what might be helpful. If they don't understand this, if they misattribute motives and values to clients, hoped-for outcomes and related factors may not be accurately identified. This illustrates the closeness between good qualitative research and a sound contextual assessment—a clinician's attempts to contextually describe the factors that influence client concerns. Examples of different kinds of qualitative research include participant observation, unstructured interviews, and hermeneutic reading of texts. For example, Bourgois and his fellow investigators (Bourgois, Lettiere, & Quesada, 2003) spent time with homeless people in San Francisco over a period of years. Case studies consist of detailed descriptions of individuals, groups, organizations, or neighborhoods. As Becker (1996) suggests, "we *always* describe how they [other people] interpret the events they participate in, so the only question is not whether we should, but how accurately we do it." He suggests that "it is inevitably epistemologically dangerous to guess at what could be observed directly. The danger is that we will guess wrong, that what looks reasonable to us will not be what looked reasonable to them" (p. 58). Becker notes that "The variety of things called ethnographic aren't all alike, and in fact may be at odds with each other over epistemological details" (p. 57).

Data gathered via participant-observation may be more valid than information collected on self-report surveys that people are paid to complete. Consider the question "What kinds of risks (if any) do street addicts take?" In their article describing HIV risk among homeless heroin addicts in San Francisco, Bourgois, Lettiere, and Quesada (2003) found that "Virtually all our network members have told us that they distort their risky behavior on questionnaires" (p. 270). Campbell (1996) agrees with Becker about over-stretching quantitative research: "Quantitative data often represents low-cost, mass-produced research and is often wrong. The others' meanings as inferred from questionnaire averages are overly determined by the ethnocentric subjectivity of the researcher" (p. 161). Campbell considers the "most ubiquitous source of error in efforts to know the other" to be "to interpret as a cultural difference what is in reality a failure of communication . . . I personally am convinced that many of the cultural differences reported by psychologists and others using questionnaires or tests come from failures of communication misreported as differences" (p. 165). A checklist for critically appraising a qualitative research report follows (see other sources for additional descriptions of qualitative research methods):

1. Did the article describe an important clinical problem examined via a clear answerable question?
2. Was the qualitative approach appropriate?
3. How were the setting and the subjects selected?
4. What was the researcher's perspective and has this been taken into account?
5. What methods did the researcher use for collecting data; are these described in enough detail?
6. What methods did the researcher use to analyze the data? What quality-control measures were used?
7. Are the results accurately described, and, if so, are they important?
8. What conclusions were drawn, and are they justified by the results?
9. Are the findings of the study transferable to other clinical settings? (Greenhalgh, 2001, pp. 207–208)

## QUESTIONS ABOUT DIAGNOSIS AND SCREENING

The professional literature describes scores of tests. The key question here is "Can a test accurately detect a certain condition or characteristics, such as depression in an elderly client and, at what cost?" Tests may provide helpful guidelines or be misleading—appear to inform but do the opposite, perhaps harm rather than help clients. Consider the example of the reflex dilation test. In Britain, Hobbs and Wynne (1989) (two pediatricians) suggested that a simple medical test could be used to demonstrate that buggery or other forms of anal penetration had occurred. Here is their description:

> Reflex dilation well described in forensic texts . . . usually occurs within about 30 seconds of separating the buttocks. Recent controversy has helped our understanding of what is now seen as an important sign of traumatic penetration of the anus as occurs in abuse, but also following medical and surgical manipulation. . . . The diameter of the symmetrical relaxation of the anal sphincter is variable and should be estimated. This is a dramatic sign which once seen is easily recognized. . . . The sign is not always easily reproducible on second and third examinations and there appear to be factors, at present, which may modify the eliciting of this physical sign. The sign in most cases gradually disappears when abuse stops. (Hanks, Hobbs, & Wynne, 1988, p. 153)

News of this test spread quickly, and because of this test, many children were removed from their homes on the grounds that they were being sexually abused—when this was not true. (Questions that should have been asked are described in the next section.) "Diagnostic tests are done when patients are symptomatic, whereas screening tests are done on nonsymptomatic clients" (Elmore & Boyko, 2000, p. 83). (See also Knottnerus, 2002.) Tests may be used to predict future behavior. They should be used to revise subjective estimates concerning a client—that is, to change a decision about how a client should be treated. Clinicians tend to overestimate the predictive accuracy of test results. One cause of this error is ignoring base-rate data (see Chapter 15). The predictive accuracy of a test depends on the initial risk of a condition in the person receiving the test. The probability that a client with a positive (or negative) test result for dementia actually has dementia depends on the prevalence of dementia in the population from which the client was selected—that is, on the pretest probability that a client has dementia. Because there is little appreciation of this point, predictive accuracy often is overestimated.

## CRITICALLY APPRAISING REPORTS OF DIAGNOSTIC ACCURACY

As when investigating the effectiveness of an intervention method, a variety of biases as well as incomplete reporting of how a test was developed and tested can lead to problems in interpreting accuracy. For example, classification is involved in testing—placing people into categories. Surprisingly few reference standards are clear for making unequivocal classifications. Lijmer and his colleagues (1999) reported that studies of diagnostic tests with certain kinds of design problems were biased, providing overly optimistic estimates of accuracy. The best type of evidence in relation to how test results relate to benefits of treatment is randomized controlled trials. If these are not available, cohort studies may provide information. Bossuyt and his colleagues (2003) describe standards for reporting diagnostic accuracy. Both a checklist and flow-chart are included to help readers to evaluate the potential for bias in a study and to judge the applicability of findings. Greenhalgh (2001) offers the following points for critically appraising related articles:

1. The test is potentially relevant to my practice.
2. The test has been compared with a true gold standard.
3. The validation study included an appropriate spectrum of clients.
4. Work up bias was avoided.
5. Observer bias has been avoided.
6. The test has been shown to be reproducible both within and between observers.
7. The features of the test as derived from this validation study are described.
8. Confidence intervals are given for sensitivity, specificity and other features of the test.
9. A sensible 'normal range' has been derived from those results.
10. The test has been placed in the context of other potential tests in the assessment sequence for the problem. (p. 205)

These questions were not raised in reviewing the accuracy of the reflex dilation test. As a result, many people were harmed. The false positive rate was not reported (the percentage of persons inaccurately identified as having a characteristic). Nor was the false negative rate reported (the percentage of persons inaccurately identified as not having a characteristic; see Exhibit 12.8.) Nor was sensitivity and specificity reported: key concepts in reviewing tests include the following: (See also discussion of absolute and relative risk reduction and number needed to treat, in Chapter 11.)

- *Sensitivity:* among those known to have a problem, the proportion whom a test or measure said had the problem.
- *Specificity:* among those known not to have a problem, the proportion whom the test or measure has said did not have the problem.
- *Pretest probability (prevalence):* The probability that an individual has the disorder before the test is carried out.
- *Post-test probability:* The probability that an individual with a specific test result has the target conditions (post-test odds/[1 + post-test odds]).
- *Pretest odds:* The odds that an individual has the disorder before the test is carried out (pretest probability/[1 − pretest probability])
- *Post-test odds:* The odds that a patient has the disorder after being tested (pretest odds × LR [likelihood ratio]).
- *Positive predictive value (PPV):* The proportion of individuals with positive test results who have the target condition. This equals the post-test probability, given a positive test result.

**Exhibit 12.8**

Definitions and Calculations for a Perfect ("Gold Standard") Diagnostic Test

**Definitions**

Sensitivity: A/(A + C)

Specificity: D/(D + B)

False-negative rate: C/(C + A)

False-positive rate: B/(B + D)

Positive predictive value: A/(A + B)

Negative predictive value: D/(C + D)

Pretest disease probability: (A + C)/(A + B + C + D)

Post-test disease probability, positive results: A/(A + C)

Post-test disease probability, negative result: C/(C + D)

| Test | Disorder Present | Disorder Absent | Total |
|---|---|---|---|
| Test Positive | A | B | A + B |
| Test Negative | C | D | C + D |
| Total | A + C | B + D | N = (A + B + C + D) |

**Calculations:**

Sensitivity: 100/(100 + ) = 100%

Specificity: 100/(100 + 0) = 100%

Positive predictive value: 100%

Post-test disease probability, negative test: 0%

| Test | Disorder Present | Disorder Absent | Total |
|---|---|---|---|
| Test Positive | 100 | 0 | 100 |
| Test Negative | 0 | 100 | 100 |
| Total | 100 | 100 | 200 |

*Source:* From "Assessing Accuracy of Diagnostic and Screening Tests," by J. G. Elmore and E. J. Boyko, 2000, in *Evidence-based Clinical Practice: Concepts and Approaches* (p. 85), edited by J. P. Geyman, R. A. Deyo, and S. D. Ramsey, Boston: Butterworth Heinemann. Reprinted with permission.

- *Negative predictive value (NPV):* The proportion of individuals with negative test results who do not have the target condition. This equals 1 minus the post-test probability, given a negative test result.
- *Likelihood ratio:* Measure of a test result's ability to modify pretest probabilities. Likelihood ratios indicate how many times more likely a test re-

sult is in a client with a disorder compared with a person free of the disorder. A likelihood ratio of 1 indicates that a test is totally uninformative. "A likelihood ratio of greater than 1 indicates that the test is associated with the presence of the disease whereas a likelihood ratio less than 1 indicates that the test result is associated with the absence of disease. The further likelihood ratios are from 1 the stronger the evidence for the presence or absence of disease. Likelihood ratios above 10 and below 0.1 are considered to provide strong evidence to rule in or rule out diagnosis respectively in most circumstances" (Deeks and Altman, 2004, p. 168).

- *Likelihood ratio of a positive test result (LR+):* The ratio of the true positive rate to the false positive rate: sensitivity/(1 − specificity).
- *Likelihood of a negative test result (LR−):* The ratio of the false negative to the true negative rate: (1 − sensitivity)/specificity (adapted from Pewsner et al., 2004).

These concepts can be illustrated by a four-cell contingency table (see Exhibit 12.8). "In clinical practice it is essential to know how a particular test result predicts the risk of abnormality. Sensitivities and specificities do not do this: they describe how abnormality (or normality) predicts particular test results. Predictive values do give probabilities of abnormality for particular test results, but depend on the prevalence of abnormality in the study sample . . ." (Deeks & Altman, 2004, p. 169).

Only if a test increases accuracy of understanding should it be used. Often in social work, psychology, and psychiatry, there is no gold standard against which to compare a test. An example of a "gold standard" is reviewing an X-ray to detect pneumonia when someone has a bad cough. We should distinguish between pre- and post-test estimates. (See Chapter 15.) A nomogram can be used to calculate post-test probabailities.

## Screening

Screening is a key public health strategy that has been broadened to concerns such as depression and anxiety. The President's New Freedom Commission on Mental Health (2005) recommends universal screening (see Lenzer, 2004). The benefits of a screening program should outweigh any harms. Other requirements for an ideal screening program include the following:

- "The benefit of testing outweighs the harm.
- The [disorder] is serious, with a high burden of suffering.
- The natural history of the [disorder] is understood.
- The [disorder] occurs frequently.
- Effective treatment exists, and early treatment is more effective than late treatment.
- The test is easy to administer.

- The test is inexpensive.
- The test is safe.
- The test is acceptable to participants.
- The sensitivity, specificity, and other operating characteristics of the test are acceptable." (Elmore & Boyko, 2000, p. 89; based on Jekel, Elmore, & Katz 1996; see also Gray, 2001a)

## QUESTIONS CONCERNING PROGNOSIS, RISK, AND PROTECTIVE FACTORS (PREDICTION)

Both prognosis and risk project into the future; related tests attempt to predict events in the future. For example, depending on a diagnosis of depression, one has a certain prognosis, which in turn is related to certain protective and risk factors. Risk assessment is of interest in a number of areas, including suicide and violent acts such as domestic and child abuse. Child welfare workers make predictions about future risk of abuse. Thousands of children are on "at risk" registers on the assumption that they are at a continuing risk of abuse. Thus, both prognosis and prediction have a forward orientation—they look into the future, and as with all such looks, there will be errors. We can and do make errors in identifying risks and protective factors in diagnosis and in prognosis. Errors in earlier stages (e.g., assessment), may result in errors at later stages (selection of service plans). Examples of questions here are:

- In elderly, frail clients living alone, what is the risk of hip fracture?
- In young children abused by their parents, what is the risk of future abuse?
- In young children rejected by their peers, what is the risk of developing problems in adolescence?
- In young adults who have unprotected sexual intercourse with multiple partners, what is the risk of developing AIDS?

Prognostic studies include clinical studies of variables that predict future events, as well as epidemiological studies of risk factors. In ecological (aggregate) studies, secondary data is often used to identify associations in a population group between risk factors and outcomes of interest, such as depression. Generalization from aggregate data to individuals is problematic because of the likelihood of the ecological fallacy (assuming what is true for a group is true for an individual). Actuarial methods (using the results of empirical investigations of the relationships between certain characteristics and an outcome) are superior to intuitive methods for making accurate predictions in a number of areas (e.g., see Dawes, Faust, & Meehl, 2002; Grove & Meehl, 1996). Both cohort and case control studies have been used to try to identify and quantify risk and protective factors. Problems include naturally occurring fluctuations. Accurately communicating risks to clients is a challenge (e.g., see Edwards, Elwyn, Matthews, & Pill, 2001).

## CRITICALLY APPRAISING RELATED RESEARCH

Guyatt and Rennie (2002) suggest the following questions concerning articles on prognosis:

*Are the results valid?*

- Was the sample of clients representative?
- Were the [clients] sufficiently homogeneous with respect to prognostic risk?
- Was follow-up sufficiently complete?
- Were objective and unbiased outcome criteria used?

*What are the results?*

- How likely are the outcomes over time?
- How precise are the estimates of likelihood?

*How can I apply the results to [client] care?*

- Were the study [clients] and their management similar to those in my practice?
- Was the follow-up sufficiently long?
- Can I use the results [in my setting?] (p. 144)

Both absolute and relative risk should be given. The latter often sounds impressive in relation to risk reduction compared to absolute risk reduction (see Chapter 15).

## QUESTIONS ABOUT PRACTICE GUIDELINES

Many sources purport to describe practice guidelines. Indeed, this term has become a buzzword, together with terms such as "best practice," "empirically-validated methods," and "evidence-based practice." Inflated claims are common regarding the effectiveness of practice guidelines (Grilli, Magrini, Penna, Mura, & Liberati, 2000). Thus, it is important to learn how to evaluate their quality. Most guidelines do not draw on the science of preparing rigorous reviews (see prior discussion of systematic reviews in this Chapter). There is a spirited controversy regarding the usefulness of such guidelines—for example, do they allow for variations in client characteristics? (See Norcross, Beutler, & Levant, 2006; Strupp & Anderson, 1997.) Clients may have multiple concerns, rendering use of guidelines more complex. We should also consider studies showing that the quality of the relationship yields different outcomes even when using the same practice guidelines. Division 12 of the American Psychological Association (The Division of Clinical Psychology) established a task force (1995) designed to choose criteria for identifying empirically supported interventions. This task force identified criteria for different levels of empirical support. It (1995) recommended that if two randomized controlled trials show the effectiveness of an intervention, then this method has been "established" as valid. Notice the justificationary nature of such a claim (certainty is suggested by the term "established,") when two randomized controlled trials, even though well-designed, cannot certainty make. The next two trials may show different results. Related controversy is suggested by the description of this task force by Lambert (2004) as "the most notorious effort" to bring in scientific standards for practice (p. 8). He argues that "This resulted in highly controversial lists of treatments that met the criteria for different levels of empirical support . . . and in lists of resources for training and treatment manuals" (p. 8). "The controversies generated from the initial report came mainly from practitioners who saw the report as rigid, if not dogmatic, and as having an agenda that is biased in favor of therapies promoted by Task Force members, e.g., criteria were set up that would give an advantage to highly structured short-term behavioral and cognitive behavioral treatments advocated by many Task Force members." But criticism came from psychotherapy researchers as well (e.g., Strupp, 1997). Critics suggested that "transportability" issues were downplayed (problems of using guidelines tested in controlled settings in the "real-world"). A key question is—"Is the guideline valid?" "Has it been rigorously tested regarding effects?" "Has its *effectiveness* been tested, not just its *efficacy*—that is, has it been tested in real world circumstances (e.g., clinics) in addition to research-based hospitals?" Questions that arise include the following:

- Were all important decisions, options, and outcomes clearly described? For example, has a well-tested alternative, such as the use of contingency management for altering behavior of children labeled ADHD, been ignored?
- Is there a rigorous effort to identify and locate all related research? Were studies located carefully appraised using rigorous criteria?
- Are the benefits and risks clearly described, as well as costs for each outcome of interest, including the views of different stake holders? (e.g., see Lawrie, McIntosh, & Rao, 2000).
- Does the guideline apply to your clients?

Greenhalgh (2001) recommends inquiring whether the preparation and publication of the guidelines involve a significant conflict of interest.

Lawrie, McIntosh, and Rao (2000) suggest the following questions in reviewing the potential usefulness of a clinical guideline. (1) Is the guideline valid? (2) Is it important (e.g., is there currently a large variation in practice?) Does the guideline contain new evidence or old research findings that are not acted on? Would use of a guideline have major effects on outcomes? and (3) Can I use it in caring for my clients? Questions regarding whether a guideline can be used with a particular client include: (1) Are there barriers to implementation? Can I enlist the cooperation of colleagues? and (2) Can I meet the "educational, administrative, and economic conditions necessary for implementation?" (p. 170). Gray (2001a) emphasizes that the experts regarding application barriers are staff and clients. They are in a position to identify, and indeed reflect in their behaviors, application barriers, such as beliefs about what methods are effective. Although the *efficacy* of a method may be tested under ideal conditions, this same program may not achieve the same results when used in real-life settings (when its *effectiveness* is examined).

## CONTROVERSIAL ISSUES

There are differences of opinion, even within a particular research tradition, regarding questions about evidence, best methods, and how to interpret results (e.g., see Becker, 1996). The research design used to explore a question reflects the researchers' views about knowledge and how it can be gained, and their views concerning honest brokering of knowledge and ignorance. Inflated claims suggest one of a variety of possibilities: Those who make them (1) are uninformed about the limitations of the research design in critically testing a question, (2) are aware of this, but do not care, or (3) care but need a publication. Claims may be inflated in a number of ways—claims of effectiveness or claims of no effectiveness, for example. Keep in mind that just because a program has been found to be effective or ineffective in critical tests does not warrant claims of certainty. Also, other dimensions come into play in addition to evidentiary status, such as importance of outcomes attained to clients and transferability of research findings.

## OBSTACLES

Obstacles to acquiring skills in critically appraising research and using these to enhance the quality of services include both personal and environmental ones. Research courses are given separately from practice courses in most professional education programs. This is not the case with problem-based learning, now used in many medical schools (e.g., Sackett et al., 2000). This discourages integration of practice and research. Agencies may discourage evidence-based services and purchasing and not provide needed training and tools, such as relevant educational programs and access to needed databases. Exploration of how to address application problems is an active area of research with many exciting developments, such as involving clients as informed participants in making decisions (see Coulter, 2002; Edwards & Elwyn, 2001).

## SUMMARY

Different kinds of practice and policy questions require different kinds of research methods to critically test assumptions. Different kinds of research have different goals. Some questions are exploratory and descriptive. Their intent is to describe the relationships among different variables. A question may be: "What is the relationship between certain characteristics of a helper (e.g., warmth) and service outcome?" Another question may be: "What are characteristics of single parents on welfare who succeed in getting a job and getting off welfare, compared to people who do not?" Some kinds of research (experimental studies) involve testing a hypothesis. Their aim is to identify causal relationships among variables in a rigorous manner. Research methods differ in the degree to which sources of bias are present. A key concern is the match between a question and the likelihood that the method used to test it can do so. Currently, literature in the helping professions abounds with poor matches.

Evidence-based practice encourages attention to the limitations of research designs. One of the key reasons for the origin of EBP was a concern about flaws in published research, such as inflated claims of knowledge (see Chapter 10). Bogus claims are problematic in a profession in which clients are affected by beliefs, in that such claims may result in selection of ineffective or harmful methods. A variety of tools and entire enterprises, such as the Cochrane and Campbell collaborations, have been developed to replace bogus claims with measured ones. These include user-friendly checklists for critically appraising the quality of different kinds of research.

# PART IV

# APPLYING CRITICAL THINKING SKILLS TO CLINICAL DECISIONS

# CHAPTER 13

# Making Decisions about Data Collection

C LINICIANS MAKE DECISIONS about what data to collect, how to gather it, when to stop, and how to combine data gathered. Decisions made influence the accuracy of accounts offered and thus options for achieving outcomes clients value. Preferred-practice theories direct what we look for and what we notice as well as how we process and organize data. We can describe individuals, situations, and their interactions in innumerable ways, emphasizing some characteristics and minimizing or ignoring others. Theories differ along a number of dimensions, including the attention devoted to the past and present; the unit of concern (individual, family, or community); the attention devoted to environmental and personal characteristics; and the degree of optimism concerning how much change is possible. They differ in their evidentiary status—the extent to which they have been critically tested regarding their value in helping clients attain hoped-for outcomes. This chapter offers an overview of sources of bias in collecting data; being forewarned is being prepared to avoid errors. Incorrect views of client concerns will interfere with helping clients (see Exhibit 13.1). Consider depression. Major grand narratives include biomedical views, social interactional perspectives, and psychological views. A practice theory emphasizing dispositional characteristics encourages collection of data about psychological factors, such as repressed anger based on past experiences of loss. A theory that emphasizes external causes encourages collection of data about environmental influences, such as a decrease in pleasant events and an increase in negative ones. Decisions are often made on the basis of quite limited data (e.g., see Kendall, 1973). Karen Budd and her colleagues (Budd, Poindexter, Feliz, & Naik-Polan, 2001) critically reviewed the content and legal relevance of clinical evaluations of parents conducted in child abuse and neglect ($n = 190$) mental health evaluation reports.

**Exhibit 13.1**

Common Errors in Gathering Assessment Data: Being Forewarned Is Being Prepared

---

- Gathering irrelevant data (e.g., redundant data).
- Gathering only data that support preconceived views (confirmation biases).
- Overlooking the role of environmental factors.
- Overlooking cultural differences that influence the validity and acceptability of given sources of data.
- Forgoing opportunities to observe behavior in real-life or role-plays when needed to clarify problems and options.
- Not involving significant others in collecting data.
- Vagueness (data do not clarify problems).
- Not describing setting events, antecedents, and consequences related to behavior of interest.
- Relying on unsupported opinions of other professionals.
- Relying on unsupported data in case records.
- Relying on biased, unrepresentative samples (sampling too narrowly, e.g., observing behavior on only one occasion that may not provide information about what usually occurs).
- Using invalid measures (they do not measure what they are supposed to measure).

---

> Evaluations of parents typically were completed in a single session, rarely included a home visit, used few if any sources of information other than the parent, often cited no previous written reports, rarely used behavioral methods, stated purposes in general rather than specific terms, emphasized weaknesses over strengths in reporting results, and often neglected to describe the parent's caregiving qualities or the child's relationship with the parent. (p. 93)

Many clinicians gather more data than needed; as the amount increases, so may confidence in its usefulness, even though accuracy is not increased (Oskamp, 1965). The collection of data appears to have a "self-reinforcing" function, since it is often unclear how additional data will be useful in making more accurate decisions. Our subjective uncertainty may be decreased—even though objective uncertainty is not—by collecting additional data. Irrelevant as well as relevant data may be influential.

Each source of information is subject to error. This may be random (unsystematic, varying) or systematic (biased in one direction). Sources of random error include measurement changes (observers may fluctuate in their ratings) and changes in client characteristics (for example, in mood). Sources of systematic error include *demand characteristics* (characteristics of a situation that encourage responses in one direction). For example, we tend to present ourselves in a good light. This is known as *the social desirability effect*. Both random and systematic error may interfere with discovering a client's "true score" on a measure. Many errors involve or result in inappropriate speculation (assuming that what is can be discovered simply by thinking about it). The question is: What method will offer information that will help you to help your clients? Selection of assessment methods may be based on sound reasons, such as feasibility (what is possible) and empirical research concerning the accuracy of a source. On the other hand, selection may be based on questionable grounds, such as personal preferences that are contradicted by empirical data about the accuracy of given sources of data or inaccurate assumptions from a practice theory. Objections to a procedure based on a theoretical perspective may not follow from the theory. For example, a clinician may prefer a psychoanalytic perspective; nothing inherent in this approach requires complete reliance on self-report data, and neglect of other methods, such as observation.

Mistaken beliefs about a source of data may limit selections. You may believe that observation of interaction in structured or natural contexts is useless, since this drastically alters usual interaction patterns, when this is not necessarily true (see later discussion of use of observation). Some data may be collected from existing sources, such as case records; other material is gathered during interviews. Regardless of the source, the process of data collection is influenced by the clinician's knowledge and related beliefs, their goals (motivation), resources available, and their relationship skills. Clinicians differ in how much information they seek before the search process is stopped. Flexibility increases the likelihood that helpful—in contrast to misleading or irrelevant—data will be obtained. "Flexibility affects the criteria used to decide if an idea, piece of information, or alternative is relevant to the problem at hand. A very narrow view of the situation or problem can produce very narrow criteria and thus limit the generation and production of potentially useful information" (Yinger, 1980, p. 21). Skill in posing well-formed answerable questions regarding assessment needs that allow you to search effectively and efficiently for related research will be valuable. Kinds of questions include description, assessment, and risk/prognosis (see Chapters 10 and 11).

## DECISIONS AND OPTIONS

Knowledge of and skill in selecting and using feasible, informative assessment methods are essential. These methods may be used to classify clients, to make predictions about them, or to describe clients (see Turner, DeMers, Fox, & Reed, 2001). Required decisions include the following:

- What data will be most helpful in making evidence-informed decisions—for example, about factors related to hoped-for outcomes and about how to achieve desired outcomes and whether they can be achieved?
- How can I obtain such data?
- How will I decide when I have enough information?
- What should I do if I obtain contradictory data?

- What criteria should I use to check the accuracy of data?
- How can I avoid inaccurate and incomplete accounts?

Because life-affecting decisions are made based on data collected during assessment, you should critically evaluate this data; assessment methods can be harmful as well as helpful. For example, they may provide misleading estimates of problem severity and misleading directions for accurate understanding of a client's concerns. Have you relied on self-reports? Do these provide a sound basis for decisions? Should you check their accuracy by observing related behaviors in real life? Will this provide a sounder basis for decisions? Here, as well as in other helping phases, specialized knowledge may be required and critical thinking skills needed to weigh the accuracy of claims and soundness of different views and to integrate different kinds of information, such as findings from external research and the unique circumstances and characteristics of a client. Informed selection of assessment methods maximizes opportunities to discover alternative behaviors that will successfully compete with disliked behaviors.

Knowledge about the potential risks and benefits of different assessment frameworks and measures will help you to select referral sources that use evidence-informed methods and to evaluate assessment data gathered by others. Informed consent obligations may be violated by not sharing uncertainties regarding possible harms and benefits associated with use of an assessment method (such as a screening test for depression). Not sharing uncertainties may hide the fact that decisions involve a value judgment about how to balance risks and harms.

- Does a risk assessment measure accurately predict further likelihood of child abuse?
- Does an anxiety measure accurately identify clients who have a level of anxiety that warrants referral to counseling?
- Does a measure designed to assess the effects of traumatic life experiences accurately identify those who could benefit from counseling?

Evidence-informed selection requires skill in critically appraising the relevance and accuracy of different kinds of data in relation to different kinds of questions (e.g., description, assessment, and risk). Judging whether a particular method provides reliable and valid data requires skills in locating related research as well as knowledge and skill in critically appraising what is found. Such skills will help you to decide whether a particular source may provide accurate data about your client. Your decisions will be influenced by your knowledge, client preferences, your practice framework, and feasibility (whether it is possible to use a method). Clients may not be willing to use certain methods. You may not have skills in administering and interpreting a measure. Some sources, such as self-report, are easy to use and are flexible in the range of content provided; however, accuracy varies considerably. In addition to deciding on *sources* of data (e.g., self-report, observation), you and your clients will decide on a *type* of measure (e.g., frequency, duration, latency). What is best will depend on the outcome focused on.

## FACTORS THAT INFLUENCE WHAT CLINICIANS SEE AND REPORT

Perception is selective. As a consequence, we may not see all there is to see and may see what is not present. As discussed in Chapter 8, experts see more compared to novices in an area.

*Availability: Preferred Theories, Vividness, Frequency, and Chance*    We seek information that is consistent with our preferred theories and preconceptions and tend to disregard contradictory information, as suggested in earlier chapters, (although this does not apply to experts in an area, see also Chapter 9). People who are informed that an instructor is warm perceive him quite differently than people who are told that the same instructor is cold (Kelley, 1950). Because of preconceptions and biases, events that are not present may be reported and those that are present overlooked. The more ambiguous a situation, the more preconceptions and biases affect what is seen. Abercrombie (1960) describes a radiologist who examined an X-ray of a child with a persistent cough. The radiologist discounted a button observed on the X-ray, assuming that the button was on the boy's vest—in fact, the button was inside of the boy and was causing his cough. We are influenced by the vividness of material. It is easy to recall bizarre behavior and pay excessive attention to this, ignoring less vivid appropriate behavior. We overestimate the frequency of data that are available. Chance availability may affect our decisions—that is, certain events may just happen to be present when thinking about a problem, and these influence what we attend to (Hogarth, 1987). Clinicians in certain settings are exposed to particular kinds of clients, which may predispose them to make certain assumptions. For example, if you see many depressed individuals you may be primed to attend to signs of depression. Baserate data that is abstract tend to be ignored, which increases the probability of inaccurate inferences (see Chapter 15).

*Motivational and Emotional Influences*    Whether we make use of data affects what we perceive. For example, people are often incorrect in their answers about which way Lincoln's profile faces on a penny because they do not normally use this information. This example illustrates the difference between perceiving and noticing; perceiving is prior to noticing. Noticed information can be verbally reported, whereas perceived data that are not noticed cannot be reported. We may perceive without noticing; that is, just because something is perceived does not mean that it is noticed, and something can be noted without appreciating its significance in terms of how it affects behavior. Individual differences in valued goals (to help clients and avoid harm, to get through a busy day early) may influence what is noticed and what is not. So, too, may our emotional responses (see also Chapter 9).

*Insensitivity to Sample Size* Clinicians must often make generalizations from single instances to larger populations. For example, a psychologist may make generalizations about a person on the basis of one meeting. Generalizations about a mother's parenting skills may be made on the basis of her self-report during one interview. A lack of appreciation for sample size and sample bias can lead to incorrect judgments. The larger the sample, the more likely it is to reflect the characteristics of the population from which it is drawn. People have little appreciation of the importance of the *law of large numbers*. We are willing to make strong inferences based on few data. This tendency offers one explanation for disagreements about how to describe certain events—each person may be using a different sample to generalize from, and each sample may be small (as well as biased). Some clinicians use verbal report in the interviews as their only data source, neglecting other sources such as role play and observation in real-life settings. They have but a tiny sample of behavior and a tiny sample in just one situation—the interview—which is not a real-life setting. Yet they may remain confident in their ability to make accurate generalizations about clients on the basis of small, biased samples. The empirical literature does not support this belief (see later discussion of method variance). The size of the sample on which decisions are based can often be substantially increased by drawing on samples collected by others that are described in professional journals and books. For example, consider a clinician who is working with a client who is having trouble finding a job, but the clinician has only worked with a handful of such clients previously. Becoming familiar with related research, using the process of evidence-based practice, may reveal promising programs.

*Sample Bias* The samples to which we have access are usually biased. Few samples are random, in which each element of the population has an equal chance of being selected. Only a small percentage of people who experience distress or who engage in deviant behavior may seek help from a clinician. Those with such problems who do seek help or are referred to clinicians thus represent a biased sample of the total population of individuals who evidence certain behaviors. If a sample is randomly selected, there is less likelihood that it will be biased. The general failure to understand this is illustrated by the cabinet officer who did not accept the results of a poll that he did not like because people were chosen at random (Tversky & Kahneman, 1971).

*Agency Policy/Social Pressures/Resources* Agency administrators have preferred practice beliefs and policies that influence the kind of staff they hire and, consequently, the kind of data gathered. These preferences are revealed in steps that are taken to facilitate (or hamper) collection of certain kinds of data. For example, agencies may discourage home visits and observation of family members at home because of related costs. Peers and supervisors may exert pressures to gather certain kinds of data and to ignore other sources. Staff may not have access to relevant databases allowing speedy searches for research findings regarding the most valid assessment method for a client with a given concern. They may not be able to search for research regarding these questions:

- Mrs. Compana is worried that because her mother has Alzheimer's disease, she herself will be so diagnosed.
  Question: In people with a parent who has Alzheimer's disease, what is their risk of developing this?
- Mrs. Leader has been accused of physically abusing her child.
  Question: In parents alleged to have physically abused their child, are actuarial or consensus based measures most accurate in predicting future abuse?
- Ms. Green is caring for her elderly aunt.
  Question: In caregivers of the elderly, what scale of caregiver burden best predicts burnout?

*The Quality of Feedback*   The timing and relevance of feedback obtained about the accuracy of observations influence descriptions offered. Helpful feedback provides opportunities to correct initial assumptions. Corrective feedback is vital to development of expertise; to the development of "informed intuition" (see Chapter 8).

*Ignoring Nonoccurrences*   Events that do not occur tend to be ignored, even though these events may be highly relevant. We fail to note that a certain bizarre behavior does not occur in 95 percent of situational contexts, attending instead to the small percentage of situations in which it does occur. Certainly, such unusual behavior is a concern. However, overlooking situations in which it does not occur deprives clinicians of valuable information about environmental influences on behavior.

*Temporary Biases*   Unexamined assumptions influence our perception, sometimes with tragic results—as illustrated by hunters who mistakenly shoot people instead of deer. Our temporary moods, either positive or negative, affect our decisions, as illustrated in Chapter 9. Different decisions may be made about a client who is seen at the end of a hectic day than may be made if the same client had been interviewed at the beginning of that day.

*Not Distinguishing between Description and Inference*   A basic distinction in collecting data is between inference and description. A descriptive statement can be confirmed by reference to the real world. For example, if a counselor states "the teenager sat between his parents," she could point to evidence for this. An inference involves extrapolation; it cannot be confirmed or rejected without other information that is not present via observation. If this counselor said, "The youth purposely sat between his parents in order to separate them as a team" or "because of his unresolved Oedipal complex," she would be making inferences. Although distinguishing between descriptions and inferences sounds easy, in fact some clinicians may lack this skill; that is, they cannot distinguish between descriptions and inferences. This may cloud their thinking in a number of ways, including confusion between what actually happened in a situation and interpretations of what happened. For example, a clinician might say that a husband is hostile toward his wife. When asked to give examples, he may say that "He does not like her." A further question may yield "He is aggressive and punishing toward his wife." Note that we still do not have any clear example of the referents for the term *hostile*.

The difficulty of distinguishing between descriptions and inferences is shown by Abercrombie's (1960) efforts to enhance the critical thinking skills of medical students. (Her description of the diplomatic skills required to succeed in this task is fascinating.) She showed the students X-rays of two hands and asked them to list the differences between them. The students typically reported that one X-ray showed an older hand than did the other. This inference was made swiftly on the basis of certain preconceptions related to the fact that one X-ray was smaller than the other. "During the discussion it became clear that the apparently 'factual' statement that 'B is an older hand than A' is an inference which had been arrived at as a result of picking up a number of clues, calling on past experience and information which was more or less relevant, ignoring the limitations of their knowledge, and inadequately testing hypotheses to estimate the probability of their being correct. The inferences the students had made were not arrived at as a result of a series of logical steps, but swiftly and almost unconsciously. The validity of the inferences was usually not inquired into, indeed the process was usually accompanied by a feeling of certainty of being right, and consequently the discussion of incompatible views sometimes became very heated" (Abercrombie, 1960, p. 105).

*Communication Skills*   The quality of a clinician's relationship skills influence what clients share (see Chapter 2). The better such skills, the more likely clients will be to share relevant material. Thus, skill in forming positive alliances with clients influences quality of information gathered.

## DIFFERENT KINDS OF EVIDENCE

Clinicians draw on various kinds of evidence in making decisions. Each type of evidence has strengths and weaknesses in relation to accuracy.

*Real Evidence*   Actual objects may be "offered to prove their own existence or to allow an inference to be drawn from their existence" (Smith & Hunsaker, 1972, p. 112), as in circumstantial evidence described subsequently. Staff may show an attending psychiatrist broken objects in a patient's room to support their statement that the patient is "out of control."

*Hearsay Evidence*   This refers to reports that are based on what someone heard someone else say; the presenter of the information did not see the event himself, he is merely reporting what someone else told him. There are elaborate rules concerning acceptance of hearsay evidence in courts of law. Hearsay evidence is relied on extensively in clinical practice. Sources of inaccuracy include limitations in the perception of the original witness and bias on the part of the "reporter." A major problem with hearsay evidence is that the original witnesses cannot be interviewed to probe the credibility of their perceptions. Clinicians often discount sources of error in accepting hearsay evidence.

*Expert Witnesses*   An expert witness is assumed to have special knowledge concerning a particular matter, which allows her to offer well-founded, authoritative opinions (conclusions based on facts). Clinicians are often called on to testify as experts in hearings concerning child custody and allegations of sexual abuse. Weighty consequences rest on the accuracy of such testimony. Experts testify regarding psychological characteristics of a person, for example: Did they have road rage? Do they have a personality disorder? How expert such individuals really are has been the subject of many spirited discussions. Questions should be raised as to whether "experts" have knowledge that allows them to make accurate assertions (see, for example, critiques of expert testimony by Gigerenzer, 2002a, McCann, Shindler, and Hammond, 2003, Sherden, 1998, and Ziskin, 1995). The topic of expert testimony has received considerable critical attention over the past years (e.g., see Ceci & Hembrooke, 1998; Dawes, 1994a). Consider the overturning of murder convictions because of flawed expert testimony (Sally Clark, 2003). We can protect ourselves from being misled by alleged "expert testimony" by being informed about factors that influence the accuracy and reliability of such reports (e.g., see Lindsey, 2004). This also applies to eyewitness accounts. Being informed about related research should increase skepticism among all involved parties about the accuracy of such reports.

   The *Daubert v. Merrell Dow Pharmaceuticals, Inc.* (1993) ruling describes requirements for expert testimony (see also *Frye v. United States*, 1923). The American Psychological Association provides ethical codes for clinicians who serve as expert witnesses (2002). The rules of hearsay evidence are less stringent in expert testimony, in which a clinician may rely on data gathered from significant others as well as archival records. Lawyers and judges may raise questions about the reliability and validity of such evidence. Whether these questions will be profitable depends partly on whether an expert has insider knowledge that cannot be checked. For example, only a psychiatrist may have access to a patient's behavior in the hospital, or other witnesses may be present who also have insider knowledge and who may confirm or contradict the psychiatrist's testimony. The excerpts below illustrate the importance of access to insider knowledge. This hearing involved a patient who was committed for assault with intent to commit murder and for breaking and entering into an automobile (Decker, 1987). The patient was characterized as a model patient during the psychiatrist's introductory testimony. The psychiatrist's argument for recommitment was based on the patient's criminal record and "his refusal to talk about his past troubles to gain insight and emotional control" (p. 167).

> Then the public defender asked if there was "any recent history . . . of violent be-havior." Again, the psychiatrist did not answer the question but shifted to the pa-tient's reluctance to discuss the past, stating in part that . . . the fact that he (the patient) is "touchy" on any discussion of the past, you know, and sort of pushes it aside is not, you know, that favorable a symptom. People that try to gain insight do not feel vulnerable to discuss, you know, the past.
>
> The psychiatrist's responses framed the public defender's concerns as irrele-vant to the patient's disposition. At this point in the hearing, the psychiatrist was not confronted by "new facts" or an alternative construction of biography. How-ever, the psychiatrist eventually lost these advantages of "insider" knowledge over the remainder of the hearing.
>
> Following the psychiatrist's response to his question about recent violence, the public defender asked the patient if he would like to ask the psychiatrist any ques-tions. The patient began by explaining why he is "very lazy about speaking about something of the past," stating in part, "I'm more concerned about my future and how to get it structured so that I can live and cope with it. I can't cope with it con-stantly antagonizing myself and think that I have done something wrong and I must always remember it and discuss it with anyone very freely at hand."
>
> Then the patient stated that the statements in the clinical summary about past charges were wrong. The clinical summary indicated he was arrested for carry-ing a concealed weapon, but the patient said he actually "was shooting birds with a BB pistol. The weapon was not concealed. The charges were all thrown out." He also pointed out that the history of incarceration depicted in the clinical summary was inaccurate. This led to the following exchange between the psy-chiatrist and the patient:
>
> *Psychiatrist:* I'm not a lawyer.
>
> *Patient:* I realize that.
>
> *Psychiatrist:* I'm really stating what's behind. It looks very bad when you say well, "He had concealed weapons." Everyone's first thought in mind was well, "He had a .38 or a Saturday Night Special or something." This is not so. It was a BB pistol.
>
> Here the psychiatrist was not asked about the substance of the criminal record but was told. She could not gloss over the patient's revelations as irrelevant with-out reopening the earlier dialogue over the criminal record. Also, since the psy-chiatrist had already characterized the patient's hospital behavior in favorable terms—as a "model patient"—she could not readily refer to other hospital be-havior to support a theme of violence or delusional thinking without contradict-

ing her earlier testimony. Faced with this situation, the psychiatrist apparently tried to maintain—but qualify—her professional authority by placing responsibility for the accuracy of the criminal record with the legal profession.

Before terminating the hearing, the hearing officer asked the psychiatrist if she had any additional testimony to offer. The psychiatrist stated that even though she said favorable things about the patient's hospital behavior, the patient's hearing behavior (i.e., his rebuttal of the psychiatrist's testimony) demonstrated how the patient is vulnerable to sudden changes, "emotional upheaval," and the "same trigger reaction" when discussing past troubles. The hearing officer then asked if this would lead the psychiatrist to a conclusion that the patient "would be likely to injure other persons if released"—adding that "it seems that would be a long step." This led to the following exchange between the psychiatrist, hearing officer, and public defender:

*Psychiatrist:* I mean, we witnessed it. It happened before your very eyes, and with these certain situations—well, whatever they might be—he can be triggered very suddenly and unexpectedly. I cannot predict what other circumstances might produce this kind of reaction.

*Hearing Officer:* Well certainly—let's let the record be clear on this, that Mr. [patient's name] did seem agitated when talking about the previous charges, uh, which he maintains are untrue. Let me say further that by agitated, I don't think anyone in the room thought that he was going to explode and cause damage to any of us.

*Psychiatrist:* True, but nevertheless, it was such an abrupt change from the previous, very smooth general tone.

*Public Defender:* If I could comment. Uh, Mr. [patient's name] is the center of attention here. Uh, he is the subject matter and in his defense, I don't find it that irregular that he might speak a little forceful in defending himself and trying to correct, uh, what he feels are inaccuracies or untruths in a current record that concerns himself.

At that point, the hearing officer stated his agreement with the public defender and stated his [intention] to order the patient returned to court for a new disposition.

Although the psychiatrist attempted to document her earlier biographical theme of "dangerousness" by referring to the patient's hearing behavior, she could no longer rely on her privileged organizational location as a resource for this interpretative work. In this instance, other hearing participants shared direct observational knowledge of the referenced patient behavior. (Decker, 1987, pp. 167–168)

*Circumstantial Evidence*   Here, the existence of an object or the occurrence of certain circumstances provides a basis for inferring that certain facts are true. Only one person may have had an opportunity to start a fire on a certain occasion. Thus, although no one witnessed a youth starting a fire, opportunity may be used as circumstantial evidence that he is guilty.

*Reluctant Evidence*   Information may be provided under duress; that is, re-spondents may be reluctant participants in offering information. Intentional misrepresentation or denials may be offered. The circumstances under which data are collected should be considered when weighing the accuracy of data. This sounds like, and is, a truism; however, in the everyday world of clinical practice, the demand characteristics of settings in which data are collected are often overlooked.

*Factual Evidence*   This refers to potentially verifiable statements that describe people or objects. Factual evidence is descriptive rather than evaluative or ex-planatory. Statistics may be used to support a claim, or observational data de-scribing interaction may be offered.

*Firsthand Reports (Testimonials)*   Clinicians have to evaluate the accuracy of reports provided by eyewitnesses. These reports may include descriptions of facts directly witnessed by a client, as well as descriptions of opinions. The possibility of inaccurate accounts is of major concern in courts of law, in which special procedures such as cross-examination and use of multiple witnesses have been developed to reveal inaccurate accounts. Consider the following ex-ample concerning a young freelance photographer:

> Dillen's initial arrest was little more than a misunderstanding. What is significant is the fact that the arrest resulted in a mug-shot photograph of Robert Dillen in the files of the Dormont police. By chance, one investigating officer thought he noticed an uncanny resemblance between Dillen and a composite sketch made by holdup victim, Diane Jones. Several weeks after the holdup, Diane Jones was asked to look at a set of ten mug-shot photographs, one of which was Dillen's. It was Dillen's that she identified.
>
> Copies of Dillen's photographs were then sent to other police departments, where they were identified by the witnesses and victims of 13 different crimes, leading subsequently to the identification of Dillen in a live lineup by several witnesses and finally to an identification in court by a 16-year-old victim of rape and abduction. Dillen was eventually proved innocent. (Hall, Loftus, & Tousig-nant, 1984, pp. 124–25)

Errors in observation can be revealed by staging an interaction and asking wit-nesses to describe what they saw. This kind of demonstration is often used in law schools to illustrate the limitations of eyewitness testimony—a kind of tes-timony that is considered superior to other kinds of evidence. Many studies demonstrate that false memories can be created (Loftus, 2004). The accuracy of witness reports may differ because of characteristics of the event itself (such as exposure), characteristics of the witness (such as amount of stress or fear) and instructions. As Loftus (1980) points out, someone who is thinking "How can I get myself out of this situation?" (p. 32) will be less attentive to charac-teristics of faces than will someone who observes people carefully. Prior knowledge and the expectations of the witness influence what is perceived. Testimony may be discounted on faulty grounds. For example, if a person cannot recall peripheral details of an incident, his testimony regarding identification of a suspect in a lineup may be discredited, even though memory for such details is not correlated with accurate identification (Wells & Lindsay, 1983). The confidence with which memories are reported is a predictor of whether the report will be believed (but not of how accurate the report is). This confidence in turn is influenced by response biases when reporting memories. Some people have a conservative bias; they are reluctant to identify someone unless they are very sure of the identification. Other people have the opposite tendency—they act more certain than they actually are. Greater credibility is accorded to an account if a person has previously freely admitted a memory failure on another item (p. 51). Verbal qualifiers (such as "I think" or "I guess") increase skepticism on the part of listeners concerning accuracy of reports. These qualifiers are cues that a "reporter is in a state of reconstructive memory" (p. 32). The research on eyewitness testimony is relevant to the concerns of clinicians in evaluating the accuracy of reports. As we have seen, there are many paradoxes in this area—all is not what it seems. Confidence does not necessarily reflect accuracy and hesitancy does not necessarily reflect a lack of accuracy. Memory changes, false memories may be created, and the very review of its contents may create changes in our memories (see later discussion of self-report data).

## NOT FOR RESEARCHERS ALONE: CONCERNS ABOUT RELIABILITY AND VALIDITY

Concerns about validity and factors that influence this (e.g., reliability) are not confined to researchers. They are also relevant to everyday practice. If you rely on irrelevant or inaccurate measures, you may select ineffective or harmful plans because of faulty assumptions. If you rely on an inaccurate measure of social skill, you may assume incorrectly that a client has the skills required to succeed in certain situations when he does not, resulting in punishing consequences such as rejection. Method variance (use of different methods to assess a given factor) has been found to account for 50 percent of observed variation in descriptions of parenting behavior (Dishion, Burraston, & Li, 2003). Method variance can occur because of different views and reporting styles of different respondents using different methods to gather data (e.g., self-report, self-monitoring, observation). Dishion and Granic (2004) emphasize the value of naturalistic observation (observation in real-life contexts such as the playground) in decreasing misleading effects of relying on one method (e.g., self-report); "When only one method is used, one introduces a mono method bias" (p. 146; see also Cook & Campbell, 1979).

*Validity* concerns the question: Does the measure reflect the characteristic it is supposed to measure? For example, does behavior in a role-play correspond to what a client does in similar real-life situations? A measure is valid to the extent to which it reflects the concept or object it is supposed to measure. Consider, for example, the Beck Depression Inventory. To what extent does a client's score reflect his or her depression? What is the likelihood that a client who scores high on a suicide potential scale will attempt suicide in the next 6 weeks? (See discussion of the predictive value of tests in Chapter 15.) There are many different kinds of validity and it is helpful to be familiar with these (Campbell & Stanley, 1963). *Direct* (e.g., observing teacher-student interaction) in contrast to *indirect* measures (e.g., asking a student to complete a questionnaire assumed to offer information about classroom behavior) are typically more valid. Confusion sometimes arises about issues of validity and the extent to which measures from different sources offer similar accounts. Different responses (overt behavior, thoughts) may or may not be related to certain events. Clients may report being anxious but show no physiological signs of anxiety. This does not mean that their reports are inaccurate. For these individuals, the experience of anxiety may be cognitive rather than physical. Types of *validity* and *reliability* include the following:

- *Predictive validity:* This refers to the extent to which a measure accurately predicts behavior at a later time. For example, how accurately does a measure of suicidal potential predict suicide attempts?
- *Concurrent validity:* This refers to the extent to which a measure correlates with a validated measure gathered at the same time; for example, do responses on a questionnaire concerning social behavior correlate with behavior in real-life contexts? Concurrent and predictive validity are sometimes referred to as *criterion validity.* In both, scores on a measure are compared to a criterion that is assumed to be accurate. For example, scores on a self-report measure of social skill could be compared with behavior in a role-play simulation.
- *Content validity:* This reflects the degree to which a measure adequately samples the domain being assessed. For example, does an inventory used to assess parenting skills include an adequate sample of such skills?
- *Construct validity:* This term refers to the degree to which a measure successfully measures a theoretical construct—the degree to which results of a measure correspond with assumptions about the measure. The finding that depressed people report more negative thoughts on the Automatic Thoughts Questionnaire (Hollon & Kendall, 1980) compared to nondepressed people adds an increment of construct validity to this measure. Evidence should be available showing that different methods of assessing a construct (e.g., direct observation and self-report) yield similar results (convergent validity) and that similar methods of measuring *different* constructs (e.g., aggression and altruism) yield different results (discriminant validity). That is, evidence should be available that a construct can be distinguished from other different constructs. For a description of different ways in which construct validity can be explored, see, for example, Anastasi and Urbina (1996).

- *Face validity:* This term refers to the extent to which items included on a measure make sense "on the face of it." Can you accurately guess the meaning (purpose) of an item?
- *Convergent validity:* This refers to the extent to which different measures of the same construct correlate with each other. Measures of the same construct should correlate with each other.
- *Discriminant validity:* Measures of divergent constructs should not be highly correlated. For example, if a measure of depression correlates highly and positively with a measure of happiness, something is wrong.
- *Reliability:* This term refers to the consistency of results (in the absence of real change) provided by the same person at different times (time-based reliability, -stability), by two different raters of the same events (individual-based reliability, as in inter-rater reliability), or by parallel forms or split-halves of a measure (item-bound reliability). For example, the reliability of the Automatic Thoughts Questionnaire (Hollon & Kendall, 1980) could be evaluated by asking people to complete this at two different times. As noted in the discussion of eyewitness testimony, inter-rater reliability is often low. Sources of error include changes in ratings due to fatigue, lack of sufficient training, and different preconceptions. Homogeneity is a kind of item-bound reliability assessing the degree to which all the items on a test measure the same characteristics. Homogeneity of a test is important if all items are supposed to measure the same characteristics. If a scale is *multidimensional* (many dimensions are assumed to be involved in a construct, such as "loneliness" or "social support"), then homogeneity would *not* be expected.

Reliability places an upward boundary on validity. For example, if responses on a questionnaire vary from time to time (in the absence of real change), it will not be possible to use results of a measure to predict what a person will do in the future. Reliability can be assessed in a number of ways, all of which yield some measure of consistency. In test-retest reliability, the scores of the same individuals at different times are correlated with each other. Correlations may range from +1 to −1. The size of the correlation coefficient indicates the degree of association. A zero correlation indicates a complete absence of consistency. A correlation of +1 indicates a perfect positive correlation. The stability (reliability of a measure at different times) of some measures is high. That is, you can ask a client to complete a questionnaire this week and 5 weeks from now and obtain similar results (in the absence of real change). Other measures have low stability. Coefficients of reliability are usually sufficient if they are .80 or better. However, the higher the better.

The degree to which different sources provide similar or identical reports is typically used as a sign that a description is accurate. Both a husband and a wife may offer identical reports concerning the husband's drinking pattern. Both staff members in a retirement home, as well as other residents, may offer similar reports about a resident's behavior. Inconsistent reports call for further investigation; they may indicate that one or more of the sources is inaccurate. Agreement between two or more witnesses of an event is often considered indicative of accuracy; however, all these witnesses may have been influenced by a similar biasing effect that distorted the accuracy of all descriptions. For example, the appearance of a suspect in a particular lineup may influence all observers' reactions similarly (Wells, Lindsay, & Ferguson, 1979). Talking together about an event may increase agreement but not accuracy. A major concern in relation to the consistency of data is that it results in overestimation of the informativeness of material. Reliability of measures used and of psychiatric diagnosis is often low (Kutchins & Kirk, 1997). Agreement between different clinicians and agreement between different ratings of the same person at different times may be modest in other fields, such as medicine.

Other important characteristics include sensitivity, utility, and feasibility. The *sensitivity* of measures is important to consider; that is, will a measure reflect changes that occur? Insensitive measures will not offer information about progress or factors related to presenting problems. The *utility* of a measure is determined by its cost (time, effort, expense) balanced against information provided. *Feasibility* is related to utility. Some measures will not be feasible to gather. For example, clients who cannot read will not be able to complete written questionnaires. Utility may be compromised by the absence of empirically derived norms for a measure.

*Norms* offer information about the typical (or average) performance of a group of individuals. You can compare your clients' results with those of similar clients. Cut points may be used to decide whether a client is in the typical range on a given characteristic or to make predictions about future behavior. Their placement will affect the rate of false positives and false negatives. Placing people into categories based on cut-points may encourage errors, such as pathologizing clients because what is in reality a continuous dimension (e.g., number of tantrums per week), is shifted to a categorical description. Be sure to consider the representativeness of norms in relation to your client. How similar is the client to the people whose norms were obtained? Are there cultural differences? The more representative the sample is to your client, the greater the utility of the measures in relation to a client. Thus, nomothetic approaches to assessment (standardized across clients) may not offer the most accurate, relevant information for individuals. Norms may reflect low levels of hoped-for behavior (e.g., a low rate of positive feedback). They may not offer the detail needed to understand a client; what is 'anger' for a particular client? Third, they may not take account of cultural differences. Idiographic measures (those specific to an individual) may offer more accurate information—those uniquely designed for a given client.

## QUESTIONABLE ASSESSMENT METHODS

Here too, as when making decisions regarding selection of service plans, we should inquire about the evidentiary status of the method being considered in comparison with alternatives. Many tests used by professionals are pseudo-scientific; that is, that there is no evidence that they are accurate and do more good than harm; there is no evidence that they contribute to accurate assessment. If this is true, they waste money and time. If we read a claim that a measure is reliable and valid, is this true and what kind of reliability and validity were assessed? Are claims made about its usefulness sound? As readers, we should be skeptical, because limitations are often not candidly acknowledged. Criteria to consider include: (1) reliability; (2) validity; (3) sensitivity; (4) utility; (5) feasibility; and (6) relevance. A fluid understanding of reliability and validity concerns as they apply to practice methods will help you to critically appraise measures. For example, standardization in how a measure is administered and interpreted is important, not just for scientific purposes, but also to increase the accuracy with which a test is used. (See, for example, guidelines of the American Psychological Association regarding use of tests.) Rarely will you find a statement such as the following: "We only examined inter-item reliability (correlation among items). We do not know if the measure is stable. That is, we do not know whether a person who takes the inventory today, will get a different score four weeks from now in the absence of intervention."

Unstable measures cannot accurately reflect change that may result from provision of services. Thus, if a measure is unstable, feedback from the test may be misleading. It may be assumed that positive changes have occurred when there has been no change. Has the validity and reliability of a test been independently investigated? Have only the creators of a test investigated its reliability and validity? And to what extent does a measure provide accurate information about clients in real-life situations? Responsibility for gathering such evidence falls, not to those who raise questions regarding the accuracy and reliability of a measure, but to those who forward claims about it. Hunsley, Lee, and Wood (2003) describe a number of assessment techniques which they regard as questionable based on a review of related empirical literature. These tests include the Rorschach inkblot test, the Thematic Apperception Test, projective drawings, anatomically detailed dolls, and the Meyers-Briggs type indicator (see also Lilienfeld, Wood, & Garb, 2000). They conclude that the Meyers-Briggs lacks convincing validity data, although they argue that it is potentially reliable, and suggest that there are some promising uses of the TAT (p. 65).

## SOURCES OF DATA

No matter what our preferred practice framework, we have a limited number of sources of information: (1) various forms of self-report (e.g., what clients or others say, written measures), (2) self-monitoring (clients or significant others keep track of some behaviors, thoughts, feelings, or events in real-life), (3) observation in role-plays or real life, and (4) physiological measures. Case records contain information based on one or more of these sources. Each method has advantages and disadvantages and certain requisites. Some clinicians depend on self-report as their main source of information. Clinicians who supplement self-report data with observation and who are trained how to maximize the likelihood of obtaining accurate data through observation are less likely, compared to those who rely solely on self-report, to fall prey to inaccurate self-reports. Inaccurate assumptions about helpful methods may discourage their use. For example, some clinicians reject self-monitoring as a potential source of information (see later discussion) on the grounds that clients will not do it. True, some will not, but others will. As with any source of data, self-monitoring will not be suitable for all clients, and has disadvantages as well as advantages. Another source of data that is often neglected is observation of interaction between a client and his or her significant others (student and teacher, peers on a playground).

## Self-Report

Self-report gathered during interviews is the most widely used assessment method. Computerized interviewing programs have been developed for a variety of presenting problems. Self-reports may not be accurate (e.g., Dishion & Andrews, 1995; Schnelle, 1974). (See also earlier discussion of method variance.) The more specific the question is, the more likely the answer is to be correct if the responder has no reason to hide the truth. Familiarity with sources of bias and error will be helpful in reducing distortion in self-reports of events that may be obtainable no other way (e.g., see Stone et al., 1999). Disadvantages of self-report include the possibility that clients cannot provide the requested information, are not willing to provide it, or present inaccurate views. Information may not be accessible to clients. Perhaps they forgot some sequence of events or never noted a sequence of events accurately. Clients may not understand a question and so report incorrect information. Inaccurate accounts may be offered because of embarrassment over a lack of information or fear about the consequences of providing accurate accounts. Reports are influenced by clients' perception of how they are expected to behave.

*Thinking Critically about Self-Report Data*    When assessing the accuracy of self-reports consider the following questions:

- Does the situation encourage an honest answer?
- Does the client have access to the information?
- Can the client comprehend the question?
- Does the client have the verbal skills required to answer questions?
- Is the interviewer familiar with and skilled in avoiding interviewer biases?

Often, people do not accurately observe the relationship between behavior and environmental events and instead offer reports based on biased assumptions. Self-reports may tell us more about what people think they have perceived rather than about what actually happened. Weiss and Brown (1977) investigated the accuracy with which women identified factors that influenced their mood. For a 2-month period, subjects recorded their mood twice a day and also kept track of several factors that might affect mood (for example, amount of sleep, the weather, health, sexual activity, and day of the week). The subjects reported their views about the relative influence of these factors on their mood at the end of the 2-month period. Multiple regression analyses were performed on the mood score of each subject to derive objective weights for each factor. Analysis of the results indicated that there were large discrepancies between these objective weights and the average subjective weights. In fact, the overall correlation between objective and subjective weights was slightly negative. Weiss and Brown (1977) also examined data for individual subjects. This analysis revealed a similar pattern; subjects were not accurate in assessing the relative effects of certain factors on their mood; they mistook strong influences for weak ones, and weak influences for strong ones. In some cases, they failed to distinguish between positive and negative influences. This study was followed by another one in which undergraduate students were asked to estimate the impact of the same factors on a person's mood. The relative weights obtained were identical to those reported by the women in the original study. "Participants' daily experience of emotional ups and downs and their concomitants, even the daily recording of these events—gave them no advantage in estimating the correlates of their moods. These data seem inevitable given our difficulty in detecting covariations. That is, weak covariations are difficult, if not impossible, to detect in the absence of a previous theory, and illusory correlations reflecting one's theoretical biases are quite apt to be falsely 'detected'" (Nisbett & Ross, 1980, pp. 222–223).

A great deal of information is available on some subjects, such as parents' reports about the behavior of their children. For example, "Social desirability influences parental reports in terms of placing the information in a positive light, showing precocity of development, or tending to be in line with socially accepted childrearing practices" (Evans & Nelson, 1977, p. 616). Parents give different reports at different times (Brekstad, 1966), and their perceptions may shift over time in line with cultural stereotypes and popular books. Parents cited problems with "sibling rivalry" more often after Dr. Spock's (1945) book appeared (Robbins, 1963). Certainly, people have unique knowledge about themselves; what they have done in the past, and their future hopes and fears. That is, "the actor enjoys privileged access to many 'clues'" (Nisbett & Ross, 1980, p. 224), which, depending on the situation, may or may not be shared with clinicians. However, actors, like observers, are influenced by availability and representativeness of data that may or may not be related to causal importance. Research on memory offers some intriguing explanations of why clients often find it difficult to offer specific examples. One way large amounts of information can be handled is to summarize inconsistencies in experiences. A wife who has had difficulty with her husband for months or years may focus on certain regularities in her experience and relate them to a theme that represents these ("He is bad tempered"). (See other sources for more details, e.g., Baddeley, 2001; Woll, 2002.)

Repeated suggestions that a certain event occurred (when it did not) may result in inaccurate reports. For example, 58 percent of preschool children produced false stories to at least one fictitious event after 10 weeks of thinking about both real and fictitious events (Ceci, Crotteau-Huffman, Smith, & Loftus, 1994). Consider the report from Bill, a 4-year-old.

> My brother Colin was trying to get Blowtorch [an action figurine] from me, and I wouldn't let him take it from me, so he pushed me into the wood pile where the mousetrap was. And then my finger got caught in it. And then we went to the hospital. And my mommy, daddy, and Colin drove me there, to the hospital in our van, because it was far away. And the doctor put a bandage on this finger (indicating). (Ceci & Bruck, 1995, p. 219)

As this example suggests, the very process of thinking about a question may alter our memories (see also Loftus & Ketcham, 1994). Consider critiques of recovered memory therapy. Scholars such as Richard Ofshe present a compelling argument that not only may these alleged memories be false, they create havoc in people's lives, as well as in the lives of those they accuse (see Ofshe & Watters, 1994). This is not to say that all memories of past abuse are false. It is to say that some are, especially those that violate what we know about how memory works. Also, we must examine all four possible relationships between whether someone who reports being abused as a child remembers abuse, and whether it really occurred (Dawes, 1994b). This is usually *not* done, resulting in false estimates.

*The Importance of the Questions Asked.* Questions are used to clarify client statements and to refine and confirm clinical assumptions. Preferred-practice models influence choice of questions, as do other factors, such as biases and expectations about which clinicians may or may not be aware. Which questions are asked, how they are asked, and when they are asked all have an effect on the response received. The accuracy of self-reports is influenced by questions asked and characteristics of the interviewer. Familiarity with sources of interviewer bias may help you to avoid them:

- Questions or terms may be vague or ambiguous.
- A particular sequence of questions may suggest certain answers.
- Too many questions may be asked (the inquisitor).
- Unwarranted assumptions may be implicit in questions asked, as in leading questions.
- More than one question may be embedded in a single question.
- Interviewer preferences, emotional reactions, and biases may influence what is noted.
- Answers may be misunderstood.
- Recording errors may be made.

Client characteristics also influence self-reports.

- Desire to give socially desirable answers
- Lack of understanding of questions
- Faulty memory
- Anxiety
- No true opinions/preferences
- Distracted because of poor timing of interview
- Misunderstandings about the purpose of the interview

The questions you ask reflect your beliefs about what is and is not important. We tend to ask questions that confirm our beliefs. This *confirmatory bias* may result in overlooking contradictory data and alternative (more accurate) views. The response format used influences what is reported. Clients may give different reports if you ask closed-end questions calling for a "yes-no" answer than if you ask open-ended questions. Some people have an *acquiescent response set* (a tendency to say "yes"). Use of inexact adjectives such as "often" or "seldom" can give an illusion of precision and agreement that does not exist. We differ in our interpretation of vague terms such as "frequent" or "seldom" (Pepper, 1981; Teigen, & Brun, 2003).

Questions asked reflect preconceptions about clients. How questions are asked (for example, wording, order, concreteness) influences both the expression and formulation of values by affecting how we define problems, and how confident we are in our judgments (Fischhoff, Slovic, & Lichtenstein, 1980; see Exhibit 13.2). Identification of values and goals is a key concern in counseling. Given the influence of subtle social psychological processes in therapy, it could be argued that nondirective methods are the most manipulative of all methods; predispositions and preconceptions of the inquirer are unanalyzed and unshared, without even a courtesy warning of this to the respondents (p. 124). One way to overcome subtle priming effects on clients is to ask about values and goals in a variety of ways, to coax out inconsistencies that can then be clarified. This method of proceeding will be helpful in preventing an imposition of values on clients. We often do not know what we want, as suggested by the saying "Be careful what you want, because you might get it," and by research showing a marked discrepancy between what we say we want (our preferences) and the actions we take (or do not) to attain related goals. For example, thousands of people pay for advice they do not follow.

Maguire and Rutter (1976) found that medical students often avoided personal issues; accepted jargon; were imprecise in relation to dates and other key events; needlessly repeated topics; overlooked clues; failed to confront patients with inconsistencies or gaps in accounts; allowed patients to talk about irrelevant matters; often buried their heads in their notes; gave little encouragement to patients to continue talking; asked leading questions, and assumed there was only one illness. Only 10 percent of the students ended their

**Exhibit 13.2**
Ways an Elicitor May Affect a Respondent's Judgments of Value

Defining the issue

Is there a problem?

What options and consequences are relevant?

How should options and consequences be labeled?

How should values be measured?

Should the problem be decomposed?

Controlling the respondent's perspectives

Altering the salience of perspectives

Altering the importance of perspectives

Choosing the time of inquiry

Changing confidence in expressed values

Misattributing the source

Changing the apparent degree of coherence

Changing the respondent

Destroying existing perspectives

Creating perspectives

Deepening perspectives

*Source:* From *Cognitive Processes in Choice and Decision Behavior* (p. 123), edited by B. Fischhoff, P. Slovic, and S. Lichtenstein, 1980, Hillsdale, NJ: Erlbaum. Copyright 1980 by Lawrence Erlbaum Associates. Reprinted with permission.

interviews on time, and only 8 percent checked to determine if the history they had gathered was correct. Inconsistent reports on the part of clients may be due to differences among interviewers. "When two different examiners get variations in a history from the same patient, they often assume that the patient is unreliable or perverse. In many instances, however, the fault lies with the examiners, not with the patient. The differences in history may arise from many aspects of the examining procedure. Among the major sources of variability is the specificity with which details of symptoms are noted" (Feinstein, 1967, p. 318). Research concerning witness testimony indicates that allowing people to offer an open narrative account results in greater accuracy than does asking many questions. The demand characteristics of the situation (what clients think others want to hear) influence reports.

Memories may be modified during the process of an interview. Question comprehension and information retrieval through memory search are related. Alteration of memories is an integral part of comprehension because it is necessary to correct erroneous inferences and change unfulfilled expectations created during the process of understanding (Robertson, Black, & Lehnert, 1985, p. 191). This assumes that a client is trying to comprehend a question. An example of the influence of questions on memory changes is provided by a study of Loftus and Palmer (1974). Subjects watched a film of a traffic accident at an intersection; they were later asked "How fast was [the car] going when it ran the stop sign?" For some subjects, no stop sign appeared in the film. However, many of these subjects reported that they had seen a stop sign in the pictures viewed. This misleading question introduced information that was not initially available into reconstructed memory. More recent research supports the creation of false memories (e.g., Loftus, 2004). Memories are not permanent—they are altered as new information is introduced and motivations change. Each time a memory is retrieved the potential is there for substitution or alteration; "the contents of the interview may not reflect a person's earlier experience and attitudes so much as their current picture of the past" (Loftus, 1980, p. 50); "misinformation can alter memory by creating new visual memories for details that were presented only verbally" (Belli & Loftus, 1996, p. 165).

*Checklists and Personality Inventories.* Checklists and personality inventories (e.g., see Corcoran & Fischer, 2000; Hersen & Turner, 2003) are forms of self-report, and are susceptible to sources of error and bias similar to those described in the discussion of verbal reports. The use of self-report inventories typically involves the assumption that the client's report provides accurate accounts of feelings, attitudes, behaviors, and related events. In fact, they may not reflect experiences either in the past or present. The particular scale that is used to assess a client may influence decisions. For example, scales allowing only yes or no answers may yield different decisions from those that allow a wider range of answers; open interviews yield different answers from interviews using multiple-choice questions (Slovic, Fischhoff, & Lichtenstein, 1982b). Concerns about personality tests are similar to those used in educational settings. That is, tests may be used for both predictive as well as prescriptive purposes; however, they may not offer correct predictions concerning future behavior, nor may they offer guidelines about how to achieve desired outcomes (Campione, 1989). For example, test results may offer no information about the reasons for a given score, whether correct or incorrect, "healthy" or "pathological."

There may be no available normative data that allow comparison of a client with other people. Another disadvantage of checklists is their tendency to emphasize problems rather than resources (see, for example, Eyberg & Ross, 1978). Overall scores are often used to describe a client, encouraging trait conceptions that obscure the situational variability of behavior (Mischel, 1968). Personality tests, as well as intelligence tests, may be used in a "static" manner to describe a client at a given time, rather than in a "process" manner, to reflect where the client can go. Tests are subject to faking of responses (see, for example, Albert, Fox, & Kahn, 1980; Faust, Hart, & Guilmette, 1988). Problems of reliability and validity are often overlooked, and personal experiences in using tests are given greater weight than are empirical data concerning tests (Wade & Baker, 1977). Computer programs are available for administering and scoring many personality tests, including the Beck Depression Inventory and the Michigan Alcohol Screening Test. Options for enhancing the accuracy and utility of computerized testing include item branching, speech analyzers, and physiological monitoring during testing.

## Self-Monitoring

Self-monitoring, in which clients keep track of behaviors, thoughts, feelings, and the conditions related to them in real-life settings offers another potential source of information (e.g., see Bloom, Fischer, & Orme, 2003; Watson & Tharp, 2001). Depressed clients may keep track of negative thoughts as well as the situations in which they occur; clients who complain about anxiety may note the circumstances related to changes in anxiety level and rate their subjective anxiety level. Benjamin Franklin used self-monitoring to keep track of various virtues he wanted to increase, such as temperance (that is, eat not to dullness) and tranquility (that is, be not disturbed by trifles; Silverman, 1986). Handheld computers may facilitate self-monitoring. For example Newman, Consoli, and Taylor (1999) requested clients with Generalized Anxiety Disorder to gather data via handheld computers. Such data can be loaded into a desktop computer and plotted for review. Handheld computers have been used to gather data regarding other problems, such as binge eating (Greeno, Wing, & Shiffman, 2000; see also overview in Richard & Lauterbach, 2004). Advantages of self-monitoring include lack of expense, lack of intrusion by outside observers, and helping clients to explore the relationship of behaviors, thoughts, and feelings to environmental events such as the reactions of other people. Whether clients will gather information and how representative this information will be depends partly on whether a feasible data-gathering method is designed that matches client skills and opportunities and whether the client understands the procedures involved in and the purpose of monitoring.

Variables that influence the reactivity of self-recording (that is, the degree to which recording a behavior alters how often it occurs) include the motivation the client has to change a behavior and the nature of the behavior monitored. The timing of self-recording (whether it occurs before or after a behavior of concern, such as smoking) and the kind of recording device used also influence reactivity. Setting performance goals and offering reinforcement for attaining these increase the reactive effects of self-monitoring. Many steps can be taken to increase the accuracy of self-monitoring, such as clearly defining what is to be recorded. Self-anchored scales are often used to measure thoughts, feelings, and behaviors. These are individually tailored for each client. Advantages include flexibility in designing a scale that matches the unique circumstances of each client. Self-anchored scales can be used to assess events (such as urges and negative thoughts) that cannot be determined by other means. Disadvantages include lack of norms. Because these are individually constructed, no norms are available allowing comparison of the client's responses with those of others. In addition, no information may be available about reliability and validity. (For further details see Korotitsch & Nelson-Gray, 1999.)

## MONITORING THE BEHAVIOR OF SIGNIFICANT OTHERS

Another way in which assessment information may be gathered is by asking a client to observe and record behaviors of significant others. The same factors that may affect accuracy of self-monitoring may affect the accuracy of information noted about the behavior of others. If people know their behavior is being observed there may be reactive effects, as there are in self-monitoring. Another effect that may occur is a change in the observer's behavior as a result of observing someone else.

## THE USE OF STRUCTURED ANALOGUES

Analogues (role-plays) include those in which clients interact together but do so in an artificial setting (such as the office), as well as contexts in which clients participate in role-playing with someone other than a real-life participant (such as with a psychologist rather than a parent; Heyman & Slep, 2004; Kerig & Lindahl, 2004). Structured situations may be used to increase access to relevant interactions. Indeed, these may provide the most accurate and efficient way to explore interaction patterns of interest. Dismissal of such data because of concerns about faking of behavior during these tasks has been found to be unbased. Dishion and Granic (2004) observe that: "In fact, it appears that a hallmark of a disturbed relationship is the inability to fake good under the watchful eye of outside observers" (p. 145).

Advantages of the use of analogues include convenience and efficiency. Information can be gathered without going into the natural environment. The more similar the artificial situation is to real-life conditions, the more likely behavior will be representative of that in real life. Analogue situations are used both in assessment of social behaviors as well as in developing effective social skills.

## OBSERVATION IN THE NATURAL ENVIRONMENT

Advantages of observation in real-life settings include the opportunity to view clients in their natural environments. Disadvantages include cost and inconvenience, restriction of observed data to overt behavior, intrusiveness, and reactive effects of observation (that is, being observed may alter interaction). For example, when parents were aware they were being observed, they played more, were more positive in their verbal behaviors, and structured their children's activities more than when they were unaware of being observed (Zegiob, Arnold, & Forehand, 1975). Such effects are usually temporary, and many steps can be taken to increase the likelihood of gaining representative data (Hartman, Barrios, & Wood, 2004). Detailed observation of family interaction is a key data collection method used by researchers at the Oregon Research Institute in their research concerning antisocial behavior of children and adolescents (Reid, Patterson, & Snyder, 2002). The *Living in Familiar Environments* (LIFE) Coding System is used to describe both depressive and aggressive behaviors (Hops, Davis, & Longoria, 1995). The latter include behaviors indicating anger or irritability, such as yelling and verbal criticism and threats. The former include crying, looking down, and self-derogatory and complaining behaviors. These two classes of aversive behavior are viewed as distinct forms of conflict behavior (Davis, Sheeber, & Hops, 2002, p. 176).

Many clinicians are not trained how to carefully observe interaction; to identify specific behaviors, as well as related cues and consequences. We are often unaware of the ambiguity of a situation (various ways in which it could be viewed). Use of handheld computers allows coding and analysis of interaction patterns in a time-efficient manner; these can be used in a variety of settings, including at home and school (Richard & Lauterbach, 2004). Lack of training increases the likelihood of biased observation. The same objective situation may create different emotional reactions; because of different past experiences two people may see an event quite differently. Thus, gathering accurate data by observation in the natural environment usually requires training (e.g., see Hartman, Barrios, & Wood, 2004). Decisions must be made about what, when, where, how long, and whom to observe, as well as how to remain unobtrusive. The more vague the categories used to describe behaviors, the lower the reliability in coding behaviors; vague terms make it difficult or impossible for observers to agree on referents. Overlooking the value of observation contributes to the *fundamental attribution error,* in which problems are incorrectly attributed to clients' personal characteristics and related environmental circumstances are overlooked. No matter how good our reasoning skills are, if we base our decisions on inaccurate data we will be less likely to help clients. (For further information see Rosenbaum, 2002; Reid, Patterson, & Snyder, 2002.) Criteria for observing and judging observational reports suggested by Ennis (1987) include:

- Minimal inferences required
- Short time interval between observation and report
- Report by observer, rather than someone else (that is, not hearsay)
- If a report is based on a record, it is generally best that: (1) The record was close in time to the observation, (2) The record was made by the observer, (3) The record was made by the reporter, (4) The statement was believed by the reporter, either because of a prior belief in its correctness or because of a belief that the observer was habitually correct
- Corroboration
- Possibility of corroboration
- Conditions of good access
- Competent use of technology, if technology is useful
- Satisfaction by observer (and reporter, if a different person) of credibility criteria. (p. 13)

## CASE RECORDS

Case records are often consulted to gather assessment information. Deficiencies of case records include missing or vague information, a focus on pathology, and neglect of client assets. Written reports are based on one or more sources of information already discussed and so may reflect errors associated with them. Often, the source of information is not noted. If a case record states "Mrs. M. is an alcoholic," does it give the source of this information? Did the author of this report directly witness related behavior? If so, where? How often did he or she witness it? What does alcoholic mean? Clinicians are often willing to accept vague statements in case records without asking such questions. Tallent (1988) has written an engaging and valuable book on psychological report writing in which pitfalls in recording are described. As he notes, these are remarkably persistent over time. His research is based on a survey of psychologists, psychiatrists, and social workers concerning problems with psychological reports. Pitfalls in recording are divided into five categories, as described next, in the hope that being forewarned will be helpful in avoiding these limitations. After all, records take time to write and to read and have important purposes—such as facilitating clinical decisioning.

1. Problems of content include omission of essential information, inclusion of irrelevant data, and unnecessary duplication.
2. Problems of interpretation. This category refers to irresponsible interpretation, overspeculation, unlabeled speculation, and inadequate differentiation. Examples of unlabeled speculation include drawing conclusions from insufficient data, expressing theory as fact, and not relating inferences to the tests they presumably are derived from. Overspeculation is a kind of irresponsible interpretation, and seemed to irritate readers. "Facts, inferences, speculations are often mixed and not labeled" (Tallent, 1988, p. 31). "The distinctions between reasonable deduction from the data, speculative extrapolations from the data, and the psychologist's clinical impression are not clear" (p. 31). Inadequate differentiation refers to reports that deal in generalities: "They tend to present generalizations that might apply to anyone rather than to the particular individual" (p. 32): "They tend to rely on vague, psychoanalytically-oriented phrases which fail to convey an individualized picture of the client" (p. 32).
3. Problems of attitude and orientation include complaints about lack of practical use, exhibitionism, excessive authoritativeness, test oriented rather than client oriented, and overly theoretical. Concerns included the following: "A lack of humility. I never cease to be amazed by the confidence some psychologists have in their tests and in their own abilities to interpret them. To accept such reports the psychiatrist would have to lose what little intelligence he or she is supposed to have" (1988, pp. 33–34).

"They often are too theoretical or academic in language to be comprehensible or meaningful in terms of future treatment goals for the client. They occasionally give us the feeling that no client was present at the time" (1988, p. 34).

4. Problems of communication included vagueness, unnecessary length (wordiness), too technical and complex, style problems, poor organization, and hedging. Complaints included the following: "Often padded with meaningless multi-syllable words to lengthen report" (1988, p. 36). "They are too often written in a horrible psychologese—so that clients 'manifest overt aggressive hostility in an impulsive manner'—when, in fact, they punch you on the nose" (p. 36). "They suffer mainly from vagueness, double-talk and universality without enough of an attempt being made to specify more precisely what sets this person off from other people (and what does not)" (p. 37). "Too often they are so poorly organized that the reader has a difficult time to get a clear psychological picture of the client" (p. 39). "When several tests have been administered, many psychologists cannot integrate the findings without giving separate results for each test" (p. 39). "They too often are riddled with qualification—'it appears that,' 'it may well be,' 'the test reports indicate.' This is fine when speculation is being introduced, but many reports merely convey the inadequacy and timidity of the writer" (p. 39).

5. Problems of science and profession refer to criticism based on characteristics of research and professions rather than of individuals. Examples include lack of agreement as to how reports should be written, inadequate theories of behavior, and unreliability of diagnostic categories. Problems of role conduct were also mentioned: "They frequently do not mind their own business and go beyond their ken—invading territory properly allocated to the MD" (1988, p. 41). Many social workers reported that psychologists invaded the realm of the psychiatrist.

These various pitfalls become downfalls, as Tallent suggests (1988, p. 233), in the courtroom, when lawyers critique a clinician's credibility and conclusions. Problems with validity and reliability that are overlooked by clinicians are often the focus in court. Errors that are especially common include over-interpretation, omission of needed information, and hedging. Ziskin (1981) states, "I have almost invariably found the clinician's report to be a goldmine of material with which to challenge his conclusions" (quoted by Tallent, 1988, p. 233). (See also Ziskin, 1995.)

## PHYSIOLOGICAL AND BIOLOGICAL MARKERS (DNA) MEASURES

Physiological measures are often used for assessment and evaluation of progress, especially in behavioral medicine. Measures include pulse rate, blood pressure, muscle tension, respiration rates, Palmer sweat index, and urine analysis. Here, too, questions of reliability and validity are important. For example, accuracy of urine analysis in relation to drug use varies widely over different laboratories. Reports may be deliberately falsified.

## ARCHIVAL DATA

Police reports, school records, and other sources of archival data may be used. Sources of error here include missing information and changes in procedures that may result in spurious increases or decreases in reported frequency.

## DATA PROVIDED BY OTHER PROFESSIONALS

Clients may be referred to other professionals—for example, to evaluate special skills or abilities. Critically review data they provide, using the same questions you would use to review material from any source: How valid are tests used? Are inferences well reasoned? Are claims made on questionable grounds (e.g., what's usually done)? Don't be intimidated by credentials and degrees. If you are working with people who are indeed professionals, they will welcome questions about their assumptions and will take the initiative in telling you about any limitations of tests used and assumptions made.

## WEIGHING THE VALUE OF DATA

We make decisions about the value of data collected. Variables that influence judgments about the accuracy of data include recency (how recent was an observation), the source, and the capability of the source to offer the data presented. Other criteria include:

- Expertise
- Lack of conflict of interest
- Agreement among sources
- Reputation
- Use of established procedures
- Known risk to reputation
- Ability to give reasons
- Careful habits

*Reliability*   As discussed earlier in this chapter, reliability places an upward boundary on validity; a measure cannot be accurate if the responses vary inconsistency (see earlier discussion in this chapter). Claims of reliability should be accompanied by facts and figures: (What *kind* of reliability was measured? Was this appropriate? Were other kinds assessed? Were reliability ratings .80 or above?)

*Validity*   What evidence is there that a measure accurately assesses what it is purported to measure? Here too, we should be given information regarding the *kind* of validity assessed (see prior discussion), as well as facts and figures, such as the correlation between a gold standard and a measure that should be .80 or higher (for example, between role-played exchanges and a self-report instrument). Here, too, as with reliability, published reports often make claims about validity but provide no related information.

*Relevance*   "So what?" Are data collected relevant? Do they help to clarify hoped-for outcomes and related factors? Clinical decisions are influenced by irrelevant as well as by relevant data. Thus, collection of additional material is not necessarily helpful and in fact may decrease accuracy, as well as take time to gather and record (Sisson, Schoomaker, & Ross, 1976). Asking "so what?" when thinking about collecting data should help to minimize collection of irrelevant data.

*What's Missing?*   Another helpful rule is to ask "What is missing?" For example, data for all four cells in a contingency table are often missing (see Chapter 14). We tend to collect data that support our preconceptions and favored theories unless we make it a habit to explore alternative well-argued views.

Relying on the criteria just discussed will help you to select accurate, relevant data. Resist the temptation to rely on measures that are available and easy to use but are irrelevant or misleading. Compromises will often be necessary between feasibility and accuracy. You will often have to settle for measures that, although imprecise, provide helpful guidelines. You can improve accuracy by using multiple methods, relying especially on those most likely to offer accurate, relevant data. Using clinical expertise to integrate data from various sources, including information about a client's characteristics and circumstances, such as their values and preferences, is a key step in evidence-based practice. Decisions about trade-offs between harms and benefits of particular methods usually involves subjective judgments that cannot be answered solely on evidentiary grounds. (Challenges in integrating data are discussed in Chapter 11.)

## RECORDING AND STORING INFORMATION

Clinicians are required to keep records, and, depending on where they work, may spend considerable time "recording." Lapses in memory highlight the value of records. The importance of case records is affirmed by court rulings that inadequate records hinder the development of treatment plans (see, for example, *Whitree v. New York State*, 1968). Records are helpful to the extent to which they fulfill the purposes of recording: These include administrative, case planning, and supervisory functions. For example, they may be used in audits of process and outcome (Øvretveit, 1995). Information should be easy

**Exhibit 13.3**
Quality Check of Psychological Reports

|  | Yes | No |
|---|---|---|
| 1. Does the report meet all responsibilities, ethical and legal, to the client, and community, and (as applicable), to other professionals and agencies? | ☐ | ☐ |
| 2. Is material up-to-date? | ☐ | ☐ |
| 3. Are presenting concerns and how the client arrived at your office clearly described (for example who referred the client)? | ☐ | ☐ |
| 4. Are clear examples of client concerns and related circumstances included? | ☐ | ☐ |
| 5. Are sources of assessment data relied on clearly described? | ☐ | ☐ |
| 6. Is the evidentiary status of assessment and intervention methods used clearly described? | ☐ | ☐ |
| 7. Are hoped-for outcomes clearly described? | ☐ | ☐ |
| 8. Are conclusions supported by data? | ☐ | ☐ |
| 9. Are measures used to describe progress clear and relevant? | ☐ | ☐ |
| 10. Does the record include clear description of degree of progress? | ☐ | ☐ |
| 11. Is speculation within reason? | ☐ | ☐ |
| 12. Is speculation labeled as such? | ☐ | ☐ |
| 13. Is there an absence of jargon, stereotypes, overly technical, or complex language? | ☐ | ☐ |
| 14. Is language used clear and unambiguous? | ☐ | ☐ |
| 15. Is the report concise and well organized? | ☐ | ☐ |
| 16. Are uninformative labels avoided? | ☐ | ☐ |
| 17. Is important information missing? | ☐ | ☐ |

*Source:* Items 1, 8, and 11–14 from *Psychological Report Writing* (3rd ed., p. 244), by N. Tallent, 1988, Englewood Cliffs, NJ: Prentice Hall. Copyright 1988 by Prentice Hall.

to locate. Information retrieval skills are vital to evidence-based practice to gain swift access to information needed in case records (for example, about progress) as well as access to research findings related to important decisions that must be made. Well-designed forms permit ready location of material as well as reminders to include helpful data. Computerized recording is becoming common. Problems with case records were discussed in a previous section. Guidelines for recording are offered in Exhibit 13.3.

## SUMMARY

Gathering data is a key step in clinical decision making. Decisions are made about what data to collect, how to gather data, and when to stop. Sources of information include self-report, self-monitoring, observation (in interviews, analogue situations, or in real life), personality inventories, physiological measures, and case records. Each source has advantages and disadvantages.

Familiarity with the strengths and weaknesses of each will be helpful in selecting those which offer accurate data. Some clinicians confine their attention to self-report, forgoing other valuable sources such as self-monitoring and observation in real-life settings that may correct biases in self-report data.

Practice theories guide how client concerns are viewed, which in turn affects what data are gathered. We are influenced by our preconceptions and by the vividness of data; we often pay undue attention to data that are vivid and ignore material that does not have this quality yet nevertheless may be helpful. Broad generalizations may be based on small samples, reflecting an insensitivity to the size of the samples on which inferences are based. Many studies highlight the difficulty of distinguishing between inferences and descriptions; when descriptions are asked for, inferences are often offered. Clinicians often gather too much data, and they tend to be overly confident of the accuracy of data gathered and assumptions made. Combining data from different sources is a challenge. Taking advantage of related research findings regarding the accuracy of different sources, including errors associated with different kinds of data, will be helpful in avoiding errors. The value of data is related to its reliability, validity, and completeness. As in other problem-solving situations, "what's missing" may not be obvious—but may be critical in understanding client concerns and potential for change.

# CHAPTER 14

# Discovering Causes of Clients' Problems: Common Biases

C LINICAL PRACTICE REQUIRES making judgments about the causes of clients' concerns. Assessment is integrally related to intervention; that is, how concerns are structured and what causal factors are assumed to be important should influence selection of intervention methods. Indeed, if plans are not successful, assessment errors could be a reason. Cues that may be used to infer causality include temporal order, contiguity in time and space, similarity of cause and effect, covariation, and availability of alternative possibilities (Einhorn & Hogarth, 1986). The presumed cause must occur before the presumed effect; the correlation must be consistent; and it must be shown that a third variable is not responsible for the relationship between the two variables. Attention to only one of these conditions can result in post hoc reasoning—the assumption that because one event follows another, it is caused by it (the post hoc ergo proc fallacy—or the fallacy of the consequent). Haynes (1992) argues that *constant conjunction* (two events always occur together) is not applicable to the social sciences because of the complexity of causes related to behavior; past events may influence current behaviors (Haynes & O'Brien, 2000). Variables related to client concerns may be *necessary* (a condition that must be present if the effect occurs), *sufficient* (a condition that by itself will bring about change), or *necessary* and *sufficient* (a condition that must be present for an effect to occur and one that by itself will bring about an effect). Assessment is an ongoing feature of clinical practice; additional information concerning causal factors usually is gained as counseling proceeds. Additional data may or may not require changes in intervention decisions. Focusing on incorrect causes of a problem such as depression will result in cutting off a search for alternative explanations and may result in no improvement or even a worsening of the situation. Consider the client who complained about abdominal pains at bedtime (Valins & Nisbett, 1972). The therapist interpreted these as pains related to sexual anxiety. As a result, the client became concerned about her emotional stability. Her anxiety and her negative image of herself increased. Later, a relative suggested that her pain might be caused by an allergic reaction to tomatoes; the client stopped eating tomatoes, and the pains disappeared.

The history of public health, medicine, psychiatry, and psychology is strewn with fascinating examples of skilled (and not so skilled) detective work in the identification of causes. Consider the assumption that dyslexia was a medical problem. "In all likelihood, nothing has done more to hinder the scientific study of reading disability than unwarranted popularization of medical explanations for the condition. It has taken this field decades to rid itself of the many incorrect physiological explanations that sprouted from the few uncontrolled case studies that were at one time introduced into the medical literature" (Stanovich, 1986, p. 169). The time lag between identification of a causative factor and acceptance of this information is often discouragingly long. Consider the lag in implementing knowledge that scurvy could be prevented by eating citrus fruit (Carpenter, 1986) or that fatal infections could be avoided by having physicians wash their hands after examining each patient (Sinclair, 1909). Consider also the belief that tuberculosis was inherited.

Elstein and his colleagues (1978) found that physicians generated hypotheses early in the process of thinking about a problem, and that only a few were considered. Expert physicians use only factors considered particularly relevant about a case; they restrict their attention to a relatively small model (Kuipers & Kassirer, 1984). Research describing how decisions are made in the natural environment (e.g., Zsambok & Klein, 1997) shows that experts in an area do not review a variety of alternatives before reaching a decision; they quickly arrive at an option based on situation awareness (on the recognition of patterns) as discussed in Chapter 9. However, in novel situations in which an option is not readily obvious, a process of problem solving may be required. Such research raises questions about programs that recommend a long search in order to locate helpful strategies. The implications of such findings is not that long searches are bad per se, but that they do not account for expertise in an area and may not improve performance (Perkins, 1985). This should be reassuring to clinicians who must make decisions in a timely manner without all the evidence that might be desirable. Causal rules derived from practice knowledge may be used to identify relationship between variables. Our background knowledge influences the accuracy of the rules we use.

## CHALLENGES

Clients often have multiple problems that are interrelated in a variety of ways. Such interrelationships may change in accordance with different people in different situations. The same form or structure of behavior may be due to quite different functions (be maintained by different contingencies). A given problem may develop via different pathways and manifest itself in a variety of ways (see Exhibit 14.1). (For a detailed discussion of the complexity of causal relationships see Haynes, 1992, and Haynes & O'Brien, 2000.) A given cause

**Exhibit 14.1**
A Model Illustrating Extended Systems Variables Affecting a Child's Behavior Problems

*Source:* From *Principles and Practice of Behavioral Assessment* (p. 188), by S. N. Haynes and W. H. O'Brien, 2000, New York: Kluwer Academic/Plenum Publishers. Reprinted with permission.

may affect behavior differently at different times and places. Rarely can we point to necessary and sufficient conditions related to problems. Contributory causes often come into play that create the total set of conditions necessary and sufficient for an effect. The strength of causal variables differs among individuals with the same concerns. People differ on

- The number of variables, which influence a behavior.
- Variables that influence the onset, magnitude, and duration of behavior.
- The relative strength of individual causal variables.
- The role of mediating variables.
- Predispositions and vulnerability to particular events.
- The setting generality of causal relationships.
- The paths through which causal effects occur. (Haynes, 1992, p. 108)

Ideally, intervention should focus on key causal variables. This requires estimating the weights of different factors. Identification of causes is not necessarily explanatory; that is, the cause of an illness (such as cancer) may be known, and the symptoms and associated pathology may be identifiable, but the etiology may not be understood. Thus, causes differ in the level of explanatory completeness they offer. People use different criteria to decide when an explanation is at hand (e.g., it allows accurate prediction—it "makes sense"; see Chapters 3 and 4). What is best depends on your purpose. The goal of helping clients highlights the value of explanations that help us to select plans that result in hoped-for outcomes. Beliefs about causes differ in the extent to which they are compatible with empirical findings about behavior; for instance, claims of "levitation" (the ability to float in the air) are not compatible with the laws of gravity. Causes may be difficult to identify because of a lag in effect, as between smoking and the development of lung cancer.

The causal rules derived from practice knowledge may not be accessible to awareness or correctly derived from a theory. Clinicians differ in their knowledge base, which influences the accuracy of the strategies they use. For example, Patel and Groen (1986) presented a case to seven specialists in cardiology and asked them to describe the underlying pathophysiology and to provide a diagnosis. The four physicians who arrived at the correct diagnosis used a different set of production rules than did the three physicians who did not find the correct diagnosis. Identifying the causes of behavior is difficult because (1) they may be unknown, (2) they occur at different levels (e.g., physiological, psychological, sociological), (3) they interact in complex or simple ways, (4) they change over time, and (5) they are influenced by chance occurrences (Haynes, 1992). Assessment requires the integration of diverse sources of data, which is difficult. Different aspects of a concern (onset, duration, intensity) may be influenced by different causes.

## DIFFERENT PRACTICE PERSPECTIVES EMPHASIZE DIFFERENT CAUSES

Assumptions about the causes associated with problems are influenced by practice theories; these theories guide selection and organization of material. If a theory stresses the importance of personal characteristics, environmental variables may be neglected. Explanations differ in the system level(s) to which they appeal (e.g., biological, psychological, sociological) and how integrative they are (the extent to which relationships among different causes are recognized) (see Exhibit 14.2). Contextual theories encourage a broad search for causes, including attention to the role of significant others (individuals who influence clients) and community characteristics (e.g., see Gambrill, 2006). For example, Wahler (1980) found that the nature of a mother's social contacts outside the home influenced the quality of her interaction with her children at home. Reid, Patterson, and Snyder (2002) describe the effect of environmental factors such as poverty on family interaction patterns and resulting behaviors, such as antisocial behavior of children and adolescents. An ecological view of excessive alcohol use would entail far more than a description of individual characteristics that may encourage related behaviors. A given theory may be applied to an increasing range of concerns over time, even though it may not be the most appropriate one in these many instances. Seeking information about the effectiveness of a theory in helping clients should decrease this tendency.

**Exhibit 14.2**
Ways in Which Theories of Behavior Differ

---

Degree to which behavior is viewed as knowable.

Goals pursued (e.g., explanation and interpretation alone, understanding based on prediction and influence).

Criteria used to evaluate claims (e.g., tradition, consensus, scientific).

Range of problems addressed with success.

Causal importance attributed to psychological factors (e.g., feelings/thoughts).

Causal importance attributed to biomedical factors (e.g., genetic and/or brain differences.)

Attention devoted to evolutionary influences.

Importance attributed to developmental stages.

Range of environmental factors considered (e.g., family, community, society).

Importance attributed to past experiences.

Degree of optimism about how much change is possible.

Degree to which related assumptions can be critically tested.

Degree of empirical support (evidence for and against a theory).

---

*Note:* The terms *explanation* and *theory* are used interchangeably.

Different views of behavior have different consequences in relation to how people are treated. Controversies include the relative importance attributed to biological, psychological, and environmental factors, and how the "environment" is defined. Consider different views concerning the cause of ADHD. Some investigators assume that related causes are based in the brain (Barkley et al., 2002). Others argue that disturbing behaviors on the part of children are due to changes in work and family life, such as less time spent by parents with their children and dulling school environments (Timimi & Taylor, 2004). These views have different intervention implications (e.g., medication compared to altering environmental circumstances). Some systems and beliefs are institutionalized in a society and have been referred to as "grand narratives"—for example, the great religions of the world, major political ideologies, such as capitalism, and biomedicine (Davey & Seale, 2002). There is general agreement that behavior varies, that it is influenced by a variety of variables, that it can be analyzed at different levels (e.g., physiological, psychological, sociological) and that there is a great deal of individual variation in response to different environmental risks, resulting in different degrees of vulnerability and resilience. Examples of variables that may come into play include temperamental and other genetic influences, past experiences, risk experiences and how we view them, protective features that counteract risks, and later circumstances. Views that emphasize the interaction among genes, organisms, and their environments differ in how reciprocal these relationships are assumed to be and in the range of environmental events considered.

A biomedical grand narrative dominates practice in many areas. The client is viewed as having an illness (mental) in need of a diagnosis and treatment. Hallmarks of a "disease" include a known etiology (cause), a predictable course, and a progression in severity if left untreated. Factors focused on may include biochemical changes, brain damage, and genetic differences (e.g., see Conrad, 2001). Beliefs that "something in the blood" or "something in the food" is related to mental illness have a long history and are reflected in current treatments, some of which are of dubious value (Skrabanek, 1990). The finding of biochemical abnormalities related to certain behavior patterns only establishes that abnormalities in biochemistry are present, not that they cause the behavior. (See also critiques of neuroimaging methods, Leo & Cohen, 2003.) And the finding that medication decreases anxiety or depression does not show that biomedical factors are responsible for anxiety and depression. Mirowsky and Ross (1989) argue that biochemical changes may result from stress caused by limited opportunities due to discrimination. In 1999 the U.S. Surgeon General concluded that there was no anatomical, biochemical, or functional sign that reliably distinguishes between the brains of mental patients and those of others. Physical abnormalities in the brain are often assumed to be responsible for certain kinds of troubled or troubling behavior. Even when brain damage can be detected, it does not necessarily indicate that it causes any particular behavioral pattern. Problems with these kinds of explanations include limited intervention knowledge and predictive validity.

> To say that Rachel can't walk, talk, or feed herself because she is retarded tells us nothing about the conditions under which Rachel might learn to perform these behaviors. . . . Even apparently constitutional differences in temperament are so vulnerable to environmental influences as to provide only limited information about how a child is apt to behave under given conditions. (Alberto & Troutman, 1990, p. 9)

Premature acceptance of one kind of explanation interferes with discovering alternative well-argued views that yield intervention knowledge. Alberto and Troutman (2002) argue that biophysical explanations give teachers excuses not to teach. It is not that such explanations are not accurate, but that they often are incomplete. For instance, environmental factors may also be important. (For a critique of biomedical approaches to deviant behavior, see Boyle, 2002; Gorenstein, 1992.)

Currently there is great interest in searching for genetic markers for physical and psychological signs and symptoms. Some argue that genotype (genetic makeup) can never be separated from phenotype (visible characteristics that result from the interaction between the genotype and the environment), because both the environment and random developmental factors affect how genotype is expressed (Lewontin, 1991, 1995; Strohman, 2003). People with a common genetic history often share a similar environmental history. Even when a genetic influence is found, it may account for only a small portion of the variance in understanding a problem or behavior. Although many people accept the findings of twin studies purporting to show a strong hereditary component to developing schizophrenia, others do not, pointing out methodological flaws (see for example Boyle, 2002).

> Certainly genes are essential for defining any phenotype but by themselves they remain just inert materials. In order for genetic information to be replicated or "decoded" and used to assemble phenotypes, the DNA must first be manipulated by systems of enzymes and small molecules that constitute the efficient cause for constructing phenotypes. Nearly all biologists now acknowledge that reality—an *epigenetic* system, so named because of its ability to activate and silence elements of DNA and thereby to produce specific patterns of gene expression and proteins in a context-dependent (time and place) manner. (Strohman, 2003, p. 190)

In developmental explanations there is an "unfolding" metaphor, in which the role of internal characteristics is emphasized (e.g., see Sameroff, Lewis, & Miller, 2000). The term *development* refers to "the process of continual change during the lifetime of an organism" (Lewontin, 1995, p. 121). Some argue that what are viewed as developmental changes in fact reflect changing environments. Variables such as age and social class are "marker variables" that correlate with many problems but do not explain them or provide service guidelines (Baer, 1984, 1987). The similarities of circumstances for many people at a given age in a society may lead one to assume (incorrectly) that biological development is responsible, overlooking the role of similar contingencies. Acceptance of a stage theory of development may get in the way of identifying environmental factors that can be rearranged. That is, it may be incorrectly assumed that a person "is stuck" in a given stage and there is nothing to do but wait for time to pass. Some scholars suggest that acceptance of Piagetian stages resulted in withholding valuable learning experiences from children, on the grounds that they were "not ready."

Psychoanalytic views emphasize the role of early childhood experiences and related unconscious influences on behavior, thoughts, and feelings. In cognitive explanations, a causal role is attributed to thoughts. There is an interest in identifying and altering mental events such as expectations, schemas (views of the self and world), and attributions. In behavioral views, including social learning theory, actions, thoughts, and feelings are considered to be largely a function of our learning history. Varied social histories result in a wide range of behavior. Thus, behavior always "makes sense." Behavior that may seem quite bizarre typically serves adaptive functions, but only when contingencies of reinforcement (relationships between behaviors and their consequences) are clarified may they become apparent. Biochemical and genetic influences are assumed to play a role; however, their interaction with learning variables is emphasized. Variations in behavioral views reflect different assumptions about the causes of behavior and what intervention should focus on (e.g., thoughts and/or environmental factors), and also different preferred methodologies (the intensive study of individuals or the study of group differences). Social learning theory (Bandura, 1986) accepts cognitive explanations, in contrast to applied behavior analysis and behavioral approaches emphasizing changes in learning histories as explanatory. In social learning theory it is assumed that we present an important part of our environment through our expectations, goals, and standards. Thoughts are considered to play an important role in the complex processes that affect attention and in the degree to which different kinds of interventions are effective. In a radical behavioral view, rather than appealing to feelings and thoughts as explanations for behavior, they are viewed as requiring explanation themselves.

Lewontin (1994) emphasizes the importance of examining the "metaphors" we use to think about behavior, such as potential, fitness, development, and adaptation. He contends that common metaphors such as *potential* and *innate capacity* are wrong. "There are differences among genotypes, with different consequences in different environments, but there is no way in general, over environments, to rate these innate or intrinsic properties from 'bad' to 'good,' 'high' to 'low,' 'small' to 'big.' There is complete environmental contingency" (1994, p. 19). Furthermore, we play a great role in creating our environments. Lewontin notes that the metaphor of adaptation implies that there is an autonomously determined world to which we change in order to fit. He suggests that based on what little we know about genes, organisms, and environment, a more accurate metaphor is that of construction. "If we want to understand evolution, we must understand it as construction because the actual situation is that organisms make their own environments. They define them. They create them. They change them. They interpret them" (1994, p. 36).

## ASSESSING COVARIATIONS

Clinical assessment involves the description of covariations among behaviors, environmental events, or personality traits, depending on preferred practice model. You may note that only when a client fails to state her preferences in a number of social exchanges do angry outbursts occur. We have beliefs (which may or may not be correct) about what kind of traits go together. A clinician may believe that dependent people have a high need for social approval. Beliefs about covariations (what events tend to go together) influence selection of presumed causes, and beliefs about causes influence judgment of covariations. Assumptions about the strength of association between variables is influenced by their correlation as well as by the implied causal clues in how variables are labeled (Einhorn & Hogarth, 1985). For example, when people were asked to assess the relationship between two variables on a scatterplot, the correlation had to be high to enable a relationship to be perceived (Jennings, Amabile, & Ross, 1982). However, when variables were given labels, the degree of correlation required to see a relationship was much lower.

Confusions between covariation and causation are often easy to spot. That both swimming and ice cream consumption increase in the summer does not mean that one leads to the other. Mistaken assumptions of covariations may not be so easy to spot if they complement beliefs about what events go together, as in the assumption that parental substance abuse will result in similar behavior on the part of their children. In the first example, there is no cultural or professional belief to support a causal relationship between ice cream consumption and swimming. In the second example, representativeness (the tendency to make judgments based on similarity) may influence judgment and result in an overestimate of the correlation between two similar events and the assumption of a causal connection. The history of science is a fascinating compendium of faulty assumptions of causal effects based on correlations. Even the great British statistician Pearson assumed that a correlation of .50 between a parent's tendency to develop tuberculosis and his or her children's tendency to contract tuberculosis reflected evidence for a hereditary cause of this disease (Blum, 1978). Another example of confusion between covariations and causation can be seen in superstitious behavior. A client may be convinced, for example, that because she had a dream that her mother would die, she is in some way responsible for the death of her mother, which happened shortly after the dream. Thus, mistaken assumptions about covariations may result in incorrect causal assumptions as reflected in superstitious beliefs, including those related to the effectiveness of the services we offer.

Terms that describe personality traits, such as *dependent* and *aggressive*, supposedly convey information about the consistency of behavior. The search for cross-situational behavioral dispositions has been disappointing. Hypothesized traits often account for a small proportion of individual differences (Mischel, 1968, 1973); method variance may be larger than person variance. That is, differences found may be more a result of different methods used to describe events (self-report and observation) than a reflection of differences in behaviors. (See also Mischel, Shoda, & Mendoza-Denton, 2002.)

## THE INFLUENCE OF PRECONCEPTIONS/PRACTICE THEORIES

Assumed covariations are influenced by preconceptions about the origins of given behaviors that may have no relation to the true level of covariation of two events. Practice theories are one important source of preconceptions. Clinicians selectively attend to factors that are compatible with their favored practice theory. A clinician favoring cognitive accounts who interviews a depressed woman will attend to her thoughts—what she says to herself. A clinician who emphasizes the role of environmental contingencies will gather information about what the client does; what events she enjoys; what recent changes have occurred in the frequency of these events, and recent factors in her life that may relate to a change in pleasant events. A psychiatrist who favors medical explanations may emphasize a client's medication regime—

what medication she is taking (if any), and what changes should be made. A psychoanalytic clinician might concentrate on exploring her past, searching for material that may relate to current complaints. Knowledge about research findings pertinent to client complaints will influence what questions are asked, what is noticed, and therefore what data are at hand when assessing co-variations and making causal analyses. Thus, we are influenced by the avail-ability of material as well as by representativeness—beliefs about what goes together. Lack of knowledge about the relationship between certain signs and underlying causes may result in incorrect decisions.

## ILLUSORY CORRELATIONS

The influence of preconceptions is highlighted by research on illusory cor-relations. Clinicians tend to overestimate the degree of covariation between variables, resulting in illusions of validity and reliability. Studies by Chapman and Chapman (1967, 1969) illustrate that expectations based on theories and semantic associations overwhelm the influence of data that do not match these expectations or even refutes them. They started with the question of how cli-nicians can persist in reporting associations between certain responses on pro-jective tests and specific clinical symptoms, when research has shown that there is little or no association between these signs and symptoms. In one study, the reports of 32 practicing clinicians who analyzed the Rorschach pro-tocols of homosexual men were reviewed (1969). These clinicians listed signs that had face validity but were empirically invalid as responses characteristic of homosexual men. That is, they selected signs based on "what seemed to go together"—on what ought to exist—rather than on empirically determined associations between signs and the criteria. Clinicians were more likely to re-port illusory correlations than were lay observers.

Illusory correlations are influenced by assumptions about what goes together: "Everyone possesses what might be called 'data' on the degree of co-variation between various socially relevant dimensions and behavior dimen-sions, but the data are usually skimpy, hit-or-miss, vague, and subject to bias and distortion in both encoding and recall" (Nisbett & Ross, 1980, p. 98). We tend to overestimate the size of correlations between factors we believe go together and to underestimate the degree of covariation when we do not have any preconceptions about the relationship between two or more factors (Jen-nings, Amabile, & Ross, 1982). Incorrect estimates often persist in spite of first-hand experience with data that do not confirm them. For example, a clinician may insist that a woman is schizophrenic because she was once labeled a schizophrenic, even though no evidence obtained for the past 3 years supports this diagnosis. This tendency is increased by the confirmation bias (not at-tending to data that do not support a position—ignoring negative instances) and not reviewing all four cells of a contingency table (see later discussion). Clinicians who believe that behavior is determined mostly by personal char-acteristics will be less likely to notice correlations between environmental factors and behavior. Some researchers have been so struck with our limited ability to use correlation appropriately in making decisions that they believe that we lack an intuitive concept of correlation (Shweder, 1977) and that we tend to blur the distinction between likeness and co-occurrence. This blurring is at the heart of the representative heuristic—the tendency to be influenced by the similarity of events. Consider, for example, that, when people were asked to make estimates of the relative frequency of tense and tolerant people (Shweder, 1977), one person estimated that of 100 people, 70 individuals would be tense and 75 would be tolerant. When asked about co-occurrence, the subject estimated that 10 percent (7) of the people who are tense would be tolerant. "Given the earlier estimate of the judge that 75 persons out of 100 are tolerant, it follows that 68 (75 minus 7) must be both tolerant and *not tense*. This is a contradiction. The judge first claims that only 30 persons out of 100 are *not tense*. Then she makes a conditional-probability estimate that requires that there actually be at least 68 (out of 100) who are *not tense*" (p. 643). Others argue that such research does not reflect real-life circumstances and that given the proper experience, fast and frugal strategies based on the recognition heuristic are quite effective in helping us make rapid, good decisions most of the time (see Chapter 9).

Expectations of consistency encourage illusory correlations. That is, we tend to assume that people behave in trait-consistent ways when, in fact, correlations between personality traits and behavior are relatively low. One reason for this is that "we tend to see most people in a limited number of roles and situations and thus are exposed to a more consistent sample of behavior than we would obtain from a true random sample of a person's behavioral repertoire" (Nisbett & Ross, 1980, p. 107; see also discussion of actor-observer differences in Chapter 9). Apparent discrepancy is readily explained away. Subjective feelings of control are enhanced by the belief that other people are consistent in their traits and thus are predictable. So, we are not very good at detecting covariations based on experience unless the experience has provided corrective feedback (see Chapter 8). This highlights the importance of arranging feedback about our assumptions as well as the importance of helpful theories. As Nisbett and Ross (1980) note, the ability to detect covariations in specific domains may be greater because we have more opportunities to observe such covariation. Take, for example, the relation between making certain changes in steering when driving a car. In this situation, we benefit from immediate feedback about the effects of our actions. Experience offers an opportunity to observe covariations and thus may help to correct the influence of inaccurate preconceptions in relation to what "ought" to go together. (See discussion of "fast and frugal" heuristics in Chapter 9.) However, if preconceptions are rigid and feedback is vague or irrelevant, experience may do little to change incorrect notions, especially in areas such as clinical practice, in which indicators of progress are often vague and not agreed upon and practice often is not systematically monitored (see also discussion of experience in Chapters 4 and 8).

## Misunderstanding Probabilities

People tend to focus on "hits" when estimating covariation; negative instances tend to be disregarded. Consider the belief that there is a relationship between worry about an event and the event occurring. Parents may worry about their teenage children arriving home safely, without getting in a car accident. So, if a mother worries and then her daughter is involved in an accident, the mother (as well as the press) may attribute this coincidence to clairvoyance or some other mystical power. Headlines may read: "Mother Worries—Daughter Injured." As Jensen (1989) notes, only the "hits" (worry followed by accident) receive attention; false alarms, misses, and correct rejections are ignored. In fact, no judgment of association can legitimately be made without considering all four of the possibilities illustrated in Exhibit 14.3. The risk of an accident if the mother worried would have to be compared to the risk in the absence of worry. In assessing covariations, pointing only to particular cases is misleading. The tendency to discount negative instances is responsible for beliefs in suspect causes such as prayer and worry. People who say that their prayers are answered may not pay attention to times when their prayers were not answered. That is, they may not keep track of *all* the times they prayed, noting the outcome of each. "Answered prayers" are more vivid—they may say, "What a coincidence." The confirmation bias (the tendency to selectively search only for evidence that supports preconceptions) encourages a focus on hits. (See Roberts, Ahmed, & Hall, 2004.)

In clinical practice, covariations (and thus causal relationships) often are assumed between certain personal and environmental characteristics (for example, personality traits or recent life changes and problems), and also between certain symptoms and diagnostic categories (for example, between

**Exhibit 14.3**
Contingency Table

|  |  | Worry | |
| --- | --- | --- | --- |
|  |  | Yes | No |
| Accident | Yes | Hit (Correct Positive) (a) | Miss (Incorrect Negative) (b) |
|  | No | False Alarm (Incorrect Positive) (c) | Correct Rejection (Correct Negative) (d) |

*Source:* Based on Jensen (1989, p. 158). Pathologies of science, precognition and modern psychophysics. *The Skeptical Inquirer*, 13, 147–160. Reprinted with permission.

**Exhibit 14.4**

Correlation-Relevant Frequency Information on the Relationship between a Hypothetical Symptom and a Hypothetical Disease in 100 Hypothetical Patients

|  |  | Disease | | |
|---|---|---|---|---|
|  |  | Present | Absent | Total |
| Symptoms | Present | 37 | 33 | 70 |
|  | Absent | 17 | 13 | 30 |
|  | Total | 54 | 46 |  |

*Source:* Based on Smedslund (1963).

vigilance and scanning and Generalized Anxiety Disorder). Decisions about the association between variables often are made without considering the necessary probabilities. The result is overestimation of pathology. The use of the terms *symptom* and *disease* in this section does not imply acceptance of a biomedical model of personal problems. These terms are used here because many clinicians use this grand narrative to understand psychological problems. The *DSM-IV-R* (*Diagnostic and Statistical Manual of Mental Disorders*, 2000) is based on the assumption that the hundreds of problems described in this source reflect a "mental disorder" (McReynolds, 1989). Considerable data on the diagnostic value of some medical tests are available. Even when such data are available this is often overlooked, resulting in incorrect decisions. Consider overestimates of the accuracy of screening tests (e.g., Thornton, Edwards, and Baum, 2003). Smedslund (1963) found that nurses tended to focus on joint occurrences of symptom and disease when they were asked to determine whether there was a relationship between symptoms and the disease. Each nurse received a pack of 100 cards, which supposedly depicted excerpts from the files of 100 patients. The presence or absence of the symptom and the presence or absence of the disease were noted on each card in the ratios shown in Exhibit 14.4. Eighty-five percent of the nurses said that there was a relationship between the symptoms and the disease, and most justified their claims by noting the number of cards in which both the symptom and the disease were present (37); that is, they tended to focus on joint occurrences of symptom and disease and to ignore other combinations.

The probability of A given B is usually not equal to the probability of B given A. For example, the probability of being a male if a person is a head of state is quite different than the probability of being a head of state if a person is a male (Bar-Hillel, 1983). The probability of being a chronic smoker if a person develops lung cancer is about .99; the probability of developing lung cancer if a person is a chronic smoker is .10 (people probably die of something else first; Dawes, 1982, p. 42). Not distinguishing between two such probabilities is known as "the confusion of the inverse."

**Exhibit 14.5**
Venn Diagram to Summarize the Judgment Situation (Sample Space) to Answer Questions
about the Probability That a Pot Smoker Is Also a Hard Drug User

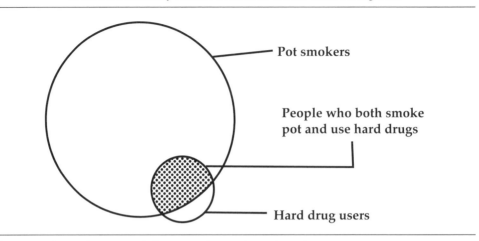

*Source:* Hastie and Dawes (2001). Reprinted with permission (p. 184).

Another source of incorrect estimates is not distinguishing between compound probabilities (the probability of this and that) and conditional probabilities (the probability of this given that). A second principle is as follows: $P(A \mid B)$ = $P(A,B)/P(B)$. "Simple, and hence conditional, probabilities can be inferred from compound probabilities, but not vice versa. But compound probabilities can be inferred via principle 2 only when both conditional and simple probabilities are known. If just simple or just conditional probabilities are known, however, no other type of probability can be inferred" (Dawes, 1982, pp. 43–44). Consider the probability of being addicted to heroin (A) if a person smokes marijuana (B). This equals the probability of being addicted both to heroin and smoking marijuana (A,B) divided by the probability of smoking marijuana (B). "It is decidedly not *equal* to $P(A,B)/P(A)$— the probability of both smoking pot and being addicted divided by the probability of being addicted; hence the fact that most heroin addicts (A) also smoke pot (A,B) is an irrational justification for draconian marijuana laws" (Dawes, 1982, p. 43; see Exhibit 14.5).

A third principle is that "the probability of a symptom is equal to the compound probability of the symptom and the disease plus the compound probability of the symptom without the disease: $P(S) = P(S,D) + P(S, \overline{D})$. Dawes uses the example that "the probability of seeing dragonflies on the Rorschach (S) is equal to the probability of seeing dragonflies and being schizophrenic (S,D) plus the probability of seeing dragonflies and not being schizophrenic (S,$\overline{D}$; p. 43). If the probability of the sign without the problem—$P(S,\overline{D})$—is quite high, the probability of the problem given the sign—$P(D \mid S)$—may be very low, even though $P(S \mid D)$ is high. This can be presented in a contingency table (see Exhibit 14.3). Determining the probability of a sign given the problem and the probability of the sign without the problem involves comparisons between the columns, whereas the probability of the problem given the sign and probability of the problem without the sign involve row comparisons. Thus, as Dawes notes, if it were known that all schizophrenic patients in a clinic saw dragonflies on the Rorschach and only 10 percent of nonschizophrenic clients did, but the proportion of clients who were schizophrenics were *not* known, then there would be no way to assess the likelihood that someone who saw dragonflies was schizophrenic.

The probability of a sign or symptom is greater than the probability of a disease or problem because signs are common to many problems; that is, $P(S|D)$ > $P(D|S)$. Dawes (1982) points out that it is only because so many women have neither cancer nor a positive reading that there is such high agreement between mammogram results and the occurrence of breast cancer. Agreement is often confused with accuracy. People may believe that the probability of cancer given a positive mammogram is equal to the probability of a positive reading given cancer (Dawes, 1982). Diagnosis is confused with prognosis (Einhorn, 1988). So a positive mammogram is less diagnostic than presented by some professionals. This results in the performance of too many biopsies (Thornton, Edwards, & Baum, 2003; see also discussion of using frequencies to correctly interpret test results, in Chapter 15). Barratt and her coauthors (2005) describe a procedure to estimate the benefits and harms of biennial screening mammography for women in different age groups. The research that clinicians draw on may overestimate the correlation between variables (spurious correlations) or underestimate this (causalation; Einhorn & Hogarth, 1985, p. 320). Consider also reports of being abused as a child and whether an individual was in fact abused. We must examine all four cells (Dawes, 1994b). We must consider who have and have not reported abuse, and who have actually been and those who have not been abused. In everyday practice, only one row of a four-cell contingency table is available to counselors. We do not know who would be represented in the other row (not caught). As Dawes points out, we do not think in comparative terms. "We match (often from memory) rather than compare" (p. 4). Statements that sound convincing may in fact be quite inaccurate. The only way to avoid these errors, as Dawes notes, is to make it a habit to elaborate joint probabilities (to use the information in all 4 cells of a 2 × 2 contingency table; see also Hastie & Dawes, 2001, and the discussion of sensitivity and specificity in Chapter 12).

## CAUSAL ANALYSIS

Different cues draw "attention to different aspects of causal strength" (Einhorn & Hogarth, 1985, p. 323). Constant conjunction is represented by cells *a* and *d* in Exhibit 14.3; cells *b* and *c* represent instances that disconfirm constant conjunction or support alternative accounts (1985). Temporal order is reflected in which variable is selected as causative. Inaccurate assumptions may occur because of a failure to consider alternative explanations or because of false assumptions based on contiguity in time and space. The *fallacy of false cause* is committed when an event is inaccurately assumed to be the cause of some other event. Consider the case of Clever Hans, the wonder horse (reported by Stanovich, 1986). Clever Hans supposedly could solve mathematical problems. When presented with a problem by his trainer, he would tap out the answers with his hoof. Many testimonials were offered in support of his amazing ability. A psychologist, Oskar Pfungst, decided to study the horse's ability. He systematically altered conditions to search for alternative explanations. This exploration revealed that Clever Hans was an astute observer of human behavior. He watched the head of his trainer as he tapped out his answer. His trainer would tilt his head slightly as Hans approached the correct answer, and Clever Hans would then stop. What are in fact the results of self-selection are often mistakenly attributed to other factors, as in the assumption that since student achievement is superior in private school, private schools are better than public schools. Conflicts between degree of statistical correlation and cues to causality (such as similarity between two variables) may result in either spurious correlation or incorrect assumption that variables are not related, based on low or no correlation. Although much attention is often devoted during graduate training to sources of and warnings about spurious correlations, little attention may be given to the opposite concern. Quite different causes may be identified by changing which "causal field" is emphasized (Mackie, 1974). For example, clinicians who emphasize dispositional causes focus on a different causal field than do systems-oriented clinicians, who attend to environmental as well as personal causes.

Beliefs about which events are causally related to each other influence data selection, as well as data processing and organization. If you believe that childhood experiences account for a client's feelings of loneliness, insight therapy may be selected to increase awareness of how past experiences relate to this concern. Based on this causal analysis, recent environmental changes (such as loss of friends) may be overlooked. A focus on one cause alone may result in inaccurate judgments. This is one reason for holding interdisciplinary case conferences, in which the biases of one kind of professional may be neutralized by the biases of other kinds of professionals. For example, many factors are related to relapse in depression. A focus on only one may result in incorrect assumptions. Clinicians, like other people, are adept at creating explanations. Once an account is offered, it may bias subsequent search for data. When asked to explain which factors affect their behavior in a situation, people often overlook correct sources of influence and identify irrelevant ones (Nisbett & Ross, 1980). The particular causes identified depend partly on how advanced knowledge is in an area. For example, causes proposed for explaining variations in behavior change over time; few, if any, clinicians now rely on examination of bumps on the head (see discussion of phrenology in Gamwell & Tomes, 1995). Widespread belief in the occult (Schultz, 1989) and the popularity of a variety of other beliefs illustrate the readiness with which suspect causes are accepted (e.g., see Shermer, 1997). Rules of thumb (heuristics) may increase or decrease the likelihood of identifying accurate causal assumptions.

There is nothing odd or negative about weighing data in relation to causal theories. "The problem arises only when flimsy, ad hoc theories are invented for the purpose at hand, and causal mechanisms that would have predicted other events or relationships are both initially overlooked and never reconsidered when the individual's initial presumptions are discredited or challenged by new data" (Einhorn, 1980a, p. 28). This tendency may be heightened in an eclectic approach to practice, which increases the likelihood of holding many ad hoc theories or notions. The more tenuous a theory is, the less it should be relied on when assessing data and the more attention should be focused on data—that is, we "should become less theory-driven and more data-driven" in making judgments (Einhorn, 1980a, p. 32). Just as a causal model may not be used in situations in which it is appropriate, it may be applied in situations in which it is inappropriate (Nisbett & Ross, 1980, p. 135). For example, transactional analysis may not have much to offer in dealing with a homeless young single parent addicted to crack cocaine. Being influenced by initial impressions of a client (anchoring effects), as well as overlooking the unreliability of sources of data about clients and their situations, may result in errors. A deterministic causal relationship may be assumed in situations in which the relations are probabilistic (statistical), as in the Gambler's fallacy (see Chapter 15). Lack of knowledge of cause-effect relationships compromises the quality of judgments. For example, a clinician may be unaware of the ways in which schedules of reinforcement influence behavior and misattribute the cause of a child's misbehavior in the classroom to personal characteristics—overlooking the role of scheduling effects in the environment. Lack of knowledge about the effects of prescribed drugs may result in incorrect assumptions about the cause of an elderly client's confusion.

## SOURCES OF ERROR

Sources of error that interfere with thinking critically about the causes of client concerns are discussed in the sections that follow. Errors described result from and in missing or ignored causal assumptions (see Exhibit 14.6). They may influence both diagnosis of a client as well as assessment.

### MISUSE OF RESEMBLANCE CRITERIA

One source of error in inferring causal relationships is the assumption that factors related to an event resemble that event. (See Chapter 9.) We have strong beliefs about what types of causal factors are associated with certain effects and "are far more confident than is warranted in [our] ability to judge the plausibility of a specific cause-effect relationship based on superficial resemblance of features" (Nisbett & Ross, 1980, p. 117). Beliefs about how events are related stem from many sources. Some originate from summaries of empirical data; some rest on informed expert opinion or systematic observation; others are based on myths, fables, metaphors, and maxims that may or may not reflect reality. In reality, "causes and effects may bear little or no resemblance to one another" (p. 117). Everyday explanations of deviant reactions often rely on

**Exhibit 14.6**
Sources of Error That May Result In Inaccurate or Incomplete Problem Structuring

| Source | Description |
| --- | --- |
| 1. Partiality in the use of evidence. | Overlooking, distorting, or discounting contradictory evidence. Giving favored treatment to favored beliefs (see, for example, items 2 to 7). |
| 2. Rationalizing rather than reasoning (justifying rather than critiquing). | Focusing on building a case for a position rather than gathering information impartially. This is an example of item 1. |
| 3. Focusing on irrelevant or incorrect reasons (fallacy of false cause). | Selecting irrelevant or marginally relevant "evidence" to support beliefs or actions. The conclusion may have nothing to do with the reasons provided. |
| 4. Jumping to conclusions. | Failing to treat a belief or conclusion as a hypothesis requiring scrutiny. |
| 5. Unwarranted persistence. | Not changing your mind even when there is compelling evidence to do so. |
| 6. Categorical rather than probabilistic reasoning. | Reducing options to two possibilities (either_____ or _____). |
| 7. Confusing naming with explaining (e.g., "diagnosing" rather than contextually assessing). | Assuming that giving something a name (e.g., Bipolar Personality Disorder) explains it and offers intervention leverage. |
| 8. Confusing correlation with causation. | Assuming that an association between two or more events indicates causation. |
| 9. Confusing shared with distinguishing characteristics. | Focusing on characteristics that may not distinguish among different groups/causes. |
| 10. Faulty generalization. | Relying on small or biased samples; assuming that what is true of the whole is true of the parts, or vice versa. |
| 11. Stereotyping. | Incorrectly estimating the degree of variability in a group. |
| 12. Influence by consistent data. | Being influenced by data that do not offer any new information but are merely consistent with data already available. |
| 13. Lack of domain-specific knowledge. | Not having information needed to clarify and understand problems (e.g., facts, concepts, theories). This source of error is related to many others in this list. |
| 14. Confusing form and function. | Mistakenly assuming that similar forms of behavior have similar functions and different forms of behavior reflect different functions. |
| 15. Simplistic accounts. | Relying on accounts that ignore important causes and/or overlook uncertainties. |
| 16. Vagueness. | Vaguely describing problems, causes, and hoped-for outcomes. |

**Exhibit 14.6** *Continued*

| | |
|---|---|
| 17. Uncritical acceptance of explanations. | Accepting explanations without evaluating them and comparing them with well-argued alternative accounts; not checking whether a belief is consistent with known facts; selecting untestable beliefs. |
| 18. Assuming that a weak argument is not true. | Assuming that because you cannot offer a convincing argument, a claim is false. |
| 19. Reliance on ad hoc explanations. | Making up explanations as you go along, even though they may contradict one another or be circular (explain nothing). |
| 20. Incorrect weighing of different contributors. | Not weighing contributing factors in relation to their importance. |
| 21. Misuse of speculation. | Believing that you can find out what is going on just by thinking about it. |
| 22. Overcomplex accounts. | Relying on needlessly complicated accounts that obscure causes. |
| 23. Ecological fallacy. | Assuming that an association between two variables on a group level is also true on an individual level. |
| 24. Confusing correlations and baserates. | Incorrectly assuming that a correlation reflects the baserate. |
| 25. Relying on questionable criteria for evaluating the accuracy of claims. | Examples include consensus, anecdotal experience, and tradition. |
| 26. Using a general rule that is not applicable to a particular situation. | Assuming that because agency administrators are usually fair that a particular administrator was fair on a certain occasion. |

*Note:* The sources of error described may be (and usually are) not related to intentions; caring about people is not enough to avoid them.

causal assumptions based on resemblance, as in bad seed arguments. Nisbett and Ross (1980) note that many causal assumptions within psychoanalytic theory rely on crude forms of the representative heuristic, as in the assumption that symptoms may have identical or opposite characteristics to their psychic causes. Timidity may be presumed to reflect underlying aggressive or hostile tendencies. In actuality, the form of a behavior may not reveal its function.

## PRACTICE THEORIES

Preconceptions and practice theories influence selection of causes. For example, many clinicians believe in the disease model of substance abuse, as well as in the addictive personality. Other perspectives focus more on identifying environmental as well as personal factors that may be related to substance abuse, and do not view it as a disease (e.g., Fingarette, 1988; Peele, 1999). A counselor who accepts the disease model will focus on dispositional causes (see later section on dispositional bias). Theories that are appropriate in some situations may be inappropriately applied in other contexts. Theories that are familiar are more available and are therefore more likely to be influential than are unfamiliar theories. The tendency to be more confident than there is good reason to be about theories compounds the distorting effects of preconceptions. The following quote from Popper (1959) is apt:

> I found that those of my friends who were admirers of Marx, Freud, and Adler, were impressed by a number of points common to these theories, and especially by their apparent explanatory power. These theories appeared to be able to explain practically everything that happened within the fields to which they referred. The study of any of them seemed to have the effect of an intellectual conversion or revelation, opening your eyes to a new truth hidden from those not yet initiated. Once your eyes were thus opened, you saw confirming instances everywhere: the world was full of verifications of the theory. A Marxist could not open a newspaper without finding on every page confirming evidence for his interpretation of history; not only in the news, but also in its presentation—which revealed the class bias of the paper—and especially of course in what the paper did not say. The Freudian analysts emphasized that their theories were constantly verified by their "clinical observations."

Preconceptions influence what we recall as well as what data we note and how we organize that data. The influence of preferred practice theories is illustrated by a study (Plous & Zimbardo, 1986) in which clinicians were asked to list the most likely explanations for three different problems—a sleep disturbance involving nightmares, severe headaches, and depression—variously portrayed by actors in a series of vignettes. Some referred to the therapist, some to the client, and some to the therapist's closest friend of the same sex. Psychoanalysts made more dispositional attributions and fewer situational or mixed attributions than did behavioral therapists. Nontherapists (college students) made the highest number of both dispositional and situational or mixed attributions. Psychoanalysts made significantly more dispositional attributions in relation to their friends and clients than they did for their own behavior. Medical training was associated with the attributional bias of psychoanalysts; that is, those with medical training gave more dispositional attributions than did clinicians without medical training. Using only one method of approaching client problems over a long period increases the likelihood of using this method with all clients, whether or not it is appropriate. (See also Chapter 9.)

## Metaphors We Use

Metaphors and similes influence how we conceptualize our experiences (Lakoff & Dean, 2004; Lakoff & Johnson, 1980). If we think of arguments as war, we may respond to arguments by trying to win and we may view others as opponents. (See also prior discussion of Lewontin's critique of the metaphor of adaptation.) Advertisers take advantage of metaphors and myths (e.g., see Scott, Stanford, & Thompson, 2004). The tendency to personify objects is one type of metaphor, such as in "Her past finally caught up with her." The sickness metaphor is prevalent in clinical practice, in such statements as "They have a sick relationship," and "She is an alcoholic." Metaphors may be helpful in revealing factors related to clients' concerns and how best to attain related outcomes, or may result in negative outcomes both for society and for clients, such as medicalizing moral dilemmas and imposing unwanted services on people (MacCoun & Reuter, 2001; Schur, 1971; Szasz, 1994). For example, because of the use of the illness metaphor, dispositional attributions may be made ("alcoholism as disease" metaphor) or people who have committed violent crimes may be excused on the grounds that they are mentally ill and thus not responsible for their behavior.

## PARTIALITY IN THE USE OF EVIDENCE—THE CONFIRMATION BIAS

Attending to only some important data and overlooking other data is perhaps the most common source of error in clinical decision making (see Exhibit 14.6). Physicians who are not accurate tend to discount evidence that contradicts a favored hypothesis (Elstein et al., 1978). New information is assigned to a favored hypothesis rather than offering a new causal account that could more effectively account for this data (1978). Terms referring to this tendency include conservation, overinterpretation, and assimilation. Diagnoses based on the *DSM-IV-R (Diagnostic and Statistical Manual of Mental Disorders, 2000)* are usually made as a result of attending to a few prototypic characteristics. Other characteristics not in accord with decisions may be ignored. Vested interest in a view compromises the ability to weigh evidence and sample data objectively. For example, research that offers mixed evidence in relation to a favored hypothesis increases belief in initial views (Lord, Ross, & Lepper, 1979). Decisions made by journal reviewers of manuscripts are in the direction of preferred-practice theories (e.g., see Mahoney, 1977). Nor are researchers immune to the influence of their assumptions—elaborate precautions are taken to avoid this influence. (See Chapter 12.) The study of experimenter effects has yielded a great deal of information about such influences (Rosenthal, 1988).

Oversimplifications may also result in errors. The belief that there is only one cause of behavior when there are many may result in faulty causal assumptions. The best-guess strategy, in which complex situations are simplified by ignoring or discounting uncertainties, encourages this source of error. Consider depression. Often both personal and environmental factors are related to depression. Ignoring important causative factors decreases the likelihood of successful intervention. The use of predigested thinking (see Chapter 5) and the tendency to think in either/or terms involve misguided parsimony.

## MISTAKING CORRELATION AND CAUSATION

The fallacy of false cause may occur because correlations are mistaken for causes (e.g., see Shanks, 2005). We may assume that because two variables (brain and foot size) covary, one causes the other. Although we may scoff at the idea that brain size causes foot size, other mistaken assumptions based on confusions between correlations and causation may not be so obvious. The history of the professions provides many illustrations of the confusion between correlation and causation. For example, people used to think that tuberculosis was inherited because people who lived together often got it. Consider also the common assumption that low self-esteem causes problems such as depression. In fact, both low self-esteem and depression may be related to other variables (e.g., a high frequency of punishing experiences and a low frequency of positive feedback in the past and the present). Our tendency to overestimate correlations heightens our susceptibility to this error.

## CONFUSING CAUSES AND THEIR EFFECTS

Is depression a cause of marital conflict, or is marital conflict a cause of depression? Is cognitive disorientation a result of being homeless, or does being homeless contribute to cognitive disorientation? Tavris (1992) argues that the depression that many women complain of is often a result of gender role expectations (e.g., that women be the major caretaker of children) that limit women's opportunities for well-paid work. Can you think of any other examples? The fundamental attribution error may result in mistaking effects for causes. Consider Jimmy, a 12-year-old African American student referred because of apathy, indifference, and inattentiveness to classroom activities (Sue & Sue, 1990, p. 44). The counselor believed that Jimmy harbored repressed rage that needed to be ventilated and dealt with. He believed that Jimmy's inability to express his anger led him to adopt a passive-aggressive means of expressing hostility (i.e., inattentiveness, daydreaming, falling asleep) and recommended that Jimmy be seen for intensive counseling to discover the basis of his anger. After 6 months of counseling, the counselor realized the basis of Jimmy's problems. He came from a home of extreme poverty, where hunger, lack of sleep, and overcrowding sapped his energy and motivation. His fatigue, passivity, and fatalism were a result of poverty.

## THE FUNDAMENTAL ATTRIBUTION ERROR

The fundamental attribution error (the tendency to attribute behavior to enduring qualities of people rather than to situational events) results in blaming people for problems and overlooking relevant environmental events. "Everyday, people make harmful and damaging judgments about themselves, or harmful judgments about their spouses even to the point of severing marriages, because they wrongly attribute current crisis to stable personal dispositions instead of transient pressures" (Nisbett & Ross, 1980, p. 252). An example of the willingness to ascribe behavior to stable dispositions is offered by a study conducted by Jones and Harris (1967). People who read an essay advocating or opposing Castro's leadership of Cuba inferred that the author of the essay believed in the view described even when they were told that the theme of the essay was dictated by someone else. One effect of preconceptions is the tendency to perceive greater consistency in behavior than exists.

Behavior is quite inconsistent across situations and "slight differences in situations often produce large differences in the behavior of most people in those situations" (Nisbett & Ross, 1980, p. 120). In one study that highlights our tendency to seek internal causes and data to justify these causes and to ignore or underestimate situational influences, subjects were recruited for a game involving tests of general knowledge (Ross, Amabile, & Steinmetz, 1977). They took part either as participants or as observers and were randomly assigned to these roles. Subjects were aware of this random distribution. Questioners could ask any questions as long as they knew the answer themselves. After completing the game, the observers, contestants, and questioners were all asked to rate contestants and questioners on their general knowledge and other competence-related items. The contestants received lower ratings by all parties despite the fact that they had little opportunity to display their knowledge because of the situational factor of random distribution. The influence of the context in which exchanges occur is often overlooked by clinicians who blame lack of honesty on the part of clients on personal characteristics. For example, it is to the advantage of clients who seek eligibility for social security payments on the grounds of mental handicap to conceal information that may weaken their request and to exaggerate information that may strengthen it. (See also discussion of biases in self-report data in Chapter 13.) Both availability and resemblance encourage the fundamental attribution error. When clinicians observe clients their behavior is often more vivid than are environmental variables, and thus behavior is more available when clinicians think about causes. The situation is the reverse from the actor's point of view; that is, to the actor, it is the situation that is more vivid. This probably explains why actors attribute a greater role to environmental variables when offering reasons for their own behavior than do people who observe the actors (see discussion of observer-actor difference in Chapter 9).

## THE READINESS TO EXPLAIN COINCIDENCES: LACK OF APPRECIATION FOR THE ROLE OF CHANCE

Many events simply happen by chance; chance and randomness are natural aspects of our everyday world and are much more likely to occur than people think (Falk, 1981). Most people, however, do not appreciate the prevalence of randomness, and readily offer explanations for events that are actually a result of chance. "Subjects appear to underestimate the ease with which virtually *any* outcomes, even mutually contradictory ones, can adequately be explained. They underestimate their own fecundity as causal theorists, and hence are overly convinced of the veridicality of their beliefs by the ease with which they were able to postulate relevant causal linkages" (Einhorn, 1980a, p. 28; see also Paulos, 1988). Our need for control encourages a search for explanations for events that offer an illusion of control (Langer, 1975). One of the problems with offering explanations is that they influence what we see and assume on subsequent occasions, even when they are incorrect. Outcomes that are really the result of chance tend to be attributed to personal characteristics, such as skill or its lack. For example, Langer (1975) found that subjects who selected a lottery ticket insisted on more money to buy back their tickets ($8.67) than did subjects who had been handed a ticket ($1.96). This illustrates a basic confusion about chance, skill, and responsibility.

## VIVIDNESS

People who are unusually prominent in some way are more likely to be considered to have a causal role. Someone who is visually prominent in a discussion is viewed as having an influential role in the outcome of the discussion (Taylor & Fiske, 1975). The proximity of one event to another may lead us to believe that a causal relationship exists. The effects of repeated affirmation of a point and the use of emotional terms on judgments offer additional examples of the role of vividness (see Chapter 6). Clinicians tend to select their most vivid case examples when discussing causal attribution. Such biased selection (attempted proof by selected instances) may result in incorrect inferences. Events that have a small probability (they occur rarely) tend to be overestimated (Tversky & Kahneman, 1981). If a rare event is associated with a particularly negative outcome, it may receive undue attention. As Elstein (1988) points out, it is often difficult to separate probability and utility. Attention may be focused on situations in which excessive drinking occurs; situations in which it does not occur may be ignored. This biased focus encourages an overemphasis on problems and limits understanding of situations in which problematic drinking does not occur. (See also Chapter 15.) Yet another source of error is primacy effects; we tend to be influenced by what is first heard or read.

## IGNORING BASERATE INFORMATION

Information about how many people act a certain way in a certain situation is often disregarded when trying to determine why a particular person acts in a certain manner. For example, in Milgram's study of obedience (1963), data on the percentage of subjects who delivered high shocks to people had little impact on judgments made by individual subjects; even though they knew that delivering high shocks was the modal response, they still made strong negative dispositional inferences about people who delivered high shocks (Miller, et al., 1973). Information about normative behavior may be dismissed even though such information would be helpful. Consensus information is also underutilized in self-perception. Subjects who were informed that feelings of depression such as the "Sunday blues" were the rule, not the exception, were no less inclined to inaccurately attribute their mood to personal inadequacy and weakness (Nisbett, Borgida, Crandall, & Reed, 1976). Nisbett and Ross (1980) suggest that consensus information is ignored because it is less vivid than information about events or people. In the *false consensus effect*, we make the assumption that the percentage of people who would act and believe as we would is higher than it actually is. The more other people's behavior differs from our own, the more likely we are to regard their behavior as unusual and as revealing of personal dispositions (Ross, Greene, & House, 1977). The tendency to associate with people who are similar and the greater ease of recalling our own beliefs and actions encourage this false consensus. Since the practice of many clinicians involves clients who are quite different from themselves, such effects are likely to encourage incorrect inferences of pathology.

### THE SELF-FULLILLING PROPHECY

There is a self-fulfilling prophecy—our expectations influence what befalls us. Clinicians often have advance descriptions of a client, perhaps from a referral source or case record. These descriptions may create expectations about a client, which then influence the exchange that occurs. For example, consider the study by Snyder, Tanke, and Berscheid (1977), in which men were asked to speak to an unknown woman over the phone. Men in one group were told that the woman was very attractive; the men in the other group were told that she was unattractive. After speaking to the woman, they rated the woman on a number of traits. The conversations were recorded, and the interactions were rated by observers who could hear only the man or only the woman and knew nothing about the attractiveness manipulation. The observers rated the "attractive woman" as being more confident and more animated, enjoying the conversation, and liking the partner. The "unattractive woman" was rated as more sensitive, trusting, kind, genuine, and modest. Men who were told they were speaking to an "attractive woman" were rated as more sociable, sexually warm, interesting, independent, permissive, bold, outgoing, humorous, socially adept, and pleased with the conversation. These results indicated that the men behaved differently in the two different conditions. Snyder and Thomsen (1988) suggest that self-fulfilling prophecies are especially likely to occur in situations of unequal power, such as therapist-client relationships. Many clients can readily be persuaded that the therapist's impressions are accurate. Some clients may even fall in love with their therapists or develop a dependence on them, which increases the probability of accepting views presented by therapists.

### OVERCONFIDENCE

We are often overconfident concerning the accuracy of our causal assumptions; this discourages a search for disconfirming data (e.g., see Arkes, 2001, and Exhibit 14.7). Einhorn (1980a) suggests that overconfidence "is a result

**Exhibit 14.7** Diagnostic overconfidence resulting from misuse of the representativeness heuristic. The patient describes her pain with several redundant descriptions that are often found in coronary artery disease. The physician assumes that this multiplicity of cues means that the patient is highly representative of patients with the disease.

*Source:* From *Medical Decision Making* (p. 44), by H. C. Sox, M. A. Blatt, M. C. Higgins, and K. I. Martin, 1988, Boston: Butterworth Heinemann.

of the way in which feedback is used to evaluate and learn from judgmental accuracy" (p. 2). For example, clinicians may rely on their anecdotal experience in judging the effectiveness of services they offer. The main effect of experience may be to support inaccurate assumptions if feedback provided is irrelevant or inaccurate (see Chapter 9). Personnel managers, for example, do not see how applicants they reject would have performed. Customs inspectors do not know about "false negatives"—travelers who had illegal or declarable goods and who passed through customs unnoticed—and are thus overconfident of their skills in spotting contraband. Clinicians usually do not find out how effective other intervention methods would have been with a client. (See also Klayman, Soll, Gonzales-Vallejo, & Barlas, 1999.) Dawes (1993) notes that predicting the future is quite different from understanding the past, and that lack of appreciation of this difference is responsible in large part for the overconfidence many clinicians have in their intuitive abilities. There is an "overestimation of contingency" (the assumption of particular causal relationships). "There is an essential difference between the consequent-antecedent process of looking backward versus the antecedent-consequence process of looking forwards." Retrospective memory is biased—"we interpret past events in a manner consistent with our present beliefs concerning stability and change in the human life course. The result is gross overestimation of the strength and consistency of the 'patterns' we observe retrospectively—hence, overconfidence in what we 'know.'" Thus, as others have noted, prediction is not equivalent to understanding and explanation. In retrospective review (looking back from a consequent—a client has been labeled a schizophrenic), we are free to search for enumerable antecedent causes resulting in post hoc reasoning. (See Dawes, 1993 for more detail.) Dawes uses the example of examining the black box after an airplane crash to discover causes. As he suggests, we do not know how many planes arrived safely in which similar factors occurred, and there is no way to find out. Our theory of what happened or what are causes of an outcome (such as being depressed) encourages an organization of memories that fits this theory, as demonstrated in research regarding retrospective memory (e.g., see Loftus, 2004).

## CONFUSING NAMING AND EXPLAINING

Naming (offering a diagnosis for an observed pattern of behavior) is often confused with explaining. That is, it is assumed that because something has been named, it has also been explained (see discussion of empathic "explanations" in Chapter 3). This is rarely the case in the field of psychology, although it may be so in the field of medicine (such as when a physician determines that a patient has tuberculosis). Pseudoexplanations involve a confusion of naming and explaining and can result in frustration, because although helpful data now seem to be on hand about how to resolve a clinical question, in fact, none has been added.

## CONFUSING CONTENT AND STRUCTURE (FORM AND FUNCTION)

Errors may occur because of confusion between content and structure. Content may differ while structure remains the same; this is difficult to appreciate (Einhorn, 1980a). The distinction between form (the typology of a behavior) and function (what maintains the behavior, why it occurs) is a basic one in some practice theories, such as applied behavior analysis (Austin & Carr, 2000). Focusing on the form of behavior (hitting) and overlooking its function (removing demands) may result in incomplete accounts. This error is less likely if practice theories emphasize the distinction between form (the typology of behavior) and function (what maintains the behavior—why it occurs). Simply describing behavior does not provide information about its function (why it occurs). The context in which behavior occurs must also be explored. If you know the circumstances in which a client is likely to engage in certain behaviors, you have information about how you might alter the environment to influence these behaviors. Ignoring the context encourages excessive focus on psychological causes. For example, individual counseling may be recom-

mended for an adolescent having problems at school that are related to the reactions of her peers and teachers as well as to the economic stress experienced
by her single parent. A problem-oriented curricular design (e.g., aging, health,
anxiety, depression, family violence) may encourage the confusion of form
and function. It may discourage recognition of similar contingencies of reinforcement that apply to different concerns. This error is less likely to occur in
practice theories that emphasize this distinction. There are no courses in the
physics department on the physics of refrigerators, the physics of air condi-
tioners, and so forth, because there is agreement on a certain core of structural
relationships (Blalock, 1984). Many graduate programs do not require students to take a course in basic behavioral principles that cuts across all problem areas in terms of potential application. This is not to say that specialized
content, for example, about developmental tasks or changes at different ages
is unimportant.

## DEAD-END AND INCOMPLETE ACCOUNTS

*Dead-end accounts* are those that do not provide guidelines for achieving valued outcomes. They get in the way of discovering promising options. An example is attributing a client's troubling behavior to angry feelings without
discovering factors such as environmental contingencies related to these feelings. "After-the-fact" accounts describing what people did (and why) may
sound profound, but do not provide "before-the-fact" information that helps
you and your clients to select effective plans. Dead-end accounts may be incomplete (omit crucial causes). *Incomplete accounts* include only some pieces of
a puzzle. They may focus on thoughts without relating them to what people
do in specific situations. Another kind of incomplete account is assuming that
behavior causes another behavior, without asking about the causes of both.
Self-esteem is often accepted as a cause of behavior. But where does self-
esteem come from? You may assume that your success in a job interview is due
to high self-efficacy (an expectation that you will succeed). A more complete
account would include information about your history in related situations
(e.g., past successful experiences; Baumeister et al., 2003). We feel confident in
situations in which we do well.

## PROBLEMS WITH MEMORY

Events may not be accurately noted in the first place. And just because a sequence of events is accurately observed does not mean that the memory of
these events will remain accurate. Distortions may and do creep in over time.
Errors of construction occur (see Chapter 9). Effective information storage and
retrieval skills are vital in allowing us to check the accuracy of our memory
(see Chapters 10 and 11).

## OTHER SOURCES OF ERROR

An event is more likely to be selected as a cause if it is presented as the subject of a sentence than as the object (Pryor & Kriss, 1977). "Thus, Sue is more likely to be identified as the causal agent in her preference for a restaurant if subjects are told that she likes the restaurant than if they are told that the restaurant is liked by Sue" (Nisbett & Ross, 1980, p. 127). The influence of surface wordings on clinical judgments needs further investigation. There is every reason to suppose that such influences occur in clinical practice as they do in other settings.

Inconsistent use of rules may result in errors. A rule may be used appropriately in some instances but be overlooked in other situations in which it would be helpful. This tendency toward inconsistency offers an advantage to actuarial methods of prediction compared with clinical inference (see Chapter 15). Errors may occur because areas of uncertainty are overlooked or ignored. Sources of uncertainty in clinical practice include potential effectiveness of intervention methods, validity of measures, and longevity of gains. As discussed in Chapter 10, evidence-based practice and policy is designed to deal with uncertainty in an ethical manner. Causal inferences may be incorrect because premises are untrue or because the form of the argument is incorrect. The factual soundness of an argument (its plausibility) as well as its logical soundness should be considered (see Chapter 3).

## A DISPOSITIONAL BIAS

Clinicians make decisions about what the problem is, where it lies, and what causes it. Although some writers make a distinction between causal attributions (what caused a problem) and locus attributions (where the problem lies), these two kinds of attributions could also be viewed as causes at different points in time. Dispositional bias refers to the tendency to attribute the cause and locus of problems to the client rather than to environmental events or to the interaction of personal and environmental factors (see earlier discussion of the fundamental attribution error). The dispositional bias of clinicians has received a great deal of attention. The following discussion of factors related to this source of error is based on Batson, O'Quin, and Pych (1982). More recent research supports this earlier discussion. Four factors involve characteristics of the observer (the clinician) and three result from being in a helper role.

1. *In their role as an observer, clinicians tend to focus on the client.* It is the client who is interviewed; the client is salient in the interview context, and such focus encourages dispositional attributions. Many studies support this. For example, Storms (1973) found that when observers of an interaction were shown a replay of the situation from a participant's point of view, they made more situational attributions. In another study, undergradu-

ates listened to an audiotape of a peer-counseling session (Snyder, Shenkel, & Schmidt, 1976). The client depicted on the tape presented her problem as being related to her situation. Her problem was viewed as more situational by observers asked to take the client's role and was viewed in more dispositional terms by subjects instructed to take the role of a peer counselor. "These results are quite consistent with the suggestion that people who identify with the helper role are prone to adopt an observer set and, as a result, to make more dispositional attributions" (Batson, O'Quin, & Pych, 1982, p. 65). Such findings are compatible with self-other differences described in Chapter 9.

2. *Information gathered is selective, or the "office-bound helper."* Many counselors see their clients only in the office, which may result in incorrect assumptions about the consistency of behavior. They do not see clients in other situations, in which behavior may differ considerably from that seen in the interview. Behavior that is the direct result of the unusual situation of being in a client role may be inaccurately assumed to reflect behavior in other situations. Agency policy may prohibit home visits. Reasons offered for this policy include the views that (1) clients should be motivated for treatment (that is, motivation is shown by their willingness to come to the agency) and (2) observation in the home does not offer helpful information because of reactive effects caused by the presence of the observer. Even when home visits do occur, the sample of behavior gathered may be small, and little care may be exercised to ensure that a representative sample is gathered. This is not to say that real-life observation is always relevant or ethical. It is to say that, even though it might be both relevant and ethical, it is often not used as a source of assessment information (see, for example, Budd et al., 2001). In some agencies, one clinician may see a child and another clinician may see the child's parents. This practice discounts the mutual influence processes between children and their parents.

3. *Practice theories influence attributions.* The preferred practice theories of many clinicians encourage dispositional attributions. Many clinicians favor *a sign approach* to assessment, in which behaviors are viewed as signs of hypothetical internal dispositions. This contrasts with *a sample approach* to assessment, in which behaviors are viewed as important in their own right as a sample of a broader class of actions. Compared to behaviorally oriented clinicians, psychodynamically oriented clinicians viewed a person as significantly more maladjusted and viewed his problems in more dispositional terms when the person was labeled a patient than when he was referred to as a job applicant (Langer & Abelson, 1974). The label "patient" created a dispositional bias on the part of psychodynamically oriented counselors.

4. *Situational information provided by the client is discounted.* Information that clients provide about situations related to their concerns may be discounted. Batson and his colleagues (1982) suggest that counselors are

especially likely to discount information that indicates the problem is situational. They identify three factors that contribute to this tendency. First, clinicians are aware of people's tendency to make situational attributions for their behaviors, and there may be an attempt to correct for this bias by emphasizing dispositional causes. Second, labels and diagnoses applied to clients encourage dispositional attributions by compromising the client's credibility as a provider of accurate information. A clinician may have read in a case record that a client has a history of being hospitalized for schizophrenia, and subsequently emphasize personal limitations as causal factors. Many studies illustrate the influence of third-party information on clinical decisions. In a study by Batson (1975), counselors who received information that a client had low scores on self-awareness and high scores on manipulation made fewer situational attributions, even though this client presented evidence that the problem was situational. Third, offering a situational attribution for a problem is usually less damaging to one's self-esteem. Thus, a client who blames a problem on the situation may be assumed to be acting in his own best interest and, for this reason, his statements may be discounted.

5. *Professional training encourages dispositional attributions.* Trained helpers are more likely to make dispositional attributions concerning clients' problems than are untrained helpers. Batson and his colleagues (1982) found this true of different types of helpers; for example, clinical psychologists as well as social workers. They conclude that there is "a pervasive tendency for trained helpers, however trained, to perceive clients' problems as more dispositional than do people without training" (p. 69). As the authors note, such differences in attribution may be due to selection effects (people who are prone to make such attributions choose helper roles) rather than to socialization effects of training. Most clinicians are trained how to use the classification of "mental disorders" in the *DSM*. Such training increases use of these categories (Pottick, Wakefield, Kirk, & Tian, 2003); such labels are required for third-party payment. They focus on alleged characteristics of the individual.

6. *Calling a healthy person sick is less serious than calling a sick person healthy.* Clinicians are supposed to protect society from people who may be dangerous. Physicians are trained to be conservative; they are trained that it is better to call a healthy person sick than to call a sick person healthy. If a social worker attributes child abuse to dispositional characteristics of a mother and removes a child, at least the child will not be harmed by the parent (although harm may result from the foster parents and/or from the trauma of separation; e.g., see DePanfilis, 2003). On the other hand, if a situational cause is assumed (such as stress, which could be relieved) and the child is left in the home and abused, there may be an uproar in the press. In this kind of situation, possible problems with other living contexts, such as the foster home, are much less vivid at the point of making a decision about whether to remove a child, since the foster home is

often unknown. On the other hand, the injuries to the child, the child's reactions to these injuries, and a parent who may be uncooperative and angry are all very vivid.

7. *Resources available relate mostly to changing the client.* Batson and his colleagues (1982) argue that helpers want to succeed but are aware that success is more likely if they change the client's situation. However, they realize that often this will not be possible. This is especially true in social work, in which many problems are related to environmental problems over which social workers have little control, such as poor housing, poor education, lack of day care, and unemployment. So helpers concentrate instead on dispositional accounts; accounts that may enable them to help. Batson, O'Quin, and Pych (1982) base their views on the assumption that clinicians believe that they are better able to help with dispositional than with situational problems. They cite three reasons for their beliefs. One is that helpers have more immediate access to clients than to their clients' environments. A second reason is that changing the environment is more difficult: "to change a sick situation may involve legal or political action affecting many people and costing much money and time" (p. 71). The third reason is that resources available are geared toward personal characteristics rather than situational causes. "The majority of our societal resources are directed toward helping individuals adapt to their social environments; far fewer are directed toward changing the social environments that breed poverty, crime, depression, and despair" (p. 71). Currently we are infatuated with taking pills to solve problems, focusing on presumed biochemical characteristics of individuals, and overlooking environmental circumstances. Most residents in the United Kingdom take some kind of medication.

Availability of resources influences attributions for client's problems. For example, in a study by Batson, Jones, and Cochran (1979), some of the subjects received a list of referral sources that emphasized the dispositional nature of problems, such as a mental hospital, a residential treatment center, a mental health clinic, group therapy, and a family counseling service. Other subjects received a list of resources emphasizing environmental contributors, such as a career information center, an ombudsman, and a community coalition. Subjects who received the former list were more likely to view the client's problems in dispositional terms. Again, vividness is an influential factor: the client's presence compared with an unseen environment. This tendency is compounded by the fact that many clinicians are not trained how to carry out contingency analyses in order to identify environmental factors that contribute to problems (Austin & Carr, 2000). Not having such skills, the influence of environmental contingencies may be overlooked. The long-term effects of decisions made, based on resources available, produces a vicious cycle; the more problems are viewed in dispositional terms, the more services compatible with this view will be requested.

## USE AND MISUSE OF INTUITION

Intuition involves a "responsiveness to information that is not consciously represented, but which nevertheless guides inquiry toward productive and often profound insights" (Bowers, 1987, p. 73; see also Chapters 4 and 8). This view is compatible with the differences found between experts and novices. Experts use mental simulations and patterns they may no longer be able to easily describe. Lack of awareness of knowledge used encourages attributions for productive solutions to intuition. When intuition is used in place of any input from related research findings, what "feels right" is relied on, rather than what has been found to be effective (or ineffective) in helping a client. "Real clinical expertise based on sound, concrete, situational understanding must be distinguished from arbitrary subjectivity, guessing, mystical intuition, instinct, routine, or habit" (Gordon, 1988, p. 278). Sole reliance on intuition is ethically questionable when better decisions could be made by drawing on related research findings (see discussion of evidence-based practice in Chapter 10 and actuarial versus clinical prediction in Chapter 15).

> There is no contradiction between the intuitive model of thinking and the behavioral model, nor do the two models represent alternative modes of thought residing in different cerebral hemispheres and competing for control over the mind. All serious thinking calls on both modes, both search-like processes and the sudden recognition of familiar patterns. Without recognition based on previous experience, search through complex spaces would proceed in snail-like fashion. Intuition exploits the knowledge we have gained through our past searches. Hence we would expect what in fact occurs, that the expert will often be able to proceed intuitively in attacking a problem that requires painful search for the novice. And we would expect also that in most problem situations combining aspects of novelty with familiar components, intuition and search will be cooperative in reaching solutions. (Simon, 1990, p. 203)

## IMPROVING THE ACCURACY OF CAUSAL ASSUMPTIONS

Guidelines suggested include the following: getting the total picture, questioning initial assumptions, paying attention to anomalies, and changing representations (restructuring situations). Tools and rules of thumb that can be used to improve the accuracy of causal assumptions share a focus of increasing awareness of the reasoning process we use—making implicit processes explicit, so that we can examine our assumptions. Examples include asking questions such as, "What's missing?" or "Do I need more information?"

*Take Advantage of Helpful Tools*   Take advantage of computer programs (see Richard & Lauterbach, 2004) as well as statistical tools such as actuarial models and Bayes Theorem; use frequency in place of probability (see Chapter 15).

Once statistical methods are mastered, their use becomes "fluid" (more efficient) and they are more accurate than intuitive reasoning (Nisbett et al., 1983; see discussion of actuarial methods in Chapter 15). Helpful tools in understanding client concerns and highlighting important content include decision aids such as algorithms. Palm Pilot decision aids are widely used in health care. Depiction of a problem is a good indication of how well it is comprehended (Greeno, 1978). Drawing a graph of the presumed relationship between two characteristics (daily mood and daily number of pleasant events) or making a contingency table may help to identify assumptions and alternative possibilities (see Exhibit 14.3). Cognitive maps, flowcharts, contingency tables, and tree structures can be used to describe the relationships among variables. Flowcharts and algorithms can be used to illustrate the sequence of steps involved in making a decision and to highlight the data needed and common errors at each point (e.g., see Rzepnicki & Johnson, 2005). Venn diagrams provide an aid for analysis of arguments (see Exhibit 14.5).

*Make Assumptions Explicit*   If we do not make our assumptions explicit, we cannot examine their accuracy. Drawing cognitive maps of possible interrelationships among concepts may be helpful in clarifying implicit assumptions that influence decisions (Novak & Gowin, 1984).

*Clearly Describe Relevant Events*   Clinical decisions often involve estimating probabilities—for example, the likelihood that a client's depression is related to recent environmental changes. Probabilities may be easier to estimate if relevant events are clearly described—for example, the exact nature of recent environmental changes. Clear description of concerns and related factors are vital to clarifying vague terms such as depression, anxiety, and poor communication (Wolpe, 1986). Vague descriptions of client concerns may make it impossible to discover related factors. Another way to get bogged down is to focus on problems rather than related factors; for example, focusing on elder abuse per se, rather than identifying and addressing related factors.

*Watch Out for the Fundamental Attribution Error*   We tend to focus on attributes of the person and to overlook environmental variables (i.e., fall into the fundamental attribution error). This, combined with the greater vividness of negative behaviors, often results in pathologizing clients. To avoid doing this, be sure to consider the context in which behaviors of concern occur (or their lack). The more clearly you describe this, the more information you will have about client concerns. You may overlook environmental influences because you focus on psychological characteristics and rely solely on self-report data that do not reflect what is happening. Our thoughts and feelings are often more vivid than associated environmental contingencies, so it is easy to focus on them as causes and to overlook environmental influences.

*Be Data Focused*   Speculative thinking may be relied on "to solve problems which can only be solved by the observation and interpretation of facts. . . . The belief that one can find out something about real things by speculation alone is one of the most long-lived delusions in human thought" (Thouless, 1974, p. 78). We often are guilty of the contrary-to-fact hypothesis, in which we state "with an unreasonable degree of certainty the results of events that might have occurred that did not" (Seech, 1993, p. 131). An example is, "She felt sad because of her neighbor's family problems. If only she hadn't gotten married at such an early age, she would be a happier woman today" (p. 131). Speculation is valuable in discovering new possibilities but it does not offer information about whether these insights are correct. What is cannot be deduced from what ought to be. Speculation is not without its effects, since our beliefs influence what we look for.

Studies illustrate illusory correlations. Such studies illustrate that expectations based on theories and semantic associations may overwhelm the influence of data that do not match these expectations or even refute them. This tendency is encouraged by confirmation biases (seeking data that confirm our beliefs and overlooking data that do not). For example, we often attend to only the positive-positive cell of a four-cell contingency table (see earlier discussion in this chapter). There is nothing odd or negative about weighing data in relation to available theories. The problem arises when we invent ad hoc accounts for the purpose at hand and overlook points of view (causes) that would have predicted other events or relationships, and never reconsider them when our initial beliefs are shown to be incorrect (Einhorn, 1980a). This tendency may be heightened in eclectic practice, in which we use ad hoc theories or notions that may contradict each other. Being data focused rather than theory focused will help you to avoid premature and excessive reliance on dubious accounts (Einhorn, 1980a). The more tenuous a theory is, the less you should rely on it when reviewing data, and the more attention you should pay to the data. What exactly is the problem? Exactly how is it manifested? What factors have been found to be associated with it in related high-quality research reports?

*Focus on Informative Data*   The data you gather could be (1) relevant (help you and your clients select effective service plans), (2) irrelevant, or (3) misleading. Focus on relevant data. Irrelevant data may lead you astray. A few worthless items can dilute the effect of one helpful item. In thinking about what a particular person might do in a situation, we tend to disregard data that describe how people usually act, even though this may help us to predict what an individual would do. Ask: "Is this data relevant here?" How so? We tend to focus on vivid events and to overlook those that are important but not vivid. We tend to recall vivid examples that may mislead us about factors related to a problem.

*Assess Rather Than Diagnose; Explain Rather Than Name*   Problem solving can be likened to walking along an unknown path with many dead ends. One kind of dead end is simply naming (e.g., labeling) something (a problem or behavior of interest). Suppose that you see a homeless person on the street gesturing oddly and talking to himself. You may think, "He is mentally ill." Is this label helpful? Does it decrease uncertainty about how you might be able to be of help?

> Intervention programs cannot be based solely on a diagnostic or classification category such as "depression" or "attention-deficit disorder" because such topographically based [description of form] diagnoses do not identify which of many possible determinants are operational for a particular client. Diagnoses typically provide only an array of possible causal factors. The generalizability of the suggested variables and weights to a particular client cannot be presumed.
>
> Diagnosis can facilitate the design of intervention programs only if any of three conditions are met: (1) specific causal paths are invariably associated with specific diagnostic categories, (2) a hierarchy of the most probable paths or their weights is associated with specific diagnostic categories, and/or (3) effective interventions are available for specific diagnostic categories regardless of within-category variance in causality. These conditions are seldom met. (Haynes, 1992, p. 109)

Assessing rather than diagnosing will help you avoid explanatory fictions (terms that seem to offer information but do not). Pseudoexplanations (circular accounts) are prime examples. In a circular account, we use a behavior to infer an explanation and appeal to the same behavior to support our explanation (no additional information is provided). For example, a teacher may "explain" a student's hitting other children by stating that he is aggressive and, when asked how she knows, may say, "Because he hits other children." A lack of situation awareness—"failing to elaborate the "problem space" (to pursue a contextual analysis) is a principal cause of ineffective problem solving (Nickerson, Perkins, & Smith, 1985; Salas & Klein, 2001; Zsambok & Klein, 1997).

*Avoid the Single-Cause Fallacy: Ask "What's Missing?"*   Just as an explanation may be overly complex and obscure options, it also may be incomplete (overlook causes) and obscure options. We may assume (incorrectly) that different problems have one cause. Rarely is behavior related to one cause. For example, investigations of relapse in depression suggest many related factors. Simplistic accounts in which complex problems such as family violence are attributed to one factor (e.g., past history of violence) can be misleading. Thinking in either/or terms and ignoring or discounting important uncertainties encourage selection of simplistic accounts. Ask yourself, Does my account consider major influences? Have I left out important influences?

*Avoid Unnecessarily Complex Accounts*   Just as an account may be overly simple (overlook causes related to a problem), it may be overly complex (unnecessary concepts may be used that get in the way of discovering causes). This is why parsimony is emphasized in science (see Chapter 4). Although general "sensitizing concepts" can be helpful in the exploratory stage of problem solving, they must be clarified to obtain a fuller understanding of clients' concerns and options for resolving them. We tend to believe that vague, jargon-filled accounts are more profound than clearly stated ones (Armstrong, 1980).

*Watch Out for Illusory Correlations* Mistaken assumptions about causes may be due to incorrect estimates of the degree to which two or more events covary. (See prior discussion of assessing covariations.) Covariations (and thus causal relationships) are often assumed between certain characteristics (e.g., personality traits or recent life changes) and problems or between certain symptoms and diagnostic categories (e.g., vigilance for danger and Generalized Anxiety Disorder). Corrective feedback offers an opportunity to change misleading beliefs about what "ought" to go together. However, if our preconceptions are rigid and the feedback is vague or irrelevant, experience may do little to alter incorrect beliefs.

*Pay Attention to Base Rates* Base rates indicate the prevalence of a behavior or event in a population. Only some parents who were abused as children abuse their own children (estimates range from 40 to 60 percent). We tend to rely on data about a particular case and to ignore base rate probabilities. Imagine that you have just left a staff position in a shelter for battered women where 90 percent of clients seeking services had been abused. You are now working in a community mental health center in which the base rate of battered women is much lower, say 10 percent. Ignoring differences in base rates may result in incorrect assumptions—that clients have been battered when they have not been. Base rate data are not as vivid as characteristics of the client whom you see during interviews. It thus is easy to overlook this information, even though it is important to consider when making decisions. If we rely on resemblance criteria (similarity) to evaluate probability, we may overlook prior probability (base rate data; Tversky & Kahneman, 1974, p. 1124; see also Chapter 15).

*Watch Out for Sample Bias* Practice decisions are made on the basis of samples of behavior or conditions. We may often make generalizations about what clients do in real-life contexts based on how they act during interviews. Inaccurate assumptions may result from *overgeneralizations* based on small, biased samples. We often overlook *selection bias.* Consider the assumption that since students' achievement in private, compared with public, schools is superior, private schools are better. What do you think?

*Avoid Influence by Anchoring Effects* We tend to be influenced by what we first see or think of. This influences later judgments. Make it a habit to question initial impressions.

*Search for Alternative Accounts*   We tend to seek data that confirm our views and not to look for evidence against them. This is known as the *confirmatory bias* or *self-fulfilling prophecy.* This style of search often results in faulty judgments (Nickerson, 1998). Studies of medical decisions show that overinterpretation is a key source of error (contradictory evidence is ignored or is incorrectly assumed to support preferred views; Elstein et al., 1978). We use different standards to criticize evidence against our views than we use to evaluate evidence that supports them. Evidence that is mixed (it provides some support for and some against favored views) increases the confidence of believers of both views (Lord, Ross, & Lepper, 1979). We readily think up causes. We have an investment in understanding and predicting what happens around us. A premature focus on one possibility will get in the way of considering alternative views. Unless your assumptions about causes provide guidelines for removing complaints, or unless you must act quickly ("shoot from the hip"), consider alternative possibilities.

*Enhance Your Understanding of Probabilities*   Misunderstanding about probabilities may result in faulty problem structuring. Different kinds of probabilities include: (1) *compound* (probability of X *and* Y), (2) *conditional* (probability of X *given* Y), and (3) *simple* (X). In the conjunction fallacy, we overlook the fact that the probabilities of A and B *both* occurring must be less than the simple probability of A or the simple probability of B. Consider the example given by Tversky and Kahneman (1983) in which subjects received the following facts about Linda, a 31-year-old single, outspoken, bright student who majored in philosophy. She was very concerned with issues regarding discrimination and social justice and took part in anti-nuclear demonstrations. Subjects were asked to evaluate the following:

a. Linda works in a bookstore and takes Yoga classes.
b. Linda is active in the feminist movement.
c. Linda is a psychiatric social worker.
d. Linda is a bank teller.
e. Linda is an insurance salesperson.
f. Linda is a bank teller and is active in the feminist movement.

Statement (f) is the conjunction of (b) and (d). The probability of (f) cannot be greater than either (b) or (d). However, most subjects believe that (f) is more probable than (d), perhaps because of the representative heuristic. Because we are influenced by representativeness (the similarity of events) we often make inferences with no reference to known or estimated base rates of the characteristic in question. Dawes (1988) gives the example of assuming that low self-esteem (*c*) results in problems (*P*) because people who consult counselors regarding problems have low self-esteem. This confuses $p\,(c\,|\,S)$—the probability of low self-esteem, given problems—and $(p\,S\,|\,c)$ the probability of problems given low self-esteem. As Dawes points out, we do not know $(p\,S\,|\,c)$ is high "because clients come to [counselors] because they have problems" (p. 76). The counselors' experience is conditional on *S*. Also, as Dawes points out, people's self-esteem may be poor *because* they have problems. Readers of books on sexual abuse are often asked to review a long list of symptoms to check for indicators of sexual abuse. One problem here is assuming that the probability of a symptom (e.g., suicidal thoughts) is the same as the probability of an underlying problem or experience (e.g., sexual abuse as a child; Ofshe & Watters, 1994). Symptoms such as depression are much more common than any one underlying cause. When we do not consider this, we are subject to illusory correlations (e.g., between symptoms and presumed causes). Another problem is that certain symptoms may not be independent but are assumed to be so when making an overall estimate. (See also prior discussion of probabilities in this chapter.)

*Watch Your Language*   The role of language is discussed at many points in this book. Language influences how successful we are in communicating with ourselves as well as with clients and colleagues. Some uses of language have an almost magical quality, as when we label a behavior and think that we have explained it when we have not (see the earlier discussion of naming compared to explaining). It is easy to slip from describing someone (She complains about being lonely) to a causal inference that provides little or no intervention leverage (She has a dependent personality). We tend to convert trait names (e.g., aggressive) into presumed causes (e.g., aggressive personality) that get in the way of searching for problem-related factors. *Psychobabble* (vague, excessively abstract concepts) obscures rather than clarifies.

*Acquire Domain-Specific Knowledge and Skills*   Specialized content knowledge and skills may be necessary to accurately assess concerns and related circumstances and options in order to help a client achieve hoped-for outcomes. You may have to search for and critically appraise related research findings to discover promising options. If you are unaware of the influence of schedules of reinforcement on behavior you may mistakenly attribute the cause of problems to personal characteristics (low self-esteem), overlooking the role of scheduling effects. Lack of knowledge about the psychological effects of certain physical illnesses or drugs may result in incorrect assumptions about the cause of an elderly client's "depression."

*Be Aware of What You Don't Know (Ignorance as a Kind of Knowledge)*   Be honest about gaps in your knowledge related to decisions you and your clients must make. Available knowledge about how to help clients attain certain outcomes is usually incomplete. Sources of uncertainty include potential effectiveness of different methods, the accuracy of assessment and evaluation measures, and the future course of certain behavior patterns. Recognizing our ignorance and the uncertainties involved in making decisions can help us to avoid misleading influences of overconfidence. Witte, Witte, and Kerwin (1994) offered a course on medical ignorance at the University of Arizona School of Medicine to highlight the importance of knowing what is not known as well as what is. Carroll (2001) has his students ask "ignorance" questions based on their reading of texts. These highlight what they do not know or what the text may not include.

*Watch Out for Redundant Data*   Our tendency to collect redundant information encourages a false sense of overconfidence. You may, for example, ask a client who complains of depression about her past history of depression. In selectively scanning for depression, you may overlook periods of happiness and related factors (see Exhibit 14.7).

*Be Rational (Flexible)*   One definition of rationality is changing your mind when data indicate that you should. Our tendency to be overconfident of our judgments and to look for data that confirm our views (confirmatory biases), contributes to unwarranted persistence. Change your mind when you have good reason to do so.

*Avoid False Dilemmas*   We often think in either/or terms when searching for causes and selecting plans. We may think it must be either x or y when in fact there may be a number of possibilities. Thinking in either/or terms may result in overlooking promising options.

*Restructure the Problem*   Restructuring problems may be useful with ill-defined goals. Let us say that you accept a client's goal of "being happier" but feel stymied as to how to pursue this goal. Recognizing that this goal is the outcome of a number of different behaviors and situations encourages a focus on pursuit of these changes as a route to being happier.

*Use Multiple Metaphors and Analogies*   Different kinds of metaphors and analogies can be used to simplify problems and to avoid a fixation on one problem structure or view that hinders solution of a problem.

*Decrease Compartmentalization*   Repeated practice in clinical decision making with corrective feedback with a focus on the process as well as the product should encourage generalization of helpful skills. (See discussion of problem-based learning in Chapter 10.) Questions that encourage generalization of content and procedural knowledge from one domain to another include "How could I apply that to this?" and "Could I use that to understand this problem?"

*Use Effective Troubleshooting Skills*   Skill in troubleshooting is one of the competency clusters that distinguishes effective from ineffective decision makers. Setbacks and mistakes are responded to as opportunities to use helpful strategies, such as asking questions that allow us to get unstuck (for example, "Why did I make this mistake?" "How could I avoid it in the future?" "How can I break this down into smaller steps?" "What do I need to know here?" "How can I rearrange information here?").

*Cultivate Positive Moods*   Research suggests that the mood of the therapist influences the decisions made (Salovey & Turk, 1988). Negative moods increase a focus on negative events and may thus encourage clinicians to pathologize clients. Biasing effects of positive moods include underplaying the severity of concerns and encouraging clients to take risks they are not ready for. Given research that suggests that many clinicians err in seeing too much pathology, and that positive support and belief in client's potential for change facilitates progress, if we have to err, a positive bias may result in the fewest and least damaging errors. Turk and Salovey (1986) suggest the use of a bias inoculation procedure in which clinicians receive experience in how their moods influence their memories. Clinicians could briefly reflect on their mood before each interview, as a check on possible bias and as a cue to alter their mood or at least be aware of it. Mood could be noted in a log to identify mood-generated influences on work with clients.

*Use Helpful Rules of Thumb*   Rules of thumb that can be useful in avoiding errors in causal assumptions are described next.

1. *Search for alternative explanations.* Causal assumptions may be retained even though they do not fit the data, as illustrated in the failure of debriefing described in Chapter 9 (see also the classic study by Ross and Lepper, 1980). Use the rule to "never rely on one way of asking" (Edwards & Von Winterfeldt, 1986, p. 657) to counteract this tendency. Incomplete or inaccurate assumptions may be discovered by searching for alternative explanations; this will counteract tendencies to focus on vivid but misleading cues and to look only for evidence that confirms favored assumptions. Bromley (1977) recommends inclusion of a heading—*Alternative Accounts*—in case records.
2. *Pay attention to sources of uncertainty.* Clinical decisions are made in a context of uncertainty. Overlooking uncertainty does not make it go away. Decisions are more likely to be accurate if it is recognized. The process of evidence-based practice is designed to reveal and if possible decrease uncertainty, such as attending to the false positive rate of an assessment measure.
3. *Seek disconfirming information.* Our tendency to discount contradictory information highlights the value of seeking disconfirming information. Let's say that a psychologist believes that problems with children are always related to marital difficulties and is confronted with a family in which no evidence of marital difficulties can be found. Reasons to discount this lack of evidence may be readily created. It may be said, "They *seem* happy, but there are problems—I just haven't found them," rather

than using disconfirming data to question assumptions. A belief that a certain effect always occurs is usually an oversimplification. Although marital problems may accompany child problems in many cases, in other instances they may not.

4. *Attend to environmental causes.* The influence of environmental variables often is overlooked, resulting in faulty selection of practice methods (see earlier discussion of the dispositional bias). Use a rule to explore the possible role of environmental variables related to client concerns. Axis IV of the *DSM* focuses on psychosocial and environmental problems such as housing problems, poverty, inadequate access to health resources, and unemployment. Inclusion of a title *Environmental Causes* on case record forms can be a useful reminder. Such causes tend to be noted more frequently from the actor's perspective than from the observer's perspective as described in Chapter 9. Make it a habit to consider relevant events from the client's point of view; this may help you to discover important environmental factors (Jordan, Harvey, & Weary, 1988; Regan & Totten, 1975). Using different sources of data will help you to counteract the fundamental attribution error, especially observation in real-life settings. Relying on self-report alone encourages a dispositional bias (see Chapter 13).

5. *Examine all four cells of contingency tables.* Incorrect assumptions about causes often occur because attention is focused on one cell (usually the positive-positive cell) of a four-cell contingency table.

6. *Ask "what if."* Asking "what if" questions should help you to avoid errors due to premature closure about causes. These include questions such as "What if X caused Y, rather than Y caused X?" or "What if X had never happened; would Y still have occurred?" If well-argued alternative explanations can readily be offered, the original account is questionable.

## SUMMARY

A key aspect of clinical practice is identifying the cause of client concerns. Effective searches for causes may require specialized knowledge based on experience providing corrective feedback as well as critical thinking skills and creativity. Practice theories guide both the collection and the processing of data in this search. Causal analysis in clinical contexts requires the integration of different kinds of data, a task that is subject to a variety of errors. We can take advantage of helpful tools such as flowcharts and heuristics to decrease the mental effort involved. Research on clinical decision making indicates that hypotheses about client concerns are arrived at quite early and that, although a great deal of data is collected, decisions are based on a modest amount of data; that is, we do not use all the data gathered. Decisions are influenced by irrelevant as well as by relevant data. Assumptions about covariations—what events go together and how strongly they are associated—influence our assumptions. Common errors in assessing how closely two or more events are related include ignoring nonoccurrences, preconceptions about which events are related, and attempted proof by selected instances (attending to observed rather than relative frequency). Here, too, as when making other decisions, we are influenced by availability and representativeness.

The fundamental attribution error in which causes are mistakenly attributed to the client rather than to situational variables is common. We often assume that behavior will be more consistent than it actually is; we overlook the variability of behavior in different situations. In exploring the relationship between personal characteristics and environmental variables and client concerns, we tend to give undue attention to the present-present cell of contingency tables, the cell that represents having both a presumed characteristic and the problem. This results in overestimates of pathology. Our interest in having control over our environment encourages a readiness to offer explanations for chance occurrences. We are influenced by vivid events, which gain undue attention in terms of their possible causative role. We tend to be overconfident in our assumptions. We may underestimate our knowledge and attribute wise decisions to our uninformed intuition; one of the hallmarks of becoming expert in a field is difficulty in identifying exactly how one arrived at a decision. An important distinction here is between "informed" intuition and the kind that relies on "inspiration without perspiration"; views that are *not* based on knowledge of content and procedure. Research concerning sources of error in assessing covariations and making causal assumptions can be used to suggest guidelines for improving accuracy. Such guidelines include making assumptions explicit, searching for alternative explanations, and taking advantage of tools such as diagrams, decision aids, notes, and computer programs.

# CHAPTER 15

# Predictions about Clients and Treatment Effectiveness: Improving the Odds

**M**AKING CHOICES AND PREDICTIONS is a routine part of clinical practice. Choices are made between different views of client concerns, different interventions, and different outcomes to pursue. These choices involve implicit or explicit predictions as to which alternatives are best. Many kinds of predictions are made. Some concern what clients will do in the future, such as: Will this man rape again if released from jail? Will a client kill herself over the weekend? Will this father participate in treatment plans? Other predictions concern the potential effectiveness of intervention methods: Will cognitive-behavioral therapy help this depressed client? How long will positive gains be maintained? Decisions about which intervention to use should be based on predictions about a client's likely future in response to different procedures or without any intervention, and an evaluation of the acceptability of each alternative to the client. Often, there is no access to such information. Different kinds of effects that are important to consider include both short-term and long-term consequences for clients as well as for their significant others (those who interact with and influence clients). Treatment methods focused on the individual usually do little or nothing to alter social, political, and economic factors that contribute to clients' concerns, as many critics of psychotherapy have emphasized (see Chapter 2). For clinicians who work in agencies, vague policies allow wide discretion in making choices in accord with each clinician's unique beliefs about criteria that should be relied on (e.g., expert opinion, evidentiary status as revealed by critical appraisal, personal preferences). Consider the reply of a field instructor to one of my students, who asked her "Do we know anything about how effective play therapy is?" (This was the method offered to all clients at this agency.): "I don't care about research. I am here doing this because it is what I like to do."

Predictions are closely related to causal assumptions, and typically concern the prediction of some clinical variable of interest, such as prognosis or recidivism based on characteristics such as history, age, and quality of social support available. "Other things being equal, the greater the predictive validity of some variable, the greater its causal relevance" (Einhorn & Hogarth, 1985, p. 320). Correlation coefficients often are used as measures of predictive accuracy. Possible misinterpretations of correlations were discussed in Chapter 14. Predictions differ in complexity and the nature of feedback required and available to check their accuracy. The more complex they are, the more likely it is they can be made only with aids such as Bayes's Theorem or actuarial models (see later discussion). The more vague and delayed the feedback is, the less help it offers in improving future predictions. Unlike medical practice, in which the outcome of a decision often can be checked against a pathologist's report, there is often no such agreed-on criterion in psychological prediction. Clinicians disagree about the criteria that should be used to assess the effectiveness of therapy.

Measures used to make predictions include self-reports, test scores, ratings based on observation, and impressions gathered in interviews. Problems of reliability may be overlooked when evaluating the usefulness of data. For instance, you might assume that a small difference in scores reflects a true difference, when the difference is a result of an unreliable measure. This might result in inaccurate classification of clients (such as assuming that clients are clinically depressed when they are not) or faulty selection of an intervention method (for example, deciding to intervene because it is assumed that a measure indicates pathology when no such condition exists). The predictive accuracy of a measure, such as a suicide potential scale, may be unknown. Judgments are made under considerable uncertainty in attempts to maximize some values while minimizing associated costs. How much we value an outcome is often confused with the probability that it will occur (Elstein, 1988). It is not surprising, given the high degree of uncertainty in making predictions and choices, that clinicians may protest that they do not make predictions or avoid making them through delay, inattention, or refusal (Corbin, 1980). The tendency to put off difficult decisions was one of the major reasons for the development of permanency planning procedures in child welfare—procedures designed to encourage social workers to arrive at a case plan for children in a timely manner (Stein & Gambrill, 1985 ).

We should weigh evidence in relation to its predictive value—how informative is it? Research shows that we do not do so. Rather, we weigh information in terms of whether we think it is causally related to a criterion. We ask "Is it meaningful to us?" rather than "Does it help us to predict which clients will benefit most from a service?" Clinicians choose practice methods on the basis of what they believe will work. But what does that mean? Does it mean that it is helpful to the people who believe in it? If this criterion is used, then we would have to say that appeal to many beliefs, including astrology, is valuable. The popularity of astrology would leave no doubt that it does work: "to most people astrological ideas have undeniable beauty and appeal, the birth chart is nonjudgmental, the interpretation is unfalsifiable, and astrologers tend to be nice people." The distinction between utility and validity explains the conflict between astrologers and critics of astrology. "Critics see a lack of factual evidence and conclude it doesn't work, whereas astrologers see that it helps people and conclude that it does work" (Dean, 1987, p. 178). Both are right and both are guilty of not wanting to know what the other is talking about.

Explanations do not necessarily yield predictions, and predictions may not yield accurate explanations, even when the predictions are accurate. Some treatment procedures in medicine are effective but the process through which success is achieved is unknown. Accurately predicting an individual's future may not be possible, even though considerable information is available about his developmental history. Consider the following case report (based on Pilpel, 1976; Morgan, 1982).

### CASE WORKER'S REPORT

SUBJECT: The "C" Family

1. R. C., male, age forty-three. Unstable personality. Irregular employment during last 8 years; frequently makes unreasonable demands of employer and threatens to resign. Very bitter toward former coworkers. Easily irritated. Has minimal contact with his children, but evinces marked hostility toward eldest son. Appears to be in poor health. (CONFIDENTIAL: Medical records reveal condition of advanced tertiary syphilis, date of infection unknown.)
2. J. C., female, age thirty-eight. Unemployed. Known to have had many extramarital affairs. Estranged from R. C. for a number of years. (CONFIDENTIAL: Medical records reveal no sign of venereal infection.) Shows only an erratic interest in her children. Has difficulty handling money matters.
3. W. C., male, age eighteen. Weak constitution; bouts of respiratory illness. Disciplinary problems in school. Poor student. Frequently fails examinations despite special tutoring. Evinces self-destructive tendencies.
4. J. S. C., male, age twelve. May be son of J. C. and one of her lovers. Submissive and indecisive. Appears intimidated by rest of family. Does well in school, however. Appears to hero-worship his brother.

ANALYSIS

1. The Cs present clear symptoms of family disintegration. R. C. and J. C. married despite initial strong opposition from the former's parents, who did not attend the wedding; latter's parents seem to have been unenthusiastic about the union even though they acquiesced to it. The birth of W. C. 7$\frac{1}{2}$ months after the marriage ceremony did nothing to ameliorate

the situation, and his "premature" arrival may be partly responsible, along with Oedipal factors, for R. C.'s obvious hostility to him.

2. Both J. C. and R. C. move in a subculture of sexual promiscuity not at all conducive to family stability. Extramarital adventures appear probable for the period between births of W. C. and J. S. C. and certain for the years following. Cohabitation within the marriage seems to have ceased at least 9 or 10 years ago.

3. Parental neglect of the children in terms of psychological and emotional nurture has been fairly chronic throughout. It has been aggravated by blatant favoritism toward the younger child on the part of both J. C. and R. C. W. C. shows clear signs of maladjustment. His misbehavior at his first school is said to have become "legendary." In his secondary school he was usually at the bottom of his class. He appears to have repressed his anger (understandable) toward his parents and turned it against himself. Seems prone to depression. Recently he jumped off a thirty-foot high bridge while playing with his brother and a cousin, on the theory, as he explained it, that he would grab onto the top of a nearby fir tree and thereby break his fall. Instead, he fell thirty feet to the bottom of the ravine, rupturing a kidney, which caused him to be laid up for 6 weeks.

4. J. S. C. suffers from a marked lack of self-direction. He tries very hard to please and be agreeable, sensing himself inadequate to deal with the three high-powered personalities around him. His autonomy seems seriously impaired.

PROGNOSES

Poor. R. C.'s health will continue to deteriorate. J. C.'s indiscreet sexual dalliance seems likely to continue also. In any case, the neglect of the children will not abate. J. C. and R. C. essentially lead separate lives now, observing only the formalities of a marriage relationship. Neither has a compelling interest in their sons, and neither seems competent to handle family finances. W. C. seems certain to have further severe problems of adjustment ahead of him, and he is ill-equipped to cope with them. J. S. C. seems to have a chance for healthy development, but he must overcome his timidity and avoid mimicking his brother's dubious exploits.

*Summary*
For all practical purposes this family has ceased to exist as a viable social unit.
—26 September 1893

*Updates*
R. C. died in 1895.
J. C. died in 1921.
J. S. C. became a stockbroker in 1900.
W. C. became Prime Minister of Great Britain in 1940.

## ACTUARIAL VERSUS CLINICAL JUDGMENT

Diagnosis, assessment, and prediction are interrelated. That is, predictions about a client (such as degree of dangerousness, likelihood of relapse, likelihood that a given intervention will be successful) are related to how problems and desired outcomes are defined and related assumptions about causal factors. For example, responses on the MMPI (as well as other sources of data) may be used to decide whether a client is schizophrenic. This decision may result in selection of a certain intervention. To be sure, many clinicians do not use test results in their work with clients. Still, whether tests are used or not, different sources of data are considered in thinking about problems and related factors; clinicians arrive at assessments of their clients in attempting to understand them, and they make predictions (implicit or explicit) about the clients' future behavior. Both assessment and prediction require the integration of diverse sources of data and the selection of relevant rather than irrelevant variables. Here is where many sources of inaccuracy creep in. Prediction involves *forward inference* (reasoning from present causes to future outcomes), whereas assessment (or diagnostic inference) often involves *backward inference* (reasoning from symptoms and signs to prior causes). Assessment and prediction are closely related in that "success in predicting the future depends to a considerable degree on making sense of the past" (Einhorn & Hogarth, 1985, p. 313). Errors in assessment may result in incorrect predictions as a result of a confusion between "diagnostic and prognostic probabilities" (Einhorn, 1988; see later section on use of test results).

One of the oldest controversies in the field of psychology concerns clinical versus statistical judgment. Meehl's classic book appeared in 1954, and this has been an active area of inquiry since that time. (See Quinsey, Harris, Rice, and Cormier, 1998, for 15 arguments against acturial risk appraisal and responses to these.) Statistical or actuarial judgement involves the systematic combination of data from a variety of sources, including life history data, test scores, ratings of behavior, and subjective judgments based on information gained during interviews. Judgments are based on empirically determined relationships between sources of data and an outcome, such as job success. Clinical judgment also draws on a variety of data sources, including impressions gained during interviews; however, judgments are intuitively arrived at on the basis of assumptions that often (if not typically) remain implicit rather than explicit. Meehl (1954) made a persuasive case for the superiority of actuarial methods over intuition, and an even more persuasive case can be made today in relation to many different kinds of judgments. There are over 136 studies demonstrating the superior predictive accuracy of actuarial methods in a variety of areas (Grove & Meehl, 1996; Grove, Zald, Lebow, Snitz, & Nelson, 2000). Areas investigated include diagnosis of medical versus psychiatric disorders; description of personality; and prediction of treatment outcome, violent behavior, length of hospitalization, and future child maltreatment (e.g., see Baird & Wagner, 2000). Actuarial judgments have been found to be superior to clinical judgments in many areas, even though they rely on linear models for what may be nonlinear relationships among variables. In many instances there is no evidence that clinicians can take advantage of additional knowledge that is not captured in linear models, when making predictions that are superior to those based on actuarial methods (Fischhoff, Goitein, & Shapira, 1983). Clinicians are better at selecting and coding information than they are at integrating it, and this may be one of the reasons why decisions made by actuarial methods are often more accurate than decisions based on clinical inference. It is difficult to combine different sources of information, as must be done in clinical contexts in which environmental, psychological, developmental, and biological factors all may be considered. Fortunately, there are some helpful tools that can be used to integrate different kinds of data (e.g., see later discussion).

The prediction paradigm used in clinical practice uses a set of predictor variables that are combined, resulting in a predicted score that is then compared with a criterion to assess validity. Several methods have been used to explore how clinicians combine data and which data they use. One method is to ask them to describe what they do and why they do it as they make decisions. Kleinmuntz (1984) attempted to find out how experts make judgments based on responses on the MMPI. An expert was asked to describe what he was doing and thinking as he evaluated the adjustment of college students from MMPI profiles. A flowchart of rules was derived based on these descriptions, and a computer program was developed. The programs developed following such procedures rely on interpretations made by clinicians: They are "not based on known empirical relationships between predictor and criterion scores" (Wiggins, 1984, pp. 8–9). So these kinds of systems are not actuarial or statistical; they are automated clinical-prediction systems. One problem with this approach is that experts may not be able to describe how they arrived at decisions (see discussion of experts and novices in Chapter 8), or may identify incorrect decision rules and models. That is, expert systems may "incorporate biases and ineffectiveness as well as true expertise" (Elstein, 1988, p. 22).

Another approach is to ask clinicians to review a set of profiles that include a set number of input variables and to predict the criterion status (for example, psychotic) of the people who produced these profiles. The data used are reviewed over a series of profiles, and regression weights are determined by correlations. A "bootstrapping" approach can be used to generate programs that make more accurate decisions than the clinicians whose data were used to develop the programs. For example, Goldberg (1970) asked clinicians to predict known criterion scores based on a set of profiles. These judgments were then regressed on the input variables to determine a rating system, and the resulting equation was then used as a prediction model to forecast scores on a new sample. This model outperformed the clinicians whose responses were used to create it, probably because it was applied more consistently than were the predictions made by clinicians in the simulated model.

Reliability influences the predictive validity of measures (the extent to which a measure corresponds to the real position of a client on whatever dimension is being measured). It does this by increasing the variability of the data source; that is, scores will be different from time to time if measures are unreliable. Some studies have found that models based on randomly determined regression weights and unit weighting (using coefficients with equal weights) outperform clinical predictions and models based on these (Dawes & Corrigan, 1974; Wainer, 1976). So what has research in this area told us? The summary offered by Wiggins in 1981 remains true today: "(a) Is there something special about clinical judgment as manifested in *performance*? That is, are clinicians any better or worse than ordinary folk at forecasting uncertain outcomes? (Answer: probably not.) (b) Is there something special about clinicians' judgmental *processes*? That is, are clinicians more or less configural in combining information or do they weigh cues differently than do nonprofessionals? (Answer: probably not.) (c) Are the judgmental shortcomings and biases of clinicians distinctively different from those of other professional decision makers? That is, have these *same* shortcomings been demonstrated in groups of stockbrokers, physicians, intelligence analysts, electrical engineers, etc.? (Answer: definitely yes). (d) Given that all of us—laypersons, clinicians and other professionals—are in the same boat, how would you evaluate our characteristic judgmental and inferential strategies with reference to the formal canons of scientific inference? (Answer: C−)" (p. 14; for a more optimistic view see later discussion in this chapter as well as description of decision making in naturalistic contexts in Chapter 9).

Certainly there are many areas in which actuarial methods are not available. Still, the question must be asked: What are the implications for clinicians in relation to areas in which actuarial methods are available and have been shown to be superior in accuracy to clinical judgments? The implication in terms of benefits to clients is that they should be used when they are superior to clinical judgments. That is, clinicians can improve the accuracy of their judgments in relation to some decisions by taking advantage of known empirical relationships in combining diverse sources of data. The topic of actuarial versus clinical judgment is a hot one, and those who advocate use of actuarial methods when they are superior in accuracy to clinical inference often are attacked as advocating complete reliance on such methods. This is not what is being argued here, nor is this the position of those who have reviewed the literature in this area (e.g., Dawes, Faust, & Meehl, 1989). In the actuarial approach, error is accepted, which decreases the likelihood that it will be ignored. Acceptance of error decreases possibilities of lost opportunities (assuming there is no way to predict an outcome when there is) and the illusion of control (assuming that accurate predictions can be made when they cannot). A key advantage of actuarial methods is increased reliability of predictions.

## PREDICTION, CHOICE, AND PROBABILITY

Making predictions and choices requires the assessment of probabilities. Probability can be viewed as a quantified opinion. The probability assigned to an event represents a subjective degree of belief that it will occur, and can be expressed on a continuous scale ranging from 0 to 1. Only the endpoints of the scale are certain; degrees of uncertainty are represented by the points in between. A psychiatrist may predict that there is a 70 percent probability that a patient admitted to a psychiatric emergency service is a danger to others if released. In some cases, information is available about past relative frequencies that can be used to make estimates. Practice-related research may provide empirically based guidelines for making predictions (see discussion of actuarial methods). In most cases probabilities based on reliable statistical data are not available in clinical practice. Clinicians may have to rely on *subjective* probabilities—their estimates of the likelihood of given outcomes that reflect their personal beliefs about the degree of uncertainty related to a decision, such as whether a depressed client will make another suicide attempt in the near future. Typically, they can only guess at the relative importance of different "predictors." Subjectivists would argue that assigning probabilities always requires an interpretation; that there is no such thing as an objective probability (Fischhoff, Goitein, & Shapira, 1983).

Clinicians differ in the kinds of data used and in the weighting of these data. One clinician may base predictions on perusal of genograms, another may base them on a contingency analysis of family interactions. Staff who make parole decisions consider different types of data important and view information in different ways (Wilkins, Gottfredson, Robison, & Sadowsky, 1973). Decisions may reflect discrimination based on race or gender. African Americans receive heavier sentences for crack cocaine compared to whites who use powdered cocaine. These differences have been so striking and viewed as so discriminatory that some judges have refused to act on mandated sentencing rules. Even in areas in which extensive research has been carried out to identify criteria of value in making predictions—for example, about future child abuse—results may be disappointing. Current actuarial systems, although superior to consensus-based systems for predicting risk of future harm to children (Baird & Wagner, 2000), increase accuracy by classifying children into categories of potential harm: high, medium, and low. And this occurs with only a certain degree of accuracy. Next, a careful assessment is needed.

Clinicians often have to consider results from different sources when making decisions. A variety of models have been developed for making choices. In the *compensatory model*, weights are assigned to each variable and the weighted values are summed. Another model is the *conjunctive model*, in which cut-points are set in relation to each dimension, and any alternative that falls below these points is dropped. The placement of the cut-point will influence the relative number of successes and failures that occur; the higher the cut-point is, the greater is the proportion of successes to failures. The lower the criteria of success is, the more successes will be observed, regardless of predictive ability and the location of the cut-point. In the *disjunctive model*, a high score on one or several dimensions compensates for a low score on a variable. Past decisions can be used to create a model for current decisions. Clinical rather that actuarial judgments are typically used in combining test results with other sources of data to arrive at judgments. That is, clinicians do not use predictive equations in combining different sources of information, even when these are available (see prior discussion of clinical versus actuarial judgment).

Clinicians and clients must also assign value or worth *(subjective utilities)* to outcomes. These represent the relative desirability of different outcomes. How much weight should be given to protecting potential rape victims and how much to maximizing freedom of those who have a history of rape? How much weight should a client give to the probability of a false positive on a diagnostic test such as a mammogram? Helping clients to clarify their values is often a goal of psychotherapy. Accurate descriptions of personal values is a difficult process that is influenced by many variables, including the questions asked, their sequence, and how responses are obtained (Slovic, Fischhoff, & Lichtenstein, 1982b; Soman, 2005). Such efforts are complicated by confirmation biases and by the fact that clients often do not know what they want. Indeed, the gap between clients' statements of their preferences and related actions is so great that it is considered a major concern in evidence-based practice (see Chapter 10). Often, there is a conflict between minimizing costs and maximizing gains. Ideally, gains would be maximized and costs minimized as well as efficiency maintained in terms of time, money, and effort devoted to making a decision.

Clinicians differ in the outcomes they pursue as well as in the probabilities and values placed on different outcomes. The assessment of probabilities and subjective utilities are interdependent. For example, certain outcomes are assessed as more valuable than uncertain outcomes. We believe that we are more likely than other people to have good things befall us and less likely to experience maladies. Potential losses are more influential than are potential gains. That is, we are "risk-adverse"—we worry more about what we will lose than what we will gain. An illustration of this tendency can be seen in a study by McNeil, Pauker, Sox, and Tversky (1982) concerning preference for surgery or radiation therapy for lung cancer. One group of subjects received statistics that showed the percentage of patients that survived for different lengths of time after treatment. The other group received mortality statistics (percentage of patients who died). When the choice was posed in terms of mortality, 42 percent selected radiation therapy; only 25 percent of patients who received survival statistics selected radiation therapy. The advantages of surgery relative to radiation therapy loomed larger in the minds of respondents when framed in terms of the probability of survival than they did when stated in terms of the probability of death. The observed effect occurred with physicians as well as patients.

## CHALLENGES IN ASSESSING RISK

Prediction of risk is of concern in many different areas, ranging from flying in airplanes, building nuclear plants, deciding whether to leave a child in a home in which he has been neglected, or deciding whether to get a mammogram. Risks differ in the degree of certainty that they will occur, knowledge about how to reduce them, and their severity, timing, and type (e.g., see Martinic & Leigh, 2004). Individual risk may differ from population-derived risks. We fall into the ecological fallacy when we assume that what is a risk factor to most people is a risk factor for an individual. People differ in how they evaluate different kinds of risks. Most people are risk-averse; that is, they make decisions in a way that minimizes risk of negative consequences such as losses. At the other end of the pole are those who seek risks—they engage in risky behavior. Examples include skydivers, mountain climbers, and high-stake gamblers. Research regarding risks shows that:

1. Voluntary risks are viewed as less risky than those that are not voluntary.
2. Natural risks are assumed to be less hazardous than artificial risks (p. 298).
3. We tend to overestimate the risks of events that kill or injure a great number of people and underestimate the risks associated with less vivid conditions or events that in fact affect many more people, such as asthma.
4. We tend to think that risks are less if we think that we have control over them.
5. We tend to think that things that we cannot see and that are associated with dreaded outcomes, such as radioactive waste and AIDS, are riskier than events that involve known risks or less dreaded outcomes such as auto accidents (Halpern, 2003, p. 299).

Thus, as Halpern (2003) notes, "personal risk perceptions are not the same as scientific risk estimates" (p. 299).

Selection of interventions is influenced by the perceived risk associated with different options. Over the last few decades, there has been enormous interest in identifying risk factors for certain diseases, including alleged mental illnesses. A public health perspective seeks to identify risks for certain future conditions—for example, through screening programs—and promotes behaviors to decrease them. The importance of some screening programs is suggested by the fact that you could have an illness without feeling ill or you may feel ill without having an illness (Gray, 2001a). It is estimated that in general practice medically unexplained, physical symptoms comprise up to half of all new referrals. But do screening programs do more good than harm? Will, for example, the government plan to screen all residents of the United States for mental illness do more good than harm? (Lenzer, 2004; President's New Freedom Commission on Mental Health, retrieved 9/9/05).

Making risk estimates understandable is a challenge (e.g., see Heller, et al., 2003). "We need to convert information regarding relative and absolute risk into language that helps clients understand 'Is this likely to happen to me?'" (p. 299; see also excellent description of evaluating the accuracy of test results, including tests for AIDS in Gigerenzer, 2002a). And clinicians must convert such questions into answers for particular clients; "Is this likely to happen to this client?" Different ways to present benefits/risks include the following:

*Absolute risk reduction:* The absolute risk reduction is the proportion of patients who die without treatment (placebo) minus those who die with treatment. Pravastatin reduces the number of people who die from 41 to 32 in 1,000. That is, the absolute risk reduction is 9 in 1,000, which is 0.9 percent.

*Relative risk reduction:* The relative risk reduction is the absolute risk reduction divided by the proportion of patients who die without treatment. For the present data, the relative risk reduction is 9 divided by 41, which is 22 percent. Thus, Pravastatin reduces the risk of dying by 22 percent.

*Number needed to treat:* The number of people who must participate in the treatment to save one life is the number needed to treat (NNT). This number can be easily derived from the absolute risk reduction. The number of people who needed to be treated to save one life is 111, because 9 in 1,000 deaths (which is about 1 in 111) are prevented by the drug.

The relative risk reduction looks more impressive than the absolute risk reduction. Relative risks are larger numbers than absolute risks and therefore suggest higher benefits than really exist. Absolute risks are a mind tool that makes the actual benefits more understandable (Gigerenzer, 2002a, p. 35).

## THE FALLACY THAT PREVENTION IS ALWAYS BETTER THAN CURE

This fallacy is highlighted by Skrabanek and McCormick in *Follies and Fallacies in Medicine* (1998). They point out that prevention has a price and that this price may be more costly than any subsequent problems (p. 87). In his article *The Arrogance of Preventive Medicine,* Sackett (2002) emphasizes (1) aggressive assertiveness (e.g., pursuing healthy asymptomatic individuals for intervention), (2) presumption (confidence that the preventive interventions will, on average, do more good than harm), and (3) attacking those who question the value of prevention. Many kinds of preventive advice encourage us to avoid certain behaviors, such as smoking, eating fats, and so on. Prevention efforts in public health make heavy use of screening measures. "This activity, usually regarded as prevention is nothing of the sort: it is the early diagnosis of disease." (Skrabanek & McCormick, 1998, p. 88). They highlight the original requirements by Wilson and Jungner (1968), which include that the disease should be both common and serious and that an effective treatment is available. They also note that "If a disease is uncommon in the population being screened even good tests will throw up a large number of false positives; each of these has to be further investigated and carries a direct cost" of overdiagnosis and overtreatment and related burdens of unnecessary anxiety (p. 88). "It has become usual to describe diseases for which there is no known necessary or sufficient cause as multi-factorial in origin" (p. 91). Each measure carries with it a variety of possibilities for error during the process of screening. This applies to medical as well as to psychological tests. For example, Skrabanek and McCormick (1998) note that an incorrect sample may be included on a smear, which misses cancer cells. This could result in false negatives. Abnormalities are much more common than one would think, and they are much more common than the disease (Strohman, 2003, p. 105).

## USING TEST RESULTS

Clinicians use tests to decrease uncertainty. Tests may be used to assess risk or to predict future behavior. Professionals estimate the likelihood that a person has a certain problem, such as depression or tuberculosis. This is known as the initial *base rate probability*. They then may consider whether asking a client to take a test will be of value. The question here is: "To what extent is taking a certain test likely to decrease uncertainty about a particular assessment or diagnostic picture?" Tests should be used to revise subjective estimates concerning a client—that is, to change a decision about how a client should be treated (Eddy, 1982; Einhorn, 1988). If, for example, you suspect, based on an interview, that an elderly client has Alzheimer's disease and you obtain psychological test results as well, the test results should be used to choose among different intervention options in light of the new estimate based on the test results. That is, estimates of the probability that the client has Alzheimer's disease will be revised.

It serves little purpose to ask a client to take a test that will not change the base rate probability of the person *prior* to taking the test, or if there is no change in what would be done, depending on what the test reveals, perhaps because there is no effective intervention. Thus, as many authors note, taking a test is only useful if it moves a client across an *"action threshold."* This refers to the point at which a different action will be taken, depending on what is revealed in assessment. In making this decision it is important to consider where a test has been normed. Has it been tested for validity on clients with a known condition? For example, has a test of depression been normed using a sample of people known to be depressed by criterion indicators? A test will have different accuracy readings in a population in which there is a much smaller percentage of individuals with known depression. If used in such a population there will be a high *false positive rate*. That is, there will be a high rate of individuals labeled with the condition (depression) who do not have it. This has been found in many tests in the medical area, including mammograms, used to diagnose breast cancer. This also applies, for example, to measures used to assess risk of further child abuse (Munro, 2004). Let's say a social worker works in an agency where staff see a high frequency of children who have been sexually abused. If such a test is used in an agency that sees a wide variety of children with a much lower base rate of sexual abuse, there will be a high rate of false positives. Thus, you should ask: "How will this test perform with my clients? Does the pretest probability for my clients differ from the pretest probability of clients who were subjects in the study for which the test was developed?" We can estimate a test's performance in distinguishing between clients with and without a certain condition by using likelihood ratios. A likelihood ratio of 1 indicates that a test is totally uninformative. The consequence of a positive or negative test will be different depending on the pre-test probability of a condition. Cut-points are used to try to balance the kinds of errors that occur. A Receiver Operating Characteristics analysis (ROC) can be used.

Professionals tend to make certain kinds of misinterpretations of test results. *Test sensitivity* (the test's accuracy in correctly identifying people who have a disorder) may be confused with *test specificity* (accuracy of a test in correctly identifying people who do *not* have a disorder), resulting in incorrect predictions; test sensitivity is often incorrectly equated with the predictive value of a positive test result and test specificity is incorrectly equated with the predictive value of a negative test result (Beck, Byyny, & Adams, 1981; Elstein, 1988; see Chapter 12). Steurer and his colleagues (Steurer, Fischer, Bachman, Koller, & ter Riet, 2002) found that Swiss general practitioners "were unable to interpret correctly numerical information on the diagnostic accuracy of the screening test." Only 22 percent of these doctors selected the correct answer for the post-test probability of a positive screening test. They grossly over-estimated the value of a positive result alone. They also found that "adding information on the test sensitivity and specificity moderated these over-estimates, and expressing the same numerical information as a positive likelihood ratio in simple, non-technical language brought the estimates still closer to their true values." They found that "doctors tend to overestimate information derived from such tests and underestimate information from a client's clinical history." Thus clinicians tend to overestimate the predictive accuracy of test results. One cause of this error is ignoring base-rate data. The predictive accuracy of a test depends on the initial risk of a condition in the person receiving the test. The probability that a client with a positive (or negative) test result for dementia actually has dementia depends on the prevalence of dementia in the population from which the patient was selected—that is, on the pretest probability that a client has dementia. Because there is little appreciation of this point, predictive accuracy is often overestimated. What percentage of applicants would succeed on the job anyway—without any testing procedure? If 90 percent would, then testing does not add much information. As highlighted in this book, the availability of information (data that decrease uncertainty), is no guarantee that it will be used (and used accurately). Such gaps were a key reason for the development of evidence-informed practice (see Chapter 10).

Sources of innumeracy to which we are prone, such as the illusion of certainty, were highlighted in Chapter 2—our difficulties in reasoning correctly about uncertainty. Consider the example described by Eddy (1982), in which a physician thinks that there is a 99 percent probability that a breast mass is not cancerous. The subjective probability at this point is 1 percent that this woman has cancer. What should the new estimate be if a positive mammogram is obtained? The accuracy of mammogram results must be considered in answering this question. In a study reported in 1966, it was found that 79.2 percent of 475 malignant lesions were correctly diagnosed and 90.4 percent of 1,105

**Exhibit 15.1**
Accuracy of Mammography in Diagnosing Benign and Malignant Lesions

| Results of X-ray | Malignant lesion (cancer) | Benign lesion (no cancer) |
|---|---|---|
| Positive | .792 | .096 |
| Negative | .208 | .904 |

*Source:* Data are from "Mammography: Contributions and Limitations in the Management of Cancer of the Breast," by R. Snyder, 1966, *Clinical Obstetrics and Gynecology, 9.* Copyright 1966 by Lippincott/Harper & Row. Reprinted with permission.

benign lesions were accurately diagnosed, for an overall accuracy of 87 percent (Snyder, 1966; see Exhibit 15.1).

Bayes's formula, as applied to this example, is as follows:

$$P(ca \mid pos) = \frac{P(pos \mid ca)P(ca)}{P(pos \mid ca)P(ca) + P(pos \mid benign)P(benign)}$$

where
$P(ca \mid pos)$ is the probability that the patient has cancer, given that she has a positive X-ray report (the posterior probability)
$P(pos \mid ca)$ is the probability that, if the patient has cancer, the radiologist will correctly diagnose it (the true-positive rate, or sensitivity).
$P(ca)$ is the probability that the patient has cancer (prior probability)
$P(benign)$ is the prior probability that the patient has benign disease $[P(benign) = 1 - P(ca)]$
$P(pos \mid benign)$ is the probability that, if the patient has a benign lesion, the radiologist will incorrectly diagnose it as cancer (the false-positive rate; Eddy, 1982, p. 253).

The results are as follows, using the new information and the 1 percent estimate of the prior probability that the mass is malignant.

$$P(ca \mid pos) = \frac{(0.792)(0.01)}{(0.792)(0.01) + (0.096)(0.99)} = 0.077$$

Thus, clinicians may either fail to revise or incorrectly revise their probability estimates when thinking about additional data. These kinds of problems are harder than we realize. They are also typical of the problems clinicians confront, although in fields such as psychiatry, social work, and psychology, less information is available about base rates and test accuracy. Two kinds of odds should be considered (Arkes, 1981). One kind consists of prior odds—odds before additional information about a client is available. Obtaining more information (data that are useful in decreasing uncertainty) should change these prior odds. Bayes's Theorem can help clinicians to improve the accuracy of judgments in situations in which base rate data (that is, prior odds) tend to be ignored. It can help clinicians to appropriately consider the effect of case-related data, such as the results of a diagnostic test, on assessment of a client in determining the posterior odds. This does not mean to say that use of Bayes's Theorem in making predictions will always result in more accurate decisions; it may not. Both astute clinical judgments and use of this aid may be needed in many instances.

Errors concerning the predictive accuracy of tests are also a result of confusion between two different conditional probabilities. That is, we tend to confuse *retrospective accuracy,* the probability of a positive test given that the person has a condition, and *predictive accuracy,* the probability of a condition given a positive test result. Retrospective accuracy is determined by reviewing test results after the true condition is known. Predictive accuracy refers to the probability of having a condition given a positive test result and the probability of not having a condition given a negative test. It is predictive accuracy that is important to the clinician confronted with a test result on an individual (see Chapter 14 for further discussion).

Another source of error in making predictions is the assumption that the accuracy of a test can be represented by one number. In fact, test accuracy will vary greatly, depending on whether a test is used as a screening device in which there are large numbers of people who do not have some condition of interest or whether it is used for clients with known signs or symptoms. In the latter case, the true positive and true negative rates are much higher than in the broad screening situation, and so there will be fewer false-positives and false-negatives. Overlooking this difference results in gross overestimations of test accuracy in screening situations, resulting in a high percentage of false-positives. Consider an example described by Elstein and Bordage (1979). Assume that school officials want to use a screening test to identify children who will be abused by their parents, and that about 3 percent of school-age children are abused. Officials claim that 95 percent of abused children will be detected and that 10 percent of nonabused children will be false positives. What is the probability that a child is abused if the screening test is positive? The following information is available: (1) the probability of a child who is abused being identified by the test is $P$(Test + Child Abuse) = .95; (2) the probability of a false positive, $P$(Test + Normal Child) = .10; and (3) the prior probability of a randomly selected child being abused is the population base rate, .03. According to Bayes's Theorem (p. 359):

$P$(Child Abuse/Test + ) =

$$\frac{P(\text{Test + Child Abuse})P(\text{Child Abuse})}{P(\text{Test + Child Abuse})P(\text{Child Abuse}) + P(\text{Test + Normal Child})P(\text{Normal Child})}$$

$$\cdot \frac{.95 \times .03}{(.95 \times .03) + (.10 \times .97)} = \frac{.0285}{.1255} = .227$$

So the probability that a child who is positively identified by the test is actually an abused child is .0285/.1255 = .227. If 10,000 children are screened, the

**Exhibit 15.2**
Accuracy of Test in Identifying Abuse

| | | True State | | |
| --- | --- | --- | --- | --- |
| | | Abused | Not Abused | |
| Test | Abused | 285 | 970 | 1,255 |
| | Not Abused | 15 | 8,730 | 8,745 |
| | | 300 | 9,700 | 10,000 |

*Source:* From "Psychology of Clinical Reasoning," by A. S. Elstein and G. Bordage, 1979, in *Health Psychology* (p. 359), edited by G. C. Stone, F. Cohen, N. E. Adler, and Associates, San Francisco: Jossey-Bass. Copyright 1979 by Jossey-Bass. Reprinted with permission.

resulting data can be represented in a 2 x 2 contingency table (see Exhibit 15.2). Note the large number of false-positives. The moral is, consider base-rate information in evaluating test accuracy.

## OVERVIEW OF SOURCES OF ERROR

There are many sources of error in trying to make accurate predictions, including overlooking the effects of confounding causes, such as the play of chance and misleading effects of small biased samples (see also Chapter 11).

### AVAILABILITY

Predictions are made based on concepts and data that are available; here again we are influenced by practice theories and preconceptions. Hearing a persuasive causal explanation of an event increases a belief that an outcome associated with that event will occur. For example, Tversky and Kahneman (1983) asked a group of professional forecasters to indicate the probability of a complete suspension of diplomatic relations between the United States and the Soviet Union in 1983. Another group was asked to estimate this same outcome occurring simultaneously with another event, "a Russian invasion of Poland and a complete suspension of diplomatic relations between the U.S.A. and the Soviet Union." The probability of the second description was evaluated as more likely than the first. The causal coherence of a scenario is used to assess the likelihood of its occurrence; that is, causal persuasiveness is confused with outcome (Hogarth, 1987, p. 49). Availability is a useful guide if it encourages us to think of cues that are helpful in making predictions, or if an accurate estimate of the frequency of an event is provided. Behaviors that have occurred with a high frequency in a certain situation in the past are likely to do so again, other factors being equal. It is when available cues do not reflect the true frequency of an event or result in ignoring the importance of other events (such as nonoccurrences) that these result in errors. An illustration is reliance on the number of times an event occurs (*absolute frequency*) rather than the relative number of occurrences (the *relative frequency*).

*Influence by Anchoring*   The manner in which data are presented influences predictions. In addition to primacy effects (items early in a series gain our attention), recency effects (items last in a series gain our attention) also occur; information in the middle tends to be ignored. Anchoring effects are influential in all stages of decision making, including making predictions. Since initial judgments are often wrong, actions taken based on these may be incorrect. Initial judgments can be remarkably resistant to change. For example, even though subjects were told that initial estimates they received were based on random information such as the throw of dice, they did not alter their estimates (Tversky & Kahneman, 1974). Adjustments in predictions are often made on the basis of information that is initially available, thus compounding possible biasing effects of initial judgments (Hogarth, 1980, p. 47).

*Framing Effects*   Posing a decision in a certain way influences our decisions (e.g., Sonen, 2005). Emphasizing potential benefits of a choice increases the likelihood that the decision maker will say "yes." Conversely, we are more likely to say "no" when possible negatives are emphasized (Dawes, 1988, pp. 34–36). Framing effects are more powerful where important decisions are being made, such as whether to undergo a surgical procedure. Consider the following example:

> *Counselor:* Perhaps I can help you with your decision. We know that two-thirds of those who get treatment at Anderson Hospital for the Chemically Dependent remain chemical-free for two years. We also know that one-third of those treated at Luther Hospital's Chemical Dependency Unit return to chemicals within two years.
> *Client:* I think I'll choose Anderson because, from what you have said, my chances seem better there.

## REPRESENTATIVENESS

We are influenced by the degree of similarity between the characteristics of an event, object, person, and the class to which it belongs. Psychologists who work in personnel departments have images, for example, of what successful people are like in certain jobs. These images are used as a guide in evaluating the qualities of applicants. This stereotyping effect is shown in a study by Kahneman and Tversky (1973). Subjects received the following description, written by a psychologist. "Tom W. is of high intelligence, although lacking in true creativity. He has a need for order and clarity and for neat and tidy systems in which every detail finds its appropriate place. His writing is rather dull and mechanical, occasionally enlivened by somewhat corny puns and by flashes of imagination of the sci-fi type. He has a strong drive for competence.

He seems to have little feel and little sympathy for other people and does not enjoy interacting with others. Self-centered, he nonetheless has a deep moral sense." They were informed that Tom was a graduate student and were asked to indicate in what area he would probably specialize in graduate school.

- Business administration
- Computer science
- Engineering
- Humanities and education
- Law

- Library Science
- Medicine
- Physical and life sciences
- Social science and social work

Subjects selected computer science and engineering as most likely and education, social science, social work, and the humanities as least likely. These choices were influenced by the consistency of data offered, which supposedly favored this selection (see discussion of the conjunction fallacy). Representativeness is a valid indicator only to the extent that data sources are not redundant or that it does not result in ignoring other information (Hogarth, 1980, p. 31). Information that is inconsistent with our stereotypes of what characteristics are predictive of a given event is often ignored.

*Overlooking the Importance of Base Rate Data*   The earlier discussion highlighted the importance of considering base rate data (the general prevalence of a behavior or event in the population) in making predictions. Normative data tends to be ignored in making predictions, not only in relation to other people but in relation to self-perception as well. If we are informed that most other individuals act in a certain way in a situation and are then asked what a particular person will do in that context, we tend to ignore normative data in arriving at a judgment. A helpful rule of thumb is to find out what is known about the most frequent outcome in a situation and to attend to these data when making predictions. Because of preconceptions about what things go together, clinicians often overlook base rate data, assuming that they have nothing to do with case data. Often, clinicians do not have access to base rate information; such data may be difficult or impossible to acquire. Ignoring base rate data when they are available can result in overestimating clinical success; the question of how many cases would be successful anyhow is overlooked (see later section on feedback).

The attention topics receive in the media influence estimates of the prevalence of events. For example, the relative frequencies of cancer and homicides are overestimated, whereas the relative frequencies of asthma and diabetes, which receive less media attention, are underestimated (Lichtenstein, Slovic, Fischhoff, Layman, & Coombs, 1978). If the media and the professional literature devote a great deal of attention to children of alcoholics, this may lead clinicians to overestimate their prevalence. Consider also the attention given to stranger-abduction of children. A review article in *Public Interest* indicated that the prevalence of abductions by strangers has been grossly overestimated by special-interest groups and that once correct figures become available, later correction of inflated figures may do little or nothing to correct initial, inaccurate estimates (Best, 1988). Overestimating the prevalence of a problem is not without effects. The result may be redistribution of clinical and other resources away from areas where need is greater. We tend to worry about what has recently happened and to let events slip from our minds as the events recede into the past. Clinicians may worry more about whether they should report a threat by a client against a significant other immediately after a lurid description of a crime committed by another client when the clinician did not warn the involved party. The purchase of earthquake insurance increases right after an earthquake (Slovic, Kunreuther, & White, 1974).

*Overlooking Regression Effects*   Overlooking regression effects can result in errors. Extreme effects will usually not be so extreme when they are reassessed. If a client does unusually well on a test, she is likely to do less well the next time around; or conversely, if she does very poorly, she is likely to do better the next time around. "The implication of the regression phenomenon is that when prediction is based on sources with imperfect predictive ability, predictions should be less extreme than the information generated by the sources. The term 'regression phenomenon' simply means that in the presence of imperfect predictive sources, predictions should be regressed toward the mean" (Hogarth, 1980, p. 35). Both reliability and validity problems add to the regression effect. For example, lack of reliability may lead to predictions that are too extreme. This is a special problem in clinical contexts in which clinicians are heavily influenced by cues that have an extreme value; extremes stand out, they are vivid. Essentially, "a failure to understand chance fluctuations leads to judgmental errors" (Hogarth, 1980, p. 35). Expecting extreme values to be less marked on repeated assessment helps avoid this source of error. Superstitious beliefs may result from overlooking regression effects. Superstitions are beliefs about the causal relation between two or more events (for example, carrying a rabbit's foot, and avoiding bad luck) that are not true. An interesting example described by Kahneman and Tversky (1973) concerns Israeli flight instructors who were encouraged to use positive reinforcement and to avoid punishment to help pilots learn to fly. After doing so, they argued that these methods were not effective since it was their experience that praise of superior performance resulted in less effective outcomes on the next efforts, while criticism of poor performance produced improved performance on subsequent attempts. They concluded that punishment was more effective than positive reinforcement in increasing desired behaviors. Some argue that unwarranted belief in the effectiveness of most practices are superstitious in nature, given that there is no evidence that most practices do more good than harm.

## ERRORS IN ESTIMATING JOINT PROBABILITIES

Clinical practice often requires the assessment of joint probabilities. Let's say that a psychologist in a student counseling center wants to determine the probability that a student (a) will select journalism as a college major, (b) become unhappy with his choice, and (c) change to engineering. This involves estimating the probability of conjunctive events. Such events are usually overestimated. For example, when different groups of subjects were asked to estimate the probabilities of (a), both (a) and (b), and the probability of all three, they gave the following average estimates: .21 for (a); .39 for (a) and (b); and .42 for all three (a, b, and c; Slovic, Fischhoff, & Lichtenstein, 1976). The joint probability of two events cannot be greater than the smaller of the probabilities that are associated with the events (see section on overlooking important probabilities in Chapter 14).

## RELYING ON IRRELEVANT DATA

Irrelevant data increase the probability of incorrect predictions; a few worthless items can dilute the effect of one helpful item. The influence of irrelevant data is illustrated in a study in which social work graduate students were asked to estimate the likelihood that some people were child abusers. Inclusion of information that the person "fixes up cars in his spare time" and "once ran away from home as a boy" decreased the effects of data that he has "sadomasochistic sexual fantasies" (see Nisbett & Ross, 1980, p. 155). Irrelevant material about this person tended to make him less similar to someone who might abuse his child. A rule of thumb here is to ask whether data have any real predictive value.

## INFLUENCE BY REDUNDANT DATA

Sources of assessment data are not necessarily independent. Take, for example, the prediction of intelligence. Data concerning grade point average, intelligence test scores, recommendations, and past employment are not independent sources of information; they are related, which decreases the amount of information each source offers. Clinicians often overlook the consistency of redundant data in making predictions; that is, the more data sources they have available, even though these are not independent, the more confident they feel in their predictions. Consider the study of Oskamp (1965), in which the judgments of clinical psychologists were studied as a function of the amount of data they received. These clinicians were asked to make a prediction based on a case study and to indicate their degree of confidence in these judgments under different conditions in relation to the amount of data they received. As the data they received increased, so did their confidence in their judgments. There was, however, no increase in predictive accuracy. Kahneman and Tversky (1973) refer to the influence by the consistency of redundant data and the influences of extreme values of predictive cues as the *illusion of validity*—both increase confidence in judgments even though both are inversely related to the predictive accuracy of data sources. Our tendency to overestimate the degree of covariation between variables adds to the illusion of validity.

## Vague and Shifting Criteria

Errors may occur because of vague and shifting criteria for judging alternatives. Being overloaded with information reduces the consistency of judgments; one form of presentation (such as charts) is usually selected and others (such as the text) are ignored. This lack of consistency is one of the reasons that actuarial judgments are often superior to clinical judgments.

## Underestimation of the Play of Chance

Errors in prediction often occur because of misperception of chance fluctuations. Clinicians tend to overestimate their ability to make accurate predictions. For example, they often fail to appreciate the random variability in behavior that may be beyond any current models of explanation. People believe that the immediate future will compensate for unusual outcomes by reversing these patterns, and they base predictions on such beliefs (Nisbett & Ross, 1980). This source of error is known as the gambler's fallacy, because gamblers often make this error. The *gambler's fallacy* refers to the belief that the next event in a sequence that is probabilistic in nature, such as flipping a coin, will redress prior imbalances. It is assumed, for example, that the outcome of tossing a coin on one occasion influences the outcome on the next occasions; that if three heads in a row appear, the next flip will yield tails. This belief is exploited by gambling casinos as well as by those who claim to have paranormal power. Clinicians are also subject to this source of error. Making predictions can lead to an illusion of control; a feeling that there is control over a future that is indeed uncertain (see later discussion of feedback).

## Confusion of the Inverse

The confusion between a conditional probability and its inverse (confusion of the inverse) is likely to result in inaccurate predictions of pathology. The probability of a sign given a disorder is not necessarily equal to the probability of the disorder given the sign; the probability of the sign is usually higher than the probability of the disorder. If $P(S \mid D)$ and $(D \mid S)$ are confused, many more clients will be falsely diagnosed as having a disorder that they do not have (Eddy, 1982).

## Hindsight Bias

We have a tendency to say that we "knew it all along" when a certain outcome occurs, especially when it is consistent with our preconceptions. In fact, we often cannot recall what we predicted before an outcome is known, or miss-recall in a biased direction. This encourages overestimates of predictability (e.g., overestimating the relationship between returning a child to the home of his biological parents and subsequent child abuse). Knowledge of an outcome encourages the view that it was inevitable—that we should have known what the outcome would be, even though there was no way we could have known the outcome beforehand. We tend to assume that outcomes are consistent with our preconceptions—"I knew it all along." Another characteristic of hindsight bias is a tendency to assume a direct relationship between an outcome and certain causes when, in fact, no evidence is offered for or against such an assumption (Fischhoff, 1975). Since explanations are readily created, possible accounts are usually always at hand. Hindsight bias often results in blaming people for what appear to be errors that could have been avoided; looking back, knowing the outcome that occurred, it is assumed that "he should have known." It also results in praising people for what were just lucky guesses (Hastie & Dawes, 2001; Hogarth, 1980). There are benefits from hindsight bias; it helps us to remember associations that work as well as ones that do not work.

## OUTCOME BIAS

We tend to judge the quality of a process by its outcome. Those who have been told there is a poor outcome evaluate the decision or action more negatively. This is referred to as outcome bias. For example, an inverse relationship has been found between the severity of outcome and the judgments on the part of anesthesiologists concerning the appropriateness of care (see Caplin, Posner, & Cheney, 1991). Cases in which there were bad outcomes were rated as substandard while the very same behaviors, if they resulted in neutral outcomes, were rated as being up to standard. As Woods and Cook (1999) point out, "The information about outcome biased the evaluation of the process that was followed" (p. 146). People view an outcome as more probable when they are given knowledge of an outcome. Research concerning physicians' decisions about whether to recommend estrogen replacement therapy for menopausal women suggests that physicians feel more responsible for negative outcomes that are a result of their direct actions (for example, cancers that result from the treatment) than they do for negative outcomes that just happen (for example, bone fractures due to osteoporosis; see Elstein, 1988). Preferences for methods that have the smallest maximum loss may decrease attention to methods that would result in maximum gains. These kinds of biases, including hindsight bias referred to earlier, show that we tend to confuse and overlook differences between information available as to outcome at one time and information available at another time. Thus, "experiments on the hindsight bias have shown that: (1) people overestimate what they would have known in foresight, (2) they also overestimate what others knew in foresight, and (3) they actually misremember what they themselves knew in foresight" (Woods & Cook, 1999, p. 146). As these authors note, all three have implications for error analysis (see also Hershey & Baron, 1995).

The studies of hindsight and outcome bias reveal the play of social and psychological processes, as Woods and Cook (1999) note. When we think about error, we typically reflect on prior circumstances after an error has occurred. Thus, there is much room for incorrect memories and incorrect estimates of what information was available when the decision was made and what information is available after we know that an error has occurred. Hindsight bias results in misperceptions as well as incorrect analysis of the reasons why the mistake was made in the first place, that is, of "The factors that influence the behavior of the people working in the situation before the outcome was known" (p. 147).

> In general, we react after the fact as if the knowledge we now possess was available to the operators then. This oversimplifies or trivializes the situation confronting the practitioners, and masks the processes affecting practitioner behavior before the fact. As a result, hindsight and outcome bias block our ability to see the deeper story of systematic factors that predictably shape human performance (Woods & Cook, 1999, p. 147).

## Overconfidence

The tendency to be overconfident about the accuracy of our predictions is as common among experts as it is among other people (Baron, 2000; Slovic, Fischhoff, & Lichtenstein, 1982a). Overconfidence resulting from flawed self-assessments influences decisions in many areas including our heath and how much we "know" (Dunning, Heath, & Suls, 2004). Use of vague or irrelevant feedback obscures the true relationship (or lack thereof) between predictions and outcomes. Success tends to be attributed to personal skill, and failure tends to be attributed to chance.

## Faulty Memory

Faulty memory influenced by preconceptions may result in errors in recall about factors related to an outcome. These errors will obscure the relationship between predictor variables and outcomes. Trying to recall events is an active process in which accounts are often reconstructed. Feedback may be ignored, especially if this contradicts predictions and favored value systems on which these predictions are based.

## Overlooking the Interaction between Predictions and Related Actions

The interactive nature between the actions we take as a result of the predictions we make may obscure the true relationship between the effects of our actions and outcomes (Einhorn, 1988). We tend to forget that actions taken as a result of predictions influence the outcomes. Consider the prediction that the banks will fail, followed by a run on the banks and their subsequent failure. If you believe you can help a group, you may extend greater effort, which may increase the probability of a positive outcome. If an applicant is accepted for a job, opportunities on the job may ensure future success. Those who are rejected do not have these opportunities.

## WISHFUL THINKING

Clinical predictions are also influenced by preferences for certain outcomes; the probability of desired outcomes is judged to be higher than is justified by information available. This has been called wishful thinking (Hogarth, 1980).

## OTHER FACTORS

Predictions as well as causal analyses differ depending on question format. Thus, the response mode influences the judgment (Slovic, Fischhoff, & Lichtenstein, 1982b). Data presented in the form of "no" (negative terms) is more difficult to comprehend than data presented in positive terms.

## INCREASING THE ACCURACY OF PREDICTIONS

One step you can take to enhance the accuracy of predictions is to clearly describe possible risks and gains of alternatives and to make explicit predictions. Few clinicians offer specific probabilities in making predictions, even though predictions become more accurate if this is done (Einhorn & Hogarth, 1978). Rather than offering vague predictions (such as "I think insight therapy will be effective"), you could predict that there is an 80 percent chance that a certain intervention will be successful in increasing positive exchanges in a family. Comparison of outcomes with specific predictions offers more fine-grained feedback about accuracy than do vague predictions, such as "There will be improvement." Considering maximum possible gains from a given method may help counteract undue attention to minimizing risks associated with different options.

Visual representations can be helpful. Some writers recommend the use of decision trees (see Exhibit 15.3). Attending to base rate data when these are available, as well as to reliability and validity of measures, will enhance accuracy. Taking advantage of statistical tools will increase the accuracy of predictions. Many of the problems clinicians confront are complex, requiring tools to overcome cognitive limitations and to counter tendencies to make certain kinds of errors, such as ignoring base rates. Use of actuarial methods will increase the consistency with which known relationships between predictors and an outcome, such as the risk of future abuse, are considered. Although some clinicians believe that reliance on a predictive equation dehumanizes clients, this view ignores the human costs of error that result from not using these tools (Dawes, Faust, & Meehl, 1989). The compelling vividness of personal experience in "what works" will continue to discourage clinicians from using actuarial methods that are more accurate than clinical judgments. The tendency to focus on the conjunction of two events (such as certain kinds of dreams and negative events) may be checked by paying attention to *dis*confirming combinations in a four-cell contingency diagram (see Chapter 14). Asking about all four cells of a contingency table should help to

**Exhibit 15.3**
Subjective Probabilities Associated with Various Outcomes Following
a Pre-Retirement Decision

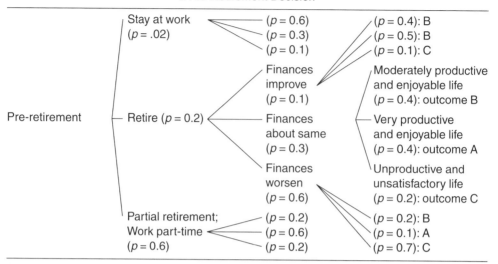

*Source:* From *The Case-Study Method in Psychology and Related Disciplines* (p. 284), by D. B. Bromley, 1986, New York: Wiley. Copyright 1986 by John Wiley & Sons. Reprinted with permission.

counter the focus on "hits." Keeping in mind harm done by not asking hard questions about diagnostic tests, or claims about the effectiveness of intervention methods, should motivate clinicians to raise such questions. Consider, for example, the harm done to children and their families by premature actions (removing children from their homes) based on invalid tests (Hobbs & Wynne, 1989). Consider harm done by placing troublesome youth in groups composed of other troublesome youth (Poulin, Dishion, & Burraston, 2001).

Decreasing reliance on memory will increase the accuracy of predictions. Because of confirmation biases, we tend to remember data that support our assumptions and may even recall data that were not present that support assumptions, and we may forget data that were present that do not support our views. These tendencies encourage excessive confidence in our judgments (Arkes, 1981). Keeping good records will decrease errors due to memory lapses. Collecting data about degree of progress will improve the quality of feedback and therefore improve the accuracy of predictions. Treatment manuals increase the fidelity with which interventions are implemented, which should enhance the accuracy of predicted outcome if this is related to fidelity. Being aware of the influence of the types of questions asked and responses requested on clients' expressed preferences may be helpful in accurately identifying preferences. Asking questions in different ways may be useful in attempting to clarify client values by revealing inconsistencies.

## Use Natural Frequencies: "Represent and Solve"

Bayes' Theorem is a key tool because it takes account of baserate probability of a condition in a population. The diagnostic value of a test is related to the base rate, as suggested earlier. Gigerenzer, here and in the following examples, (2002a) shows us how to make easier use of this tool. He and others have demonstrated that thinking in terms of natural frequencies rather than probabilities can help us to overcome sources of innumercy. They function as a "mind tool." Let's say that "The following information is available about asymptomatic women aged 40 to 50 in a given region who participate in mammography screening":

> The probability that one of these women has breast cancer is 0.8 percent. If a woman has breast cancer, the probability is 90 percent that she will have a positive mammogram. If a woman does not have breast cancer, the probability is 7 percent that she will still have a positive mammogram. Imagine a woman who has a positive mammogram. What is the probability that she actually has breast cancer?

Here is the problem in natural frequencies:

> Eight out of every 1,000 women have breast cancer. Of these 8 women with breast cancer, 7 will have a positive mammogram. Of the remaining 992 women who don't have breast cancer, some 70 will still have a positive mammogram. Imagine a sample of women who have positive mammograms in screening. How many of these women actually have breast cancer? (p. 42)

Here is the depiction of both natural frequencies and probabilities (p. 45):

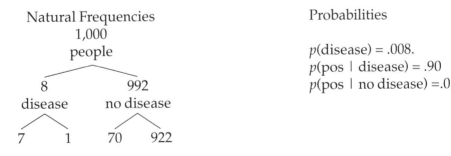

Natural Frequencies

1,000 people

8 disease      992 no disease

7    1       70    922

$P$(disease | positive)

$$= \frac{7}{7 + 70}$$

Probabilities

$p$(disease) = .008.
$p$(pos | disease) = .90
$p$(pos | no disease) =.0

$P$(disease | positive)

$$\frac{.008 \times .90}{008 \times .90 + .992 \times .07}$$

Let's take another example:

To diagnose colorectal cancer, the hemoccult test—among others—is conducted to detect occult blood in the stool. This test is used from a particular age on, but also in routine screening for early detection of colorectal cancer. Imagine you conduct a screening using the hemoccult test in a certain region. For symptom-free people over 50 years old who participate in screening using the hemoccult test, the following information is available for this region (p. 104):

### Conditional Probabilities Format—First 24 Participants

The probability that one of these people has colorectal cancer is 0.3 percent. If a person has colorectal cancer, the probability is 50 percent that he will have a positive hemoccult test. If a person does not have colorectal cancer, the probability is 3 percent that he will still have a positive hemoccult test. Imagine a person (over age 50, no symptoms) who has a positive hemoccult test in your screening. What is the probability that this person actually has colorectal cancer? ____ percent.

### Natural Frequencies Format—Remaining 24 Participants

Thirty out of every 10,000 people have colorectal cancer. Of these 30 people with colorectal cancer, 15 will have a positive hemoccult test. Of the remaining 9, 970 people without colorectal cancer, 300 will still have a positive hemoccult test. Imagine a sample of people (over age 50, no symptoms) who have positive hemoccult tests in your screening. How many of these people actually have colorectal cancer? ____ out of ____ ( pp. 104–105)

Here we have the natural frequency depicted (p. 107).

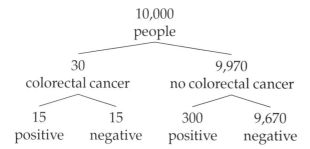

### THE IMPORTANCE OF FEEDBACK

One of the many choices you make is how (or if) to explore the accuracy of your decisions including predictions. Judgments in clinical work typically involve continuous rather than discrete evaluation, and thus many opportunities for gaining corrective feedback are available. The more rapid and continuous the feedback, the more sensitive and valid the measures of progress; the more closely outcomes are related to decisions made, the more opportunities we have to learn how to make better decisions in the future.

Feedback may be irrelevant to learning; outcomes observed may offer inaccurate or incomplete data about predictions, which may result in overconfidence in judgments. (See discussion of wicked environments in Chapter 8.) Clearly describing objectives and keeping track of progress on an ongoing basis will be helpful in assessing the accuracy of judgments. If feedback is delayed, for example, whether a rapist will rape again when released from prison, a precursor of later behavior, such as urges, could be monitored. What and how to measure outcome is a hotly debated issue. Choices are influenced by practice perspectives. Measures used include therapist opinions, self-report of clients, self-monitoring, role-playing, observation of behavior in real-life settings, and archival records, such as hospital admissions (see Chapters 11 and 13). Feedback that is vague, irrelevant, or delayed gets in the way of discovering relationships between predictions made and outcome. Selection of sensitive, relevant outcome indicators often requires creativity, as well as a knowledge of practice-related literature about possible options. (See Chapter 11 for further detail.)

## SUMMARY

Predictions are one of the products of clinical judgments. The predictions made are related to causal assumptions and typically involve the prediction of a criterion variable, such as likelihood of relapse, based on a number of factors. For example, a psychiatrist may have to predict whether a homeless, mentally ill person will make another suicide attempt in the near future. Clinical prediction involves the integration of different kinds of data—a task that is difficult. Predictions must be made under considerable uncertainty in terms of the relationship between predictor variables and a criterion such as the likelihood that an intervention will be effective. There is controversy over what criteria to use to evaluate outcome (for example, client self-report, opinion of the clinician, changes in real-life behavior). Comparison of statistical versus clinical prediction shows that actuarial methods usually are more accurate than clinical inference. Competing values must be considered; for example, to protect potential victims from assault, and maximize individual freedom of the potentially assaultive individual. Given the importance and uncertainties of the predictions that clinicians make, it is not surprising that they often say they do not make predictions or that they delay or avoid making them.

Making predictions and choices requires the assessment of probabilities. We are prone to make certain kinds of errors, such as the "confusion of the inverse" (assuming that the probability of a sign given a disorder is the same as the probability of the disorder given the sign). Other sources of error include overlooking the unreliability of data, being influenced by the consistency of redundant data, and using vague and shifting criteria for evaluating options. Ignoring consensus information and baserate data are common sources of error. Relevant data are often ignored because of our limitations in considering many different sources. We are also prone to hindsight bias; that is, knowledge of an outcome encourages a view that it was inevitable. Undue weight often is given to observed outcome rather than to examining all four cells of a contingency table; in addition, errors may arise from irrelevant, delayed, or vague feedback concerning the accuracy of decisions. Here, too, being forewarned is being prepared; that is, if we are aware of common sources of error, we are more likely to avoid them. Aids such as Bayes's Theorem can be used to combine subjective beliefs with objective data to arrive at probabilities. We can use frequency rather than probability to estimate risk. Visual representations can help us to attend to sources of uncertainty. The quality of feedback about the accuracy of predictions can be increased by making precise estimates of the probable success of intervention methods, by identifying clear objectives, and by monitoring progress in an ongoing fashion.

# CHAPTER 16

# Enhancing the Quality of Case Conferences, Team Meetings, and Organizational Culture

MAKING CLINICAL DECISIONS often involves discussions with other professionals, as well as with clients and their significant others. Sources of error discussed in previous chapters may occur during such conversations. A physician, social worker, physical therapist, occupational therapist, and nurse may all contribute to serving frail elderly clients. Social workers and nurses work closely together in hospice work. The involvement of different professionals with different helping approaches, and perhaps interests, highlights the potential for misunderstandings and conflict. Many decisions are made in case conferences, a setting that does not necessarily enhance the accuracy of decisions. The classic article by Paul Meehl, "Why I Do Not Attend Case Conferences" (1973), describes reasons why this occurs. Meehl believes that "many intelligent, educated, sane, rational persons seem to undergo a kind of intellectual deterioration when they gather around a table in one room" (p. 227); that group situations bring out the worst in many people in terms of intellectual functioning. The impressions that Meehl offered in 1973 have been supported by in-depth studies of dialogue in case conferences. For example, a study of decisions made in case conferences concerning child abuse found that, rather than a balanced search for the truth, these involved premature closure in assignment of responsibility for the abuse (Dingwall, Eekelaar, & Murray, 1983).

Case conferences represent a complex social situation in which participants have different goals, skills, values, styles of interaction, practice theories, prejudices, and biases. The setting in which they take place influences what occurs, as do the tasks addressed, the physical environment (for example, comfortable or uncomfortable, noisy or quiet), and the particular pressures (for example, to contain costs). The overall agency climate and culture influences the nature of team meetings and case conferences—for example, do administrators model critical appraisal of practices and policies in their agencies? (See Gray, 2001a.) Conferences are an ideal setting for the use of persuasion strategies that are not likely to further the quality of discussion. Emotional language may be used to create positive or negative views of clients. Opinions may be changed and actions taken on the basis of appeals to emotion rather than in response to sound arguments. Meehl (1973) suggests that clinicians take on questions to which they would never consider offering blithe answers in other contexts (for example, suggesting complex psychodiagnostic accounts even though they have had only a brief exposure to a client and little evidence has been offered to support their accounts). Sharing the values and skills of evidence-based practice should facilitate decision making in interdisciplinary teams. This will contribute to a culture of thoughtfulness in which everyone participates, agreed-on tasks are clear, differences of opinion are viewed as learning opportunities, and there is a sincere interest in understanding other points of view and critiquing all views in order to help clients.

## CHARACTERISTICS OF CASE CONFERENCES THAT DECREASE THE QUALITY OF DECISIONS

Questionable practices that occur in conferences are discussed in the sections that follow. Other concerns that encourage inaccurate decisions, such as the sick-sick fallacy and use of pseudoauthority, which also occur in case conferences, are discussed in Chapter 7. Many of these practices should be decreased in evidence-based organizations, which reflect a keen interest in and value informed decision making involving critical appraisal of different views based on relevant research findings and consideration of client values and preferences as well as those of other involved groups (see Chapters 10 and 11).

### Attributing Value to All Contributions

There may be a reluctance to criticize anyone's views, even though these may be uninformative or inaccurate. Practice-related research may be ignored or disregarded: "the prestigious thing to do is to contribute ideas to the conference . . . whether or not the quality of evidence available is adequate to support the view offered" (Meehl, 1973, p. 235). The tendency to be impressed by plausible-sounding but uninformative explanations is encouraged by not asking such questions as "What evidence is there for this view?" or "How does this help us understand and know what to do about this problem?" "In order to maintain the fiction that everybody's ideas are worthwhile, it is necessary to lower the standards for what is evidential. As a result, a causal anecdote about one senile uncle remembered from childhood is given the same group interest and intellectual respect that is accorded to the citation of a high quality experimental or field actuarial study" (p. 228).

Participants may abandon ordinary rules of scientific inference and principles of human development. Meehl offers an example of a nurse equating a childhood imaginary companion with an adult's visual hallucination. Trivial statements that are uninformative may be made because they are true of all people (Kadushin, 1963). This has been called the Barnum effect. Examples are: "She has intrapsychic conflicts," or "He has problems with object relations." Along the same lines, the vagueness of astrological descriptions allows readers to see themselves in such accounts and so consider them accurate and meaningful. Tolerance for feeble statements will occur if these statements, even though flawed, succeed in persuading others to accept a favored position. Fallacies may be recognized but not pointed out because their acceptance will bolster a favored position. Asking pointless questions slows down the process of decision making. Questions can be divided into three categories in terms of encouraging helpful answers: (1) irrelevant, (2) of possible relevance, and (3) highly relevant. So, we should ask, "Will the answer make any difference in helping clients attain outcomes they value?" Asking "and therefore?" following irrelevant questions may, as Meehl suggests, encourage participants to think more carefully before asking questions. Questions sometimes are posed not to advance toward an informed decision based on sound arguments and evidence, but to do the opposite—for example, to sidetrack a discussion by encouraging biasing emotional reactions. Such questions have a point, but it is not to arrive at informed decisions.

## CONFUSING INCLUSION AND EXCLUSION TESTS

One kind of decision clinicians make is whether to assign a diagnosis to a client. Some characteristics may indicate that a client is not an X (an exclusion test) whereas others indicate that if the client has certain characteristics he is an X (an inclusion test). These two kinds of criteria are confused when it is incorrectly argued that because Mr. A does not have a certain characteristic, he is not an X when, in fact, this characteristic may not be associated with a particular diagnosis (that is, it is not *critical* to the diagnosis). Meehl (1973) uses the example of a trainee who argues that a patient is not schizophrenic because he does not have "delusions or hallucinations with clear sensorium" (p. 230). Meehl argues that not all schizophrenics have these accessory symptoms.

## CONFUSING THE CONSISTENCY OF AND DIFFERENTIAL WEIGHT OF A SIGN

Another kind of statement that does not advance well-reasoned decisions is pointing out that a certain diagnosis is consistent with a characteristic when it is also consistent with other possibilities among which the group is trying to distinguish. For example, if a group is trying to decide which of two parents abused a child and each of the parents has a history of abuse as a child, pointing out that the mother has a past history of abuse is not informative, since the father also has such a history. This sign has no diagnostic relevancy at this point. This error "illustrates one of the generic features of case conferences in psychiatry, namely, the tendency to mention things that don't make any difference one way or the other" (Meehl, 1973, p. 231).

## NEGLECT OF STATISTICAL LOGIC

Unreliability of measures may be neglected when interpreting score changes or difference scores. Relatively small differences (for example, in before-and-after measures) may reflect unreliable measures rather than a true difference. (Whether the measures are valid is another question.) If the reliability of a measure is questionable, then small differences should be interpreted with caution or ignored. Ignoring the size and representatives of samples used to infer traits or tendencies is a common error made in arriving at clinical decisions. Inferences are often based on small, unrepresentative samples of behavior. For example, a judgment about a resident of a nursing home may be based on a 15-minute observation in an interview (see the discussion of the law of large numbers in Chapter 13). There are many ways in which samples may be unrepresentative. Behavior may have been sampled in a context that differs considerably from the one in which the problems occur. Aggressiveness of a child at home may be the problem, but perhaps the only observational data available may have been gathered at school. Behavior in this situation may not reflect behavior at home. Furthermore, since no information is offered about the antecedents and consequences of behavior labeled *aggressive,* little is known about the circumstances in which such behavior takes place. Errors may occur because of lack of understanding about how probability logic applies to individual cases. Estimates of prior probability (for example, the base rate for a diagnosis of schizophrenia in a particular population) and the degree of leverage added by a given characteristic (such as history of hospitalization) often are neglected. Actuarial data often are ignored and decisions based on intuition, even though research supports the superiority of actuarial methods (see Chapter 15). A clinician may decide to rely on intuition even though no other outstanding factors offer sound reasons for overriding actuarial data. When a decision must be made about whether to accept an applicant for clinical training who has a low college grade point average, it is not rare for someone to say, "Let's interview him," assuming an interview would yield better predictions, when actuarial data shows that it will not. This is called the "interview error" (Dawes, 1994a). Clearly, there are instances in which other factors should be considered. However, disregard for empirical data results in more misclassifications than correct classifications.

## INAPPROPRIATELY MINIMIZING SIGNS OR SYMPTOMS

This fallacy occurs when a behavior is excused on the grounds that anyone would do it. The question is—would anyone do it? Thinking about doing something and doing it are two different things. Clinicians are influenced by personal biases when selecting characteristics viewed as normal as well as when identifying what is pathological. This fallacy is the opposite of the sick-sick fallacy, and is illustrated by the nurse who attempted to belittle the importance of a patient's hallucinations by telling the group that she herself had an imaginary companion as a child (Meehl, 1973). Both tendencies result from the inappropriate imposition of personal biases in relation to what is "healthy" and what is not. Both tendencies are encouraged by lack of knowledge about norms and a reluctance to seek such data (see also discussion of the rule of optimism in Chapter 7).

### IDENTIFYING THE SOFTHEADED WITH THE SOFTHEARTED

A regard for critical appraisal of a claim may be viewed as cold, unemotional, and unfeeling, whereas a regard for vagueness, non sequiturs, and tolerance of fallacies may be considered a mark of caring and compassion. Actuarial methods for making decisions (see Chapter 15) may be abandoned because of a concern that a client will not receive optimal treatment—even though, over all clients, research suggests that more accurate decisions result from actuarial decision methods than from relying on consensus, for example (e.g., Grove & Meehl, 1996; see also earlier section on neglect of statistical logic). Such a departure from what practice-related research suggests is best may not only increase the chances of making a mistake for an individual client, but increase inaccurate predictions for other clients as well (Meehl, 1973). Unless there is a sound method that allows you to discriminate between cases in which intuition or consensus would be the optimal method for making a decision, and cases in which it would be more accurate to rely on actuarial methods, neglect of actuarial methods that have a better success rate will decrease the accuracy of decisions. Sympathy is not a sound reason to abandon well-tested actuarial methods for making predictions.

### OTHER PROBLEMS

Different standards of evidence may be used to support a favored position than are used to critique opposing views; that is, more rigorous evidence may be requested when considering perspectives other than our own. For example, inferences based on projective tests may be offered with no corroborative evidence to support a preferred diagnosis. In contrast, data based on observation of behavior in real-life settings may be requested in support of alternative views of a client's problem. It may be assumed that only a certain kind of professional is qualified to offer certain information. Psychiatrists may assume that the role of psychologists is mainly to offer assessment data based on psychological tests, and that they have little else to contribute. Actually, the particular degree that a professional has does not necessarily indicate areas of competence.

The "spun glass theory of the mind" refers to the belief that people are very fragile and should be treated as such; that relatively minor deprivations, rejections, or failure experiences play a causative role in major traumas (Meehl, 1973, p. 253). As Meehl (1973) notes, such a belief may have counter-therapeutic effects in protecting clients from reality or not offering them effective intervention methods. For example, one clinician objected to interviewing a client about to be discharged in a new setting on the grounds that this unusual situation might undo the successful effects of therapy.

The *fallacy of uncertain consequences* involves the argument that because the consequences related to an option (such as selection of a given intervention) are uncertain, it should not be used—it would be too risky. Indeed, uncertainty is an inevitable part of most decisions. If no data are offered showing a high likelihood of anticipated risks, the fallacy of uncertain consequences has been made (Michalos, 1971, p. 100). The *crummy criterion* fallacy occurs when the criteria used to assess the soundness of an argument are weak or inappropriate. Meehl (1973) offers the example of dismissing psychological test results on the basis that these do not agree with the assessment of a psychiatrist who held a 10-minute interview with a client.

## CHEAP SHOTS

Some tactics can be called cheap shots because of their failure to advance informed decision making. Like other kinds of strategies, they may be subtle or obvious (e.g., see Edwards, 1938). Such cheap shots often are used by people in power positions. Negative labels (such as "nitpicker"), may be used to refer to someone in order to discredit a position. This unimaginative ploy is made more effective by including actions that attempt to convince listeners that the person using the negative labels does so only because he or she has been forced to by the supposed "facts." A sad expression of inevitability may be assumed or a joking manner used so that the negative label will leave its mark but the name caller can deny that he meant it that way. A possible remedy here is to ignore the cheap shot and reintroduce the question at hand. This remedy is suitable unless the name calling has a negative effect on the decision-making process. There are two situations in which it may have such an effect. One is when the recipient of the name is a client or significant other who may be stigmatized in terms of decisions made about her or him. Another such situation is when the negative name is attached to one of the decision makers, whose views are then ignored as a result, even though they are sound.

Ridicule may be communicated in how something is said as well as by what is said. A roll of the eyes may change the impact of a statement. A look of shared commiseration and strained long-suffering directed toward other participants (a raise of the eyebrows and a sigh) may accompany a statement. Remedies here include restating a position clearly, noting why it should be taken seriously (for example regarding possible consequences for clients). If the ridicule is offered by a person in authority, others in the group could ask for more appropriate criticism of the position. The success of these remedies depends on several factors, such as the cogency of a point, the views of others, and the status of the ridiculer. Those who use ridicule may attempt to make the target appear pedantic for continuing to uphold an "ill-advised" position. A more subtle but no more admirable tactic is to make negative innuendoes about a position without offering any evidence for them—to imply, for example, that a certain action will have bad effects. Emotional appeals and innuendoes may be used to encourage others to discount disliked cogent points. Force or intimidation is sometimes used to gain compliance in place of offering sound reasons to create conviction. Threats of removal of resources or punishing consequences, such as loss of a job, may be made. There is, of course, no assurance that decisions based on this foundation are sound.

## WHY IS THE QUALITY OF DISCUSSION IN CASE CONFERENCES OFTEN POOR?

Reasons for the poor quality of many case conferences are related to the factors discussed at the beginning of this chapter, namely that case conferences represent complex social contexts in which people have different goals, values, styles, and skills, and in which they are influenced by the particular setting and the pressures within this setting. Reluctance to hurt or embarrass people encourages some of the problems described in the previous sections. Meehl calls this the "buddy-buddy syndrome." It results from the false belief that high-quality discussions cannot occur unless harsh or discourteous methods are used. This is not so.

> If it is argued that you can't prevent people who have nothing significant to contribute from talking without being cruel or discourteous, I submit that this is empirically false. I point to case conferences in other specialties like neurology and internal medicine, where, so far as I have observed, there is no social discourtesy or cruelty manifested by those in charge; but the general atmosphere is nevertheless one which says, in effect, "Unless you know what you are talking about and have reason to think that you are saying something really educational for the rest of us or beneficial to the patient, you would be well advised to remain silent. Mere yakking for yakking's sake is not valued in this club." I have rarely had to listen to trivia, confused mentation, plain ignorance, or irrelevancies when I have attended case conferences in internal medicine or neurology or the clinicopathological conference on the medical service. If an atmosphere of decent intellectual scholarly standards can be created and maintained on those services, I cannot think it is impossible to approximate the same thing in clinical psychology and psychiatry. (p. 284)

Participants have different goals. These may be explicit or implicit and may be shared or competitive (if some goals are achieved, others may not be). The explicit goal of case conferences is to make decisions, such as what treatment should be recommended for a client or whether to transfer a client to another facility. The manifest purpose of the group may not be the real one. Take "rubber stamp groups," for example. Here, the ostensible purpose is to arrive at a decision. In reality, the decision has already been made; the purpose of the meeting is to simply go through the motions of having a discussion about a matter that has already been decided. Strains and differences among goals account for some of the odd happenings at group meetings. Personal goals that often do not contribute to the process of decision making include the following: show how bright you are, avoid anyone knowing you don't know what you are doing, impress your superiors, be as invisible as possible (a chair potato), skewer your boss or most disliked colleague, and win your point. Goals in most groups include maintaining positive relations, regulating intimacy and accessibility, appearing normal, maintaining claims to roles, and controlling information presented.

If participants have different values, misunderstandings may occur. For example, a psychologist may focus on harm done to a victim of rape whereas a lawyer may focus on protecting the rights of the accused. Fallacies that occur may not be recognized, even blatant ones. Case material is often presented in a disorganized fashion, which makes sound decision making difficult or impossible. An agreed-on format for case presentations can encourage descriptions that make it easier to catch errors. This should include a description of how the client came to the attention of an agency or clinician. Although this may be obvious in some contexts, in other settings, such as schools, child protection, and community mental health centers, it is not obvious. For example, significant others (those who interact with and influence a client) may have encouraged a client to seek help against the client's wishes. Such information is important in recognizing coercive elements in initial contacts. Topics in need of discussion can be noted on the form.

Disagreements and differences of opinion are inevitable; however, many clinicians do not learn to discuss differences in a helpful fashion. For those who lack skills and positive experiences with discussions of differences, disagreements may create feelings of anxiety or anger. For example, master's degree students in the School of Social Welfare at Berkeley had been interested for years in forming a panel of clinicians with different perspectives and having these individuals discuss a case or some common questions. Some instructors who were approached turned them down on the grounds that a discussion of differences would be divisive. The terms *discussion* and *debate* seemed to be associated with *oppositional, destructive,* and *confrontational,* rather than with *inquiring* and *stimulating.* Some people react to disagreements as if these are altercations or may lead to altercations or fights. The term *argument* as used in lay language typically refers to a disagreement between two people—emotions are high, language may be abusive. There is disregard for the feelings of others. Winning is the object, rather than finding the truth, and there is a resistance to new ideas. Discussions, dialogues, and debates are centered on issues rather than on people. The purpose of a discussion is not to protect the self-esteem of the head of the psychology department—it is to determine if Mr. Richards is ready to be discharged from the hospital or whether Mr. Sansom, who is dying of AIDS, requires a more protective setting. The focus should be on finding the best route to achieving outcomes valued by clients. There is an openness to new ideas rather than a resistance to these, no matter what their source—whether offered by a low-status person, perhaps a social worker in a medical conference, or by a high-power person, perhaps the head physician on a service unit. Emotion is at a functional level.

Participants may not realize that their biases encourage them to ignore contradictory information. Consider the prevalence of *group think* (overlooking deficits in a preferred view because of lack of consideration of disadvantages and well-argued alternatives). Symptoms suggested by Janis and Mann (1977) include the following:

1. *Illusion of Invulnerability:* Members ignore obvious danger, take extreme risk, and are overly optimistic.
2. *Collective Rationalization:* Members discredit and explain away warnings contrary to group thinking.
3. *Illusion of Morality:* Members believe their decisions are morally correct, ignoring the ethical consequences.
4. *Excessive Stereotyping:* The group constructs negative stereotypes of rivals outside the group.
5. *Pressure for Conformity:* Members pressure any in the group who express arguments against the group's stereotypes, illusions, or commitments, viewing such opposition as disloyalty.
6. *Self-Censorship:* Members withhold their dissenting views and counter-arguments.
7. *Illusion of Unanimity:* Members perceive falsely that everyone agrees with the group's decision; silence is seen as consent.
8. *Mindguards:* Some members appoint themselves to the role of protecting the group from adverse information that might threaten group complacency.

Group characteristics that contribute to group think include high cohesiveness, an insulation from outside influence, authoritarian leadership styles, and high stress. Pressure for conformity has long been studied with sobering findings (e.g., Asch, 1956). Recognizing the value of minority views in discovering solutions should lessen tendencies to squelch them (e.g., see Nemeth & Goncalo, 2005).

Pfohl (1978) found that diagnostic team members usually passed over contradictory information and, when directly confronted with contradictory evidence, would ask the group "to look beyond this irrelevant 'fact,' to grasp the whole picture of a patient's problem" (p. 175). Contradictory evidence to a position may be transformed into additional evidence for a preferred diagnosis;

for example, by interpreting a client's statements as denials that yield further evidence for a diagnosis. Errors are particularly likely when a practice theory is used that can account for anything—even contradictory claims. The high status of some participants in case conferences increases the probability that errors they make will be accepted. Decker (1987) suggests that even if defense lawyers are present at commitment hearings, reliance on knowledge about the patient's behavior in the hospital (to which lawyers do not have access unless they locate and use another insider) gives the upper hand to psychiatrists. False biographical material may be used to bolster a position, and this may remain standing unless challenged.

Fallacies may be recognized but not commented on because of past failures to improve the quality of discussions. The power structure in a group may be such that no matter how cogent a point, it will not be persuasive because of the apathy and fear of most participants. Or diplomatic skills that are useful in countering or neutralizing fallacies may be lacking. A history of harsh criticism for speaking up in case conferences or fear of negative evaluation discourages participation. Silence, when confronted with faulty assumptions that may harm clients, no matter what the cause—including a past history of being harshly criticized in a group—calls for thinking about the possible implications for clients. (See discussion of the ethics of excuses in Chapter 17.) Feeling helpless and saying nothing in a group setting, even though understandable in terms of an unpleasant past history, is an ethical concern if this may result in decisions that harm clients. Participants may lack skills in focusing on shared goals (see Fisher & Ury, 1991). Ideological biases may interfere with balanced consideration of different perspectives. If there are no incentives to alter such biases, the level of discourse may remain at a low level. Some discussions are not so much arguments but an exchange of opinions. That is, there may be so little clarification of claims and grounds for these, that no one knows what is being discussed. Topics discussed may be of little or no interest to participants. There may be little shared sense of working together toward helping clients receive high-quality services.

The fact that people sit around a table does not necessarily mean that they will be listened to if they speak. Whether others listen and whether an opportunity to speak is even given depends on factors such as status in a group. Studies of decision making in predicting the dangerousness of psychiatric patients suggest that effective neutralizing of information contradictory to a preferred diagnosis is based largely on the authority and control of the psychiatrist over other team members (Pfohl, 1978). Psychiatrists used a variety of tactics to control interaction, including interruption of team members in the process of interviewing a patient and disrupting the timing of the presentation of information. Participants often have different frames of reference and knowledge bases for viewing a concern. A psychiatrist may focus on biomedical causes; a social worker may emphasize environmental causes. An administrator may be concerned about the precedent a decision may set. Use of different frames of reference may result in misunderstandings.

## DENUNCIATIONS AND PITCHES

Some investigators who have made detailed examinations of case conferences conclude that these can most accurately be described as contexts in which someone is prematurely assumed to be responsible for an act, such as child maltreatment, and then a denunciation effort is made to bolster this account. "A successful denunciation establishes the act as one typically committed by persons of a 'bad' character and constructs a biography of the actor that indicates such a character. A successful pitch normalizes the act and the biography" (Emerson, 1969, p. 156). Opinions may be changed and actions taken based on appeals to emotion rather than in response to well-thought-out arguments that offer sound reasons. The following excerpts show how participants who disagree with a position are ignored and illustrates the use of emotional language to encourage acceptance of a preferred position. It is based on a transcript of a case conference held to determine whether a child's injuries resulted from maltreatment and, if so, who was responsible (Dingwall, Eekelaar, & Murray, 1983).

## AN EXAMPLE OF A CASE CONFERENCE[1]

The participants in this conference included a social worker (SW), her senior (SSW), a health visitor (HV), her nursing officer (NO), a medical social worker (MSW), two policemen (PC1 and PC2), two physicians (Cons 1 and Cons 2), a registrar (Reg), a medical student, and a secretary. The family involved in this case included the mother, Mrs. Hancock; her live-in boyfriend, Mr. Finnegin; Mary Walsh, who lived with the family and helped out with the children following the mother's recent accident; Lindy Oates, the eight-month-old baby brought to the hospital; and three other children (pp. 152–53; all names used throughout this case are fictitious).

> The child came to casualty at 5 p.m. . . . The boyfriend had come home and said that he had held the child up because it was crying and had discovered a lot of bruises. He didn't know how they had got there and he called the GP [general practitioner]. The GP had said that he had been called only because of a cough and a runny nose. The only prior admitted incident was that the child fell off the sofa and had a bruised cheek. The mother was living with a twenty-six-year-old boyfriend called Finnegan but the child was a child of her former boyfriend. The mother had had her hand in plaster because she had broken her wrist after falling on ice. They were living with three other children in the house. There was somebody else living in the house as a kind of help for them who was known to

1. *Source:* From *The Protection of Children: State Intervention and Family Life* (pp. 152–65), by R. Dingwall, J. Eekelaar, and T. Murray, 1983, Oxford, England: Basil Blackwell. Copyright 1983 by Basil Blackwell, R. Dingwall, J. Eekelaar, and T. Murray. Reprinted with permission.

the social services. On examination the baby was crying. She had a torn upper frenulum . . . and was covered in bruises . . . . These were on the mouth, the chest and the upper abdomen and they were usually circular. Some of them were recent, only a few hours old but others had been there a few days. No other abnormality had been found and there was no bone injury. The child had been admitted for observation. . . . Everybody commented how wary the child was when anyone approached the cot. . . . She looked suspicious and afraid . . . and sometimes she cried if anybody tried to touch her. (pp. 153–154)

There was agreement based on the clinical evidence as well as on the social context (that is, irregular cohabitation, previous contact with social services) that the injuries resulted from maltreatment. The discussion then focused on identifying the person guilty of this abuse.

*MSW:* This is complicated by the fact that there are three adults in the house. No one knows very much about Finnegan. She (Mrs. Hancock) claims that she wants to marry him and that he is wonderful with children. Mary Walsh is a vulnerable person who has been known to the social services and she has been the main caretaker of the child. It's a complicated situation.

*SSW:* Yes, she was known to us a long time ago but we have had no contact since then.

*CONS1:* Does the present cohabitee have a police record?

*PC1:* We don't know.

*HV:* He is a divorcee with children aged six and four whom he visits. He looks to be in his 20s. He's Irish, he comes from Belfast.

*PC1:* Could the injuries have been due to a fall from a cot?

*REG:* No.

*SW:* I know the priest to whom Mary goes when she is in trouble. I had a phone call on Monday from him saying that Mary has been upset about the baby. Mary's version, and she is a person who tends to drift around with problem families, is that four weeks ago she was worried about the baby's chest but the parents would not call a doctor. She knows that she is under suspicion, and her explanation is that they didn't call the doctor because of the bruises and she thought that the boyfriend used to grip the baby too tightly. When asked who gets up when the baby cries at night, she says it is the boyfriend. She thinks the bruises come from the boyfriend's holding the baby too tightly. (p. 155)

The authors note that Mary Walsh is discredited by references to her vulnerability as well as by her previous contact with social services, which offer evidence of an uncertain mental state and impairment of responsibility. She is also presented as the person with the greatest opportunity to injure the children, given her role as their main caretaker. On the other hand, Finnegan and the mother are presented as considering marriage and Finnegan's skills with children are praised.

This debate runs through the conference as the area team social workers attempt to make a pitch for Mary Walsh and the others denounce her. After the MSW's initial proposal, the senior from the area team makes a rather weak attempt to dispute the first two references: her contact with social services was a long time ago and it is therefore wrong to stigmatize her as a current client and as someone who is so vulnerable as to need frequent help. The following utterances generally contribute to the favorable view of the cohabitee: he has no known police record; he is of mature age; and although divorced, he visits his children. . . . Mary Walsh's social worker than comes in with another challenge to the MSW's formulation of the household. She links Mary to her parish priest, as someone who might be thought to have a special competence as a receiver of true statements and might be a candidate for the status of 'reputable sponsor,' to assert that Finnegan and Mrs. Hancock are colluding to cover up Finnegan's rough handling of the child. . . . The consultant pediatrician points to the limitations of this (second-hand) story in accounting for the clinical presentation. (pp. 156–157)

> *CONS1:* That doesn't account for the torn lip.
> *SW:* No . . .
> *CONS1:* It seems as if the torn lip was caused by a blow to the face but (Cons2) is more expert at this.
> *CONS2:* There could have been no other way.
> *SW:* Mary is rather dim but very fond of babies. She says that she has had too much put on her of late. She has always looked after other people's children. (p. 157)

Dingwall points out that the social worker "does not have a license to challenge the statement of the consultant." The MSW asks the senior social worker about previous contacts with the family. The senior social worker noted that the first contact with the family was in 1973, when Mrs. Hancock and her husband were homeless and that occasional contacts occurred at other times for financial difficulties and marital problems. "Her husband had left and came back with another woman and tried to turf her out" (p. 157). He was evicted by order of the County Court. The health visitor then spoke:

> *HV:* I saw Mrs. Hancock yesterday. . . . She said she didn't know how the bruises had happened. She said that on Friday her boyfriend said that she should call a doctor and that he was cross when this was not done when he had come home. There was no mention of the bruises to the doctor but the doctor noticed it when he came. She said she didn't know how they had happened and said that Mary had baby sat the previous day and said that she hadn't broached the subject with Mary because Mary was upset due to the death of an aunt. About the lip she said she thought it was simply teething. She said that Mary had been looking after the child the day before. She also said that it was only occasionally that the children were left in a room with the baby but they were not left alone in

the house with [the baby]. I asked Mary if she knew how the bruises came and she said no. I asked if she had seen them before and she said that she had seen them on Wednesday. I asked why she hadn't mentioned it and she said she didn't want to cause trouble. I had met them just before the baby was born. Mother/baby interactions always seemed to be good. Mr. Oates wasn't living with them at the time. He was divorced and had custody of his own children. They originally had planned to get married when they got a four-bedroomed house. Mrs. Hancock came to the clinic in January and then I heard that she had now got a new boyfriend who was Mr. Finnegan—I visited her—Lindy looked well and went to both Mrs. Hancock and her boyfriend readily and cuddled with them and that was the last I saw of them. (pp. 157–58)

The authors comment: "This sequence continues the character work on three adults. The senior social worker runs over Mrs. Hancock's record. She is known to the department but not as a persistent or highly dependent client. The most recent contacts with her have been as the victim of her husband's attempt to prise her out of the matrimonial home and as a self-referral for help with her children's behavior." The health visitor "depicts Mrs. Hancock as worried about the baby's health, as a reliable source of data on her boyfriend's concern and as a kindly woman who had not liked to ask Mary about the bruising on the child because of Mary's recent bereavement" (p. 158).

> *CONS1:* Has anybody else have anything to say? (There is a long silence.) I think it appears to be a child who by persons unknown has been subject to repeated assaults over a period of time. I would feel that the child should not be allowed to return home when further damage might occur. . . . Does anybody feel that they would like the child to go home?
> *SW:* Whoever caused the injury, it's quite clear that the others have colluded with it. Because of the relationship, it is not possible to point the finger.
> *MSW:* Mary might be being used as a scapegoat (p. 159).

The authors note that nobody is yet firmly identified as the agent of the abuse. The consultant still holds out the possibility that Mrs. Hancock was responsible, but whoever had done it, as the social worker and her colleague point out, all the adults may be responsible. The consultant shuts out the possibility of disagreement with his conclusion about returning the child. A view is stated and the obligation placed on the hearers to show why it should not prevail, an exercise which would involve breaching a strong interactional preference for agreement, an act which is capable of discrediting the speaker as a person of sound judgment. By her partial agreement, however, the social worker gets into a position where she can renew her attempts to defend her client. (p. 159)

The discussion continues.

> *SW:* Mary is leaving this weekend. She has known the baby since it was born and she has looked after the older children when Mrs. Hancock had her baby. . . .

What might happen is that if a child is miserable for four weeks with a cold this could be a trigger.

*PC2:* Was Mary married?

*SW:* Yes to Matt Walsh, an inadequate person who drank a lot.

*PC2:* What's her age?

*SW:* 28 and she is fairly dim.

*PC1:* Could the children have been responsible? The eldest is seven.

*HV:* I don't think that she would leave them alone with the baby. Maureen's a tearaway; she has set light to a bedroom.

*REG:* But they are adult fingertips.

*PC2:* Has anybody seen them separately?

*SW:* Not really.

*PC2:* Mary hasn't been seen about it?

*HV:* No. She has gone to her GP this morning. (pp. 159–60)

Another possible cause of the injuries, the other children, is discussed. The discussion continues, and some additional evidence of the abuse is brought forward.

*CONS2:* Is this Mrs. Walsh part of the famous Walsh family? There is a sub-culture, of which the Walshes are a part, who have been battering their children for 30 years.

*SW:* He is the brother of Bridget.

*CONS2:* That's right, she was a Walsh, she flung her baby across the room in front of me. The first time I actually saw classic baby-battering myself. They all belong to a subculture of batterers. My God, a bloody Walsh, God help us.

*SW:* But she is a Walsh by marriage only.

*NS2:* Oh it doesn't matter. It isn't a question of the genes. Well I am very doubtful of taking them on with any hope for success. (There is some further muttering along these lines.)

*PC1:* Are there any signs of neglect, for example, nappy rash?

*HV:* No.

*CONS2:* All this is very recent. A very recent intrusion and we have now an intruder with an ominous name.

*PC1:* It is one for us?

*CONS2:* Yes, it is for you gentlemen. When the mother broke her wrist, someone intervened.

*PC1:* So long as we have a statement of complaint we can act. Is the baby being taken into care? (pp. 161–62)

The authors comment that this passage is the key to the conference outcome; that it "opens up the possibility of . . . a 'total denunciation,' which overrides all possible defenses by declaring that the person's character is so irremediably damaged as to eliminate all chance of successful voluntary intervention. By linking Mary Walsh to a known child abuser, her sister-in-law,

Bridget, she is tied into a group for whom child mistreatment is a natural way of life. As such, she must be the agent of these particular injuries. Moreover, the actions involved are so intrinsic to her moral nature as a member of this 'subculture of batterers' that there is little prospect of changing them without compulsion or punishment." Mary's social worker still attempts to test the analysis.

> *CONS2:* It doesn't seem as if the mother neglected her.
> *SW:* But she colluded.
> *CONS2:* Yes, that is a matter for the police. (p. 162)

The authors note that the absence of neglect of the child is being tied to the children's mother rather than being used as evidence on Mary's behalf. "Again, we have the 'facts' being assembled to support a particular characterization. Debate on this is quickly shut down" (p. 162).

> *PC1:* How long will the child stay here?
> *CONS1:* We could keep her a week.
> *PC1:* That'll give us time to do our business.
> *SW:* Has the mother visited the child? How does the baby react?
> *REG:* She has. . . .
> *MSW:* So we should wait to hear from the police and then consult with you.
> CONS2: Yes, I will do some research.
> *SW:* Yes, it is relevant. She has looked after children before.
> *CONS2:* I'm not accusing her. The link-up is a necessary piece of knowledge.
> MSW: I could find out from the social workers where she looked after children before.
> *NO:* What if the parent wanted to take the child home?
> *CONS2:* You should get a place of safety . . .
> *CONS1:* Is there anything else?
> *PC2:* I need some personal details of Walsh.
> *SW:* Is there any way of finding out a bit about Martin Finnegan?
> *PC1:* We will. (laughter) (pp. 162–63)

The authors note that even though "the social worker asks about the child's reaction to her mother, points to Mary Walsh's record of satisfactory child care-taking and to their ignorance of Martin Finnegan's past . . . none of these challenges is picked up. The registrar attempts to deal with the first and is cut off, the second is ignored, and the third . . . is treated as a joke. . . . By the end of the conference the police are already referring to 'Walsh' in the way they would characteristically talk of a suspect. Mary Walsh is to be prosecuted and the children left at home" (p. 163).

This case conference illustrates an effort to determine who is responsible for the maltreatment of a child—who is capable of such an action. The authors believe that the selection of Mary was the predictable outcome of a process that permeates the whole system for the identification and management of mistreatment. She seemed to be the person least responsible for her actions and therefore most likely to have been responsible for the abuse. Identification of Mary as the culprit allows the family to remain intact and minimizes the amount of coercion involved. Dingwall and his colleagues note how difficult it would be to challenge the preferred account "without calling one's own competence into question" (p. 164). When a "total denunciation is initiated, those who hold other views must be brought into line or discredited" (Emerson, 1969, pp. 140–41). Dingwall, Eekelaar, and Murray are also aware of the long-term effects of being discredited; these professionals will see each other again in the future.

And what was the outcome? Mary Walsh was arrested and was prosecuted on a charge of bodily harm. The case was dismissed. "About two weeks after this hearing, Lindy Oates was admitted to hospital with two skull fractures, a broken arm, and three broken ribs. Her brother had bruising in nineteen separate places. It emerged that Martin Finnegan had, five years previously, been convicted of causing grievous bodily harm to his own daughter. He pleaded guilty to the assaults on Lindy and her brother and was jailed for four years. Mrs. Hancock continued to insist on his competence as a stepfather and announced her intention of standing by him" (p. 165).

The authors believe that the identification of Mary Walsh as the person responsible for the abuse was the expected outcome of the reasoning process that characterizes the system in which these kinds of cases are reviewed. "Once Lindy Oates had been adequately characterized as a victim, Mary seemed to be the person least responsible for her own actions and therefore most likely to have perpetrated the injuries. Moreover, her prosecution left Mrs. Hancock's household / family intact and the children out of state care. The decision gives effect to the liberal principles on which child protection operates" (p. 165; see Chapter 7 for a discussion of the rule of optimism).

## ENHANCING THE QUALITY OF CASE CONFERENCES AND TEAM MEETINGS

Steps that can be taken to enhance the quality of team meetings and case conferences are described in the following.

### USE EFFECTIVE INTERPERSONAL SKILLS

Effective use of critical thinking skills in group contexts requires complementary social skills. This became clear shortly after I had introduced material on critical thinking in my classes for graduate students. For example, one student said that the chief psychiatrist became quite irritated when she questioned the clarity of a term he used during a conference. Rather than clarify the term, he asked the student "Don't they teach you that at Berkeley?" He attempted to use his prestige and authority in an ad hominem attack on the student's school. So, colleagues may not appreciate others who ferret out vagueness and identify fallacies in reasoning, even though this is helpful in avoiding clinical errors that may harm clients. You should be prepared that you may be liked less by questioning dubious statements, even when you are very diplomatic. Cultural differences may limit critical feedback. Familiarity with common fallacies and social persuasion strategies will be valuable in identifying and countering methods others may use to discourage active involvement in a discussion (see Chapter 6). Gaining the attention of the group will require skill in identifying appropriate opportunities to enter a discussion. Holding the floor against interruption attempts is an important skill (see Gambrill and Richey, 1988). Humor can be used for many different purposes, including encouraging others to feel relaxed, defusing aggressive reactions, relieving embarrassment, reminding people of social rules, introducing risky topics, and unmasking pretensions. A sense of humor helps to keep things in perspective.

## PRESENT IDEAS CLEARLY AND PERSUASIVELY

Guidelines offered by Rieke and Sillers (1984) for the use of evidence include using detailed persuasive examples that relate to the experience of the audience, noting exceptions to a position, and selecting representative examples. How ideas are presented as well as what is said influences the persuasiveness of a message. Practice helps in presenting views clearly and persuasively. Staff who use brief words or phrases can increase their effectiveness by using elaborated opinion statements when expressing their views. An elaborated opinion statement starts with a pronoun and contains a compound sentence, such as "Well, I think _____ because of . . ." Smiling or giggling when discussing a serious topic will dilute the impact of what is said. Seating position may influence persuasiveness. Past research found that even avowed feminists did not perceive women who sat at the head of a table as leaders (Porter & Geis, 1981). Eye contact with others will enhance the credibility of statements. Preparation of Critically Appraised Topics (CATS) will facilitate sharing of important information (see Chapter 11).

The "humble inquirer and doubter" approach that Benjamin Franklin found so useful in having others consider his views may be effective in some groups. Franklin "resolved never to advance any view as certainly correct, but rather to express himself in terms of 'modest diffidence'" (Silverman, 1986, p. xix). In other groups, phrases that minimize the importance of what is said (such as, "I don't know if this is important, but" or "this may not be significant, but") may encourage others to tune out rather than tune in.

## PRESENT IDEAS POSITIVELY

Presenting ideas in a positive manner involves avoiding unnecessary negative comments about other views, recognizing common interests, and praising other people's good ideas. Avoid temptations to make hostile or sarcastic comments. Points can be persuasively made without resorting to put-downs which, although they may temporarily impress people by their wit, may not win friends or influence people.

## Do Not Take Things Personally

Assuming the best rather than the worst about other people's intentions can help us to identify and move beyond fallacies and stratagems without becoming overly emotional. Stressful work environments may encourage harsh, inappropriate reactions. Certainly there are times when a direct request for a behavior change is called for; one of the reasons unconstructive behaviors persist, such as belittling and ad hominem comments, is because no one does anything to discourage them.

## Prepare for Meetings

You can prepare for meetings by posing answerable questions regarding decisions that must be made at case conferences, and searching for and critically appraising related external research. For example, perhaps a decision must be made about what services would be best for an elderly woman with recurring depression. An answerable question might be "For an elderly woman with depression related to lack of social contacts, is cognitive behavioral or interpersonal intervention most effective in decreasing depression?" Posing relevant questions and seeking related research allows you to bring what you find to the conference—or even better, to distribute it beforehand so participants can read it before they arrive. This kind of preparation will be helpful in weighing the evidentiary status of different views during meetings.

The likelihood of offering sound arguments can be increased by practicing how to present views, anticipating counterarguments, and being prepared with responses. A search for accurate explanations requires an open exploration and critique of well-argued alternatives. Those with privileged access to relevant data will have an advantage, since their statements cannot be checked. During a commitment hearing, a psychiatrist may be the only one present with knowledge of a patient's behavior in the hospital (Decker, 1987). If the psychiatrist's report cannot be corroborated, there is no way of knowing whether it is accurate or not. Studies of periodic commitment hearings show that evidence offered is not always accurate (see, for example, Decker, 1987). Other staff members may have access to a patient's behavior, and their reports may be sought. Case records should be reviewed before case conferences to check statements based on these records for accuracy. Memories of what was contained in case records may be altered by confirmation biases. That is, deliberate misreporting is probably not the reason for false reports. However, whatever the reason, inaccurate accounts may result in decisions that do more harm than good. It is much easier to distort positions if these do not appear in writing. People who use an authoritarian decision-making style and who make use of propaganda methods are aware of this and will try to discourage putting things in writing, usually by claiming that it is unnecessary, foolish, a waste of time, or dangerous. This is not to say that noting things in writing is always a good idea. Clearly it is not, for example, if a policy is to be flexibly implemented.

## Clarify Vague Terms and Evaluations

General terms and vague evaluations often occur in case conferences. Unless these are clarified, their relevance and validity cannot be judged. Metaphors should be clarified in terms of how they apply to a discussion. The same is true for fables and descriptions of personal experiences. Such descriptions may be psychologically moving but may not help in making accurate decisions. Vague statements such as "she's mentally ill," and vague labels such as "borderline personality" or "depressive syndrome" should be clarified. Abstractions sometimes hide a lack of related evidence.

## Distinguish between Strong Opinions and Bias

Strong opinions often are mistaken for bias (Scriven, 1976). People can accurately be called biased only if their reasons for holding a position are matters of prejudice and they cannot be convinced to alter their position when presented with more accurate premises or inferences. The style of presentation may be misleading in distinguishing between someone who is biased and someone who has strong opinions. Strong bias may pass unchallenged because of the style of presentation. For example, someone who is biased may disguise this by acting as if he has been forced into accepting a position against his will; that it is the last thing he would do if his hands were free (which they are). Conversely, someone who is open to a discussion of different perspectives may appear biased because of strong assertion of a point of view. People with a point of view who are interested in discovering what is true will be interested in hearing criticism and diverging views. "Someone can be said to represent a point of view rather than a bias if s/he strives to (a) identify his/her interests; (b) open them to examination; (c) encourage discussion; and (d) take into serious consideration dissenting points of view" (MacLean, 1981, p. 148).

## Focus on Common Goals

Fisher and Ury (1991) stress the importance of focusing on common goals, especially in contentious atmospheres. They suggest that this is helpful in encouraging understanding of other views and in keeping anger and anxiety in reasonable bounds, even in response to people who are masters of giving others "aggro" (aggravation). Rather than dwelling on a troubling reaction, such as name calling, the common goal (to arrive at well-reasoned decisions) guides the discussion.

## Increase Knowledge of Group Process

Many behaviors that occur in groups are the result of particular kinds of group process and structure. For example, groups have different leadership patterns and different norms. Being familiar with group process and structure should increase your effectiveness in groups (e.g., see Garvin, Gutierrez, & Galinsky, 2003). This should decrease tendencies to "take things personally" or blame others (reactions that get in the way of cooperative problem solving) because you will recognize the role of group structure or process. Knowledge of group process highlights the importance of setting an agenda at the beginning of the meeting to ensure that important topics are discussed. This also suggests the prevalence of the "buddy-buddy syndrome" and should encourage group members to agree on norms that encourage open critical appraisal of different views that, if acted on, will affect clients' wellbeing—for example to seek information about the evidentiary status of recommended methods. Strategies suggested by Janis and Mann (1977) to avoid group think include the following:

1. The group should be aware of the causes and consequences of group think.
2. The leader should be neutral when assigning a decision-making task to a group, initially withholding preferences and expectations. This practice will be especially effective if the leader consistently encourages an atmosphere of open inquiry.
3. The leader should give high priority to airing objections and doubts, and be accepting of criticism.
4. Groups should always consider well-argued unpopular alternatives, assigning the role of devil's advocate to several strong members of the group.
5. Sometimes it is useful to divide the group into two separate deliberative bodies as options are evaluated.
6. Spend a sizable amount of time surveying all warning signals from rival groups and organizations.
7. After reaching a preliminary consensus on a decision, all residual doubts should be expressed and the matter reconsidered.
8. Outside experts should be included in vital decision making.
9. Tentative decisions should be discussed with trusted colleagues not in the decision-making group.
10. The organization should routinely follow the administrative practice of establishing several independent decision-making groups to work on the same critical issue or policy.

Agreeing on an agenda is useful in clarifying the goals of a meeting and increasing the probability that they are met. Such agreement offers an opportunity to reaffirm the focus of a discussion if people get off the track. Agreeing on norms that facilitate well-reasoned ethical decisions is another valuable practice. Examples include the following: (1) no one should interrupt another speaker, (2) no one person should hog the floor, (3) speakers are responsible for describing how points raised relate to the topic being discussed, and (4) assumptions should be accompanied by a description of related research.

Agreement on a well-designed case presentation format should save time by clearly presenting relevant data, decreasing discussion of extraneous data, and helping to ensure inclusion of data that contribute to well-reasoned decisions, such as information about environmental factors related to hoped-for outcomes. Another helpful norm is to take a vote on controversial issues; otherwise, a consensus in favor of a position may be assumed when there is none, or there may be a consensus, but in favor of a competing position. One group member can be selected to introduce alternative perspectives in groups in which there tend to be premature closure, and to remind the group that they should not attack (or ignore) people who introduce different views but respond to points raised in a constructively critical manner (Janis, 1982). This role can be assumed by a different person each month.

## KNOW WHOM YOU ARE DEALING WITH: BE POLITICALLY SAVVY

It helps to know whom you are dealing with—that is, to be familiar with preferred decision making and interactional styles of participants (e.g., see French and Raven, 1959; Jehn, 2004). One purpose of group meetings may be to discuss a change in procedure or policy. Decisions discussed in group meetings may really be made outside the group. For example, a small cohort may run things in a hospital by laying the groundwork for support of preferred positions prior to meetings. This may be done by meeting together and agreeing on a position and by seeking the support of others who are sympathetic to a position prior to the group meeting. Seeking solutions to difficult clinical questions may be hampered by naysayers who may comment, "It won't work," "We've tried that in the past and it failed," "There's no time," "We don't have the resources," "You don't understand our system," or "That's the way we've been doing it for years." Typically, no evidence—or only weak support—is provided for such statements. Such statements may be made not because a solution is not desired, but because no possible solution can be envisioned. It may not be possible to change a disliked or dysfunctional style; however, critical thinking skills and related interpersonal competencies can be used to mute the effects of styles that compromise the quality of decision making. Group members can become more active in modeling effective decision-making behaviors, such as asking about the evidentiary status of recommended methods. Some people possess critical thinking skills as well as helpful interpersonal competencies, but use these only when they must, in order to reach their goals. I have been quite amazed to see that someone who is usually attacking and demeaning in a discussion, and who makes use of dishonest strategies (such as misrepresenting positions), can act quite differently (courteous, attentive, even ingratiating) in settings in which such offensive strategies would be quickly identified and countered. Rather than assuming a pained, patronizing expression when colleagues speak, there is attentive interest with an expression that wise words are being spoken.

The preferred style of some individuals is to make unsupported pronouncements and to act as if support is offered for the pronouncement when it is not (begging the question). This method is used mostly by those who occupy a power position in the group—taking advantage of participants' reluctance to question a person in such a role. Pronouncers may assume a patronizing or offended stance if asked to support their views. Some people try to encourage others to go along with a position by forecasting vague negative outcomes if disliked options are selected. If others are not swayed by one negative forecast, additional scare tactics may be invoked to create fear and worry. Intimidators may first try to neutralize disliked positions (for example, by ignoring them or by using patronizing responses) and, if this fails, then try to intimidate participants. A colleague may say that if cognitive-behavioral methods are used to treat depression, rather than medication, the client may make another suicide attempt. The question is: Is there evidence that such an attempt would be more likely if the former method were used? Is there counterevidence?

## ENHANCE CRITICAL THINKING SKILLS

Being familiar with formal and informal fallacies increases the likelihood that you can identify them and move the discussion to sounder points. Having names or numbers for the fallacies helps in recognizing them, and may even be of value in discouraging a fallacy with humor. When I pointed out to one of my colleagues who had the habit of distorting positions and then attacking the distorted version, that he had just committed number 19 of Thouless's (1974) list of 38 dishonest tricks of debate, everyone laughed, and he dropped his straw man argument. Case conferences provide one of many opportunities to hone critical thinking skills and related interpersonal competencies. Fallacies are bound to occur. A "fallacy or stratagem of the week" can be selected for special focus.

## TRY TO UNDERSTAND OTHER POINTS OF VIEW

Only if you understand another point of view can you accurately identify flaws and strengths in a position. If this guideline had been used by participants in the case conference described earlier in this chapter, the true culprit might have been identified as being responsible for the abuse of Lindy, and subsequent abuse avoided. And we can offer cogent counterarguments only if we understand other views. A focus on common goals (helping clients) encourages attention to other perspectives. We are less likely to blame others for actions, statements, and styles that we do not like if we try to see things from their points of view. Empathic reactions increase recognition of environmental factors that influence others (Regan & Totten, 1975), and reduce prejudice toward others (Batson et al., 1997).

## THE INFLUENCE OF ORGANIZATION CULTURE AND CLIMATE

Organizations develop cultures and climates. Certain values are preferred and certain norms and rules are followed. Components of culture include his-

**Exhibit 16.1**

Factors That Influence Clinical Practice

| Source | Influencing contributory factors |
|---|---|
| Agency context | Funding sources |
| | Legal and administrative regulations |
| | Economic and regulatory context |
| Organizational policies and management practices | Financial resources and constraints |
| | Organizational structure |
| | Policy standards and goals |
| | Safety culture and priorities |
| Work environment | Staffing levels and skills mix |
| | Workload and shift patterns |
| | Design, availability and maintenance of equipment |
| | Administrative and managerial support |
| Team characteristics | Verbal communication |
| | Written communication |
| | Supervision and seeking help |
| | Team structure (congruence, consistency, leadership, etc.) |
| Individual (staff) factors | Competence (knowledge and skills) |
| | Physical and mental health |
| Task requirements | Task design and clarity of structure |
| | Availability and use of protocols |
| | Availability and accuracy of test results |
| Client characteristics | Complexity and seriousness of concerns |
| | Language and communication |
| | Personality and environmental circumstances |

*Source:* Adapted from "The Investigation and Analysis of Clinical Incidents," by C. Vincent and S. Taylor-Adams, 2001, in *Clinical Risk Management: Enhancing Patient Safety* (p. 442), edited by C. Vincent, London: BMJ. Reprinted with permission.

tory, contingencies in effect, patterns of communication, decision making styles, philosophy, myths, and stories. Organizations are influenced by their external environments, including funding sources and legal regulations (see Exhibit 16.1). Staff are influenced by accepted policies and preferred management practices—for example, a "top down" or participatory decision-making style. Policies influence staffing levels, adequacy of training, and overall workload, which in turn affects staff stress levels. Organizations differ in the quality of services offered, and in the quality of training opportunities and supervision provided to staff. A recent report of services in Wales and England reported that half of the patients in intensive care receive suboptimal care (Kmietowicz, 2005). Agencies differ in their policies about introducing inno-

**Exhibit 16.2**
How Different Organizational Cultures Handle Safety Information

| Pathological culture | Bureaucratic culture | Generative culture |
|---|---|---|
| • Don't want to know. | • May not find out. | • Actively seek it. |
| • Messengers (whistleblowers) are 'shot.' | • Messengers are listened to if they arrive. | • Messengers are trained and rewarded. |
| • Responsibility is shirked. | • Responsibility is compartmentalized. | • Responsibility is shared. |
| • Failure is punished or concealed. | • Failures lead to local repairs. | • Failures lead to far-reaching reforms. |
| • New ideas are actively discouraged. | • New ideas often present problems. | • New ideas are welcomed. |

*Source:* From *Managing the Risks of Organizational Accidents* (p. 38), by J. Reason, 1997, Aldershot, England: Ashgate. Reprinted with permission.

vative technologies and in how well they match the competence of staff to the tasks they confront. All these factors influence the overall task environment, which in turn influences decisions made (see Exhibit 16.1). Although status (ranking) is important in all organizations, the criteria on which it is based differ in different organizations—for example, longevity of service, charisma, expertise, or coercive power. Contingencies may not support behaviors that forward evidence-informed decisions and related critical thinking skills. Organizations have different ways of handling conflict and uncertainty and less-than-hoped-for success. They differ in the extent to which they seek clear, accurate information about service outcomes and use this information to improve services, and in the extent to which they encourage a culture of thoughtfulness, in which critical discussion is valued (see Exhibit 16.2).

If we can have worker incompetence, is there such a thing as organizational incompetence? Examples include: 1. lack of any means of checking whether key tasks are carried out; 2. not checking the quality of communication with clients; 3. lack of feedback on important decisions, so staff cannot learn how to improve future performance; 4. not using interventions that have been shown to be effective; 5. continuing to use services that have been shown to be ineffective; and 6. using interventions that have been found to harm clients. Of course, what is considered incompetence will depend on the goals of the individual. For example, a chief administrator who values only his salary and doesn't care about clients will not consider harm to clients a sign of organizational incompetence. To what extent are errors tolerated, or glossed over, because of callousness? Are some planned with knowledge that clients will be harmed? Singer (1978) suggests that incompetence, callousness, and planned error explain organizational error behavior. He suggests that "In cases where there is an unwillingness to take action, the second category occurs, errors of callousness" (p. 31). "When key people within organizations or institutions are made aware of a problem, persistent or exceptional, and do not take steps to correct it or to rectify injustices, we have errors of callousness" (p. 31). We frequently rationalize our behavior, that is, give a reason as to why it occurred. When are such rationalizations unethical? We should ask these questions regarding bureaucrats—those who are in high-level administrative places, as well as line staff.

## CREATING A LEARNING ORGANIZATION

Knowledge can grow only in an open environment, in which clients and staff are free to raise questions (express criticism) about practices and policies and their outcomes. Criticism provides information that may help to minimize avoidable mistakes. Learning organizations are characterized by ongoing improvement in the quality of decisions as well as the development of new knowledge, including new ways of using and managing knowledge developed by others. Gray (2001a) suggests that knowledge in an organization can be increased by transforming tacit into explicit knowledge (see discussion of intuition in Chapter 4). The notion of a learning organization suggests an active pursuit of the flow of knowledge and developing more knowledge, rather than a passive stance that characterizes many organizations. An evidence-informed organization is one in which staff at all levels "are able to find—appraise, and use knowledge from research evidence" (p. 249). Gray (2001a) characterizes the evidence-based organization as having "an obsession with finding, appraising, and using research-based knowledge as evidence in decision making" (p. 250). In an evidence-based organization, practices and policies are selected based on their track record of success in attaining outcomes that clients value. "The aim is to allocate resources equitably, and in ways in which resources can do the most good for the least cost, and to ensure that providers do the same, where it is appropriate . . . to prescribe provider actions" (Øvretveit, 1995, p. 121). Evidentiary status alone does not imply that a practice or policy should be adopted; there are many other considerations, such as client preferences, needs of different populations, and resources available. Adoption of an intervention depends on whether the benefit is sufficiently large relative to related risks and costs (see also discussion of "What is Evidence?" in Chapter 9.) Administrators have a responsibility to create a work environment in which behaviors that contribute to positive outcomes for clients are maximized and behaviors that diminish such outcomes are minimized.

*Learning from Errors*   Settings differ in how easy it is to make, recognize, cover up, and remedy mistakes. In discussing errors we should consider the extent to which employees control their own work life. Some agencies take advantage of opportunities to learn how to improve services from a review of factors related to adverse events. Others ignore such opportunities. Research regarding error highlights its inevitability and its many related causes:

- Human fallibility can be moderated up to a point, but it can never be eliminated entirely. It is a fixed part of the human condition, partly be-

cause errors, in many contexts, serve a useful function (for example, trial-and-error learning in knowledge-based situations).
- Different error types have different psychological mechanisms, occur in different parts of the organization and require different methods of management.
- Safety-critical errors happen at all levels of the system, not just at the sharp end.
- Measures that involve sanctions, threats, fear, appeals and the like have only a very limited effectiveness. And, in some cases, they can do more harm—to morale, self-respect and a sense of justice—than good.
- Errors are a product of a chain of causes in which the precipitating psychological factors—momentary inattention, misjudgement, forgetfulness, preoccupation—are often the last and least manageable links in the chain.
- The evidence from a large number of accident inquiries indicates that bad events are more often the result of error-prone situations and error-prone activities than they are of error-prone people. Such people do, of course, exist, but they seldom remain at the hazardous sharp end for very long. Quite often, they get promoted to management. (Reason, 1997, p. 129)

Staff willingness to identify mistakes is influenced by agency culture. Ineffective error management strategies include:

- They 'firefight' the last error rather than anticipating and preventing the next one.
- They focus on active failures rather than latent conditions.
- They focus on the personal, rather than the situational contributions to error.
- They rely heavily on exhortations and disciplinary sanctions.
- They employ blame-laden and essentially meaningless terms such as 'carelessness,' 'bad attitude,' 'irresponsibility.'
- They do not distinguish adequately between random and systematic error-causing factors.
- They are generally not informed by current human factors, knowledge regarding error, and accident causation. (Reason, 1997, p. 126)

Reason (1997) identified a variety of factors that influence how safety is handled. These include *safety-specific factors*, such as policy concerning incident and accident reporting and emergency resources. *Management factors* include how change is handled, quality of leadership, and communication. Other factors include policies regarding hiring and placement, purchasing, and degree of control over purchasing. *Technical factors* also influence how safety is handled, such as compatibility of human and system interfaces. *Procedural factors* include standards, rules, and operating procedures. *Training characteristics* also influence safety. For example, is there a close match between training offered and competencies required? If reporting mistakes is pun-

**Exhibit 16.3**
Making Adverse Incident Reporting Work

1. Training for all staff on risk management and incident reporting.

2. Continuing education on the aims and importance of risk management and incident reporting.

3. A clear statement that all staff are responsible for reporting.

4. A clear description of reportable incidents/indicators, drawn up in consultation with staff.

5. User-friendly incident reporting forms.

6. Clear description of reporting procedures.

7. Encouragement of staff to report an incident even if they are not sure whether it is necessary to do so.

8. A designated person on shift who is responsible for making sure that any incident that occurs during that time is reported.

9. A policy of no blame and no disciplinary action except in cases of gross misconduct, repeated errors despite retraining, or criminal negligence.

10. Regular feedback to staff describing the action taken as a result of their reports.

11. Design of corrective strategies to reduce undesirable incidents in the future.

12. Inclusion in clinical practice of specific corrective strategies by general consensus.

13. Evaluation of the efficacy of corrective strategies.

*Source:* Adapted from "Clinical Incident Reporting," by J. Secker-Walker and S. Taylor-Adams, in *Clinical Risk Management: Enhancing Patient Safety* (p. 434), edited by C. Vincent, London: BMJ. Reprinted with permission.

ished, few will do it. On the other hand, if agency policy recognizes that mistakes will be made and that they are vital for learning how to do better in the future, and staff are encouraged to discuss them with their supervisors at an early point, they are less likely to result in further negative effects, and provide an opportunity to learn how to decrease avoidable mistakes. Strategies suggested to make incident reporting work are illustrated in Exhibit 16.3. A key reason errors and mistakes continue to occur is that no one takes any steps to identify them, bring them to people's attention, discover their causes, and involve others in trying to minimize avoidable ones. Social organizations have a great deal to gain in the short term by encouraging the view that errors are caused by a particular individual in an organization, but much to lose in the long run in terms of helping clients. Consider, for example, the many instances in which the death of a child in state care is attributed to a single staff person. This hinders a systematic exploration of agency culture and climate to identify related factors. The causes of errors are systemic. We cannot understand them, in most cases, by looking solely at one individual.

*Encourage Accountability*   The prevalence and variety of avoidable errors that decrease quality of services clients receive are related to agency policies regarding accountability. Assumed responsibilities of different parties have implications for opportunities to make these visible and to decrease avoidable errors. To what extent are known errors tolerated? To what extent do staff fail to acknowledge and rectify known errors? Related forms of denial Singer (1978) proposes include blaming the victim, trivializing error, nonresponse, outright cover-ups, reinterpreting errors as correct, and bureaucratic diffusion of responsibility. Staff could suggest that errors are unavoidable when indeed they are avoidable, or protest that errors have only minor consequences, when they have major consequences, including killing people. "Hidden by bureaucratic complexity, decision-makers increasingly take overt chances with the lives of individuals, groups, or whole populations, themselves shielded from the consequences of their actions by various forms of organizational assumed liability" (Singer, 1978, p. 31). That is, most corporations have legal wings used to protect the corporation and those in it from adverse events, such as lawsuits. What is the responsibility of those in leadership positions to honestly represent the quality of services provided? To what extent are they complicit participants in cover-ups that prevent improvement in services? In a helplessness/hopelessness point of view, we deny that we have a choice. However, as many suggest, we *do* have a choice. Indeed, existentialists argue that our entire life is about making choices in the absence of knowledge as to what lies ahead, including nothing. Singer (1978) suggests that "probabilism"—the view that most bad things won't happen—has replaced the view that we have a choice. He argues that this is used as a substitute for thinking and to obscure moral responsibility. Consider continuing to offer services that have been found to harm clients. Is this ethical? Is it an example of "planned tolerable error"—the view that not that many people will be hurt?

## SUMMARY

One setting in which clinical decisions are made, discussed, or rubber-stamped is case conferences. The case conference has been the subject of some excellent and lively critiques, such as the classic chapter by Meehl, in which he identified a number of characteristics that dilute the quality of decisions made, including the tolerance for feeble inferences and rewarding gold and garbage alike. Factors that encourage the use of low-level appeals and irrelevant statements include the buddy-buddy syndrome (people are reluctant to hurt or embarrass others), a feeling of powerlessness, social anxiety, lack of effective social skills, vested interests, ideological biases, and failure to recognize fallacies. Rather than being a setting in which there is a reasoned discussion of well-argued alternatives, case conferences may reflect emotional denunciations and pitches for or against particular individuals. Effective interpersonal skills, considering other perspectives, and assuming the best about the intentions of others are an important complement to critical thinking skills. An emphasis on shared values (helping clients) will encourage consideration of different perspectives, as will staying focused on the task at hand—making decisions that benefit clients. Other steps that can be taken to increase effectiveness in case conferences include learning to identify and counter fallacies (such as polarized thinking, straw person arguments, and appeals based on emotion rather than reason) and encouraging helpful group practices, such as setting agendas. Sharing the values, knowledge, and skills as well as the products (e.g., CATS) of evidence-informed practice will facilitate effective team decision making.

PART V

# THE FUTURE

# CHAPTER 17

# Overcoming Personal Obstacles to Critical Thinking

A VARIETY OF PERSONAL OBSTACLES may interfere with making sound decisions, including lack of content and procedural knowledge (Nickerson, 1986a). Errors may occur because of inadequate knowledge. You may not keep up-to-date with new developments or may overlook important client characteristics or circumstances. Errors in communication may occur that result in inaccurate accounts of client concerns. Lack of self-knowledge is an obstacle. This includes knowledge of personal strengths and limitations that influence decision making. For example, awareness of how you tend to respond to certain kinds of clients may help you to avoid dysfunctional countertransference reactions. Blau (1988) suggests that errors may occur because of clinicians' character flaws or neurotic conflicts, such as inappropriate intimacy with clients, breaches of confidentiality, lying to clients, and not seeking consultation when needed. Concerns related to personal obstacles include becoming too busy to properly conduct practice, being inappropriately confrontative, overresponding to threats, not setting appropriate limits, not dealing with depletion, and becoming cynically resigned to poor practice standards. These may reflect dysfunctional work environments and/or life-styles. Lack of interest in having a carefully thought out position or a wish to appear decisive may compromise the quality of clinical reasoning. Brookfield (1987) suggests that adult learners may view learning to think critically as a journey into ambiguity and uncertainty.

Other obstacles include a low tolerance for ambiguity, a tendency to make premature judgments, unrealistic expectations, and a desire for quick success (Adams, 1974). Examples of barriers to the development of intelligence suggested by Sternberg (1987) include the following (pp. 212–221):

- Lack of motivation
- Lack of impulse control

- Lack of perseverance
- Inability to translate thought into action
- Lack of follow-through
- Procrastination
- Distractibility and lack of concentration
- Spreading yourself too thick or too thin
- Lack of goal orientation
- Fear of failure
- Excessive self-pity
- Excessive dependency
- Wallowing in personal difficulties
- Inability to see the forest for the trees
- Lack of balance between critical, analytic thinking and creative, intuitive thinking
- Flawed self-assessments (e.g., overconfidence)

You may be too invested to quit (Teger, Cary, Katcher, & Hillis, 1980), that is, continue on in ineffective ways because that is what you have done—it is too painful to think of change (see discussion of sunk costs in Hastie & Dawes, 2001).

Attitudes many authors view as vital for critical thinking include intellectual curiosity and honesty, objectivity, skepticism, open-mindedness, and a disposition to be both systematic and flexible. (See list of intellectual traits in Chapter 1.) A comparison of good and poor problem solvers suggests that good problem solvers are more attentive to situational details, and are more tenacious. Poor problem solvers are more likely to rely on unreasoned guessing and rationalizations, and not to attend to detail. (For further discussion of differences in styles of reasoning see Suedfeld & Tetlock, 2001; Stanovich & West, 2002.) The term *style* refers to a way of approaching problems that is used in many different situations (Yinger, 1980). A preferred style may not be seen in all areas; for example, you may be imprecise about goals, but precise about scheduling appointments. Ennis (1987) suggests that being sensitive to the feelings, level of knowledge, and degree of sophistication of others, as well as seriously considering other views, is important.

## ENCOURAGE VALUES COMPATIBLE WITH ETHICAL OBLIGATIONS TO CLIENTS

Thinking critically about practice and policy decisions may require changes in how you weigh certain outcomes. Values that encourage well-reasoned decisions include an interest in mastery over mystery, helping clients and avoiding harming them, and honoring professional codes of ethics. Valuing discovery of accurate accounts and an appreciation for originality increase the likelihood of creative solutions to problems, as does tolerance for differences (Perkins, 1988). Some clinicians read what they feel like reading, giving little thought to the potential usefulness of material to helping clients attain outcomes they value. That is, they value entertainment more than gaining knowledge that can help them to help their clients and to avoid harm. Some are more concerned with appearing expert than they are with learning from their colleagues.

## CHANGE A PREFERENCE FOR MYSTERY TO ONE FOR BEING WELL INFORMED

One indicator of a preference for mystery is a disinterest in practice-related research findings that, if drawn on, would improve the quality of services offered. A preference for mystery and apparent profundity in contrast to clear description and accurate appraisal of the evidentiary status of claims partly explains the neglect by clinicians of research findings concerning the effectiveness of different practice methods. "If a solution can actually be found, it is often judged to have little value, regardless of its practical importance for people's lives" (Thompson, 1988, p. 400). "Findings that would be considered fascinating, if not unprecedented, in other areas of the applied sciences are viewed as pedestrian" (p. 400). A disinterest in clear description of the evidentiary status of procedures and outcomes is partly the result of professional education programs that emphasize mystery over mastery; obscurity in place of transparency. Some clinicians receive more of an indoctrination than an education, in which critical appraisal of claims is encouraged, including seeking disconfirming evidence regarding preferred views (Gambrill, 1997).

A disinterest in using available knowledge may be related to a search for final answers, or the false belief that drawing on practice-related research allows no room for individual creativity and judgment. On the contrary, drawing creatively on clinical expertise is needed to fill in gaps in knowledge. Keep in mind that evidence-based practice entails recognizing knowledge, ignorance, and uncertainty related to decisions that must be made. A preference for mystery may be related to the imposter syndrome, the feeling on the part of therapists that they are not therapists. Gibbs and DeVries found that about a fifth of a sample of 62 clinicians frequently feel like fakes (reported in DeAngelis, 1987, p. 14). If clinicians do not draw on practice-related research, as required by professional codes of ethics—if they do not seek and use empirically based content and procedural knowledge concerning outcomes their clients hope to attain, don't they indeed misrepresent themselves?

## OFFER CLIENTS THE SAME QUALITY OF SERVICES YOU WOULD LIKE

One of the striking characteristics about human beings is their compartmentalization of standards. For example, clinicians who rely on intuition want their physician to rely on results of randomized controlled trials when making treatment recommendations (see Chapter 1 for results of the "gooseygander test"). Does this apply to you? If so, should you correct this mismatch? (See later discussion of excuses.)

## REVIEW COMPROMISES AND RECOGNIZE SIGNS
## OF DEPLETION

The realities of day-to-day practice may result in changes in what you hope to accomplish. A mismatch between our skills and the tasks we confront may result in a mentality of powerlessness—or an unrealistic sense of omnipotence. Nattering (complaining without trying to improve things) is an indicator of the former. Signs of the latter include making no attempt to draw on practice and policy-related research, and a view of therapy as totally an art. The distinction between collective and individual ignorance is overlooked by clinicians who accept the latter path. Some clinicians turn to private practice after becoming disenchanted with the potential for helping clients in agency-based practice. Clinical students usually start graduate education with ideals and enthusiasm, perhaps believing that they will achieve greater success than former helpers who were less motivated, received less-adequate training, and cared less. After encountering limited progress, they may revise their expectations downward—especially in relation to social reform goals. Original standards may become dimmer, harder to recall, or even forgotten, as new, less hopeful ones replace them. Related factors include lack of high-quality supervision, lack of resources, lack of time, and heavy caseloads. Clinicians may decide that clients are really worse off than they thought—sicker and harder to change. Graduate training may encourage this view (see Chapter 7). Blaming the client or the agency for limited success removes responsibility from clinicians' shoulders.

Previous interests in increasing equity in the world by helping those who struggle with poverty, poor housing, high-crime neighborhoods, lack of health care, and poor education may be abandoned as it becomes obvious that individually focused counseling results in little or no headway in decreasing these problems. Ashton and Webb (1986) studied teachers' sense of efficacy and its relation to student achievement, and found marked changes over a few years, even in idealistic students. "As a student, Linda was full of vitality and fueled by a sense of purpose and personal efficacy. The teacher we observed had none of these characteristics. She went through her days mechanically, and no longer spoke of social problems or individual development as motivating her work. Linda appeared unaware that her teaching had become just the kind of monotonous activity she had once been determined to avoid. Her classroom was drab, without decorations or examples of students' work. Visitors could not easily tell what subject was taught in her room, and could see no physical evidence that those who worked within its walls shared a common commitment to their daily activities" (p. 56).

Efforts to systematically improve practice competencies may be abandoned because of a lack of effective learning skills, including identification of specific goals, intermediate steps, and progress indicators. Personal control tends to be abandoned when performance demands and risks associated with this control are excessive (Bandura, 1986, p. 449). Incorrect beliefs about the conditions required for learning may get in the way. Education programs differ in opportunities offered to evaluate whether skills have been acquired (see Dunning, Heath, & Suls, 2004). Everyone gets stuck sometimes; plans are not successful or the assessment picture is cloudy. Consultation may have been eagerly used when it was readily available (for example, during an internship), but may no longer be sought or available. Many clinicians give up trying to stay abreast of practice-related research. It is difficult for busy practitioners to keep up with research findings in one area. Indeed, this was a key reason for developing tools such as rigorous, routinely updated reviews of research related to specific clinical questions. You may say: "It's not possible," "No one does it," or "There's nothing I can learn." Another way to give up is not to evaluate client progress in any systematic way; to accept a feeling of what works rather than gathering data to explore degree of progress. You may believe that careful evaluation of progress will be very time consuming or cannot offer helpful information. Neither of these beliefs is true (see Chapter 11).

Considerable attention has been given to burnout in the literature on psychotherapy. Symptoms of burnout include cynicism, depression, a loss of motivation and energy, and a numbing of feeling (Maslach et al., 2001). Three components often emphasized include emotional exhaustion, depersonalization, and reduced personal accomplishment. There may be a cynical resignation to poor practices and policies. Burnout results from an imbalance between the strains of clinical practice and the available skills and resources for handling these strains—it is sometimes referred to as an *overload* (Blau, 1988). Indicators include sleepiness during sessions; drifting attention; being late for therapy sessions with increasing frequency; annoyance with patients; overzealous relief at the end of the workday; feelings of relief when a client cancels; sardonic or humorous references to clients; psychophysiological responses; increased irritability with staff, family, and clients; and disillusionment with work (p. 284). We may even become numb to the misery of others (Fetherstonhaugh, Slovic, Johnson, & Friedrich, 1997). These indicators can be used as cues that something should be changed in your personal or work life to create a more positive balance. For example, perhaps you do not carefully evaluate progress with your clients; it is easy to become discouraged when our effectiveness is unknown. Burnout is associated with a higher frequency of mistakes (see Campbell & Cornett, 2002). Evidence-based practice emphasizes the importance of lifelong learning, which can enliven everyday practice as well as contribute to positive outcomes, which enhances work satisfaction.

## INCREASE EFFECTIVE REACTIONS TO UNCERTAINTY AND AMBIGUITY

Uncertainty is an inherent part of life itself (Marris, 1996). A search for final answers is at odds with an approach to knowledge in which certainty is viewed as unachievable. In opting for all, some clinicians opt for ignoring what information is available (see discussion of essentialism in Chapter 4). Practice methods must typically be chosen in the face of uncertainty, perhaps due to lack of data about the effectiveness of different methods. Hallmarks of evidence-based practice include recognizing the uncertainty involved in making decisions and in taking steps to reduce it, such as drawing on practice- and policy-related research. Evidence-based practice requires sharing ignorance and uncertainty as well as knowledge about decisions that must be made. It is a way to handle the inevitable uncertainty in the helping process in an ethical, informed, and participatory manner (see Chapter 10). Consider the following questions: How accurate is this client's self-report? Will this client really carry out agreed-on tasks required for a successful outcome? Will this treatment be more (or less) effective than another for this client? How long should follow-up services be provided in order to maintain gains? Even when well equipped with knowledge and tools that facilitate evidence-based practice, lack of time to locate needed information may contribute to avoidable uncertainty. Uncertainty breeds a temptation to deny itself, perhaps fearing that its recognition would stifle needed action. How uncertainty is handled influences the quality of decisions. It can be denied or ignored. Ignoring uncertainty may result in overlooking valuable options. We may deny uncertainty by ignoring individual differences or redefining a problem in a way that dismisses uncertainty. Cassell (1991) suggests that "to disengage from the patient [for example by ignoring knowledge about their unique circumstances and characteristics] is to lose the ultimate source of knowledge in medicine" (p. 232). We do not see what is there to be seen. Inflated estimates of judgmental accuracy may in part be an adaptive reaction to uncertainty; overconfidence encourages needed action, despite doubts about outcomes (Fischhoff, 1975).

Acknowledging uncertainty does not mean that decisions are not made: it means that steps are taken to decrease it. Focusing on helping clients, including what to do when resources are not available, will help us to choose the best course of action in difficult circumstances. As Archie Cochrane (1992) noted, outcome "is certainly not the whole story" (p. 95). The manner in which services are provided, including kindliness and the ability to communicate, matter also. Quality is a complex concept. He suggests that "We all recognize quality when we see it and particularly when we receive it" (p. 95). Consider the example he gives in *Effectiveness and Efficiency* (1999). As a prisoner of war during World War II Archie Cochrane took care of other prisoners of war. He was with a dying soldier who was in great pain. Neither spoke a word of the other's language. He had no pain medication. He took the man in his arms and held him until he died. "In despair, and purely instinctively, I sat on his bed and took him in my arms. The effect was almost magical; he quieted at once and died peacefully a few hours later. I was still with him, half asleep and very stiff. I believe that by personal intervention I improved the quality of care dramatically in this case, and I know it was based on instinct and not on reason" (pp. 94–95).

## ACQUIRE FACILITATING VIEWS ABOUT KNOWLEDGE AND HOW TO GET IT

We each have a personal epistemology—beliefs about what knowledge is and how to get it (e.g., see Hofer & Pintrich, 2002). Our beliefs about how we can learn and how much control we have over what we learn are integrally related to our potential to learn (Hofer, 2001). A belief that we have little control over what we learn will hinder lifelong learning, as will lack of knowledge about how to do so. Beliefs that acquiring new knowledge requires little effort will interfere with learning, as will the belief that others (rather than ourselves) are responsible for what we learn. Intuitive beliefs are often remarkably difficult to modify. For example, many students emerge from introductory physics courses with their original incorrect ideas of motion unchanged, and with new knowledge incorporated into old intuitive beliefs so as to preserve those ideas and beliefs (McCloskey, 1983). Properties of beliefs that influence how difficult it may be to alter them include their strength (confidence in a belief—willingness to act on a belief), longevity (how long it has been held), and value (how important it is to us). The stronger a belief, the more it is valued, and the longer it has been held, the harder it may be to change. These factors are not necessarily related to accuracy (Nickerson, 1986a, pp. 23–24). Public commitment to a belief makes it more resistant to change (Levy, 1977). Once a belief is formed, we are likely to fall prey to confirmation bias—a selective search for confirming data.

## VIEW LEARNING AS AN ACTIVE PROCESS

There is a remarkable concordance within the areas of problem solving, professional decision making, critical thinking, and education, on the value of active learning, in which we focus on problem solving (e.g., see King & Kitchener, 2002; see critique of the *bucket theory* and discussion of problem-based learning in Chapter 8). In problem-based learning, the focus is on the *process* of decision making.

## VALUE ERRORS AND LACK OF SUCCESS AS LEARNING OPPORTUNITIES

Assumptions may not be questioned because of fear of discovering errors. Clinical errors and lack of success are inevitable in professional practice. The constructive way to view mistakes is as an opportunity to learn. Indeed, making mistakes is an integral aspect of learning. We learn by "risking" and then responding to feedback on our performance. This feedback helps us to discover what we understand and what we do not, what we can do and what we cannot. Some argue that we learn more from our mistakes than from our successes (but only if we have the required attitudes and skills to do so). Changing one's view of errors as rare and as occasions for blame to one of recognizing their frequency and using them as learning opportunities is vital. Skill in troubleshooting is one of the cluster of skills that distinguishes novices from experts. Responding to setbacks as opportunities to learn focuses attention on problem solving. Our reactions to feedback, including recognition of errors, are influenced by how secure we feel; secure individuals are more receptive to both positive and negative feedback than are insecure people (Snyder & Clair, 1977; see also Chanowitz & Langer, 1985). Recognizing the inevitability of lack of success in some (or many) situations should encourage reactions to regret over negative outcomes that help us to learn how to make better decisions in the future (see research on counterfactual thinking, e.g., Kahneman, 1995). For further discussion of fear of failure on the part of clinicians see Kottler and Blau (1989). Lifelong learning requires arranging opportunities to critically assess the quality of clinical knowledge and skills and using corrective feedback to enhance future success. A clinician who is skilled in a certain assessment or intervention method can review a colleague's use of this method and offer corrective feedback. Select colleagues who are skilled in offering constructive feedback, for example, who know how to identify specific knowledge and skills related to the use of a particular practice method, and who offer clear instructions concerning helpful changes (see Gambrill, 2006).

## NURTURE DISSATISFACTION WITH YOUR CURRENT KNOWLEDGE

We are unlikely to be interested in acquiring new knowledge if we are satisfied with our current knowledge. Dissatisfaction with current views is a vital source of motivation for looking further; for example, for alternative, more effective services. What we say we do or know does not necessarily match our behavior. (See later discussion of self-efficacy and self-esteem.) I often have been told "I already do that" when I am discussing the topic of identifying clear objectives. Further inquiry often reveals that the speaker does not have the related skills. A belief that a skill is already present will get in the way of acquiring new competencies. Perkinson (1993) as well as others stresses that "students must become critical of their own performances and their own understandings—while remaining confident in their ability to do better if they are to continue growing" (pp. 40–41). The importance of thinking about why theories do not work has been emphasized by many writers (e.g., Argyris & Schon, 1974). "Developing theories in use is one of the most important ways critical thinking can be practiced at the workplace. It requires practitioners to reflect on the reasons why espoused theories are not working and to seek alternative forms of practice" (Brookfield, 1987, p. 154). It requires us to distinguish between which theories we think we rely on and which ones we actually use—which may be a surprising revelation.

## CULTIVATE AN OPEN MIND

Of all the beliefs about why people think, feel, and act as they do; what is aberrant, what is normal, and what can be done to change behavior—some are based on sound reasons, others are based on unsupported hunches or misinformation. That is, beliefs vary in their accuracy (their evidentiary status).

Some clinicians believe that growing up with an alcoholic parent usually results in a damaged adult. Does it? At a recent presentation on children of schizophrenic parents, the presenter made the comment that growing up with a schizophrenic parent inevitably results in damage to the person. Data concerning resilient children (children who do well despite very difficult environments) were dismissed by the presenter with the statement, "I don't believe it's possible." Here we see an example of the preeminence of personal opinion over evidence in arriving at conclusions. Many writers stress the relationship between effective reasoning and an attitude toward the truth. Effective reasoning "presupposes a questioning attitude, an openness to both arguments and facts, and a willingness to modify one's beliefs in the light of evidence that they should be modified. In other words, it presupposes a commitment to the truth insofar as the truth can be ascertained" (Nickerson, 1986a, p. 12). Integral to this commitment is the understanding that beliefs should be reexamined from time to time, and that there will be no clear answers for many questions, or no way to find out what the answers are. "That is not to say that reasoning serves no purpose in such cases, but simply to suggest that some issues must be decided on the basis of preferences, tastes, or weakly held opinions regarding what the truth might be. The reasonable person will surely reason about such issues, but having reasoned, will recognize the tenuous nature of the basis of any conclusions drawn or decisions reached" (Nickerson, 1986a, pp. 12–13).

To offer high-quality services, new knowledge will have to be used and old assumptions winnowed out. Correcting faulty self-assessment will require an openness to reviewing background knowledge and skills and candidly comparing these with what the literature suggests is needed to help clients.

> Intellectually, critical thinking is challenging because we must prepare the way for new ideas by rooting out old ones, by breaking down remnants from popular, if incoherent, illogical and insupportable ideologies and prejudices of the day. Until we have thought deeply and critically we are apt to be persuaded by deeply flawed ideas. . . .
>
> We must learn in other words, something quite new to us: to identify not with the content of our beliefs but with the integrity of the process by which we arrived at them. We must come to define ourselves, and actually respond in everyday contexts, as people who reason their way into, and can be reasoned out of, beliefs. Only then will we feel unthreatened when others question our beliefs, only then will we welcome their questions as a reminder of the need to be ready to test and retest our beliefs daily at the bar of reason, only then will we learn to think within multiple points of view, with a sense of global perspective. (Paul, 1993, p. xii)

Basic to this process is a willingness to challenge ideas and conceptions, to adopt a view of knowledge as tentative, and a view of theories as tools rather than dogma to be guarded. People differ in how open they are to examining their beliefs. This topic has been of interest in psychology for many years, as illustrated by Rokeach's book—*The Open and Closed Mind* (1960). Those with closed minds are more limited in their reactions to messages than are individuals with open minds. They are limited to alternatives 1 and 4 in the following list (Hayakawa, 1978, p. 232): "1. he may accept the speaker and accept his statement; 2. he may accept the speaker but reject his statement; 3. he may reject the speaker but accept his statement; 4. he may reject the speaker and reject his statement." There is a relationship between dogmatism and making uncritical inferences (Tobacyk & Milford, 1982). There is also a relationship between rigidity, intolerance of ambiguity, and stress (see, for example, Hellman, Morrison, & Abramowitz, 1987).

Beliefs differ in their evidentiary status as well as in how clearly they are formulated and how accessible they are in our consciousness. Data tend to be interpreted in ways that make it consistent with current views; information that is not consistent tends to be resisted or "assimilated" (made to fit preferred views). Whether a belief is true or false may have great or little impact on the tenability of other beliefs. If knowledge of a subject is quite limited, inconsistencies in beliefs may not be recognized. One way to avoid inconsistencies is not to recognize them; to simply add new beliefs without altering old ones. This has been called the *add on* principle (Harmon, 1986). The principle of *negative undermining* states that we should stop believing something whenever we do not have adequate reasons to do so (p. 39). The principle of *positive undermining* states, "you should stop believing something whenever you believe that your reasons for believing it are not good" (p. 39). Harmon suggests that we are also influenced by the principle of *clutter avoidance*—the mind should not be cluttered with trivialities (p. 55). Practice-related beliefs are often difficult to alter because they are linked to a worldview; a preferred approach to understanding reality. Conceptions of behavior and how it can be changed form a basic part of our beliefs about the nature of human beings, and thus have emotional connotations attached to them. If a view is proposed that differs from an accepted view in significant ways, the new perspective may be rejected out of hand. The strength of feelings about different views can be seen by reactions to Skinner's views. The more clearly an issue or situation is described, the easier it is to identify related beliefs, such as practice theories. Often it is only when specific situations are considered that differences emerge. For example, we may agree on the value of client self-determination, but disagree as to how this should be implemented in specific cases.

A willingness to question beliefs requires curiosity and an interest in discovering what is true. It requires a move away from "motivated skepticism" that favors preferred views (Ditto & Lopez, 1992) to an open-minded, even-handed review of evidence. A disinterest in examining practice beliefs may be related to a reluctance to accept responsibility for decisions. Attributing responsibility for decisions to someone (a supervisor) or to some entity (the legal system, the administration), relieves clinicians from assuming responsibility. It is not unusual to hear clinicians say, "I don't make decisions. Clients make their own decisions." This stance overlooks the social-influence process inherent in clinical practice (see discussion in Chapter 2). A belief on the part of clinicians that they do not make decisions is a key indicator of a sense of powerlessness that develops when we lack decision-making skills. (See later section concerning compromises and excuses.)

## IMPROVE SELF-MANAGEMENT SKILLS

The first 10 obstacles to the full development of intelligence, described at the beginning of this chapter, are related to a lack of self-management skills. Self-management involves rearranging the environment and behavior in order to attain valued goals (Skinner, 1974). Steps include identifying specific goals, planning how to achieve these, acting on plans, and monitoring progress. For example, if you want to be more consistent and timely in replying to referral sources, thanking them and offering information about progress—you could have e-mail addresses and phone numbers readily available. The Premack Principle can be used to increase desired behaviors; high-probability behaviors can be used to reinforce low-probability behaviors (Premack, 1965). Rather than having a cup of coffee before starting a disliked task (such as recording), a modest amount of recording should first be completed (close to baseline). Precommitment strategies can be used to avoid future temptations such as momentary moods and distractions. For example, you could make a commitment to spend 1 hour each week seeking practice-related research on relevant databases, and this time could be protected from interruptions by planning ahead. Skills such as self-monitoring are a valuable component of effective problem solving. Self-change methods have been used to help clients attain a wide range of hoped-for outcomes; clinicians can also take advantage of these methods (Watson & Tharp, 2001).

### INCREASE TIME-MANAGEMENT SKILLS

People who are productive engage in metaplanning. A review of your schedule often reveals room for improvement (Maher & Cook, 1985). Helpful guidelines include the following:

1. Distinguish between tasks that must be done and discretionary tasks that do not have to be completed on a given day.
2. Delegate responsibilities to others.
3. Select a pleasing variety of tasks each day—some that can be easily accomplished and some that will be more challenging.
4. Arrange some distraction-free time each day.

5. Make realistic daily plans.
6. If possible, allow time for recording between interviews.

You may assume that your workdays must have a crisis mentality; this attitude will interfere with systematic attention to clients. A closer examination may reveal opportunities for some distraction-free time; rearranging your schedule or making trades with coworkers may offer some timeouts from phone calls and other interruptions. Feeling disorganized may be a result of not planning the day in terms of priorities; what must be done versus what could be done (discretionary activities)—being careful not to overload the "must-do" category. Arranging the day so that planned activities can be completed offers a sense of achievement and may permit a free period at the end of the day for discretionary activities. If procrastination is a problem, develop self-management skills to overcome it. If delegating responsibility is difficult, explore the reasons for this. Using a computer as a tool to ease work tasks may take up time in the beginning, but save time in the long run.

### ENHANCE STRESS-MANAGEMENT SKILLS

Stress may result from too much work, personal problems, a job that is boring or too demanding in terms of the match between required and available skills, or an oversensitivity to negative evaluations (see Exhibit 17.1). Differ-

**Exhibit 17.1**
Sources of Stress and Remedies

| Source | Remedy |
| --- | --- |
| • Negative thoughts | Replace with positive task-oriented thoughts |
| • Ineffective social skills | Acquire effective skills |
| • Overwork | Plan more manageable work load (for instance, delegate responsibility), acquire needed resources |
| • Fatigue | Check balance between work and recreation |
| • Lack of positive feedback from colleagues | Arrange support group |
| • Lack of self-reinforcement for accomplishments | Increase self-reinforcement |
| • Muscle tension | Use relaxation skills |
| • Lack of knowledge | Acquire needed information |
| • Lack of clinical skills | Acquire helpful skills |
| • Lack of positive feedback from clients | Enhance evaluation skills |
| • Lack of needed resources | Problem-solve to determine if added resources can be acquired. |

ent stressors may influence our problem-solving capability in different ways (e.g., see Hammond, 2000; Matthews, 2001). Too little or too much interest, anxiety, or anger can get in the way of making informed decisions. Excessive interest in an outcome may interfere with the careful weighing of evidence and make it difficult to manage impatience, anxiety, or anger. Both behavioral and cognitive coping skills can be of value in avoiding and regulating arousal (see Exhibit 17.2). Stressors differ in how easily they can be controlled. They differ in how much control we have over their frequency, timing, intensity, and duration. Excessive workloads may continue in spite of repeated requests for more help, as illustrated by the comments of an overloaded, underresourced pediatrician accused of exaggerating abuse. "A consultant pediatrician facing allegations of misconduct in overstating and exaggerating reports of child abuse was running a unit that was grossly understaffed at the time, the General Medical Council heard last week" (Dyer, 2005, p. 1105; see also Barling, Kelloway, & Frone, 2004). Situations initially appraised as threatening can be reframed as unimportant by asking questions such as "Does this really matter?" and 'Will it make any difference ten years from now?" Ignoring minor irritations and acquiring skills in requesting behavior changes and responding to criticism will decrease reactions of anger that interfere with making well-reasoned decisions. Expressing anger in an abusive manner only makes matters worse (Averill, 1982). Emotional reactions can be regulated by keeping things in perspective. "Whenever you are in doubt or when the self becomes too much with you, try the following experiment: Recall the face of the poorest and most helpless man you have ever seen and ask yourself if the step you contemplate is going to be of any use to him. Then you will find your doubts and your self melting away" (Ghandi in Burgess, 1984, p. 38). Social anxiety may be related to a lack of social skills. If this is the case, the most effective way to alter such reactions is to acquire and use helpful skills. One advantage of being a clinician is that assessment skills can be used to determine how to achieve a desired change, such as decreasing personal anxiety or anger.

## INCREASE RELATIONSHIP SKILLS

Clinical practice involves exchanges with clients, their significant others, fellow workers, clerical help, and various other professionals who may become involved in a case. Examples of relevant social skills include praising others and offering encouragement; offering criticism in a constructive manner; disagreeing with others in a nonabrasive manner; supporting positive alternatives to negative behaviors; requesting changes in annoying behavior without becoming unpleasant, and effectively responding to criticism (see Gambrill, 2006). The quality of your skills for handling challenges that arise in social situations will influence the quality of your decisions. The importance of relationship skills has been highlighted by research in psychotherapy (see discussion in Chapter 2). Premature termination by clients may be related

**Exhibit 17.2**

Coping Skills Used by Hospice Nurses

*Rational Action*

Identified a couple of different solutions

Accepted my limitations

Did what I knew had to be done

Tried to learn from the situation

Discussed the situation with peer or team member

Drew on past experience of similar situation

Tried not to act too hastily

Told myself I had done well

Told myself that I was not responsible

*Fantasized Action*

Wished that I could change the way I felt

Wished that I could change what happened

Imagined a better time or place than the one I was in

Wished that the situation would go away or be over

Wished I were a stronger person

*Emotional Avoidance*

Kept my feelings to myself

Tried to forget the whole thing

*Professionalism*

Assured myself that the dying are needy

Told myself that dying is a natural process

Chose my words carefully with the patient

*Emotional Response*

Took deep breaths and/or meditated

Waited to see what would happen

*Anticipated Coping*

Anticipated difficulty and prepared myself emotionally

Talked to someone to find out more about the situation

Made up a plan of action and followed it

Tried to appreciate some humorous aspect of the situation

Asked someone I respected for advice and followed it

Examined my goals regarding the patient

Just took one step at a time

**Exhibit 17.2** *Continued*

*Conflicted Behavior*

   Avoided being with people for a while

   Slept more than usual

   Felt better by eating, drinking, or smoking

   Turned to some other activity to take my mind off things

   Sought emotional support from family and friends

*Meditation*

   Prayed

   Hoped a miracle would happen

   Looked for the "silver lining"

   Rediscovered what is important in life

   Examined my goals regarding the patient

   Focused on what I might learn about life from the patient

   Blamed myself

   Talked to a patient about my feelings

*Concerned Behavior*

   Went over the problem trying to understand it

   Talked to someone who could do something

*Source:* Adapted from "Stress and Coping among Hospice Nurses: Test of an Analytic Model," by D. A. Chiriboga, G. Jenkins, and J. Bailey, 1983, *Nursing Research, 32,* pp. 294–299. Reprinted with permission.

to mistakes in how clinicians interact with clients. Examples described by Kottler and Blau (1989, pp. 80–81) are shown in the following:

- Distracting mannerisms or facial expressions
- Poor attending skills and eye contact
- Difficulty following and focusing the direction of the client's statements
- The use of closed-ended questions and an interrogative style that puts the client on the defensive
- Frequent interruptions of the client
- Noting surface messages of what is said rather than deeper-level messages
- Relying exclusively on the content of communications rather than on affect or process
- Using excessive self-disclosure and inappropriately putting the focus on oneself
- Exaggerated passivity in therapeutic style
- Difficulty tolerating silence
- Appearing unduly cold, aloof, and wooden in appearance
- Appearing too friendly, seductive, and informal
- Being aggressive or punitive in confrontations

Negative outcomes, such as an intensification of symptoms, may be related to inappropriate or ineffective ways of relating to clients (Strupp & Hadley, 1985).

Effective relationship skills will add to your confidence and comfort in exchanges, even difficult ones. In their review, Horvath and Bedi (2002) found an average correlation between alliance and outcome of .21 (median effect size .25). Beutler and his colleagues (2004) argue that "Although the causal role of relationship is still unproven, there can be no doubt that relationship quality is one of the stronger correlates of outcome" (p. 292; for a less positive appraisal see Wampold, 2005; see also Chapter 2). There is a rich literature you can draw on to enhance your understanding of social behavior and to hone your relationship skills (e.g., see Schlenker, 2003). Knowledge about cultural differences in interactional styles may be needed to respond effectively. Empathy and warmth create a context in which other important elements of effective services are offered, such as clarifying goals and planning services. Empathy is positively associated with outcome, perhaps by increasing client satisfaction and so increasing participation, including disclosure (Bohart, Elliott, Greenberg, & Watson, 2002). Lapses in empathy include (1) telling people what they should feel (e.g., "That's not the way to feel when you see her"), (2) an interrogative interview style, (3) overinterpretation, (4) self-disclosure, which distracts attention from service goals, and (5) encouragement of dependence by offering excessive help ("Call me if you ever want to talk"). Examples of physicians' poor attempts at empathy, when they must deliver bad news to patients, are as follows:

> One 72-year-old woman with breast cancer confided to her consultant surgeon that she did not want to lose her breast, only to be told, "At your age, what do you need a breast for?"

> A woman of 40 with the same disease asked a different hospital consultant if there was any way she could avoid a mastectomy. He said, "There is not much there worth keeping, is there?"

> An elderly man with terminal lung cancer was asked by a junior hospital doctor why he was crying, and [he] explained that he did not want to die. The house officer's unsympathetic response was: "Well, we all have to die some time." (Collins, 1988, p. A7)

Effective social skills can be used to avoid conflicts during team meetings as well as to resolve conflicts in a constructive manner. Clear description of the exact nature of a conflict (for example, what does each party want, what indicators will be used to determine whether goals are met) is helpful (Fisher & Ury, 1983). A troubleshooting checklist for reviewing situations is offered in Exhibit 17. 3. Some clinicians overreact when they are criticized; they become anxious or angry, and are less able and willing to consider alternative views. Confrontational rather than cooperative methods may be used to persuade

**Exhibit 17.3**
Troubleshooting Checklist

___ 1. Were my goals achievable? Did I focus on common goals?

___ 2. Did I plan how to achieve my goals?

___ 3. What thoughts and behaviors did I attend to? Were they relevant or irrelevant? Distracting or helpful?

___ 4. What should I have done more of?

___ 5. What should I have done less of?

___ 6. Did I consider other perspectives?

___ 7. Were special skills required that I don't have?

colleagues to accept favored positions. Questions raised by clients or colleagues about the effectiveness of proposed methods or degree of progress may be met with defensive responses rather than informed answers. Oversensitivity to negative feedback decreases the likelihood that divergent views will be shared or defended in the face of criticism, and increases the likelihood of overreactions to criticism. Excessive reactions to negative evaluation or to being ignored may be related to unrealistic expectations, such as expecting to please everyone. Schlenker and Leary (1982) suggest that all social anxiety is related to fear of negative evaluation. One reason people do not speak up in case conferences is because of a concern about what others will think of their ideas, of their style of presentation, or of the way they look. People differ in how concerned they are with pleasing others; concern about disapproval may get in the way of expressing opinions. Focusing on the benefits to clients of taking an active role in discovering and critiquing assumptions in order to arrive at well-reasoned decisions will encourage participation; independence of judgment is one characteristic of creative individuals (Weisberg, 1986).

## SHARPEN AWARENESS OF TRANSFERENCE AND COUNTERTRANSFERENCE EFFECTS

One of the goals of clinical training programs is to help clinicians become aware of transference effects (how clients respond to clinicians, based on their past experiences) and countertransference efforts (how clinicians tend to relate to different clients). Not recognizing such effects may result in errors such as misattributing a lack of progress to environmental obstacles and overlooking relationship factors. Kottler and Blau (1989) discuss a number of errors that may result from lack of awareness of countertransference effects, including premature termination of treatment due to an unrecognized dislike for clients. Thus, either underinvestment or overinvestment in clients may result in poor decisions: Examples of errors described by Herbert Strean in one of his cases that he attributed to his negative attitude toward a client appear in the following (cited in Kottler & Blau, 1989, p. 132).

- He lost his objectivity and let himself be pulled into the client's manipulative ploys.
- Because of feelings of threat, jealousy, and competition, he perpetuated a continual power struggle.
- He often made the "correct" interpretation or said the "right" words, but in a tone of voice that was more hostile than empathic.
- He spent much of the time trying to prove to the client (flashbacks to his father) that he knew what he was doing.
- Although he was aware that his countertransference feelings were getting in the way, he could not monitor or confront them sufficiently, nor did he seek supervision or therapy to resolve them.
- He retreated behind the mask of cold, objective analyst in order to be punitive, rather than adopting a posture of empathy and support.

## DECREASE UNREALISTIC EXPECTATIONS

Clinicians are not immune to unrealistic expectations. These may concern colleagues ("I have to please everyone"), as well as clients ("I have to help everyone"). Ellis has offered a variant on his classic list of irrational assumptions that applies to practitioners:

- I have to be successful with all of my clients practically all of the time.
- I must be an outstanding therapist, clearly better than other therapists I know or hear about.
- I have to be greatly respected and loved by all my clients.
- Since I am doing my best and working so hard as a therapist, my clients should be equally hardworking and responsible, should listen to me carefully and should always push themselves to change.
- Because I am a person in my own right, I must be able to enjoy myself during therapy sessions and to use these sessions to solve my personal problems as much as to help clients with their problems. (Cordes, 1983, p. 22)

A belief that "I must be successful with all my clients" may contribute to burnout. Unrealistic beliefs may be due to expectations for success that cannot be realized, because individual counseling cannot alter problems (such as homelessness) as suggested in Chapter 2. They may be due to intemperate expectations on the part of government officials, such as "Ensure that no child be harmed in care." Waiting for an ideal alternative may result in unnecessary delays in choosing among available options. Realistic expectations should increase our readiness to seek consultation when needed (when stuck or concerned about a high-risk, such as potential suicide).

## AVOID SELF-HANDICAPPING REACTIONS AND DEVELOP POSITIVE ALTERNATIVES

One of your greatest sources of discouragement may be the discrepancy between services needed and services available. For example, money may not be provided for in-home services, requiring clients to go into institutions. Neither money nor services may be available to help an abusive parent lessen external stresses related to her abusive behavior. What can be done in such situations? As with any problem, it can be handled in a constructive or a dysfunctional manner. One dysfunctional response assumes that what is must always be. There is a fatalism that nothing can be done to alter conditions. I have been struck by the prevalence of reactions such as "There is nothing we can do"; "We have too many cases"; "We have no power"; "We have to make decisions quickly." There is a feeling of hopelessness and helplessness, even among graduate students. *Goal displacement* is another kind of dysfunctional reaction. This involves focusing on concerns that are not of key importance to clients. For example, you may recommend that a client participate in counseling, even though this will do nothing to address environmental circumstances related to problems. If you do this often enough, you may convince yourself that this is appropriate. Constructive ways of handling discrepancies between services needed and those available include: (1) offering what help you can related to the problems of greatest concern to clients; (2) taking what steps you can to decrease discrepancies (e.g., bringing them to the attention of administrators and legislators and forming a group of other interested colleagues to pursue a specific change). We may create self-imposed obstacles to high-quality performance (consistently get insufficient sleep) to avoid failure. Such strategies help us to preserve self-esteem and personal control. They help us "to negotiate reality" (Higgins, Snyder, & Berglas, 1990). Alternatives to self-handicapping reactions are suggested in Exhibit 17.4.

## WHAT ABOUT SELF-EFFICACY AND SELF-ESTEEM?

Considerable attention has been devoted to examining the influence of judgments of efficacy on performance (Bandura, 1986; 1997). "A lack of confidence in our ability to solve problems can manifest itself in a variety of ways; for example it may be reflected by a lack of interest, fear of exploring new domains, and fear of criticism. These feelings can interfere with solving a problem and can prevent us from engaging in activities that might improve our problem-solving skills. . . . The tendency to avoid new areas becomes especially strong when others are performing well while we experience considerable difficulty. A common way to define such difficulties is simply to assume we are inept or slow and others are talented. An alternative perspective is that *everyone* experiences difficulty when first learning about a new area" (Bransford & Stein, 1984, p. 123). Fatigue that is a natural result of hard work may be

**Exhibit 17.4**

Self-Handicapping Strategies and Constructive Alternatives

| Self-Handicapping Strategies | Constructive Alternatives |
|---|---|
| • Become fatalistic; focus on problems. Natter (complain without taking action to correct disliked situations). | • Seek positive alternatives. Identify the specific changes you would like, as well as how these could be attained and take steps in that direction. |
| • Blame others/blame yourself. | • Same as above. |
| • Decide there is little help that can be offered and do your job in a "routinized" uncaring manner. | • Offer whatever help you can to clients and meet with others to explore what changes could be made to improve services. |
| • Assume a self-congratulatory position (congratulate yourself on services offered even though none have been provided). | • Carefully evaluate progress and be honest about results. |
| • Claim you do not make decisions. | • Recognize the decisions you make, identify factors that limit your options and meet with others to see how obstacles could be decreased. |
| • Struggle on by yourself. | • Involve others in seeking positive changes; form coalitions. A group has more power than an individual. |

misperceived as reflecting personal limitations. *Performance efficacy* refers to the belief that a certain behavior can be performed. *Outcome efficacy* is a judgment of the likely effect of a behavior. Judgments of efficacy influence motivation—how long we persist at a task and how much effort we make. Success in real-life situations is the most influential source of accurate efficacy expectations (see Baumeister et al., 2003). Perceptions of self-efficacy influence thoughts and emotions as well. A valued goal may not be pursued because required skills are not available, or because use of skills has not lead to success in achieving hoped-for outcomes in the past. Some people have a "let me out of here" approach when confronting difficult problems. "Over time, the let me out of here approach can result in self-fulfilling prophecies. For example, people who initially have difficulty solving math problems may come to believe that they have no math ability; they may therefore avoid situations in which they must deal with math problems. Since such individuals receive little practice with math because they avoid it, their initial hypothesis about not being able to solve math problems is likely to come true. In general, it seems clear that people who avoid dealing with problems place limitations on themselves that are not necessarily there to begin with" (Bransford & Stein, 1984, p. 4). Mental escapes such as drifting while reading or listening may be signs of the "let me out of here" attitude. "It can be very difficult to focus attentively on a problem while concerned with competing thoughts about personal problems or about fears that we may fail" (p. 6).

Self-efficacy and self-esteem are not necessarily correlated with actual skill levels. (See research related to flawed self-assessment in Dunning, Heath, and Suls, 2004.) Simply raising self-esteem is unlikely to improve skilled performance, as suggested in the title of Baumeisler et al.'s review (2003): "Does self-esteem cause better performance, interpersonal success, happiness, or healthier lifestyles? Answer: No, no, probably, sporadically." (See also Foxx & Roland, 2005.) Self-assessment on the part of physicians is not highly correlated with actual performance (e.g., see Tousignant & DesMarchais, 2002). Facilitators tend to overestimate the skills of their students (Whitfield & Xie, 2002). Thus, as Baumeisler and his colleagues (2003) conclude, raising self-esteem should not be an end in itself. Self-efficacy can be enhanced by acquiring additional skills, and diminished by magnifying negative qualities and minimizing positive qualities.

Low levels of outcome efficacy pose an obstacle to decision making in several ways. Helpful views may not be presented in a case conference, or may be presented in an ineffective manner. Just as the boldness with which comments are made does not necessarily reflect their soundness, so too, the diffidence with which comments are made does not necessarily reflect a lack of cogency. Low self-efficacy is associated with negative affect, which reduces the quality of problem solving. Positive emotions encourage flexibility and creativity and enhance helpfulness and generosity, which should add to effectiveness in both interviews and case conferences (see Isen, 1987). Low self-efficacy increases vulnerability to fears of negative evaluation and embarrassment (Edelmann, 1987, p. 130). Both extremes of self-esteem, excessive and limited, may interfere with making well-informed decisions, by encouraging a reluctance to examine beliefs. Evaluations of personal efficacy and self-esteem are not necessarily related (Bandura, 1986). If clinicians are effective in certain situations but do not value their related skills, they may still have low self-esteem.

## EXAMINE RATIONALIZATIONS/EXCUSES

When our skills and resources do not match the challenges we confront, we seek reasons. Difficult situations may breed excuses that preserve self-esteem and help us live with our limitations (Snyder, Higgins, & Stucky, 1983; see also section on self-handicapping reactions). Excuses can be defined as "explanations or actions that lessen the negative implications of an actor's performance, thereby maintaining a positive image for oneself and others" (p. 45). There are many ways to deny responsibility. Offering rationalizations and excuses is an everyday part of life, and there is a valuable literature in this area. It overlaps with literature concerning self-protection, self-deception, and the deception of others. This literature suggests challenges to the ethical components of EBP, as well as possible remedies. There are many ways in which we create a disconnect between our actions and the harm we create or contribute to (Bandura, 1999). Popular excuses for avoiding responsibility for harming others are: (1) I didn't know, (2) I was just following orders (from my supervisor, or from an evil administrator), and (3) I was just doing what others do; using the same standards of care (even though abysmal). We could deny there is a problem. We can offer an excuse and provide what we know to be merely "bandaid" help. Excuses given by social workers for less-than-optimal service include lack of resources and high caseloads. These may reflect reality. Caseloads may be high. Many objectives are difficult to attain. Resources are often lacking. We may deny that we make decisions. I am often told by social workers that "I don't make decisions." We may reframe negative outcomes as deserved because of moral lapses on the part of the harmed. (They deserve it.) We may use "cleansing" language that obscures suffering and coercion.

We may resort to pseudoscientific practices, such as assigning uninformative diagnostic labels to clients in order to relieve our discomfort when confronted with unsolvable problems (Houts, 2002). If an incorrect decision is made, one or more of the following accounts could be offered:

- It was not possible to get all the information.
- This was a difficult case; anyone would have had trouble.
- I was pressed for time.
- I didn't have the authority to make a decision.
- I was tired.
- My graduate education didn't prepare me for this kind of client.
- Other people make the same mistakes.

Examples of excuses that astrologers offered when they made a wrong statement about a client include the following (Dean, 1986–1987, p. 173):

1. Client does not know himself.          This shifts the blame from astrology to the participants.
2. Astrologer is not infallible.
3. Another factor is responsible.         This puts the blame on the ambiguity of the birth chart.
4. Manifestation is not typical.

We tend to attribute our successes to our own efforts and abilities and our failures to external influences, such as luck or test difficulty (Davis & Davis, 1972). Excuses are especially likely to occur when we hold ourselves responsible for a negative outcome but still want to believe that we are good people. Excuses serve many functions, including preserving self-esteem, smoothing social exchanges, and helping people to live with their limitations; they function as self-handicapping strategies if they reduce options for achieving valued clinical goals. To the extent that excuses relieve us from assuming undue responsibility for clients and encourage reasonable risk taking, they are helpful. To the extent that they prevent us from recognizing limitations that could be altered—for example, by keeping up with practice-related research—they are not helpful. Reframing strategies may be used to mute the negative consequences of an action; harm may be underestimated ("He wasn't really harmed"), victims may be derogated ("He's not worth helping"), or the source of the negative feedback may be attacked ("My supervisor doesn't have experience with such clients"; Bandura, 1999). Such strategies are encouraged by our tendency to question the accuracy of negative feedback. Acts of omission may be excused by denying there was any need for action, as in the famous Kitty Genovese case, in which witnesses who observed the slaying of a young woman did not become involved; they said they thought it was a "lovers' quarrel," or that it was not their responsibility (Rosenthal, 1964). "Transformed responsibility excuses" decrease responsibility for actions. For example, consensus-raising tactics may be used; a clinician can protest that others would have acted in the same way. He can say that he was coerced, or shortcomings can be attributed to others to avoid threats to himself—that is, projection can be used (Snyder, Higgins, & Stucky, 1983, p. 97). Use of projection is illustrated by research that shows that when people receive negative feedback they describe others as having the negative characteristics (Holmes, 1978).

A temporary inconsistency in performance may be appealed to in order to decrease responsibility. Variations include the intentionality plea ("I didn't mean to do it") and effort-lowering statements ("I didn't try"); for a detailed description of different kinds of accounts, see Semin & Manstead, 1983). Self-handicapping strategies, such as expecting to fail, may be used to remove responsibility for possible low performance (Arkin & Oleson, 1998). Excuses may save time in the short term, but will cost time in the long run. For example, not evaluating practice and not keeping up with practice-related research saves time in the short run but may cost time in the long run, both for clients and clinicians, because the most effective practice methods may not be used.

Excuses are self-handicapping if they pose an obstacle to detecting and acting on options for achieving goals clients value (if they get in the way of recognizing limitations that could be altered). So, when you offer an excuse, ask "Does this work for me (and my clients) or against me (and my clients)?"; "Does this increase or decrease the likelihood of providing needed services and liking my work?" Professional codes of ethics provide a guide here. When confronted with demonstrably poor services, we can refer to our ethical obligations to discover our professional responsibility. For example, codes of ethics obligate us to perform competently. If our agency culture prevents such practice (it is incompetent), aren't we obligated to do something about it? When are rationalizations unethical? Is it okay just to throw up our hands and say we cannot do anything?

> Failure to perform competently as a professional means two different things. First, there is failure to apply correctly the body of theoretic knowledge on which professional action rests. Failures of this sort are errors in techniques. For surgeons, we have identified two varieties of this type of error—technical and judgmental. Second, there is failure to follow the code of conduct on which professional action rests. Failures of this sort are moral in nature. (Bosk, 1979, p. 168)

## EXCUSES AND SELF-DECEPTION

Richard Paul (1993) suggests that we consistently deceive ourselves about the state of, the degree of, and the nature of our knowledge, our freedom, and our character (Paul, 1993, xiii). If the essence of self-deception is not knowing when we are deceiving ourselves, as Baron (2000) suggests, what is possible? For example, when confronted with evidence that they use different standards of evidence when making decisions about their own health than they do with clients, some professionals dismiss this discrepancy by saying "medicine is different" (from psychology or social work); (Gambrill & Gibbs, 2002). Is it different? Is it so different that we do not have to concern ourselves with informed consent obligations—sharing with a client that recommended practices and policies have been found to be harmful or ineffective, or are of unknown effectiveness? The self-deceived could be classified into two categories: (1) those whose values match their self-deception, and (2) those whose values do not match their self-deception. The latter, unlike the former, can be enlightened (enlightened according to their own values), whereas the former, because there is a match between their self-deception and their values, cannot be changed by appealing to (revealing) the lack of correspondence between their beliefs and their actions.

There are those who want to help clients but do not know how. And there are those who really do not care about clients. Other methods will be required, such as evidence-informed organizational cultures, to alter the behavior of those who do not care. I suggest that self-deception in the two different instances described above serves different functions, is created by different histories, and requires different remedies. Self-deception can be viewed as a form of self-propaganda. (See discussion of propaganda in Chapter 4.) Possible remedies when our values do not match our actions include both those designed to decrease our vulnerability to sociological propaganda (including material from professional organizations), and those that allow us to break out of self-propaganda—self-deceptions that do not match our values (see Chapter 18). We can increase empathy for clients by attending to data illustrating harming in the name of helping and ignoring of client perspectives to discourage self-deceptions that harm clients (e.g., see Rose, Fleischmann, Wykes, Leese, & Bindman, 2003). Some authors argue that we have multiple selves developed in relation to multiple contexts (e.g., work, home, and recreational life) that we routinely inhabit, and that these multiple selves may not communicate with each other. For example, we may not compare the professional self and the moral self to determine if we act consistently (honor certain obligations in different contexts).

## SUMMARY

A variety of personal obstacles may hinder sound decision making. Making well-reasoned decisions may be hampered by a lack of self-knowledge. This includes knowledge of personal strengths and limitations that influences decision making. Motivational and attitudinal obstacles may compromise the quality of reasoning. These include carelessness, lack of interest in having a well-reasoned position, a wish to appear decisive, and a vested interest in a certain outcome. You may have a preference for mystery over mastery, unconstructive reactions to mistakes and lack of success, a low tolerance for ambiguity, and a desire for quick success. Ideals about what can be accomplished may be replaced by a pessimistic view. Once-valued goals, such as taking small steps to rectify inequities in service delivery, may be abandoned. Some obstacles to critical thinking, such as procrastination and distractibility, are related to a lack of self-management skills. Effective stress-management and time-management skills are important in providing a facilitative setting for making decisions. Interpersonal skills are needed to manage social exchanges involved in making decisions. Perhaps the most important obstacle is a reluctance to examine competencies and the accuracy of beliefs. This reluctance may be related to overconfidence and other self-handicapping reactions. Lack of awareness of the relationship between our preferred views and preferences and related political, economic, and social influences is an obstacle to critically examining beliefs—we assume that we have created them, and overlook external influences. The excuses we use for lack of success may be a barrier to offering clients high-quality services. Guidelines describing how to alter the personal obstacles discussed in this chapter are available; indeed, many clinicians often use these with their clients.

# CHAPTER 18

# Maintaining Critical Thinking Skills

B OTH PERSONAL AND ENVIRONMENTAL obstacles may chip away at critical thinking values and skills that contribute to evidence-based practice. There are formidable barriers to encouraging use of evidence-based practices and policies. These include characteristics of the practice environment, such as funding patterns, vested interests in current power networks and related contingencies, limited resources, and preferred practice theories. There may be conflicts between professional values and agency practices. Agency administrators may pressure staff to continue use of ineffective or harmful methods rather than practices and policies that have been critically tested and found to help clients. We are bombarded with inflated claims from professional newsletters, colleagues, and the media. Prevailing opinion is another obstacle—influence by standards of practice, opinion leaders, professional education, and advocacy (for example, by pharmaceutical companies). Other barriers suggested by Oxman and Flottorp (1998) include knowledge and attitudes regarding uncertainty, feelings of incompetency regarding new practices, need to act, information overload, and client values and expectations. Some people may be absorbed in their own lives and care little about the effect of services on clients. Suggestions for maintaining helpful values and skills that contribute to life-long learning are offered in this chapter.

## GENERALIZING AND MAINTAINING CRITICAL THINKING SKILLS

Having critical thinking knowledge and skills does not mean that they will be used. Cultivating related values and arranging for the generalization and maintenance of such knowledge and skills is also needed (e.g., see Halpern, 1998). The distinction between learning and performance is just as true in the area of evidence-based practice and related critical thinking skills and knowledge as in other areas; it is just as important to arrange for the generalization and maintenance of new skills as it is to develop them in the first place. Without transfer training and arrangement of supportive tools and contingencies, the use of new knowledge and skills may be confined to the specific situations in which training was offered. Valuable knowledge may be used to solve a problem in one context, but may fail to be applied in other situations in which it would be of value. Including a variety of situations in training and acquiring useful self-questioning skills, such as asking "Could I be wrong?" "How am I doing?", encourages transfer (Belmont, Butterfield, & Ferretti, 1982; Halpern, 2003; Haskell, 2001; Stokes & Baer, 1977). Some instructional methods, such as discovery learning, which require review and revision of plans, are more effective than are others in encouraging generalization. In this kind of learning the emphasis is on the process rather than on the product of problem solving. This emphasis on process is also seen in problem-based learning, as described in Chapter 18.

## REMEMBER THE BENEFITS OF CRITICAL THINKING

Remembering the benefits of critical thinking—arriving at well-reasoned decisions that contribute to helping clients and avoiding harm should encourage you to take advantage of critical thinking skills. Large variations in helping efforts and harming in the name of helping contributed to the development of evidence-based practice. Use of critical thinking knowledge, and skills will help you to avoid variations that are ineffective or harmful. For example, awareness of informal fallacies and persuasion strategies that advertisers, politicians, professional organizations, and colleagues use to create beliefs in certain claims that affect clients can help you to avoid their influence. Clinical decision making is an ethical as well as a practical enterprise. The decisions made affect people; they offer or limit opportunities for clients and significant others to enhance the quality of their lives. The history of the helping professions clearly indicates the need for boundaries on the individual discretion of clinicians in the selection of objectives (making sure clients value them) and procedures (choosing those that, while least intrusive, are most effective and efficient and acceptable to clients), and in being accountable to clients by monitoring progress, so that timely, sound decisions can be made about "what to do next." As we have more information about what practices and policies are effective and which ones are ineffective or harmful, lack of knowledge about this research becomes ever more problematic.

Clients will benefit from critical thinking values, knowledge, and skills by receiving effective assessment and intervention methods. Clinicians will benefit by increased success in helping clients attain outcomes they value. Whether colleagues will be thankful will depend on your skills in diplomacy, their values (e.g., avoiding harm to clients) and beliefs about knowledge (how or if it can be gained) and on other personal and environmental factors discussed in previous chapters. They are more likely to value and support critical appraisal that contributes to high-quality services if goals are shared (e.g., to involve clients in decision making as informed participants). How about those in positions of authority? A quote from Nickerson (1987) is apt here. "I believe that often, when people in positions of authority (parents, teachers, managers, military leaders) say that they wish that the people over whom they have authority (children, students, employees, subordinates) could think, they mean that they wish their charges or subordinates were more skillful at accomplishing goals set, or at least endorsed, by their superiors. Seldom do they have in mind a concept of thinking that is sufficiently broad to include the questioning of the goals themselves and the authorities that have set them" (p. 34). Use of sound decision-making methods can move clinical practice further along the continuum of effectiveness, which includes deterioration effects, neither harming nor helping, and offering the best help that could be attained anywhere. Research in psychotherapy shows that deterioration effects occur with some clients (Lambert & Ogles, 2004). Some may be unavoidable. Other negative effects may be avoidable—for example, by minimizing reactions that contribute to them. Many clients are content with half the glass when they could have, if not the whole glass, at least three-quarters.

## PAY ATTENTION TO PROCESS AS WELL AS TO OUTCOME

Process and outcome are integrally related in clinical practice. Without a process that maximizes opportunities to help clients, including facilitating relationships with clients, achieving hoped-for outcomes is less likely. Evidence-based practice describes a process for integrating evidentiary (e.g., Does it work?), ethical (e.g., Is it acceptable to clients?) and application (e.g., Are needed resources available?) issues. It is hoped that this process will contribute to helping clients and avoiding harm. Research concerning personal control suggests the advantages of focusing on process (How can I do it?) rather than outcome (Can I do it?; Langer, 1983). Focusing solely on outcome may increase anxiety and divert attention from exploring *how* problems can be solved. And if the skills required to enhance the quality of decision making are absent, increasing calls for accountability will not improve practice and, indeed, may have a negative effect (Lerner & Tetlock, 1999). A *process* orientation encourages active involvement in grappling with the challenges of practice; it highlights the relation between process and outcome, and in so doing, should be more fruitful in generating valuable ideas. A sole focus on outcome may encourage a sense of incompetence—a belief that there is no relationship between what we can do (our behavior) and what may be achieved (hoped-for outcomes); it may encourage a mindless approach to problems that results in lost opportunities to help clients. "Since the attention of outcome-oriented individuals is directed toward the goal of the task and their own ability to accomplish it, they may be relatively 'mindless' concerning actual methods of performing the task, at least in comparison to process-oriented individuals. The latter individuals, in contrast, focus their attention on methods of task performance and are probably more mindful about different feasible solutions" (Langer, 1983, p. 131).

## ENCOURAGE GOALS AND BELIEFS INTEGRAL TO CRITICAL THINKING AND EVIDENCE-INFORMED PRACTICE

For some people, it is more important to avoid doubt and to appear consistent than it is to discover the best answer to a question. Some people do not believe in the value of thinking. "If people do not believe that thinking is useful, they will not think. This is perhaps the major argument we hear against thinking about things like nuclear war, religion, and morals: 'These matters are beyond me. They are best left to experts who are capable of thinking about them—if anyone'" (Baron, 1985b, p. 259). Beliefs that encourage critical thinking include the following (p. 254): thinking often leads to better results; difficulties may be overcome through critical thinking; good thinkers are open to new possibilities and to evidence against views they favor; and in most cases, nothing is wrong with being undecided or uncertain for a while. Beliefs that discourage critical thinking include: changing one's mind is a sign of weakness; being open to alternatives leads to confusion and despair; quick decision making is a sign of strength or wisdom; truth is determined by authority; we cannot influence what happens to us by trying to understand events; and intuition is the best guide to making decisions. An interest in being informed, curiosity, and a "will to doubt" all encourage use of critical thinking skills. Only when we clarify our beliefs can we critically examine them. Research on human judgment shows that we are often *un*aware of how we are influenced. Propaganda strategies take full advantage of this fact—even creating beliefs that we have arrived at a certain view ourselves, when indeed our views are created by others (Ellul, 1965). We may change our opinions without knowing we have done so. For example, listeners' opinions on bussing of school children could be altered from pro to con or from con to pro by an eloquent speaker, without listeners realizing that their opinion had shifted (Goethals & Reckman, 1973). Clearly describing the reasoning process involved in making a decision may increase the likelihood of avoiding errors and identifying values that influence decisions.

## ARRANGE A SUPPORTIVE ENVIRONMENT

Even the strongest repertoire can be eroded in an unsupportive environment. Unless there are prompts and incentives to use critical thinking skills and related evidence-based steps, they may not be used. Gray (2001a) has written an excellent guide for arranging supportive practice environments. He describes what is required at the administrative and management levels to create an evidence-based agency. Not all will warm to his recommendations. For example, he suggests that such an agency must "have an obsession for evaluation." Such an "obsession" is viewed as essential to integrate practice and research as required by professional codes of ethics. Arranging and maintaining a supportive environment will be easier with expertise in contingency analysis—knowledge and skill in rearranging the relationships between behaviors of interest and environmental events (e.g., see Austin & Carr, 2000; Malott, Malott, & Trojan, 1999). Prompts and incentives should be provided for use of knowledge and skills that encourage high-quality decision making, such as posing well-formed questions related to information needs and searching effectively and efficiently for related research, preparing clear, up-to-date records, and using valid sources of assessment data and effective intervention programs that are acceptable to clients.

Kindred spirits can be wooed to work together to create conditions that contribute to EBP and care. If competencies start to drift downward, this knowledge can be used to discover how to reverse the trend. Helpful questions include: What consequences support desired behaviors? What events punish these? How can I increase reinforcement of critical thinking skills? What prompts could I arrange? You can place a reminder to question initial assumptions on your desk and include a heading for alternative hypotheses on recording forms. Are necessary tools available? Are undesired behaviors reinforced? You can evaluate your progress in using evidence-based knowledge and skills by reviewing the list of items in Exhibit 11.8 in Chapter 11. Are personal obstacles getting in the way (see Chapter 17)? If so, what kind, and how can you minimize them? Monthly meetings can be held to review decisions with others who model critical appraisal of claims and assumptions as a route to ethical practices and policies. The payoffs of critical thinking and related evidence-informed practices in greater success with clients should be a major incentive to enhance and use related skills. You could start a journal club in which you take turns searching for external research findings related to clinical questions, share new research reports (for example by preparing CATS—see Chapter 11), and practice critical appraisal skills—by using a well-designed checklist to appraise the quality of a new review (see Chapter 12).

## BE POLITICALLY AND ORGANIZATIONALLY SAVVY

Some clinicians forgo having a voice in what happens in an organization or in their community because they believe that politics are beneath them. This decision will be a welcome one to those who wield power. Skill in recognizing various kinds of political tactics is useful in anticipating and exerting countercontrol against these. Politics—the effort to gain or maintain power—is an integral part of everyday life; political action is often necessary to achieve desired goals. Political skills are important, especially those in working with others toward mutually valued aims, such as enhancing the quality of services offered to clients. We have a choice about how to react in settings in which low-level appeals are tolerated or even encouraged—appeals that diminish opportunities to provide evidence-informed practices and policies (e.g., see Hyde, 2003). Conditions that undermine and compromise the quality of decisions may be ignored; disliked situations may be tolerated with little or no effort made to improve matters. Or we can work together with others to create an environment that encourages high-quality services. True, such action requires time and effort—however, in the long run, if we value helping clients and avoiding harm, this is more satisfying than just complaining. And it is the road emphasized in professional codes of ethics. Let's say there is a policy against observing clients and significant others in real-life settings, such as classrooms and playgrounds, and research suggests that such naturalistic observation provides valuable guidelines for selecting promising plans (e.g., see Reid, Patterson, & Snyder, 2002). Not gathering such data when possible and needed may increase the likelihood of the *fundamental attribution error* (attributing behaviors to personality dispositions of clients and overlooking environmental causes). You and your colleagues could lobby to change the policy based on evidentiary grounds. You can give copies to your colleagues of the results of studies showing that observation of interaction between clients and significant others can provide valid data (see Chapter 13).

A request for change is more likely to receive a favorable reaction if it involves a small change and is compatible with current beliefs and goals; you will be more successful if you focus on shared goals, such as helping clients (Fisher & Ury, 1991). Anticipate objections and prepare counterarguments and seek the support of colleagues. If many people work together to achieve a change, it is more likely to occur than if one person pursues it alone. Understanding organizations—how they work, how they change, and why change is often difficult—will offer information about options for introducing valuable innovations. Examine both the formal (e.g., written agency policies) as well as the informal (e.g., preferred communication styles) systems to explore options for change. The informal system includes contingencies that are not formally codified in writing—for example, informal rules such as "Keep records general to protect confidentiality." An example of a formal rule would be the written requirement that there must be a recorded service agreement in each case. The implementation of a formal rule may not reflect its intention. For example, written service agreements may be prepared but may not contain ingredients that facilitate case planning and clarify expectations, such as clear description of hoped-for outcomes and progress indicators.

You also have a choice as to how involved to be in professional organizations—for example, to work together with others to enhance the extent to which such organizations promote evidence-informed practice. Professional organizations should assume greater responsibility for clarifying vague ethical guidelines related to clinical practice. Professionals are mandated to honor codes of ethics. Typically these codes are vague, requiring (and allowing) varied and discretionary interpretations. Take, for example, the statement in the NASW Code of Ethics (National Association of Social Workers, 1999) that "The social worker should accept responsibility or employment only on the basis of existing competence or the intention to acquire the necessary competence." What criteria are to be used to evaluate competence? Does "competence" imply being up-to-date with practice-related empirical literature and use of this information in making decisions? Or does it mean using services consistent with standards in a community (which may be quite poor)? You could join an organization which encourages integration of research and practice.

## CULTIVATE REALISTIC EXPECTATIONS

Critical thinking values and skills will enhance recognition of the limits and potentials of clinical practice—of the inevitable uncertainty associated with decisions. The expectation to succeed all the time can only be satisfied by ignoring lack of success. Problems differ in their potential for resolution, even by expert clinicians. It is unrealistic to expect clinicians to resolve problems such as poverty, lack of access to medical care, and lack of job opportunities, which are the result of structural factors that require redistribution of economic or political resources. An understanding of social, political, and economic factors related to social and personal problems protects you from assuming potentials for change via individually based services such as counseling and therapy that do not exist and that may result in the demoralization associated with burnout.

## CREATE A PLAN OF ACTION FOR CONTINUED LEARNING

Continued learning over your career is one of the joys of being a professional. Identifying obstacles such as misconceptions that hinder well-reasoned decisions is one matter; minimizing their influence is another. We typically carry out everyday tasks with the help of scripts and decision strategies (Hamm, 2003; Schank & Abelson, 1977) that occur relatively automatically in specific contexts; for example, greeting clients, ending interviews, reviewing alternative case formulations, or requesting services from other professionals. Questioning these strategies takes time and requires effort. Enhancing the quality of decisions requires changing thoughts and actions when in clinical situations. If new information is simply added to old information, both the old and the new will be used; "misconceptions must be altered in some way by demonstrating their falseness" (Green, McCloskey, & Caramazza, 1985, p. 137). Related thoughts and actions must be reviewed and altered; there must be some "deep processing" (see Chapter 8). If, for example, you tend to focus on pathology and to neglect client assets, then client assets are less likely to be explored. Work together with others to review your skills in evidence-informed practice, drawing on empirical knowledge about behavior change, such as identifying and using realistic approximations to current performance levels (see list of self-development competencies in Chapter 10).

George Kelley (1955) suggested that clients approach change as personal experiments—trying out a new path for a limited time to see if it is more productive and pleasing. You can design personal experiments to enhance decision-making skills (Neuringer, 1981). These are more likely to succeed if you take advantage of self-management skills such as identifying clear goals and progress indicators and planning a step-by-step agenda. Being your own personal change agent is not easy. However, you can take advantage of guidelines to make this a successful adventure (Watson & Tharp, 2001). You can consult sources that publish evidence-informed articles in your area (e.g., Evidence-Based Mental Health) that may call into question findings from previous research (e.g., see MacMillan, Thomas, Jamieson, Walsh, Boyle, Shannon, & Gafni, 2005) and select continuing education program wisely. (For a critique of the latter see Wright, 2005.)

*Increase Feedback, Which Provides Learning Opportunities*   Much of clinical practice is unknown; there are few opportunities for others to check what actually occurs. Most clinical exchanges take place in private. Disadvantages that result from the privacy of professional exchanges range from lost opportunities to gain corrective feedback from colleagues to the practice of outright quackery and sexual abuse of clients. Experience is valuable only if it is accompanied by corrective feedback (see Chapter 9). Arranging for such feedback is thus vital. Monitoring progress will improve the quality of decisions, since detailed data on which to base decisions will be available. Methods that can be used to keep track of progress are described in a number of sources (see also Chapter 11). Colleagues who have content and procedural knowledge about particular practice methods can help others to improve treatment fidelity and client participation, based on observation of interviews or review of audio or video-taped exchanges with clients.

*Take Advantage of Helpful Tools and Training Programs*   Attention to application obstacles is a hallmark of evidence-based practice. This includes the creation of tools to facilitate the integration of practice and research, such as systematic reviews, and the sharing of what is found with clients in a way that they can understand, as called for in informed consent requirements. The very creation of evidence-based practice was enabled by the Internet revolution and the invention of the systematic review and related enterprises, such as the Cochrane and Campbell Collaborations. These inventions allow rapid access to practice- and policy-related research findings. Additional tools include diagrams, flow-charts, contingency tables, and computerized decision aids, as described in this book and other sources. Note taking and reminders can be helpful in remembering important steps. Treatment manuals describing effective intervention can be used to guide practice. Ways explored to encourage dissemination include workshops, interactive computer programs, and use of aids such as Palm Pilots and role models (Greenhalah et al., 2004). Traditional methods of dissemination, such as continuing education programs, do little to change professional behavior (Davis et al., 1999; Thomas O'Brien et al., 2003). Related research includes investigation of how to increase the effectiveness of professional education programs in developing needed skills and values. Efforts to integrate evidence-based practice into professional education programs range from shifting entirely to a problem-based format (e.g., see

Barrows, 1994; Sackett et al., 2000) to more modest efforts, such as mini-courses and workshops. Although results of research regarding the effectiveness of problem-based learning (PBL) and teaching critical appraisal skills have been in the positive direction (e.g., Coomarasamy & Khan, 2004; Norman & Shannon, 1998; Parkes, Hyde, Deeks, & Milne, 2004), such efforts are not without their critics (e.g., Williams, 2004). Outcomes assessed may be confined to changes in attitudes and knowledge, forgoing evaluation of change in real-life practice situations. Workshops and books designed to enhance critical appraisal skills are readily available (see Chapter 11).

Perkins (1987) suggests putting up a poster that lists important components of a *thinking frame* (a guide to organizing and supporting thought processes; p. 47). Effective *meta-decision skills* (decisions about which strategies to use in making decisions and how much time to devote to a decision) will save time and effort. Aids such as actuarial methods can be used to manage information overload and to increase the likelihood of well-informed decisions. Time can be saved by taking advantage of computer testing and graphing of data concerning progress when appropriate (see Richard & Lauterbach, 2004). Even brief programs may be helpful in counteracting error-producing strategies (e.g., see Gigerenzer, 2002a; Larrick, 2005). Fong, Kravitz, and Nisbett (1986) found that brief instruction concerning the law of large numbers helped subjects to improve their statistical reasoning. Experts' judgments can be improved by training in how to ignore irrelevant data (Gaeth & Shanteau, 1984). (See also Agrawal, Saluja, & Kaczorowski, 2004.) Baron (1985b) suggests that lack of helpful schemas (useful ways of analyzing a problem) is the main reason why people do not think more carefully about issues and tasks. (See discussion of pattern recognition in Chapter 8.)

### BE VIGILANT FOR PROPAGANDA (SELF AND OTHER)

Interrelated kinds of propaganda include deep propaganda that obscures political, economic, and social contingencies that influence troubled and troubling behaviors, and the questionable accuracy of some common assumption; for example, that hundreds of such behaviors are caused by biomedically based mental disorders requiring the help of experts (see Chapters 1 and 2). Related literature highlights the prevalence of propaganda and our vulnerability to it (Gilovich, 1991; Mansfield, 1997; Pratkanis & Aronson, 2001). If harm results from influence by human service propaganda (e.g., choosing services that harm rather than help clients), it is important to develop ways to avoid its effects. We can keep a copy of Carl Sagan's *Baloney detection kit* on our desk or a cue card listing Hugh Rank's (1984) common propaganda cues: *Hi, Trust Me, You Need, Hurry, Buy.* We can become familiar with informal fallacies, such as glittering generalizations, name calling, plain folks appeal, and card stacking, and their use to encourage beliefs and actions with the least thought possible (Gibbs & Gambrill, 1999); we can read Thousless's *Straight and Crooked*

*Thinking: Thirty-Eight Dishonest Tricks of Debates* (1974). We can join others who share our interest to spot bogus claims—for example, the most outrageous pitch of the month. All professional schools should offer courses on human service propaganda to help professionals avoid unwanted influence (Wilkes & Hoffman, 2001). Professional education programs should also offer courses on the history of harming in the name of helping in the professions, and ignorance in social work/psychiatry/psychology. At least one school offered a course on Medical Ignorance (Witte, Witte, & Kerwin, 1994).

We can decrease self-propaganda by making the effects of our decisions and criteria on which we base them more visible. We can:

- Question rather than assume.
- Thank others for pointing out mistakes in our thinking.
- Become informed about common informal fallacies and cognitive biases, such as wishful thinking and hindsight bias, and learn how to avoid them (Flannelly & Flannelly, 2000).
- Examine the correspondence between our values and our actions by taking the Goosey-Gander test (see Chapter 1).
- Take time for empathic reflection (what if I were in her shoes?) and correct empathic dysfunctions (under- or overinvolvement) that contribute to a detachment that harms clients (Halpern, 2001). We can read client narratives and view photographs of harmful consequences that result from poor decisions.
- Explore personal excuses that result in and hide harms to others. (See Chapter 17.) Excuses include bogus objections to the process and philosophy of EBP, such as "It is a cookbook approach," "It ignores clinical expertise," and "It ignores clients' values"—all untrue.

## PRACTICE CRITICAL THINKING SKILLS

Both our personal and work environments offer many opportunities to practice critical thinking skills—reading the newspaper and professional journals, watching TV, attending case conferences (e.g., see Frankfurt, 2005). As many have noted (e.g., Tuchman, 1989) we are a public that is brought up on deception through advertising. Watch how others handle situations in which fallacies occur, to discover options. Having names for the different kinds of fallacies will make it easier to identify them. Practice will make the use of critical thinking skills more fluid. Structural factors related to personal and social problems often are not mentioned in newspaper reports or professional sources, which focus on "blaming the victim" (see Chapter 2). Ownership of the major media by a few companies is not encouraging in terms of describing views that are not compatible with vested interests (Bagdikian, 2004). Many writers both past and present, such as Foucault (1981), emphasize the extent to which influence is not necessarily consciously used. That is, there may not be a conspiracy to suppress information about structural sources of influence (Ellul, 1965). Conspiracy or not, the media influence our views about factors related to problems.

## USE HELPFUL RULES

Many tips have been described in previous chapters. Key examples are highlighted here:

1. *Place clients' interests front and center.* A focus on helping clients and avoiding harm should serve as a key centering point that will help you to avoid directions that do not match related values.
2. *Look for disconfirming evidence.* Make it a habit to search for disconfirming evidence, such as counterexamples and counterarguments (Mussweiler, Strack, & Pfeiffer, 2000). Bromley (1977) recommends inclusion of an Alternative Hypotheses heading in clinical records. This may help to counter the influence of initial assumptions, which may be incorrect. Take advantage of websites that question claims such as Committee for the Scientific Investigation of Claims of the Paranormal (CSICOP) and AdWatch (see Mansfield, 2003).
3. *Increase intellectual and emotional empathy: Try to understand other points of view and experiences.* Understanding other points of view has several advantages. One is identifying flaws in your thinking. If this rule had been used by participants in the case conference described in Chapter 16, the person responsible for the abuse of Lindy may have been identified earlier and subsequent abuse might have been avoided. Misunderstandings are less likely and cogent counterarguments are more likely when other well-argued perspectives are understood and considered. A focus on common goals (for example, to help clients) will encourage attention to other positions. Here too, take advantage of websites that highlight costs of bogus claims and corruption such as www.transparency.org
4. *Watch out for the fundamental attribution error.* The tendency to attribute client concerns to dispositional causes has been often noted in this book. This tendency deflects attention from environmental factors related to client concerns and may result in incorrect inferences. One way to combat this bias is to enhance empathic reactions—that is, to "put yourself in other people's shoes" (Regan & Totten, 1975). This may decrease the observer-actor bias (see Chapter 9). Another is to become informed about environmental causes of personal problems.
5. *Pay attention to words.* Different meanings for words and failure to clarify these or to recognize their emotional influences can result in errors and muddled discussions. Both spoken and written language in clinical settings (such as written records and case conferences) should be used to inform. Nickerson (1986a) argues that "It is never inappropriate to ask what someone means by a specified word in a particular context"

(p. 130). On the other hand, Popper warns us about being more precise than we need to be and about trying to arrive at "the truth" by arguing about the definition of words. Research on the helping process reveals how clinicians use words to influence patients' decisions:

> Doctors realized that the words they chose to present the evidence could have a strong influence on the patient's decision. They effectively limited the options while seeming to invite the patient to make the decision. The contributors framed these themes with phrases such as 'It's how you put it over,' and 'It depends on how you feed information to people.' The semantics then affect the way in which evidence is implemented by swaying the patient in a particular direction. (Freeman & Sweeney, 2001)

6. *Watch out for vivid data.* The more vivid the data, the more caution should be exercised in assigning it weight. We tend to overlook the importance of nonoccurrences that may be important. It is easy to ignore "good behavior" and focus on more vivid disliked behaviors. Make it a habit to ask about events that do not occur.

7. *Beware of personally relevant data.* One of the themes throughout this book is the influence of emotions and self-interest on judgments. "Perhaps there are no greater impediments to effective reasoning than those that derive from a confusion between reasoning and rationalizing, or, to make the same distinction in other terms, between weighing evidence on the one hand and defending a position or making a case on the other. This is the problem of our frequent failure, perhaps our inability, to assess evidence objectively and without bias when we have a vested interest in the outcome of a debate" (Nickerson, 1986b, p. 362). Use emotional and personally relevant material as a reminder to be especially vigilant. Being informed about research findings regarding the influence of mood and emotional arousal on our judgments may increase the likelihood that this source of error will be avoided (e.g., see Slovic, Finucane, Peters, & MacGregor, 2002). Research suggests the need for deep processing of new ways of thinking, especially when there are strong incentives for maintaining current biases and prejudices—what Paul and Elder (2002) refer to as "activated ignorance" (p. 82)—that may neutralize new ways of thinking. Without deep processing, new knowledge about reasoning may be used to bolster current biases and prejudices.

8. *Complement critical thinking skills with knowledge.* Familiarity with relevant knowledge in a domain is often vital in making accurate decisions. "The first rule of effective reasoning is to get your facts straight" (Nickerson, 1986a, p. 132). Critical thinking skills, as well as good intentions and supportive skills, may be enough when little is known about how to help a client with a problem (that is, when either nothing is known or research indicates that it does not matter what is done as long as you talk and listen to the person). Offering support is not enough, however,

when more can be done. For example, I recently saw a client who had been seeing a therapist for depression for over a year. She reported that her therapist was using supportive counseling and that there was no focus on acquiring skills that could be used in daily life to decrease depression. A careful assessment revealed many specific changes that could be made to decrease her depression; that is, far more help than supportive counseling was needed and was available. Evidence-based practice offers a variety of tools and resources for taking advantage of relevant knowledge. Effective learning skills and the process of evidence-based practice make it possible to gain maximum payoff for time spent locating and appraising practice-related content (see Chapters 8 and 10).

9. *Ask about test accuracy.* Some errors result from reliance on unreliable and invalid psychological tests. Questions here include, How sensitive is the test? What is the false-positive rate? What is the false-negative rate? What is the number needed to harm? (see Chapter 11). Be sure to ask about all four cells of a four-cell contingency table. We tend to pay attention to the present-present cell and to ignore the other three cells (see Chapter 14). This results in overestimates of the effectiveness of services and overestimates of pathology.

10. *Ask questions with a high payoff value.* Questions differ in the likelihood that helpful information will be revealed by the answers. Asking questions that have maximum utility will save time. One helpful question is "What's missing?" What is not discussed may be most important in identifying factors related to hoped-for outcomes.

11. *Move beyond the illusion of understanding.* Some assumptions contribute real understanding; others provide merely a feeling of understanding and are not helpful when applied to real-life problems. Accepting beliefs based on a feeling of understanding is encouraged by the expectation that we should have explanations on hand for almost anything, without significant effort to arrive at these accounts. Pressures on clinicians, often self-imposed, to appear more expert than is warranted encourage this tendency. Accepting views only because they "make sense" may result in a fragmented eclectic approach to practice—an unintegrated, unevidence-informed mix of assumptions that is used to make decisions rather than a cohesive, empirically informed practice theory.

12. *Be your own best critic.* We learn how to do better only by being willing to candidly examine our limitations as well as our strengths. Only in this way can we correct flaws in our self-assessment that may get in the way of offering high quality services to clients.

13. *Catch and counter reemerging falsehoods that diminish the quality of services.* Certain key beliefs discourage acquisition and maintenance of critical thinking skills. One of the most common and hardy is the belief that reason and caring are incompatible. The rational individual is painted as

cold, unfeeling, and missing the boat in relation to understanding the qualitative, subjective, rich-textured side of life. It is argued that one cannot be a critical thinker and a caring person at the same time. Reason and passion are pitted against one another as if they were adversaries. An argument can be made that caring without careful reasoning is not caring at all, especially in professions such as social work, psychology, psychiatry, medicine, dentistry, and counseling. Indeed, the history of harming in the name of helping in some "helping professions" shows that good intentions do not protect people from harm (e.g., Valenstein, 1986; Wright & Cummings, 2005). "A passionate drive for *clarity*, accuracy, and fair-mindedness, a fervor for getting to the bottom of things, to the deepest root issues, for listening sympathetically to opposition points of view, a compelling drive to seek out evidence, an intense aversion to contradiction, sloppy thinking, inconsistent application of standards, a devotion to truth as against self-interest—these are essential commitments of the rational person" (Paul, 1987, p. 142).

Another hardy falsehood is that because there is no such thing as total objectivity (for example, our interpretation of the meanings of events intrudes between what is in the world and what we see), science is no better than and not as valuable as a subjective intuitive approach in arriving at knowledge (tentative assumptions about what is true). Objective methods are painted as sterile, narrow, and unfaithful to reality, and subjective methods are presented as rich, meaningful, and representative of reality. Objective methods are sometimes discussed as if their use requires a belief that total objectivity is possible. In fact, the elaborate methodologies used in scientific investigation are because of concern with the very issue subjectivists claim is ignored in scientific inquiry —a concern to tease out misleading, biasing effects that may result in faulty conclusions (see Chapter 4). Methods of inquiry differ in the kinds of questions that can be answered and in the kinds of answers that are offered (see Chapter 12). Science deals with questions that are possible to critically test. This is not to say that other kinds of questions and related methods do not have value or that intuition is not vital for coming up with ideas and how to test them. (See also discussion of informed intuition in Chapter 9.)

Yet another falsehood that keeps people uninformed is the belief that critical thinking is difficult. This view may be accepted because of an interest in decreasing effort and avoiding indecision and failure. A related myth is the belief that you have to be an expert in an area to critically evaluate related claims. On the contrary, critical thinking values, knowledge, and skills can be applied to any area if authors and speakers clearly describe methods used to arrive at assumptions. Some clinicians believe that the therapeutic process is essentially unknowable, implying that it is useless to try to identify specific elements that contribute to success. Indeed, the rich literature related to the therapeutic process belies this assumption (e.g., Norcross, 2002a). In moments of discouragement, it may be tempting to slip into this belief and to abandon efforts to discover what is knowable in this complex area. A belief that there are no answers discourages a search for answers; "any advance, personal or scientific, depends on the assumption that what is not yet known is knowable" (Langer, 1983, p. 119). The influence of Basagalia in changing the pattern of service delivery to psychiatric patients in Italy offers an example of what is possible to achieve (Basaglia, in Scheper-Hughes & Lovell, 1987) as does the creation of the Cochrane and Campbell Collaborations. Yet another belief is that if errors are inevitable there is no use trying to avoid them. Indeed, errors are part and parcel of how we learn to refine our skills and are more likely to be avoided if we accept the inevitability of error. The need to act may encourage excessive belief in the appropriateness of actions taken.

## REVIEW PREFERRED PRACTICE THEORIES

Not all answers to a question are equally good, as revealed by the history of harming in the name of helping. Decisions are more likely to be accurate if practice theories are selected that offer sound causal assumptions about how to attain outcomes clients value. Some clinicians do not distinguish between theories of different empirical status—embracing those with none as readily as those with considerable evidentiary status (Meehl, 1978). A helpful theory consists of a set of concepts and proposed interrelationships that are of value in understanding a broad array of phenomena. Confusing theories of different breadths of application may result in frustration, as efforts are made to apply a narrow model to events that are too complex to be handled within such a limited framework.

## TAKE OCCASIONAL TIME-OUTS TO REFLECT ON YOUR WORK

Those who work in agencies in which most hoped-for outcomes are related to social, political, and economic factors and who emphasize dispositional attributions often believe, with good reason, that they are providing a Band-Aid function; no real changes are possible that can improve the quality of life for clients. Clients are often resistant—especially in nonvoluntary settings such as child protection agencies. Many clinicians believe that nothing can be done about social conditions and the personal problems they create until there are societal and economic changes. You may focus on dispositional characteristics and ignore environmental causes of client concerns because of a lack of resources (see Chapter 14). The excuses you adopt for offering inadequate services (see Chapter 17) may result in overlooking opportunities for change that can be made within the constraints of a given setting, as well as small steps that can be taken outside work—for example, lobbying legislators. Excuses reflect a resignation to a less-than-optimal work life. A review of your career goals as well as a realistic appraisal of the potential of given intervention methods to help your clients may encourage a redistribution of effort in terms of the balance between individual practice and participation in collective efforts to seek changes in service-delivery patterns that would benefit clients. Indeed, in describing the philosophy of evidence-based practice, Guyatt and Rennie (2002) suggest that when physicians observe that their patients' well-being is influenced by the quality of their environment they have an obligation to advocate for positive changes.

## SUMMARY

Maintaining critical thinking values, knowledge, and skills that contribute to evidence-informed practice should not be left to chance. Transfer of new skills to other areas can be facilitated by developing useful self-management skills, by focusing on the process rather than on the product of thinking (using the steps in evidence-based practice), and by practicing skills in many different situations. Reviewing the benefits of critical thinking and awareness of the prevalence of propaganda in the helping professions (e.g., suppressed information), both in the mass media and in professional sources should be a reminder to take advantage of critical thinking skills in day-to-day practice. Increasing the quality of feedback about degree of progress offers fine-grained data on the accuracy of clinical decisions. Arranging a supportive environment and cultivating realistic standards of success will be helpful in maintaining valued skills. Rules, such as asking, "What's the accuracy of this test?," as well as tools, such as access to needed databases, are vital. Focusing on helping clients and avoiding harm should contribute to the courage to ask "hard questions." Increasing the quality of clinical reasoning skills may encourage a reconsideration of the potential of pursuing valued goals that have been abandoned. Most importantly, it will enhance the quality of services offered to clients.

# References

Abbott, A. (1988). *The system of professions: An essay on the division of expert labor.* Chicago: University of Chicago Press.

Abercrombie, M. L. J. (1960). *The anatomy of judgement.* New York: Basic Books.

Abramowitz, S. I., Berger, A., & Weary, G. (1982). Similarity between clinician and client: Its influence on the helping relationship. In T. A. Wills (Ed.), *Basic processes in helping relationships* (pp. 357–379). Orlando, FL: Academic Press.

Abramowitz, S. I., & Murray, J. (1983). Race effects in psychotherapy. In J. Murray & P. R. Abramson (Eds.), *Bias in psychotherapy.* New York: Praeger.

Ackerman, S. J., & Hilsenroth, M. J. (2003). A review of therapist characteristics and techniques positively impacting the therapeutic alliance. *Clinical Psychology Review, 23,* 1–33.

Adams, J. L. (1974). *Conceptual blockbusting: A guide to better ideas.* New York: W. H. Freeman.

Addis, M. E., & Krasnow, A. D. (2000). A national survey of practicing psychologists' attitudes towards psychotherapy treatment manuals. *Journal of Consulting and Clinical Psychology, 68,* 331–339.

Advertisement for professional liability insurance. (1987, April). *NASW News, 32,* 17.

Agrawal, S., Saluja, I., & Kaczorowski, J. (2004). A prospective before-and-after trial of an educational intervention about pharmaceutical marketing. *Academic Medicine, 79,* 1046–1050.

Albert, S., Fox, H. M., & Kahn, M. W. (1980). Faking psychosis on the Rorschach: Can expert judges detect malingering. *Journal of Personality Assessment, 44,* 115–119.

Alberto, P. A., & Troutman, A. C. (1990). *Applied behavior analysis for teachers* (5th ed.). Columbus, OH: Merrill.

Altman, D. G. (2002). Poor-quality medical research: What can journals do? *Journal of the American Medical Association, 287,* 2765–2767.

Altman, D. G., Machin, D., Bryant, T. N., & Gardner, M. J. (Eds.). (2000). *Statistics with confidence: Confidence intervals and statistical guidelines.* London: BMJ Books.

Altman, D. G., Schulz, K. F., Moher, D., Egger, J., Davidoff, F., Elbourne, D., et al. for the CONSORT Group. (2001). The revised CONSORT statement for reporting randomized trials: Explanation and elaboration. *ANNALS of Internal Medicine,* 134(8), 663–694. Available at www.soncort-statement.org

American Psychiatric Association. (2000). *Diagnostic and statistical manual of mental disorders* (4th ed. rev.). Washington, DC: Author.

American Psychological Association. (2002). *Ethical principles of psychologists and code of conduct,* Draft 6, The Code of Ethics Project Task force (Available from the APA Center for Ethics and Human Rights; 2002, available APA website 10/7/04).

Anastasi, A., & Urbina, S. (1996). *Psychological testing* (7th ed.). Upper Saddle River, NJ: Prentice Hall.

Angell, M. (2004). *The truth about drug companies: How they deceived us and what to do about it.* New York: Random House.

Anthony, E. J., & Cohler, B. J. (1987). *The invulnerable child.* New York: Guilford.

Antman, E. M., Lau, J., Kupelnick, B., Mosteller, F., & Chalmers, T. C. (1992). A comparison of results of meta-analyses of randomized controlled trials and recommendations of clinical experts: Treatments for myocardial infarction. *Journal of the American Medical Association, 268,* 240–248.

Antonuccio, D. O., Burns, D. D., & Danton, W. G. (2002). Antidepressants: A triumph of marketing over science. *Prevention & Treatment, 5,* 1–17.

Argyris, C., & Schön, D. A. (1996). *Organizational learning II: Theory, method, and practice.* New York: Addison-Wessley.

Argyris, C., & Schön, D. A. (1974). *Theory in practice: Increasing professional effectiveness.* San Francisco: Jossey-Bass.

Arkes, H. (1981). Impediments to accurate clinical judgment and possible ways to minimize their impact. *Journal of Consulting and Clinical Psychology, 49,* 323–330.

Arkes, H. R. (2001). Overconfidence in judgmental forecasting. In J. S. Armstrong (Ed.), *Principle of forecasting handbook* (pp. 495–515). Boston: Kluwer.

Arkin, R. M., & Oleson, K. C. (1998). Self-handicapping. In J. M. Darley & J. Cooper (Eds.), *Attribution and social interaction: The legacy of Edward E. Jones* (pp. 313–347). Washington, D.C.: American Psychological Association.

Armstrong, J. C. (1980). Unintelligible management research and academic prestige. *Interfaces, 10,* 80–86.

Aronson, J. K. (2003). Anecdotes as evidence: We need guidelines for reporting anecdotes of suspected adverse drug reactions. *British Medical Journal, 326,* 1346.

Asch, S. E. (1956). Studies of independence and conformity: Minority of one against a unanimous majority. *Psychological Monographs, 70*(9, Whole No. 416).

Ashton, P. T., & Webb, R. B. (1986). *Making a difference: Teachers' sense of efficacy and student achievement.* New York: Longman.

Asimov, I. (1989). The relativity of wrong. *The Skeptical Inquirer, 14,* 35–44.

Austin, J. & Carr, R. J. (Eds.). (2000). *Handbook of applied behavior analysis.* Reno, NV: Context Press.

Averill, J. (1982). *Anger and aggression: Implications for theories of emotion.* New York: Springer-Verlag.

Bacon, F. ([1620] 1985). (Appendix 4: Idols of the mind). In J. Pitcher (Ed.), *Francis Bacon: The essays.* New York: Penguin Books.

Baddeley, A. D. (1997). *Human memory: Theory and practice* (rev. ed.). Hove, UK: Psychology Press.

Baddeley, A. D. (2001). Is working memory still working? *American Psychologist, 56,* 851–864.

Baddeley, A. D., Conway, M. A., & Aggleton, J. P. (2002). *Episodic memory: New directions in research.* New York: Oxford.

Badinter, E. (1980). *Mother love, myth and reality.* New York: Macmillan.

Baer, D. M. (1984). Future directions: Or, is it useful to ask, "Where did we go wrong?: before we go? In R. F. Dangel & R. A. Polster (Eds.), *Parent training: Foundations of research and practice* (pp. 547–557). New York: Guilford.

Baer, D. M. (1987). Weak contingencies, strong contingencies, and many behaviors to change. *Journal of Applied Behavior Analysis, 20,* 335–337.

Baer, D. M. (2003). *Program evaluation: Arduous, impossible, or political?* In H. E. Briggs & T. L. Rzepnicki (Eds.), *Using evidence in social work practice: Behavioral perspectives* (pp. 310–322). Chicago: Lyceum.

Bagdikian, B. H. (2004). *The new media.* Boston: Beacon Press.

Baird, C., & Wagner, D. (2000). The relative validity of actuarial and consensus-based risk assessment systems. *Child and Youth Services Review, 22,* 839–871.

Baldwin, S. (1999). Applied behavior analysis in the treatment of ADHD: A review and reapproachment. *Ethical Human Sciences and Services, 1,* 35–60.

*Bandolier.* (2003a). Magnetic insoles for foot pain: Randomized trial results. Comment on M. H. Winemiller, et al. (2003). Effect of magnetic vs sham-magnetic insoles on plantar heel pain: A randomized controlled trial. *Journal of the American Medical Association, 290,* 1474–1478.

*Bandolier.* (2003b). Homeopathy: Systematic review of systematic reviews. Oct., 116–118.

Bandura, A. (1978). On paradigms and recycled ideologies. *Cognitive Therapy and Research, 2,* 79–103.

Bandura, A. (1986). *Social foundations of thought and action.* Englewood Cliffs, NJ: Prentice Hall.

Bandura, A. (1997). *Self-efficacy: The exercise in control.* New York: W. H. Freeman.

Bandura, A. (1999). Moral disengagement in the perpetration of inhumanities. *Personality and Social Psychology Review, 3,* 193–209.

Bar-Hillel, M. (1983). The base-rate fallacy controversy. In R. W. Scholz (Ed.), *Decision making under uncertainty* (pp. 39–62). New York: Elsevier.

Barkley, R. A., Cook, E. H., Diamond, A., Zametkin, A., Thapar, A., Teeter, A., et al. (2002). International Consensus Statement on ADHD. *Clinical Child and Family Psychology Review, 5,* 89–111.

Barling, J., Kelloway, E. K., & Frone, M. R. (2004). *Handbook of work stress.* Thousand Oaks, CA: Sage.

Barnett, R., & Rivers, C. (2004). *Same differences: How gender myths are hurting our relationships, our children, and our jobs.* New York: Basic Books.

Baron, J. (1981). Reflective thinking as a goal of education. *Intelligence, 5,* 291–309.

Baron, J. (1985a). What kind of intelligence components are fundamental? In S. F. Chipman, J. W. Segal, & R. Glaser (Eds.), *Thinking and learning skills: Vol. 2. Research and open questions.* Hillsdale, NJ: Erlbaum.

Baron, J. (1985b). *Rationality and intelligence.* Cambridge, England: Cambridge University Press.

Baron, J. (1994). *Thinking and deciding.* New York: Cambridge University Press.

Baron, J. (1997). Biases in the quantitative measurement of values for public decision. *Psychological Bulletin, 122,* 72–88.

Baron, J. (1998). *Judgment misguided: Intuition and error in public decision making.* New York: Oxford University Press.

Baron, J. (2000). *Thinking and deciding* (3rd ed.). New York: Cambridge University Press.

Baron, J. (2005). Normative models of judgment and decision making. In D. J. Koehler & N. Harvey (Eds.), *Blackwell handbook of judgment and decision making* (pp. 19–36). Malden, MA: Blackwell.

Baron, J. B. & Sternberg, R. J. (1993). *Teaching thinking skills: Theory and practice.* New York: Freeman.

Barratt, A., Howard, K., Irwig, L., Salkeld, G., & Houssami, N. (2005). Model of outcomes of screening mammography: Information to support informed choices. *British Medical Journal, 330,* 936.

Barrett, S., Jarvis, W. T., Kroger, M., & London, W. H. (2002). *Consumer health: A guide to intelligent decision* (7th ed.). New York: McGraw-Hill.

Barrows, H. S. (1994). *Practice-based learning: Problem-based learning applied to medical education.* Springfield, IL: Southern Illinois University School of Medicine.

Batson, C. D. (1975). Attribution as a mediator of bias in helping. *Journal of Personality and Social Psychology, 72,* 455–466.

Batson, C. D., Jones, C. H., & Cochran, P. J. (1979). Attributional bias in counselors' diagnosis: The effects of resources on perception of need. *Journal of Applied Social Psychology, 9,* 377–393.

Batson, C. D., O'Quin, K., & Pych, V. (1982). An attribution theory analysis of trained helpers' inferences about clients' needs. In T. A. Wills (Ed.), *Basic processes in helping relationships* (pp. 59–80). New York: Academic Press.

Batson, C. D., Polycarpoum, P., Harmon-Jones, E., Imhoff, H. J., Mitchener, E. C., Bednar, L. L., Klein, T. R., & Highberger, L. (1997). Empathy and attitudes: Can feeling for a member of a stigmatized group improve feelings toward the group? *Journal of Personality and Social Psychology, 72,* 105–118.

Baumeister, R. F., Campbell, J. D., Krueger, J. I., & Vohs, K. D. (2003). Does high self-esteem cause better performance, interpersonal success, happiness, or healthier lifestyles? *Psychological Science in the Public Interest, 4,* 1–44.

Beck, A. T. (1976). *Cognitive therapy and the emotional disorders.* New York: International Universities Press.

Beck, A. T., Steer, R. A., Kovacs, M., & Garrison, B. (1985). Hopelessness and eventual suicide: A 10-year prospective study of patients hospitalized with suicidal ideation. *American Journal of Psychiatry, 152,* 559–563.

Beck, P., Byyny, R. L., & Adams, K. S. (1981). *Case exercises in clinical reasoning.* Chicago: Yearbook Medical.

Becker, H. S. (1996). The epistemology of qualitative research. In R. Jessor, A. Colby, & R. A. Shweder (Eds.), *Ethnography and human development: Context and meaning in social inquiry* (pp. 53–71). Chicago: University of Chicago Press.

Beit-Hallahmi, B. (1987) The psychotherapy subculture: Practice and ideology. *Social Science Information, 26*, 475–492.

Bekelman, J. E., Li, Y., & Gross, C. P. (2003). Scope and impact of financial conflicts of interest in biomedical research: A systematic review. *Journal of the American Medical Association, 289*, 454–465.

Bell, T., & Linn, M. C. (2002). Beliefs about science: How does science instruction contribute? In B. K. Hofer & P. R. Pintrich (Eds.), *Personal epistemology: The psychology of beliefs about knowledge and learning* (pp. 321–346). Mahwah, NJ: Erlbaum.

Belli, R. F., & Loftus, E. F. (1996). The pliability of autobiographical memory: Misinformation and the false memory problem. In D. C. Rubin (Ed.), *Remembering our past: Studies in autobiographical memory* (pp. 157–179). New York: Cambridge University Press.

Belmont, J. M., Butterfield, E. C., & Ferritti, R. P. (1982). To secure transfer of training instruct self-management skills. In D. K. Detterman & R. J. Sternberg (Eds.), *How and how much can intelligence be increased* (pp. 147–154). Norwood, NJ: Ablex.

Bennett, K. J., Sackett, D. L., Haynes, R. B., Neufeld, V. R., Tugwell, P., & Roberts, R. (1987). A controlled trial of teaching critical appraisal of the clinical literature to medical students. *Journal of the American Medical Association, 257*, 2451–2454.

Bereiter, C., & Scardamalia, M. (1985). Cognitive coping strategies and the problems of "inert" knowledge. In S. F. Chipman, J. W. Segal, & R. Glaser (Eds.), *Thinking and learning skills: Vol. 2. Research and open questions.* San Francisco: Jossey-Bass.

Berger, P. L., & Luckman, T. (1966). *The social construction of reality.* New York: Doubleday.

Bergin, A. E., & Garfield, S. L. (Eds.). (1994). *Handbook of psychotherapy and behavior change* (4th ed.). New York: Wiley.

Berk, R. A., & Rossi, P. H. (1990). *Thinking about program evaluation.* Newbury Park: Sage.

Best, J. (1988). Missing children, misleading statistics. *Public Interest, 92*, 84–92.

Best, J. (2004). *More damned lies and statistics: How numbers confuse public issues.* Berkeley, CA: University of California Press.

Beutler, L. E. (2000a). Empirically based decision making in clinical practice. *Prevention and Treatment, 3.*

Beutler, L. E. (2000b). David and Goliath: When empirical and clinical standards of practice meet. *American Psychologist, 55*, 997–1007.

Beutler, L. E., Malik, M., Alimohamed, S., Harwood, T. M., Talebi, Z. H., Noble, S., & Wong, E. (2004). Therapist variables. In M. J. Lambert (Ed.), *Bergin and Garfield's Handbook of psychotherapy and behavior change* (5th ed., pp. 227–306). New York: Wiley.

Beyerstein, B. L. (1990). Brainscams: Neuromythologies of the new age. *International Journal of Mental Health, 19*, 27–36.

Bhandari, M., Busse, J. W., Jackowski, D., Montori, V. M., Schünemann, H., et al. (2004). Association between industry funding and statistically significant pro-industry findings in medical and surgical randomized trials. *Canadian Medical Association Journal, 170*, 477–480.

Black, N. (1994). Experimental and observational methods of evaluation. *British Medical Journal, 309*, 540.

Blackard, M. K., & Barsh, E. T. (1982). Parents' and professionals' perceptions of the handicapped child's impact on the family. *Journal of the Association for Person's with severe handicaps, 7,* 62–70.

Blackmore, S. (1987). The elusive open mind: Ten years of negative research in parapsychology. *The Skeptical Inquirer, 11,* 244–255.

Blackmore, S. (1991). Keynote annual meeting CSI-COP (Committee for the Scientific Investigation of Claims of the Paranormal).

Blalock, H. M, Jr. (1984). *Basic dilemmas in the social sciences.* Beverly Hills, CA: Sage.

Blau, P. M. (1960). Orientation toward clients in a public welfare agency. *Administrative Science Quarterly, 5,* 341–361.

Blau, T. H. (1988). *Psychology tradeoff: The technique and style of doing therapy.* New York: Brunner/Mazel.

Blenkner, M., Bloom, M., & Nielson, M. (1971). A research and demonstration project of protective services. *Social Casework, 52,* 483–499.

Bless, H. (2001). The consequences of mood on the processing of social information. In A. Tesser & N. Schwarz (Eds.), *Blackwell handbook of social psychology: Intraindividual processes* (pp. 391–421). Oxford, UK: Blackwell.

Bloom, M., Fischer, J., & Orme, J. G. (2003). *Evaluating practice: Guidelines for the accountable professional* (4th ed.). Boston: Allyn & Bacon.

Blum, J. (1978). *Pseudoscience and mental ability.* New York: Monthly Review Press.

Bodenheimer, T. (2000). Disease management in the American market. *British Medical Journal, 320,* 563–566.

Bogner, M. S. (Ed.). (1994). *Human error in medicine.* Hillsdale, NJ: Erlbaum.

Bohart, A. C., Elliott, R., Greenberg, L. S., & Watson, J. C. (2002). Empathy. In J. C. Norcross (Ed.), *Psychotherapy relationships that work: Therapist contributions and responsiveness to patients* (pp. 89–108). New York: Oxford University Press.

Bond, M. H. (Ed.). (1986). *The psychology of the Chinese people.* New York: Oxford University Press.

Boren, J. H. (1972). *When in doubt, mumble: A bureaucrat's handbook.* New York: Van Nostrand Reinhold.

Borgida, E., & Nisbett, R. E. (1977). The differential impact of abstract vs. concrete information on decisions. *Journal of Applied Social Psychology, 7,* 258–271.

Bosk, C. L. (1979). *Forgive and remember: Managing medical failure.* Chicago: University of Chicago Press.

Bossuyt, P. M., Reitsma, J. B., Bruns, D. E., Gatsonis, C. A., Glasziou, P. P., Irwig, L. M., Ligmer, J. G., Moher, D., Rennie, D., & de Vet, H. C. (2003). Towards complete and accurate reporting of studies of diagnostic accuracy: The STARD initiative. *British Medical Journal, 326,* 41–44.

Bourgois, P., Lettiere, M., & Quesada, J. (2003). Social misery and the sanctions of substance abuse: Confronting HIV risk among homeless heroin addicts in San Francisco. In J. D. Orcutt & D. R. Rudy (Eds.), *Drugs, alcohol, and social problems* (pp. 257–278). New York: Oxford University Press.

Bower, G. H., & Cohen, P. R. (1982). Emotional influences in memory and thinking: Data and theory. In M. S. Clark & S. T. Fiske (Eds.), *Affect and cognition* (pp. 291–332). Hillsdale, NJ: Erlbaum.

Bowers, K. S. (1984). On being unconsciously influenced and informed. In K. S. Bowers & D. Meichenbaum (Eds.), *The unconscious reconsidered* (pp. 227–272). New York: Wiley.

Bowers, K. S. (1987). Intuition and discovery. In P. Stern (Ed.), *Theories of the unconscious and theories of the self* (pp. 71–90). Hillsdale, NJ: Analytic Press.

Boyle, M. (2002). *Schizophrenia: A scientific delusion?* (2nd ed.). London: Routledge.

Braddock, C. H., Edwards, K. A., Hasenberg, N. M., Laidley, T. L., & Levinson, W. (1999). Informed decision making in outpatient practice. Time to get back to basics. *Journal of the American Medical Association, 282,* 2313–2320.

Bransford, J. D., Brown, A. L., & Cocking, R. R. (Eds.). (1999). *How people learn: Brain, mind, experience, and school.* Washington, DC: National Academy of Sciences.

Bransford, J. D., & Stein, B. S. (1984). *The IDEAL problem solver: A guide for improving thinking, learning, and creativity.* New York: W. H. Freeman.

Brekstad, A. (1966). Factors influencing the reliability of anamnestic recall. *Child Development, 37,* 603–612.

Brewer, D. D., Brody, S., Drucker, E., Gisselquist, D., Minkin, S. F., Potterat, J. J., Rothenberg, R. B., & Vachon, F. (2003). Mounting anomalies in the epidemiology of HIV in Africa: Cry the beloved paradigm. *International Journal of STD & AIDS, 14,* 144–117.

Broad, W., & Wade, N. (1982). *Betrayers of the truth.* New York: Simon & Schuster.

Brock, T. C., & Green, M. C. (Eds.). (2005). *Persuasion: Psychological insights and perspectives* (2nd ed.). Thousand Oaks, CA: Sage.

Bromley, D. B. (1977). *Personality description and ordinary language.* New York: Wiley.

Bromley, D. B. (1986). *The case-study method in psychology and related disciplines.* New York: Wiley.

Brookfield, S. (1995). *Becoming a critically reflective teacher.* San Francisco: Jossey-Bass.

Brookfield, S. D. (1987). *Developing critical thinkers: Challenging adults to explore alternative ways of thinking and acting.* San Francisco, CA: Jossey-Bass.

Brounstein, P. J., Emshoff, J. G., Hill, G. A., & Stoil, M. J. (1997). Assessment of methodological practices in the evaluation of alcohol and other drug (AOD) abuse prevention. *Journal of Health and Social Policy, 9,* 1–19.

Bryant, G. D., & Norman, G. R. (1980). Expressions of probability: Words and numbers. *New England Journal of Medicine, 302,* 411.

Budd, K. S., Poindexter, L. M., Feliz, E. D., & Naik-Polan, A. T. (2001). Clinical assessment of parents in child protection cases: An empirical analysis. *Law and Human Behavior, 25,* 93–108.

Buie, J. (1987). Newspaper's tone, errors irk sources. *APA Monitor, 18,* 23.

Buie, J. (1989). Psychologists defend reimbursement rights. *APA Monitor, 20,* 25.

Bullmore, E., Joyce, H., Marks, I. M., & Connolly, J. (1992). A computerized quality assurance system (QAS) on a general psychiatric ward: Towards efficient clinical audit. *Journal of Mental Health, 1,* 257–263.

Bunge, M. (1984). What is pseudoscience? *The Skeptical Inquirer, 9,* 36–47.

Bunge, M. (2003). The pseudoscience concept, dispensable and professional practice, is required to evaluate research projects: A reply to Richard J. MacNally. *The Scientific Review of Mental Health Practice, 2,* 111–114.

Burgess, P. H. (1984). *The sayings of Mahatma Gandhi.* Singapore: Graham Brash.

Burnham, J. C. (1987). *How superstition won and science lost. Popularizing science and health in the United States.* New Brunswick, NJ: Rutgers University Press.

Burns, D. D. (1999). *Feeling good: The new mood therapy* (2nd ed.). New York: Avon.

Busfield, J. (Ed.). (2001). *Rethinking the sociology of mental health.* Malden, MA: Blackwell.

Bynum, W. F., Browne, E. J., & Porter, R. (Eds.). (1985). *Dictionary of the history of science.* Princeton: Princeton University Press.

Campbell, D. A., & Cornett, P. L. (2002). How stress and burnout produce medical mistakes. In M. M. Rosenthal & K. M. Sutcliffe (Eds.), *Medical error: What do we know? What do we do?* (pp. 1137–57). San Francisco, CA: Jossey-Bass.

Campbell, D. T. (1969). Reforms as experiments. *American Psychologist 24,* 409–429.

Campbell, D. T. (1996). Can we overcome worldview incommensurability/relativity in trying to understand the other? In R. Jessor, A. Colby, & R. A. Shweder (Eds.), *Ethnography and human development: Context and meaning in social inquiry* (pp. 153–172). Chicago: University of Chicago Press.

Campbell, D. T., & Stanley, J. C. (1963). *Experimental and quasi-experimental design for research.* Chicago: Rand-McNally.

Campbell, J. A. (1988). Client acceptance of single-system evaluation procedures. *Social Work Research and Abstracts, 24,* 21–22.

Campione, J. C. (1989). Assisted assessment: A taxonomy of approaches and an outline of strengths, and weaknesses. *Journal of Learning Disabilities, 22,* 151–165.

Cantor, J. R, Zillmann, D., & Bryant, J. (1975). Enhancement of experienced sexual arousal in response to erotic stimuli through misattribution of unrelated residual excitation. *Journal of Personality and Social Psychology, 32,* 69–75.

Cantor, N. (1982). "Everyday" versus normative models of clinical and social judgment. In G. Weary & H. L. Mirels (Eds.), *Integrations of clinical and social psychology* (pp. 27–47). New York: Oxford University Press.

Caplin, R. A., Posner, K. L., & Cheney, F. W. (1991). Effect of outcome on physician judgments of appropriateness of care. *Journal of the American Medical Association, 265,* 1957–1960.

Carpenter, K. J. (1986). *The history of scurvy & vitamin C.* New York: Cambridge University Press.

Carr, E. G., Levin, L., McConnachie, G., Carlson, J. I., Kemp, D. C., & Smith, C. E. (1994). *Communication-based intervention for problem behavior: A user's guide for producing positive change.* Baltimore: Paul H. Brookes.

Carroll, D. W. (2001). Using ignorance questions to promote thinking skills. *Teaching of Psychology, 28,* 98–100.

Carroll, L. (1946). *Alice in wonderland and through the looking glass.* Kingston, TN: Kingsport Press.

Cassell, E. J. (1991). *The nature of suffering and the goals of medicine.* New York: Oxford University Press.

Ceci, S. J., & Bruck, M. (1995). *Jeopardy in the courtroom: A scientific analysis of children's testimony.* Washington, D.C.: American Psychological Association.

Ceci, S. J., Crotteau-Huffman, M., Smith, E., & Loftus, E. W. (1994). Repeatedly thinking about non-events. *Consciousness and Cognition, 3,* 388–407.

Ceci, S., & Hembrooke, H. (Eds.). (1998). *Expert witnesses in child abuse cases*. Washington, DC: American Psychological Association.

Center for Reviews & Dissemination, University of York, UK.

Chalmers, I. (1983). Scientific inquiry and authoritarianism in perinatal care and education. *Birth, 10,* 151–166.

Chalmers, I. (1990). Underreporting research limitations is scientific misconduct. *Journal of the American Medical Association, 263,* 1405–1408.

Chalmers, I. (2003). Trying to do more good than harm in policy and practice: The role of rigorous, transparent, up-to-date evaluations. *The ANNALS of the American Academy of Political and Social Science, 589,* 22–40.

Chalmers, I. (2004). Well informed uncertainties about the effects of treatment. *British Medical Journal, 328,* 475–476.

Chanowitz. B., & Langer, E. J. (1985). Self-protection and self-inception. In M. W. Martin (Ed.), *Self-deception and self-understanding: New essays in philosophy and psychology* (pp. 117–135). Lawrence: University of Kansas Press.

Chapman, G. B. (2000). Preferences for improving and declining sequences of health outcomes. *Journal of Behavioral Decision Making, 13,* 203–218.

Chapman, L. J. (1967). Illusory correlation in observational report. *Journal of Verbal Learning and Verbal Behavior, 6,* 151–155.

Chapman, L. J., & Chapman, J. P. (1967). Genesis of popular but erroneous diagnostic observations. *Journal of Abnormal Psychology, 72,* 193–204.

Chapman, L. J., & Chapman, J. P. (1969). Illusory correlation as an obstacle to the use of valid psychodiagnostic signs. *Journal of Abnormal Psychology, 74,* 271–280.

Chase, W. G., & Simon, H. A. (1973). Perception in chess. *Cognitive Psychology, 1,* 55–81.

Chelton, L. G., & Bonney, W. C. (1987). Addiction, affects, and self object theory. *Psychotherapy, 2,* 40–46.

Chi, M. T. H., Feltovich, P. J., & Glaser, R. (1980). Categorization and representation of physics problems by experts and novices. *Cognitive Science, 5,* 121–152.

Chiriboga, D. A., Jenkins, G., & Bailey, J. (1983). Stress and coping among hospice nurses: Test of an analytic model. *Nursing Research, 32,* 294–299.

Choi, I., Choi, J. A., & Norenzayan, A. (2005). Culture and decisions. In D. J. Koehler & N. Harvey (Eds.), *Blackwell handbook of judgment decision making* (pp. 504–524). Malden, MA: Blackwell.

Christensen, A., & Jacobson, N. S. (1994). Who (or what) can do psychotherapy: The status of and challenge of nonprofessional therapies. *Psychological Science, 5,* 8–14.

Cialdini, R. B. (1984). *Influence: The new psychology of modern persuasion.* New York: Quill.

Cialdini, R. B. (2001). *Influence: Science and practice* (4th ed.). New York: Harper.

Cialdini, R. B., & Sagarin, B. J. (2005). Principles of interpersonal influence. In T. C. Brock & M. C. Green (Eds.), *Persuasion: Psychological insights and perspectives* (2nd ed., pp. 143–170). Thousand Oaks, CA: Sage.

Cirino, R. (1971). *Don't blame the people.* New York: Random House.

Clarke, A., Shim, J. K., Mamo, L., Fosket, J. R., & Fishman, J. R. (2003). Biomedicalization: Technoscientific transformations of health, illness, and U.S. biomedicine. *American Sociological Review, 658,* 161–194.

Clarkin, J. F., & Levy, K. N. (2004). The influence of client variables on psychotherapy.

In M. J. Lambert (Ed.), Bergin and Garfield's *Handbook of psychotherapy and behavior change* (5th ed., pp. 194–226). New York: Wiley.

*Clinical Evidence: The international source of the best available evidence for effective health care* (2002 [7th Issue]). London: BMJ Publishing Group.

Cochrane, A. L. (1999). *Effectiveness and efficiency: Random reflections on health services.* Cambridge, England: The Royal Society of Medicine Press, and The Nuffield Trust, Cambridge University Press. (Originally published 1972)

Cohen, J. (1977). *Statistical power analysis for the behavioral sciences.* New York: Academic Press.

Cohen, D. & Jacobs, D. (1998). A model consent form for psychiatric drug treatment. *International Journal of Risk & Safety in Medicine, 11,* 161–164.

Cohen, L., Sargent, M., & Sechrest, L. (1986). Use of psychotherapy research by professional psychologists. *American Psychologist, 41,* 198–206.

Cohen, M. S., Freeman, J. T., & Thompson, B. (1998). Critical thinking skills and tactical decision-making: A model and a training method. In J. Cannon-Bowers & E. Salas (Eds.), *Making decisions under stress: Implications for individual and team building* (pp. 155–159). Washington, DC: APA Press.

Cohen, R. S., Simpson, K. L., & Bride, B. E. (2004). Treatment anorexia nervosa and bulimia nervosa. *Journal of Evidence-Based Social Work, 1,* 27–39.

Cole, J. R. (2005, September 9). The new McCarthyism. *The Chronicle Review,* B7–B8.

Collins, R. (1988, August 7). Lessons in compassion for student doctors. *Sunday New York Times,* A7.

Colliver, J. A. (2000). Effectiveness of problem-based learning curricula: Research and theory. *Academic Medicine, 75*(3), 259–266.

Colman, A. M. (1987). *Facts, fallacies, and fraud in psychology.* London: Hutchinson.

Committee for the Scientific Investigation of Claims of the Paranormal (CSICOP). www.csicop.org.

Connelly, T., & Beach, L. R. (2000). The theory of image theory: An examination of the central conceptual structure. In T. Connolley, H. R. Arkes, & K. R. Hammond (Eds.), *Judgment and decision making: An interdisciplinary reader* (2nd ed., pp. 755–766). New York: Cambridge University Press.

Conrad, P. (2001). Genetic optimism: Framing genes and mental illness in the news. *Culture, Medicine and Psychiatry, 25,* 225–247.

Conrad, P., & Schneider, J. W. (1992). *Deviance and medicalization: From badness to sickness.* Philadelphia: Temple University Press.

Cook, T. D., & Campbell, D. T. (1979). *Quasi-experimentation: Design analysis issues for field settings.* Boston: Houghton & Mifflin.

Coomarasamy, A., & Khan, K. S. (2004). What is the evidence that postgraduate teaching in evidence-based medicine changes anything? A systematic review. *British Medical Journal, 329,* 1017–1021.

Corbin, R. M. (1980). Decisions that might not get made. In T. S. Wallsten (Ed.), *Cognitive processes in choice and decision behavior* (pp. 47–67). Hillsdale, NJ: Erlbaum.

Corcoran, K., & Fischer, J. (2000). *Measures for clinical practice: A sourcebook* (3rd ed.), Vol. 1: *Couples, families, and children.* Vol. 2: *Adults.* New York: Free Press.

Cordes, C. (1983). Don't be your most difficult client. *APA Monitor, 14*(11), 22.

Cottle, M. (1999). Selling shyness. *New Republic, 221*(5), 24–29.

Coulter, A. (2002). *The autonomous patient: Ending paternalism in medical care.* London: Nutfield Trust.

Cowan, N. (2005). *Working memory capacity.* Psychology Press. New York: Taylor and Francis.

Crombie, E. K. (1996). *The pocket guide to critical appraisal: A handbook for health care professionals.* London: BMJ Pub.

Crone, D. A., & Horner, R. H. (2003). *Building positive behavior support systems in schools: Functional behavioral assessment.* New York: Guilford.

Dallas, M. E., & Baron, R. S. (1985). Do psychotherapists use a confirmatory strategy during interviewing? *Journal of Social and Clinical Psychology, 3,* 106–122.

Damer, T. E. (1995). *Attacking faulty reasoning: A practical guide to fallacy free argument* (3rd ed.). Belmont, CA: Wadsworth.

Darley, J. M., & Cooper, J. (Eds.). (1998). *Attribution processes, person perception, and social interaction: The legacy of Edward E. Jones.* Washington, DC: American Psychological Association.

Darley, J. M., & Gross, P. H. (1983). A hypothesis-confirming bias in labeling effects. *Journal of Personality and Social Psychology, 44,* 20–37.

Daubert vs. Merrell Dow Pharmaceuticals, Inc. (1993).

Davey, B., & Seale, C. (Eds.). (2002). *Experiencing and explaining disease* (3rd ed.). Open University Press.

Davies, P. (2004, February 19). *Is evidence-based government possible?* Jerry Lee lecture, 4th Annual Campbell Collaboration Colloquium, Washington DC.

Davis, B., Sheeber, L., & Hops, H. (2002). Coercive family processes and adolescent depression. In J. B. Reid, G. R. Patterson, & J. Snyder (Eds.), *Antisocial behavior in children and adolescents: A developmental analysis and model for intervention* (pp. 173–192). Washington, DC: American Psychological Association.

Davis, D., O'Brien, M. A., Freemantle, N., Wolf, F. M., Mazmanian, P., & Taylor-Vaisey, A. (1999). Impact of formal continuing medical education. *Journal of the American Medical Association, 282,* 876–874.

Davis, W. L, & Davis, D. E. (1972). Internal-external control and attribution of responsibility for success and failure. *Journal of Personality, 40,* 123–136.

Dawes, M., Davies, P., Gray, A., Mant, J., Seers, K., & Snowball, R. (1999). *Evidence-based practice: A primer for health care professionals.* New York: Churchill Livingstone.

Dawes, M., Summerskill, S. W., Glasziou, P., Cartabellotta, A., Martin, J., Hopayian, K., Porzsolt, F., Burls, A., & Osborne, J. (2005). Sicily statement on evidence-based practice. *BMC,* Medical Education, Vol. 5, No. 1.

Dawes, R. (1997). Behavioral decision making and judgment. In D. Gilbert, S. Fiske, & G. Lindzey (Eds.), *Handbook of social psychology* (pp. 497–548). New York: MacGraw Hill.

Dawes, R. M. (1982). The value of being explicit when making clinical decisions. In T. A. Wills (Ed.), *Basic processes in helping relationships* (pp. 37–58). Orlando, FL: Academic Press.

Dawes, R. M. (1988). *Rational choice in an uncertain world.* Orlando, FL: Harcourt, Brace Jovanovich.

Dawes, R. M. (1993). Prediction of the future versus an understanding of the past: A basic asymmetry. *American Journal of Psychology, 106*, 1–24.

Dawes, R. M. (1994a). *House of cards: Psychology and psychotherapy built on myth*. New York: Free Press.

Dawes, R. M. (1994b). On the necessity of examining all four cells in a 2 × 2 table. In *Making better decisions* (Vol. 1, pp. 2–4). Pacific Grove, CA: Brooks/Cole.

Dawes, R. M. (2001). *Everyday irrationality: How pseudo-scientists, lunatics and the rest of us systematically fail to think rationally*. Boulder, CO: Westview Press.

Dawes, R. M., & Corrigan, B. (1974). Linear models in decision making. *Psychological Bulletin, 81*, 95–106.

Dawes, R. M., Faust, D., & Meehl, P. E. (1989). Clinical versus actuarial judgment. *Science, 243*, 1668–1674.

Dawes, R. M., Faust, D., & Meehl, P. E. (2002). Clinical versus actuarial judgment. In T. Gilovich & D. Griffin (Eds.), *Heuristics and biases: The psychology of intuitive judgment* (pp. 716–729). New York: Cambridge University Press.

Dean, G. (1986–1987). Does astrology need to be true? Part 1: A look at the real thing. *The Skeptical Inquirer, 11*, 166–185.

Dean, G. (1987). Does astrology need to be true? Part 2: The answer is no. *The Skeptical Inquirer, 257*–273.

DeAngelis, T. (1987). Therapists who feel as if they're not therapists: The imposter syndrome. *APA Monitor, 18*, 14.

Decker, F. H. (1987). Psychiatric management of legal defense in periodic commitment hearings. *Social Problems, 34*, 156–171.

Deeks, J. J., & Altman, D. G. (2004). Diagnostic tests 4: Likelihood ratios. *British Medical Journal, 329*, 168–169.

DeMott, B. (1990). *The imperial middle: Why Americans can't think straight about class*. New York: William Morrow.

DePanfilis, D. (2003). Review of IAIU investigations of suspected child abuse and neglect. In *DYFS out-of-home care settings in New Jersey*. Final Report. Baltimore: School of Social Work. College Park: University of Maryland.

DePanfilis, D., & Girvin, H. (2005). Investigating child maltreatment in out-of-home care: Barriers to effective decision-making. *Children and Youth Services Review, 27*, 353–374.

Dewey, J. (1933). *How we think: A restatement of the relation of reflective thinking to the education process*. Boston: Heath.

Deyo, R. A., Simon, G., & Omenn, G. S. (1997). The messenger under attack—intimidation of researchers by special interest groups. *New England Journal of Medicine, 336*, 1176–1180.

DeYoung, M. (2004). *The day care ritual abuse moral panic*. Jefferson, NC: McFarland.

Diaz, F. J., & de Leon, J. (2002). Excessive anti-psychotic dosing in two US state hospitals. *Journal of Clinical Psychiatry, 63*, 998–1003.

Didi-huberman, G. (2003). *Invention of hysteria: Charcot and the photographic iconography of the Salpêtrière*. Mass: MIT Press. (Originally published 1982)

Dillard, J. P., & Pfau, M. (Eds.). (2002). *The persuasion handbook: Developments in theory and practice*. Thousand Oaks, CA: Sage.

Dillinger, D. (1988, March). Playing with prisoners' minds. *Fellowship, 54*, 18–20.

Dingwall, R., Eekelaar, J., & Murray, T. (1983). *The protection of children: State intervention and family life.* Oxford, England: Basil Blackwell.

Dishion, T. J., & Andrews, D. W. (1995). Preventing escalation in problem behaviors with high-risk young adolescents: Immediate and one-year outcomes. *Journal of Consulting and Clinical Psychology, 63*, 538–548.

Dishion, T. J., & Bullock, D. (2001). Parenting and adolescent problem behavior: An ecological analysis of the nurturant hypothesis. In J. G. Borkowski, S. Rayney, & M. Bristol-Power (Eds.), *Parenting and the child's role: Influences on intellectual academic and social-emotional development* (pp. 231–249). Mahway, NJ: Erlbaum.

Dishion, T. J., Burraston, B., & Li, F. (2003). A multimethod and multitrait analysis of family management practices: Convergent and predictive validity. In Z. Sloboda, & W. J. Bukoski (Eds.), *Handbook of drug abuse prevention: theory, science and practice* (pp. 587–608). New York: Kluwer Academic/Plenum Press.

Dishion, T., & Granic, I. (2004). Naturalistic observation of relationship processes. In S. N. Haynes & E. M. Heiby (Eds.). *Comprehensive handbook of psychological assessment* (Ed. M. Hersen). *Vol. 3 Behavioral Assessment* (pp. 143–161). Hoboken, NJ: Wiley.

Ditto, P. H., & Lopez, D. F. (1992). Motivated skepticism: Use of differential decision criteria for preferred and nonpreferred conclusions. *Journal of Personality and Social Psychology, 62*, 568–584.

Di Iulio, J. J., Jr. (1988). What's wrong with private prisons? *Public Interest, 92*, 66–83.

Dixon, R. A., Munro, J. F. L., & Silcocks, P. B. (1998). *The evidence based medicine workbook.* Woburn, MA: Butterworth Heinemann.

Djulbegovic, B. (2004). Lifting the fog of uncertainty from the practice of medicine. *British Medical Journal, 329*, 1419–1420.

Dobson, K. S., Backs-Dermott, B., & Dozois, D. (2000). Cognitive and cognitive-behavioral therapies. In R. E. Ingram & C. R. Snyder (Eds.), *Handbook of psychological change: Psychotherapy processes and practices for the 21st century* (pp. 409–428). New York: Wiley.

Domenighetti, G., Grilli, R., & Liberati, A. (1998). Promoting consumers' demand for evidence based medicine. *International Journal of Technology Assessment in Health Care, 14*(11), 97–105.

Donovan, P. (2004). *No way of knowing: Crime, urban legends, and the Internet.* New York: Routledge.

Doust, J., & Del Mar, C. (2004). Why do doctors use treatments that do not work? For many reasons—including their inability to stand idle and do nothing. *British Medical Journal, 328*, 474–475.

Dreyfus, H. L., & Dreyfus, S. E. (1986). *Mind over machine: The power of human intuition and expertise in the era of the computer.* New York: Free Press.

Druckman, D., & Bjork, R. A. (Eds.). (1991). *In the mind's eye: Enhancing human performance.* Washington, D.C.: National Academy Press.

Duncan, B. (1976). Differential social perception and attribution of intergroup violence: Testing the lower limits of stereotyping blacks. *Journal of Personality and Social Psychology, 34*, 590–598.

Dunning, D., Heath, C., & Suls, J. M. (2004). Flawed self-assessment: Implications for health, education, and the work place. *Psychological Science in the Public Interest, 5,* 69–106.

Dunning, D., Van Boven, L., & Loewenstein, G. F. (2001). Egocentric empathy gaps in social interaction and exchange. *Advances in group processes, 18,* 65–97.

Durso, F. T., & Gronlund, S. D. (1999). Situation awareness. In F. T. Durso, R. S. Nickerson, R. W. Schvaneveldt, S. T. Dumais, D. S. Lindsay, & M. T. H. Chi (Eds.), *Handbook of applied cognition* (pp. 283–314). New York: Wiley.

Dyer, C. (2005). News roundup. Doctor was "near to breaking point" when she exaggerated abuse. *British Medical Journal, 330,* 1105.

Eddy, D. M. (1982). Probabilistic reasoning in clinical medicine: Problems and opportunities. In D. Kahneman, P. Slovic, & A. Tversky (Eds.), *Judgment under uncertainty: Heuristics and biases.* New York: Cambridge University Press.

Eddy, D. M. (1990). Comparing benefits and harms: The balance sheet. *Journal of the American Medical Association, 263,* 2493, 2498, 2501.

Eddy, D. M. (1993). Three battles to watching the 1990s. *Journal of the American Medical Association, 270,* 520–526.

Eddy, D. M. (1994a). Principles for making difficult decisions in difficult times. *Journal of the American Medical Association, 271,* 1792–1798.

Eddy, D. M. (1994b). Rationing resources while improving quality. *Journal of the American Medical Association, 373,* 817–824.

Edelmann, R. J. (1987). *The psychology of embarrassment.* New York: Wiley.

Edmondson, R. (1984). *Rhetoric in sociology.* New York: Macmillan.

Edwards, A., & Elwyn, G. (2001). *Evidence-informed patient choice: Inevitable or impossible?* New York: Oxford University Press.

Edwards, A., Elwyn, G., & Mulley, A. (2002). Explaining risks: Turning numerical data into meaningful pictures. *British Medical Journal, 324,* 827–830.

Edwards, A. G., Elwyn, G., Matthews, E., & Pill, R. (2001). Presenting risk information—A review of the effects of "framing" and other manipulations on patient outcomes. *Journal of Health Communication, 6,* 61–82.

Edwards, V. (1938). *Group leader's guide to propaganda analysis.* New York: Institute for Propaganda Analysis.

Edwards, W., & von Winterfeldt, D. (1986). On cognitive illusions and their implications. In H. R. Arkes & K. R. Hammond (Eds.), *Judgment and decision making: An interdisciplinary reader* (pp. 642–679). Cambridge, England: Cambridge University Press.

Ehrenreich, B., & Ehrenreich, J. (1977). The professional managerial class. *Radical America, 11,* 7–31.

Einhorn, H. J. (1980a). Overconfidence in judgment. In R. A. Shweder (Ed.), *New directions for methodology in social and behavioral science: No.4. Fallible judgment in behavioral research* (pp. 1–16). San Francisco: Jossey-Bass.

Einhorn, H. J. (1980b). Learning from experience and suboptimal rules in decision making. In T. S. Wallsten (Ed.), *Cognitive processes in choice and decision behavior* (pp. 1–20). Hillsdale, NJ: Erlbaum.

Einhorn, H. J. (1988). Diagnosis and causality in clinical and statistical prediction. In D. C. Turk & P. Salovey (Eds.), *Reasoning, inference and judgment in clinical psychology* (pp. 51–72). New York: Free Press.

Einhorn, H. J., & Hogarth, R. M. (1978). Confidence in judgment: Persistence of the illusion of validity. *Psychological Review, 85,* 395–416.

Einhorn, H. J., & Hogarth, R. M. (1985). Prediction, diagnosis, causal thinking in forecasting. In G. Wright (Ed.), *Behavioral decision making* (pp. 311–328). New York: Plenum.

Einhorn, H. J., & Hogarth, R. M. (1986). Judging probable cause. *Psychological Bulletin, 99,* 3–19.

Ellis, A., & Dryden, W. (1996). *The practice of rational-emotive therapy* (2nd ed.). New York: Springer.

Ellis, A., & Grieger, R. (1977). *Handbook of rational-emotive therapy.* New York: Springer.

Ellis, J., Mulligan, I., Rowe, J., Sackett, D. L. (1995). Inpatient general medicine is evidence based. *Lancet, 346,* 407–10.

Ellul, J. (1965). *Propaganda: The formation of men's attitudes.* New York: Vintage.

Elmore, J. G., & Boyko, E. J. (2000). Assessing accuracy of diagnostic and screening tests. In J. P. Geyman, R. A. Deyo, & S. D. Ramsey (Eds.), *Evidence-based clinical practice: Concepts and approaches* (pp. 83–93). Boston: Butterworth Heinemann.

Elstein, A. S. (1988). Cognitive processes in clinical inference and decision making. In D. C. Turk & P. Salovey (Eds.), *Reasoning, inference, and judgment in clinical psychology* (pp. 17–50). New York: Free Press.

Elstein, A. S. (2000). Clinical problem solving and decision psychology: Comment on "the epistemology of clinical reasoning." *Academic Medicine, 75*(Supplement 10), S134–136.

Elstein, A. S., & Bordage, G. (1979). Psychology of clinical reasoning. In G. C. Stone, F. Cohen, N. E. Adler, & Associates (Eds.), *Health psychology-a handbook: Theories, applications and challenges of a psychological approach to the health care system* (pp. 333–368). San Francisco: Jossey-Bass.

Elstein, A. S., & Schwartz, A. (2002). Clinical problem solving and diagnostic decision making: A selective review of the cognitive research literature. In J. A. Knottnerus (Ed.), *The evidence base of clinical diagnosis* (pp. 179–195). London: BMJ Books.

Elstein, A. S., Shulman, L. S., Sprafka, S. A., Allal, L., Gordon, M., Jason, H., Kagan, N., Loupe, M., & Jordan, R. (1978). *Medical problem solving: An analysis of clinical reasoning.* Cambridge, MA: Harvard University Press.

Elwyn, G., Edwards, A., Wensing, M., Hood, K., Atwell, C., & Grol, R. (2003). Shared decision making: Developing the OPTION scale for measuring patient involvement. *Quality and Safety of Health Care, 12,* 93–99.

Ely, J. W., Osheroff, J. A., Ebell, M. H., Bergus, G. R., Levy, B. T., Chambliss, M. L., & Evans, E. R. (1999). Analysis of questions asked by family doctors regarding patient care. *British Medical Journal, 319,* 358–361.

Ely, J. W., Osheroff, J. A., Ebell, M. H., Chambliss, M. L., Vinson, D. C., Stevermer, J. J., & Pifer, E. A. (2002). Obstacles to answering doctors' questions about patient care with evidence: Qualitative study. *British Medical Journal, 324,* 710–718.

Emerson, R. M. (1969). *Judging delinquents: Context and process in juvenile court.* New York: Aldine.

Engel, S. M. (1982). *With good reason: An introduction to informal fallacies* (2nd ed.). New York: St. Martin's Press.

Engel, S. M. (1994). *With good reason: An introduction to informal fallacies* (5th ed.). New York: St. Martin's Press.

Ennis, B. J., & Litwak, T. R. (1974). Psychiatry and the presumption of expertise: Flipping coins in the courtroom. *California Law Review, 62,* 693–752.

Ennis, R. H. (1987). A taxonomy of critical thinking dispositions and abilities. In J. B. Baron & R. J. Sternberg (Eds.), *Teaching thinking skills, theory, and practice* (pp. 9–26). New York: W. H. Freeman.

Entwistle, N. (1987). A model of the teaching-learning process. In J. T. Richardson, M. W. Eysenck, & D. W. Piper (Eds.), *Student learning: Research in education and cognitive psychology* (pp. 13–28). Milton Keynes, England: Society for Research into Higher Education and Open University Press.

Entwistle, V. A., Renfrew, M. J., Yearley, S., Forrester, J., & Lamont, T. (1998). Lay perspectives: Advantages for health research. *British Medical Journal, 316,* 463–466.

Entwistle, V. A., Sheldon, T. A., Sowden, A. J., & Watt, I. A. (1998). Evidence-informed patient choice. *International Journal of Technology Assessment in Health Care, 14,* 212–215.

Erault, M. (1994). *Developing professional knowledge and confidence.* London: The Falmer Press.

Ericsson, K. A., & Smith, J. (Eds.). (1991). *Toward a general theory of expertise: Prospects and limits.* New York: Cambridge University Press.

Evans, I. M., & Nelson, R. O. (1977). Assessment of child behavior problems. In A. R. Ciminero, K. S. Kalhoun, & H. E. Adams (Eds.), *Handbook of behavioral assessment* (pp. 601–630). New York: Wiley.

Expert Group on Learning From Adverse Events in the NHS. (2000). An organization with a memory. The Stationary Office.

Eyberg, S. M., & Ross, A. W. (1978). Assessment of child behavior problems: The validation of a new inventory. *Journal of Clinical Psychology, 16,* 113–116.

Eysenck, H. J., & Nias, D. K. B. (1982). *Astrology: Science or superstition.* New York: St. Martin's Press.

Fabrigar, L. R., Smith, S. M., & Brannon, L. A. (1999). Applications of social cognition: Attitudes as cognitive structures. In F. T. Durso (Ed.), *Handbook of applied cognition* (pp. 173–206). New York: Wiley.

Faden, R., Beauchamp, T., & King, N. (1986). *A history and theory of informed consent.* New York: Oxford.

Falk, R. (1981). On coincidences. *The Skeptical Inquirer, 6,* 18–31.

Farrington, D. P. (2003). Methodological quality standards for evaluation research. *The ANNALS of the American Academy of Political and Social Science, 587,* 49–68.

Faust, D., Hart, K., & Guilmette, T. J. (1988). Pediatric malingering: The capacity of children to fake believable deficits on neuropsychological testing. *Journal of Consulting and Clinical Psychology, 56,* 578–582.

Fearnside, W. W., & Holther, W. G. (1959). *Fallacy: The counterfeit of argument.* Englewood Cliffs, NJ: Prentice Hall.

Fehrenbach, P. A., & O'Leary, M. R. (1982). Interpersonal attraction and treatment decisions in inpatient and outpatient psychiatric settings. In T. A. Wills (Ed.), *Basic processes in helping relationships* (pp. 13–36). Orlando, FL: Academic Press.

Feinstein, A. R. (1967). *Judgment.* Baltimore: Williams & Wilkins.

Feltovich, P. J., Johnson, P. E., Moller, J. H., & Swanson, D. B. (1984). The role and development of medical knowledge in diagnostic expertise. In W. J. Clancey & E. H. Shortliffe (Eds.), *Readings in medical artificial intelligence: The first decade* (pp. 275–319). Reading, MA: Addison-Wesley.

Feltovich, P. J., Spiro, R. J., & Coulson, R. (1989). The nature of conceptual understanding in biomedicine: The keep structure of complex ideas and the development of misconceptions. In D. A. Evans & V. L. Patel (Eds.), *Cognitive science in medicine: Biomedical modeling* (pp. 113–172). Cambridge, MA: MIT Press.

Feltovich, P. J., Spiro, R. J., & Coulson, R. L. (1993). Learning, teaching, and testing for complex conceptual understanding. In N. Frederickson, R. Mislevy, & I. Bejar (Eds.), *Test theory for a new generation of tests* (pp. 181–218). Hillsdale, NJ: Lawrence Erlbaum.

Fetherstonhaugh, D., Slovic, P., Johnson, S. M., & Friedrich, J. (1997). Insensitivity to the value of human life: A study of psychophysical numbing. *Journal of Risk and Uncertainty, 14*(3), 282–300.

Fingarette, H. (1988). *Heavy drinking: The myth of alcoholism as a disease.* Berkeley: University of California Press.

Finucane, M. L., Alhakami, A., Slovic, P., & Johnson, S. M. (2000). The affect heuristic in judgments of risk and benefits. *Journal of Behavioral Decision Making, 13,* 1–17.

Firestone, R. W., & Seiden, R. H. (1987). Microsuicide and suicidal threats of everyday life. *Psychotherapy, 24,* 31–39.

Fischhoff, B. (1975). Hindsight foresight: The effect of outcome knowledge on judgment under uncertainty. *Journal of Experimental Psychology: Human Perception and Performance, 1,* 288–299.

Fischhoff, B., Goitein, B., & Shapira, Z. (1983). Subjective expected utility: A model of decision-making. In R. W. Scholz (Ed.), *Decision making under uncertainty* (pp. 183–208). New York: Elsevier.

Fischhoff, B., Slovic, P., & Lichtenstein, S. (1980). Knowing what you want: Measuring labile values. In T. S. Wallsten (Ed.), *Cognitive processes in choice and decision behavior* (pp. 117–141). Hillsdale, NJ: Erlbaum.

Fisher, R., & Ury, W. (1991). *Getting to yes: Negotiating agreement without giving in* (2nd ed.). New York: Penguin.

Flannelly, L. T., & Flannelly, K. J. (2000). Reducing people's judgment bias about their level of knowledge. *Psychological Record, 50,* 587–600.

Flew, A. (1985). *Thinking about social thinking.* Oxford: Blackwell.

Fong, G. T., Kravitz, D. H., & Nisbett, R. E. (1986). The effects of statistical training on thinking about everyday problems. *Cognitive Psychology, 18,* 253–292.

Foucault, M. (1981). *Power-knowledge: Selected interviews and other writings, 1972–1977.* New York: Pantheon.

Fowler, S. A. (1988). The effects of peer-mediated interventions on establishing, maintaining, and generalizing children's behavior changes. In R. H. Horner, G. Dunlap, & R. L. Koegel (Eds.), *Generalization and maintenance in applied settings* (pp. 143–170). Baltimore: Paul H. Brookes.

Fox, R. C., & Swazey, J. P. (1974). *The courage to fail: A social view of organ transplants and dialysis.* Chicago: University of Chicago Press.

Foxx, R. M., & Roland, C. E. (2005). The self-esteem fallacy. In J. W. Jacobson, R. M.

Foxx, & J. A. Mulick (Eds.), *Controversial therapies for developmental disabilities: Fad, fashion, and science in professional practice* (pp. 101–112). Mahwah, NJ: Erlbaum.

Frank, J. D., & Frank, J. B. (1991). *Persuasion and healing: A comparative study of psychotherapy* (3rd ed.). Baltimore: John Hopkins Press.

Frankfurt, H. G. (2005). *On bullshit*. Princeton, NJ: Princeton University Press.

Frazer, J. G. (1925). *The golden bough: A study in magic and religion*. London: Macmillan.

Freeman, A. C., & Sweeney, K. (2001). Why general practitioners do not implement evidence: qualitative study. *British Medical Journal, 323,* 1100–1102.

French, J. R. P., Jr., & Raven, B. (1959). The bases of social power. In D. Cartwright (Ed.), *Studies in social power* (pp. 150–167). Ann Arbor: University of Michigan, Institute for Social Research.

Friedson, E. (Ed.). (1973). *Professions and their prospects*. Beverly Hills, CA: Sage.

Friedson, E. (1994). *Professionalism reborn? Theory, prophecy, an policy*. Chicago: University of Chicago Press.

From the president. (1986, November). *NASW News, 31,* 2.

From the president. (1987, April). *NASW News, 32,* 2.

Fromm, E. (1963). *Escape from freedom*. New York: Holt, Rinehart & Winston.

Frye v. United States, 293 F 1013 (DC Cir. 1923).

Furnham, A. F. (1988). *Lay theories: Everyday understanding of problems in the social sciences*. New York: Pergamon.

Furukawa, T. A. (1999). From effect size into number needed to treat. *Lancet, 353*(9165), 1680.

Gaeth, G. J., & Shanteau, J. (1984). Reducing the influence of irrelevant information on experienced decision makers. *Organizational Behavior and Human Performance, 33,* 263–282.

Gahagan, J. (1984). *Social interaction and its management*. London: Methuen.

Gallup Organization, The Americans' belief in psychic and paranormal phenomena is up over the last decade. [Retrieved 2001, July 3].

Gambrill, E. D. (1997). Social work education: Possible futures. In M. Reisch & E. Gambrill (Eds.), *Social work in the 21st century* (pp. 317–327). Thousand Oaks, CA: Pine Forge Press.

Gambrill, E. D. (1999). Evidence-based practice: An alternative to authority-based practice. *Families in Society: Journal of Contemporary Human Services, 80,* 341–350.

Gambrill, E. (2001a). A client focused definition of social work practice. *Research on Social Work Practice, 13,* 310–323.

Gambrill, E. (2001b). Social work: An authority-based profession. *Research on social Work Practice, 11,* 166–175.

Gambrill, E. (2002). Bibliotherapy. In M. Hersen & W. Sledge (Eds.), *Encyclopedia of psychotherapy* (pp. 309–315). New York: Academic.

Gambrill, E. (2003a). Evidence based practice: Sea change or the emperor's new clothes? *Journal of Social Work Education, 39,* 3–23.

Gambrill, E. (2003b). Evidence based practice: Implications for knowledge development and use in social work. In A. Rosen & E. K. Proctor (Eds.), *Developing practice guidelines for social work interventions: Issues, methods and research agenda* (pp. 37–58). New York: Columbia University Press.

Gambrill, E. (2006). *Social work practice: A critical thinker's guide* (2nd ed.). New York: Oxford.

Gambrill, E. D,. & Gibbs, L. (2002). Making practice decisions: Is what's good for the goose good for the gander? *Ethical Human Sciences & Services, 4,* 31–46.

Gambrill, E., & Richey, C. (1988). *Taking charge of your social life.* Berkeley, CA: Behavioral Options.

Gambrill, E. & Shlonsky, A. (2001). The need for comprehensive risk management systems in child welfare. *Children and Youth Services Review, 23,* 79–107.

Gamwell, L. & Tomes, N. (1995). *Madness in America: Cultural and medical perceptions of mental illness before 1914.* Ithaca, NY: Cornell University Press.

Ganzach, Y. (2000). The weighing of pathological and non-pathological information in clinical judgment. *Acta Psychologica, 104,* 87–101.

Garb, H. N. (1998). *Studying the clinician: Judgment, research and psychological assessment.* Washington, DC: American Psychological Association.

Gardner, M. (1957). *Fads and fallacies in the name of science.* New York: Dover.

Garvin, C. D., Gutierrez, L. N., & Galinsky, M. J. (2003). *Handbook of social work with groups.* New York: Guilford.

Geddes, J., Tomlin, A., & Price, J. (1999). *Practicing evidence-based mental health.* Abington, Oxon, England: Radcliffe Medical Press.

Gelles, R. J. (1982). Applying research on family violence to clinical practice. *Journal of Marriage and the Family, 44*(1), 9–20.

Gellner, E. (1992). *Postmodernism, reason, and religion.* New York: Routledge.

Gergen, K. J. (1987). Introduction: Toward a metapsychology. In H. J. Stam, T. B. Rogers, & K. J. Gergen (Eds.), *The analysis of psychological theory: Metapsychological perspectives* (pp. 115–130). Cambridge, MA: Hemisphere.

Geyman, J. P., Deyo, R. A., & Ramsey, S. D. (2000). *Evidence-based clinical practice: Concepts and approaches.* Boston: Butterworth Heinemann.

Gibbs, L. (1991). *Scientific reasoning for social workers.* New York: McGraw Hill.

Gibbs, L. (2003). *Evidence-based practice for the helping professions.* Pacific Grove, CA: Brooks/Cole.

Gibbs, L., & Gambrill, E. (1999). *Critical thinking for social workers: Exercises for the helping professions* (2nd ed.). Thousand Oaks, CA: Pine Forge Press.

Gibbs, L,. & Gambrill, E. (2002). Evidence-based practice: Counterarguments to objections. *Research on Social Work Practice, 14,* 452–476.

Gigerenzer, G. (1998). Ecological intelligence: An adaptation for frequencies. In D. D. Cummins & C. Allen (Eds.), *The evolution of mind* (pp. 9–29). New York: Oxford.

Gigerenzer, G. (2002a). *Calculated risks: How to know when numbers deceive you.* New York: Simon & Schuster.

Gigerenzer, G. (2002b). *Reckoning with risk: Learning to live with uncertainty.* New York: Penguin.

Gigerenzer, G. (2003). The adaptive tool box and life span development: Common questions? In E. M. Staudinger & U. E. R. Lindenberger (Eds.), *Interactive minds: Life-span perspectives on the social foundations of cognition* (pp. 319–346). New York: Cambridge University Press.

Gigerenzer, G. (2005). Fast and frugal heuristics: The tools of bounded rationality. In

D. J. Koehler & N. Harvey (Eds.), *The Blackwell Handbook of judgment and decision-making* (pp. 62–88). Malden, MA: Blackwell.

Gigerenzer, G., & Goldstein, D. G. (1999). Betting on one good reason: The take the best heuristic. In G. Gigerenzer, P. M. Todd, & the ABC Research Group, (Eds.), *Simple heuristics that make us smart* (pp. 75–95). New York: Oxford University Press.

Gilbert, P. (1994). Male violence: Toward an integration. In J. Archer (Ed.), *Male violence* (pp. 352–389). London: Routledge.

Gilovich, T. (1991). *How we know what isn't so: The fallibility of human reason in everyday life.* New York: Macmillan.

Gilovich, T., & Griffin, D. (2002). Introduction—Heuristics and biases: Then and now. In T. Gilovich, D. Griffin, & D. Kahneman (Eds.), *Heuristics and biases: The psychology of intuitive judgement* (pp. 1–18). New York: Cambridge .

Gilovitch, T., & Savitsky, K. (2002). Like goes with like: The role of representativeness in erroneous and pseudo-scientific beliefs. In T. Gilovich, D. Griffin, & D. Kahneman (Eds.), *Heuristics and biases: The psychology of intuitive judgment* (pp. 616–624). New York: Cambridge.

Glasziou, P., Del Mar, C., & Salisbury, J. (2003). *Evidence-based medicine workbook.* London: BMJ Books.

Glasziou, P., & Irwig, L. M. (1995). An evidence-based approach to individualizing treatment. *British Medical Journal, 311,* 1356–1359.

Glasziou, P., Vandenbroucke, E. J., & Chalmers, I. (2004). Assessing the quality of research. *British Medical Journal, 328,* 39–41.

Glattborn, A. A., & Baron, J. (1991). The good thinker. In A. L. Costa (Ed.), *Developing minds: A resource book for teaching thinking. Vol. 1* (Rev. ed., pp. 63–67). Alexandria, VA: Association for Supervision and Curriculum Development.

Glazener, C. M. A., Evans, J. H., & Petro, R. E. (2005). Alarm interventions for nocturnal enuresis in children. *Cochrane Library,* Issue 2. Chichester, UK: John Wiley & Sons.

Glazer, M. P., & Glazer, P. M. (1991). *The whistle-blowers: Exposing corruption in government and industry.* New York: Basic Books.

Goethals, G. R., & Reckman, R. F. (1973). The perception of consistency in attitudes. *Journal of Experimental Social Psychology, 9,* 491–501.

Goffman, I. (1961). *Asylums.* New York: Anchor Press.

Goldberg, L. R. (1959). The effectiveness of clinicians' judgements: The diagnosis of organic brain damage from the Bender-Gestalt test. *Journal of Consulting Psychology, 23,* 25–33.

Goldberg, R. L. (1970). Man vs. model of man: A rationale, plus some evidence, for a method of improving on clinical inference. *Psychological Bulletin, 73,* 422–432.

Goldiamond, I. (1984). Training parent trainers and ethicists in nonlinear analysis of behavior. In R. F. Dangel & R. A. Polster (Eds.), *Parent training: Foundations of research and practice* (pp. 504–546). New York: Guilford.

Goldman, R. K, & Mendelsohn, G. A. (1969). Psychotherapeutic change and social adjustment: A report on a national survey of psychotherapists. *Journal of Abnormal Psychology, 74,* 164–172.

Goldstein, A. P. (1980). Relationship enhancement methods. In F. H. Kanfer & A. P. Goldstein (Eds.), *Helping people change: A textbook of methods* (pp. 18–57). Elmsford, NY: Pergamon.

Goldstein, D. G. & Gigerenzer, G. (1999). The recognition heuristic: How ignorance makes us smart. In G. Gigerenzer, P. M. Todd, & the ABC Research group. *Simple heuristics that make us smart* (pp. 37–58). New York: Oxford.

Gollwitzer, P. M. (1999). Implementation intentions: Strong effects of simple plans. *American Psychologist, 54,* 493–503.

Gollwitzer, P. M, Bayer, U. C., & McCulloch, K. C. (2005). The control of the unwanted. In R. R. Hassin, J. S. Uleman, & J. A. Bargh (Eds.), *The new unconscious* (pp. 485–515). New York: Oxford.

Gondolf, E. W., & Fisher, E. R. (1988). *Battered women as survivors: An alternative to treating learned helplessness.* Lexington, MA: Lexington Books.

Gordon, D. R. (1988). Clinical science and clinical expertise: Changing boundaries between art and science in medicine. In M. Lock & D. R. Gordon (Eds.), *Biomedicine examined (culture, illness, and healing)* (pp. 257–295). New York: Springer.

Gorenstein, E. E. (1992). *The science of mental illness.* New York: Academic Press.

Gorman, D. M. (1998). The irrelevance of evidence in the development of school-based drug prevention policy, 1986–1996. *Evaluation Review, 22*(1), 118–146.

Gorman, P. N., & Helfand, M. (1995). Information seeking in primary care: How physicians choose which clinical questions to pursue and which to leave unanswered. *Medical Decision Making, 15,* 113–119.

Gottlieb, S. (2003). One in three doctors don't tell patients about services they can't have. *British Medical Journal, 327,* 123.

Gøtzsche, P. C., Liberati, A., Torri, V., & Rossetti, L. (1996). Beware of surrogate endpoints. *International Journal of Technology Assessment in Health Care, 12,* 238–246.

Goulding, R. (2004). One in twelve older people are prescribed the wrong drug. *Archives of Internal Medicine, 164,* 305–312.

GRADE Working Group. (2004). Grading quality of evidence and strength of recommendations. *British Medical Journal, 328,* 1490.

Gray, J. A. M. (1997). *Evidence-based health care: How to make health policy and management decisions.* New York: Churchill Livingstone.

Gray, J. A. M. (1998). Where is the chief knowledge officer? *British Medical Journal, 317,* 832.

Gray, J. A. M. (2001a). *Evidence-based health care: How to make health policy and management decisions* (2nd ed.). New York: Churchill Livingstone.

Gray, J. A. M. (2001b). Evidence-based medicine for professionals. In A. Edwards & G. Elwyn (Eds.), *Evidence-based patient choice: Inevitable or impossible?* (pp. 19–33). New York: Oxford.

Gray, W. D. (1991). *Thinking critically about new age ideas.* Belmont, CA: Wadsworth.

Gray-Little, B., & Kaplan, D. (2000). Race and ethnicity in psychotherapy research. In C. R. Snyder & R. E. Ingram (Eds.), *Handbook of psychological change* (pp. 591–613). New York: Wiley.

Green, B. F., McCloskey, M., & Caramazza, A. (1985). The relation of knowledge to problem solving, with examples from kinematics. In S. F. Chipman, J. W. Segal, & R. Glaser (Eds.), *Thinking and learning skills: Vol. 2. Research and open questions* (pp. 127–140). Hillsdale, NJ: Erlbaum.

Greenhalgh, T. (2001). *How to read a paper: The basis of evidence-based medicine* (2nd ed.). London: BMJ Press.

Greenhalgh, T., & Hurwitz, B. (1998). *Narrative based medicine: Dialogue and discourse in clinical practice.* London: BMJ Press.

Greenhalgh, T., Robert, G., Macfarlane, F., Bate, P., & Kyriakidou, O. (2004). Diffusion of innovations in service organizations: systematic review and recommendations. *The Milbank Quarterly, 82,* 581–629

Greenhalgh, T., & Young, G. (1998). Applying the evidence to patients. In C. Silagy & A. Haines (Eds.), *Evidence-based practice in primary care* (pp. 44–58). London: BMJ Books.

Greeno, C. J., Wing, R. R., & Shiffman, S. (2000). Binge antecedents in obese women with and without binge eating disorder. *Journal of Consulting and Clinical Psychology, 68,* 95–102.

Greeno, J. G. (1978). Nature of problem-solving abilities. In W. K. Estes (Ed.), *Handbook of learning and cognitive processers: Vol. 5. Human information processing* (pp. 239–270). Hillsdale, NJ: Erlbaum.

Gresham, F., & MacMillan, D. (1997). Denial and defensiveness in the place of fact and reason: Rejoinder to Smith and Lovaas. *Behavioral Disorders, 22*(4), 219–230.

Grilli, R., Magrini, N., Penna, A., Mura, G., & Liberati, A. (2000). Practice guidelines developed by specialty societies: The need for a critical appraisal. *Lancet, 355,* 103–106.

Groen, G. J., & Patel, V. L. (1988). The relationship between comprehension and reasoning in medical experts. In M. T. H. Chi, R. Glaser, & M. J. Farr (Eds.), *The nature of expertise* (pp. 287–310). Hillsdale, NJ: Erlbaum.

Gross, P. R., & Levitt, N. (1994). *Higher superstition: The academic left and its quarrels with science.* Baltimore: Johns Hopkins University Press.

Grove, W. M., & Meehl, P. E. (1996). Comparative efficiency of informal (subjective, impressionistic) and formal (mechanical, algorithmic) prediction procedures: The clinical-statistical controversy. *Psychology, Public Policy & Law, 2,* 293–323.

Grove, W. M., Zald, D. H., Lebow, B. S., Snitz, B. E., & Nelson, C. (2000). Clinical vs. mechanical prediction: A meta-analysis. *Psychological Assessment, 12,* 19–30.

Grunebaum, H., & Chasin, R. (1978). Relabeling and retraining reconsidered: The beneficial effects of a pathological label. *Family Process, 17,* 449–455.

Gusfield, J. R. (2003). Constructing the ownership of social problems: Fun and profit in the welfare state. In J. D. Orcutt & D. R. Ruby (Eds.), *Drugs, alcohol, and social problems* (pp. 7–18). New York: Rowman & Littlefield.

Guyatt, G. H., & Rennie, D. (2002). *Users' guides to the medical literature: A manual for evidence-based clinical practice.* The Evidence-Based Medicine Working Group JAMA & Archives. Chicago: American Medical Association.

Guyatt, G. H., Meade, M. O., Jaeschke, R. Z., Cook, D. J., & Haynes, R. B. (2000). Practitioners of evidence-based care: Not all clinicians need to appraise evidence from scratch but need some skills. *British Medical Journal, 320,* 954–955.

Hagert, G., & Waern, Y. (1986). On implicit assumptions in reasoning. In T. Myers, K. Brown, & B. McGonigle (Eds.), *Reasoning and discourse* (pp. 95–115). Orlando, FL: Academic Press.

Hakel, M. D. (1997). What we must learn from Alverno. *About Campus, 2–3,* 16–21.

Hall, D. F., Loftus, E. F., & Tousignant, J. P. (1984). Post-event information and changes in recollection for a national event. In G. L. Wells & E. F. Loftus (Eds.), *Eyewitness testimony: Psychological perspectives* (pp. 124–141). Cambridge, England: Cambridge University Press.

Halpern, D. F. (1998). Teaching critical thinking for transfer across domains: Dispositions, skills, structure, training, and meta-cognitive monitoring. *American Psychologist, 53,* 449–455.

Halpern, D. F. (2003). *Thought & knowledge: An introduction to critical thinking* (4th ed). Mahwah, NJ: Erlbaum.

Halpern, J. (2001). *From detached concern to empathy: Humanizing medical practice.* New York: Oxford.

Hamblin, C. L. (1970). *Fallacies.* London: Methuen.

Hamm, R. M. (2003). Medical decisions scripts: Combining cognitive scripts and judgment strategies to account fully for medical decision making. In D. Hardman & L. Macchi (Eds.), *Thinking: Psychological perspectives on reasoning, judgment and decision making* (pp. 315–345). New York: John Wiley.

Hammond, K. R. (1996). *Human judgment and social policy: Irreducible uncertainty, inevitable error, and unavoidable injustice.* New York: Oxford.

Hammond, K. R. (2000). *Judgments under stress.* New York: Oxford.

Hanks, H., Hobbs, C. J., & Wynne, J. M. (1988). Early signs and recognition of sexual abuse in the pre-school child. In K. Browne, C. Davies, & P. Stratton (Eds.), *Early prediction and prevention of child abuse* (pp. 139–160). Chichester, UK: Wiley.

Hanley, B., Truesdale, A., King, A., Elbourne, D., & Chalmers, I. (2001). Involving consumers in designing, conducting, and interpreting randomised controlled trials: Questionnaire survey. *British Medical Journal, 322,* 519–523.

Handlin, C. L. (1970). *Fallacies.* London: Methuen.

Hansen, H. V., & Pinto, R. C. (Eds.). (1995). *Fallacies: Classical and contemporary readings.* University Park, PA: The Pennsylvania State University Press.

Harmon, G. (1986). *Change in view: Principles of Reasoning.* Cambridge, MA: MIT Press.

Harris, G. (2004, May 14). Pfizer to pay $439 million over promoting drug to doctors. *The New York Times,* 1.

Hartman, D. P., Barrios, B. A., & Wood, D. D. (2004). Principles of behavioral observation. In S. M. Haynes & E. M. Heiby (Eds.), *Comprehensive handbook of psychological assessment.* Vol 3. Behavioral assessment. New York: Wiley.

Haskell, R. E. (2001). *Transfer of learning: Cognition, instruction, & reasoning.* San Diego, CA: Academic Press.

Hastie, R., & Dawes, R. (2001). *Rational choice in an uncertain world: The psychology of judgment and decision making.* Thousand Oaks, CA: Sage.

Hathaway, S. R. (1948). Some considerations relative to nondirective counseling. *Journal of Clinical Psychology, 4,* 226–231.

Hayakawa, S. I. (1978). *Language in thought and action* (4th ed.). New York: Harcourt Brace Jovanovich.

Hayes-Roth, F., Klahr, P., & Mostow, D. J. (1981). Advice taking and knowledge refinement: An iterative view of skill acquisition. In J. R. Anderson (Ed.), *Cognitive skills and their acquisition* (pp. 231–253). Hillsdale, NJ: Erlbaum.

Haynes, R. B., Devereaux, P. J., & Guyatt, G. H. (2002). Editorial. Clinical expertise in the era of evidence-based medicine and patient choice. *ACP Journal Club, 136*(A11), 1–2.

Haynes, S. N. (1992). *Models of causality and psychopathology: Toward dynamic, synthetic and nonlinear models of behavior disorders.* New York: Macmillan Publishing Co.

Haynes, S. N., & O'Brian, W. H. (2000). *Principles and practice of behavioral assessment.* New York: Kluwer Academic/Plenum.

Healy, D. (2003). Lines of evidence on the risk of suicide with selected Serotonin re-uptake inhibitors. *Psychotherapy and Psychosomatics, 72,* 71–79.

Hellman, L. D., Morrison, T. L., & Abramowitz, S. I. (1987). Therapist flexibility/rigidity and work stress. *Professional Psychology, 18,* 21–27.

Henggeler, S. W., & Lee, T. (2003). Multisystemic treatment of serious clinical problems. In A. E. Kazdin & J. R. Weisz (Eds.), *Evidence-based psychotherapies for children and adolescents* (pp. 301–324). New York: Guilford.

Herbert, R. (2002). We'd like to thank the academy. *Observer, 15,* p. 1/23–28. Washington, DC: American Psychological Association.

Herbst, A. L., Ulfelder, H., & Poskanzer, D. C. (1971). Adnocarcinoma of the vagina: Association of maternal stilbestrol therapy with tumor appearances in young women. *New England Journal of Medicine, 284,* 878–881.

Herron, W. G., & Rouslin, S. (1984). *Issues in psychotherapy.* Washington, DC: Oryn Publications.

Hersen, M., & Turner, S. M. (Eds.). (2003). *Diagnostic interviewing* (3rd ed.). New York: Kluwer Academics/Plenum.

Hershey, J. C., & Baron, J. (1995). Judgment by outcomes: When is it warranted? *Organizational behavior and human decision processes, 62,* 127.

Heyman, R. E., & Slep, A. M. S. (2004). Analogue behavioral observation. In S. N. Haynes & E. M. Heiby (Eds.); M. Hersen (Editor in chief), *Comprehensive handbook of psychological assessment.* Vol. 3 *Behavioral assessment* (pp. 162–180). New York: Wiley.

Higbee, K. L. (1977). *Your memory: How it works and how to improve it.* Englewood Cliffs, NJ: Prentice Hall.

Higgins, R. L., Snyder, C. R., & Berglas, S. (1990). *Self-handicapping: The paradox that isn't.* New York: Plenum Press.

Hillebrandt, D., & Imray, C. (2004). Minerva. *British Medical Journal, 328,* 1210.

Hinds, P. J. (1999). The curse of expertise: The effects of expertise and debiasing methods on prediction of novice performance. *Journal of Experimental Psychology: Applied, 5,* 205–221.

Hobbs, C. J., & Wynne, J. M. (1989). Sexual abuse of English boys and girls: The importance of anal examination. *Child Abuse and Neglect, 13,* 195–210.

Hobbs, N. (1975). *The futures of children: Recommendations of the Project on Classification of Exceptional Children.* San Francisco: Jossey-Bass.

Hockey, R. (1984). Varieties of attentional state. In R. Parasuraman & D. R. Davies (Eds.), *Varieties of attention* (pp. 449–484). Orlando, FL: Academic Press.

Hodgkinson, G. P., & Sparrow, P. R. (2002). *The competent organization: A psychological analysis of the strategic management process.* Buckingham, England: Open University Press.

Hofer, B. K. (2001). Personal epistemology research: Implications for learning and teaching. *Journal of Educational Psychology Review, 13,* 353–383.

Hofer, B. K., & Pintrich, P. R. (Eds.). (2002). *Personal epistemology: The psychology of beliefs about knowledge and knowing.* Mahwah, NJ: Erlbaum.

Hogarth, R. M. (1980). *Judgment and choice: The psychology of decisions* (1st ed.). New York: Wiley.

Hogarth, R. M. (1981). Beyond discrete biases: Functional and dysfunctional aspects of judgemental heuristics. *Psychological Bulletin, 90,* 197–217.

Hogarth, R. M. (1987). *Judgement and choice: The psychology of decision* (2nd ed.). New York: Wiley.

Hogarth, R. M. (2001). *Educating intuition.* Chicago: University of Chicago Press.

Hoge, M. A., Tomdora, J., & Stuart, G. W. (2003). Training in evidence-based practice. *Psychiatric Clinics of North America, 26,* 851–865.

Holland, J. H., Holyoak, K. J., Nisbett, R. E., & Thagard, P. R. (1986). *Induction: Processes of inference, learning, and discovery.* Cambridge, MA: MIT Press.

Hollingshed, A. B., & Redlich, R. C. (1958). *Social class and mental illness.* New York: Wiley.

Hollon, S. D., & Kendall, P. C. (1980). Cognitive self-statements in depression: Development of an automatic thoughts questionnaire. *Cognitive Research and Therapy, 4,* 382–395.

Holmes, D. S. (1978). Projection as a defense mechanism. *Psychological Bulletin, 85,* 677–688.

Hops, H., Davis, B., & Longoria, N. (1995). Methodological issues in direct observation: Illustrations with the Living in Familiar Environments (LIFE) coding system. *Journal of Clinical Child Psychology, 24,* 193–203.

Horvath, A. O., & Bedi, R. P. (2002). The alliance. In J. C. Norcorss (Ed.), *Psychotherapy relationships that work: Therapists' contributions and responsiveness to patients* (pp. 37–69). New York: Oxford.

Houts, A. C. (1984). Effects of clinical, theoretical orientation and patient explanatory bias on initial clinical judgments. *Professional Psychology: Research and Practice, 15,* 284–293.

Houts, A. C. (2002). Discovery, invention, and the expansion of the modern diagnostic and statistical manuals of mental disorders. In L. E. Beutler & M. L. Malik (Eds.), *Rethinking the DSM: A psychological perspective* (pp. 17–65). Washington, DC: American Psychological Association.

Houts, A. C., & Galante, M. (1985). The impact of evaluative disposition and subsequent information on clinical impressions. *Journal of Social and Clinical Psychology, 3,* 201–212.

Howitt, D. (1992). *Child abuse errors: When good intentions go wrong.* New York: Harvester Wheatsheaf.

Hoyle, R. H., Harris, M. J., & Judd, C. M. (2002). *Research methods in social relations.* Pacific Grove, CA: Wadsworth.

Hrobjartsson, A., & Goetzsche, P. C. (2001a). Is the placebo powerless? An analysis of clinical trials comparing placebo with no treatment. *New England Journal of Medicine, 344,* 1594–1602.

Hrobjartsson, A., & Gotzsche, P. C. (2001b). Placebo interventions for all clinical conditions. (Cochrane Review). In *Cochrane Library,* Issue 3. Chichester, UK: Wiley.

Hubble, M. A., Duncan, B. L., & Miler, S. D. (Eds.) (1999). *The heart & soul of change: What works in therapy.* Washington, DC: American Psychological Association.

Huck, S. W., & Sandler, H. M. (1979). *Rival hypotheses: Alternative interpretations of data based conclusions.* New York: Harper & Row.

Huber, R. B. (1963). *Influencing through argument.* New York: David McKay.

Huff, D. (1954). *How to lie with statistics.* New York: Norton.

Hunsley, J., Lee, C. M., & Wood, J. M. (2003). Controversial and questionable assessment techniques. In S. O. Lilienfeld, S. J. Lynn, & J. M. Lohr (Eds.), *Science and pseudoscience in clinical psychology* (pp. 39–76). New York: Guilford.

Hyde, C. A. (2003). More harm than good? Multicultural initiatives in human service agencies. *Social Thought, 22,* 23–40.

Hyman, R. (1961). On prior information and creativity. *Psychological Reports, 9,* 151–161.

Illich, I. (1976). *Limits to medicine: Medical nemesis, The expropriation of health.* London: Boyars.

Illich, I., Zola, I. K., McNight, J., Caplan, J. A., & Shaiken, H. (1978). *Disabling professions.* New Hampshire: Marion Boyers.

Isaacs, D., & Fitzgerald, D. (1999). Seven alternatives to evidence based medicine. *British Medical Journal, 319,* 1618.

Isen, A. M. (1987). Positive affect, cognitive processes, and social behavior. In L. Berkowitz (Ed.), *Advances in experimental social psychology* (pp. 203–254). (Vol. 20). Orlando, FL: Academic Press.

Isen, A. M., Shalker, T. E., Clark, M., & Karp, L. (1978). Affect, accessibility of material in memory, and behavior: A cognitive loop? *Journal of Personality and Social Psychology, 36,* 1–12.

Jacobs, J. (1985). "In the best interests of the child": Official court reports as an artifact of negotiated reality in children's assessment centers. *Clinical Sociology Review, 3,* 88–108.

Jacobson, R. B., & Humphrey, R. A. (1979). Families in crisis: Research and theory in child mental retardation. *Social Casework, 12,* 597–601.

Jacobson, J. W., Foxx, R. M., & Mulick, J. A. (Eds.). (2005). *Controversial therapies for developmental disabilities: Fad, fashion, and science in professional practice.* Mahwah, NJ: Erlbaum.

Jacobson, J. W., Mulick, J. A., & Schwartz, A. A. (1995). A history of facilitated communication: Science, pseudoscience, and antiscience working group on facilitated communication. *American Psychologist, 50,* 750–765.

James, W. (1975). *Pragmatism.* Cambridge, MA: Harvard University Press.

Janis, I. L., (1982). *Group think: Psychological studies of policy decisions and fiascos* (2nd ed.). Boston: Houghton Mifflin.

Janis, I. L., & Mann, L. (1977). *Decision making: A psychological analysis of conflict, choice and commitment.* New York: Free Press.

Janofsky, M. (2001, June 19). Therapists are sentenced in girl's "rebirthing" death. *New York Times,* p. A12.

Janson, D. (1988, April 22). End to suit denied in shooting death. *New York Times,* pp. AI, B2.

Jarvis, W. T. (1990). *Dubious dentistry: A dental continuing education course.* Loma Linda

University School of Dentistry, Loma Linda, CA : Loma Linda University School of Dentistry.

Jehn, K. A. (2004). A qualitative analysis of conflict types and dimensions in organizational groups. *Administrative Science Quarterly, 42*(3), 530–557.

Jekel, J., Elmore, J. G., & Katz, D. (1996). *Epidemiology, biostatistics, and preventive medicine*. Philadelphia: Saunders.

Jennings, D. L., Amabile, T. M., & Ross, L. (1982). Informal covariation assessment: Data-based versus theory-based judgments. In D. Kahneman, P. Slovic, & A. Tversky (Eds.), *Judgment under uncertainty: Heuristics and biases* (pp. 211–230). New York: Cambridge University Press.

Jensen, D. D. (1989). Pathologies of science, precognition and modern psychophysics. *The Skeptical Inquirer, 13,* 147–160.

Johnson, D. M. (1972). *A systematic introduction to the psychology of thinking*. New York: Harper & Row.

Johnson, E. J. (1988). Expertise and decision under uncertainty: Performance and process. In M. T. H. Chi, R. Glaser, & M. J. Farr (Eds.), *The nature of expertise* (pp. 209–228). Hillsdale, NJ: Erlbaum.

Johnson, W. (1946). *People in quandaries: The semantics of personal adjustment*. New York: Harper & Row.

Johnson-Laird, P. N. (1983). *Mental models: Towards a cognitive science of language, inference, and consciousness*. Cambridge, MA: Harvard University Press.

Johnson-Laird, P. N. (1985). Logical thinking: Does it occur in daily life? Can it be taught? In S. F. Chipman, J. W. Segal, & R. Glaser (Eds.), *Thinking and learning skills: Vol. 2. Research and open questions* (pp. 293–318). Hillsdale, NJ: Erlbaum.

Jones, E. E., & Harris, V. A. (1967). The attribution of attitudes. *Journal of Experimental Social Psychology, 3,* 1–24.

Jordan, C., & Franklin, C. (2003). *Clinical assessment for social workers: Quantitative and qualitative methods* (2nd ed.). Chicago: Lyceum.

Jordan, J. S., Harvey, J. H., & Weary, G. (1988). Attributional biases in clinical decision making. In D. C. Turk & P. Salovey (Eds.), *Reasoning, inference, and judgement in clinical psychology* (pp. 93–106). New York: Free Press.

Jørgensen, K. J., & Gøtzsche, P. C. (2004). Presentation on websites of possible benefits and harms from screening for breast cancer: Cross sectional study. *British Medical Journal, 328,* 148–155.

Judson, H. F. (2004). *The great betrayal: Fraud in science*. New York: Harcourt.

Jüni, P., Altman, D. G., & Egger, M. (2001). Assessing the quality of controlled clinical trials. *British Medical Journal, 323,* 42–46.

Jüni, P., Witschi, A., Bloch, R., & Egger, M. (1999). The hazards of scoring the quality of clinical trials for meta analysis. *Journal of the American Medical Association, 282,* 1054–1060.

Kadushin, A. (1963). Diagnosis and evaluation for (almost) all occasions. *Social Work, 8,* 12–19.

Kahane, H. (1971). *Logic and contemporary rhetoric: The use of reason in everyday life*. Belmont, CA: Wadsworth.

Kahane, H. (1995). *Logic and contemporary rhetoric: The use of reason in everyday life* (7th ed.). Belmont, CA: Wadsworth.

Kahane, H., & Cavender, N. (1998). *Logic and contemporary rhetoric: The use of reason in every day life.* (8th Ed.). New York: Wadsworth.

Kahneman, D. (1995). Varieties of counterfactual thinking. In N. J. Roese & J. M. Olsen (Eds.), *What might have been: Social psychology of counterfactual thinking* (pp. 375–396). Mahwah, NJ: Erlbaum.

Kahneman, D., & Tversky, A. (1973). On the psychology of prediction. *Psychological Review, 80,* 237–251.

Kahneman, D., & Tversky, A. (1984). Choices, values, and frames. *American Psychologist, 39,* 341–350.

Karger, H. J. (1983). Science, research and social work: Who controls the profession? *Social Work, 28,* 200–205.

Kassirer, J. P. (1994). The quality of care and the quality of measuring it. *New England Journal of Medicine, 329,* 1263–1265.

Kassirer, J. P. (2004). *On the take: How medicine's complicity with big business can endanger your health.* New York: Oxford.

Kassirer, J. P., & Kopelman, K. I. (1989). Cognitive errors in diagnosis, instantiation, classification, and consequences. *American Journal of Medicine, 86,* 433–441.

Kassirer, J. P., & Kopelman, R. I. (1991). *Learning clinical reasoning.* Baltimore: Williams and Wilkins.

Kazak, A. E., & Marvin, R. S. (1984). Differences, difficulties and adaptation: Stress and social networks in families with a handicapped child. *Family Relations, 33,* 67–77.

Kazdin, A. E., & Weisz, J. R. (2003). *Evidence-based psychotherapies for children and adolescents.* New York: Guilford.

Keefe, R. (2000). *Theories of vagueness.* New York: Cambridge University Press.

Kelley, G. A. (1955). *The psychology of personal constructs.* New York: Norton.

Kelley, H. H. (1950). The warm-cold variable of first impressions of persons. *Journal of Personality, 18,* 431–439.

Kelly, I. W., Culver, R., & Loptson, P. J. (1989). Astrology and science: An examination of the evidence. In S. K. Biswas, D. C. V. Malik, & C. V. Vishveshwara (Eds.), *Cosmic perspectives.* New York: Cambridge University Press.

Kendall, R. E. (1973). Psychiatric diagnoses: A study of how they are made. *British Journal of Psychiatry, 122,* 437–445.

Kenrick, D. T., & Gutierres, S. E. (1980). Contrast effects in judgments of attractiveness: When beauty becomes a social problem. *Journal of Personality and Social Psychology, 38,* 131–140.

Kerig, P. K., & Lindahl, K. M. (Eds.). (2004). *Family observational coding systems: Resources for systemic research.* Mahwah, NJ: Erlbaum.

Kerr, N., MacCoun, R. J., & Kramer, G. (1996). Bias in judgment: comparing individuals and groups. *Psychological Review, 103,* 687–719.

Kessler, R. C., Ustun, T. B., et al. (2004). Prevalence, severity, and unmet need for treatment of mental disorders in the World Health Organization world mental health surveys. The WHO World Mental Health Survey Consortium. *Journal of the American Medical Association, 291,* 2581–2590.

Kiesler, D. J. (1966). Some myths of psychotherapy research and the search for a paradigm. *Psychological Bulletin, 65,* 110–136.

King, L. S. (1981). *Medical thinking: A historical preface.* Princeton, NJ: Princeton University Press.

King, P. M., & Kitchener, K. S. (2002). The reflective judgment model: Twenty years of research on epistemic cognition. In B. K. Hofer & P. R. Pintrich (Eds.), *Personal epistemology: The psychology of beliefs about knowledge and knowing* (pp. 37–61). Mahwah, NJ: Erlbaum.

Kirk, S. A., & Kutchins, H. (1992a). *The selling of DSM: The rhetoric of science in psychiatry.* New York: Aldine de Gruyter.

Kirk, S. A., & Kutchins, H. (1992b). Five arguments for using DSM-III-R and why they are wrong. In E. Gambrill & R. Pruger (Eds.), *Controversial issues in social work* (pp. 146–154). Boston: Allyn & Bacon.

Kirk, S., Osmalov, M., & Fischer, J. (1976). Social workers' involvement in research. *Social Work, 21,* 121–132.

Kirsch, I., & Sapirstein, G. (1999). Listening to prozac but hearing placebo: A meta-analysis of antidepressant medications. In I. Kirsch (Ed.), *How Expectancies Shape Experience* (pp. 303–320). Washington, DC: American Psychological Association.

Kitchener, K. S. (1986). The reflective judgment model: Characteristics, evidence and measurement. In R. A. Mines & K. S. Kitchener (Eds.), *Adult cognitive development: Methods and models* (pp. 76–91). New York: Praeger.

Klayman, J. (1995). Varieties of confirmation bias. *Psychology of learning and motivation, 32,* 385–418.

Klayman, J., Soll, J. B., Gonzales-Vallejo, C., & Barlas, S. (1999). Overconfidence: It depends on how, what, and whom you ask. *Organizational Behavior and Human Decision Processes, 79,* 216–247.

Klein, G. (1998). *Sources of power: How people make decisions.* Cambridge, MA: MIT Press.

Klein, H. S., Ross, F. V., Adams, D. L., & Gilbert, C. M. (1994). Effect of online literature searching on length of stay and patient care costs. *Academic Medicine, 69,* 489–495.

Kleinmuntz, B. (1984). The scientific study of clinical judgment in psychology and medicine. *Clinical Psychology Review, 4,* 111–126.

Klemp, G. O., & McClelland, D. C. (1986). What characterizes intelligent functioning among senior managers. In R. G. Sternberg & R. K. Wagner (Eds.), *Practical intelligence: Nature and origins of competence in the everyday world* (pp. 31–50). Cambridge, England: Cambridge University Press.

Kluger, M. P., Alexander, G., & Curtis, P. A. (2002). *What works in child welfare.* Washington, DC: CWLA Press.

Kmietowicz, Z. (2005). Half of patients in intensive care receive suboptimal care. *British Medical Journal, 330,* 1101.

Knishinsky, A. (1982). *The effects of scarcity of material and exclusivity of information on industrial buyer perceived risk in provoking a purchase decision.* Unpublished doctoral dissertation, Arizona State University, Tempe.

Knottnerus, J. A. (Ed.). (2002). *The evidence base of clinical diagnosis.* London: BMJ.

Koberg, D., & Bagnall, J. (1976). *The universal traveler: A soft system guide to creativity, problem-solving and the process of reaching goals.* Los Altos, CA: Kaufman.

Koehler, D. J., & Harvey, N. (Eds.). (2005). *The Blackwell handbook of judgment and decision making.* Oxford, England: Blackwell Publishing.

Kohn, A. (1988). *False prophets: Fraud and error in science and medicine.* New York: Basil Blackwell.

Kondro, W., & Sibbald, B. (2004). Drug company experts advised staff to withhold data about SSRI use in children. *Canadian Medical Association, 170*(5), 783.

Kopta, S. M., Newman, F. L., McGovern, M. P., & Sandrock, D. (1986). Psychological orientations: A comparison of conceptualizations, interventions, and treatment plan costs. *Journal of Consulting and Clinical Psychology, 54,* 369–374.

Korotitsch, W. J., & Nelson-Gray, R. O. (1999). An overview of self-monitoring research in assessment and treatment. *Psychological Assessment, 11,* 415–425.

Korzybski, A. (1980). *Science and sanity: An introduction to nonaristotelian systems and general semantics* (4th ed.). Lakeville, CT: Institute of General Semantics.

Kottler, J. A., & Blau, D. S. (1989*). The imperfect therapist: Learning from failure in therapeutic practice.* San Francisco: Jossey Bass.

Kruger, J., & Dunning, D. (1999). Unskilled and unaware of it: How difficulties in recognizing one's own incompetence lead to inflated self-assessments. *Journal of Personality and Social Psychology, 77,* 1121–1134.

Kruglanski, A., & Webster, D. (1996). Motivated closing of the mind: Ceasing and freezing. *Psychological Review, 103,* 263–278.

Kruskal, W., & Mosteller, F. (1981). Ideas of representative sampling. In D. Fiske (Ed.), *New Directions for methodology of social and behavioral science: No.9. Problems with language imprecision* (pp. 3–24). San Francisco: Jossey-Bass.

Kuhn, T. S. (1996). Logic of discovery or psychology of research? In I. Lakatos & A. Musgrave (Eds.), *Criticism and the growth of knowledge* (pp. 1–23). Cambridge, MA: Cambridge University Press.

Kuipers, B., & Kassirer, J. P. (1984). Causal reasoning in medicine: Analysis of a protocol. *Cognitive Science, 8,* 363–385.

Kuno, E., & Rothbard, A. B. (2002). Racial disparities in anti-psychotic prescription patterns for patients with schizophrenia. *The American Journal of Psychiatry, 159,* 567–572.

Kunst, H., Groot, D., Latthe, P. M., Latthe, M., & Khan, K. S. (2002). Accuracy of information on apparently credible websites: Survey of five common health topics. *British Medical Journal, 324,* 581–582.

Kurasaki, K. S., Okazaki, S., & Sue, S. (Eds.). (2002). *Asian American mental health: Assessment, theories, and methods.* New York: Kluwer Academic/Plenum.

Kutchins, H., & Kirk, S. A. (1997). *Making us crazy: DSM: The psychiatric bible and the creation of mental disorders.* New York: Free Press.

LaBerge, D. (1995). *Attentional processing: The brain's art of mindfulness.* Cambridge, MA: Harvard University Press.

Lacasse, J. R., & Gomory, T. (2003). Is graduate social work education promoting a critical approach to mental health practice? *Journal of Social Work Education, 39,* 383–408.

Lakoff, G., & Dean, H. (2004). *Don't think of an elephant! Know your values and frame the debate: The essential guide for progressives.* White River Junction, VT: Chelsea Green.

Lakoff, G., & Johnson, M. (1980). *Metaphors we live by.* Chicago: University of Chicago Press.

Lakoff, R. T. (2001). *The language war.* Berkeley, CA: University of California Press.

Lambert, M. J. (2004). Introduction and historical overview. In *Bergin and Garfield's Handbook of psychotherapy and behavior change* (5th ed., pp. 3–15). New York: Wiley.

Lambert, M. J., & Barley, D. E. (2002). Research summary on the therapeutic relationship and psychotherapy outcome. In J. C. Norcross (Ed.), *Psychotherapy relationships that work: Therapists' contributions and responsiveness to patients* (pp. 17–32). New York: Oxford.

Lambert, M. J., & Ogles, B. M. (2004). The efficacy and effectiveness of psychotherapy. In M. J. Lambert (Ed.), *Bergin and Garfield's handbook of psychotherapy and behavior change* (5th ed., pp. 139–293). New York: Wiley.

Lambert, M. J., Whipple, J. L., Vermeersch, D. A., Smart, D. W., Hawkins, E. J., Nielsen, S. L., & Goates, N. (2002). Enhancing psychotherapy outcomes via providing feedback on client progress: A replication. *Clinical Psychology & Psychotherapy, 9,* 91–103.

Landers, S. (1987). LD definition disputed. *APA Monitor, 18*(12), 35.

Langer, E. J. (1975). The illusion of control. *Journal of Personality and Social Psychology, 32,* 311–328.

Langer, E. J. (1983). *The psychology of control.* Newbury Park, CA: Sage.

Langer, E. J., & Abelson, R. P. (1974). A patient by any other name: Clinician group difference in labeling bias. *Journal of Consulting and Clinical Psychology, 42,* 4–9.

Larrick, R. P. (2005). Debiasing. In D. J. Koehler & N. Harvey (Eds.), *Blackwell handbook of judgement and decision making* (pp. 316–337). Malden, MA: Blackwell.

Larson, M. S. (1977). *The rise of professionalism: A sociological analysis.* Berkeley: University of California Press.

Last, J. M. (1988). *A dictionary of epidemiology* (2nd Ed.). New York: Oxford.

Lawrie, S. M., McIntosh, A. M., & Rao, S. (2000). *Critical appraisal for psychiatry.* New York: Churchill Livingstone.

Leape, L., Lawthers, A. G., Brennan, T. A., et al. (1993). Preventing medical injury. *Qualitative Review Bulletin, 19,* 144–149.

Lehman, A. F., Goldman, H. H., Dixon, L. B., & Churchill, R. (2004). *Evidence-based mental health treatments and services: Examples to inform public policy.* New York: Milbank Memorial Fund.

Leiby, J. (1978). *A history of social welfare and social work in the United States.* New York: Columbia University Press.

Leichtman, M. D., & Ceci, S. J. (1995). The effects of stereotypes and suggestions on preschoolers' reports. *Developmental Psychology, 31,* 568–578.

Lemert, E. M. (1951). *Social pathology.* New York: McGraw-Hill.

Lenrow, P. (1978). Dilemmas of professional helping: Continuities and discontinuities with folk helping roles. In L. Wipse (Ed.), *Altruism, sympathy and helping: psychological and sociological principles* (pp. 263–290). Orlando, FL: Academic Press.

Lenzer, J. (2004). Bush plans to screen whole U. S. population for mental illness. *British Medical Journal, 328,* 1458.

Leo, J., & Cohen, D. (2003). Broken brains or flawed studies? A critical review of ADHD neuroimaging research. *Journal of Mind and Behavior, 24,* 29–56.

Lerner, J. S., & Tetlock, P. E. (1999). Accounting for the effects of accountability. *Psychological Bulletin, 125,* 255–75.

Lesgold, A., Rubinson, H., Feltovich, P., Glaser, R., Klopfer, D., & Wang, Y. (1988). Expertise in a complex skill: Diagnosing x-ray pictures. In M. T. H. Chi, R. Glaser, & M. Farr (Eds.), *The nature of expertise* (pp. 311–342). Hillsdale, NJ: Erlbaum.

Levy, C. J. (2002, December 13). State to survey mentally ill in residences. *The New York Times*, p. 1.

Levy, R. L. (1977). Relationship of an overt commitment to task compliance in behavior therapy. *Journal of Behavior Therapy and Experimental Psychiatry, 8*, 25–29.

Lewontin, R. C. (1991). *Biology as ideology: The doctrine of DNA.* New York: HarperCollins.

Lewontin, R. C. (1994). *Inside and outside: Gene, environment, and organism.* Worcester, MA: Clark University Press.

Lewontin, R. C. (1995). Genes, environment and organisms. In R. B. Silvers (Ed.), *Hidden histories of science* (pp. 115–139). New York: New York Review Book.

Lichtenstein, S., Slovic, P., Fischhoff, B., Layman, M., & Coombs, C. (1978). Judged frequency of lethal events. *Journal of Experimental Psychology: Human Learning and Memory, 4*, 551–578.

Lijmer, J. G., Mol, B. W., Heisterkamp, S., Bonsel, G. J., Prins, M. H., van der Meulen, J. H., et al. (1999). Empirical evidence of design-related bias in studies of diagnostic tests. *Journal of the American Medical Association, 282*, 1061–1066.

Lilienfeld, S. O. (2002). When worlds collide: Social science, politics, and the Rind et al. (1998) child sexual abuse meta-analysis. *American Psychologist, 57*, 176–188.

Lilienfeld, S. O., Lynn, S. J., & Lohr, J. M. (2003). *Science and pseudoscience in clinical psychology.* New York: Guilford.

Lilienfeld, S. O., Wood, J. M., & Garb, H. N. (2000). The scientific status of projective techniques. *Psychological Science in the Public Interest, 1*, 27–66.

Lindsey, D. S., Hagen, L., Read, J. D., Kimberley, A. W., & Garry, M. (2004). True photographs and false memories. *American Psychological Society, 15*, 149–154.

Lindsey, D., Martin, S., & Doh, J. (2002). The failure of intensive casework services to reduce foster care placements: An examination of family preservation studies. *Children and Youth Services Review, 24*, 743–775.

Lindsey, S. (2004). Statistical scientific evidence and expertise in the courtroom. In E. Kurz-Milcke & G. Gigerenzer (Eds.), *Experts in science and society* (pp. 269–279). New York: Kluwer Academic/Plenum.

Lipman, M. (2003). *Thinking in education* (2nd ed.). Cambridge: Cambridge University Press.

Lipsey, M. W. (2003). Those confounded moderators in meta-analysis: Good, bad and ugly. *The ANNALS of the American Academy of Political and Social Science, 587*, 69–81.

Lipshitz, R. (1997). Naturalistic decision making perspectives on decision making. In C. Zsambok & G. Klein (Eds.), *Naturalistic decision making* (pp. 151–162). Mahwah, NJ: Erlbaum.

Lipton, J. P., & Hershaft, A. M. (1985). On the widespread acceptance of dubious medical findings. *Journal of Health and Social Behavior, 26*, 336–351.

Littell, J. (2005). Lessons from a systematic review of effects of multisystemic therapy. *Children and Youth Services Review, 27*, 429.

Lock, M. (1982). Popular conceptions of mental health in Japan. In A. J. Marsella & G. M. White (Eds.), *Cultural conceptions of mental health and therapy* (pp. 215–234). Norwell, MA: D. Reidel.

Lock, M. (1993). *Encounters with aging: Mythologies of menopause in Japan and North America.* Berkeley: The University of California Press.

Loftus, E. F. (1979a). *Eyewitness testimony.* Cambridge, MA: Harvard University Press.

Loftus, E. F. (1997b). Creating false memories. *Scientific American, 277,* 70–75.

Loftus, E. F. (1980). *Memory: Surprising new insights into how we remember and why we forget.* Reading, MA: Addison-Wesley.

Loftus, E. F. (2004). Memories of things unseen. *Current Directions in Psychological Science, 17,* 145–147.

Loftus, E. F., & Guyer, M. J. (2002). Who abused Jane Doe? The hazards of the single case history Part 1. *Skeptical Inquirer, 26,* 22–32.

Loftus, E. F., & Ketcham, K. E. (1983). The malleability of eyewitness accounts. In S. M. A. Lloyd-Bostock & B. R. Clifford (Eds.), *Evaluating witness evidence: Recent psychological research and new perspectives* (pp. 159–172). New York: Wiley.

Loftus, E., & Ketcham, K. (1994). *The myth of repressed memory: False memories and allegations of abuse.* New York: St. Martin's Press.

Loftus, E., & Palmer, J. (1974). Reconstruction of automobile destruction: An example of the interaction between language and memory. *Journal of Verbal Learning and Verbal Behavior, 13,* 585–589.

Lord, C., Ross, L, & Lepper, M. R. (1979). Biased assimilation and attitude polarization: The effects of prior theories on subsequently considered evidence. *Journal of Personality and Social Psychology, 37,* 2098–2109.

*Los Angeles Times.* The shrinking family doctor in California. (1979, August 5, p. 3).

Luborsky, L., Diguer, L., Seligman, D. A., Rosenthal, R., Krause, E. D., Johnson, S., Halperin, G., Bishop, M., Burman, J. S., & Schweizer, E. (1999). The researchers' own therapy allegiances: A "wildcard" in comparisons of treatment efficacy. *Clinical Psychology: Science and Practice, 6,* 95–106.

Luck, J., & Peabody, J. W. (2002). Using standardized patients to measure physicians' practice: Validation study using audio recordings. *British Medical Journal, 325,* 67–92.

Ludmerer, K. M. (1999). *Time to heal.* New York: Oxford University Press.

Lynn, S. J., Lock, T., Loftus, E. E., Krackow, E., & Lilienfeld, S. O. (2003). The remembrance of things past: Problematic memory recovery techniques in psychotherapy. In S. O. Lilienfled, S. J. Lynn, & J. M. Lohr (Eds.), *Science and pseudoscience in clinical psychology* (pp. 250–239). New York: Guilford.

MacCoun, R. J. (1998). Biases in the interpretation and use of research results. *Annual Review of Psychology, 49,* 259–287.

MacCoun, R. J. (2001). American distortion of Dutch drug statistics. *Society, 38,* 23–26.

MacCoun, R. J., & Reuter, P. (2001). *Drug war heresies: Learning from other vices, times, & places.* New York: Cambridge University Press.

Mackie, J. L. (1974). *The cement of the universe: A study of causation.* Oxford, England: Clarendon Press.

MacLean, E. (1981). *Between the lines: How to detect bias and propaganda in the news and everyday life.* Montreal: Black Rose Books.

MacLehose, R. R., Reeves, B. C, Harvey, I. M., Sheldon, T. A., Russell, I. T., & Black,

A. M. (2000). A systematic review of comparisons of effect sizes derived from randomized and non-randomized studies. *Health Technology Assessment, 4*(34), 1–154.

Maclure, M. (1985). Popperian refutation in epidemiology. *American Journal of Epidemiology, 121,* 28–35.

MacMillan, H. L., Thomas, B. H., Jamieson, E., Walsh, C., Boyle, M. H., Shannon, H. S., & Gafni, A. (2005). Effectiveness of home visitation by public-health nurses in prevention of the recurrence of child physical abuse and neglect: A randomized controlled trial. *Lancet, 365,* 1786–1793

Magee, J. (1985). *Philosophy in the real world.* LaSalle, IL: Open Court.

Maguire, G. P., & Rutter, D. R. (1976). History-taking for medical students. I. Deficiencies in performance. *Lancet, 11,* 556–560.

Maher, C. A., & Cook, S. A. (1985). Time management. In C. A. Maher (Ed.), *Professional self-management: Techniques for special service providers* (pp. 23–43). Baltimore: Brooks.

Mahoney, M. J. (1977). Publication prejudices: An experimental study of confirmatory bias in the peer review system. *Cognitive Therapy and Research, 1,* 161–175.

Malott, R. W., Malott, M. E., & Trojan, E. A. (1999). *Elementary principles of behavior* (4th ed.). Upper Saddle River, NJ: Pearson.

Manning, N. P. (Ed.). (1985). *Social problems and welfare ideology.* Aldershot, England: Gower.

Mansfield, P. R. (1997). How does pharmaceutical company promotion affect prescribing? Retrieved September 16, 2005, from http://mednet3.who.int/icium/icium1997/posters/4P7_fintext.html .

Mansfield, P. R. (2003). Healthy skepticism's new ad. AdWatch: Understanding drug promotion. *Medical Journal of Australia, 179,* 644–645.

Margo, C. E. (2005). A pilot study in ophthalmology of inter-rater reliability in classifying diagnostic errors: An under-investigated area of medical error. *Quality and Safety of Health Care, 12,* 416–420.

Margolin, L. (1997). *Under the cover of kindness: The invention of social work.* Charlottesville: University of Virginia Press.

Marketing: A lifeline for private practice. (1987, October). *NASW News, 32,* 5.

Marlatt, G. A., & Gordon, J. R. (Eds.). (1985). *Relapse prevention: Maintenance strategies in the treatment of addiction.* New York: Guilford.

Marris, P. (1996). *The politics of uncertainty: Attachment in private public life.* New York: Routledge.

Marshall, J. G. (1992). The impact of the hospital library on clinical decision making: The Rochester Study. *Bulletin of the American Medical Association, 80,* 169–178.

Martin, D. J., Garske, J. P., & Davis, K. N. (2000). Relation of the therapeutic alliance with outcome and other variables: A meta-analytic review. *Journal of Consulting and Clinical Psychology, 68,* 438–450.

Martin, G., & Pear, J. (1988). *Behavior modification: What it is and how to do it* (3rd ed.). Englewood Cliffs, NJ: Prentice Hall.

Martinic, M., & Leigh, B. (2004). *Reasonable risk: Alcohol in perspective.* New York: Routledge.

Maslach, C., & Pines, A. (1979). "Burn out": The loss of human caring. In A. Pines &

C. Maslach (Eds.), *Experiencing social psychology* (pp. 245–252). New York: Random House.

Maslach, C., Schaufeli, W., & Leiter, M. P. (2001). Job burnout. *Annual Review of Psychology, 52,* 397–422.

Masson, J. M. (1984). *The assault on truth: Freud's suppression of the seduction theory.* New York: Farrar, Straus & Giroux.

Masson, J. M. (1988). *Against therapy: Emotional tyranny and the myth of psychological healing.* New York: Atheneum.

Matthews, G. (2001). Levels of transaction: A cognitive science framework for operator stress. In P. A. Hancock & P. A. Desmond (Eds.), *Stress, workload, and fatigue* (pp. 5–33). Mahwah, NJ: Erlbaum.

Mazzoni, G. A. L., Loftus, E. F., Seitz, A., & Lynn, S. J. (1999). Changing beliefs and memories through dream interpretation. *Applied Cognitive Psychology, 13*(2), 125–144.

McCann, J. T., Shindler, K. L., & Hammond, T. R. (2003). The science and pseudoscience of expert testimony. In S. O. Lillienfeld, S. J. Lynn, & J. M. Lohr (Eds.), *Science and pseudoscience in clinical psychology* (pp. 77–108). New York: Guilford.

McCloskey, M. (1983). Intuitive physics. *Scientific American, 248,* 122–130.

McCord, J. (1978). A thirty-year follow-up of treatment effects, *American Psychologist, 33,* 284–289.

McCord, J. (2003). Cures that harm: Unanticipated outcomes of crime prevention programs. *The ANNALS of the American Academy of Political and Social Science, 587,* 16–30.

McCormick, J. (1996). Health scares are bad for your health. In D. M. Warburton & N. Sherwood (Eds.), *Pleasure and quality of life* (pp. 189–199). New York: Wiley.

McCoy, R. (2000). *Quack! Tales of medical fraud from the museum of questionable medical devices.* Santa Monica, CA: Santa Monica Press.

McDaniel, P. A. (2003). *Shrinking violets and caspar milquetoasts.* New York: New York University Press.

McFall, R. M. (1991). Manifesto for a science of clinical psychology. *The Clinical Psychologist, 44,* 75–88.

McGimsey, J. F., Greene, B. F., & Lutzker, J. R. (1995). Competence in aspects of behavioral treatment and consultation: Implications for service delivery and graduate training. *Journal of Applied Behavioral Analysis, 28,* 301–315.

McGovern, M. P., Newman, F. L., & Kopta, S. M. (1986). Metatheoretical assumptions and psychotherapy orientation: Clinician attributions of patients' problem causality and responsibility for treatment outcome. *Journal of Consulting and Clinical Psychology, 54,* 476–481.

McGrath, E., Keita, G. P., Strickland, B. R., & Russo, N. F. (Eds.). (1990). *Women and depression: Risk factors and treatment issues.* Washington, DC: American Psychological Association.

McIntyre, N., & Popper, K. (1983). The critical attitude in medicine: The need for a new ethics. *British Medical Journal, 287,* 1919–1923.

McLellan, D. (1986). *Ideology: Concepts in social thought.* Minneapolis: University of Minnesota Press.

McNeil, B. J., Pauker, S. G., Sox, H. C., Jr., & Tversky, A. (1982). On the elicitation of preferences for alternative therapies. *New England Journal of Medicine, 306,* 1259–1262.

McReynolds, P. (1989). Diagnosis and clinical assessment: Current status and major issues. In M. R. Rosenzweig & L. W. Porter (Eds.), *Annual Review of Psychology, 40,* 83–108.

Medawar, P. (1979). A bouquet of fallacies from medicine and medical science with a sideways glance at mathematics and logic. In R. Duncan & M. Weston-Smith (Eds.), *The encyclopedia of delusions: A critical scrutiny of current beliefs and conventions* (pp. 97–105). New York: Simon & Schuster.

Medawar, P. B. (1984). *Pluto's republic.* Oxford, England: Oxford University Press.

Medical ethics—Should medicine turn the other cheek? (1990). *Lancet, 336,* 846–847.

Medin, D. L. (1989). You have to almost know something in order to learn it. *Contemporary Psychology, 34,* 445–447.

Meehl, P. E. (1954). *Clinical versus statistical prediction: A theoretical analysis and a review of the evidence.* Minneapolis: University of Minnesota Press.

Meehl, P. E. (1973). Why I do not attend case conferences. In P. E. Meehl (Ed.), *Psychodiagnosis: Selected papers* (pp. 225–304). Minneapolis: University of Minnesota Press.

Meichenbaum, D., & Asarnow, J. (1979). Cognitive behavior modification and metacognitive development: Implications for the classroom. In P. Kendall & S. Hollon (Eds.), *Cognitive behavioral interventions: Theory, research, and procedures* (pp. 11–36). Orlando, FL: Academic Press.

Meier, B. (2004, July 21). Some professional groups demand public listing of all test outcomes. *New York Times,* p. C-1.

Mennerick, L. L. (1974). Client typologies: A method of coping with conflicts in the service worker-client relationship. *Sociology of Work and Occupations, 1,* 396–418.

Mercer, J. R. (1973). *Labeling the mentally retarded.* Berkeley: University of California Press.

Merrell, K. & Walker, H. M. (2004). Deconstructing a definition: Social maladjustment versus emotional disturbance and moving the EBD field forward. *Psychology in the Schools, 41,* 899–910.

Michael, M., Boyce, W. T., & Wilcox, A. J. (1984). *Biomedical bestiary: An epidemiologic guide to flaws and fallacies in the medical literature.* Boston: Little, Brown.

Michalos, A. C. (1971). *Improving your reasoning.* Englewood Cliffs, NJ: Prentice Hall.

Midanik, L. T. (2006). *Biomedicalization of alcohol studies: Ideological shifts and institutional challenges.* New Brunswick, NJ: Aldine/Transaction.

Milgram, S. (1963). Behavioral study of obedience. *Journal of Abnormal and Social Psychology, 67,* 371–378.

Mill, J. S. (1911). *A system of logic. Book 3: Of induction. Chapter 5: Of the law of universal causation,* pp. 211–242.

Miller, A. G., Gillen, B., Schenker, C., & Radlove, S. (1973). Perception of obedience to authority. *Proceedings of the 81st Annual Convention of the American Psychological Association, 8,* 127–128.

Miller, D. (1994). *Critical rationalism: A restatement and defense.* Chicago: Open Court.

Miller, D. J., & Hersen, M. (1992). *Research fraud in the behavioral and biomedical sciences.* New York: Wiley.

Miller, J. D. (1987). The scientifically illiterate. *American Demographics, 9,* 26–31.

Mills, C. W. (1959). *The sociological imagination.* New York: Grove Press.

Mirowsky, J., & Ross, C. E. (1989). *Social causes of psychological distress.* New York: Aldine de Gruyter.

Mischel, W. (1968). *Personality and assessment.* New York: Wiley.

Mischel, W. (1973). Toward a cognitive social learning reconceptualization of personality. *Psychological Review, 80,* 252–283.

Mischel, W., Shoda, Y., & Mendoza-Denton, R. (2002). Situation-behavior profiles as a locus of consistency in personality. *Current Directions in Psychological Science, 11,* 50–54.

Miser, W. F. (1999). Critical appraisal of the literature. *Journal of the American Board of Family Practice, 12,* 315–333.

Miser, W. F. (2000a). Applying a meta-analysis to daily clinical practice. In J. P. Geyman, R. A. Deyo, & S. D. Ramsey (Eds.), *Evidence-based clinical practice: Concepts and approaches* (pp. 57–64). Boston, MA: Butterworth & Heinemann.

Miser, W. F. (2000b). Critical appraisal of the literature: How to assess an article and still enjoy life. In J. P. Geyman, R. A. Deyo, & S. D. Ramsey (Eds.), *Evidence-based clinical practice: Concepts and approaches* (pp. 41–56). Boston: Butterworth-Heinemann.

Moncrieff, J. (2003). Is psychiatry for sale? An examination of the influence of the pharmaceutical industry on academic and practical psychiatry. Maudsley Discussion Paper, June 2003. Available from Institute of Psychiatry, de Crespigny Park, London, SE5 8AF.

Montenegro, M. (1988). Human subjects at risk of torture U.S. style: California. *NASW News, 14,* 5.

Monteith, M. J., Sherman, J. W., & Devine, P. G. (1998). Suppression as a stereotype control strategy. *Personality and Social Psychology Review, 2,* 63–82.

Moore, K. D. (1986). *Inductive arguments: A field guide.* Dubuque, IA: Kendall/Hunt.

Moran, G. (1998). *Silencing scientists and scholars in other fields: Power, paradigm controls, peer review and scholarly communication.* Greenwich, CT: Ablex.

Morawski, J. G. (1987). After reflection: Psychologists' uses of history. In H. J. Starn, T. B. Rogers, & K. J. Gergen (Eds.), *The analysis of psychological theory: Metapsychological perspectives* (pp. 157–174). New York: Hemisphere.

Morgan, M. G., Fischhoff, B., Bostrom, A., & Atman, C. (2001). *Risk communication: The mental models approach.* New York: Cambridge University Press.

Morgan, R. F. (Ed.). (1983). *The iatrogenics handbook.* Toronto: IPI Publications.

Morgan, T. (1982). *Churchill: Young man in a hurry 1874–1915.* New York: Simon & Schuster.

Morrissey, J., & Monahan, J. (1999). *Coercion in mental health services: International perspectives.* Stamford, CT: JAI Press.

Morrow-Bradley, C., & Elliot, R. (1986). Utilization of psychotherapy research by practicing psychotherapists. *American Psychologist, 41,* 188–197.

Moynihan, R. (2003a). Claims by charity exaggerate dangers of osteoporosis. *British Medical Journal, 327,* 358.

Moynihan, R. (2003b). The making of a disease: Female sexual dysfunction. *British Medical Journal, 326,* 45–47.

Moynihan, R., Heath, I., Henry, D., & Gøtzsche, P. C. (2002). Selling sickness: The pharmaceutical industry and disease mongering. *British Medical Journal, 324,* 886–891.

Munro, E. (1996). Avoidable and unavoidable mistakes in child protection work. *British Journal of Social Work, 26,* 793–808.

Munro, E. (2004). A simpler way to understand the results of risk assessment instruments. *Children and Youth Services Review, 26,* 873–883.

Munz, P. (1985). *Our knowledge of the growth of knowledge: Popper or Wittgenstein.* London: Routledge & Kegan Paul.

Munz, P. (1992). What's postmodern, anyway? *Philosophy and Literature, 16,* 333–353.

Mussweiler, T., Strack, F., & Pfeiffer, T. (2000). Overcoming the inevitable anchoring effect: Considering the opposite compensates for selective accessibility. *Personality and Social Psychology Bulletin, 26,* 1142–1150.

Nadelmann, E. A. (1988). The case for legalization. *Public Interest, 92,* 3–31.

Naftulin, D. H., Ware, J. E., & Donnelly, F. A. (1973). The Doctor Fox lecture: A paradigm of educational seduction. *Journal of Medical Education, 48,* 630–635.

Najavits, L. M., & Strupp, H. H. (1994). Differences in the effectiveness of psychodynamic therapists: A process-outcome study. *Psychotherapy, 31,* 114–123.

Natale, J. A. (1988). Are you open to suggestion. *Psychology Today, 22,* 28–30.

Nathan, P. E., & Gorman, J. M. (2002). *A guide to treatments that work* (2nd ed.). New York: Oxford.

National Assessment of Educational Programs (NAEP). (1981). *Reading, thinking, and writing.* Denver, CO: Educational Commission of the States.

National Association of Social Workers. (1999). NASW code of ethics. Washington, DC: NASW.

National Campaign to Abolish the Lexington Women's Control Unit. (n.d.). *Buried alive in the Lexington Women's Control Unit.* New York: National Campaign to Abolish the Lexington Women's Control Unit.

National Science Foundation. (2002). Science and technology: Public attitudes and public understanding. See website.

Naylor, R. (2002). *Medication errors: Lessons for education and health care.* Abingdon, UK: Radcliffe Medical Press.

Nemeth, C. J., & Goncalo, J. A. (2005). Influence and persuasion in small groups. In T. C. Brock & M. C. Green (Eds.), *Persuasion: Psychological insights and perspectives* (2nd ed., pp. 171–194). Thousand Oaks, CA: Sage.

Nettler, G. (1970). *Explanations.* New York: McGraw-Hill.

Nettleton, S., & Bunton, R. (1995). *Sociological critiques of health promotion.* In R. Bunton, S. Nettleton, & R. Burrows (Eds.), *The sociology of health promotion: Critical analysis of consumption, lifestyle and risk* (pp. 41–59). London and New York: Routledge.

Neuringer, A. (1981). Self-experimentation. *Behaviorism, 9,* 79–94.

Newman, M. G., Consoli, A. J., & Taylor, C. B. (1999). A palmtop computer program for the treatment of generalized anxiety disorder. *Behavior Modification, 23,* 597–619.

New report opens old debate about the nature of mental illness. (2005). *The National Psychologist,* p. 23. July/August.

Nickerson, R. S. (1985). Reasoning. In R. F. Dillon, & R. J. Sternberg (Eds.), *Cognition and instruction*. Orlando, FL: Academic Press.

Nickerson, R. S. (1986a). *Reflections on reasoning*. Hillsdale, NJ: Erlbaum.

Nickerson, R. S. (1986b). Reasoning. In R. F. Dillon & R. J. Sternberg (Eds.), *Cognition and instruction* (pp. 343–374). Orlando, FL: Academic Press.

Nickerson, R. S. (1987). Why teach thinking? In J. B. Baron & R. J. Sternberg (Eds.), *Teaching thinking skills: Theory and practice* (pp. 27–37). New York: W. H. Freeman.

Nickerson, R. S. (1988–1989). On improving thinking through instruction. In E. Z. Rothkopf (Ed.), *Review of research in education* (pp. 3–57). Washington, DC: American Educational Research Association.

Nickerson, R. (1998). Confirmation bias: A ubiquitous phenomena in many guises. *Review of General Psychology, 2*, 175–220.

Nickerson, R. S., Perkins, D. N., & Smith, E. E. (1985). *The teaching of thinking*. Hillsdale, NJ: Erlbaum.

Nisbett, R. E. (2003). *The geography of thought: How Asians and Westerners think differently . . . and why*. New York: Free Press.

Nisbett, R. E., Borgida, E., Crandall, R., & Reed, H. (1976). Popular induction: Information is not necessarily informative. In J. S. Carroll & J. W. Payne (Eds.), *Cognition and social behavior* (pp. 113–134). Hillsdale, NJ: Erlbaum.

Nisbett, R. E., Krantz, D. H., Jepson, C., & Kunda, Z. (1983). The use of statistical heuristics in everyday inductive reasoning. *Psychological Review, 90*, 339–363.

Nisbett, R. E., & Ross, L. (1980). *Human inference: Strategies and shortcomings of social judgement*. Englewood Cliffs, NJ: Prentice Hall.

Norcross, J. C. (Ed.). (2002a). *Psychotherapy relationships that work: Therapists' contributions and responsiveness to patients*. New York: Oxford.

Norcross, J. C. (2002b). Empirically supported therapy relationships. In J. C. Norcross (Ed.), *Psychotherapy relationships that work: Therapists' contributions and responsiveness to patients* (pp. 3–16). New York: Oxford University Press.

Norcross, J. C., Beutler, L. E., & Levant, R. F. (Eds.). (2006). *Evidence-based practices in mental health: Debate and dialogue on the fundamental questions*. Washington, DC: American Psychological Association.

Norman, G. R., & Shannon, S. L. (1998). Effectiveness of instruction in critical appraisal (evidence-based medicine) skills: A critical appraisal. *Canadian Medical Association Journal, 158*(2), 177–181.

Nosek, B., Banaji, M., & Greenwald, T. (2002). Harvesting implicit group attitudes and beliefs from a demonstration website. *Group Dynamics: Theory, Research and Practice, 6*, 101–115.

Novak, J. D., & Gowin, D. B. (1984). *Learning how to learn*. New York: Cambridge University Press.

Nye, M. J. (1980). N-rays: An episode in the history and psychology of science. *Historical Studies in the Physical Sciences, 11*, 125–156.

Oakes, M. (1986). *Statistical inference: A commentary for the social and behavioral sciences*. New York: Wiley.

Oakley, A. (1976). *Women's work: The housewife, past and present*. New York: Vintage.

O'Connor, A. M. (2001). Using patient decision aids to promote evidence-based decision making. *ACP Journal Club, 135*(1) A11–12.

O'Connor, A. M., Stacey, D., Rovner, D., Homes-Rovner, M., Tetroe, J., Llewellyn-Thomas, H., Entwistle, V., Rostom, A., Fiset, V., Barry, M., & Jones, J. (2002). Decision aids for people facing health treatment or screening decisions (Cochrane Review). In *Cochrane Library*, Issue 2, Oxford: Update Software.

O'Donohue, W., & Szymanski, J. (1994). How to win friends and not influence clients: Popular but problematic ideas that impair treatment decisions. *Behavior Therapist, 178*(2), 29–33.

Ofshe, R., & Watters, E. (1994). *Making monsters: False memories, psychotherapy, and sexual hysteria*. New York: Charles Scribner's.

O'Hagan, P. E. (2003). Fraudulent misrepresentation and eating disorder. *International Journal of Law and Psychiatry, 26*, 713–717.

Olds, D., Henderson, C. R., Jr., Cole, R., Eckenrode, J., Kitzman, H., Luckey, D., et al. (1998). Long-term effects of nurse home visitation on children's criminal and antisocial behavior: 15-year follow-up of a randomized controlled trial. *Journal of the American Medical Association, 280*, 1238–1444.

Opotow, S., & Weiss, L. (2000). Denial and the process of moral exclusion in environmental conflict. *Journal of Social Issues, 56*, 475–490.

Orasanu, J., & Connolly, T. (1993). The reinvention of decision making. In G. Klein, J. Orasanu, R. Calderwood, & C. E. Zsambok (Eds.), *Decision making in action: Models and methods* (pp. 3–20). Norwood, NJ: Ablex.

Orlinsky, D. E., Grave, K., & Parks, B. K. (1994). Process and outcome in psychotherapy: Noch Einmal. In A. E. Bergen & S. L. Garfield (Eds.), *Handbook of psychotherapy and behavior change* (pp. 270–376). New York: Wiley.

Ortiz de Montellano, B. (1992). Magic melanin: Spreading scientific illiteracy among minorities: Part II. *Skeptical Inquirer, 16*, 162–166.

Orwell, G. ([1946] 1958). Politics and the English language. In S. Orwell & I. Angus (Eds.), *The collected essays, journalism and letters of George Orwell: Vol. 4. In front of your nose, 1945–1950* (pp. 127–140). London: Secker & Warburg.

Oskamp, S. (1965). Overconfidence in case-study judgments. *Journal of Consulting Psychology, 29*, 261–265.

Øvretveit, J. (1995). *Purchasing for health: A multi-disciplinary introduction to the theory and practice of health purchasing*. Philadelphia: Open University Press.

Oxford English Dictionary. (1994).

Oxman, A. D., Thomson, M. A., Davis, D. A., & Haynes, R. B., (1995). No magic bullets: A systematic review of 102 trials of interventions to improve clinical practice. *Canadian Medical Association Journal, 153*, 1423–1431.

Oxman, A. D., & Flottorp, S. (1998). An overview of strategies to promote implementation of evidence based health care. In C. Silagy & A. Haines (Eds.), *Evidence based practice in primary care* (pp. 91–109). London: BMJ Books.

Oxman, A. D., & Guyatt, G. H. (1993). The science of reviewing research. In K. S. Warren & F. Mosteller (Eds.), *Doing more good than harm: The evaluation of health care interventions* (pp. 125–133). New York: New York Academy of Sciences.

Oxman, A. D., Cook, D. J., & Guyatt, G. M. (1994). Users' guides to the medical literature. V1: How to use an overview. *Journal of the American Medical Association, 272*, 1367–1371.

Oxman, A. D., Thomson, M. A., Davis, D., & Haynes, R. B. (1995). No magic bullets: A systematic review of 102 trials of interventions to improve professional practice. *Canadian Medical Association Journal, 153,* 1423–1443.

Palincsar, A. S., & Brown, A. L. (1984). Reciprocal teaching of comprehension-fostering and comprehension-monitoring activities. *Cognition and Instruction, 1,* 117–175.

Parkes, J., Hyde, C., Deeks, J., & Milne, R. (2004). Teaching critical appraisal skills in health care settings (Cochrane Review). In *Cochrane Library,* Issue 3. Chichester, UK: Wiley.

Parloff, M. B., Waskow, I. E., & Wolf, B. E. (1978). Research on therapist variables in relation to process and outcome. In S. L. Garfield & A. E. Bergin (Eds.), *Handbook of psychotherapy and behavior change: An empirical analysis* (2nd ed., pp. 233–282). New York: Wiley.

Parry, V. (2003). The art of branding a condition. *Medical marketing and Media, 38,* 43–49.

Parsons, T. (1951). *The social system.* England: RKP.

Patai, D., & Koertge, N. (2003). *Professing feminism: Education and indoctrination in women's studies* (new ed.). Lanham, MD: Lexington Books.

Patel, V. L., & Groen, G. J. (1986). Knowledge based solution strategies in medical reasoning. *Cognitive Science, 10,* 91–116.

Patterson, G. R., & Forgatch, M. S. (1985). Therapist behavior as a determinant for client noncompliance: A paradox for the behavior modifier. *Journal of Consulting and Clinical Psychology, 53,* 846–851.

Paul, G. L. (2000). Evidence-based practices in inpatient and residential facilities. *The Clinical Psychologist, 53,* 3–11.

Paul, R. W. (1987). Critical thinking and the critical person. In D. N. Perkins, J. Lochhead, & J. Bishop (Eds.), *Thinking: The second international conference* (pp. 373–404). Hillsdale, NJ: Erlbaum.

Paul, R. W. (1992). *Critical thinking: What every person needs to survive in a rapidly changing world* (2nd ed.). Foundation for Critical Thinking. www.criticalthinking.org.

Paul, R. W. (1993). *Critical thinking: What every person needs to survive in a rapidly changing world* (3rd ed.). Foundation for Critical Thinking. www.criticalthinking.org.

Paul, R. W., & Elder, L. (2004). *Critical thinking: Tools for taking charge of your professional and personal life.* Upper Saddle River, NJ: Prentice Hall.

Paul, R. W., Elder, L., & Bartell, T. (1997). *California teacher preparation for instruction in critical thinking: Research findings and policy recommendations.* Sacramento, CA: California Commission on Teacher Credentialing, March.

Paulos, J. A. (1988). *Innumeracy: Mathematical illiteracy and its consequences.* New York: Vintage.

Payne, J. W., & Bettman, J. R. (2005). Walking with the scarecrow: The information processing approach to decision research. In D. J. Koehler & N. Harvey (Eds.), *Blackwell handbook of judgment and decision making* (pp. 110–132). Malden, MA: Blackwell.

Pear, R. (2004, April 26). US finds fault in all 50 states' child welfare programs, and penalties may follow. *New York Times,* A27.

Peele, S. (1999). *Diseasing of America: How we allowed recovery zealots and the treatment industry to convince us we are out of control.* San Francisco: Jossey-Bass.

Pekkala, E., & Merinder, L. (2004). Psychoeducation for schizophrenia (Cochrane Review). In *Cochrane Library,* Issue 4. Chichester, UK: Wiley.

Pepper, C. (1984). *Quackery: A $10 billion scandal.* Subcommmittee on health and long-term care of the Select Committee on Aging. U.S. House of Representatives. No. 98-435. Washington, DC: U.S. Government Printing House.

Pepper, S. (1981). Problems in the quantification of frequency experiences. In D. Fiske (Ed.), *New directions for methodology of social and behavioral science: No. 9. Problems with language imprecision* (pp. 25–42). San Francisco: Jossey-Bass.

Perkins, D. N. (1985). General cognitive skills, why not? In S. F. Chipman, J. W. Segal, & R. Glaser (Eds.), *Thinking and learning skills: Vol. 2. Research and open questions* (pp. 339–364). Hillsdale, NJ: Erlbaum.

Perkins, D. N. (1987). Thinking frames: An integrative perspective on teaching cognitive skills. In J. B. Baron & R. J. Sternberg (Eds.), *Teaching thinking skills: Theory and practice.* New York: W. H. Freeman.

Perkins, D. N. (1988). Creativity and the quest for mechanism. In R. J. Sternberg & E. E. Smith (Eds.), *The psychology of human thought* (pp. 309–336). Cambridge, England: Cambridge University Press.

Perkins, D. (1992). *Smart schools: From training memories to educating minds.* New York: Free Press.

Perkins, D. (1995). *Outsmarting IQ: The emerging science of learnable intelligence.* New York: Free Press.

Perkins, D. N. (2002). The engine of folly. In R. J. Sternberg (Ed.), *Why smart people can be so stupid* (pp. 64–85). New Haven, CT: Yale University Press.

Perkins, D. N., Allen, R., & Hafner, J. (1983). Difficulties in everyday reasoning. In W. Maxwell (Ed.), *Thinking.* Philadelphia: Franklin Institute Press.

Perkinson, H. (1993). *Teachers without goals, students without purpose.* New York: McGraw-Hill.

Peterson, C. L., Navarro, V. & Peterson, C. (Eds.). (2003). *Work stress: Studies on the context, content, and outcomes of stress: A book of readings.* Amityville, NY: Baywood Publishing.

Petrosino, A., Turpin-Petrosino, C., & Buehler, J. (2003). Scared straight and other juvenile awareness programs for preventing juvenile delinquency: A systematic review of the randomized experimental evidence. *The ANNALS of the American Academy of Political and Social Science, 589,* 41–62.

Petrosino, A., Turpin-Petrosino, C., & Finckenauer, J. O. (2000). Well-meaning programs can have harmful effects! Lessons from experiments of programs such as Scared Straight. *Crime & Delinquency, 46,* 354–379.

Petty, R. E., & Cacioppo, J. T. (1986). The elaboration likelihood model of persuasion. In L. Berkowitz (Ed.), *Advances in experimental social psychology* (pp. 124–206) (Vol. 19). Orlando, FL: Academic Press.

Petty, R. E., Cacioppo, J. T., Strathman, A. J., & Priester, J. R. *To think or not to think: Exploring two routes to persuasion.* In T. C. Brock & M. C. Green (Eds.), *Persuasion: Psychological insights and perspectives* (2nd ed., pp. 81–116). Thousand Oaks, CA: Sage.

Pewsner, D., Pattaglia, M., Minder, C., Marx, A., Bucher, H. C., & Egger, M. (2004). Ruling a diagnosis in or out with "SpPIn" and "SnNOut": A note of caution. *British Medical Journal, 329,* 209–213.

Pfohl, S. J. (1978). *Predicting dangerousness: The social construction of psychiatric reality.* Lexington, MA: Heath.

Phillips, D. C. (1987). *Philosophy, science and social inquiry: Contemporary methodological controversies in social science and related applied fields of research.* New York: Pergamon Press.

Phillips, D. C. (1990). Postpositivistic science: Myths and realities. In E. G. Guba (Ed.), *The paradigm dialog* (pp. 31–45). Thousand Oaks, CA: Sage.

Phillips, D. C. (1992). *The social scientist's bestiary: A guide to fabled threats to, and defenses of, naturalistic social studies.* New York: Pergamon.

Phillips, J. K., Klein, G., & Sieck, W. R. (2005). Expertise in judgment and decision making: A case for training intuitive decision skills. In D. J. Koehler & N. Harvey (Eds.), *Blackwell handbook of judgment and decision making* (pp. 297–315). Malden, MA: Blackwell.

Phillips, P. (2005). *Censored 2005: The top 25 censored stores (censored).* New York: Seven Stories Press.

Pilpel, R. H. (1976). *Churchill in America.* New York: Harcourt Brace Jovanovich.

Plato. ([1954] 1993). *The last days of Socrates.* (H. Tredennick & H. Tarrant, Trans.). New York: Penguin.

Pliske, R. M., McCloskey, M. J., & Klein, G. (2001). Decision skills training: Facilitating learning from experience. In E. Salas & G. Klein (Eds.), *Linking expertise and naturalistic decision making* (pp. 37–54). Mahwah, NJ: Erlbaum.

Plous, S. (1993). *The psychology of judgement and decision making.* New York: McGraw-Hill.

Plous, S., & Zimbardo, P. G. (1986). Attributional biases among clinicians: A comparison of psychoanalysts and behavior therapists. *Journal of Clinical and Consulting Psychology, 54,* 568–570.

Pope, K. S. (1998). Pseudo-science, cost-examination, and scientific evidence in the recovered memory controversy. *Psychology, Public Policy, & Law, 4,* 1160–1181.

Popper, K. (1998). *The world of Parmenides: Essays on the pre-Socratic enlightenment.* New York: Routledge.

Popper, K. R. (1959). *The logic of scientific discovery.* London: Hutchinson.

Popper, K. R. ([1963] 1972). *Conjectures and refutations: The growth of scientific knowledge* (4th ed.). London: Routledge & Kegan Paul.

Popper, K. R. ([1957] 1983). The aim of science. In D. Miller (Ed.), *A pocket Popper* (pp. 162–170). London: Fontana Press.

Popper, K. R. (1992). *In search of a better world: Lectures and essays from thirty years.* London: Routledge & Kegan Paul.

Popper, K. R. (1994). *The myth of the framework: In defense of science and rationality.* Edited by M. A. Notturno. New York: Routledge.

Porter, N., & Geis, F. (1981). Women and nonverbal leadership cues: When seeing is not believing. In C. Mayo & N. M. Henley (Eds.), *Gender and nonverbal behavior* (pp. 39–61). New York: Springer-Verlag.

Porter, R. (2002). *Quacks: Fakers & charlatans in English medicine*. Charleston, SC: Tempus.

Poses, R. M., Cebul, R. D., & Wigton, R. S. (1995). You can lead a horse to water—Improving physicians' knowledge of probabilities may not affect their decisions. *Medical Decision Making, 15*, 65–75.

Pottick, K. L., Wakefield, J. C., Kirk, S. A., & Tian, X. (2003). Influence of social workers' characteristics on the perception of mental disorder in youths. *Social Service Review, 77*, 431–454.

Poulin, F., Dishion, T. J., & Burraston, B. (2001). 3-year iatrogenic effects associated with aggregating high-risk adolescents in cognitive-behavioral preventive interventions. *Applied Developmental Science, 5*, 214–224.

Pratkanis, A. R., & Aronson, E. (2001). *Age of propaganda: The everyday use and abuse of persuasion* (revised ed.). New York: W. H. Freeman and Company.

Premack, D. (1965). Reinforcement therapy. In D. Levine (Ed.), *Nebraska symposium on motivation* (pp. 23–180). Lincoln: University of Nebraska Press.

President's New Freedom Commission on Mental Health. Retrieved 9/9/05, from www.mentalhealthcommission.gov.

Pressley, M., Borkowski, J. G., & O'Sullivan, J. T. (1984). Memory strategy instruction is made of this: Metamemory and durable strategy use. *Educational Psychologist, 9*, 94–107.

Pronin, E., Kruger, J., Savitsky, K., & Ross, L. (2001). You don't know me, but I know you: The illusion of asymmetric insight. *Journal of Personality and Social Psychology, 81*, 36.

Pronin, E., Puccio, C., & Ross, L. (2002). Understanding misunderstanding: Social psychological perspectives. In T. Gilovich, D. Griffin, & D. Kahneman (Eds.), *Heuristics and biases: The psychology of intuitive judgment* (pp. 636–665). New York: Columbia University Press.

Pronin, E., & Ross, L. (1999). Two views of romantic break-ups: Biased perceptions of the clarity of intimate communication. Unpublished manuscript. Stanford University.

Prosser, M. (1987). The effects of cognitive structure and learning strategy on student achievement. In J. T. E. Richardson, M. W. Eysenck, & W. Piper (Eds.), *Student learning: Research in education and cognitive psychology* (pp. 29–38). Milton Keynes, England: Society for Research into Higher Education and Open University Press.

Prounis, C. (2004). The art of advertorial. *Pharmaceutical Executive, 24*(5), 152–164.

Pryor, J. B., & Kriss, M. (1977). The cognitive dynamics of salience in the attribution process. *Journal of Personality and Social Psychology, 35*, 49–55.

Pryor, K. (1984). *Don't shoot the dog*. New York: Bantam.

Pyszczynski, T., & Greenberg, J. (1985). Depression and preferences for self-focusing stimuli after success and failure. *Journal of Personality and Social Psychology, 49*, 1066–1075.

Pyszczynski, T., & Greenberg, J. (1987). Toward an integration of cognitive and motivational perspectives on social inference: A biased hypothesis-testing model. In L. Berkowitz (Ed.), *Advances in experimental social psychology, Vol. 20* (pp. 297–340). Orlando, FL: Academic Press.

Quinsey, V. L., Harris, G. T., Rice, M. E., & Cormier, C. A. (1998). *Violent offenders: Appraising and managing risks.* Washington, D C: American Psychological Association.

Raghunathan, R., & Pham, M. T. (1999). All negative moods are not created equal: Motivational influences of anxiety and sadness on decision making. *Organizational Behavior and Human Decision Performance, 79,* 56–77.

Rank, H. (1984). *The peptalk: How to analyze political language.* Park Forest, IL: The Counter-Propaganda Press.

Ravitch, D. (2003). *The language police: How pressure groups restrict what students learn.* New York: Alfred A. Knopf.

Reason, J. (1997). *Managing the risks of organizational accidents.* Aldershot, England: Ashgate.

Reason, J. (2001). Understanding adverse events: The human factor. In C. Vincent (Ed.), *Clinical risk management: Enhancing patient safety* (2nd ed., pp. 9–30). London: BMJ Books.

Regan, D. T., & Totten, J. (1975). Empathy and attribution: Turning observers into actors. *Journal of Personality and Social Psychology, 32,* 850–856.

Regehr, G., Freeman, R., Robb, A., Missiha, N., & Heisey, R. (1999). OSCE performance evaluations made by standardized patients: Comparing checklist and global ratings scores. *Academic Medicine, 74,* S135–S137.

Reid, J. B., Patterson, G. R., & Snyder, J. (Eds.). (2002). *Antisocial behavior in children and adolescents: A developmental analysis and model for intervention.* Washington, DC: American Psychological Association.

Reiman, J. (2004). *The rich get richer and the poor get prison* (7th ed.). Boston: Allyn & Bacon.

Renaud, H., & Estess, F. (1961). Life history interviews with one hundred normal American males: "Pathogenicity" of childhood. *American Journal of Orthopsychiatry, 31,* 796–802.

Renstrom, L., Andersson, B., & Marton, F. (1990). Students' conceptions of matter. *Journal of Educational Psychology, 82,* 555–569.

Rhoads, S. E. (2004). *Taking sex differences seriously.* San Francisco, CA: Encounter Books.

Richard, D. C., & Lauterbach, D. (2004). Computers in the training and practice of behavioral assessment. In S. N. Haynes & E. M. Heibey (Eds.), *Comprehensive handbook of psychological assessment. Vol. 3. Behavioral assessment* (pp. 222–245). New York: Wiley.

Richman-Hirsch, W. L. (2001). Post-training interventions to enhance transfer: The moderating effects of work environments. *Human resource development quarterly, 12,* 105–120.

Rieke, R., & Sillers, M. (1984). Argumentation and the decision making process (2nd ed.). Glenview, IL: Scott, Foresman.

Robbins, L. C. (1963). The accuracy of parental recall of aspects of child development and child-rearing practices. *Journal of Abnormal and Social Psychology, 66,* 216–270.

Roberts, I., Kramer, M. S., & Suissa, S. (1996). Does home visiting prevent childhood injury? A systematic review of randomized controlled trials. *British Medical Journal, 312,* 29–33.

Roberts, L., Ahmed, I., & Hall, S. (2004). Intersessionary prayer for the alleviation of ill health. *Cochrane Review. The Cochrane Library,* Issue 3. Chicester, UK: Wiley.

Robertson, S. P., Black, J. B., & Lehnert, W. G. (1985). Misleading question effects as evidence for integrated question understanding and memory search. In A. C. Graesser & J. B. Black (Eds.), *The psychology of questions* (pp. 191–218). Hillsdale, NJ: Erlbaum.

Roediger, H. L., & Bergman, E. T. (1998). The controversy over recovered memories. *Psychology, Public Policy, & Law, 4,* 1091–1109.

Roese, N. J., & Olson, J. M. (Eds.). (1995). *What might have been: The social psychology of counterfactual thinking.* Mahwah, NJ: Erlbaum.

Rokeach, M. (1960). *The open and closed mind.* New York: Basic Books.

Rook, K. S. (1984). The negative side of social interaction: Impact on psychological well being. *Journal of Personality and Social Psychology, 46,* 1097–1108.

Rose, D., Fleischmann, P. Wykes, T., Leese, M., & Bindman, J. (2003). Patients' perspectives on electro-convulsive therapy: Systematic review. *British Medical Journal, 326,* 1363–1367.

Rose, S., Bisson, J., & Wessely, S. (2004). Psychological debriefing for preventing post traumatic stress disorder (PTSD). (Cochrane Review). In *Cochrane Library.* Issue 3. Chichester: Wiley.

Rosen, A., Proctor, E. K., Morrow-Howell, N., & Staudt, M. (1995). Rationales for practice decisions: Variations in knowledge use by decision task and social work service. *Research on Social Work Practice, 15,* 501–523.

Rosen, G. M. (1982). Self-help approaches to self-management. In K. R. Blankstein & J. Polivy (Eds.), *Self-control and self modification of emotional behavior* (pp. 183–200), (Vol. 7). New York: Plenum.

Rosenau, P. M. (1992). *Post-modernism and the social sciences: Insights, inroads, and intrusions.* Princeton, NJ: Princeton University Press.

Rosenbaum, P. R. (2002). *Observational studies (Springer series in statistics)* (2nd ed.). New York: Springer-Verlag.

Rosenhan, D. L. (1973). On being sane in insane places. *Science, 179,* 250–258.

Rosenthal, A. M. (1964). *Thirty-eight witnesses.* New York: McGraw-Hill.

Rosenthal, R. (1988). *Experimenter effects in behavioral research.* New York: Irvington.

Rosenthal, R. (1994). On being one's own study: Experimenter effects in behavioral research—30 years later. In W. R. Shadish & S. Fuller (Eds.) *The social psychology of science* (pp. 214–229). New York: Guilford.

Rosenthal, R., & Jacobson, L. (1992). *Pygmalian in the classroom: Teacher expectations and pupils' intellectual development.* New York: Irvington.

Rosenthal, T. (1994). Science and ethics in conducting, analyzing, and reporting psychological research. *Psychological Science, 5,* 127–134.

Rosenthal, T. (2001). *Workshop on meta-analysis.* Berkeley: University of California.

Ross, L., Amabile, T., & Steinmetz, J. (1977). Social roles, social control and biases in social perception processes. *Journal of Personality and Social Psychology, 35,* 485–494.

Ross, L., Greene, D., & House, P. (1977). The false consensus phenomenon: An attributional bias in self-perception and social perception processes. *Journal of Experimental Social Psychology, 13,* 279–301.

Ross, L., & Lepper, M. R. (1980). The perseverance of beliefs: Empirical and normative considerations. In R. A. Schweder (Ed.), *New directions for methodology of social and behavioral science: No.4. Fallible judgment in behavioral research* (pp. 17–36). San Francisco: Jossey-Bass.

Ross, L., Lepper, M. R., & Hubbard, J. (1975). Perseverance in self perception and social perception: Biased attributional processes in the debriefing paradigm. *Journal of Personality and Social Psychology, 32,* 880–892.

Ross, L., & Ward, A. (1996). Naïve realism in everyday life: Implications for social conflict and misunderstanding. In T. Brown,. E. Reed, & E. Turiel (Eds.), *Values and knowledge* (pp. 103–135). Hillsdale, NJ: Erlbaum.

Ross, W. D. (Trans. ed.). *The works of Aristotle.* Oxford, England: Clarendon Press. (Cited in Hamblin, 1970.)

Rossi, P. H., Lipsey, M. W., & Freeman, H. E. (2003). *Evaluation: A systematic approach* (7th ed.). Thousand Oaks, CA: Sage.

Ryan, W. (1976). *Blaming the victim* (rev. ed.). New York: Vantage.

Rycroft, C. (1973). *A critical dictionary of psychoanalysis.* Towata, NJ: Littlefield, Adams.

Rzepnicki, T. L., & Johnson, P. R. (2005). Examining decision errors in child protection: A new application of root cause analysis. *Children and Youth Services Review, 27,* 393–407.

Sackett, D. L. (1979). Bias in analytic research. *Journal of Chronic Disease, 32,* 51–63.

Sackett, D. L. (2002). The arrogance of preventive medicine. *Canadian Medical Association Journal, 167,* 363–364.

Sackett, D. L., & Haynes, R. B. (2002). The architecture of diagnostic research. *British Medical Journal, 324,* 539–541.

Sackett, D. L., & Oxman, A. D. (2003). Harlot plc: amalgamation of the world's two oldest professions. *British Medical Journal, 327,* 1442–1445.

Sackett, D. L., & Straus, S. E. (1998, October 21). Finding and applying evidence during clinical rounds. The "Evidence Cart." *Journal of the American Medical Association, 280*(15).

Sackett, D. L., Richardson, W. S., Rosenberg, W., & Haynes, R. B. (1997). *Evidence-based medicine: How to practice and teach EBM.* New York: Churchill Livingstone.

Sackett, D. L., Rosenberg, W. M. C., Gray, J. A. M., Haynes, R. B., & Richardson, W. S. (1996). Evidence-based medicine: What it is and what it isn't. *British Medical Journal, 312,* 71–72.

Sackett, D. L., Straus, S. E., Richardson, W. S., Rosenberg, W., & Haynes, R. B. (2000). *Evidence-based medicine: How to practice and teach EBM* (2nd ed.). New York: Churchill Livingstone.

Sagan, C. (1987). The burden of skepticism. *The Skeptical Inquirer, 12,* 38–74.

Sagan, C. (1990). Why we need to understand science. *Skeptical Inquirer, 14,* 263–269.

Sagan, C. *The fine art of baloney detection.*

Salas, E., & Klein, G. (Eds.). (2001). *Linking expertise and naturalistic decision making.* Mahwah, NJ: Erlbaum.

Sally Clark freed after appeal court quashes her convictions. (2003) *News British Medical Journal, 326,* 304.

Salovey, P., & Turk, D. C. (1988). Some effects of mood on clinicians' memory. In D. C.

Turk & P. Salovey (Eds.), *Reasoning, inference and judgement in clinical psychology* (pp. 107–123). New York: Free Press.

Sameroff, A. J., Lewis, M., & Miller, S. M. (Eds.). (2000). *Handbook of developmental psychopathology* (2nd ed.). Dordrecht, Netherlands: Kluwer Academic.

Sampson, E. E. (1977). Psychology and the American ideal. *Journal of Personality and Social Psychology, 35,* 767–782.

Sanford, A. J. (1985). *Cognition and cognitive psychology.* Hove, East Sussex, England: Erlbaum.

Sarnoff, S. K. (2001). *Sanctified snake oil: The effect of junk science on public policy.* Westport, CT: Praeger.

Schacter, D. L. (1999). The seven sins of memory: Insights from psychology and cognitive neuroscience. *American Psychologist, 54*(3), 182–203.

Schank, R., & Abelson, R. (1977). *Scripts, plans, goals, and understanding: An inquiry into human knowledge.* Hillsdale, NJ: Erlbaum.

Scheff, T. F. (1963). Decision rules, types of errors, and their consequences in medical diagnosis. *Behavioral Science, 8,* 97–107.

Scheff, T. J. (1984a). *Labeling madness* (2nd ed.). Englewood Cliffs, NJ: Prentice Hall.

Scheff, T. J. (1984b). *Being mentally ill: A sociological theory* (2nd ed.). New York: Aldine.

Scheper-Hughes, N., & Lovell, A. M. (Eds.). (1987). *Psychiatry inside out: Selected writings of Franco Basaglia.* New York: Columbia University Press.

Schlenker, B. R. (2003). Self-presentation. In M. R. Leary & J. P. Tangney (Eds.), *Handbook of self and identity* (pp. 492–518). New York: Guilford.

Schlenker, B. R., & Leary, M. R. (1982). Social anxiety and self-presentation: A conceptualization and model. *Psychological Bulletin, 92,* 641–669.

Schnaitter, R. (1986). Behavior as a function of inner states and outer circumstances. In T. Thompson & M. D. Zeiler (Eds.), *Analysis and integration of behavioral units* (pp. 247–274). Hillsdale, NJ: Erlbaum.

Schneider, D. J. (2004). *The psychology of stereotyping.* New York: Guilford.

Schnelle, J. F. (1974). A brief report on invalidity of parent evaluations of behavior change. *Journal of Applied Behavior Analysis, 7,* 341–343.

Schoenfeld, A. H. (1982). Measures of problem-solving performance and of problem-solving instruction. *Journal for Research on Mathematics Education, 13,* 31–49.

Schön, D. (1990). *Educating the reflective practitioner* (new ed.). San Francisco, CA: Jossey-Bass.

Schopenhauer, A. (1942). The art of controversy. In A. Schopenhauer, *The essays of Arthur Schopenhauer* (T. B. Saunders, Trans.). New York: Wiley.

Schulz, K. F., Chalmers, I., Hayes, R. J., & Altman, D. G. (1995). Empirical evidence of bias. Dimensions of methodological quality associated with estimates of treatment effects in controlled clinical trials. *Journal of the American Medical Association, 273*(5), 408–412.

Schultz, T. (Ed.). (1989). *The fringes of reason: A whole earth catalog.* New York: Harmony Books.

Schur, E. M. (1971). *Labeling deviant behavior.* New York: Harper & Row.

Schwartz, I. M. (1989). *(In)justice for juveniles: Rethinking the best interests of the child.* Lexington, MA: Lexington.

Schwartz, N. (2002). Feelings as information: Moods influence judgments and processing strategies. In T. Gilovich, D. Griffin, & D. Kahneman (Eds.), *Heuristics and biases: The psychology of intuitive judgment* (pp. 534–547). New York: Cambridge University Press.

Scott, S., Knapp, M., Henderson, J., & Maughan, B. (2001). Financial cost of social exclusion: Follow-up study of anti-social children into adulthood. *British Medical Journal, 323,* 191–194.

Scott, T., Stanford, N., & Thompson, D. R. (2004). Killing me softly: Myth in pharmaceutical advertising. *British Medical Journal, 329,* 1484–1487.

Scriven, M. (1976). *Reasoning.* New York: McGraw-Hill.

Scull, A. (2005). *Madhouse: A tragic tale of megalomania and modern medicine.* New Haven, CT: Yale University Press.

Secker-Walker, J., & Taylor-Adams, S. (2001). Clinical incident reporting. In C. Vincent (Ed.), *Clinical risk management: Enhancing patient safety* (2nd ed., pp. 419–438). London: BMJ.

Sedgwick, P. (1982). *Psycho Politics.* New York: Harper & Row.

Seech, Z. (1993). *Open minds and everyday reasoning.* Belmont, CA: Wadsworth Publishing Co.

Segal, S. P., Bola, J. R., & Watson, M. A. (1996). Race, quality of care, and antipsychotic prescribing practices in psychiatric emergency services. *Psychiatric Services, 47,* 282–286.

Semin, G. R., & Manstead, A. S. R. (1983). *The accountability of conduct: A social psychological analysis.* Orlando, FL: Academic Press.

Shadish, W. R., Cook, T. D., & Campbell, D. T. (2002). *Experimental and quasi-experimental designs for generalized causal inference.* Boston: Houghton-Mifflin.

Shahar, E. (1997). A Popperian perspective of the term "evidence-based medicine." *Journal of Evaluation in Clinical Practice, 3,* 109–116.

Shahar, E. (1998). Evidence-based medicine: A new paradigm or the emperor's new clothes? *Journal of Evaluation in Clinical Practice, 4,* 277–282.

Shanks, D. R. (2005). Judging covariation and causation. In D. J. Koehler & N. Harvey (Eds.), *Blackwell handbook of judgment and decision making* (pp. 220–239). Malden, MA: Blackwell.

Shanteau, J. (1992). How much information does an expert use? Is it relevant? *Acta Psychologica, 51,* 75–86.

Shanteau, J., Grier, M., Johnson, J., & Berner, E. (1991). Teaching decision-making skills to student nurses. In J. Baron & R. V. Brown (Eds.), *Teaching decision-making to adolescents* (pp. 185–206). Hillsdale, NJ: Erlbaum.

Sharpe, V. A , & Faden, A. I. (1998). *Medical harm: Historical, conceptual, and ethical dimensions of iatrogenic illness.* New York: Cambridge University Press.

Sheldon, B., & Chilvers, R. (2000). *Evidence-based social care: A study of prospects and problems.* Lyme Regis: Russell House Publishing.

Sheldon, T. A., Guyatt, G. H., & Haines, A. (1998). Getting research findings into practice: When to act on the evidence. *British Medical Journal, 317,* 139–142.

Sherden, W. A. (1998). *The fortune sellers: The big business of buying and selling predictions.* New York: Wiley.

Sherman, L. W., Farrington, D. P., Welsh, B. C., & MacKenzie, D. L. (Eds.). (2002). *Evidence-based crime prevention*. London: Routledge.

Shermer, M. (1997). *Why people believe weird things: Pseudoscience, superstition, and other confusions of our time*. New York: W. H. Freeman.

Shin, J. H., Haynes, R. B., & Johnston, M. E. (1993). Effect of problem-based, self-directed undergraduate education on life-long learning. *Canadian Medical Journal, 148*, 969–976.

Shorter, E., & Tyrer, P. (2003). Separation of anxiety and depressive disorders: Blind alley in psychopharmacology and classification of disease. *British Medical Journal, 327*, 158–160.

Shweder, R. A. (1977). Likeness and likelihood in everyday thought: Magical thinking in judgments about personality. *Current Anthropology, 18*, 637–658.

Shweder, R. A., & Miller, J. G. (1985). The social construction of the person: How is it possible? In K. J. Gergen & K. E. Davis (Eds.), *The social construction of the person* (pp. 41–72). New York: Springer-Verlag.

The Sicily Statement on Evidence-based Healthcare. (2004). *British Medical Journal*.

Sigel, I. E. (1979). On becoming a thinker. A psychoeducational model. *Educational Psychologist, 14*, 70–78.

Silverman, K. (1986). *Benjamin Franklin: The autobiography and other writings*. New York: Penguin.

Silverman, W. A. (1980). *Retrolental fibroplasia: A modern parable*. New York: Grune & Stratton.

Silverman, W. A. (1998). *Where's the evidence?: Debates in modern medicine*. New York: Oxford.

Simon, H. (1955). A behavioral model of rational choice. *Quarterly Journal of Economics, 69*, 99–118.

Simon, H. (1982). *Models of bounded rationality*. Cambridge, MA: MIT Press.

Simon, H. A. (1983). *Reason in human affairs*. Oxford, England: Basil Blackwell.

Simon, H. A. (1990). Alternative visions of rationality. In P. K. Moser (Ed.), *Rationality in action: Contemporary approaches* (pp. 189–204). New York: Cambridge University Press.

Sinclair, J. C., Cook, R. J., Guyatt, G. H., Pauker, S. G., & Cook, D. J. (2001). When should an effective treatment be used? Deviation of the threshold number needed to treat and the minimum event rate for treatment. *Journal of Clinical Epidemiology, 54(3)*, 253–262.

Sinclair, W. J. (1909). *Semmelweis, his life and his doctrine: A chapter in the history of medicine*. Manchester, England: University Press.

Singer, B. D. (1978). Assessing social errors. *Journal of Social Policy, 9*, 27–34.

Singh, I. (2002). Bad boys, good mothers, and the "miracle" of Ritalin. *Science in Context, 15*, 577–603.

Singh, I. (2004). Doing their jobs: Mothering with Ritalin in a culture of mother blame. *Social Science & Medicine, 59*, 1193–1205.

Sisson, J. C., Schoomaker, E. B., & Ross, J. C. (1976). Clinical decision analysis: The hazard of using additional data. In H. R. Arkes & K. R. Hammond (Eds.), *Judgment and decision making: An interdisciplinary reader* (pp. 354–363). Cambridge, England: Cambridge University Press.

Skinner, B. F. (1974). *About behaviorism.* New York: Knopf.

Skrabanek, P. (1990). Reductionist fallacies in the theory and treatment of mental disorders. *International Journal of Mental Health, 19,* 6–18.

Skrabanek, P., & McCormick, J. (1998). *Follies and fallacies in medicine* (3rd ed.). Whithorn, Scotland: Tarragon Press.

Slovic, P. (1987). Perception of risks. *Science, 236,* 280–285.

Slovic, P., Finucane, M., Peters, E., & MacGregor, D. G. (2002). The affect heuristic. In T. Gilovich & D. Griffin (Eds.), *Heuristics and biases: The psychology of intuitive judgment* (pp. 397–420). New York: Cambridge University Press.

Slovic, P., Fischhoff, B., & Lichtenstein, S. (1976). Cognitive processes and societal risk taking. In J. S. Carroll & J. W. Payne (Eds.), *Cognitive and social behavior* (pp. 165–184). Hillsdale, NJ: Erlbaum.

Slovic, P., Fischhoff, B., & Lichtenstein, S. (1982a). Facts versus fears: Understanding perceived risk. In D. Kahneman, P. Slovic, & A. Tversky (Eds.), *Judgment under uncertainty: Heuristics and biases.* New York: Cambridge University Press.

Slovic, P., Fischhoff, B., & Lichtenstein, S. (1982b). Response mode, framing, and information-processing effects in risk assessment. In R. M. Hogarth (Ed.), *New directions for methodology of social and behavioral science: No. 11. Question framing and response consistency* (pp. 21–36). San Francisco: Jossey-Bass.

Slovic, P., Kunreuther, H., & White, G. F. (1974). Decision processes, rationality, and adjustment to natural hazards. In G. F. White (Ed.), *Natural hazards: Local, national, and global* (pp. 187–205). Oxford, England: Oxford University Press.

Smedley B. D., Stith, A. Y., & Nelson, A. R. (Eds.) (2003). *Unequal treatment: Confronting racial and ethnic disparities in health care.* Institute of Medicine. Washington, DC: National Academy Press.

Smedslund, J. (1963). The concept of correlation in adults. *Scandinavian Journal of Psychology, 4,* 165–173.

Smith, R. (2003). Do patients need to read research? *British Medical Journal, 326,* 1307.

Smith, R. (2005). Investigating the previous studies of a fraudulent author. *British Medical Journal, 331,* 288–291.

Smith, C. R., & Hunsaker, D. M. (1972). *The bases of argument: Ideas in conflict.* Indianapolis, IN: Bobbs-Merrill.

Smits, P. B. A., Verbeek, J. H. A., & de Buisonjé, C. D. (2002). Problem based learning in continuing medical education: A review of controlled evaluation studies. *British Medical Journal, 324,* 153–156.

Snowden, L. R. (2003). Bias in mental health assessment and intervention: Theory and evidence. *American Journal of Public Health, 93,* 239–243.

Snyder, C. R., & Clair, M. S. (1977). Does insecurity breed acceptance? Effects of trait and situational insecurity on acceptance of positive and negative diagnostic feedback. *Journal of Counseling and Clinical Psychology, 45,* 843–850.

Snyder, C. R., Higgins, R. L., & Stucky, R. J. (1983). *Excuses: Masquerades in search of grace.* New York: Wiley.

Snyder, C. R., Shenkel, R. J., & Schmidt, A. (1976). Effects of role perspective and client psychiatric history on locus of problem. *Journal of Consulting and Clinical Psychology, 44*, 467–472.

Snyder, M., & Swann, W. B. (1978). Behavioral confirmation in social interaction: From social perception to social reality. *Journal of Experimental Social Psychology, 14*, 148–162.

Snyder, M., Tanke, E. D., & Berscheid, E. (1977). Social perception and interpersonal behavior: On the self-fulfilling nature of social stereotypes. *Journal of Personality and Social Psychology, 35*, 656–666.

Snyder, M., & Thomsen, C. J. (1988). Interactions between therapists and clients: Hypothesis testing and behavioral confirmation. In D. C. Turk & P. Salovey (Eds.), *Reasoning, inference, and judgement in clinical psychology* (pp. 124–152). New York: Free Press.

Snyder, R. E. (1966). Mammography: Contributions and limitations in the management of cancer of the breast. *Clinical Obstetrics and Gynecology, 9*, 207–220.

Soares, H. P., Daniels, S., Kumar, A., Clarke, M., Scott, C., Swann, S., & Djulbegovic, B. (2004). Bad reporting does not mean bad methods for randomized trials: Observational study of randomized controlled trials performed by the Radiation Therapy Oncology Group. *British Medical Journal, 328*, 22–24.

Sobell, M. B., & Sobell, L. C. (1982). Controlled drinking: A concept coming of age. In K. R. Blankstein & J. Polivy (Eds.), *Self-control and self-modification of emotional behavior* (pp. 143–162). New York: Plenum.

Sokal, A. D. (1998). What the social text affair does and does not prove. In N. Koertge (Ed.), *A house built on sand: Exposing postmodernist myths about science* (pp. 9–22). New York: Oxford University Press.

Soman, D. (2005). Framing, loss aversion, and mental accounting. In D. J. Koehler & N. Harvey (Eds.), *Blackwell handbook of judgment and decision making* (pp. 379–398). Malden, MA: Blackwell.

Sontag, S. (1991). *Illness as a metaphor and AIDS and its metaphors.* London: Penguin.

Sox, H. C., Blatt, M. A., Higgins, M. C., & Marton, K. I. (1988). *Medical decision making.* Boston: Butterworth-Heinemann.

Sparrow, M. (2000). *License to steal: How fraud bleeds America's health care system.* Boulder, CO: Westview Press.

Spector, A., Orrell, M., Davies, S., & Woods, B. (2004). Reality orientation for dementia (Cochrane Review). In *Cochrane Library*, Issue 3. Chichester, UK: Wiley.

Spiro, R. J., Coulson, R. L., Feltovitch, P. J., & Anderson, D. K. (1988). Cognitive flexibility theory: Advance knowledge acquisition in ill-structured domains. Proceedings of the 10th annual conference of the Cognitive Science Society. Hillsdale, NJ: Erlbaum.

Spittlehouse, C., Acton, M., & Enock, K. (2000). Introducing critical appraisal skills training in the UK social services: Another link between health and social care? *Journal of Interprofessional Care, 14*, 397–404.

Spock, B. (1945). *Baby and child care.* New York: Pocket Books.

Staats, A. W., & Staats, C. K. (1963). *Complex human behavior: A systematic extension of learning principles.* New York: Holt, Rinehart & Winston.

Stanovich, K. E. (1986). *How to think straight about psychology.* New York: Harper-Collins. (See also 7th Ed. 2004).

Stanovich, K. E., & West, R. F. (2002). *Individual differences in reasoning: Implications for the rationality debate?* In T. Gilovich, D. Griffin, & D. Kahneman (Eds.), *Heuristics and biases: The psychology of intuitive judgment* (pp. 421–440). New York: Cambridge University Press.

Starcevic, V. (2002). Opportunistic rediscovery of mental disorders by the pharmaceutical industry. *Psychotherapy and Psychosomatics, 71,* 305–310.

Stein, T. J., & Gambrill, E. D. (1985). Permanency planning for children: The past and present. *Children and Youth Services Review, 7,* 83–94.

Sternberg, R. J. (1986). *Intelligence applied: Understanding and increasing your intellectual skills.* San Diego, CA: Jovanovich.

Sternberg, R. J. (1987). Teaching intelligence: The application of cognitive psychology to the improvement of intellectual skills. In J. B. Baron & R. J. Sternberg (Eds.), *Teaching thinking skills: Theory and practice* (pp. 182–218). New York: W. H. Freeman.

Sternberg, R. J., & Kagan, J. (1986). *Intelligence applied: Understanding and increasing your intellectual skills.* San Diego, CA: Harcourt Brace Jovanovich.

Sternberg, R. J., & Wagner, R. K. (Eds.). (1986). *Practical intelligence: Nature and origins of competence in the everyday world.* Cambridge, England: Cambridge University Press.

Sterne, J. A., Egger, M., & Smith, G. D. (2001). Investigating and dealing with publication and other biases. In M. Egger, G. D. Smith, & D. G. Altman (Eds.), *Systematic Reviews in Healthcare: Meta-analysis in Context* (2nd ed.) (pp. 189–210). London: BMJ Books.

Steurer, J., Fischer, J., Bachmann, L. M., Koller, M., & ter Riet, G. (2002). Communicating accuracy of tests to general practitioners: A controlled study. *British Medical Journal, 324,* 824–826.

Stevens, P., Jr. (1988). The appeal of the occult: Some thoughts on history, religion, and science. *The Skeptical Inquirer, 12,* 376–385.

Stokes, T. F., & Baer, D. M. (1977). An implicit technology of generalization. *Journal of Applied Behavior Analysis, 10,* 349–367.

Stone, A. A., Turkkan, J. S., Bachrach, C. A., Jobe, J. B., Kurtzman, H. S., & Cain, V. S. (Eds.). (1999). *The science of self-report: Implications for research and practice.* Mahwah, NJ: Erlbaum.

Stone, G. C. (1979). Patient compliance and the role of the expert. *Journal of Social Issues, 35,* 34–59.

Storms, M. (1973). Video-tape and attribution process: Reversing actors' and observers' points are viewed. *Journal of Personality and Social Psychology, 27,* 165–174.

Straus, S. E., & McAlister, D. C. (2000). Evidence-based medicine: A commentary on common criticisms. *Canadian Medical Journal, 163,* 837–841.

Strohman, R. C. (2003). Genetic determination as a failing paradigm in biology and medicine: Implications for health and wellness. *Journal of Social Work Education, 39,* 169–191.

Strong, P. M. (1979). *The ceremonial order of the clinic.* London: Routledge & Kegan Paul.

Strupp, H. (1976). The nature of the therapeutic influence and its basic ingredients. In

A. Burton (Ed.), *What makes behavior change possible* (pp. 96–112). New York: Brunner/Mazel.

Strupp, H. H. (1997). On the limitation of therapy manuals. *Clinical Psychology, Science, & Practice, 4,* 76–82.

Strupp, H. H. (1958). The therapists' contribution to the treatment process. *Behavior Science, 3,* 34–67.

Strupp, H. H., & Anderson, T. (1997). On the limitations of therapy manuals. *Clinical Psychology: Science and Practice, 4,* 76–82.

Strupp, H. H., & Hadley, S. W. (1979). Specific versus nonspecific factors in psychotherapy: A controlled study of outcome. *Archives of General Psychiatry, 36,* 1125–1136.

Strupp, H. H., & Hadley, S. W. (1985). Negative effects and their determinants. In D. T. Mays & C. M. Franks (Eds.), *Negative outcome in psychotherapy and what to do about it* (pp. 20–55). New York: Springer.

Sue, D. W., & Sue, D. (1990). *Counseling the culturally different: Theory and practice* (2nd ed.). New York: Wiley Interscience.

Sue, D. W., & Sue, D. (2002). *Counseling the culturally different: Theory and practice* (4th ed.). New York: Wiley-Interscience.

Suedfeld, P., & Tetlock, P. E. (2001). Cognitive styles. In A. Tesser & N. Schwartz (Eds.), *Blackwell international handbook of social psychology: Intra-individual processes* (pp. 284–304). Vol. 1. London: Blackwell.

Summerfield, D. (2001). The invention of post-traumatic stress disorder and the social usefulness of a psychiatric category. *British Medical Journal, 322,* 95–98.

Swann, W. B., Jr., & Guiliano, T. (1987). Confirmatory search strategies in social interaction: How, when, why, and with what consequences. *Journal of Social and Clinical Psychology, 5,* 511–524.

Swartz, R. J., & Perkins, D. N. (1990). *Teaching thinking: Issues and approaches.* Pacific Grove, CA: Critical Thinking Press and Software.

Szasz, T. S. (1961). *The myth of mental illness: Foundations of a theory of personal conduct.* New York: Harper & Row.

Szasz, T. S. (1970). *The manufacture of madness: A comparative study of the inquisition and the mental health movement.* New York: Harper & Row.

Szasz, T. S. (1987). *Insanity: The idea and its consequences.* New York: Wiley

Szasz, T. S. (1994). *Cruel compassion: Psychiatric control of society's unwanted.* New York: Wiley.

Szasz, T. S. (2001). *Pharmacracy: Medicine and politics in America.* Westport, CT: Praeger.

Szasz, T. S. (2003). *Liberation by oppression: A comparative study of slavery and psychiatry.* New Brunswick, NJ: Transaction Press.

Tallent, N. (1988). *Psychological report writing* (3rd ed.). Englewood Cliffs, NJ: Prentice Hall. (See also 4th Ed. 1993).

Task Force. (1995). Training in and dissemination of empirically validated psychological treatment: Report and recommendations of the task force on Promotion and Dissemination of Psychological Procedures of Division 12 (Clinical Psychology). American Psychological Association. *Clinical Psychologist, 48,* 3–23.

Tavris, C. (1989). *Anger: The misunderstood emotion.* New York: Simon & Schuster.

Tavris, C. (1992). *The mismeasure of women.* New York: Simon & Schuster.

Tavris, C. (2001). *Psychobabble & biobunk: Using psychology to think critically about issues in the news* (2nd ed.). Upper Saddle River, NJ: Prentice Hall.

Tavris, C. (2003). Mind games: Psychological warfare between therapists and scientists. *Chronicle of Higher Education,* B7–B9. Feb. 28.

Taylor, R. B. (1999). The incivilities thesis: Theory, measurement, and policy. In R. Langworthy (Ed.), *Measuring what matters* (pp. 65–90). Washington DC: US Department of Justice, National Institute of Justice.

Taylor, E., & Rutter, M. (2002). Classification. Conceptual issues and substantive findings. In M. Rutter & E. Taylor (Eds.), Child and adolescent psychiatry (4th ed., pp. 3–17). Malden, MA: Blackwell.

Taylor, S. E., & Fiske, S. T. (1975). Point of view and perceptions of causality. *Journal of Personality and Social Psychology, 32,* 439–445.

Taylor, S., Fiske, S., Close, M., Anderson, C., & Ruderman, A.(1979). *Solo status as a psychological variable: The power of being distinctive.* Unpublished manuscript, Harvard University. (Discussed in Gahagan (1984), p. 87.)

Teasdale, J. D., & Fogarty, S. J. (1979). Differential effects of induced mood on retrieval of pleasant and unpleasant events from episodic memory. *Journal of Abnormal Psychology, 88,* 248–257.

Teger, A. I., with Cary, M., Katcher, A., & Hillis, J. (1980). *Too much invested to quit.* New York: Pergamon Press.

Teigen, K. H., & Brun, W. (2003). Verbal probabilities: A question of frame? *Journal of Behavioral Decision Making, 16,* 53–72.

Teigen, K. H., & Brun, W. (2003). Verbal expressions of uncertainty and probability. In D. Hardman & L. Macchi (Eds.), *Thinking: Psychological perspectives on reasoning, judgment and decision making* (pp. 125–145). New York: Wiley.

Temerlin, M. K. (1968). Suggestion effects in psychiatric diagnosis. *Journal of Nervous and Mental Disease, 147,* 349–357.

Terry, D. R. (1973). Structure of argument in debate. In D. R. Terry (Ed.), *Modern debate case techniques* (pp. 95–101). Skokie, IL: National Textbook.

Tesh, S. N. (1988). *Hidden arguments of political ideology and disease prevention policy.* New Brunswick, NJ: Rutgers University Press.

Tetlock, P. E. (2003). Correspondence and coherence: Indicators of good judgment in world politics. In D. Hardman & L. Macchi (Eds.), *Thinking: Psychological perspectives on reasoning, judgment and decision making* (pp. 233–250). New York: Wiley.

Thomlison, B. (2003). Characteristics of evidence-based child maltreatment interventions. *Child Welfare, 82,* 541–569.

Thompson, J. B. (1987). Language and ideology. *Sociological Review, 35,* 517–536.

Thompson, T. (1988). Retrospective review: Benedictus behavior analysis: B. F. Skinner's magnum opus at fifty. *Contemporary Psychology, 33,* 397–402.

Thomson O'Brien, M. A., Freemantle, N., Oxman, A. D., Wolf, F., Davis, D. A., & Herrin, J. (2003). Continuing education meetings and workshops: effects on professional practice and health care outcomes (Cochrane Review). In *Cochrane Library,* Issue 1. Oxford: Update Software.

Thornley, B., & Adams, C. (1998). Content and quality of 2000 controlled trials in schizophrenia over 50 years. *British Medical Journal, 317,* 1181–1184.

Thorngate, W., & Plouffe, L. (1987). The consumption of methodological psychological knowledge. In H. J. Stam, T. B. Rogers, & K. G. Gergen (Eds.), *The analysis of psychological theory: methodological perspectives* (pp. 61–92). New York: Hemisphere.

Thornton, H., Edwards, A., & Baum, M. (2003). Women need better information about routine mammography. *British Medical Journal, 327*, 101–103.

Thouless, R. H. (1974). *Straight and crooked thinking: Thirty-eight dishonest tricks of debate.* London: Pan Books.

Timimi, S. (2002). *Pathological child psychiatry and the medicalization of childhood.* London: Brunner-Routledge.

Timimi, S., & Taylor, E. (2004). ADHD is best understood as a cultural construct. *British Journal of Psychiatry, 184*, 8–9.

Tobacyk, J., & Milford, G. (1982). Criterion validity for Ellis' irrational beliefs: Dogmatism and uncritical inferences. *Journal of Clinical Psychology, 38*, 605–607.

Todd, J. T., & Morris, E. K. (1983). Misconception and miseducation: Presentations of radical behaviorism in psychology textbooks. *The Behavior Analyst, 6*, 153–160.

Toulmin, S. E. (2003). *The uses of argument.* Cambridge: Cambridge University Press. (Orig. pub. 1958).

Toulmin, S. E., Rieke, R., & Janik, A. (1979). *An introduction to reasoning.* New York: Macmillan.

Tousignant, M., & DesMarchais, J. E. (2002). Accuracy of student self-assessment ability compared to their own performance in a problem-based learning medical program: A correlation study. *Advances in Health Sciences Education, 7*, 19–27.

Transparency International. www.transparency.org

Trotter, W. (1916). *Instincts of the herd in peace and war.* London: T. F. Unwin.

Truax, C. (1966). Reinforcement and nonreinforcement in Rogerian psychotherapy. *Journal of Abnormal Psychology, 71*, 1–9.

Truzzi, M. (1976). Sherlock Holmes: Applied social psychologist. In W. B. Sanders (Ed.), *The sociologist as detective: An introduction to research methods* (2nd ed.) (pp. 50–86). New York: Praeger.

Tuchman, B. W. (1984). *The march of folly: From Troy to Vietnam.* New York: Ballantine.

Tuchman, B. (1989). In *Bill Moyers', A world of ideas: Conversations with thoughtful men and women about American life today and the ideas shaping our future.* New York: Doubleday.

Tuffs, A. (2004). Only 6% of drug advertising material is supported by evidence. *British Medical Journal, 328*, 485.

Tufte, E. R. (1983). *The visual display of quantitative information.* Cheshire, CT: Graphics Press.

Tufte, E. R. (1990). *Envisioning information.* Cheshire, CT: Graphics Press.

Turk, D. C., & Salovey, P. (1986). Clinical information processing: Bias inoculation. In R. Ingram (Ed.), *Information processing approaches to psychopathology and clinical psychology* (pp. 306–324). Orlando, FL: Academic Press.

Turner, S. M., DeMers, S. T., Fox, H. R., & Reed, G. M. (2001). APA's guidelines for test user qualifications: An executive summary. *American Psychologist, 56*, 1099–1113.

Tversky, A., & Kahneman, D. (1971). Belief in the law of small numbers. *Psychological Bulletin, 76*, 105–110.

Tversky, A., & Kahneman, D. (1973). Availability: A heuristic for judging frequency and probability. *Cognitive Psychology, 5,* 207–232.

Tversky, A., & Kahneman, D. (1974). Judgment under uncertainty: Heuristics and biases. *Science, 185,* 1124–1131.

Tversky, A., & Kahneman, D. (1981). The framing of decisions and the psychology of choice. *Science, 211,* 453–458.

Tversky, A., & Kahneman, D. (1983). Extensional versus intuitive reasoning: The conjunction fallacy in probability judgment. *Psychological Review, 90,* 293–315.

Tweed, R. G., & Lehman, D. R. (2002). Learning considered within a cultural context: Confucian and Socratic approaches. *American Psychologist, 57,* 89–99.

U.S. Department of Health and Human Services. (1999). Mental Health: A report of the surgeon general. Rockville, MD: U.S. Department of Health and Human Services Substance Abuse and Mental Health Service Administration, Center for Mental Health Services, National Institutes of Health, National Institute of Mental Health.

Valenstein, E. S. (1986). *Great and desperate cures: The rise and decline of psychosurgery and other medical treatments for mental illness.* New York: Basic Books.

Valenstein, E. S. (1988). *Blaming the brain: The truth about drugs and mental health.* New York: Free Press.

Valins, S., & Nisbett, R. E. (1972). Attributional processes in the development and treatment of emotional disorders. In E. E. Jones, D. E. Kanouse, H. H. Kelley, R. E. Nisbett, S. Vallins, & B. Weiner (Eds.), *Attribution: Perceiving the causes of behavior* (pp. 137–150). Morristown, NJ: General Learning Press.

Verhave, T., & Van Hoorn, W. (1984). The temperalization of the self. In K. J. Gergen & M. M. Gergen (Eds.), *Historical social psychology* (pp. 325–346). Hillsdale, NJ: Erlbaum.

Villanueva, E. V., Burrows, E. A., Fennessy, P. A., Rajendran, M., & Anderson, J. N. (2001). Improving question formulation for use in evidence appraisal in a tertiary care setting: A randomized controlled trial. *BMC Medical Informatics and Decision Making, 1:4.*

Vincent, C., & Taylor-Adams, S. (2001). The investigation and analysis of clinical incidents. In C. Vincent (Ed.), *Clinical risk management: Enhancing patient safety* (2nd ed., pp. 439–460). London: BMJ.

Voss, J. F. (1989). Problem solving in the educational process. In A. Lesgold & R. Glaser (Eds.), *Foundations for a psychology of education* (pp. 251–294). Hillsdale: Lawrence Erlbaum.

Wade, T. C., & Baker, T. B. (1977). Opinions and use of psychological tests: A survey of clinical psychologists. *American Psychologist, 32,* 874–882.

Wahler, R. G. (1980). The insular mother: Her problems in parent child treatment. *Journal of Applied Behavior Analysis, 13,* 207–219.

Wainer, H. (1976). Estimating coefficients in linear models: It don't make no nevermind. *Psychological Bulletin, 83,* 213–217.

Waitzkin, H. (1991). *The politics of medical encounters: How patients and doctors deal with social problems.* New Haven, CT: Yale University Press.

Wakefield, J. C. (2003). Dysfunction as a factual component of disorder: Reply to Houts, Part 2. *Behavior Research and Therapy, 41,* 969–990.

Walker, S. (1994). *Sense and nonsense about crime and drugs: A policy guide* (3rd ed.). Belmont: Wadsworth.

Walter, H., & Gilmore, S. K. (1973). Placebo versus social learning effects in parent training procedures designed to alter the behaviors of aggressive boys. *Behavior Therapist, 4,* 361–377.

Wampold, B. E. (2001). *The great psychotherapy debate: Models, methods, and findings.* Mahwah, NJ: Erlbaum.

Wampold, B. E. (2006). The psychotherapist. In J. C. Norcross, L. E. Beutler, & R. F. Levant (Eds.), *Evidence-based practices in mental health: Debate and dialogue on the fundamental questions* (pp. 200–208). Washington, DC: American Psychological Association.

Wandersman, A. H., & Hallman, W. K. (1993). Are people acting irrationally? Understanding public concerns about environmental threats. *American Psychologist, 48,* 681–686.

Ward, M., Gruppen, L., & Regehr, G. (2002). Measuring self-assessment: Current state of the art. *Advances in Health Sciences Education, 7,* 63–80.

Watkins, R. S., & Kimberly, J., Jr. (2004). What residents don't know about physician-pharmaceutical industry relations. *Academic Medicine, 79,* 432–437.

Watson, D. L., & Tharp, R. G. (2001). *Self-directed behavior: Self-modification for personal adjustment* (8th ed.). Monterey, CA: Brooks/Cole.

Watson, T. S., & Steege, M. W. (2003). *Conducting school-based functional behavioral assessments.* New York: Guilford.

Webb, S. A. (2001). Some considerations on the validity of evidence-based practice in social work. *British Journal of Social Work, 21,* 57–59.

Webster, Y. O. (1992). *The racialization of America.* New York: St. Martin's Press.

Webster, Y. O. (1997). *Against the multicultural agenda: A critical thinking alternative.* Westport, CT: Praeger.

Webster, Y. O. (2002). A human-centric alternative to diversity and multicultural education. *Journal of Social Work Education, 38,* 17–38.

*Webster's New World Dictionary* (3rd ed.). (1988). New York: Simon & Schuster.

Weiner, B. (1985). "Spontaneous" causal thinking. *Psychological Bulletin, 97,* 74–84.

Weinstein, C. E., & Rogers, B. T. (1985). Comprehension monitoring as a learning strategy. In G. d'Ydewalle (Ed.), *Cognition, information processing, and motivation* (pp. 619–629). New York: Elsevier.

Weisberg, R. (1986). *Creativity, genius and other myths.* New York: W. H. Freeman.

Weisburd, D., Lum, C. M., & Petrosino, A. (2001). Does research design affect study outcomes in criminal justice? *The ANNALS of the American Academy of Political and Social Science, 578,* 50–70.

Weisburd, D., Lum., C. M., & Yang, S-M. (2003). When can we conclude that treatments or programs "Don't Work"? *The ANNALS of the American Academy of Political and Social Science, 587,* 31–48.

Weiss, J., & Brown, P. (1977). *Self-insight error in the explanation of mood.* Unpublished manuscript, Harvard University.

Weisz, J., Suwanlert, S., Chaiyasit, W., & Walter, B. R. (1987). Over- and undercontrolled referral problems among children and adolescents from Thailand and the

United States: The Wat and Wai of cultural differences. *Journal of Consulting and Clinical Psychology, 55,* 719–726.

Wells, G. L., & Lindsay, R. C. L. (1983). How do people infer the accuracy of eyewitness memory? Studies of performance and a metamemory analysis. In S. M. A. Lloyd-Bostock & B. R. Clifford (Eds.), *Evaluating witness evidence: Recent psychological research and new perspectives* (pp. 41–56). New York: Wiley.

Wells, G. L., Lindsay, R. G. L., & Ferguson, T. J. (1979). Accuracy, confidence, and juror perceptions in eyewitness identification. *Journal of Applied Psychology, 64,* 440–448.

Wells, G. L., & Loftus, E. F. (1984). *Eyewitness testimony.* Cambridge, England: Cambridge University Press.

Wennberg, J. E. (2002). Unwarranted variations in healthcare delivery: Implications for academic medical centers. *British Medical Journal, 325,* 961–964.

Westen, D., Novotny, C. N., & Thompson-Brenner, H. (2004). The empirical status of empirically supported psychotherapies: Assumptions, findings, and reporting in controlled clinical trials. *Psychological Bulletin, 130,* 631–663.

Westermeyer, J. (1987). Cultural factors in clinical assessment. *Journal of Consulting and Clinical Psychology, 55,* 471–478.

When Drug Companies Hide Data. (2004, June 6). *The New York Times,* p. 12.

Whitehead, A. (1929). *The aims of education and other essays.* New York: Dutton.

Whitfield, C. F., & Xie, S. X. (2002). Correlation of problem-based learning facilitators = scores with student performance on written exams. *Advances in Health Sciences Education, 7,* 41–51.

Whitman, R. M., Kramer, M., & Baldridge, B. (1963). Which dreams does the patient tell? *Archives of General Psychiatry, 8,* 277–282.

*Whitree v. New York State,* 290 N.Y. 5. 2d 486 (Ct. Claims 1968).

Wiggins, J. (1984). Clinical and statistical prediction: Where are we and where do we go from here? *Clinical Psychology Review, 1,* 3–18.

Wilkes, M. S., & Hoffman, J. R. (2001). An innovative approach to educating medical students about pharmaceutical promotion. *Academic Medicine, 76,* 1271–1277.

Wilkins, L. T., Gottfredson, D. M., Robison, J. O., & Sadowsky, A. (1973). *Information selection and use in parole decision-making* (Supp. Rep. 5). Davis, CA: National Council on Crime and Delinquency Research Center.

Williams, M., (2004). A brave new paradigm? *British Medical Journal, 329,* 357.

Wills, T. A. (1978). Perceptions of clients by professional helpers. *Psychological Bulletin, 85,* 968–1000.

Wills, T. A. (1982). Nonspecific factors in helping relationships. In T. A. Willis (Ed.), *Basic processes in helping relationships* (pp. 381–404). Orlando, FL: Academic Press.

Wills, T. A., Weiss, R. L, & Patterson, G. R. (1974). A behavioral analysis of the determinants of marital satisfaction. *Journal of Clinical and Consulting Psychology, 42,* 802–811.

Wilson, J. A. (2001). Pseudoscientific beliefs among college students. *Reports of the National Center for Science Education, 21,* 9–36.

Wilson, J. M. G., & Jungner, G. (1968). Principles and practice of screening for disease. *WHO Public Health Papers No. 34.* Geneva, Switzerland: World Health Organization.

Witte, C. L., Witte, M. H., & Kerwin, A. (1994). Suspended judgment: Ignorance and the process of learning and discovery in medicine. *Controlled Clinical Trials, 15,* 1–4.

Woll, S. (2003). *Everyday thinking: Memory, reasoning and judgment in the real world*. Mahwah, NJ: Erlbaum.

Wolpe, J. (1986). Individualization: The categorical imperative of behavior therapy practice. *Journal of Behavior Therapy and Experimental Psychiatry, 17*, 145–154.

Wood, D. F. (2003). Clinical review. ABC of learning and teaching in medicine. Problem based learning. *British Medical Journal, 326*, 328–330.

Woods, D. D., & Cook, R. I. (1999). Perspectives on human error: Hindsight biases and local rationality. In F. T. Durso, R. S. Nickerson, R. W. Schzaneveldt, S. T, Dumais, D. S. Lindsay, & M. T. Chi (Eds.), *Handbook of Applied cognition* (pp. 141–171). New York: Wiley.

Woods, D. D., & Patterson, E. S. (2001). How unexpected events produce an escalation of cognitive and coordinative demands. In P. Hancock & P. A. Desmond (Eds.), *Stress, workload, and fatigue* (pp. 290–302). Mahwah, NJ: Erlbaum.

Woodward, K. L. (2004). A politial sacrament. *New York Times,* May 28, Sect. A, p. 21.

Woolf, S. H., Kuzel, A. J., Dovey, S. M., & Phillips, R. L. (2004). A string of mistakes: The importance of cascade analysis in describing, counting, and preventing medical errors. *Annals of Family Medicine, 2*, 317–326.

Wosinka, W., Cialdini, R. B., Barrett, D. W., & Reykowski, J. (Eds.). (2001). *The practice of social influence in multiple cultures*. Mahwah, NJ: Erlbaum.

Wright, R. H. (2005). The myth of continuing education: A look at some intended and (maybe) unintended consequences. In R. H. Wright & N. A. Cummings (Eds.), *Destructive trends in mental health: A well-intentioned path to harm* (pp. 143–151). New York: Routledge.

Wright, R. H., & Cummings, N. A. (Eds.). (2005). *Destructive trends in mental health. The well-intentioned path to harm*. New York: Routledge.

Wu, A. W., Cavanaugh, T. A., McPhee, S. J., & Micco, G. P. (1997). To tell the truth: Ethical and practical issues in disclosing medical mistakes to patients. *Journal of General Internal Medicine, 12*, 770–775.

Wu, A. W., Folkman, S., McPhee, S. J., & Lo, B. (2003). Do house officers learn from their mistakes? *Quality and Safety in Health Care, 12*, 221–226.

Ying, Y. (2002). The conception of depression in Chinese Americans. In K. S. Kurasaki, S. Okazaki, & S. Stanley (Eds.), *Asian American mental health: Assessment theories and methods* (pp. 173–183). New York: Kluwer Academic/Plenum Publishers.

Yinger, R. J. (1980). Can we really teach them to think? In R. E. Young (Ed.), *New Directions for teaching and learning: No. 3. Fostering critical thinking* (pp. 11–32). San Francisco: Jossey-Bass.

Young, J. H. (1992). *American health quackery*. Princeton, NJ: Princeton University Press.

Zatz, M. J. (1984). Race, ethnicity, and determinate sentencing: A new dimension to an old controversy. *Criminology, 22*, 147–175.

Zegiob, L., Arnold, S., & Forehand, R. (1975). An examination of observer effects in parent-child interaction. *Child Development, 46*, 509–512.

Zilbergeld, B. (1983). *The shrinking of America: Myths of psychological change*. Boston: Little, Brown.

Zimbardo, P. G. (1989). *Shyness: What it is, what to do about it*. Boston: Addison Wesley.

Ziskin, J. (1981). *Coping with psychiatric and psychological testimony* (3rd ed., two vols.). Venice, CA: Law and Psychology Press.

Ziskin, J. with chapters by Faust, D., et al. (1995). *Coping with psychiatric and psychological testimony.* (5th Ed.). Law and Psychology Press.

Zsambok, C. E., & Klein, G. (Eds.). (1997). *Naturalistic decision making.* Mahwah, NJ: Erlbaum.

# Author Index

# Subject Index

Absolute risk reduction (ARR), 307–308
Abuse:
  child
    limited access to information and, 45
    preferred view of clients and, 46
  domestic, 41
  sexual, 12
  vagueness of terms and, 23
Abstraction, differences in, 136
Acceptability principle, 79
Accountability, encouraging, 494–495
Acquiescent response set, 383
Acquired immunodeficiency syndrome
    (AIDS), 44
Action threshold, 449
Actuarial judgments, 442–444
Addiction, vagueness of terms and, 23
Ad Hominem argument, 148–150, 163
Ad Populum argument, 163
Adverse incident reporting, 494
Adversarial arguments, 77, 78
AdWatch, 534
Affect:
  heuristic, 225
  persuasion and, 139
  *See also* Emotions, sources of influence
Affirming the consequence error, 71
*Against Therapy*, 148
Agency culture/climate. *See* Organizational
    culture/climate
Agency for Healthcare Research and Quality
    (AHRQ), 300
Agency, influences of, 42–48
Agency policy, 368
Agoraphobia, 40
Alcoholics Anonymous, 178
Alcoholism, problem definition, 36
AMED, 301
American Psychiatric Association:
  influence of language and, 134
  problem definition and, 31, 33

American Psychological Association:
  expert witnesses and, 371
Analogies, 202
  forced, 158
  inappropriate use of, 157–158
  reasoning from, 62, 63
Analogues, 387
Anchoring effects, 19, 135, 209–210, 232,
    454
Anger as diversion, 159
Antiscience. *See* Science, antiscience
Anxiety, persuasion tactics and, 159–160
Appeals, irrelevant, 178–181
Applied behavior analysis, 402
Apriorism, 153
Argumentation, 68–73
Arguments:
  deductive and inductive, 72
  premises and, 69
Aristotle, 77–78
*The Arrogance of Preventive Medicine*, 448
Assertions, bold, 134–135
Assessment, and accuracy, 363
  causal assumptions, 367
  compared to diagnosis, 430
  dispositional bias, 423–427
  errors, sources of, 367–370
  by experts and novices, 192–198
  questionable methord, 378–379
Assessment, questions, 290, 292
Associative thinking, 234
Assumption, 69
  influence of language, 120–131
Attention-Deficit/Hyperactivity Disorder, 3
  causes of, 399
  classification and, 166–167
  problem definition, 37
Attrition bias, 329
Authority, 202
  appeal to, 163
  irrelevant, 177

# About the Author

**E**ILEEN GAMBRILL IS the Hutto Patterson Professor of Child and Family Studies in the School of Social Welfare at the University of California at Berkeley. She received her BA degree from the University of Pennsylvania, her MSW degree from Bryn Mawr School of Social Work and Social Research, and her PhD degree from the University of Michigan in Social Work and Psychology. She has been a visiting scholar at the University of Oxford and Tel Aviv Universities and received a Benjamin Meeker Fellowship from the University of Bristol in 1999. She has won two Pro Humanitate Awards from the North American Resource Center for Child Welfare, one in 2001 and another in 2004. Her areas of interest include professional decision making, ethics, and the integration of research and practice in the helping professions. Books include *Social Work Practice: A Critical Thinker's Guide* (2nd ed.; 2006), *Critical Thinking For Social Workers: Exercises for the Helping Professions* (2nd ed.; with Len Gibbs, 1999), and *Controversial Issues in Social Work, Ethics, Values and Professions* (with Robert Pruger, 1997).

Gambrill served as Editor-in-Chief of Social Work Research and Abstracts 1984–1988 and as Editor-in-Chief of the Journal of Social Work Education, 2000–2003, and currently is on the editorial boards of many journals. She was elected by Division 25 members to serve on the Council of Representatives of the American Psychological Association 2003–2005 and elected to the Board of Directors of the Council on Social Work Education 2000–2002. She is a licensed psychologist in the state of California.